PRESERVATION COMES OF AGE

*From Williamsburg to
the National Trust, 1926–1949*

Charles B. Hosmer, Jr.

PRESERVATION COMES OF AGE

*From Williamsburg to
the National Trust, 1926–1949*

VOLUME II

PUBLISHED FOR THE PRESERVATION PRESS

National Trust for Historic Preservation in the United States

BY THE UNIVERSITY PRESS OF VIRGINIA

Charlottesville

THE UNIVERSITY PRESS OF VIRGINIA
Copyright © 1981 by Charles B. Hosmer, Jr.

First published 1981

Frontispiece: *La Purisima Mission, Lompoc, Calif., in 1953. (Photography by Wilkes, Santa Barbara County Plans and Planting Branch, Community Arts Association)*

Library of Congress Cataloging in Publication Data

Hosmer, Charles Bridgham, 1932–
  Preservation comes of age.

  Bibliography: p.
  Includes index.
  1. Historic buildings—United States—Conservation
and restoration. 2. Historic buildings—United States
—Remodeling for other use. 3. Architecture—United
States—Conservation and restoration—Business community participation. I. National Trust for Historic Preservation in the United States. II. Title. NA106.H67
363.6'9'0973   80–260678
ISBN 0–8139–0712–8

Printed in the United States of America

TO JERI

who gave so much

CONTENTS

CONTENTS

VOLUME TWO

ACKNOWLEDGMENTS

THIS BOOK is a collaborative effort in every sense of that word. The author has had assistance from many of the people who saved the buildings described in the text. It is his hope that just recognition has been given to the individuals and groups that contributed to the development of a new vision of America's historical heritage. Between 1961 and 1976, eighty-five of these people willingly granted taped interviews in an effort to impart the deeper meaning of events that usually escapes the researcher who is restricted to documentary sources. Thousands of letters, reports, minutes, and memoranda were made available to the author by librarians, administrators, and archivists who managed the preservation projects of the 1970s. Many of the veteran leaders read portions of this manuscript with a selfless willingness to make the interpretations as clear as possible. Some of these individuals have made the author painfully aware of the impossibility of recreating the tensions and complexities that went into the decision-making process.

Two exceptionally well qualified historians, Charles W. Porter III and Frederick L. Rath, Jr., read the entire book in its draft form. They were able to draw on their rich experience in the preservation field for insights that could have come in no other way. Many other scholars read portions of the draft and gave the author their comments: Horace M. Albright, Edward P. Alexander, Roy E. Appleman, Joseph F. Booton, E. Milby Burton, Richard Candee, David R. Crippen, Newton B. Drury, Henry E. Edmunds, David E. Finley, E. McClung Fleming, Michael R. Hardwick, Herbert E. Kahler, Richard Lawwill, V. Aubrey Neasham, Philip Dana Orcutt, George A. Palmer, Erling Pedersen, Charles E. Peterson, Philip T. Primm, James R. Short, Albert Simons, John A. H. Sweeney, Minor Wine

ACKNOWLEDGMENTS

Thomas, Jr., Charles van Ravenswaay, Patty Whitelaw, and Samuel Wilson, Jr.

Some preservation leaders could not be interviewed in taping sessions, but they chose to share their insights by means of letters: Paul Angle, George W. Chambers, Laurence Vail Coleman, Benjamin P. Draper, Adolph J. Gondek, Allen Griffin, Ralph Happel, Paul S. Kerr, Theodore Fred Kuper, Chester G. Mayo, Edwin Small, H. V. Smith, Hillory Tolson, and Ronald L. Way.

Nearly six years of extensive travel went into the documentary research for this book. This work would have taken much longer without the assistance of archivists, administrators, and interpretive staff: at Old Sturbridge Village, Etta Falkner, Roger Parks, and Alexander J. Wall; at the Society for the Preservation of New England Antiquities, Bertram K. Little, Abbott Lowell Cummings, Mrs. Martin Goldsborough, and E. Florence Addison; at the Preservation Society of Newport County, Harold R. Talbot and Mrs. Leonard J. Panaggio; at the Archives of the Mother Church, the First Church of Christ, Scientist, in Boston, Joanne Shaw; at the New York State Historical Association, Louis C. Jones, Frederick L. Rath, Jr., Minor Wine Thomas, Jr., and Wendell Tripp; at the National Archives, Robert M. Kvasnicka; at the National Park Service offices, Robert M. Utley and Roy E. Appleman; at Independence National Historical Park, John D. R. Platt; at the Robert E. Lee Memorial Foundation, Mrs. Austin P. Leland, Helen Keller, Irving T. Duke, and Edith Healy; at the Henry Ford Museum and Greenfield Village, Donald Shelley and Robert G. Wheeler; at the Ford Archives, Henry E. Edmunds, Winthrop Sears, and David Crippen; at the Colonial Williamsburg Foundation, Edward P. Alexander, James R. Short, Paul Buchanan, Mrs. A. Lawrence Kocher, and D. Stephen Elliott; at the Vieux Carré Commission, J. H. Phillips and Wayne Collier; at the Historic New Orleans Collection, Edith Long; at the San Antonio Conservation Society, Conrad True and Pat Osborne; at the Hammond-Harwood House Association, J. H. McDonald; at La Purisima State Historical Park, M. J. Mason and Michael R. Hardwick; at Santa Barbara, Pearl Chase; at the Library of Congress, Virginia Daiker; at the Illinois Department of Conservation, John A. C. Schulte and Robert E. Sherman; at the American Institute of Architects, George Pettengill; at the Indiana State Library, Frances B. McDonald and John Selch; at the Lilly Library at Indiana University, Elfrieda Lang; at the South Carolina Historical Society, Helen McCormack; at the Historic Charleston Foundation, Frances Edmunds; for Charleston in general, Albert Simons and Mary Anderson; in Natchez, Katherine Miller; in Richmond, Mary Wingfield Scott; at the Carnegie Institution of Washington, Sheila McGough; at the Henry Francis du Pont Winterthur Museum, Charles van Ravenswaay, John A. H. Sweeney, Elizabeth Hill, Nancy Goyne Evans, and Barbara Hearn; at the Pennsylvania State Archives, Donald H. Kent and Martha Simonetti; at the National Trust for Historic Preservation, James Biddle, Helen Duprey Bullock, Terry B. Morton, and Patricia E. Williams; at the Oral History Research Library at Columbia University, Elizabeth Mason; and at the National Park Service Archives at Harpers Ferry, David H. Wallace and Richard Russell.

Professor George B. Tatum permitted the author to look over the manuscript of his book *Philadelphia Georgian* in order to understand the preservation of the Samuel Powel House.

Several of the students at Principia College helped in the research for particular portions of this book over the past decade. They were willing assistants who often did research by means of independent study courses in distant cities. They were Jane Stewart Spitzer, Paul and Leigh Daugherty, Sharon Brown Wootton, Brian Demuth, Cynthia Mathieu, and Donna Virgil Holden. Deborah Swindoll Olsen assisted greatly in the process of transcribing some of the taped interviews.

Lester J. Cappon provided some much-needed encouragement at the beginning of this research, which helped the author to focus the chronological limits of the book.

A program that required several years of research in archives all over the United States could tax the resources of several individuals, not to speak of a small college. The administrative officers of Principia College, David K. Andrews, C. Theodore Houpt, and Kenneth S.

Johnston, were most willing to grant the author a total of twenty-three months of leave time. My colleagues in the history department, Brook B. Ballard, James H. Belote, and Thomas R. Fennell, willingly took on heavy work loads to support my research and writing.

Friends and relatives permitted the author to stay with them when the research work took him and his family to distant parts of the nation: George and Christine Knadler, Floyd S. Barringer, Pearl Chase, Kenneth and Martha Hufford, Carlie Lackey, V. Aubrey Neasham, and his wife's parents, David and Dallas Wylie Prugh. The author's mother, Faye D. Hosmer, and her friend Kathryn W. Hartman assisted in many aspects of the research work as well.

The Eastern National Park and Monument Association, the National Trust for Historic Preservation, the American Philosophical Society, and the American Association for State and Local History all gave grants that covered major research and travel expenses.

National Park Service alumni and friends and relatives who wanted to remember the career of Ronald F. Lee united to create a fund that would help make possible the publication of this book. Under the leadership of George A. Palmer this group joined with the Eastern National Park and Monument Association to assist the Preservation Press of the National Trust in the task of meeting production costs. There is probably no single individual in the preservation movement before 1950 who is more deserving of this recognition than Ronald F. Lee.

With the guidance of Terry B. Morton, both Diane Maddex and Jennie B. Bull of the Preservation Press of the National Trust for Historic Preservation worked diligently to make this book a clear and comprehensive picture of the preservation field. They asked questions, debated important issues, and made vital suggestions about the arrangement of the book. A thoughtful comparison of the draft of the manuscript with the final revision would show the great help given by the dedicated editors in Washington.

Only one person was indispensable in the production of this book, my wife, Jeralyn Prugh Hosmer. She has read and reread the draft copies many times. She helped to transcribe interviews and to care for the many needs that came up during the research and travel. She has come to know the preservation field in a way that few persons could imagine. She has been patient, careful, and soundly critical through the long years of preparation and revision. This is a very considerable accomplishment, considering the demands of two children who were born during the years this book was being written.

CHARLES B. HOSMER, JR.

Ronald F. Lee Memorial Fund

IN MEMORY OF RONALD F. LEE, chief historian of the National Park Service during the expansion of the New Deal programs and the post-war years, first secretary of the National Trust for Historic Preservation, and a preservationist who was uniquely able to unite both government and private interests, the following friends contributed toward the publication of this book: Horace M. Albright, Roy E. Appleman, Ruth Aull Cerick, Verne E. Chatelain, Eastern National Park and Monument Association, Charles Edison Fund and Melvin J. Weig, Hyde Park Historical Association, T. Sutton Jett, Jean P. Lee, Ralph H. Lewis, George A. Palmer, Charles E. Peterson, Thomas J. Pitkin, Charles W. Porter III, Ann and Frederick L. Rath, Jr., Trustees of Saint-Gaudens Memorial, Edith Appleton Standen, Ben H. Thompson, and Conrad L. Wirth.

GEORGE A. PALMER

PRESERVATION COMES OF AGE

From Williamsburg to
the National Trust, 1926–1949

9

The Federal Program and
the War Years
1941-49

T HE YEARS OF expanding federal preservation activity that followed
the passage of the Historic Sites Act ended abruptly with the Japanese attack on Pearl Harbor. As the emphasis on national defense increased, the government began to restrict its historical interests in almost
every direction, and the period of retrenchment continued for about ten
years. Even after the war ended in 1945, most lawmakers were convinced that a strong defense continued to be essential to the survival of
the United States. From 1942 through 1950 the National Park Service
found itself outside the mainstream of governmental expansion, and the
appropriations voted by Congress permitted little more than a holding
operation. Gas rationing and concern about the needs of service personnel helped to turn the visiting public away from historic sites. More
serious was the threat to historic areas all over the nation as cities rapidly
expanded. Shifts of population for war industry and the resulting industrial expansion led to demolition of buildings and uprooting of Americans from the communities they had come to value.

The best way to illustrate this sudden shift in the preservation field
is to turn to a letter from President Franklin Roosevelt to Secretary of
the Interior Harold Ickes on March 28, 1942, designating the Gloria Dei

Church (1698–1700) in Philadelphia as a National Historic Site. The president began by "reluctantly" approving the old church.

> While I favor the preservation for public use of historic sites, buildings, and objects of national significance, and while a designation as an historic site frequently requires no Federal expenditure, it seems inappropriate, when the Nation is at war, to utilize the time of Government employees in conducting investigations looking to the designation of such sites. I believe that such employees could be assigned duties more closely related to the war effort.
>
> In view of the foregoing I suggest that for the duration of the war all efforts with respect to the designation of national historic sites be suspended, and that the time of employees engaged in this line of endeavor be directed into more productive channels.[1]

This presidential rearrangement of priorities should not be taken to mean that Roosevelt had lost interest in history or historic preservation; he added a note to the bottom of the letter that gave Ickes an escape clause: "In exceptional cases, please speak to me."[2]

The war was not the only factor that affected the historical program of the Park Service. Arno Cammerer's health began to fail, and on August 20, 1940, Newton B. Drury, founder of the Save-the-Redwoods League and acquisitions officer for the California State Park Commission, became the fourth director. Drury's attitude toward adding new historical properties was quite different from that of his predecessor.[3] Because federal officials looked upon the Park Service as a nonessential agency, Drury's offices were moved to Chicago early in 1942, much against the wishes of the employees and the Advisory Board.[4] In addition, the Branch of History lost the services of Ronald F. Lee to the air force from 1942 to 1946.[5] It was a bleak period for the professional group that had worked so hard throughout the late 1930s to create a national historical program.

The cumulative effect of these changes could be referred to as a direct blow to the cause of historic preservation, as each of the decisions—to change personnel, to move offices, and to cut off funds for ongoing projects—tended to convert the Park Service into a caretaker organization with a skeleton staff.[6] Drury was especially concerned about the decision to put the offices in Chicago. He estimated that the move cost at least $250,000, and a great many experienced people chose to find alternative employment in Washington rather than suffer exile to the windy city. Charles Porter and Herbert Kahler "became" the Branch of History throughout these war years. Associate director Arthur Demaray remained in Washington with a small staff so that at least one

Newton B. Drury. (National Park Service)

Park Service official could maintain communications with Congress and the secretary of the interior.[7] At a meeting in May 1942 the Interim Committee of the Advisory Board reviewed the costs of the move and then passed a motion condemning the whole operation in scathing terms: "The Interim Committee, on behalf of the Advisory Board, accordingly renews its protest against the removal of the headquarters of the National Park Service from the seat of government, as an ill-conceived, unrealistic measure, extravagantly uneconomical, unjustified by any needs of the other branches of the Government, harmful to the Service, and detrimental to the war effort and the public interest."[8] Director Drury, however, was delighted to find once he was in Chicago that members of Congress did not telephone him every day to push their pet projects, although he did find it difficult to look after the legislative needs of the Park Service.[9]

The shift in directorship was significant because Drury had a conservative approach to the acquisition and development of historic sites.

He was one of those rare individuals who managed to divide his interests equally between scenic parks and historical areas. Ronald Lee, who worked closely with the new director after the war, remembered the change in emphasis:

> Newton Drury was a very sensitive man. His primary interest has always been in the natural areas in California and the redwoods and other superb natural areas throughout the country. . . . Drury was always sympathetically interested in historic preservation. He was interested in Columbia, California, the early mining town; he was interested in Monterey; he was interested in San Juan Bautista, and in the considerable number of historic properties that belonged to California when he came to the Park Service. His interest was genuine, but his problem was that World War II was on. After the war all these matters of trying to get the Service going again were on his shoulders.[10]

It was natural that the Park Service might experience a period of conservative reaction after the spectacular achievements of the 1930s, but the hiring of Drury speeded up this process. Drury should be permitted to explain for himself the nature of his cautious approach. He had learned a great deal about historic sites and land acquisition during the years he had worked closely with Joseph Knowland in developing the California State Park System. That same desire for judicious planning came to Washington.

> Of course, a great many people felt that I was unduly conservative, and perhaps I was. I went to Washington with the concept that the National Parks were the crown jewels of the nation, and that quality was far more important than quantity. I was not particularly an advocate of adding areas of lesser caliber to the National Park System; in fact I was rather aggressive in opposing that. I was, however, considerably interested, having been a land acquisition man for many years, in rounding out the parks by acquiring in-holdings, and from the very beginning I tried to get appropriations to that end. And within two or three years before I retired, we finally got a very meager appropriation of some $300,000 a year.[11]

Another factor that made Newton Drury appear conservative was his idea about federalism. He did not share the vision of a growing National Park System that had been extended from Stephen Mather through Horace Albright to Arno Cammerer and the executive staff throughout the 1930s. California had been adding to its own park system all through these years on the basis of the Frederick Law Olmsted survey carried out in the late 1920s. So it is no wonder Drury believed that the influence of the federal government in historic preservation should be curtailed. But he appreciated the expertise that had been built up in the Park Service: "The Park Service still has a very well-organized historic section, and there's no question that there's been great advance in the United States in the consciousness of the importance of preserving symbols of the past because of the leadership that the National Park Service took. That was a function that I personally entered into wholeheartedly and believed in. But there again I felt that there should be selectivity and that, just as in the phase of state parks, it was wise to encourage the states, regions and localities to engage in the preservation of historic sites."[12]

Neither Drury's conservative approach nor the removal of the Park Service staff to Chicago could fully explain the way in which the federal government seemed to ignore historic preservation during the war years. The goals of the American people had shifted once democracy itself was on trial throughout the world. The Cold War, which began almost immediately after the Japanese surrender, generated the same concern over the future of democracy. In a period of full employment and rising defense expenditures it seemed wasteful to develop new national historic sites. Planes and ships could protect the United States; old buildings could not.

Late in World War II director Drury concluded he could counteract criticism of the National Park Service by recording the contributions it had made toward the war effort. He asked Charles Porter to assemble a comprehensive report that would include the role historical areas had to assume in a total national mobilization.[13] In his account historian Porter tried to capture the mood of urgency that influenced the interpretation of historic sites in wartime:

> The individual citizens faced by a troubled world turned in the moment of national danger to the national historical parks and shrines for a renewal of their faith in their country's traditions and their country's destiny, for encouragement, and patriotic inspiration. Many people seemed desirous of reconsecrating themselves to the ideals for which this country stands by direct emotional experience on soil made sacred by the heroism and unselfish patriotism of our forefathers. This public demand was reflected in questions and advice given to historians and public contact men in the historical parks and in increased visitation to the historical areas themselves.[14]

Almost immediately after the attack on Pearl Harbor the interpretive program of the Park Service switched to a heavy emphasis on patriotic inspiration, and men in uniform appeared in large numbers at the most accessible historical areas.[15] The Park Service was an excellent means for giving the people of the United States a sense of their destiny, but the costs of that interpretation had to be kept to a minimum.[16]

The reports that came into the Department of the Interior during the war years from the historic parks and sites show that the Park Service staff had to turn to planning and research functions almost entirely. There was no money for construction projects, and the vast pool of WPA and CCC labor did not reappear after the war. There were a few instances where the war effort (in the form of veterans' hospitals and housing shortages) seemed to menace National Historic Sites, but none of these threats ever fully materialized. The Park Service personnel, who were nearly all survivors of the great professional influx of the 1930s, had to be willing to devote their time to debates over the problems involved in interpretation and restoration. They could concentrate on working with the public and on sketching out future developments that might be carried out if the federal government should ever again choose to put substantial funds into historic preservation.

In June 1947, shortly before peacetime conditions permitted the National Park Service to move its offices back to Washington, Ronald Lee complained to director Drury that the Branch of History had been cut from six professional employees to four. Lee then noted that "the work load now exceeds its highest pre-war level." He listed for the director all of the duties that had been assigned to the History Branch—including research into new areas for the Park System. The list of responsibilities filled nearly seven pages; it included, though, no direct suggestion for the most efficient way to alleviate the situation.[17]

NEGLECTED SITES AND EXCEPTIONAL CASES

No matter how inadequate the appropriations of the war years may have been, the Park Service had already acquired a chain of historic sites it had to maintain. In a few instances projects that had been planned and funded in the prewar years were carried to completion. There were even a few additions to the National Park System—mostly "exceptional cases" that did merit the attention of President Roosevelt.

When superintendent Elbert Cox went off to war, J. C. Harrington, the staff archaeologist, took over at Colonial National Historical Park. He was not permitted to do much in the way of planning or construction because of the national emergency, but he did become the regional archaeologist in Richmond when the war ended, and that new

position permitted him to host a major conference on archaeological research at Jamestown and Yorktown in 1946.[18] From 1944 to 1949 the
Park Service staff in Washington (Arthur Demaray) and at Yorktown
worked together in an effort to win congressional approval for land acquisition at Colonial. This plan would have necessitated adding a plantation complex, such as the buildings at Carter's Grove or the ruins of
Rosewell, across the York River from the parkway. Charles Porter in the
Washington office pleaded for "a Colonial National Historical Park
which will be superlative in quality and worthy of National Park Service
standards in striving for the *superlative and best*—an exhibit able to stand
on its own feet even in the presence of the work of Rockefeller at Williamsburg."[19]

The push to make Colonial a better park area came into focus in the
spring of 1948 when Kenneth Chorley, president of Colonial Williamsburg, tried to interest Congressman Schuyler Otis Bland of Virginia in
helping to get appropriations for the National Park Service. Chorley,
who was already a major influence in the preservation movement, outlined for Bland an ambitious program for restoring Yorktown as a seaport and reconstructing Jamestown as a seventeenth-century capital. He
hinted that if Colonial could expand its research and development activities there might be a greater opportunity for cooperation between Williamsburg and the Park Service; Chorley ended his appeal to the congressman with a piece of patriotic propaganda that helps to illustrate the
inspirational tone preservationists took in the Cold War years:

> There never was a time in the history of this country or in the history of the
> world when freedom and human liberty were as important as they are today.
> The citizens of the United States, and in fact the citizens of the world, need
> a rededication to the principles of freedom and human liberty. They need a
> reawakening as to the benefits and advantages that accrue to human beings
> who live in an atmosphere of freedom and opportunity. The area embracing
> Jamestown, Williamsburg and Yorktown provides a responsibility and chal-
> lenge to carry this message forward which is without parallel anywhere in
> our country. If you, Mr. Bland, can bring such a broad-gauge program to
> fruition, I feel you will be rendering a service to present and future genera-
> tions that will be comparable to the service that your fellow Virginians—
> Washington, Jefferson, Mason, and Henry—rendered to their generation
> and future generations.[20]

Newton Drury immediately asked Bland to back the Chorley proposals
as long as there was no requirement to reconstruct Jamestown, where
the historical evidence was inconclusive.[21] Apparently these ringing ap-

peals fell on deaf ears in Congress; the war-torn economy of the United States and the priorities set up for rebuilding Western Europe did not permit substantial sums for historical projects.

At Salem Maritime National Historic Site in Massachusetts the focus of attention was the remains of an old commercial building on federal land. The structure, known as the Forrester Warehouse (1832), was really a rectangle of brick walls that would require a total reconstruction.[22] There was also some interest in museum planning at Salem, but no funds were available.[23] In 1946 the regional director agreed to assign a priority number to the restoration of the warehouse, but he admitted that the data for a good restoration were lacking.[24] Instead the Park Service resorted to the expedient of tearing down the unsightly walls and then covering the foundations with some vines and shrubs. The solution was certainly a cheap stopgap that soon contributed to the final demolition of the remaining brickwork.[25] In an era of financial starvation the Park Service had taken the only logical course of action.[26]

The impression of desolation and neglect at Fort Laramie National Monument in Wyoming was particularly depressing during the 1940s. There were debates over the master plan for the fort area, and visitors from the Park Service headquarters made recommendations about the location of the museum.[27] As World War II ended, the staff at Fort Laramie outlined a series of research projects that would give all the necessary data for a full restoration and interpretive program.[28] In the meantime custodian Thor Borresen complained that he had no equipment to keep the grass cut or to maintain the buildings.[29] A reporter for the *Denver Post* visited Fort Laramie in the spring of 1949 and encountered a situation that seemed incredible for a National Monument that had been in the Park System for over a decade. "So far, it [National Monument status] is a change in name only. That Fort Laramie is such a bedraggled orphan among our national monuments—most of them of lesser historical importance—is not the fault of the Park Service. There was the war, remember, and now its aftermath. Park Service plans for Fort Laramie include repair and rehabilitation of the historical buildings, with exhibits and facilities as required by public use."[30]

In New York the Vanderbilt Mansion occupied a unique place in the Park Service picture because it continued to receive the special attention of the president throughout World War II, and it was closely tied to the development of the Home of Franklin D. Roosevelt National Historic Site following the president's death in 1945. In 1944 there was an abortive move to use the mansion itself as a hospital, but the structural problems were great enough to keep the building as a museum.[31] As soon as Secretary Ickes was free of the restraining influence of President Roosevelt, he set out to remove Mrs. Cooper as superintendent. She had been much too eager to use her friendship with Roosevelt in administrative matters, and that procedure had tended to upset the whole chain of command in the Park Service.[32]

The situation at the National Historic Sites that had come into the Park System through cooperative agreements was not much better than the grim standstill that characterized the federally owned historical areas. At San Jose Mission in San Antonio there was even a proposal to house army families in the reconstructed Indian quarters.[33] The Park Service officials had to point out that the installation of kitchens and bathrooms in the adobe buildings would completely negate the purposes of the Historic Sites Act.[34] Throughout the later 1940s regional archaeologist Erik Reed visited San Jose Mission periodically in order to see if a master plan could be developed.[35] The policies governing the development of the San Jose property soon began to come from an advisory board that had been set up in San Antonio for the purpose of helping with the restoration of the church.[36] The Park Service could not give out sums of money for much needed repairs in the 1940s, but the Washington office and the regional offices stood ready to offer professional advice.[37]

The patriotic concerns of the war years made the Carl Schurz Memorial Foundation, tenant at the Custom House in Philadelphia, a vulnerable target. In January 1944 the Internal Revenue Service suddenly withdrew the tax exemption granted to the Schurz Foundation, claiming that there had been past contacts with Nazi leaders. The foundation went to court and won a reversal of the IRS decision.[38] At the same time the foundation discovered that maintenance was an expensive proposition.[39] Newton Drury offered to let the American Philosophical Society occupy part of the building and thus get some rental income to pay for the running expenses, but nothing came of the proposal.[40] By the later 1940s George McAneny of New York became president of the Schurz Foundation and relationships with the Park Service improved remarkably, but no money came from the federal government to help with the Custom House.[41]

JEFFERSON NATIONAL EXPANSION MEMORIAL

Two historical areas received more attention than the others during the postwar years because important decisions had to be made, decisions that related to prewar commitments: Appomatox Court House and the Jefferson National Expansion Memorial. At the latter the differences between the development favored by Luther Ely Smith (the lawyer who had originated the memorial) and the plans worked out by the historical staff of the Park Service led to a number of confrontations. The same perplexing questions that had troubled the Park Service staff in the 1930s remained to be answered in 1941.

During the war the work for the memorial continued to keep the Museum Branch of the Park Service functioning. In 1941 Ronald Lee had transferred Ralph Lewis, the principal assistant to Ned Burns of the Museum Branch, to St. Louis as a staff historian. Lewis spent his time in the Old Courthouse profitably, as he planned exhibits that would go into the great new Museum of Westward Expansion.[42] He wisely concluded that the courthouse would be used for many years as the museum for the Jefferson Memorial, so he devoted a considerable amount of time working with the fur trade theme (favored by Carl Russell) and with the architectural fragments collected by Charles Peterson.[43]

The debate over the future of the whole memorial area came into focus during the last year of the war with two unusual proposals for using the open space on the riverfront. The Park Service and the Memorial Association had to make some hasty decisions. One scheme called for the creation of a small downtown airport, and the other involved opening a municipal parking lot. The discussions that were generated by these suggestions helped to reveal the gulf that existed between Luther Ely Smith and the Park Service officials. There simply had never been an agreement on the final development of the memorial. Herbert Kahler, acting as chief historian, told director Drury that the airport idea had been proposed by means of a letter to a St. Louis paper and that the mayor was really prepared to ask the Park Service for permission to install a landing strip on the vacant memorial site. Then Kahler noted that a principal highway was supposed to run along Third Street (which is the western edge of the park area). Kahler's report to Drury concluded with strong arguments against Smith's scheme for the great building that would come from the international competition:

> With the erection of the Thomas Jefferson Memorial in Washington, there is less need to construct a second memorial structure on a grand scale honoring the achievements of Thomas Jefferson. The need for a memorial to westward expansion still exists, but such memorialization can, I believe, be handled best through museum presentation. The Old Courthouse can be used to good advantage for the purpose. It is now the heart of the project and would increase in interest and usefulness as the museum advances. Most

of the land acquired could be transferred to the City of St. Louis without jeopardizing the project. Such a program is more in keeping with Service objectives than the erection of a monumental structure.[44]

Obviously "Service objectives" would not include a large memorial, and Kahler was convinced that the river bank had already been stripped of its major historical interest during the demolition program of 1939–40. It seemed logical to turn the whole thing over to the city of St. Louis as a park. Then the Park Service could concentrate on a manageable project that the historical staff could understand: the development of a museum in the Old Courthouse dedicated to westward expansion.

Kahler was not alone in his desire to free the Park Service of the memorial area with its attendant local problems. Charles W. Porter of the Branch of History wrote a long report in the fall of 1944 covering the purpose and theme of the memorial. He frankly stated that somehow the goals of the United States Territorial Expansion Memorial Commission had to be fitted in with the desire of the Park Service to develop the area as a National Historic Site. Porter believed that the job of interpreting the Louisiana Purchase was a challenging one. He proposed that the physical remains of the street plan be maintained as a historical exhibit and that a set of six or ten bronze memorials be placed around the riverfront park as interpretive devices. But he did not sympathize with the idea of a giant central building.[45]

Kahler went to St. Louis in January 1945 with Ned Burns of the Museum Branch and Tom Vint of the architectural staff to look into the final plans for the Jefferson National Expansion Memorial. He reported that the local situation in St. Louis was confusing. Each group had a different plan for treating the huge scar facing the Mississippi. Some wanted a museum complex, a few wanted a world's fair arrangement, and several hoped for a parking lot. The most difficult group to deal with proved to be Luther Ely Smith's association. Kahler said, "The lack of a clear objective is entirely understandable when it is realized that the project was sponsored by a group which had sketches ready for execution when the area was turned over to the Service."[46] Although the project had been originally accepted by President Roosevelt under the provisions of the Historic Sites Act, the group that worked with Smith held fast to the idea of a memorial.[47] Newton Drury himself reasoned that the debate would boil down to a problem in planning and that the final solution would reflect the wording of the title for the area, especially if the memorial was to become a "National Historic Site" instead of a "memorial."

The Branch of History never had a chance in the face of the skill and determination of Smith. Drury agreed in January 1946 to permit municipal parking temporarily on sections of the memorial area.[48] He also accepted the general terms of the architectural competition as outlined by the Jefferson National Expansion Memorial Association. But he pleaded with Smith to retain the courthouse, the cathedral, and the Old Rock House. Then the Park Service director tried to head off any development that might disfigure the historical area: "You will perhaps recollect that when I was in St. Louis I expressed to you my personal opinion that the architectural aspects of the Memorial should not unduly dominate it. This might result in subordination of the historical aspects, which are the justification for administration by the National Park Service."[49] That summer Drury insisted that the specifications for the competition require the Old Cathedral and the Old Rock House to be preserved *in situ* along with the development of a major museum.[50] The Park Service staff realized that it would have to work within Smith's overall scheme, but at the same time it must try to save the two remaining buildings inside the boundary of the memorial.[51] The Park Service also fought against any long-term provision for a large parking lot there.[52]

When the guidelines for the architectural competition appeared in June 1947, it was clear that Smith had been able to get his way again. The architects who hoped to prepare the drawings for the new memorial were warned that they must preserve the Old Cathedral and the Old Courthouse at all costs, but the "preservation of the Manuel Lisa Warehouse, generally known as the Old Rock House, is considered desirable but is not mandatory if its preservation is incompatible with the Competitor's conception of the appropriate development of the Historic Site."[53] The competitors were told that they could also ignore the old street plan. The park area had to include an open-air campfire theater and a group of museums (for the fur trade and architecture), and "small buildings typical of Old St. Louis, five in number, may be reerected and reproduced from documents in an appropriate group at some place on the Historic Site at the option of the Competitor."[54] The Memorial Association responded to the wishes of many St. Louisans in calling for the reconstruction of the old village. For example, on August 24, 1947, the *Post-Dispatch* asked for a reproduction of the first fur post at St. Louis in order to keep up with the work at Williamsburg and New Salem.[55] The Park Service administrators, including Ronald Lee himself, immediately issued a memo protesting the possible elimination of the Old Rock House in the competition specifications. They maintained that the old building was the principal remnant of the era of the fur trade in St.

Louis, and with its unusual basement, it stood as the only physical evidence of the rock ledge that made possible the creation of a flood-free dock area along the levee. Most important of all, the federal government had already expended money and time in restoring the little warehouse in order to turn it into a museum.[56]

Still Luther Ely Smith patiently pushed the Jefferson National Expansion Memorial along the road to completion, undaunted by the protests of the Park Service professionals. He must have been pleased when the association announced on February 18, 1948, that Eero Saarinen had been awarded the prize money for the most successful plan for the riverfront park. The winning design called for a stainless steel arch as the central feature with the Old Rock House nestled somewhat insecurely next to one of the legs.[57] The Saarinen drawing included a history museum, an architectural museum, the Old Cathedral, the proposed frontier village, a campfire theater, a tea pavilion, and a pair of riverview restaurants. It appears that the architect originally planned to use the Rock House as the entrance to the arch.[58] But superintendent Julian Spotts, who worked closely with Saarinen in St. Louis, urged him to avoid making the little building the entrance because the historic ledge behind would be disturbed.[59] The National Park Service gracefully accepted the basic plan and asked that the Memorial Association donate funds for preliminary surveys of the area to be developed.[60]

Other obstacles slowed down the final planning for the memorial: finances and the persistent problem of removing the Terminal Railroad's elevated tracks that ran along the riverfront.[61] The city of St. Louis still hoped for a large federal appropriation that had been more or less promised in the 1930s. The mayor proposed to Secretary of the Interior Julius Krug that a corporation be formed to pool the resources of the city government and the National Park Service in planning the development of the memorial area in line with the principles of good city planning. Krug retorted that he favored municipal administration of the whole project rather than any kind of joint effort; but once more the Park Service had to accommodate itself to the goals of the Jefferson National Expansion Memorial Association.[62] On December 6, 1949, director Drury and the mayor signed an agreement with the architect, with Smith, and with the representatives of two railroads for the removal of the elevated tracks. The compromise plan called for a tunnel that would be high enough to protect the railroads against flood damage. The agreement did remove the last major legal problem in the way of the full implementation of the memorial, while at the same time it doomed the Old Rock House, which stood in the way of the grading for the railroad tunnel.[63] In 1959 the little building was taken apart as the construction crew prepared the footings for the arch. Park Service officials pledged an eventual reconstruction, but that has never been carried out.[64]

The Department of the Interior could not deflect Smith from the completion of his original plans because the Park Service was always on the defensive. A writer for the *St. Louis Star-Times* described Smith's methods in a short sketch published on March 29, 1947. "The riverfront project remains his continuing passion. He envisions it as a thing of beauty and he pooh-poohs delays in the matter as things of small moment. Top people here still don't know how he talked the federal government into allotting $9,000,000 for the riverfront and agreeing further to spend $3 for every $1 for the city. But he did. Some say he did it as persistently as he orders 'hot apple pie hot on a hot plate hot.'"[65] Smith had always seen the scheme simply as an effort to clean up the riverfront and offer a great memorial building for the people of St. Louis. The use of the National Park Service and the Historic Sites Act had only been a case of finding a means to an end. The professional staff in St. Louis was well aware of the situation, but it persisted in its efforts to use the provisions of the Historic Sites Act to assist the cause of historic preservation.

The case of the Jean Baptiste Roy House (1832) further illustrates the way in which Smith and the Park Service staff worked in opposite directions. The encounter also shows something about the way in which Smith won every battle. In January 1947 (a year before the winner of the competition design was announced) John Albury Bryan, a St. Louis architect, warned superintendent Spotts that an old stone house had been discovered just south of the memorial area. "The National Park Service could hardly justify its refusal to accept and preserve the house when the whole legal basis for its having undertaken the St. Louis project is the Historic Sites Act of 1935. Much criticism has already been made of the seeming contradictory policy on the part of the Park Service in regard to old buildings in this city; and this proposal offers an opportunity to bolster our standing with the local organizations which have been our most reliable friends during more than a decade of controversy and delays."[66] Charles Peterson immediately entered the fray and put pressure on Spotts to accept the Roy House as a gift if a private individual could be found to pay for moving it into the park.[67] Peterson had discovered that the Manufacturers' Railway had purchased the Roy House site and fully intended to use the property for business purposes. The railway company was willing to have the house dismantled and moved. Roy had been an important figure in the fur trade and his home represented a small building type that had almost disappeared in St.

Jean Baptiste Roy House, St. Louis, 1940. (Photograph by Lester Jones, National Park Service)

Louis. Peterson remarked in his report that the house would be worth more to the Jefferson National Expansion Memorial than the Tempe Wick House had been to the Morristown National Historic Park.[68]

Within a week director Drury began exploring a scheme for extending the boundaries of the memorial to include the Roy House property, but he did not fully realize that the little building could not remain on its original foundations.[69] The officials at the headquarters of Region II of the Park Service urged Drury to approve the removal and reerection of the house inside the memorial area since the railroad intended to clear the site. They did not know that Drury was a purist on the subject of removal and reconstruction, that he had said plainly that in the case of the Lisa Warehouse he favored preservation of the house *in situ*.[70] Spotts, who was much closer to the situation, warned that if the Roy House were to be preserved on its foundation, it would be completely isolated from the memorial by a railroad cut.[71]

The real situation became more apparent in February when Hillory Tolson of the Park Service called Luther Ely Smith from the Chicago offices. A transcript of the conversation hints at Smith's attitude toward historic preservation whenever it tried to attach itself to his memorial scheme:

SMITH: We have been hearing a lot of rumors; there is a lot of excitement here in the public prints about the Jean Roy House, just south of our area. It's supposed to be an old French House where a fur trader lived and also a hot dog inventor. There is a rumor that somebody might make an effort to have the boundaries of our area extended to include it.

TOLSON: Well, that was in accordance with your wish, wasn't it?

SMITH: It was *not*! First I heard of it was recently here, and there is a railroad track on Poplar Street which is the southern boundary, and I had not heard anything about extending the area. It would involve I think a good many difficulties and should not be undertaken without a very mature consideration. My offhand reaction is that it would be a mistake.[72]

Quickly the Roy House proposal came to a standstill, as had every other preservation issue connected with the development of the JNEM. Drury still strongly favored saving the building on its original site.[73] Smith clearly opposed expanding the park to include the Roy property because the house would then be physically separated from the rest of the development. Charles Peterson worked away on a plan to collect private funds for moving the building into the memorial area. Once his idea came up, Smith retreated to a secondary position: He would prefer to see the Roy House saved on its own foundations rather than have it moved into the park before the winning design had been chosen.[74] This clever move helped to insure the destruction of the troublesome little house as long as the railroad was adamant about keeping the property for development purposes. Spotts admitted that he did not think the house would be much of an "asset" to the memorial on its original site or in reconstructed form on the park grounds.[75] The American Packing Company had indeed considered moving the building to Forest Park to serve as a hot dog "shrine," but that plan had also been abandoned.[76] By April the Roy House had been safely demolished after the publicity over the hot dog exhibit subsided.[77]

Once more the most elaborate project created under the provisions of the Historic Sites Act contributed to further destruction of the historical remains of the early nineteenth-century city of St. Louis. The Jefferson Memorial had never been a preservation project, and only two buildings within the area finally survived the landscape and grading operation that prepared the way for the construction of the Gateway Arch. The debates over the historical aspects of the new memorial had been

McLean House archaeology, 1941, Appomattox Court House, Va. (National Archives)

futile because the Park Service staff never could derail Luther Ely Smith's dream. By 1950 he had won his big battle for the design, and the only remaining challenges came in the area of finance. Smith had triumphed over all of the talented people who kept trying to save portions of old St. Louis. One of the few positive elements concerning the Jefferson National Expansion Memorial was the fact that the architects managed to give some professional advice, as in the case of the restoration of the Holy Family Church in Cahokia, Ill., in 1948 and 1949.[78]

APPOMATTOX COURT HOUSE

Newton Drury and his historical lieutenants at the Park Service faced another skirmish at the village of Appomattox Court House in Virginia. Ronald Lee had failed in 1940 to convince the local people that the government should not reconstruct the McLean House, where the surrender terms had been drawn up between Generals Grant and Lee. During World War II, while all construction activity had been stopped, Drury tried again to change the plans of the determined group of Virginians. But the proponents of home rule at Appomattox had two potent weapons that made their victory inevitable: excellent research plans for the reconstruction already prepared by the Park Service before the war and a continuing congressional appropriation that had been set aside in 1935 for the work.

In the face of these impressive odds Drury's conservatism led him to propose the stabilization of the foundations of the McLean House, a move that would avoid the pitfalls of rebuilding. Herbert Kahler, Thomas Vint (chief of planning), and senior architect Albert Good agreed with Drury. While Kahler liked the idea of having the building in the little village as an interpretive device for visitors, he was concerned with some liberties that had been taken in the reconstruction plans that had been prepared.[79] At a conference on April 13, 1943, these men officially decided "not to reconstruct the McLean House."[80] Arthur Demaray, the administrative watchdog of the Park Service, quickly sent a note to Drury, reminding him that the original $100,000 appropriation had been specifically earmarked for the reconstruction. If Drury's decision were to stand, Demaray warned, "we are headed for trouble with Senators Glass and Byrd, and the Virginia members of the House of Representatives."[81] A survey of the funds on hand from the original grant revealed that a $60,000 reserve had been kept intact for reproducing the McLean House.[82] Drury made a strategic retreat. He agreed that in view of the commitments that had been made there would indeed have to be a rebuilding of the house; but he refused to approve the plans that had been drawn for the work.[83] It was possible that the controversial reconstruction could be held up administratively for a few years, but there was no chance that the people of Appomattox Court House could be denied their new McLean House indefinitely.

Two questions still remained to be settled. (1) Would the whole village of Appomattox Court House be restored as "a typical county seat community that will illustrate the background of rural social and economic life of the seaboard states in pre-war days"? (2) Was the new McLean House going to be an exact replica of the original? Herbert Evison, the associate regional director, frankly expressed the idea that the reconstruction of the McLean House would be quite enough because the little crossroads town had no historical importance beyond the fact that Lee and Grant had finally met at that point in April 1865. It seemed

to Evison and a number of other officials that restoration and interpretation of the entire community would detract from the Civil War
theme.[84]

Just before World War II the National Park Service architects had
completed a plan for reproducing the McLean House, based on considerable archaeological and historical documentation—including the detailed plans of the house, made up in 1893 when it was torn down. The
historians of the Park Service, smarting under the inaccuracies encountered at Wakefield, were saddened to discover that the architects had
taken some liberties with the original dimensions in order to include a
heating system and a stronger frame than had existed in the original
building. Newton Drury sided with his historians and insisted on a re-
study of the McLean House drawings.[85] The regional director, Thomas
Allen, disagreed with the purists, maintaining that the verisimilitude
gained by bringing back the old dimensions would not be worth the
cost.[86]

Finally Drury approved the revised plans for the reconstruction
after he had sought the advice of Fiske Kimball of the Park Service Advisory Board.[87] He asked Kimball if it was important to aim at an exact
replica in all dimensions, and Kimball replied that he thought a fireproof
McLean House with adequate heat and water could be a few inches
larger than the original without seriously affecting the validity of the
reconstruction.[88] So the Park Service finally hired the firm of C. W. Han-
cock and Son of Lynchburg, Va., to rebuild the house—the contractors
who had dismantled the little building half a century before.[89]

On April 16, 1950, Drury went to Appomattox Court House to
help dedicate the McLean House. He gave a thoughtful speech in which
he bluntly admitted that the Park Service had viewed the reconstruction
"with some misgiving." Drury confessed that he had been concerned
whether the copy would be authentic, but he could finally refer to the
operation with real pride as a "model Service project." The combined
talents of the professional staff of the Washington and Richmond offices
had put together enough data to insure one of the most careful reconstructions that had ever been done. The new McLean House even contained over five thousand bricks that had been stacked up when the original house was torn down.[90] The National Park Service had been forced
to develop a historical area in a way that pleased the local interests—but
the result also seemed to satisfy the historians, archaeologists, and architects who had participated in the numberless planning sessions all
through the 1940s. Undoubtedly the work would not have been possible
without the prewar funding and research.

NEW PROJECTS

The Park Service did take on a few new historical projects during the war years, but they fitted into the narrow category of "exceptional cases" that President Roosevelt referred to in his March 28, 1942, letter to Secretary Ickes. The remaining staff members of the Branch of History had to decide in each instance whether they were dealing with sites that possessed special merit—and then they had to guide the most promising proposals through the top-heavy bureaucracy of a war-weary Washington.

Touro Synagogue

The first of these high-priority sites came to the attention of the Park Service offices by means of an unusual suggestion advanced by Arthur Hays Sulzberger, publisher of the *New York Times*. In the winter of 1944 Sulzberger told Harold Ickes that he thought the National Park Service should create a historic church advisory board to help select and set aside one Protestant church, one Roman Catholic church, and one Jewish synagogue as evidence of American religious unity during World War II. Ickes immediately put his staff to work on the idea.[91] Francis Ronalds of Morristown National Historical Park went to Newport, R.I., to see Touro Synagogue (1763), and he also visited St. Paul's Church in Eastchester, N.Y. (1763–90), with Sulzberger.[92]

Unfortunately, Sulzberger's scheme proved to be more cumbersome than any arrangement the Park Service had worked out up to that point. His proposal called for a self-perpetuating board set up by an act of Congress to memorialize two churches and a synagogue in the original 13 colonies.[93] The Park Service personnel were more concerned about the historical and architectural importance of each religious edifice than they were in finding a formula that would give each major religious group equal representation in the field of historic preservation.[94]

The Advisory Board of the Park Service evaluated Touro Synagogue at its meeting in March 1945. Fiske Kimball quickly backed the nomination with the highest compliment he could pay: "It is one of the finest surviving examples of Colonial architecture in America." It was also the oldest synagogue still standing in the United States.[95] Herbert Kahler, who attended the meeting as chief historian, told Charles Porter that the historians should draft a letter from Secretary Ickes to the president pointing out that the synagogue was an "exceptional case."[96] Quickly the note went out with Ickes's signature, informing President

Touro Synagogue, Newport, R.I. (Photograph by Jack Boucher, National Park Service)

Roosevelt that Arthur Hays Sulzberger was behind the proposal.[97] A favorable reply came on April 19, bearing the signature of the new president, Harry Truman. Immediately acting director Hillory Tolson informed Francis Ronalds (who was the regular National Park Service emissary to prominent New Yorkers) that he could contact Sulzberger and draft a cooperative agreement that would make Touro Synagogue a National Historic Site.[98]

Sulzberger was delighted that the president was willing to grant special recognition to Touro Synagogue, but the publisher of the *New York Times* still wanted to set up a board that would commemorate the whole concept of religious freedom in the United States.[99] Ickes argued that the designation of San Jose Mission in Texas and the recognition of Gloria Dei Church in Philadelphia took care of the other major religious groups. There was no need for a board that looked for historic churches.[100] But Sulzberger would not be set aside easily. He had wanted a Catholic edifice within the area that had been the original 13 colonies—and that narrowed the field to an old church in Leonardtown, Md.[101] Ickes checked with his staff and concluded that the building in question, the Church of St. Francis Xavier (1766), did not possess true national significance in the same sense as Touro Synagogue and was undistinguished architecturally.[102] By 1945 the historians had concluded that additions to the Park System should possess considerable historical and architectural qualifications, including a high proportion of surviving original features.

The Park Service succeeded in negotiating a cooperative agreement with two Hebrew congregations—the Newport group (Congregation Jeshuat Israel), who used Touro Synagogue, and Congregation Shearith Israel in New York, owner of the property.[103] The designation of the synagogue as a National Historic Site came on March 5, 1946.[104] Superintendent Edwin Small of Salem Maritime National Historic Site began making annual visits to Newport to inspect Touro. He urged the local congregation and the Newport Historical Society to form an organization pledged to the maintenance of the property.[105] By the winter of 1948 Bernard C. Friedman, president of the synagogue, had organized the Society of Friends of Touro Synagogue National Historic Shrine.[106] Small also tried to convince the officials of the synagogue that they were going to have to extend the open hours for the building in order to take advantage of the heavy influx of summer visitors.[107] Everyone seemed to be happy because the little building had received federal recognition without a change in ownership.

Adams Mansion

The second special case had nothing to do with national unity and the war effort. On January 5, 1945, Congressman Richard Wigglesworth of Massachusetts wrote to Newton Drury in Chicago, asking if the United States government would be interested in accepting the Adams House (1731) in Quincy, Mass.[108] The homestead had been open to the public for more than a decade under the auspices of the Adams Memorial Society, comprised of twenty-two direct descendents of John Adams, second president of the United States. The active trustees of the society were two elderly members of the family who feared that "there was no one after them who really cared for the place as they did." Henry Adams II and Charles Francis Adams "were afraid there might be some danger that the house be sold and its contents disbursed after their deaths."[109]

For the second time in the history of the National Park Service a staff historian took the initiative. Roy Appleman had been the agent in setting aside Hopewell Village as a National Historic Site because it happened to be located in a Federal Recreation Demonstration Area. Charles W. Porter III now became the principal savior of the Adams Mansion as he set out to convince everyone that a most "exceptional case" had come before the Department of the Interior. Porter was located in the Chicago office where he could work closely with Drury during the crucial winter of 1945. Porter informed his colleague Herbert Kahler that he was going to push hard for the house in Quincy: "I think we should go all out to acquire this property, which includes the famous Adams Library of 10,000 volumes. I have prepared three letters, one to Congressman Wigglesworth, one to Secretary Ickes, and one to the President through the Bureau of the Budget."[110]

Porter did indeed "go all out" in his effort to assist the Adams family in turning over the old house with its splendid furnishings. He remembered the tense moments he experienced in Chicago at that time:

The question came up: what should we do. The Director of the Park Service, Newton B. Drury, was in a very bad financial bind because all Federal monies were being poured into the war effort and Park Service appropriations were ridiculously low, so when this letter came in from Wigglesworth offering us the Adams Mansion at Quincy, the Director of the Park Service was minded to say "no." Well, I think I can fairly say that it was my determination to have it that got it into the National Park System. And I argued with Newton Drury day after day long and hard, and finally Newton Drury broke down and said, "Well, if a Virginian can argue that hard for a place in

Adams Mansion, Quincy, Mass. (Photograph by Fasch Studio; National Park Service)

Massachusetts, I think maybe we ought to have it." And from then on I had clear sailing. I wrote letters which got around the stop order against the acquisition of any new areas.[111]

The letters drafted by Porter worked exactly as planned. Drury, pleading with Ickes to intercede with President Roosevelt on the Adams Mansion, said that it was an "exceptional" house because it was "undoubtedly one of the most historic in New England."[112] Another ally in Porter's battle, Edwin Small in Boston, referred to the proposed gift in glowing terms as "the most important house in New England and very likely unsurpassed elsewhere in the country."[113] Ickes dutifully asked Roosevelt to authorize the acquisition, and the tired president (who had just returned from his journey to the Crimea) signed the order on March 9, 1945.[114] The negotiations with Charles Francis Adams were not especially difficult, even when the discussions turned to touchy questions such as the disposition of the original furnishings and the contents of the library.[115]

All of the people who reported to Newton Drury spoke about the Adams Mansion in terms that bordered on the superlative. Waldo Leland, chairman of the Advisory Board, thought that the house would undoubtedly prove to be one of the "most important and precious acquisitions" of the National Park Service. He was struck by the great sense of continuity that a visitor gained by seeing the furnishings and architectural adornments left in the house by four successive generations of a prominent family.[116] Francis Ronalds, who went up from Morristown to inspect the building with the Adams family representatives, could not restrain his enthusiasm. He unhesitatingly referred to the house as possessing a historical integrity that was unique in America; and his glowing comments to Drury went on for five pages.[117] No other home offered to the Park Service during the war era won such universal acclaim. Once the negotiations over the furnishings had been completed in the fall of 1946, director Drury recommended the designation of Adams Mansion National Historic Site.[118]

The Adams Mansion was the only property that came into the Park System without long debates and some substantial push from an outside agency. Drury referred to the board as "a sort of sounding board" and "a valuable ally and a sort of buffer on occasion,"[119] and the Advisory Board did fulfill these various roles during the later 1940s. Acting director Hillory Tolson admitted in 1946 that he used the board to pass judgment on all sites, "even those of dubious value" if the recommendations came from members of Congress.[120]

Deshler-Morris House

One such instance was in 1948 when the Deshler-Morris House (1772) in Germantown, Pa., came up for consideration. The building had some historical interest because it had served as the summer residence for George Washington several times during his presidency in the 1790s. Marriott C. Morris had included in his will a codicil that called for the donation of the property to the federal government. But Newton Drury was skeptical about the proposed gift, so he asked Fiske Kimball to comment on its value.[121] Kimball believed that the Morris House might possess national historical significance and it had the added advantage of being "one of the finest examples of the characteristic roadside Germantown houses."[122] This assessment was neutral enough to make it necessary to consult the entire Advisory Board, especially at a time of great financial hardship for the National Park System. Regional historian Appleman could not see any "sound basis" for acquiring the house when there were so many memorials already set aside to commemorate Washington's career. Appleman was more than willing to see the house in the hands of a local historical or patriotic society.[123] Francis Ronalds went to see the place and proposed that it become a part of the new Independence National Historic Park by means of a cooperative agreement with the Germantown Historical Society.[124] The Historical Society officially requested an arrangement of the type proposed by Ronalds, perhaps following the model of the Carl Schurz Memorial Foundation.[125]

In April 1948 the Advisory Board formally reviewed the case of the Deshler-Morris House and performed its function as a buffer in a most interesting way. The august advisers of the secretary of the interior concluded that the house did indeed possess national significance, but "in view of the heavy burden of maintenance facing the National Park Service at the present time, the Board does not recommend Federal ownership of the property."[126] Armed with this statement Drury broke the news to Congressman Hugh Scott of Pennsylvania, a proponent of the Germantown house. Drury outlined the grim facts about the minuscule appropriations that had been voted for the Park Service, and he expressed his sincere hope that the Germantown Historical Society would quickly take over the property.[127] Although the written offer from the Morris family had not yet come in, the Park Service would soon find itself in the strange position of turning down a nationally important building.[128]

The situation changed radically when some members of Congress took the initiative. In May, Congressman Ben F. Jensen, with the cooperation of Scott, introduced an amendment to the Interior Department appropriations bill that included the sum of $15,000 for the maintenance of the Morris House. Thanks to Scott's strong support the bill passed with the amendment intact, and then the onus for the decision regarding the house lay completely with the officials of the National Park Service. Drury almost *had* to accept the property when it was offered by Elliston P. Morris as a memorial to Elizabeth and Marriott C. Morris. Drury's lack of enthusiasm is clear from the tone of his note to Secretary of the Interior Krug:

> We are hard put to take care of far more important structures, or to obtain additional funds for them, but in view of the action of the Congress in appropriating $15,000 for the administration and maintenance of the Perot-Morris House for the 1949 fiscal year, I feel that I should recommend that the Perot-Morris House be accepted as a part of Independence National Historical Park, pursuant to Public Law 795, 80th Congress. This will not entail its establishment as a distinct national historic site. Efforts will be made to obtain a cooperating agency to assist in, or to take over, the display and maintenance of the Perot-Morris House.[129]

Within a month the Park Service had begun negotiations with the Germantown Historical Society in hopes that a contract could be worked out that would relieve the government of financial responsibility for the Morris House.[130] The ratification of the new agreement freed the Park Service to expend all of the money voted by Congress on necessary repairs and remodeling operations at the Germantown property.[131]

No doubt Newton Drury would have preferred to develop a project like Harpers Ferry, a proposed National Monument that still seemed a long way from establishment. Congress passed a bill in 1944 that authorized the secretary of the interior to accept land around the West Virginia town in order to commemorate events that immediately followed John Brown's famous raid.[132] The challenge at Harpers Ferry remained the same—there was no money to cover the costs of the necessary land acquisition, and the local communities in Maryland, Virginia, and West Virginia could not handle the proposition. The president of the Washington County Historical Society in Hagerstown, Md., referred to her organization as a "most obscure Historical Society" that was already saddled with the restoration of one old house.[133] Congressman Jennings Randolph continued to push for the Harpers Ferry Monument, but he had to work closely with people in the West Virginia legislature in hopes of getting appropriations.[134] In 1950 the necessary land-purchase program still was not carried out.[135] It was no wonder that Drury was not happy about spending money on a house in Germantown. A dangerous precedent was involved in the Morris House designation, because the wishes of the National Park Service Advisory Board and the director had been thwarted by an act of Congress.

Surplus Forts

Neither the board nor Drury was being unduly cautious in this unwillingness to accept the Morris House. The Park Service had to fight off many requests from agencies that favored the creation of new National Historic Sites. In 1948 the problem intensified as the War Department declared a number of military posts surplus property. Soon committees and organizations all over the United States stood ready to pressure the Park Service and members of Congress with regard to each of these old forts. Ronald Lee, who had rejoined the Park Service in 1946 as chief historian, later described the challenge: "The War Department declared surplus a considerable number of historic forts. In the first place, many of these forts were of significant historical interest, but not enough to justify making them national monuments. On the other hand, it seemed to many people to be a great shame if they were lost. We were concerned about that as a broad general problem all over the country. There was Fort Wayne in Detroit. They were even talking about selling Fort Sumter in Charleston Harbor. There were some heated speeches made on the floor of the House and Senate about the subject."[136] The Advisory Board tried to head off a major crisis at its April 1948 meeting. It was possible that some important installations might be lost if state and local agencies were not encouraged to take them over, but there was also the danger that Congress might force the overburdened Park Service to accept some historic sites that would not measure up to the high standards being set by the Department of the Interior. During the 1930s a number of military posts had been studied as part of the national survey, so it was easy for the board to set up a list of criteria governing the evaluation of forts. In order to be judged nationally significant each surplus property had to possess the all-important mixture of historical significance, a high proportion of surviving historic buildings, and accessibility for the visiting public.[137] Although the Park Service found that only Fort Sumter met the rigorous standards set by the Advisory Board, a number of other posts did come under the control of local governmental units. It must be remembered that Congress always had the power to force the Park Service to take over sites that the Advisory Board had turned down. This danger made it imperative that the surplus sites be disposed of successfully within a reasonable amount of time and that local historical groups be given some assistance whenever possible.

The case of Jefferson Barracks (1826) in St. Louis County, Mo., serves to illustrate the way in which the National Park Service had to work to save military installations that did not come up to the exacting criteria. The old fort had been the first permanent military post west of the Mississippi, and it played a key role in conquering the West. In the 1930s, when the Jefferson National Expansion Memorial first began to take form, some people proposed that Jefferson Barracks might be made a part of the new riverfront scheme with regular boat service connecting the two areas. But the idea never came close to implementation as long as Luther Ely Smith and his association centered their attention on the development of the old levee district.[138] In March 1948 the War Department announced that Jefferson Barracks would be declared surplus property. Immediately a group of St. Louisans formed a Jefferson Barracks National Park Committee with P. Donald Fisher, the commander of a St. Louis chapter of the Disabled American Veterans, as its secretary-treasurer. Newton Drury was thoroughly alarmed after a visit from Fisher, whom he had warned that Jefferson Barracks would probably not qualify as a National Park. As a precaution Drury immediately asked the regional director in Omaha to contact the proper state authorities in Jefferson City to see if Missouri would be interested in taking over the barracks area as a state park.[139] Fisher apparently did not understand clearly what the director had told him, and he could not resist telling Drury that more and more organizations (including the Missouri House of Representatives) had passed resolutions endorsing the idea of a National Park. Drury wrote in the margin of Fisher's effusive letter, "Told Mr. Fisher plainly that we would not recommend a national park or monument."[140]

The pressure from the St. Louis group continued to mount as Fisher contacted President Truman's office in an effort to get a fellow Missourian to support National Park status for the barracks. The threat had become real enough to get Secretary of the Interior Krug to write Truman's secretary about the significance of Jefferson Barracks as a historic spot with local interest. Charles Porter, who drafted Krug's letter, noted that it was "unlikely" that the property would qualify as a National Historic Site because the Park Service could only accept areas "of supreme national importance."[141] A St. Louis delegation came to Washington in July to discuss the possible use of portions of the barracks property for recreational purposes and the preservation of the oldest parts as a historic park.[142] The visitors from Missouri informed the Park Service officials that St. Louis County (rather than the state) might want to save some of the barracks area.[143] At the same time Fisher's organization began to bombard different members of the Missouri delegation in the House and Senate with requests that Jefferson Barracks be set aside as a National Monument no matter what the Park Service might say. Ronald Lee managed to talk to a number of congressional staff members about his preference for county administration of the barracks.[144]

The Park Service did everything it could to assist the officials of St. Louis County in their efforts to make application to the War Assets Administration for the preservation of about one hundred acres of the original part of Jefferson Barracks.[145] The Service even helped the county officials draw up historical background statements and survey maps for the application forms.[146] Eventually the transfer of the barracks to St. Louis County in 1950 proved the efficacy of the research and planning done by the Park Service staff, but it had been accomplished under the threat of a possible act of Congress or a presidential order to force the secretary of the interior to take the barracks against the wishes of his Advisory Board and the Branch of History.

Shirley-Eustis House

Once the Branch of History and the Advisory Board realized the funding restrictions brought by the national war effort, they became more and more cautious. They managed to avoid taking over several questionable historic properties that individuals and groups had eagerly offered to the federal government. It is probable that even reasonably worthwhile sites stood no chance of acceptance during the war years, especially after the president had put a moratorium on all survey and research activity for acquisitions. The staff of the Branch of History gradually learned how to head off unwanted acts of Congress and presidential proclamations, even when the preservation groups outside of the Park Service were persistent in their campaigns.

William Sumner Appleton, the arch foe of federal preservation programs, took up the fight for a house he desperately wanted to save. In 1912 he had taken over the Shirley-Eustis House (the 1747 home of a colonial governor, in Roxbury, Mass.) and then created an association that managed to keep the structure more or less intact for about thirty years. Evidently Appleton thought he saw a chance in 1942 to turn the house over to the National Park Service through a cooperative agreement with the Colonial Dames. However, the Massachusetts Society of the Colonial Dames of America had different ideas from Appleton's on the final solution to the preservation of the Shirley place. Mary Caner issued a booklet in 1941 that proposed the removal of the house to a new site on the Boston Fenway, "there being nothing to recommend its present location."[147]

Mrs. Charles S. Hamlin, acting on instructions from Appleton, asked President Roosevelt to intercede personally with the Department

Shirley-Eustis House, Roxbury, Mass. (SPNEA)

of the Interior in order to save the house. The president asked Secretary Ickes to consider the restoration of the house as a postwar project. The president argued, "The only cost to the Government would be the protection of the house in the meantime."[148] Ickes reported to Roosevelt that the Advisory Board had already found that the Shirley-Eustis House possessed sufficient historical significance to become a National Historic Site, and if an agreement could be worked out with the Shirley-Eustis House Association for exhibiting the building throughout the war period, it would be possible for the government to restore the house later on (providing more land had been acquired).[149]

Appleton wrote to Newton Drury informing him that the Colonial Dames should be the organization to negotiate the cooperative agreement with the National Park Service, and he included the specific provisions regarding the care of the house. Appleton bluntly stated that his long-term goal was to return the Shirley mansion to its original site in Roxbury (which was about fifty feet away from where it stood then). He admitted that the smallness of the lot had been a great obstacle to the organizations that had shown any interest in the house.[150] Laurence B. Fletcher of the Trustees of Public Reservations asked Drury to come to Boston to look at the house in its slum setting. He believed that the director might be willing to push for federal preservation if the Colonial Dames made a gift of the house.[151] Drury had to warn Fletcher that the government almost never appropriated funds for land acquisition.[152] Drury undoubtedly realized as he studied the correspondence from Boston that the Shirley-Eustis House Association and the Colonial Dames were at odds over the issue of moving the house and that as long as the friends of the house could not unite on a plan of action, there was no hope of arriving at a successful agreement.[153] He finally took a stand that satisfied neither of the groups in Boston: The Shirley-Eustis House should not be under federal ownership. In a letter to Francis Ronalds in Morristown, Drury announced his decision and then briefly defended the cooperative agreements that had already been worked out with organizations that maintained churches and public buildings.[154] The impasse in Boston continued and made it impossible for the Park Service to take over the property even after the war was over.[155]

St. Ann's Church

Several times during the war years the staff of the National Park Service and the Advisory Board came under fire because of their unwillingness to grant National Historic Site status to places that did not possess national significance. The case of St. Ann's Church of Morrisania (1841), in the borough of the Bronx, N.Y., is a good example. The proponents of this church may well have brought more organized pressure to bear on the secretary of the interior and his Advisory Board than the supporters of any other unsuccessful proposal to come before the Park Service under the terms of the Historic Sites Act. The church of St. Ann's became a pet project for a number of patriotic and veterans organizations in the Bronx, including the American Legion. The rector of the parish, E. C. Russell, was especially eager to see his church given the same recognition that had been granted to Touro Synagogue in Newport.

The nagging problem with St. Ann's did not have much to do with cost or authenticity. The church property contained the tombs of a number of members of the famous Morris family, including one signer of the Declaration of Independence and Gouverneur Morris, the "penman" of the United States Constitution.[156] Talbot Hamlin, the architectural historian at Columbia University, informed Francis Ronalds that the church itself, which dated from the 1840s, was "a charming example of rather naive provincial work" that added something to an otherwise dreary area in the Bronx.[157] But the Park Service historians and the Advisory Board steadfastly refused to dignify the tombs of famous people with National Historic Site status.

The persistence of Russell and some members of Congress quickly forced the Park Service staff to erect defensive roadblocks. The first logical delaying strategy was a simple one: The restrictive war budgets made it necessary to defer all research studies for historic sites until peacetime.[158] But as soon as the war ended, Russell began pushing members of Congress who then put pressure on Secretary Ickes and his staff.[159] In the summer of 1946 Ronalds visited Russell and found that the whole proposal rested on the presence of the Morris tombs.[160] After that report, it was natural that the Advisory Board at its meeting on October 21, 1946, declined to accept any form of national recognition for St. Ann's Church because it had no connection with people who had fought in the Revolution and did not possess "sufficient architectural merit."[161] The illustrious members of the board may not have realized that their carefully worded motion would only serve to stir up fires among the patriots in the Bronx.

A host of angry letters followed, reflecting a broad base of interest in the little church, although most of the correspondents did not seem to understand fully why the board had been so definite in its judgment. Congressman Walter Lynch told the Department of the Interior that he had been taken to visit St. Ann's as a schoolboy. He said, "If this is not an historic site, I am afraid that I have no real conception of the term."[162] The chairman of a Bronx committee that supported the nomination made it clear by means of a telegram that historical significance of the church building had never been raised as an issue by the supporters of St. Ann's; it was those sacred graves that meant so much. The New Yorker referred to the recent designations of Touro Synagogue and Castle Clinton as nationally significant, and he thought that the final resting place of the penman of the Constitution certainly ranked above the other two sites.[163] Russell told Interior officials that even President Roosevelt had hoped that St. Ann's would receive some kind of recognition—and he volunteered to come to Washington any time to testify with regard to his church.[164] The more Russell thought about the Advisory Board action, the angrier he became. He finally wrote Assistant Secretary of the Interior Davidson:

> Many people are asking me, what is the personnel of this Advisory Board; and if it is not a secret of the Dept. of the Interior, we would like to know the names of the distinguished members of the same. Its most un-American findings in the matter of St. Ann's and the historical personages buried here, repudiating its distinguished Founding Fathers as people of scant national importance, is so flagrant that it causes any intelligent American to wonder why the whole matter cannot be brought out into the open and dealt with in the democratic American way of life. . . . Of recent date, the little Synagogue in Rhode Island, was made a National Site. As far as I can learn, this esteemed Synagogue, of very unpretentious appearance, dates back to Revolutionary days, and as far as I know, is not the resting place of any noted American connected with the history of our country. Shortly afterwards, Congressman Solomon Bloom, put through a bill in Washington, making the Aquarium a National Site; based on the fact that in its early history it was Ft. Clinton, where never a shot was fired or any revolutionary engagement took place. . . . These two samples of National Sites certainly cannot claim the galaxy of Founding Fathers buried at St. Ann's, whose ashes consecrate this place as a national spot.[165]

Arthur Demaray immediately sent Russell a list of the members of the Advisory Board with a note that politely pointed out that the National Park Service could not possibly study and mark all of the sites connected with the careers of the people who wrote the Declaration of Independence and the Constitution.[166] The attack on the Advisory Board had been unfair, because the designation of Touro Synagogue had been based largely on architectural criteria, and the board never had a chance to discuss Castle Clinton to any extent before Congress chose to make it a National Historic Site.

It was obvious that the board would have to reconsider the historical value of St. Ann's and make a general statement on the status of graves of important people. Russell kept up an almost constant barrage of letters that quoted individuals who had been impressed by the sacred memories enshrined at St. Ann's.[167] Finally, at a meeting in April 1948, the board made a second statement on the Bronx church:

> The Advisory Board recognizes that the graves of persons who have had an important part in forming the history of the United States are of public interest and hopes that they may be suitably marked and maintained under appropriate auspices, but the number of such graves is so great that, in view of the severely limited funds at the disposal of the National Park Service, it is impossible for it to mark and maintain more than a very few of them and these must of necessity be limited to those historical figures of transcendant importance. Accordingly, the Advisory Board does not recommend that the graves of Gouverneur Morris and Lewis Morris should be marked or maintained by the National Park Service.[168]

The proponents of St. Ann's found the new decision "amazing" because it implied that Gouverneur Morris lacked historical importance.[169] Unfortunately, the board had not made sufficiently clear what the financial problem really was. Under Secretary of the Interior, Oscar Chapman, informed Congressman Lynch that the National Park Service had been given $3 million less than was needed for minimal maintenance of the existing historical and natural areas in the Park System.[170] The Park Service could not afford to assign its professional staff to any survey work that involved historic graveyards when studies had to be made on structures that were already under the care of the Department of the Interior.

Russell gave up his attempts to get Interior to reverse its stand. Instead he turned to President Truman and urged him to take advantage of a crucial election year to make the people of New York happy by proclaiming St. Ann's a National Historic Site.[171] Newton Drury had tried to tell the irate clergyman that the expense of "orderly evaluation" of all the historic places that came before the Advisory Board would be staggering, but Drury was dealing with sincere patriots who viewed the whole board mechanism as a roadblock.[172] In February 1949 a local newspaper in New York reported that some youthful vandals had desecrated the Morris crypt at St. Ann's—and that the evasive National Park Service should share the blame for this outrageous act. The "repeated refusals to designate St. Ann's a shrine" had meant that no government funds could be used to assure the safety of the Morris tombs.[173] But the Department of the Interior stood behind its Advisory Board and maintained to the last that the preservation of the historic graveyard was primarily a local matter.[174] The amazing aspect of this episode is that the staff of the Park Service stood its ground in the face of the most concerted pressure that had been exerted over a long period of time. Ronald Lee, who had taken over again as chief historian, commented, "I don't know how many letters we wrote saying the same thing to the same people, too, year after year."[175]

Alexander Majors House

At times the Department of the Interior had to find ways to work with the president himself if a site happened to be familiar to him. During the late 1930s Franklin Roosevelt had been deeply interested in historic sites around Hyde Park. And Harry Truman had some concern for places around Kansas City that illustrated different facets of the Westward Movement. Before Truman became president in 1945, the Park Service had been studying ways to commemorate the Pony Express as a part of the history of transportation, and that research had brought the historical staff out to look over the Alexander Majors House in Kansas City. A Senate motion (introduced by Truman as a senator) called for the creation of a Russell-Majors-Waddell National Monument to honor the men who had formed the Pony Express. The question remained— was the Majors home the best place in the United States to memorialize the mail riders?[176] Secretary Ickes thought it might not be, and he outlined his reasons in a letter to President Truman in February 1946. Ickes urged as an alternative the preservation of a Pony Express depot, such as the station at Fort Laramie. The Majors House was fairly large and in need of considerable repair. On top of that, Alexander Majors had lived in the house no more than two years.[177]

Apparently Truman was not especially interested in the Majors House, and the Department of the Interior succeeded in convincing some members of Congress that the purchase and restoration of the property would be unnecessarily expensive.[178] In the spring of 1947 the department notified the Committee on Public Lands of the House of Representatives that exhibiting the Majors House would not be the most effective way to illustrate the contribution of the Pony Express to the development of transportation.[179] That report seemed to end the issue, and the bill calling for creation of a National Monument did not pass the House that year.

Shadwell

In August 1945 a group of people who wanted to preserve the site of Shadwell (1735, burned 1770) four miles east of Charlottesville, Va., where Thomas Jefferson was born, asked President Truman to endorse its plan. Director Drury turned to Fiske Kimball for advice on the stand the president should take with regard to the Shadwell invitation.[180] Kimball quickly answered that the Thomas Jefferson Birthplace Memorial Park Commission had purchased the site and he himself had excavated the foundations in 1942. But Kimball added that the commission hoped to reconstruct the house, a course of action that he definitely opposed.[181] Hillory Tolson of the Park Service polled the members of the Advisory Board on the same question, adding that having the president approve the work at Shadwell would ultimately increase the chances of the area becoming a National Historic Site.[182] On September 20, 1945, the Department of the Interior officially notified the White House staff that it was appropriate for the president to lend his name to the Shadwell operation as long as he stated that he did not favor "conjectural restoration" of the missing buildings.[183]

About four years later, after a successful campaign to complete the purchase of the site, the Thomas Jefferson Birthplace Commission sought the advice of the Park Service on a possible reconstruction of the main building.[184] Charles Porter of the Branch of History saw the request: "These people are exactly where the Wakefield Association was in 1926–1930. They may be presumed to own the birthplace, but have they dug it up? No 18th century stuff was found in the foundations uncovered by Fiske Kimball!!! Fiske plausibly explains this; but there remains the good chance that the real foundations are only 60 or 75 feet away and carry the correct ground plan of the birthplace house. Ergo—more archaeology is in order."[185] Naturally the Park Service offered to help, especially if all the research reports could be shared with the staff that would review the work.[186] The commission had consulted Kimball, and he had recommended that a simple shelter be erected over the old foundations. On that condition he accepted the idea of reconstructing a house fairly near the Shadwell foundations.[187] The Park Service historical staff urged that the construction work be done slowly so that historical and archaeological research could continue as long as possible.[188] Even if Congress starved the National Park Service when the appropriation bills came up, the Branch of History wanted to influence the field of historic preservation in the direction of authenticity whenever the opportunity presented itself.

Rebuilding the White House

There was one elaborate restoration project that the federal government carried out in the late 1940s that was not in any significant way influenced by the National Park Service: the rebuilding of the White House. During the fall of 1948 President Truman noticed that there were disturbing evidences of structural decay throughout the Executive Mansion, including sagging floors and ceilings. The First Family decided to move across Pennsylvania Avenue to Blair House (purchased for State Department use in 1942), and they lived there through most of Harry Truman's second term in office. At first no one could tell how serious the situation was, but competent engineers estimated that it could take as much as $1 million to make the White House stable and fireproof.[189]

Several important decisions had to be made early in 1949 with regard to the treatment of the nation's most famous public building. Would the exterior walls be permitted to stand, or should the whole structure be replaced? Would there be a special commission to oversee the renovation? Would there be a massive sale of souvenirs of debris left by the structural work done on the interior? Initial reports in the *New York Times* were written on the assumption that the mansion would be repaired, rather than removed.[190] Truman shocked some of his former colleagues in Congress in February when he made a request for about $5 million "to rebuild" the White House.[191] The president quickly noted: "It perhaps would be more economical from a purely financial standpoint to raze the building and to rebuild completely. In so doing, however, there would be destroyed a building of tremendous historical significance in the growth of our nation. I am in favor of preserving our outstanding historical structures."[192] Also in February, W. E. Reynolds, commissioner of public buildings, issued a detailed account of all the various expensive structural problems that had been found in the much repaired Executive Mansion. The Reynolds report estimated that the difficult hand labor that would be required might well run the costs of repair up to $5,412,000. Curiously enough, Reynolds absolutely ruled out any consideration of tearing down the White House and starting over with a new building. He admitted that renovation would cost more, but the demolition might trespass "upon the domains of national pride, sentiment and tradition."[193] Quickly several senators introduced a bill that specified that neither the interior room arrangement nor the exterior walls of the building could be changed.[194]

Truman saw the need for a special commission to oversee the project. He recommended that Congress set up a panel from its own membership.[195] Eventually the legislators established a Commission on Renovation of the Executive Mansion chaired by Sen. Kenneth McKellar. The group included two senators, two members of the House, and two private citizens appointed by the president.[196]

As soon as the $5.4 million appropriation came up for debate in

Congress, there were battles over the renovation.[197] Congressman Clarence Cannon proposed that the old White House be replaced by a building that would be made of steel, bronze, and marble, "that would last as long as the pyramids." He maintained that the old sandstone walls would probably not last another fifty years.[198] Sen. John Sparkman rejected the idea of demolishing the mansion completely, but he recommended that the architects consider rebuilding the interior in a way that would make it "resist atomic bombs."[199] Both Bess Truman and Eleanor Roosevelt quickly spoke out in favor of retention of the old walls.[200] The Senate Appropriations Committee approved a bill that called for the original room arrangement on the first floor and the same outside "appearance."[201]

On June 3, 1949, the Commission on the Renovation of the Executive Mansion held its preliminary meeting, and newspaper reporters detected an ominous note of discord in the proceedings. "It was reported that not all the members of the commission agreed that the present exterior should be preserved, which President Truman desires."[202] The House Appropriations Committee appeared to be delaying the approval of the money until the plans could be altered to include total demolition of the old White House. When the bill finally passed both Houses of Congress it became clear that the legislators had left the big decision on the retention of the exterior walls up to the new commission.[203]

All through June and July the commissioners heard reports from engineers and architects about the advisability of keeping the old walls. Apparently the consultants hired for this inquiry unanimously agreed that it would be both "feasible and properly economical" to retain them. The architect called in for the investigation, William Adams Delano of New York, strongly urged their preservation from the architectural standpoint.[204] On August 2, 1949, the commission finally voted to stick with tradition: "Resolved, that this Commission approve a basic plan of construction procedure predicated upon the retention of the existing exterior walls of the White House, adequately underpinned, and upon substantially relieving the walls of the load of the floors and the roof which shall be carried on an independent frame with adequate foundation."[205] The press cheered the decision as a reaffirmation of the nation's belief in history and the traditions of democracy. The *New York Times* commented, "Something imponderable, but priceless, would have been lost if the six-man Commission . . . had decided to tear it down and replace it."[206]

There still remained one more potentially controversial decision, and it concerned the disposition of souvenirs from the renovation of the interior of the building. On April 2, 1949, Lorenzo S. Winslow, the

Digging out new foundations in the White House restoration, Washington, D.C., ca. 1950. (Photograph by Abbie Rowe; National Archives)

architect for the White House, explained that several souvenir manufacturers had already proposed the purchase of surplus material from the structure, but the president would have nothing to do with the idea. Winslow insisted that all the old materials be used over again if possible. He did admit that there would be the problem of disposing of parts of the building that could not be reused.[207] Two members of the staff of the Commission for the Renovation went to see the Park Service Advisory Board in December 1949 to ask the distinguished panel what it thought should be done with the smaller fragments of stone, timbers, paneling and brickwork. The board immediately passed a resolution declaring that it would be undignified to have an organized sale of White House souvenirs, especially since it would be extremely difficult in years to come to guarantee the authenticity of objects that came on the market. The Park Service group recommended the destruction of all materials that could not be reused.[208] It realized that it was only expressing an informal opinion because the secretary of the interior had no jurisdiction over the renovation of the White House.

The White House Commission did not accept the advice of the National Park Service. Starting in the winter of 1951, portions of the White House became available to the general public in "kits" that were usable for commemorative purposes. These kits ranged in price from 50¢ for small stones or old nails up to $100 for enough bricks to build a fireplace. The commission distributed more than 30,000 kits of various sizes and realized a profit of about $10,000 after taking into account the costs of distribution. About one thousand kits containing one small piece of stone and one old nail were encased in plastic and presented to high government officials.[209] The distribution of these souvenirs did not become an undignified effort to reap a great profit from the historically minded people of the nation, but it does seem that perhaps the Park Service Board may have been right about the importance of divorcing the renovation process completely from the commercial considerations of sale and dispersion of fragments that could eventually be duplicated or faked. In any event, the White House restoration was carried out completely outside the professional staff of the National Park Service and the Department of the Interior. Winslow and two staff architects from the General Services Administration supervised the work. They correctly described the operation as a renovation and did not pretend to be restoring the Executive Mansion to any particular period. The only consultation seems to have come with the question of the disposition of the surplus building materials, and the Advisory Board did not succeed in winning the commission over to the conservative view.

Postwar Years

The years that followed the ending of World War II were busy ones for the Park Service staff. There were several new and elaborate historical projects that required attention because they had ample funding and widespread public support. Four of these sites came into the National Park System between the end of the war and the middle of 1950. Three of the four became federal property because important people outside of the Park Service knew how to mount successful preservation campaigns: Independence National Historical Park in Philadelphia, Castle Clinton in New York City, and Hampton, a country house outside of Baltimore.

F.D.R.'s Hyde Park Estate

The fourth historic site had been on the National Park Service agenda since 1939, when Congress accepted the donation of the Franklin D. Roosevelt Library at Hyde Park. In the spring of 1939, just before the Vanderbilt Mansion became the subject of a concerted preservation debate, the president officially offered several acres of land from his estate to the nation as the site for a library. The structure would be built with private funds to serve as a central point for storing all of the historical papers from his administration. It was the first time that such a plan had ever been put before the Congress, and the ensuing debate was especially vicious and partisan. The House indulged in a long analysis of the president's greatness in July. Several Republicans claimed that Roosevelt's desire to construct a memorial to himself while he was in office proved that he was completely lacking in humility. Some of the president's detractors maintained that the rising national debt was a sufficient monument to Franklin Roosevelt.[210]

The bill that the members of Congress were debating with such earnestness contained a provision that no one seemed to notice—the Roosevelt family would have the right to donate other portions of the Hyde Park estate to the government at a later date. In addition, the president's wife and children could reserve a life interest in the property, but all taxes and upkeep would have to be paid by the family while they continued to exercise their life interest. Perhaps the idea of a Franklin D. Roosevelt Library was so controversial that no one bothered to say much about the idea of turning over Roosevelt's home to the people of the United States as a historic site.[211] The bill passed easily when all of the Democrats lined up behind it.

Once the library construction project had been completed, President Roosevelt considered giving his home to the nation. In October

Home of Franklin D. Roosevelt, Hyde Park, N.Y. (Photograph by New York Times—Wide World; FDR Library Collection)

1943 the Park Service found itself involved in a study that would eventually lead to the creation of a new major historic site.[212] During that month the president met with representatives of his own legal staff and the Department of the Interior to work out the specific terms of a gift of land to the government of the United States. The agreement seemed to follow closely the terms of the joint resolution of Congress passed in 1939, including the provision for a life interest for the Roosevelt family. The conferees agreed that there must be no significant changes in the house or the grounds immediately surrounding it if the full terms of the transfer were to be binding.[213] Director Drury naturally wanted to have his Advisory Board pass on the appropriateness of the transfer, but he well knew that the 1939 act made it possible to donate the property without the consent of any governmental body as long as the president approved.[214]

Secretary Ickes apparently had no intention of telling Roosevelt that there should be a considerable period for research and evaluation before the Hyde Park residence could be declared a National Historic Site. Instead Ickes sent the president a list of possible names that could be used for the designation order. The president selected "Home of Franklin D. Roosevelt National Historic Site" because the next logical choice, "Franklin D. Roosevelt Home National Historic Site," sounded to him "like a home for discarded politicians."[215] Although the official designation of the home did not come until January 15, 1944, the *New York Times* carried a story on January 4. The *Times* informed the American people that their president had taken the unprecedented step of turning over his only home to the Department of the Interior as a National Historic Site! Although the article explained the terms of the life-interest agreement and the obligation of the Roosevelt family to pay the taxes while they occupied the estate, there was no mention of the 1939 act passed by Congress.[216]

Secretary Ickes did not hesitate to refer to the transaction as a "generous gift," but a number of his fellow Americans did not share that view.[217] Soon editorials and letters began to arrive at the Department of the Interior, ranging from denunciations of the memorialization of a living president to offers to donate historic houses under similar terms.[218] The staff of the National Park Service readily answered these irate citizens: Congress had spoken in 1939 when it approved the transfer of the land for the library. Hillory Tolson, acting director of the Park Service, could say, "President Roosevelt's gift to the Nation has been accepted in accordance with the will of the people of the United States as expressed by their representatives in the Congress."[219]

During the fall of 1944 and the early winter of 1945, there was a flurry of interest in working out an agreement on the Roosevelt furnishings that might be left in the homestead. Perhaps the president had some kind of premonition of impending doom when he asked for an interview with a Park Service representative in January 1945.[220] On January 13 superintendent Francis S. Ronalds of Morristown National Historical Park went up to Hyde Park and talked with the president for about two hours about the development of the house and its immediate surroundings. Ronalds left with the impression that the president expected to have another session in the near future, but that never came to pass.[221]

Although columnists like Westbrook Pegler continued to complain about the tax write-off permitted by the acceptance of the Roosevelt estate, all suspicion seemed to disappear with the death of the president on April 12 of that year. For several months after the funeral the fate of the Roosevelt home seemed uncertain. Several of the former president's children were overseas and did not commit themselves on their right to a life interest in the use of the estate.[222]

The National Park Service staff, sensing the great responsibility that might be cast upon it, prepared to take over the Hyde Park property in case the Roosevelts should give up all their residual rights.[223] Secretary Ickes asked for appropriations to maintain the house even if the family should decide to live there—in order to protect the long-term interests of the federal government.[224] In the summer of 1945 the Park Service began conferring with the National Archives officials at the Roosevelt Library about problems of admission fees, parking, and visitation.[225] In the fall the superintendent of Vanderbilt Mansion National Historic Site, George A. Palmer (who would soon administer the Roosevelt Home and the Vanderbilt Estate), started looking for a qualified historian to interpret Roosevelt's home to the hordes of visitors that were certain to come once the future of the property had been settled. Palmer recommended the appointment of a native New Yorker, Frederick L. Rath, Jr., a Park Service historian who had worked at Vicksburg and Morristown before World War II. Rath, who was soon to return from military duties, seemed to possess all of the necessary qualifications. He had had considerable prewar experience in site interpretation, and he was well-trained in the field of history.[226]

The Roosevelt family officially executed a quit-claim deed that transferred the homestead to the United States government in November 1945, so all of the preliminary planning had been done with a real purpose.[227] H. I. Brock, in a *New York Times Magazine* article that month, sounded an awesome note when he referred to Hyde Park as "a new shrine."[228] The historians and administrators who had been trained in the 1930s were about to have their first opportunity to interpret a site

George A. Palmer examining stuffed birds in the Home of Franklin D. Roosevelt, 1956. (National Park Service)

Frederick L. Rath, Jr., seated in a favorite chair of the president, Home of Franklin D. Roosevelt, 1946. (National Park Service)

that had suddenly become sacred in the eyes of the public. On January 31 superintendent George Palmer wrote his regional director about the scenes he witnessed at the graveside on the late president's birthday: "The first party had waited two hours for the gates to open. There was the six-year old boy who placed a small bouquet of flowers. There were tears, bowed heads, uncovered heads, the sign of the cross. There was the woman who had walked all the way from Poughkeepsie in the storm. There was the figure of a man kneeling in the snow. From it all I came away feeling that the National Park Service has a different kind of responsibility for a man's spirit."[229]

While the devout pilgrims were kneeling in the snow, the new staff historian, Frederick L. Rath, Jr., began to suspect that these people were only the advance guard of an army of tourists who would want to see the domestic side of a family that had been at the apex of power for over twelve crucial years of American history. Rath was deeply concerned about the fact that inadequate postwar funding was going to make his task enormously difficult. He noted in his diary for January 13, 1946:

Crowds waiting to tour the Home of Franklin D. Roosevelt. (National Archives)

"Thro'out the week I've thought: What a shame this isn't being done right! It's the same old story, not enough money and not enough help. When the Gov't undertakes the responsibility of these areas, it should realize and act upon the full responsibility. What sense in accepting an area like Vanderbilt Mansion or Roosevelt Home unless you maintain and operate them properly?"[230]

One of the first big decisions that director Newton Drury had made regarding Hyde Park was the setting of the date for the official dedication ceremonies. He avoided the January celebration of Roosevelt's birthday on the basis of probable weather difficulties. The next logical choice and the one he decided on, was April 12, 1945, the first anniversary of the late president's death (four months away), a proposal that left the staff at Hyde Park breathless.[231] Engineers, historians, and museum personnel looked over the rooms that had been vacated by the Roosevelt family and decided that only minimal repairs could be made in the short time that remained before the grand opening. But the rooms should mirror the life-style of the president and his family if possible.[232] Ned

Burns, chief of the Museum Division of the Park Service, tried to help Rath and Palmer in their efforts to plan labels and room arrangements that would somehow convey the atmosphere of a home to thousands of visitors who would have to be funneled through the house by a guard force.[233]

The staff began to realize that planning for the interpretation of the Hyde Park estate also included another significant factor: the physical presence of the president's public-spirited widow, Eleanor Roosevelt. She helped to compose a speech that became the nucleus of the interpretive statement for the home.[234] Her frequent visits must have given the harried staff the definite impression that it had to deal with a monument to two famous individuals instead of one. She brought distinguished guests to the house frequently—and many of the tourists recognized her as she moved around the grounds.

Harry Truman himself came to the dedication ceremonies on April 12, and along with him an enormous assembly of dignitaries and tourists. While the new president spoke of his devotion to Roosevelt's programs of reform, the former president's pet Scottie, Fala, sat at Truman's feet and stared out at the crowd.[235] Eleanor Roosevelt gave an excellent summary of the "healing quality" that the house had for her husband, whether he was dealing with the problems of the Great Depression or the agonizing decisions leading to the prosecution of the war effort.[236] She said, "His spirit will always live in this house." One columnist in the *New York Times* remarked that President Roosevelt had been sure of his place in history, judging by the careful way in which he provided for his personal papers and his home. Apparently the many people who viewed the dedication ceremonies shared Roosevelt's own judgment of his decisive role in recent history.[237]

The administration of the Home of Franklin D. Roosevelt National Historic Site presented a number of challenges that had been foreseen by George Palmer and his staff. Within a few weeks after the opening, for instance, Palmer had to remind Mrs. Roosevelt that her husband had asked in his deed of gift that the house and grounds be left without any change or modification that would detract from the atmosphere of the place. Therefore it would be imperative to decline an offer of a bust of the former president that was intended for a niche in the garden.[238]

The business of operating a shrine included working with crowds of reverent tourists. Frederick Rath noted with some desperation in his diary for June 23, 1946: "Another throng and a virtual repetition of what has been taking place each Sunday. Almost 3,900 visitors, and 2,404 through the Home. Had to put the main waiting line out under the trees. Our grass will suffer; but rather it than the waiting visitors. Got

Independence Mall area after development, Philadelphia, 1966. (Photograph by Alois Strobl, Philadelphia City Planning Commission)

the line south of the weeping elm edging the driveway and then headed N.E. Line started 12:45 and got longer until after ticket sale stopped at 3:50. My sole job—but it seems to allow very little time for sitting down—is supervisory control, straightening something out here, doing a job there and so on."[239] In July, Ronald F. Lee, chief historian, and Ned Burns of the Museum Division inspected the Home of Franklin Roosevelt and decided that Palmer, Rath, and the guards were performing as well as could be expected with an average of nearly three thousand people a day going through the building while other thousands had to be satisfied with looking only at the grave site, garden, and library exhibits. The two Park Service inspectors found that the home still exuded "an atmosphere of dignity and restraint, combined with friendly hospitality, in spite of the lines of waiting visitors." From the standpoint of interpretation, the Hyde Park staff had hit upon several helpful devices (including an excellent set of labels by Rath) that gave tourists a sense of historical reality when they looked through the house itself.[240] But by October, Rath admitted that there were not enough guides; the few who were there were showing some strain.[241] A year later superintendent Palmer reported to the Washington office that the "experiment" was still going on—and that 75,000 pilgrims had gone through the house during the month of August without doing any significant damage.[242]

The historian at Hyde Park, though overworked, found the time to do necessary research to support the efforts of those who would some-day have to interpret the home to visitors unfamiliar with the Roosevelt era. Rath spent much of his spare time reading different sources on the life of Franklin Roosevelt. He constantly sought out older people who had known and worked with the former president. George Palmer insti-gated a wire-recording program (a precursor of tape recording) in De-cember 1947 that kept both him and Rath busy interviewing people who had been close to the Vanderbilt and Roosevelt families. These inter-views provided valuable insights into such varied questions as Roose-velt's attitude toward his gardens and the groundskeepers who worked for him, or Frederick Vanderbilt's schedule for entertaining his weekend guests.[243] Before long the National Park Service staff in Washington con-sidered asking Palmer to demonstrate his oral history techniques to the Interior Department.[244]

When superintendent Palmer drafted a two-year summary of the operation and administration of the Home of Franklin D. Roosevelt in June 1948, he could look back with understandable pride over the two hectic seasons that he and Rath had weathered. The dedicated workers at Hyde Park had been able to keep visitors moving through the house and gardens in a reasonably pleasant and productive manner. Palmer's major concern for the future involved maintaining the atmosphere of the estate as it had been in 1945, the time of Roosevelt's death. That task seemed to be increasingly difficult with half a million visitors a year, and it appeared that additional staff members would be required.[245] Unfor-tunately, Rath was about to leave the Hyde Park position and take up his duties as executive secretary of the newly founded National Council for Historic Sites and Buildings in Washington, D.C. In the years that followed Palmer and his staff capably interpreted the Roosevelt home to thousands of visitors. The pattern had been set in the first few years.

Independence Park

It could be said that the whole movement to preserve Independence Hall and its historic surroundings in Philadelphia originated in the first anx-ious weeks that followed the Japanese attack on Hawaii and the German declaration of war. A number of Philadelphians who were well aware of what had happened to London's churches in 1940 during the Nazi Blitz wanted to see that the old state house in their city did not suffer a similar fate. On December 13, 1941, the *Philadelphia Record* mentioned that Howard Murphy of the bureau of city property had announced that the Liberty Bell might be shipped to Fort Knox in Kentucky for safekeeping throughout the war. At the same time the president of the Pennsylvania Society of the Sons of the Revolution, Edwin O. Lewis, set up a committee to study the problems involved in protecting the notable public buildings of downtown Philadelphia. Architect D. Knickerbacker Boyd accepted the chairmanship of the new committee.[246]

There was real fear that Independence Hall and the buildings close to it might be destroyed by a direct hit from a bomb. The immediate solution to this threat seemed to be to collect all of the measured drawings of the historic structures that various architects had made over the years.[247] Fortunately a number of drawings survived from the 1931 survey of old Philadelphia, so it was possible for the Sons of the Revolution committee to assemble these documents.[248] In addition, chairman Boyd wrote to architectural historians around the country asking for ideas on preserving the important buildings in the Independence Square area. He told the distinguished Charleston architect Albert Simons that Judge Lewis would be coming to Charleston in the spring of 1942 to attend a meeting of the Society of Colonial Wars and also to study Simons's preservation work, perhaps as a precedent for Philadelphia.[249]

At first Edwin Lewis tried to work through the Pennsylvania Committee on the Conservation of Cultural Resources, a state-sponsored survey of wartime cultural needs chaired by William Lingelbach of Philadelphia. At the May 1942 meeting of the committee Lewis announced that a number of organizations wanted to insure the preservation of Philadelphia's shrines—as a contribution to the nation's cultural resources. He proposed the creation of a historic park that would surround Independence Hall.[250] However, the experts that made up the committee thought that it was "not advisable" for their organization to become involved in a downtown preservation scheme.[251]

Lewis considered himself a leader with a cause, and no learned committee was going to derail his plan for saving Independence Hall. On June 30 he became president of a new group, which evolved out of Boyd's Sons of the Revolution committee, called An Organization for the Conservation of Historic Sites in Old Philadelphia. His new federation, seeking a broad base of support in the Delaware Valley, quickly sent out invitations to individuals and institutions that might want to cooperate in a preservation plan. About two weeks later the judge held a formal meeting of the organization and told the various constituent groups that he was planning to put pressure on several municipal and federal agencies. The next day he would ask the city council for $25,000 to permit a real survey of the historical resources of the old city. Lewis urged his listeners to come to the city council session with him in order to show the breadth of concern that existed throughout the area.

Lewis was an impressive figure as he began to bring together the diverse groups of civic-minded Philadelphians. He was intelligent, persuasive, and widely known.[252] When he took office as president of the Organization for the Conservation of Historic Sites, he bluntly told his followers, "I am not accustomed to heading up failures."[253] Some people believe that during these first few months he conceived of a vast land-clearance program in downtown Philadelphia that would rival the Jefferson National Expansion Memorial in St. Louis.[254] Whether that was true or not, Lewis was different from Luther Ely Smith. To begin with, the Lewis program (which was not so clearly spelled out as Smith's riverfront scheme) did involve historic preservation. The main goal in Philadelphia was the creation of a setting for Independence Hall and the other buildings that illustrated Philadelphia's great days as the capital and financial center of the United States. The Jefferson National Expansion Memorial also had been intended as a "shrine" for the Westward Movement; but it had been set up as a make-work project for rejuvenating a decaying downtown area. No old buildings were necessary for Smith's scheme. The Independence Square proposal involved demolition, but only for the purpose of singling out some old buildings in a congested commercial district where serious damage might come from nearby structures in the case of a bombing attack. It was to be an exercise in selective preservation. In St. Louis the Old Courthouse and cathedral were outside the memorial area, and they were to be dwarfed by a modern structure.

The Independence Hall preservation scheme required just as much personal stamina and political skill as the Jefferson National Expansion Memorial. In 1942 the organization changed its name to the Independence Hall and Old Philadelphia Association, Inc., Founded for the Preservation and Beautification of Historic Philadelphia.[255] The people who gave their support to the idea represented a broad spectrum of interests and organizations throughout the city, ranging from political clubs to universities and historical societies. Despite the national importance of the site, the movement was almost entirely limited to the greater Philadelphia area.

Sylvester K. Stevens, state historian, offered his counsel and influence. He was greatly impressed with both Judge Lewis and his organization, but Stevens quickly saw that the Philadelphians would have to turn to Washington for help:

Since I knew Drury and Ronnie Lee, I asked him [Lewis] if he would have any objections to my going down to Washington and talking to these people about it. And I remember Newton Drury in particular . . ., a short, rather vigorous firey kind of a guy. When I came into the office he of course knew what I was there for, and I explained it briefly, and he informed me in no uncertain terms that he didn't care particularly about reopening the problem of the Philadelphia people. He told me about this agreement which they had worked out with Mayor Lamberton's administration [in 1941]. He pulled a copy of it out of his drawer, and I asked him for a copy of it, which I got. . . . I said, "I think Judge Lewis has perhaps the political insight and know-how to make this thing a success."[256]

Stevens's report to Lewis on the Washington visit included a clear warning that Park Service support could only come with the consummation of a cooperative agreement with the city of Philadelphia for the administration of Independence Hall as a National Historic Site.[257] As a professional historian working in the field of historic preservation, Stevens could say with conviction that the advice of the National Park Service was essential in the fields of research and planning. Stevens also suggested that Fiske Kimball, as a member of the Park Service Advisory Board, should be encouraged to explore the idea of an agreement.

Both Lewis and Stevens went to work on Mayor Bernard Samuel with the goal of reopening negotiations with the Park Service. Stevens pointed out to the mayor that a cooperative agreement with the federal government was a necessary first step toward the accomplishment of the grand design for a renewal of the Independence Square area.[258] During a conference in the mayor's office Lewis won over Howard W. Murphy of the bureau of city property, a man who had been a "principal stumbling block" in the 1941 negotiations. Murphy had been jealous of the rights of the city of Philadelphia with regard to its major historical shrine.[259] Encouraged by the meeting of minds, Stevens and Lewis worked on a news release about the new association in another effort to weld all of the major historical and patriotic organizations into an informed group supporting the Independence Hall movement.[260]

Apparently the persuasive skill shown by Judge Lewis in Mayor Samuel's office bore fruit almost immediately in a revival of the original cooperative agreement that had been worked out by Newton Drury a year earlier. On November 9, 1942, Secretary Ickes asked President Roosevelt to treat Independence Hall as "an exceptional case" and ratify the agreement (which would not necessarily commit the Department of the Interior to expend any funds on the restoration or maintenance of Independence Hall). Roosevelt signed the letter of approval on December 2.[261] During the winter of 1943 the Park Service staff hammered out an arrangement that left the city of Philadelphia free to accept or reject the advice of the Department of the Interior.[262] The department issued a news release on March 30 that announced the establishment of Independence Hall as a National Historic Site, although the official designation would not come until May 14.[263] The notice tactfully complimented Philadelphia for the care it had lavished on the building for so many years. This was unquestionably a first important step toward the development of a sense of confidence on the part of the city officials in the abilities of the historical staff of the Park Service. Lewis had managed to create a legal relationship that would make feasible a much more elaborate cooperative scheme in the future.

By 1943 the question of preserving and interpreting Independence Hall no longer involved the fear of enemy bombing. Lewis and his allies had begun to think in broad terms about the right kind of development for downtown Philadelphia, the closer ties between the National Park Service and the city government, and the best possible interpretive treatment for the group of old buildings. There were two avenues of approach that seemed to offer some promise: the selection of a commission to set up a National Historical Park in the center of old Philadelphia and a proposal to locate the new world-peacekeeping organization near Independence Square. D. Knickbacker Boyd of the Independence Hall Association suggested that there could be no more appropriate place for the postwar negotiations than the same hall that had given birth to the government of the United States.[264]

It was at this critical point that the leadership qualities of Edwin O. Lewis began to stand out, especially his ability to unite people of many different political and economic interests. Isidor Ostroff, a lawyer who represented the Independence Hall area in the state legislature, was one of Lewis's recruits. Ostroff, a Democrat, knew that he had little in common with Lewis or the Sons of the Revolution, but when a Philadelphia lawyer received a command to see a judge, it was an order from "Mount Olympus":

> Judge Lewis sat me down and told me about the work that his group was going to do, and he suggested that we did not have to stop anything that we were doing if we didn't like what he was telling me, but that he thought that in union there is strength. . . .
>
> Judge Lewis was very persuasive, and besides that I saw that he was very intelligent and had the kind of influence that our project [a neighborhood association] lacked with me as its leader. . . . So it seemed that if we were going to accomplish something that would be substantial and that would last

beyond our lifetime and be important in the life of the United States of America, that would be something historical that the youngsters in the United States could learn about and be inspired by, that I ought to line up behind Judge Lewis and with him. . . .

I had to admire the way he played off Republicans against Democrats and Democrats against Republicans, making the other fellow feel that he'd better do something about it before the other part got credit for doing the thing, and he did it skillfully. He handled the political situation in this entire project like a master of a great orchestra. He played the right instruments and brought out the right reactions and brought out the right results.[265]

The designation of Independence Hall as a National Historic Site was only a good primary step. Lewis believed that he would have to move outside the Philadelphia area to muster support for a great mall that would terminate in front of Independence Hall. Sensing the possible influence of speculators, Lewis "stressed the Association's avoiding the taint of real estate embroilment in every way possible."[266] As one of the first moves in the new program a representative group of Philadelphians went to a top Park Service official in Washington, Arthur Demaray, to talk "boldly" about future plans. Lewis picked up Sylvester Stevens's suggestion that Independence Hall serve as a setting for the peace conference. The judge agreed that if only the formal signing ceremonies should take place in the historic old building, that would be quite enough.[267] The conference with Demaray led to the drafting of a proposal for a congressionally approved commission to study the neighborhood around Independence Hall and to sketch out a proper role for the federal government in the project. It was clear from the meeting that Demaray was sympathetic with Lewis's long-term objectives and that the creation of a new commission would closely follow the successful pattern used with the Jefferson National Expansion Memorial. It is probable that Demaray had told the Philadelphians how useful the Territorial Expansion Commission had been for Luther Ely Smith in developing congressional backing for the St. Louis project in the mid-1930s.[268]

During the final years of the war Lewis waged his campaigns successfully on all three fronts: More and more members of Congress lined up behind a proposal to create a Philadelphia National Historic Shrines Commission; the various interest groups in and out of the Philadelphia city government supported the proposed study; and the Pennsylvania legislature voted to make $4 million available to purchase a three-block area for a mall leading from Independence Hall northward toward the Delaware River Bridge. Fiske Kimball reported to the Park Service Advisory Board that the state money had been set aside in order to promote

Independence Mall area before clearance, Philadelphia, 1950. (Photograph by Lawrence S. Williams, Inc.; Philadelphia City Planning Commission)

Philadelphia as a headquarters site for the United Nations—a new twist on the peace conference idea. Lewis began to compile for the Shrines Commission a list of people who reflected the viewpoints of both political parties and the various professional groups that might be able to influence public opinion in the direction of a Philadelphia historical park. The Advisory Board noted that a full development of the area surrounding Independence Hall would require an expenditure far beyond the resources of the city or of the commonwealth. Newton Drury informed the board that he thought it would be possible to work out a three-way agreement linking the interests of the city and the state with those of the federal government.[269]

The next step came on August 9, 1946, when Congress authorized the creation of the seven-member Philadelphia National Shrines Park Commission.[270] Judge Lewis, of course, became the chairman. The panel included a most important figure in the cause of historic preservation, George McAneny of New York City, who was then deeply involved in the battle to save Castle Clinton. McAneny was a leader in the Philadelphia scene through his presidency of the Carl Schurz Memorial Foundation, which was still administering the old Custom House. The new commission met in Philadelphia on November 15. An invited guest was the director for Region I of the Park Service, Thomas J. Allen, a senior administrator who could share his views on the planning problems that would face the new commission.[271]

Apparently director Allen had the difficult task of raising with the group a sensitive issue that could have prevented the full accomplishment of its goals. He explained that the federal government would not be satisfied with a supportive role in the park development (along with the state and the city) if the administration of Independence Hall were left up to the municipal authorities. Lewis naturally defended Philadelphia's care of the old hall, and he hoped that there would be no question about the right of the city to retain control over her most sacred trust. Allen quickly added that the federal authorities could share in the administration of the hall even if the title to the property continued to rest with Philadelphia.[272]

Lewis asked Park Service director Drury about procuring professional assistance for the commission. Apparently the judge hoped to get funding from Congress to hire a local Philadelphia architect, Grant Simon, as the official planner.[273] Drury had to tell the Philadelphians how the federal government operated. Congress had approved a $15,000 appropriation to help in the preparation of the report that the commission was to present, but the funds had not been officially set aside. When the money was available, it had to be spent through the regional office in

Richmond, and only civil service personnel could carry out the necessary studies. Drury naturally recommended architect Charles E. Peterson, then of St. Louis, as the best-qualified person in the United States in 1946 to conduct an architectural inventory of Philadelphia's historic buildings.[274]

When Ronald Lee went to Harrisburg in March 1947 to confer with Gov. James Duff, the chief executive of Pennsylvania announced his full support of the state appropriation of $4 million for the purchase of the land in front of Independence Hall. At the same meeting Judge Lewis revealed that some people in Philadelphia were prepared to invest at least $7 million in an apartment development on the edge of the park area if the mall idea went through. Duff believed that land acquisition for the state mall area should begin at once because prices would certainly increase.[275]

The Philadelphia National Shrines Park Commission met on March 11 with several Park Service Officials to go over the plans for the boundaries of the proposed park. Lee noted that each time the Independence Hall area came under consideration, the district slated for federal ownership became larger. And so the commission asked the Department of the Interior to draft a bill that would set definite boundaries for the new park.[276] Although Charles Peterson came to Philadelphia to study its architectural features, the commission had also hired Grant Simon to prepare sketches for presentation to the public. The March 11 meeting included a protest from the local opposition group of displaced businesses. Park Service architect Dick Sutton reported on Lewis's expert handling of the potentially tense situation:

Opposition to the mall was voiced by an attorney, representing the merchants who occupy structures within the proposed area, on the grounds that an economic hardship would be imposed upon his clients. He was supported on aesthetic grounds by Mr. Magazini, an architect, who questioned the desirability of such a pretentious approach which might by contrast dwarf the Independence Hall group of buildings. He suggested as an alternate the clearing of approximately one-half of the square north of Chestnut fronting on Independence Hall, contending that the historic structures were essentially city in character and should be seen in restricted surroundings. The Commission dismissed the idea of reducing the size of the mall but promised that the merchants would be given as much time as possible to find other suitable quarters.[277]

There was no interest in 1947 in keeping businesses operating inside an area to be designated as a "shrine."

The Park Service staff was ready to give substantial support to the

Shrines Commission as soon as the major problems had been worked out with regard to the boundaries and final administration of the various historical areas. Lee recommended that Peterson and "our best available historian" be assigned to Philadelphia to write two technical reports on the proposed park project. The architect and the historian could help the commission with ideas on both the interpretive program and the final physical development of the Independence Hall grouping.[278] Ralph Lewis of the Museum Division of the Park Service drew up a three-page interpretive plan, with many suggestions for guiding different age groups and using various kinds of introductory lectures.[279] By mid-April, Peterson and regional historian Roy Appleman were hard at work on their technical reports.[280]

Once more Edwin Lewis's skill as a planner and harmonizer came to the fore. He worked easily with the two consultants from the National Park Service and listened carefully as they criticized the proposed boundaries for the federal area. Naturally Peterson pointed out several worthwhile buildings that could be restored, including some old houses and the Jayne "skyscraper" erected in the 1850s. At an informal meeting of the commission Lewis also gave some time to the consideration of a few proposals put forth by the city planning commission of Philadelphia.[281] Appleman quickly came to the conclusion that the American Philosophical Society should be encouraged to reconstruct the old Philadelphia Library Company Building next to the Second Bank of the United States. He also suggested the addition of two noncontiguous areas to the park, the site of Benjamin Franklin's house and the site of the building occupied by Thomas Jefferson when he drafted the Declaration of Independence.[282] Melvin Weig, the historian at Morristown, went to Philadelphia to inspect the quality of interpretation and maintenance offered by the city at Independence Hall. Naturally, Weig did not find that the city had been able to maintain the exacting standards of the National Park Service in these particular areas, but he was pleasantly surprised to find some worthwhile items on display at the hall.[283]

By May 1947 Judge Lewis became anxious that the report of the Shrines Commission might not be ready for Congress unless more assistance could be given by the Park Service personnel. He managed to convince Newton Drury to permit both Peterson and Appleman to remain in Philadelphia through most of the month of June.[284] Lewis could hardly contain himself in telling the director about the high qualifications and ability of these veteran researchers. He concluded that they had "rendered the greatest service to our Commission." Fortunately, both consultants agreed on almost all questions—boundaries, the need for Park Service administration of all the main buildings, and interpretive procedures.[285]

The Philadelphia National Shrines Park Commission submitted its final summary to Congress on December 29, 1947, complete with 337 pages of maps and historical data. The report presented arguments for the participation of the federal government in a program that would combine the historical efforts of three governmental units. It was now obvious that Lewis had gained the wholehearted support of the Philadelphia city planning commission and the commonwealth through the pledge of support from Governor Duff. The last paragraph of the introduction showed how different the Philadelphia plan was from the Jefferson National Expansion Memorial idea. The Park Commission pulled out all the stops in orchestrating its historical preservation arguments for needed funds:

> The buildings listed are the core of our spiritual heritage, representing now the hope of the entire world because of their significance in history and in ideology. The Government of the United States should act to preserve these shrines before they are destroyed by fire or other casualty, and to embellish their environment within the small area that is involved. Countless millions of our fellow-citizens, born and to come, will make pilgrimages to these shrines of Old Philadelphia, and they should be rescued from the envelope of decay that every day becomes more marked as the life of the city of Philadelphia moves away from the Delaware River neighborhood.[286]

The report gave a description of the areas that had been selected for federal acquisition and administration, with clear historical and financial justifications for each case. Then came a real masterstroke. Near the end of the document Lewis thought to include a brief essay from Mayor Bernard Samuel that outlined for the members of Congress how the city of Philadelphia approved the entire plan and intended to cooperate fully.[287] This pleasant note proved that continued municipal ownership of Independence Hall would make it possible for the National Park Service to work out a program. The city planning commission also had a chance to tell how the proposed federal park would fit in with existing plans for the rejuvenation of the whole neighborhood.[288]

Both Charles Peterson and Roy Appleman were reasonably happy with the report that went to Congress. Appleman volunteered several pointed comments to Drury about the genesis of the report. He believed that the recommendations nearly all originated in the city planning commission and not in the Philadelphia National Shrines Park Commission. Appleman bluntly said, "First, so far as I could tell, Judge Lewis was the Commission. No other member of the Commission was active or contributed in planning the report or in making decisions concerning it, so far as I could learn."[289] Peterson agreed with all the major proposals for the boundaries of the park area, but he hoped that when the bill finally emerged in Congress it would give the National Park Service a substantial amount of freedom in the development and interpretation of the project.[290]

During March and April 1948 the subcommittee of the House Committee on Public Lands held hearings on the proposed park and also went to Philadelphia to look at the real estate that the United States government was asked to purchase for the protection of the landmarks. The congressmen from the Philadelphia area had no trouble in backing up the arguments offered in support of the inspirational values of the new park—especially during the Cold War era.[291] Lewis claimed that appropriating $5 million for the acquisition of the historical area to the east of Independence Square was a sound investment in the future education of millions who would come to Philadelphia.[292] He pleaded for saving the whole picture and compared it to the great restorations at Williamsburg and in the Battery District of Charleston.[293] Lewis also admitted that he had initially favored and still wanted to see the creation of the urban park plan as a means of protecting these shrines from the danger of fire. He pointed out that a fire had broken out in an abandoned four-story structure directly across the street from Independence Hall in the brief time that had elapsed *since* the members of the House committee had visited Philadelphia.[294]

The only serious question that divided the membership of the House subcommittee involved the decisions on certain parcels of land that were not directly connected with the three blocks adjoining Independence Square to the east. Newton Drury had hinted that the acquisition of some of these small and expensive properties might be controversial. The most questionable one involved the purchase of the lot at the corner of Seventh and Market streets, once occupied by the Graff House (1775, demolished 1883) where Thomas Jefferson had drafted the Declaration of Independence.[295] When Ronald Lee testified before the committee, he could not state clearly how that piece of land would be used, but it was logical to him that a memorial should be erected there. It did not seem right to allow the sacred spot to continue to serve as a parking lot for a hamburger stand—but at the same time Lee could not imagine putting in anything larger than a small model of the Graff House.[296] The contemporary use of the site bothered the legislators greatly, especially when the commission report estimated an appropriation of $250,000 for buying that property.[297] A few members of the

House committee suggested that the same amount of money could be spent in Germantown to preserve buildings around the Morris House.[298] In the end the majority could not bring themselves to recommend paying a quarter of a million dollars for a hamburger stand, so the proposal was removed from the bill.[299] The committee members were also reluctant to purchase the secluded site of Benjamin Franklin's home, but they finally agreed that the Franklin connection was too important to ignore.[300]

On June 28, 1948, President Truman signed the bill creating Independence National Historical Park.[301] The press release from the Department of the Interior explained clearly that the federal government was about to enter into a partnership with the city of Philadelphia and the Commonwealth of Pennsylvania.[302] In accordance with the provisions of the new bill, the secretary of the interior set out to appoint several members to a new Independence National Historical Park Commission.[303] Although the actual purchasing program had not begun in 1949, Judge Lewis could see by the early part of that year that his first campaign had come to a successful conclusion. Perhaps the sense of national emergency that came with the outbreak of war in 1941 and the great renewal of interest in our national ideals that marked the formative years of the Cold War all created a political climate that made the saving of Independence Hall and its surroundings essential. Although the war generally had a devastating effect on preservation work, the Philadelphia situation consistently stood out as an "exceptional case."

Castle Clinton

At the end of World War II the National Park Service found itself involved in a bitter preservation battle over an old fort that stood at the tip of Manhattan Island. The extended fight over Castle Clinton brought the officials of the Department of the Interior into close contact with a dedicated and determined civic leader and influential businessman, George McAneny, who had already been involved in the negotiations over Federal Hall in New York City and the old Custom House in Philadelphia as president of the Carl Schurz Foundation. Because personalities and political power played such an important role in this conflict, Castle Clinton itself became nearly incidental to the whole affair. The building was a stone fortification that dated back to the period just before the War of 1812, and it had also served as a theater, an immigration depot, and an aquarium during its long career. The walls stood on the north edge of Battery Park, facing New York harbor, and they did have the historical distinction of marking the site of fortifications that had

Battery Park area showing Castle Clinton, New York City. (Photograph by Jack Boucher, National Park Service)

stood on the tip of Manhattan since the Dutch occupation early in the seventeenth century. Some of the Park Service historians who supported preservation in New York City sincerely doubted that the old ruin was worth expending any energy on.[304]

Although many other people became a part of the legal and legislative maneuvering over Castle Clinton, the battle was principally between George McAneny and the powerful park commissioner Robert Moses. Ronald Lee of the National Park Service tended to become McAneny's "second" in the duel, while Mrs. Arthur Hays Sulzberger of the *New York Times* family stood firmly behind Robert Moses. It was a protracted conflict that transformed Castle Clinton into a symbol of the opposition of preservationists to the high-handed tactics of city planners. Lee, in particular, quickly lost sight of the historical value of the stone fort as he sought to prove that the preservation community was strong and united. He was enlisting the aid of people who would charter the National Trust for Historic Preservation, and McAneny with his business and historical contacts in New York City was the kind of man who could be most helpful in bringing the right people into a nationwide preservation organization. Lee himself looked back on the Castle Clinton affair in that light: "The National Park Service has found itself in similar situations on a number of occasions, and they pose a difficult question: should you bend your viewpoint somewhat in order to uphold the hands of ardent and effective and important preservationists who find themselves with their backs against the wall? And we did it a number of times; and I hope we continue to do it."[305]

Between 1939 and 1941 McAneny and other reformers had fought a plan developed by Moses for a bridge that would connect the southern tip of Manhattan Island with Brooklyn.[306] At a city council hearing on the proposed bridge Moses ruthlessly characterized McAneny as "an extinct volcano who never expects to run for public office again."[307] Although it appeared in 1939 that the determination of Robert Moses would triumph, in the long run McAneny and his allies in New York City defeated the plan by appealing to the authorities in Washington.[308] President Roosevelt accepted the argument that a strategic risk was involved, because the new bridge could become a severe hazard to navigation if it were bombed into the harbor.[309] McAneny shifted his support to a tunnel that was to cover the same route as the proposed bridge, but that change in plans made another collision with Moses inevitable.

In all fairness to Moses it must be stated that he had had some discouraging experiences in dealing with historic buildings while serving as commissioner of parks. The new American Society of Architectural Historians published a letter from him in the July-October 1941 issue of its *Journal* that purported to study "some hard facts about practical preservation." The message was dated September 19, 1940, and in it Moses enumerated the reasons for his opposition to the preservation of the Schenck Farmhouse (1720, 1788) in Highland Park. As parks commissioner he already had to maintain thirteen historic house museums in the New York City area, and he was not anxious to take on another one. Moses had no use for preservationists who led campaigns to dump old buildings onto the city budget:

> When the so-called restoration of one of these mansions is completed and the antiquaries, historians, and architects have had their field day, the question remains as to what will be done with the completed building. I have never known such a building to be satisfactory for modern public use or for the transaction of present-day business. The alternative is a museum. If the demand for a museum is met, endless troubles arise in obtaining the proper exhibits, bearing in mind that the furniture, fixtures, decorations, and implements of living of one kind or another, which originally made the house habitable and attractive, have long since disappeared and that at best contemporary objects and replicas of such objects are the best that can be expected.[310]

Moses could be typified as an individual who considered his approach to historic preservation more practical than that of the vast majority of "antiquaries, historians, and architects" who enjoyed rescuing structures that harried public officials would eventually have to maintain.[311]

The battle over the proposed Brooklyn-Battery Bridge had been a mere skirmish in preparation for the real war between George McAneny and Robert Moses.[312] The first confrontation came on June 25, 1942, when the New York City board of estimate voted 11 to 5 to demolish the old aquarium in Battery Park. Moses had already closed the building to visitors, and all he needed was permission to tear it down in order to facilitate the construction of the ventilating system for the new tunnel. Moses simply referred to the remaining stone walls as a fort with no history. "It never fired a shot," was his epitaph for the building.[313] The staff architect for the parks department admitted that he did not have enough material for an authentic restoration. So Moses quickly disposed of the other historical claims for the old building in one sweeping statement: "The Barnum period, when it was Castle Garden, has gone. And no one wants to dwell on the period when the structure was an immigration station—that was a disgrace." True to his role as New York's defender of historical causes, McAneny appeared at the hearing. He refuted Moses's stand: "We see no necessity for the removal of the fort. Battery Park is important not only for its beauty but also because it is steeped in historical association. It is the gateway to the nation, and no one can fail to feel that there is no place to compare with it, unless it be Independence Hall in Philadelphia."[314] In spite of his best arguments McAneny lost the first round. Castle Clinton appeared to be doomed, although the duration of World War II provided a stay of execution. All through the war years he took people down to view the old fort in an effort to head off Moses's next attack.[315]

As soon as peace came, McAneny assembled a group of his most powerful friends (and there were many) to address an open letter to the *New York Times*, pleading for the preservation of Castle Clinton as one more element in "our most priceless heritage" that had been spared devastation of warfare. The letter stated that the fort needed to be saved— and after that the question of its future use as a gate to the city could be discussed. One of the well-known New York residents who added his name to the Castle Clinton letter was Horace M. Albright.[316] But Robert Moses stood his ground at the board of estimate meeting on October 11, 1945, when he declared that it would take at least $250,000 to restore the old fort, which stood in the way of his plans for the Brooklyn-Battery Tunnel.[317]

The National Park Service had not been deeply involved in this debate up through the fall of 1945, although the site had been discussed by the Interim Committee of the Advisory Board in 1944. The committee noted the impending demolition of Castle Clinton at its December meeting. Newton Drury warned the board that he and Secretary Ickes were committed to support legislation calling for the preservation of the building. Fiske Kimball said that he envisaged the fort as "an item in the urban picture of New York," but he did not consider it to be more significant than any of the other forts in seaports along the Atlantic Coast.[318]

With little hope of assistance from the Department of the Interior, McAneny and his friends hit on a new strategy that eventually won the victory over Moses: Get a judgment from Congress on the status of the remaining stone walls. The depth of the Park Service commitment to Castle Clinton became clearer in 1946 as Congress once more attempted to use the functions of the Advisory Board in declaring the fort nationally significant. New York Congressman Sol Bloom readily supported a bill that placed the federal government in the position of asking the city of New York to turn the old fort over to the Department of the Interior as a National Monument.[319] The Bloom bill did not specifically commit the government to carry out a restoration program, so Mayor O'Dwyer asked the Park Service what its plans would be for the development of a Castle Clinton National Monument. In the meantime the New York

City budget included an item of $54,000 to cover the demolition of the remaining ramparts.[320] The mayor took a halfway position on the controversial castle because he did not want to alienate the powerful people who wanted a restoration, and he also did not want to see the urban landscape defiled by a stone ruin that badly needed repairs. The bill passed the House and went on to the United States Senate.[321] There, too, McAneny had the influence necessary for pushing the bill through. Ronald Lee, who accompanied him on a journey to Capitol Hill, remembered the results:

> George McAneny also had other friends and among them was Senator Robert Wagner. I went with George McAneny to see Senator Wagner . . . and it turned out Senator Wagner's father—and Senator Wagner himself—had entered the United States as immigrants through Castle Clinton. Senator Wagner was a child then and his father and family came in through Castle Clinton or Castle Garden as it had been called. . . . And I don't know what his attitude was toward Robert Moses. After all, Wagner was a very prominent Democrat, and Moses was a Progressive Republican. I don't imagine it bothered Senator Wagner any to save Castle Clinton. If it wasn't something that Robert Moses wanted, it wouldn't bother Senator Wagner a bit probably. So he helped get the bill through.[322]

The possibility that the United States Senate might pass a bill accepting Castle Clinton brought forth protests from one of Moses's most potent allies, Mrs. Arthur Hays Sulzberger, the wife of the publisher of the *New York Times* and an officer in the Park Association of New York. Iphigene Sulzberger sent a batch of telegrams to members of the Senate asking them to vote against the Bloom bill. She maintained that a National Monument in Battery Park would destroy the vista from Broadway down toward the Statue of Liberty. Then she brought together a series of arguments that sounded suspiciously like the reasoning of Moses: "Fort Clinton does not exist as an architectural entity, nor do its original plans. It never fired a shot and its historical value is almost nil. The Aquarium building is now half way through the process of demolition due to construction of the Brooklyn-Battery Tunnel. If a replica of the fort is to be built, it will be necessary to underpin the remaining part of the structure at a considerable cost."[323] The *New York Times* carried a couple of pictures of the fort as it appeared in July 1946 with the following captions: "Exterior of landmark half demolished due to construction of Brooklyn-Battery Tunnel" and "The rubble-littered interior."

McAneny did not take this new attack with complacency. He immediately wrote Sen. James M. Mead of New York in an effort to correct "erroneous" statements in Mrs. Sulzberger's telegram. The telegram and the *Times* article had implied that the building was half destroyed and full of debris. As president of the American Scenic and Historic Preservation Society, McAneny asserted that he did not contemplate a full (and expensive) restoration of the fort—and he insisted that the walls were still there. The demolition had involved removing portions of the building that had been added to accommodate the theater and aquarium. In addition there was no evidence that the retention of Castle Clinton would interfere with the entrance to the tunnel. Once more McAneny mustered his historical arguments—the fort had been effective *because* it never fired a shot; New York had not suffered the fiery fate of Washington, D.C., in the War of 1812. The greatest leaders and artists of the nineteenth century had performed in Castle Garden. And then nearly eight million immigrants had streamed through the building that served as their "Plymouth Rock." McAneny claimed that all of the important civic organizations except the Park Association wanted to see Castle Clinton preserved.[324]

On July 30 the Senate passed the Castle Clinton bill and sent it on to President Truman for his signature.[325] There had been a few anxious moments, but McAneny's alert lobbying had won the day. Senator Wagner had wavered for a brief period in early August because people he greatly respected were on both sides of the controversy; then he withdrew any possible objections to the proposal he had initially supported. Wagner concluded that the wording was permissive: The city of New York could request to donate Castle Clinton with the assurance that the Department of the Interior would have to administer the old fort, but the New Yorkers could easily decide not to make the donation.[326] Almost immediately organizations from New York City began to put pressure on Truman to sign the bill.[327] The president did sign the measure in mid-August, bypassing any input from Park Service advisers. The new law was something of a moral commitment; the legislators who had gone on record as favoring National Monument status would eventually have to appropriate the funds for restoration and maintenance.

During the fall of 1946 it appeared that Robert Moses and the Sulzbergers had accepted the idea that Castle Clinton would become a National Monument unless they could prove that the federal government would not take proper care of it. The *New York Times* regretted that Truman had chosen to sign the bill and estimated that any federal officials who took the trouble to come to New York to look at the ruined walls would see that at least $300,000 would be required for repairs. In addition the editors sincerely questioned the historical arguments advanced to support designation of the National Monument.[328] The mayor continued to try to satisfy both groups by asking that the work on the new tunnel be speeded up no matter what might be done with Castle Clinton itself.[329] Iphigene Sulzberger asked Secretary of the Interior Julius Krug to look over the castle and assess the situation. She asserted that the new law constituted an "unwarranted interference with local self-government," which was certainly an overstatement in view of the permissive wording of the act.[330] The *Times* coordinated its editorials with Mrs. Sulzberger's attack. The editors argued that if the fort must be saved, then the federal government should get on with it. Otherwise there would be an unfair delay in the construction of the tunnel approaches.[331] In the absence of Krug, Acting Secretary of the Interior Warner W. Gardner told Mrs. Sulzberger that he admired the earnestness of the citizens on both sides of the debate, but the Department of the Interior was bound by an act of Congress to consider that Castle Clinton merited National Monument status. He pointed out that the city of New York would have the final say in the matter, since the fort was the property of the municipal government.[332] Krug told Mayor O'Dwyer the same thing a few weeks later.[333] The mayor then outlined a series of financial pledges he expected from the Department of the Interior that could serve as evidence of good faith on the future care of Castle Clinton.[334] Gardner explained that nearly all of these demands had already been met—Interior had placed several items in its future budget estimates to cover the stabilization and restoration of the fort. The total commitment over two years ran close to $350,000.[335]

The impartial and businesslike tone used by the officials of the Department of the Interior had been deceptive. Ronald Lee, as chief historian, had already committed the Park Service to a close relationship with George McAneny. Lee knew that McAneny would prove to be one of the most important allies in the formation of the National Council for Historic Sites and Buildings. On October 28, 1946, Lee had dinner with McAneny and two other friends to discuss the founding of a semiprivate preservation organization. The group covered two vital topics: the nature of the preservation crisis in the United States and the kinds of people who should be brought together to deal effectively with the forces of destruction.[336] Obviously, the new partnership with McAneny was so fundamental that the National Park Service would move heaven and earth to help him save the fort. The opponents of the National Monument idea probably did not realize the degree to which the secretary of the interior and his subordinates were bound to assist the Castle Clinton movement.

The battle over the castle continued for three more years. During the struggle it appeared that Moses's side generally took the offensive, but it never seemed to be able to overcome the momentum set by the congressional pledge that put the Department of the Interior in the curious position of being legally "prepared" to accept the property as a gift from the city of New York.

The initial strategy of the enemies of Castle Clinton was a bold one: The city board of estimate was asked to vote a $54,000 appropriation for demolition of the remaining walls of the fort on the plausible theory that the new Republican Congress elected in the fall of 1946 would never honor the financial pledge made by the previous Congress, and the ensuing standoff could cost the city the use of the Brooklyn-Battery Tunnel for several years.[337] Mayor O'Dwyer took a middle position in the fray, shifting between discouragement over the postponement of federal appropriations and a constant willingness to ask the New York legislature for permission to cede the park area to the United States government.[338] The mayor made one rather guarded statement in support of a proposed National Monument at a meeting at Fraunces Tavern in New York: "I think it should be a national shrine because I believe that any structure—even a couple of bricks—should be preserved if it represents something that the American people wanted in a time of emergency."[339] The *Times* seized on O'Dwyer's words in an editorial, warning that even if the legislature allowed the city to grant Castle Clinton to the United States, a delay of a year and a half would then ensue before any federal funds could be spent. The editorial ended on an urgent note: "We have our own emergencies today, for which a half a million dollars can be better spent than on a 'couple of bricks' laid in 1807."[340] Naturally this statement led the supporters and the opponents of the Castle Clinton National Monument to engage in a verbal duel through the letters columns of the *Times*.[341]

A curious legal impasse crept into the negotiations between the city of New York and the Department of the Interior. O'Dwyer asked Secretary Krug to promise to request the proper appropriations for the restoration so that the city could petition the legislature in good conscience for permission to cede Castle Clinton to the United States government.[342] On the other hand, the Department of the Interior did not want to push the appropriations request until there was absolute assurance that the city would turn over the property.

On July 24, 1947, the Moses group overplayed its hand, and the *New York Times* celebrated a premature victory. The board of estimate approved the sum of $54,000 for leveling Castle Clinton, because the mayor had apparently concluded that there would be an inordinate delay before the Park Service could undertake a stabilization operation, much less a restoration. The *Times* gloated, "The vote to finish the demolition of the structure was a victory for Park Commissioner Robert

Moses and the final blow to the hopes of several groups that sought to have the building restored as a Fort Clinton memorial."[343] The opponents of the castle also pointed out with justifiable concern that the federal government was not willing to vote enough money to clean up just the surroundings of the Statue of Liberty—a genuine National Monument.[344]

Within a matter of a week George McAneny was back in the fight with a new legal maneuver that promised to derail Moses. He had the Municipal Art Commission file a request with the board of estimate to delay the destruction of Castle Clinton on the grounds that the commission had not given its approval.[345] The Art Commission had "consistently" defined the fort as a monument, and the Congress of the United States had already gone on record as favoring its establishment as a National Monument. There was a section of the New York City Code that required the permission of the Art Commission before the "cleaning, restoration, repair, alteration, removal or relocation of any work of art."[346]

The Department of the Interior eased its way into the controversy by referring to the demolition order of the board of estimate as a "precipitate step" in view of the fact that the federal government had lived up to its end of the bargain. Acting Secretary Oscar Chapman (speaking for the secretary) told Mayor O'Dwyer that his department had, as agreed, requested funds from Congress for restoration and repair of the old fort. It seemed logical that the city should reconsider its decision to demolish the remaining walls.[347] Armed with the letter from Chapman and the vote of the Municipal Art Commission, the mayor requested that his board reverse its action.[348] The editors of the *Times* were furious. They argued that it was ridiculous to listen to appeals from the federal government while the 1947 appropriations for the Statue of Liberty had been cut severely. And who would dare to compare the historical significance of the Statue of Liberty with the unsightly ruin in Battery Park?[349]

The board of estimate, prodded by a letter from Chapman, backed down on August 27 and voted to put $50,000 into shoring up the sides of the walls as the tunnel construction proceeded. The *Times* referred to this strategic retreat as a delay that would give the government a chance to show its good faith.[350] The mayor said, however, that the city had been willing to give the Department of the Interior only a year to come up with a large appropriation for restoring the castle.[351]

Throughout the fall of 1947 the Interior Department played a subtle waiting game with the city of New York. Secretary Krug and his immediate staff repeatedly told the municipal officials that the federal government did not want to influence the mayor and his board in making their decisions on Castle Clinton—but that the requests for the restoration funds had gone in; Krug stood ready to honor the pledge made by Congress. By this means he put the entire onus for demolition on the mayor and the board of estimate.[352] Mrs. Sulzberger made the mistake of assuming that Krug had taken a position of impartiality, and so she urged him to end the whole controversy by simply withdrawing his request for funds. In that way, she argued, Krug could break the impasse.[353] The secretary immediately warned Mrs. Sulzberger and Mayor O'Dwyer that he had to request the funds for restoration work in view of the responsibility that had been placed upon the Department of the Interior under the 1946 act that authorized the National Monument. He still maintained that New York City was perfectly free to refuse to donate the land to the United States.[354] This clever stand made it imperative that O'Dwyer petition the New York legislature to grant permission to New York City to turn over the land.[355] Krug was powerless to accede to Mrs. Sulzberger's request to stop supporting the restoration appropriation.[356]

The opponents of the Castle Clinton development won another hollow victory in the winter of 1948 when the New York legislature appeared to deny New York City's request to donate the land to the Department of the Interior.[357] A committee of the New York State Assembly killed the bill in early March, and the *Times* issued another triumphal statement in an editorial entitled "Exit Fort Clinton!" The writer referred to the "sane appraisal" made by the Assembly Committee, for in the future people could look across an unblemished Battery Park to Fort William on Governor's Island—to a well-preserved example of military architecture.[358] George McAneny found that the state legislators he met in Albany were afraid to vote against something Robert Moses wanted and that the mayor "swayed rather easily" from one side to another.[359]

The prorestoration forces now played their trump card, which was sure to win them a stay of execution, even if it did not ultimately save the castle. McAneny announced that any move on the part of the city to demolish Castle Clinton would result in a lawsuit based on the powers of the Municipal Art Commission.[360] All through the spring McAneny undercut Robert Moses on two fronts. He campaigned vigorously to see that members of the New York delegation in Congress pushed the appropriations for Castle Clinton. At the same time he looked into the possibility that the New York City bill which had stalled in Albany was a "phoney" sacrifice that had been sent up to be killed.[361] McAneny also addressed a forceful letter to the mayor hinting that His Honor had not really worked hard enough for the passage of a simple request up in Albany. Would it not make sense to bypass the whole idea of appealing to the legislature? Apparently, said McAneny, the city of New York could turn the land over to the Department of the Interior on its own.[362]

In spite of McAneny's efforts O'Dwyer finally concluded that time had run out, and he notified Secretary Krug that he must ask for the demolition of Castle Clinton because it would delay the construction of the tunnel approaches if the city waited any longer.[363] For a brief moment McAneny believed that he had lost the fight. In a public statement the alert preservationist headed off an attempt by the mayor to blame the federal government for the delay and the decision to demolish the fort.[364] McAneny admitted to Arthur Demaray, "We are in hard luck." The House Appropriations Committee in Washington had deleted the Interior request for restoration funds. But there still remained a lawsuit blocking demolition because of the jurisdiction of the Art Commission. Ronald Lee remembered this grim moment as a turning point in the battle that convinced him that McAneny had the fortitude to win the fight. "When the New York State Legislature and Congress both acted adversely and Castle Clinton appeared irretrievably lost, I recall vividly the feelings of dismay that spread through the ranks of its supporters. It was then that George McAneny was at his best, and through a miracle of maneuvers kept the issue open until in the end Castle Clinton was saved."[365] The board of estimate once more voted to carry out the destruction of Castle Clinton.[366] The *New York Times* was so sure of victory that it tried to be magnanimous:

> Some good friends differed with us on whether Fort Clinton should be preserved. We argued that it should not be, for reasons we have stated on numerous occasions. The years that have passed since the city first ordered demolition, and the number of times that the order has been cancelled after reinstatement, testify to the ardor and eloquence with which such civic leaders as George McAneny and others associated with him have fought the battle for a landmark they believed of sufficient historical interest to preserve. We are fortunate to have such citizens, who delight in keeping the city's past fresh in memory and who are able to recite its details with lively relish. Although we did not agree with them on this issue, believing that a greater advantage to the City lay in unbroken park development, we hold nevertheless to the principle that what is of convincing historic value in the city should be saved. This should make us allies together on some future battle lines.[367]

Somehow this editorial bore the marks of an epitaph rather than a compliment.

The American Scenic and Historic Preservation Society filed suit in the New York Supreme Court to stop the demolition of Castle Clinton, basing its case on the powers and the responsibilities of the City Art Commission.[368] On December 13, 1948, Justice Samuel Null ruled in favor of the society. In the eyes of at least one jurist Castle Clinton did possess "intrinsic value as a work of art." Thus the Art Commission would have to grant permission before the old fort could ever be taken down. Both McAneny and Lee drew great satisfaction from the decision because Null had gone out of his way to establish a legal basis for historic preservation:[369] "Whatever may be said for the concept that the old must yield to the new, I think there is still room for values which, while they may fail to impress in a material sense, nevertheless make for a fuller national and community life. A people indifferent to the landmarks and monuments of its past will not long retain its capacity to achieve an honored future."[370]

McAneny telephoned Lee with the good news, but the determined New York preservationist left nothing to chance. He was sure that Robert Moses would not take the new ruling with quiet resignation, so McAneny attacked on two fronts. He asked Mayor O'Dwyer to reintroduce the bill in Albany authorizing the city to turn over Castle Clinton to the federal government. At the same time he prepared for another court battle as rumors were in circulation that Moses would appeal the decision.[371]

The friends of Castle Clinton did not have to wait long for the storm to break. The *New York Times* carried several letters to the editor that accused Judge Null of giving in to a small group of determined people who had made a sacred cause out of a fort that had never seen a battle. One anonymous correspondent urged the Art Commission to take off its "rosy glasses" and see how far the ruined hulk of Castle Clinton was from becoming a true monument.[372] Moses himself chose the Letters to the Editor column as his own forum in late December. He was irked to discover that the *Times* had chosen to publish a letter from "J.O.G." who denounced the city for threatening to tear down Castle Clinton at a time when the proper course of action would be the appointment of a commission to inventory the historic landmarks that could be found all over New York City.[373] Once more Moses utilized the "practical" argument by listing the number of early buildings that had become wards of the city: "As to historic buildings and other structures, scores have been rehabilitated at enormous expense, much of it hidden in relief appropriations during the prodigal but not unconstructive days of the depression, and some of it representing the pious gifts of good citizens. . . . Why harp on the filling of seven acres of swamp [along Riverside Drive, site of Claremont] in a city in which thousands of acres of natural beauty have been preserved, or moan over a sunken gas tank at the Battery, where so many truly historic objects are being repaired and placed in a more dignified and conspicuous setting?"[374]

Ronald Lee and Arthur Demaray tried to keep alive the Castle Clinton Fund of $195,000 while the House Appropriations Committee tried to hold up the large grant until the land had been safely transferred to the United States. Demaray asked that the appropriation be left in the bill because O'Dwyer was working on the legislature again.[375] The mayor had indeed taken the decision of the Supreme Court as a signal to reintroduce the bill granting permission to New York City to turn over Castle Clinton to the government.[376]

Fortunately for the cause of history, the field now labeled oral history was just opening up under the guidance of Allan Nevins of Columbia University. Although Frederick Rath and George Palmer had already begun their collection of Hyde Park interviews on a wire recorder a year earlier, the great Columbia University collection of taped interviews began at a session in the apartment of George McAneny. While Nevins and a graduate student plied him with questions, the old warrior recounted his life story, including the battle over Castle Clinton.[377] The comments made by McAneny during the conversation recorded early in 1949 catch the flavor of his approach to the controversy while the final decision was still some months away:

> Every newspaper in New York except the *Times* has been with us. Now, this decision [from Justice Null] has been made and the Secretary of the Interior responded with a letter which hasn't been published yet, a letter to the Mayor saying he now supposes that everything is removed in the way of the City's ceding the property and he assumed that action will be taken at once toward that end. It put the Mayor on the spot. That will be printed in a few days, but, meanwhile, Moses appealed the case, and the Mayor didn't interfere with that. The argument on the appeal is to be held on the 15th of this month, Appellate Division. If we lose there, we're put back to some other move. If we win, that will pretty well settle the whole thing. Moses is costing the city a pile of money over this; all the expense of this litigation which has been voluminous. . . . It's been a long fight but it's been well worth it. Moses' first objection was that it's an old gas tank. That's what he says, says it's sunk in the ground there, that it isn't worth it. It can be brought to life by a few strokes of work, as the old red sandstone fort, as the old twin of the one on Governor's Island. . . . Well, that's rather a long story but it conveys the idea that New York's old landmarks ought to be preserved. . . . So much for Castle Clinton. If I win that fight, I'll feel I haven't lived in vain.[378]

Although McAneny may have surmised during the taping sessions that the fight was not over, he probably did not realize that one of the most exciting aspects of it still lay ahead. He announced to the press in late February that Secretary of the Interior Krug had requested enough money to start the restoration of Castle Clinton in the next annual budget. That should have meant that the New York legislature would have no real reason for turning down New York City's request to cede the land to the National Park Service.[379] William Adams Delano, president of the New York City Art Commission, said that a brief correspondence with President Truman led him to believe that the president and the secretary of the interior really were ready to take over the site of the old fort.[380] The Castle Clinton bill moved through the legislature quite easily in March, even clearing the Committee on the Affairs of New York City, where it had been derailed the year before.[381] The bill finally passed and went to Gov. Thomas E. Dewey for his signature on March 21, 1949.[382]

The drama then shifted to the governor's office. Just after the legislature opened the way for the cession of Castle Clinton, the Appellate Division of the New York court system reversed the New York Supreme Court decision. Robert Moses had won his appeal. In the words of Justice Bernard L. Shientag, "We hold that what now remains of the Aquarium structure or the walls of the old fort which preceded it does not constitute a 'monument' or a 'work of art' within the meaning of the City Charter." Therefore the City Art Commission had no right to stop the board of estimate from carrying out a decision to demolish the old ruin.[383] McAneny knew that he could quickly win the fight if Dewey could be persuaded to sign the Castle Clinton bill that was on his desk. The trouble was, McAneny confided to Ronald Lee, that Dewey appeared to favor the views of the Sulzbergers and Moses. Suspecting this possibility, though, the American Scenic and Historic Preservation Society members had sent a "raft of telegrams and letters" to Albany.[384] The governor soon learned that many New Yorkers would view his veto of the bill as a defeat for the concept of home rule—when the measure had passed both houses of the legislature without a dissenting vote.[385] C. C. Burlingame told the readers of the *Times* in a letter printed on April 11 that the new Appellate Division ruling had not "ended the life of the fort." He boasted that Castle Clinton had "as many lives as a cat."[386] He was right, because Dewey disappointed the friends of park commissioner Moses when he signed the bill giving Castle Clinton to the federal government.[387] Dewey hastened to point out that the bill was "permissive" and New York City was still free to demolish the fort if it chose to do so.

The officials of the Department of the Interior announced that they would request at least $195,000 in the appropriations for 1950 to cover restoration of the old fort if the city would promise to turn the land over to the government.[388] Hillory Tolson of the Park Service put some pressure on members of Congress to keep the Castle Clinton restoration item alive.[389] On October 6, 1949, the House of Representatives approved an appropriation bill that included $165,000 for the "improvement and rehabilitation" of Castle Clinton.[390] On May 13, 1950, Castle Clinton became a National Monument.

At long last George McAneny could consider his campaign successful. He even issued a guarded victory statement that warmly praised the officials of the National Park Service and Mayor O'Dwyer for pushing the bill in Albany.[391] The *New York Times* responded with a testy editorial that may well have had a certain amount of prophetic vision. The headline on the column was "Even $165,750 is too much," and the anonymous writer predicted that the United States government would never commit enough money for the proper development of the old fort. (The castle did not undergo a full restoration for nearly twenty-five years.) The editorial mildly urged President Truman to reverse the decision of Congress: "We venture to say that posterity will wonder why in the world the Government decided to keep Fort Clinton."[392] On the surface this complaint seems justified. Fiske Kimball had warned the Park Service Advisory Board in 1945 that there were a number of old installations along the Atlantic Coast that rivaled Castle Clinton.

What the *New York Times* never fully understood was that the real issue was the question of preserving urban monuments all over the nation—and the need for greater unity in the preservation movement in order to accomplish this. The Sulzbergers and Robert Moses probably never realized that McAneny was not their only skilled opponent. Ronald Lee saw in McAneny and his long war for the beleaguered fort a means for uniting preservationists into an organization that could combine the strength and fervor of the private historical and preservation field with the professional skills developed by the National Park Service. Castle Clinton was not important in and of itself; it was only a means to a greater end. But the loss of the fort—once the battle had started—would have greatly upset a group of people who hoped that the Department of the Interior and the various historical organizations active in preservation work could unite in the new National Council. The survival of Castle Clinton was a visible proof that the union had been achieved.

The *New York Times* was as magnanimous in defeat as it had tried to be in victory. When George McAneny turned eighty in December 1949, his opponents greeted him with an editorial tribute that listed his political, cultural, and historical accomplishments (without mentioning the controversial fort). The article concluded, "New York is indebted to George McAneny for his unflagging work for its betterment. On this, his eightieth birthday, we salute him."[393] Frederick L. Rath, Jr., who came to work for the new National Council for Historic Sites and Buildings in 1948, remembered McAneny as a tired warrior who believed he had done enough in helping to found the new organization. McAneny did not seem to want any more responsibilities in the preservation field after the campaign for Castle Clinton: "I thought he was a towering figure. I thought he was an extraordinarily sensible and sensitive man. He amused me a good deal with his doggedness and perseverance, particularly in the Castle Clinton fight. He loved having bested Robert Moses in that one. He just loved that."[394] Castle Clinton has perhaps finally become a major historical landmark because of its position as the focal point of the most hard-fought preservation battle of the 1940s. The fort might never have fired a shot in the War of 1812, but George McAneny and Robert Moses expended enough legal ammunition over the future of the sandstone walls to fill the entire courtyard.

Hampton

The National Park Service took on very few new properties in the years following World War II because the funds provided even for the operation of the existing historic sites and monuments were inadequate. In the case of the Home of Franklin D. Roosevelt there had been a long-term commitment to the idea of a National Historic Site through a congressional resolution in 1939. The death of Roosevelt provided a focus for the visiting public who streamed to Hyde Park in such great numbers over the years. Independence National Historical Park was the product of pressure brought to bear by Edwin O. Lewis and his Independence Hall Association, along with the Pennsylvania delegation in Congress. All of the money for the purchase of land north of Independence Hall came from the Commonwealth of Pennsylvania, and the Park Service administrative staff supported the park because of its transcendant historical value. George McAneny and Ronald Lee had managed to get a bill through Congress that pledged acceptance of Castle Clinton if the state of New York would permit New York City to cede the old fort to the United States government. But there was no clear way for the Park Service to purchase any architectural monuments that might be in danger. No one seriously questioned the historical importance of Independence Hall or even President Roosevelt's home. Though some people sincerely doubted the worth of Castle Clinton, Park Service officials were mainly concentrating on building an alliance with McAneny. But when one of the great Georgian houses of America, Hampton, needed preservation, it was a different story. The building not only lacked any connection with people who had profoundly influenced the course of history, but it also had no large organization moving to save it.

It was this unlikely situation that brought the National Park Service into close contact with David Finley, director of the National Gallery of Art in Washington, D.C. Finley had been an adviser of Andrew Mellon, the former secretary of the treasury who donated the large National Gallery building to the United States government. Finley had entered the field of cultural preservation during World War II when he served on the Roberts Commission, or the American Commission for the Protection and Salvage of Artistic and Historic Monuments in War Areas.[395] From August 1943 through 1946 he must have become familiar with the efforts of a small band of fine-arts officers who tried to preserve the artistic and architectural heritage of Western Europe.[396]

Strangely enough, the search for a particular painting for the National Gallery led Finley into the center of the historic preservation community in the United States. As director, Finley had been keenly aware of the gaps in the collection of American painters, and he was especially eager to find an adequate representation of the work of Thomas Sully. Sometime in the summer of 1945 he visited Hampton (1783), the country seat of the Ridgely family in Towson, Md., just north of Baltimore. The furnishings of Hampton included two fine Sully portraits, the more important of which was a full-length picture of Eliza Ridgely, entitled *The Lady with a Harp*. Finley successfully negotiated the purchase of the paintings for the National Gallery.[397] But he realized during his visit to Hampton that John Ridgely, the owner of the estate, faced a great challenge.

> John Ridgely very kindly let me see not only this painting and his other treasures, but he also showed me Hampton, so appealing in its beauty and dignity, and practically unchanged in the midst of its rolling acres after more than a hundred and sixty years.

> Mr. Ridgely, however, knew that its integrity as a great country house was seriously threatened by encroaching developments from the neighboring city of Baltimore. He told me of his desire that Hampton should become a national monument and saved for future generations as an outstanding example of Eighteenth Century American-Palladian architecture. He was very generous in offering to do what he could in helping to bring this about, so when I got back to Washington, I talked with Mr. Drury, Mr. Demaray, and Mr. Ronald Lee.[398]

Hampton, Towson, Md. (National Park Service)

Apparently the first person Finley approached was Fiske Kimball, a member of the Park Service Advisory Board and also director of the Philadelphia Museum of Art. On December 11, 1945, Kimball asked the Advisory Board Interim Committee to recognize Hampton as "one of the great post-Revolutionary houses in the United States." He admitted that Hampton should be thought of as a superb Georgian house—not as the home of the Ridgelys. But Newton Drury recommended that the board consider carefully whether the National Park Service should acquire even "a supreme example of architecture that creates an additional financial burden for the Government." Drury was concerned over the way in which the Park Service had been making excuses to the Bureau of the Budget and the House Appropriations Committee over the government's new responsibilities in the historical parks area. Then he made the momentous suggestion that preservationists create a National Trust similar to the English organization that could care for places like Hampton. After some discussion of the idea, Kimball managed to get the Interim Committee to pass a resolution that had the unprecedented effect of putting the Park Service into the field of architectural history. Hampton received the singular distinction of being described as worthy of national recognition "on account of its outstanding merit as an architectural monument, almost perfectly preserved from the time it was built."[399] Before this meeting the Park Service had always put historical considerations first in deciding whether to grant national significance to landmarks that had architectural qualifications. Nevertheless, Kimball was in no position to push the Department of the Interior into taking over Hampton.

David Finley also talked about the situation at Hampton with Andrew Mellon's daughter, Ailsa Mellon Bruce.[400] He apparently convinced Mrs. Bruce and Donald D. Shepard of the Avalon Foundation (a Mellon family philanthropy) that the ideal way to save Hampton would be for the foundation to make a contribution of the purchase price—on the assumption that the National Park Service would take over the restoration and maintenance of the great house and its spacious grounds. The idea must have appealed to the Mellon family, and so negotiations began among John Ridgely, the Avalon Foundation board, and the Park Service.[401]

The Hampton question came up before the Park Service Advisory Board just at the time that the Washington office was about to be reorganized after the war. Ronald Lee had returned as chief historian in January 1946, after spending three years in England with the air force. Up until that time Arthur Demaray had been the only senior Park Service administrator who had maintained an office in Washington. The rest of the staff had gone to Chicago with director Newton Drury. At about the same time Donald E. Lee, an expert in real estate matters, joined the Washington office of the Park Service to plan land acquisitions.

This small staff went to work on the problem of saving Hampton with the assistance of David Finley and the Mellon family. Early in 1946 Ronald Lee went to Towson with Finley and Shepard to see if John Ridgely would be willing to come to some agreement that would permit the donation of private funds for the acquisition of the estate as a National Historic Site. Lee became convinced that Hampton was worth saving and that it was possible for the Park Service to take over the property.[402] However, he had to work hard to sell the senior administrators on the idea, because they saw in Hampton a great new "white elephant" that would require a large appropriation for a proper rehabilitation.[403] But Demaray did believe that any building that could interest Ronald Lee, Fiske Kimball, and David Finley certainly deserved extended study by the National Park Service staff.[404]

All during the spring and summer of 1946 Park Service personnel studied and debated the question of acquiring Hampton as a gift from the Mellon interests. Historian Frederick Tilberg went out to Towson in March to work up a historic-site survey-report on Hampton.[405] And in April regional director Thomas Allen noted that an "un-named donor plans to acquire the building and some of the property and then offer it to the National Park Service."[406] Somehow the whole purchase was coming into focus.

The postwar starvation of the National Park Service and the severe planning problems that came with demobilization were awesome obstacles facing those who worked to make Hampton a National Historic Site. The senior officers of the Park Service feared that they would never be able to get the project through the Bureau of the Budget, even if the mysterious donor did present the estate to the Department of the Interior.[407] It was going to be difficult to sell the hard-nosed federal bureaucracy on an architectural monument even if it came as a gift.

Demaray tried to get as much evidence as possible regarding the importance of Hampton. He began by asking Kimball for his views.[408] Once more the architectural historian was emphatic. Hampton represented "the height of opulence in the moment just at the end of the Revolution," and it deserved the care that the Park Service could give it. Kimball's final comment drew on his great knowledge: "I know of no other 18-century house of equal importance which is apt to be given to the nation in any near future, and I think, if offered as a gift, it should by all means be accepted."[409] Park Service architect Stuart Barnette was not quite so lavish in his praise, but he thought the "architectural importance" of Hampton deserved some consideration for preservation.[410]

On November 15, 1946, Ronald Lee, David Finley, Donald Shepard, and Donald Lee all went to Hampton to see if an agreement might be worked out with John Ridgely, who was confined to his sickroom. The meeting was productive because the owner of Hampton signed an option agreement that represented a figure "substantially below the market value." Armed with this crucial document Ronald Lee asked director Drury to commit himself on the acceptability of Hampton for the Park Service. Lee mentioned that the officials of the Mellon Charitable and Educational Trust were interested in presenting the property to the Department of the Interior, but they had to know how the Park Service might treat the gift before any formal transaction took place.[411] Lee went to Chicago with Arthur Demaray, and the two convinced Drury that the Park Service should go on record as favoring the purchase.[412] Drury, however, maintained that he could not act on the Hampton project until an organization could be found to ease the financial burden that would come with the maintenance of the house and grounds.[413] Demaray assured his boss that the Mellon Trust (which wished to remain anonymous) guaranteed to expend up to $90,000 for the house and its furnishings, as well as some necessary repairs. At the same time he promised that his office would contact Goucher College, in Towson, as a possible custodian.[414]

As had been so often the case in the busy years just before World War II, the National Park Service had to conduct some delicate negotiations in order to execute a cooperative agreement that would satisfy both the Bureau of the Budget and the ever-cautious Newton Drury. The discussions included questions dealing with the repair of the house, the purchase of some of the Ridgely furniture, and the running expenses that would have to be covered by some private organization.[415] Demaray and Lee worked hard to make sure that Drury did not allow the secretary of the interior to decline any offer from the Mellon interests regarding Hampton.[416] When the official offer did come, it turned out that the donor was to be the Avalon Foundation through its director, Shepard. Shepard told Secretary Krug that the foundation was willing to donate up to $90,000 to the Park Service for Hampton, some original furnishings, and necessary repairs. He was quick to add that the donation would not include any promises of assistance in the maintenance of the estate. It was essential that the secretary of the interior find some means of funding the complete restoration and exhibition of Hampton before the middle of June 1948. The Mellons obviously wanted to get Krug to obtain a congressional appropriation for the care of Hampton.[417] Krug replied to Shepard with a note of gratitude that did not commit the Park Service in any way.[418]

Drury tried to make up his mind whether to support the Hampton proposal so earnestly advocated by his chief historian and his associate director. He ordered the Park Service staff to prepare a detailed statement for the president of the United States of the probable costs of buying and maintaining the property. Drury assumed that Goucher College would be the agency that would eventually use Hampton for some historical purpose.[419] The situation became even more clouded after Park Service engineer W. E. O'Neil, Jr., visited Hampton in January 1947. He reported that he was not sure about the whole negotiation—Ridgely seemed to be in too much of a hurry to unload his great house upon the people of the United States. "Having lived quite closely to the extremely unromantic phase of trying to repair, restore, and render safe for public use, with a minimum of funds, several large and expensive historic houses, I must say that my own emotions in going over Hampton House and its immediate grounds were quite mixed. It is a rather impressive place in a not too serious state of disrepair . . ., but I am not at all sure that I am an enthusiastic supporter of the idea principally because of the improbability of our obtaining sufficient appropriated funds for its proper rehabilitation and adaption to historic site use."[420] That was just the kind of language that tended to make Drury retreat from a proposed acquisition, especially at a time when he could not figure out how the Park Service was going to maintain its far-flung empire.

While the director mulled over the situation, Ronald Lee entered into negotiations with a new organization that showed a real interest in taking over the management of Hampton—the Society for the Preservation of Maryland Antiquities.[421] Lee had already given Robert Garrett of the Maryland society a copy of the existing cooperative agreement with the Carl Schurz Memorial Foundation as an example of a successful relationship that had permitted a private organization to care for property of the federal government.[422] Quickly Lee informed Drury about the new source of support. He told Drury that Garrett was a distinguished Baltimore banker who had important civic interests in both the Walters Art Gallery and the National Recreation Association.[423] But Drury remained unimpressed by the earnestness and zeal of his chief historian. The warning contained in the O'Neil report stuck in his mind. Drury did not think the Hampton cooperative agreement would sit well with Congress in view of the "delicate" situation with the House Appropriations Committee. He quoted a passage from a famous educator: "I am also reminded of the statement that the late President Benjamin Ide Wheeler used to make to the fellows in each freshman class: 'Boys, you will have to let a lot of good things pass by.'"[424]

In all justice to Drury, it is necessary to realize that the proposed $90,000 gift from the Avalon Foundation had been broken down into the following component parts: $43,300 to purchase the house and forty acres of land, $15,000 to buy some of the Ridgely furniture, and $25,000 to repair the structure in a way that would permit the public to view it.[425] There was no provision for maintaining the estate beyond 1948.

It was Ronald Lee's enthusiasm and industry that won the first round of the battle. Lee drafted a letter for Acting Secretary Warner W. Gardner to Donald Shepard, conditionally accepting the donation from the Avalon Foundation. Gardner noted that the negotiations with the Maryland society were still under way, and several important matters with regard to the Ridgely furnishings had to be cleared up. He said that the Park Service could return almost all of the money if the actual purchase of Hampton did not go through.[426] The officers of the foundation saw that there was almost no hope of an appropriation from Congress for the long-term maintenance of Hampton, and so they were still willing to make their donation as long as the Society for the Preservation of Maryland Antiquities appeared to be a "substantial" group and if John Ridgely would agree to the idea of the cooperative agreement.[427] Shepard, speaking for the foundation, readily accepted the new arrangement after he had concluded that Garrett's organization seriously meant to discharge its obligations with regard to Hampton. On April 25, 1947, he officially transmitted to Secretary Krug the sum of $90,000 to be used for the purchase, repair, and furnishing of Hampton.[428] Krug gratefully accepted the gift.[429]

Meanwhile Lee was in Baltimore trying to work out all the necessary arrangements with Robert Garrett and the Maryland society.[430] Lee helped to draft the cooperative agreement that would leave the society in charge of the newly refurbished Hampton estate.[431] John H. Scarff, a Baltimore architect who was an officer in the society, spent some time at Hampton on an inspection trip with one of the Park Service engineers. He wanted to be sure that some kind of document had been prepared specifying repairs that the Park Service might carry out on Hampton before the agreement went into effect. The society wanted any changes that were to be made considered as part of an overall restoration program.[432]

During the summer Lee succeeded in carrying the preliminary negotiations to a successful conclusion. In August the secretary of the interior officially asked President Truman to approve a cooperative agreement with the Maryland society that would mean that Hampton could be accepted into the National Park System. On October 6 the president gave his approval;[433] in December, Assistant Secretary of the Interior C. Girard Davison consented to the actual purchase of Hampton for the sum of $43,315 and to the acquisition of the more valuable pieces of Ridgely furniture in the house.[434] At that point approximately $28,000 of the Avalon donation remained to be used for the repair of the house. Arthur Demaray outlined to Robert Garrett in some detail the priorities that had been assigned to the repair schedule by the Park Service engineers and architects, but at the same time he welcomed ideas from the Maryland society.[435] The Preservation Society quickly ratified the final form of the cooperative agreement and sent along its own list of necessary repairs. It hoped to operate Hampton from the admissions income, augmented by the proceeds from refreshments and the rental of rooms in the upper floors of the mansion.[436] Although the Park Service administrators generally did not agree with certain aspects of the approach of the Maryland society, associate regional director Elbert Cox remarked to Garrett that he liked Hampton and that he was greatly heartened by "the realistically intelligent and businesslike attitude of the officers and members of your Society."[437]

Both the Park Service staff and the officers of the Society for the Preservation of Maryland Antiquities needed all the business sense they could muster in 1948 as they studied the problems involved in presenting Hampton to the public. Elbert Cox warned that admission fees would finally prove to be the only reliable source of income. The tearoom idea and the rooms for visitors were operations that might well cost more than they would bring in—not to speak of the possible fire risks involved.[438] Throughout most of 1948 the principal problem consisted of finding a way to harmonize three apparently divergent sets of interests: The Park Service wanted to see Hampton properly restored and furnished under the auspices of the Maryland society; Congress and the Bureau of the Budget were willing to bring Hampton into the National Park System only if the federal government did not have to bear any of the regular maintenance costs; and the Society for the Preservation of Maryland Antiquities wanted to stretch whatever was left of the Avalon Foundation's gift of $90,000 as far as it could go to make Hampton usable and presentable.

Newton Drury promised John Scarff that the Park Service would render all the technical assistance it could to the Preservation Society. But Drury considered the plans for the refreshments and the use of rental space inappropriate for a National Historic Site, although the sale of postcards and a "carefully selected number of souvenir objects" might help to augment admission fees.[439] The technical assistance came to the Hampton project quite early because Ronald Lee watched over the developments in Towson as much as he could. For instance, Lee informed Garrett that the kind of research operation carried on by the Maryland society should not receive advance publicity until much of the original material had been examined by the people hired to do the basic studies on the house.[440] During most of 1948 and 1949 the museum staff of the National Park Service gave considerable assistance to the Maryland group in cataloging and restoring the furnishings selected for Hampton.[441]

When Secretary Julius Krug officially designated Hampton a National Historic Site on June 22, 1948, it appeared that Lee's carefully negotiated cooperative agreement had worked out well. The Avalon Foundation through the influence of David Finley had made it possible for the federal government to take over and repair one of the great architectural landmarks from the Georgian period. At the same time Lee had been able to locate, through his conversations with Robert Garrett, an organization that was capable of caring for the house in a responsible way.

Unfortunately, that last point led to one final crisis in the saving of Hampton. On October 1, 1948, John Scarff notified director Drury that the Society for the Preservation of Maryland Antiquities could not accept the custodianship of the property unless two critical situations could be cleared up. The house needed an adequate water supply and the second floor required considerable reinforcement. The gardens also needed some landscaping, but that was not an immediate problem.[442] Drury discovered that some members of the society had already approached the directors of the Avalon Foundation with word of the financial and structural situation at Hampton. Although the foundation had made it abundantly clear that there was to be no donation beyond the initial $90,000, the new request received some sympathetic consideration.[443] Lee conferred with some members of the Preservation Society, notably Garrett and H. Alexander Smith, Jr., about ways to pay for the necessary work at Hampton so that the house could be opened to the public. Lee hoped that the Maryland legislature might be willing to follow the lead of the Mellon family in supporting the latest federal project.[444] The whole crisis evaporated on December 29, when Donald Shepard of the foundation announced to Secretary Krug that his organization was prepared to add the sum of $40,000 to the initial Hampton donation.[445] Shepard also stated that the foundation would be willing to make available another $18,000 to help with the landscaping if the Society for the Preservation of Maryland Antiquities could raise a matching sum. The office of the secretary of the interior gratefully accepted the offer on December 31.[446]

All through the spring of 1949 the National Park Service and the society worked to prepare Hampton for visitors. People such as Charles Peterson and Ronald Lee gave the Maryland preservationists sound advice on restoration, interpretation, and historical research. Everyone involved wanted to be sure that the Hampton program was not rushed by a premature opening date, since there was so much documentary research and cataloging of furnishings that had to be done.[447] On May 2 the mansion opened to the public with enough visitors to amass $600 in admission fees.[448] Although much more research and restoration work remained to be done, the most difficult hurdles had been crossed.

Why had Ronald Lee worked so hard for a period of three or four years to insure the preservation and renovation of a large Georgian house in Maryland? He was the chief historian of the National Park Service at a time when the director was concerned about the ability of the Department of the Interior to maintain the many historic buildings already within the National Park System. Obviously, Lee had convinced Newton Drury that Hampton deserved the recognition that would come through designation as a National Historic Site. Fiske Kimball and Charles Peterson, two of the foremost architectural historians in the United States at that time, had pronounced Hampton to be a remarkably unspoiled mansion. Kimball did not hesitate to push the nomination of Hampton through the Advisory Board on architectural grounds. That was a precedent that proved that the Park Service did not restrict its interests to places associated with great people or important events.

The cooperative agreement worked out with Robert Garrett and the Society for the Preservation of Maryland Antiquities showed once more that the most successful negotiations had come in instances where the federal government owned the property and the private agency became the custodian. It was the kind of cooperation that Lee hoped would eventually unite the resources of private historical groups and the Park Service.

Most important of all, Lee saw that the acquisition of Hampton could bring new faces and new sources for funding into the preservation movement. David Finley, as a close confidant of the Mellon family, had been instrumental in consummating the purchase of Hampton. The 1950 *Report* of the Avalon Foundation showed that the Mellons had become much more important patrons of historic preservation than anyone had supposed up to that time. The foundation had also assisted the Robert E. Lee Memorial Foundation at Stratford, the Woodlawn Public Foundation in Virginia, and the Roosevelt Memorial Association in its

Dedication of Hampton National Historic Site, Towson, 1950. Left to right: *David Finley, William Lane, Robert Garrett, Newton Drury. (National Archives)*

efforts to improve Sagamore Hill, the Long Island home of Theodore Roosevelt. And so just after Henry Ford had died and the Rockefeller commitment to Williamsburg seemed to be tapering off, the National Park Service had managed to interest another of America's wealthy families in preservation.[449]

All through the Hampton negotiations Lee also worked closely with Finley to find ways to unite all interested private individuals and organizations into a National Council for Historic Sites and Buildings. Finley, in speaking at the dedication of Hampton in 1950, remembered that he and the senior Park Service officials were happy to look back over the struggle for the preservation of Hampton, "but like most people in our positions, we determined to go on to bigger and bigger things." The biggest thing of all was the end goal—the formation of an American National Trust.[450] The newly restored Hampton became the visible symbol of the rejuvenated preservation movement. The scale of the challenges that faced preservationists in 1946 had demanded a move toward an amalgamation of governmental and private organizations throughout the country, and men such as Ronald Lee and Arthur Demaray achieved that goal while they were negotiating the terms for the purchase of Hampton and its family furnishings from John Ridgely in 1946 and 1947.[451]

Part Four

Preservation Matures

10

The Formation of the National Trust for Historic Preservation

T HE PRESERVATION MOVEMENT in the United States produced a number of leaders who yearned for an organization that could operate on the national scene. The fragmented nature of preservation work worried these people because they began to see that proper financing and professional management would never come while the historic buildings of America remained mainly in the hands of amateurs. The local emphasis that had characterized preservation was an asset in that there were always many dedicated supporters around the country, but it was also a weakness because the movement seemed so aimless. By the late 1940s administrators from the National Park Service and private historical groups realized there must be a central preservation agency in the United States. They could not agree fully on the functions of the organization they wanted, but they knew the forces of destruction could only be met effectively by a national trust that combined the professionalism of the Park Service with the public support to be found in private preservation organizations. The first step would be the formation of a national headquarters. Then a committee could draft a charter, which would establish a board of trustees drawn from different federal agencies and private preservation groups. The new trust would be empowered to accept gifts and to own historic properties.

The English artist Charles R. Ashbee had come to the United States in 1901 to produce a report on the status of preservation in this country. He also hoped to found an American branch of the English National Trust, but he was disappointed to find so many active groups already at work that a truly centralized organization had no base of support. Ashbee recognized the strong backing given to different local preservation causes, and he readily admitted that all one could hope to do was try to coordinate these far-flung activities.[1]

William Sumner Appleton echoed Ashbee's lament several decades later in 1919 when the New Englander published his appeal to preservationists in the United States in the spring issue of *Art and Archaeology.* Appleton hoped that a fund could be set up to be administered by a board of trustees, operating on a national basis. His plan called for two procedures that seemed to be critical at that time: amassing larger endowments for maintaining museum properties and removing threatened buildings to outdoor museums. The idea was a workable one, but no patrons came forth to give the necessary money.[2]

Even when Verne Chatelain and Horace Albright of the National Park Service began to work on a federal program for historic preservation, there were thoughtful people who hoped that their plan might include some kind of private organization that could function on a national scale. Just as the Historic Sites Act was moving through the legislative process, Charles Merriam of the University of Chicago told the United States Territorial Expansion Memorial Commission on December 19, 1934, that there should be "a private organization or semi-private. . . . England has quite an organization for the preservation of historic sites and monuments." The commission agreed with Merriam's basic idea, but the distinguished men who attended the St. Louis meeting were really only trying to look into the validity of the Jefferson National Expansion Memorial.[3] The planning for the Historic Sites Act was quite enough in 1934 without investigating the possibility of founding a national trust in the United States.

The historians who administered the programs set up under the new law in 1935 became an elite guard of nationally minded preservationists. They were the first professional group to see the true scope of the federal program, and they quickly grasped the importance of bringing private historical organizations more strongly into the planning work being done by the federal government. Ronald F. Lee and some of the regional historians were particularly well placed to understand the problems involved in trying to conduct a national survey, while all sorts of new destructive forces tended to lessen the impact of the National Park Service. The inability of the Department of the Interior to purchase threatened buildings gravely weakened the program that did emerge after 1935. The United States was ready for a coordinated preservation plan.

The regional supervisor of historic sites in the Santa Fe office of the Park Service in 1941 was V. Aubrey Neasham, a trained historian who had had considerable experience in surveying early sites in California. Neasham wrote a paper late in 1941 that showed he clearly recognized that the Park Service could not deal with the vast number of preservation crises that came up each year. Even the money made available through the New Deal programs had not been able to stem the tide of inaction and outright destruction that seemed to be sweeping across the United States with the return of prosperity. Neasham saw that the real danger was summarized in the appealing word *progress*. He noted that the vast majority of sites considered to possess national significance in Region III of the Park Service were still in private hands. The federal government could in no way preserve all of them. What was to be done?

A national campaign pointing out the importance of preservation would do much. In addition to this, however, the most practical method would be to form a non-profit private corporation, comparable to the "Save the Redwoods League" of California [Newton Drury's old organization], having as its primary function the acquisition and preservation of historic sites of national significance which are now owned privately. The ultimate function would be to transfer the sites under its jurisdiction to qualified public agencies, when those agencies are ready to take them over.

A non-profit private corporation of the type we have in mind, let us call it Historic Sites of America, Incorporated, should not be attempted without sufficient capital to carry on its functions effectively. It is believed that there are enough people in the United States who would be interested in financing such a corporation, either by outright donations or purchase of shares of stock. Some $20,000,000 were made available by private interests for the restoration of Williamsburg, Virginia. $1,000,000, for a corporation to save the outstanding historic sites of our nation now in private hands, would be of greater service to the American people.[4]

Neasham outlined a skeleton office force for the new organization, and then he assumed that the fruits of the National Survey of Historic Sites and Buildings would make it possible to build up a priority list of the endangered sites in the United States. (A few years before 1941 such a census could not have been made.) He went on to propose that Historic

Sites of America, Inc., engage in a program of stabilization that would keep all of its newly acquired properties in good repair until a suitable organization could take over their maintenance.[5] The new private corporation could funnel the most important historical and architectural resources of the nation into the hands of public and semipublic preservation agencies.

In January 1942 Neasham wrote another report that carried his program a step further. He recognized the anarchy that existed as long as historic places remained in the hands of unsympathetic private owners. He also saw that the forces of change and progress had been temporarily stifled by the Great Depression and the outbreak of World War II: "A program formulated now can be well under way by the end of the war. This factor is important. Heaven help the historic sites of America, if such a program has not been formulated when peace does come! With the great sums of money, which will be released at the end of the war to take up the slack in employment as a result of war industries giving way to peace-time endeavors, irreparable harm may be done. Witness the mistakes of the depression years, when too much money and too few plans based upon sound principles were not uncommon."[6] Neasham outlined a system of financing the quasi-private corporation that would begin to purchase the historic sites of the future.[7] He even suggested an annual appropriation of perhaps $100,000 a year. Obviously, Aubrey Neasham had put his finger on a most significant point: There was going to be a great challenge to the preservation field after the war, but there was no certainty that there could be adequate funding (public or private) for such a confrontation unless some immediate planning were done.

A few other individuals foresaw that same challenge and offered ideas of their own in letters to the White House from time to time during the war. Unfortunately, these communications received rather perfunctory replies from the staff of the National Park Service (which was then in its Chicago exile). One restaurant owner in Chatham, N.J., wrote a long letter to Eleanor Roosevelt in 1944. Mrs. M. McCann Naef proposed that the federal government begin a vast program of registering historic buildings that could be put into adaptive use (like her restaurant) with zoning restrictions that would protect them from the highway builders and commercial developers. Mrs. Naef suggested that a property owner could enter into a contract with some branch of the government that would guarantee a certain amount of protection in return for reasonable access to the building. The Naef plan featured awesome-looking bronze plaques that would proclaim each site a "Historic Property of the United States." It is not difficult to recognize in this plea a prototype of what has since become the National Register of Historic

Places.[8] In 1944 all the Park Service officials could do was tell Mrs. Naef that state or local governments should handle all questions having to do with zoning. Newton Drury and Arthur Demaray discussed her proposal and concluded that the nation was not ready for federal intervention in local affairs.[9] On July 24, 1945, Frances Davis Bendtsen of South St. Joseph, Mo., asked President Truman to establish a separate federal agency to be called the "Department or Division for Preservation of American Heritages and Historical Sites." She proposed that all the skills of modern urban planners be used to prepare the postwar program for the new department. She envisaged an employment program for the millions of veterans who would be returning to the work force in a fairly short time. The blighted neighborhoods in large cities could be eliminated while the road builders would try to tie in rural areas with a national highway program. The whole effort would culminate in a series of "National Tours" that could become a major source of postwar prosperity. Mrs. Bendtsen showed a fair knowledge of preservation developments abroad without exhibiting much understanding of the ways in which the Historic Sites Act had been put into operation.[10] Herbert Kahler drafted a pleasant letter from Newton Drury to the concerned preservationist from Missouri, encouraging her to visit the large number of historical areas already within the National Park System, once the wartime travel restrictions had been lifted.[11]

FIRST STEPS

There were other well-informed private individuals who quickly recognized the nature of the crisis that faced historic preservation in 1945, and they began to move along paths that eventually brought them together in Washington, D.C., in 1947 to found the National Council for Historic Sites and Buildings. The organization of a national council was considered a necessary first step in creating a congressionally chartered national trust. These civic leaders included George McAneny, then president of the American Scenic and Historic Preservation Society; Horace M. Albright, former director of the National Park Service, who was president of the Borax Corporation; Ronald F. Lee, chief historian of the National Park Service, who had been in England during most of World War II; David Finley, director of the National Gallery of Art; and Christopher Crittenden, director of the North Carolina Department of Archives and History.

Horace Albright had been the first person in this group to take an interest in a national preservation program. He had visited England in

1934 and discovered the varied activities of the National Trust in that country. Upon his return to the United States, Albright had helped to interest John D. Rockefeller, Jr., in sponsoring the studies made by J. Thomas Schneider in preparation for the Historic Sites Act of 1935.[12] At the end of World War II Albright and George McAneny found themselves engaged in a battle to save a number of nineteenth-century row houses along Washington Square in New York City.[13] Although he was a hardworking businessman, Albright could not resist cooperating with McAneny as the contest over Washington Square and Castle Clinton began to take form. Albright was caught up with McAneny's enthusiasm. "I was president of a company here [in New York City] and . . . I was spread out too thin to get myself going to Washington often. . . . But McAneny was retired and he had time for it. We used to meet over in the bar-room of the old Murray Hill Hotel which is up there above Grand Central. We used to go over there and have cocktails in the evening and wait until the late train back and talk things over. George McAneny was a wonderful fellow."[14]

While McAneny and Albright discussed the strategy that would eventually defeat Robert Moses at Castle Clinton, David Finley had become concerned about the fate of Oak Hill, the former home of President Monroe that was across the highway from Finley's estate at Oatlands, near Leesburg, Va. Frank Littleton, the owner of Oak Hill, had told Finley in the summer of 1945 that he was going to have to sell the property, but he wanted to make sure that it was preserved by a board of trustees that would maintain it as an educational museum. Finley could not imagine what kind of organization could be put together to save such a large Virginia estate in a proper manner.[15] At the same time he went out to see the Sully portraits at Hampton in Towson, Md.; he quickly realized that there must be many similar country seats endangered by the forces of progress.

The National Park Service Advisory Board Interim Committee undertook the evaluation of both Oak Hill and Hampton at its December 11, 1945, meeting. Fiske Kimball told the board that he believed Oak Hill represented Monroe's most important years and that the house exemplified the president's mature taste in architecture. At that point the board discussed the proposition that homes of presidents possessed much more historical interest than did birthplaces. Director Newton Drury, the ever cautious guardian of the Park Service, retorted that the preservation of the homes of thirty-two presidents was beyond the capability of the understaffed Interior Department. Drury could agree to a motion that would declare Oak Hill to be nationally significant if those present understood such a motion to mean only approval of a cooperative

Oak Hill, Aldie, Va., ca. 1935. (Library of Congress)

agreement with a board of trustees.[16] Then the Advisory Board took up the case of Hampton. Kimball and Charles Porter used illustrations from *Great Georgian Houses of America* to show the board how important Hampton was in the evolution of architecture in the eighteenth century. Drury reiterated his concern over the inability of the government to handle properties such as Hampton. The minutes of the Advisory Board carry several sentences that bear witness to Drury's hopes for a national trust: "Possibly, a trust similar to the National Trust in England was needed to care for places like Hampton. After some further discussion of the national trust idea, the group recessed for luncheon at noon."[17]

Throughout the winter of 1946 George McAneny tried to find a logical answer to the problem of preserving the Greek Revival row houses on Washington Square (c. 1830). He contacted many institutions in New York City, including both the Metropolitan Museum of Art and the Whitney Museum. McAneny even asked Stephen Clark, who was a former member of the board of the Metropolitan Museum, if he would help to save the Rhinelander houses on Washington Square. Clark politely explained that he was deeply involved in developing the Farmers' Museum in Cooperstown and his principal interest in New York City was the Museum of Modern Art.[18] Ronald Lee and McAneny began to discuss the future of Castle Clinton, and these conversations naturally blurred into a consideration of the whole preservation picture in urban America. The two men apparently talked about different combinations of organizations that might be able to help save the old buildings in American cities, but nothing conclusive came out of these meetings until that fall.[19]

One curious incident in the early fall of 1946 shows how far preservation still had to go in order to gain the confidence necessary for founding a national organization. Mrs. George Henry Warren of Newport, R.I., stopped in to see Kenneth Chorley of Colonial Williamsburg on October 10. She wanted advice on how her new Preservation Society should proceed in trying to save the eighteenth-century buildings in Newport; and Chorley gave her his usual advice—hire a team of architects to do a survey. But somewhere in the conversation Chorley blurted out his concern about the confusion that existed on the national scene. Mrs. Warren recorded in her notes on the discussion with Chorley:

> He also reiterated from time to time that the ideal solution is private ownership of all buildings, but could see that impossible in Newport as too big. Another solution would be ownership by the National Park Commission [Service] to be held by them in the nature of a National Trust, but felt that it would be impossible to persuade Congress to appropriate the necessary

Washington Square houses, New York City, 1934. (Photograph by E. P. McFarland, HABS; Library of Congress)

funds, and that it would be a long and slow process to put through any legislation in Washington of this nature as the National Government at the moment is not interested in any such project.[20]

Chorley's pessimistic analysis of the situation with regard to the federal government was partially correct, but he had not counted on the vigorous and imaginative leadership of chief historian Ronald F. Lee. It was true that under Newton Drury the National Park Service had not been successful in getting money from Congress for the development of any new historical areas. Lee was well aware of that situation, but he had been busy during World War II while he was stationed in England: "My own personal interest in the possibility of a national council or a national trust began partly during the war years when I was in England and had some opportunity to observe the British National Trust and was stimulated by talks with Arthur Demaray after I got back, who said that he thought what we needed in this country was some kind of a council."[21]

Lee's conversations with Demaray led to one of the events that proved to be a turning point. On October 26 Lee gave a speech at a meeting of the American Association for State and Local History. This group had begun as a committee within the American Historical Association, but it had separated from the parent organization in 1940. Lee had been one of the first preservation leaders to recognize how important it was going to be to focus on local historical societies. In his address, entitled "The Effect of Postwar Conditions on the Preservation of Historic Sites and Buildings," he warned his fellow historians that the old order was changing quickly. He referred to inflation, suburban developments, highway building, exploration for oil, construction of office buildings, the possible sale of surplus forts, and the destruction of archaeological sites through water control projects.[22] Lee outlined the crisis in strong language in order to prepare his audience to accept some specific course of action:

> There can be no doubt that the United States is facing a period of unprecedented development during which the preservation of historic and pre-historic sites and buildings is in great jeopardy. No one, I believe, would be foolish enough to propose that an effort be made to resist the sweeping changes which are in progress or to save everything. However, it is certain that selected historic sites and buildings possessing cultural and patriotic value and chosen on the basis of careful surveys, must be preserved permanently as an essential part of our national historical heritage.[23]

He proposed that the AASLH appoint committees of correspondence (perhaps on the Revolutionary model) to keep local groups informed about the developments on the national scene. Then Lee hinted that ultimately a new organization might be formed:

> There must be close cooperation between national, state and local organizations concerned with the preservation of historic sites and buildings. This collaboration could and should strengthen the efforts of all. It is my belief that the time is rapidly approaching when an appropriate organization should call a special national conference similar to the very successful National Conference on State Parks to discuss problems of conserving the historic sites and buildings in the United States.
>
> Every one of us is involved in the revolutionary changes both physical and ideological, taking place all over the world today. The preservation of the physical symbols of our national growth should be regarded as an important contribution to the understanding of our own evolution as a nation and of the place of our nation in the modern world.[24]

Armed with these potent ideas, Ronald Lee went to New York City several days later to have dinner with George McAneny, Francis S. Ronalds (superintendent of Morristown National Historical Park), and Eric Gugler, a New York architect who was interested in preservation causes. On October 28, 1946, the four men sat in the dining room of the Ritz Carlton Hotel and compared two courses of action that might achieve the centralization that the private sector of the preservation community so urgently needed. The first option was the rejuvenation of the American Scenic and Historic Preservation Society, which was already half a century old. The society had become a New York based operation with only a few historic properties. Early in the twentieth century it had influenced the New York legislature in acquiring historical areas for state administration.[25] By 1946 McAneny was president of the organization, and therefore it seemed plausible that the original charter and bylaws might be just what the mounting preservation crises demanded. The four men discussed the possibility that Ronalds might become executive director if the reorganization took place, but legal obstacles prevented restructuring an existing group.[26]

The second alternative proposed that night at the Ritz Carlton was the formation of an entirely new organization. In a letter to McAneny a week later Lee summarized the need for cooperation on all levels—federal, state, local, and private. Then he recounted the real substance of their conversation: "As one possibility for a start in this direction, you and Eric and Fran Ronalds and I have talked of bringing together 12 or 15 key individuals to explore the subject. This seems to me to be an excellent approach. Should the combined judgment of these individuals indicate the importance of further steps, plans might be laid for a larger national conference on the conservation of historic sites and buildings, with perhaps 100 participants from the various parts of the country."[27] Lee listed fifteen people who had been selected and divided them into three groupings—those from private organizations, such as Kenneth Chorley; those from municipal and state conservation work, such as Edwin O. Lewis; and the National Park Service executives, including Newton Drury and Arthur Demaray. Lee hinted that David Finley of the National Gallery of Art might be a key person to bring along.[28] The Park Service officials in Chicago were eager to participate in a meeting that would include a representative group of preservation leaders.[29]

A third major event in the creation of the new National Council for Historic Sites and Buildings happened almost by accident, but it finally brought together the major figures in the preservation movement. In the fall of 1946 Christopher Crittenden, one of the founders of the AASLH, was visiting Washington and he stopped in to talk to Ronald Lee. Lee had another important visitor, who had just come in from New York. Lee remembered well how he suggested the next logical step:

> One day Mr. McAneny was down in Washington and it happened that Chris Crittenden was in Washington that day, and Mr. McAneny wanted to talk about a possible new organization. And I said, "Well, let's go over and talk with David Finley." I called Chris Crittenden and we went over. Mr. Finley was happy to talk about it and we . . . sat in his office and discussed the desirability of forming a new organization. Let me at this point emphasize the vital importance of Mr. Finley's interest in the possibility of a National Trust. . . . As Director of the National Gallery of Art, Mr. Finley was an extremely important figure in cultural affairs in the national capital and in the nation. His personal interest and the background and prestige which the National Gallery of Art gave to the initiation of the National Trust made a critical difference both in its character and its prospects for ultimate success.[30]

The four men who met in Finley's office drew up an invitation list of interested people and set a date for a conference to be held at the National Gallery. Finley agreed to write official letters to the participants in the "pre-organization meeting." The men hoped that the people at the first gathering would help to determine the type of organization that would eventually come into existence, and then set up the roster for a larger conference to be held in the spring of 1947.[31]

The ragged state of the preservation movement and David Finley's influence were strong enough to bring ten carefully selected individuals together at the National Gallery of Art on February 5, 1947. They represented a broad range of organizational and professional interests, although some of them would have to be described as comparatively recent converts to the cause of historic preservation. The veterans at the February meeting included Horace Albright (from the American Planning and Civic Association), Christopher Crittenden (who had been working with historic sites in North Carolina for about eight years), Ronald Lee, Waldo G. Leland (chairman of the Park Service Advisory Board), Judge Lewis from Philadelphia, and George McAneny. The relative newcomers were James R. Edmunds, president of the American Institute of Architects; David Finley of the National Gallery; Guy Stanton Ford, executive secretary of the American Historical Association; and John Walker, curator of paintings at the National Gallery. The men apparently tried to live up to their mandate by dutifully passing resolutions that endorsed the idea of a larger conference and a new organization that would include representatives of both private and governmental preservation groups. The report of the February 5 meeting included a list of organizations to be invited to participate in a conference to be held on April 15 at the National Gallery. Only two of the twelve learned and professional societies on the invitation list had been deeply involved in the preservation field—the Society for the Preservation of New England Antiquities and the American Scenic and Historic Preservation Society. All of the others represented historical, geographical, planning, or architectural constituencies. The small group agreed that the new National Council for Historic Sites and Buildings should have at least four goals: "(1) Mobilizing sentiment and opinion. (2) Diffusing knowledge concerning the need for such preservation and the appropriate methods and techniques. (3) Examination, appraisal and support of specific projects. (4) Conducting research and surveys on matters relating to the preservation and use of historic sites."[32] The guests also agreed that the new council must work for the establishment of a national fund that would be used to purchase historic properties, similar to the example of the English National Trust. Almost everyone wanted to see an American National Trust that had the backing of the federal government. The council was to be incorporated in the District of Columbia as a first step because the chances of obtaining a congressional charter for a national trust in a short time were not promising.[33]

Plans for the organizational meeting went well. Lee reported to McAneny that many of the people invited had accepted with a real sense of anticipation, including Fiske Kimball of the Philadelphia Museum and S. K. Stevens, the Pennsylvania state historian. Lee was certain that an enthusiastic group from all over the East Coast would assemble. His contacts throughout the scholarly and preservation communities had been centered mainly in Washington and New York.[34] The official letter of invitation included the minutes of the February meeting so that the participants would know what kinds of goals had been tentatively set for the new organization. A proposed constitution, worked out by Finley and McAneny, among others, also went out in advance of the April meeting.[35] People such as John D. Rockefeller III and William Sumner Appleton were just too concerned with other affairs to come, but Appleton expressed his interest in the idea and hoped that he could eventually contribute ideas on running the council.[36]

The meeting to establish the National Council for Historic Sites and Buildings assembled at the National Gallery of Art on April 15, 1947. After a few remarks from David Finley about the evolution of the historic preservation movement in the United States, George McAneny gave the official report of the committee that had worked on the creation of the National Council. He was quick to point out that the new permanent organization would not in any way usurp the prerogatives of existing local groups. He explained that the small subcommittee (which included Waldo Leland and Ronald Lee) had drafted bylaws and had also prepared an agenda for the meeting. Then McAneny listed what he believed to be the principal reasons for an organization that could coordinate preservation activity all over the United States. He saw two opposing trends: the growing individual and group interest in the saving of historic buildings, in sharp contrast with the "falling off of both interest and understanding of many of those entrusted with official power." World War II had shown clearly what devastation could do to world-renowned buildings in Europe, and yet the same War Department that had denounced German destruction was in the process of disposing of a group of America's historic forts. McAneny cited a few cases where private and state efforts for preservation had borne some rich results in the period since the war, but he maintained that there was a need for an organization that could "increase pressure" and help with the selection process when it came to launching preservation campaigns. He hoped that the new council could use the results of the great surveys of the 1930s carried out by architects and historians. He expected that the council could also bring some pressure to bear on Congress. Finally, McAneny revealed his dreamchild, which had been embedded in the bylaws of the new council: a national trust, qualified to receive donations of money and property. He frankly compared the proposed trust with the English National Trust, implying that the new organization might eventually turn over some of its properties to other groups or to federal and state agencies.[37]

Two distinguished professionals told the delegates at the meeting

Delegates to the organization meeting of the National Council for Historic Sites and Buildings at the National Gallery of Art, Apr. 15, 1947. Shown here are: Guy Stanton Ford, Turpin C. Bannister, Frank H. H. Roberts, Jr., David E. Finley, Solon J. Buck, Waldo G. Leland, Herbert E. Kahler, Arthur E. Demaray, Carroll L. V. Meeks, John L. Caskey, George A. McAneny, Francis S. Ronalds, U. S. Grant III, Luther H. Evans, Christopher C. Crittenden, Ronald F. Lee, Milton L. Grigg, Ella Lonn, Kenneth Chorley, J. Otis Brew, Mrs. Dwight F. Davis, Walter A. Taylor, Richard Koch, Fiske Kimball, Charles E. Peterson, Robert N. S. Whitelaw, Alexander Hamilton, Eric Gugler, Verne Chatelain, Charles Messer Stow, unidentified, Gardner Osborn, Laurence Vail Coleman. (National Trust for Historic Preservation Collection)

that the National Council could count on the support of the architectural and archaeological groups throughout the United States. Turpin C. Bannister, chairman of the American Institute of Architects' Committee on the Preservation of Historic Buildings, outlined a complete program for training and utilizing a crew of architects who would be qualified to carry out surveys and properly restore the buildings that would be dedicated to public use.[38] J. Otis Brew of Harvard University described the manner in which the archaeological profession had been working its way toward an understanding of historic buildings through work at Williamsburg and some Indian sites in the Southwest. Brew also remarked that he personally hoped the council could make the city of Washington a showcase for enlightened preservation activity, with the older buildings around the White House preserved as vital symbols of the growth of the capital city.[39]

One more professional group had to be represented—the planners and engineers, in the person of Maj. Gen. U. S. Grant III, who explained that he hoped the great buildings of Victorian America might be saved to illustrate an important style that had lost favor temporarily. Because Grant's experience had been largely in the field of planning, he, too, referred to the importance of having Washington, D. C., serve as an example of different kinds of preservation interests, including Indian sites.[40]

Then the meeting got down to serious business. After George McAneny presented a draft of the bylaws of the new council, chairman Waldo Leland told the delegates about the problems they would have to deal with in compiling the bylaws. To begin with, the council had no specified means of support. The bylaws committee had not proposed any kind of dues either from organizations or individuals, because the council had promised not to usurp the powers and responsibilities of the constituent organizations. The other major problem seemed to be the future relationship between the council (and the National Trust) and the Park Service. Leland, who had considerable experience on the Advisory Board of the Park Service, told the delegates about the weaknesses of the federal program:

> He believed that the new organization would supplement the efforts of existing organizations and provide a national focal point of their common efforts. The National Park Service, the official agency of the Federal Government for preservation of historic sites and buildings, cannot perform all the vital preservation work that is required over the country. For example, the National Park Service cannot ordinarily purchase historic sites and buildings but can only receive them by donation. Furthermore, additions to the National Park System are carefully selected on the basis of their national his-

torical significance and therefore only a limited number of properties can be accepted. A voluntary organization supported by the effective cooperation of constituent bodies and flexible in character would not be subject to the restrictions of a Federal agency.[41]

Ronald Lee repeated his warning about the preservation crisis that had been created by the surplus forts program and the construction of dams in the Missouri Valley. He argued that the great need was a "strengthening of historical preservation efforts at every level of government and organization, national, state and local."[42]

Throughout the afternoon of April 15 the delegates approved the bylaws and declaration of purpose. There were substantial areas of agreement, because so many of the people present were sure that the time had come for a national organization. They did argue over the exact wording of the name, for instance, in a spirit of friendly debate.[43] When they dispersed at the end of the meeting, the founders could confidently say that they had accomplished three things: (1) They had drafted a workable set of bylaws that called for the creation of a national trust to administer properties; (2) they had spelled out the general educational purposes of the National Council for Historic Sites and Buildings; and (3) they had elected a slate of officers that included George McAneny as chairman of the board, General Grant as president, Kenneth Chorley as vice president, and Ronald Lee as secretary.[44]

Although the National Council had no staff, budget, or office, it did have an active secretary in the person of chief historian Lee. At once he began to receive letters that showed a great desire on the part of preservationists to find a central office that could offer advice. While Lee was used to giving advice on restoration problems through his position in the Park Service, he began to tell people that by fall their council should become a significant force in preservation.[45] Eventually it would relieve the Department of the Interior of the responsibility of acting as a national preservation clearinghouse.

About three weeks after the meeting in the National Gallery the new board assembled to discuss such touchy issues as financial support and the location of an office. Lee suggested that he would approach the Ford Foundation for a grant, but several people argued that the professional organizations and preservation groups that had sponsored the original meeting could be called upon to donate some funds for operating a headquarters.[46] Lee added that there was a good chance that office space might be found in the old Ford's Theatre, along with some surplus Park Service furniture.

Within a few months the officers of the council discovered that there were many preservation crises awaiting the new organization. The announcement of the formation of the National Council received fairly wide coverage in newspapers and magazines, so it was natural that some preservationists jumped to the conclusion that a large organization had entered the field. Their reaction was reminiscent of the wave of proposals that followed the passage of the Historic Sites Act, although in this case the buildup was more gradual.

David Finley, as president of the American Association of Museums, received a desperate call for help from some citizens of Massachusetts who wanted to stop the mayor of Waltham from turning the grounds of Gore Place into a veterans' housing project.[47] On July 18 Grant, as the new president of the council, wrote his first official letter of protest. He addressed the chairman of the board of selectmen of Watertown, Mass. In ringing tones Grant outlined the unique architectural and historical importance of the Christopher Gore Mansion and its spacious grounds. While he did not deplore the idea of veterans' housing, he warned the selectmen that "once destroyed to meet a temporary need, this valuable and educational example of our nation's architecture cannot be replaced, a serious loss not only for the present generation, but for posterity." Then Grant listed the important organizations and individuals that had already allied themselves with the new council. This letter represented a significant breakthrough in the field of preservation because it was the first message to convey the awesome power that could come with arousing a national preservation organization. How could the selectmen of Watertown ignore the collective weight of opinion represented by the president of the American Scenic and Historic Preservation Society, the president of Colonial Williamsburg, the director of the National Gallery of Art, the director of the American Council of Learned Societies, the president of the American Institute of Architects, and the executive secretary of the American Historical Assocation? What did it matter in 1947 if the council had no staff or budget? Ronald Lee provided that temporary help through his Park Service offices.[48] Lee was the real force behind the organization at this point, because his position as chief historian of the Park Service made it possible to watch the progress of preservation work all across the country. He made sure that the right letters went to the right people—and he continued to hammer away at any groups that might be influenced by a letter from the council.[49]

David Finley enjoyed his role as spokesman for the National Council, but he could not promise anything specific to the people who sought aid in those early years. In August 1947 he received a letter from William

G. Wendell of Portsmouth, N.H., asking for help in preserving the MacPheadris-Warner House. Wendell explained that his mother, Mrs. Barrett Wendell, had saved the old building in the early 1930s and he had carried on the work of the Warner House Association since her death in 1938. The association was in fairly good shape, and the house did not need much restoration. Wendell was concerned about the long-term situation because he did not detect anyone within the Warner House group coming along to succeed him in a position of leadership.[50] Finley told Wendell that the National Gallery had no funds to provide for the restoration of the mural paintings on the stairway of the Warner House. He also said that he was impressed with the pictures of the house itself because they revealed an early home that had been carefully restored and maintained. All Finley could do was urge Wendell to come to Washington for a conference to be held on October 20 that would map out plans for the formation of a national trust.[51] Wendell gladly accepted the invitation.[52]

Frank Littleton, Finley's neighbor in Virginia, asked to be invited to the National Council meeting because he had just completed the final plans for an organization (known as the James Monroe Association, Inc.) that was to help save his home, Oak Hill (1820–31).[53] Just before the meeting Donald Shepard of the Avalon Foundation suggested to Finley that Helen C. Frick might be asked to help preserve the Albert Gallatin Home near Pittsburgh.[54]

The old and the new order in the history of preservation work encountered each other briefly—without much effect—in early October when Ronald Lee received a letter from William Sumner Appleton of the SPNEA. Appleton's career in New England was nearly over, but he could not resist the chance to send to the incorporators of the National Council some sage advice on correctly selecting a board of directors. Appleton had found that unwanted board members could be removed easily if the terms were staggered in such a way as to take every one off the board for a brief period. He was also concerned that the charter of the trust and the council might be too restrictive in their definitions of "historic." The New Englander noted that The Breakers in Newport might not be considered a historic building in some quarters, whereas he believed "it would be an invaluable acquisition."[55] Lee was in the midst of the final planning for the first large meeting of the National Council when he answered Appleton, so he merely thanked the New Englander politely for his ideas and said he looked forward to working with Thomas Waterman as the official representative of the SPNEA at the meeting.[56]

ORGANIZATION MEETING

Finally the big day arrived, and the delegates to the organization meeting of the National Council for Historic Sites and Buildings assembled at the National Gallery of Art on the morning of October 20, 1947. They were pleased to find that they had a great many common problems to discuss, and they must have been delighted to find that the preliminary work had already been done by George McAneny and Ronald Lee. U. S. Grant III presided, and David Finley acted as host. Finley welcomed the delegates with a speech informing them that the Avalon Foundation was about to donate Hampton to the federal government. He invited his listeners to go upstairs to the galleries at some point during this visit and pay their respects to Eliza Ridgely (the Sully portrait) because she had been the cause of the decision to preserve Hampton.[57] Finley then pointed out that he and the senior Park Service officials hoped to go on to bigger things: "The Park Service felt a great need for a national council composed of interested, able and influential persons, such as those in this room, who have not only accomplished miracles over many years in the field of historic preservation, but who are in a position to focus national attention on this subject and to rally support for the rescue of important sites and buildings threatened with destruction."[58]

As the meeting progressed it became clear that the main goal of the open sessions was purely informational. Preservation leaders invited by Lee and Finley from all over the country had their first chance to air their concerns in a national meeting. The minutes convey a feeling of genuine excitement as the delegates found that they could offer advice, denounce urban destruction, and plead for help in any form. It is almost certain that Lee chose the first speaker of the meeting, Congressman Walter G. Andrews of New York, chairman of the House Committee on the Armed Services. Andrews gave a good account of the problems connected with the disposal of the surplus forts that had been offered to public and private agencies by the War Assets Administration.[59] Grant then called for remarks from the floor, and in so doing referred to the "cumulative evidence that we who are interested in the preservation of this heritage should get together and operate together as is proposed in this Council." To get the ball rolling, Grant appropriately turned to Charles E. Peterson, who represented the National Park Service office in St. Louis. Peterson had to admit that the preservation scene in Missouri was discouraging, but he said that there was some chance of restoring the Holy Family Church in nearby Cahokia, Ill.[60] The delegates also heard about the proposed reconstruction of the home of Francis

Scott Key in Washington, D.C.; the impending destruction of a court-house in Louisville, Ky.; the local crafts movement in Waterford, Va.; and the restoration of a house in South Carolina. Thomas Waterman, the restoration architect who had made Virginia houses his specialty, gave a spirited defense of adaptive uses. He frankly told the assembly that he believed buildings "lose vitality" when they are restored only for exhibition purposes. He favored a state system of grants that would encourage private owners to maintain their properties without necessarily turning them all into museums.[61]

During the evening session of the meeting the National Council members heard from John Nicholas Brown and Louise du Pont Crown-inshield. These two philanthropists had supported preservation and restoration work for a fairly long time, and their comments showed that they had each developed a sense of sophistication about the ways in which buildings should be restored and exhibited.[62]

On the second day of the conference George McAneny presented the proposed charter for the National Trust for Historic Preservation. The evening before, the delegates had been exposed to a talk on the British National Trust in a carefully orchestrated process of preparation.[63] The crucial purpose of the new organization, according to Mc-Aneny, was the acquisition of gifts of property and sums of money for special preservation projects. McAneny predicted that private gifts would be coming in soon enough to launch the trust successfully and that it would function like the British Trust—by taking over important properties and finding ways to preserve them in the public interest.[64] In summary, he cautioned his audience against an "overheated nationalistic emphasis" that tended to stress the rightness of any particular stand the United States might take. Instead he referred to the remarks of Guy Stanton Ford of the American Historical Association. Ford had claimed that the organization meeting of the National Council was a clear sign of progress in looking at American civilization, a maturity that meant the citizens of the United States no longer belittled their own achievements.[65]

Kenneth Chorley, acting for the first time as vice president of the new council, spoke gratefully about the potential in a real national trust. He implied that Rockefeller might have turned over the entire Williamsburg Restoration to such an organization if one had existed in the early 1930s. Then Chorley hinted at the central role he had occupied in the preservation movement for a number of years: "We get letters nearly every week from all over this country requesting information about the preservation or restoration of historic sites. I hope very soon to start turning them over to the Council!"[66] He added that the delegates should heed the warning given earlier in the meeting by Luther Evans, the librarian of Congress, to stay out of the "field of scenic beauty." Chorley and a number of other people agreed that such areas belonged to the National Park System.[67] He hoped the trust would avoid the role already assigned to the Department of the Interior, thus making the American National Trust distinctly different from its English counterpart.

At the conclusion of the presentation of the National Trust charter, General Grant graphically illustrated the need for the new organization by turning the meeting back to a consideration of the problems preservation leaders faced in towns like Alexandria and Newport. Katherine U. Warren gave a fine capsule history of the Preservation Society in Newport, along with an account of the influence that Kenneth Chorley had brought to bear on the Rhode Island scene through his visit the previous spring.[68] William Phillips mentioned the recent victory in Waltham, Mass., that had insured the preservation of the grounds of Gore Place.[69]

Then Grant outlined the probable committee structure for the National Council for Historic Sites and Buildings. He told the conferees that the creation of a Committee on Standards and Surveys was essential in order to operate on the basis of good information. This was a goal that had been only partially attained by the Park Service Advisory Board.[70] Grant suggested that much of the private and governmental preservation work done up through the 1940s had been carried out without much attention to overall criteria of importance. He also hinted that the council would soon have other committees—dealing with legislation, ways and means, the creation of a manifesto, and the organization of the National Trust.[71]

The grass-roots aspect of the preservation movement was permitted to dominate the organization meeting, and it was a wise decision. Leaders such as Judge Lewis were amazed to hear how effective Mrs. Warren's small organization had been in Newport. Lewis had been so wrapped up in the difficult political battles that characterized his fight for the creation of the Philadelphia National Historic Shrines Commission that he had not been aware of similar campaigns being waged on a smaller scale in communities all over the nation. The judge spoke with feeling about his discovery that there were more than a thousand houses worthy of preservation in Charleston alone. He had been impressed with the magnitude of the challenge involved in saving Society Hill in Philadelphia—and now he found that there were people in other cities who were dealing with essentially the same problems he had encountered.[72]

The founders of the National Council had accomplished their primary objectives, but they had to spell out the goals of the new organization in a way that would attract more and more people—both professionals and amateurs—to the cause of historic preservation. Ronald Lee had to inform Kenneth Chorley and J. O. Brew of the different classes of memberships that might be included. Lee explained that a large group of interested professionals called "associates" would be assembled as a back-up informational force. He confidently predicted in November 1947: "I anticipate that we will have, within a year or so, a network, so to speak, of several hundred persons over the United States, who are in positions of leadership and influence because of their professional connections and otherwise, and situated in every state in the union. It will be one of the functions of the Council secretariat to keep these individuals informed regarding the status of major preservation efforts, such as the archaeology salvage program, the preservation of surplus forts, the ruins stabilization program in the southwest, and so on."[73]

Each of the founders of the council had in mind a predetermined aim, and these diverse objectives reflected a broad spectrum of the people in the preservation field. David Finley clearly wanted to see houses such as Oak Hill and Hampton set aside the way the great houses of England had been opened to the public in the years following World War II. George McAneny wanted to help create a strong organization with sufficient funds and political influence to become a real force in working with problems of land acquisition in places like New York City and the Princeton battlefield in New Jersey.[74] Ronald Lee, viewing the crises all over the nation as chief historian of the Park Service, had the widest vantage point of all. He later gave an account of his hopes:

One of the goals of the National Council was to organize a National Trust and set up a corporation or a chartered body of some appropriate type, you see, properly established to hold valuable historic property. That was written into the by-laws by Mr. McAneny the day before or the day of the meeting at which the National Council was organized. A second goal was to provide an instrument, a national organization, to mobilize sentiment and opinion in the United States behind the better preservation of historic sites and buildings and to speak up in Washington, D.C.—if necessary in Congress or in other ways—when emergencies arose or when crises developed, and to support efforts for preservation. There were lots of things going on, of course, problems all around the country resulting from highway construction, dam construction, and the various kinds of emergencies that developed during and after World War II. In addition, the Council contemplated gathering and disseminating information about preservation. It contemplated, I think from the beginning, training programs in this area.[75]

Lee expected to see a variety of activities that had not been coordinated in any previous preservation organization, including the National Park Service. There were particular strengths and weaknesses in both the private and public sectors of the preservation movement that could be studied and discussed in order to weld a strong national organization. Although the people who had attended the three meetings in 1947 had different goals, they certainly agreed on the need for one central focus for all of their work. The lack of a headquarters had plagued them for many years, and at long last the desperate situation produced by the postwar building boom and the financial starvation of the Park Service made progress inevitable. No single individual understood the situation more clearly than Lee, and no other person had a broader circle of acquaintances. Since 1938 he had shown considerable expertise in working with professional groups. He knew how to communicate effectively with members of Congress and executives in the Department of the Interior. The first executive secretary of the National Council, Frederick Rath, referred to Ronald Lee as the "pivot" of the whole operation.[76] Lee's graduate training and the reports and studies made by the historians of the Park Service put him in contact with the scholarly world as it affected preservation. George McAneny and David Finley helped the chief historian to understand the world of private philanthropy. The meetings of the National Council had been the first organized efforts to unite those two communities, and Lee had an appreciation for the contributions both could make. Other people like McAneny could make speeches that spelled out the great needs of the preservation field. Lee had the cool competence and the warm friendliness that made it possible to put programs into operation.

SETTING UP A CENTRAL OFFICE

Once the organization meeting of the National Council for Historic Sites and Buildings adjourned, it was time to get down to the serious business of transforming an idea into a working organization. The board met at the National Gallery in late November and set up a series of committees, possibly the largest and most important of which carried the title "Ways and Means." It included a number of wealthy people who were known to have supported preservation causes in the past, along with individuals such as Horace Albright who had proved to be helpful in working with foundations and other sources of philanthropy.[77] At first the board of the council refused to charge annual dues and instead decided to seek donations as the principal source of money. The board was concerned about the possibility that the organization might appear to be competing with existing groups that were about to become affiliated members. Lee suggested that at least $3,000 be budgeted for a secretary, and the board accepted the idea. He also reported on the situation regarding surplus forts. At the end of the meeting the trustees voted to invite several prominent individuals to become "associates" of the council. They were people of wealth as well as some well-known writers and historians.[78] The idea of using distinguished people as a committee of correspondence for the preservation movement never worked out.[79]

Throughout the fall of 1947 and the winter of 1948 both Ronald Lee and David Finley became aware of the need for a central office to handle the correspondence and other important public-relations functions of the new National Council. When requests came in for help, they were usually addressed to General Grant, and then either Lee or Grant himself personally answered them. For example, a group in Dayton, Ohio, asked for some assistance in persuading the local government to save the old Montgomery County Courthouse. The distraught historians hoped the general would push for a picture story in *Life* magazine.[80] But all Grant could do was forward their letter to Lee with a request that the Park Service draft a reply to them. Grant added, "Of course, I am always for doing what we can even if it is little and without formal authority."[81] He had correctly described the condition of the council's office in those formative months. Finally, in February 1948 Grant responded to the Dayton letter with a long note that compared the courthouse situation with the efforts of some New Yorkers to save the Rhinelander houses on Washington Square in New York City. Grant admitted that the council had no funds available to assist in preservation work. "Nevertheless, we desire to extend moral assistance and encouragement wherever and whenever we can, to those state and local societies which are fighting to protect the heritage of their own communities."[82]

The first requirement in setting up a central office was more money. Grant sent out a letter to all of the new "associates" on January 26 outlining the immediate needs of the council. He requested a "modest fund" of $16,000 to give the organization a secretary and an office and to cover the costs of publications and mailing. The letter skillfully crossed the divide between becoming a request for a donation and serving as a newsletter about the long-term plans for funding the National Council. Grant hoped that enough gifts would come in soon to finance the first year of operation while the Committee on Ways and Means thought through the difficult question of membership.[83] The committee met on February 5, and it quickly came up with a plan for categories of membership that even included life memberships of $1,000 or more. The committee urged the council to extend its list of associates in order to build up a substantial roster of members by the end of the year.[84]

The second challenge that faced the founders of the National Council was the method of staffing the office once the necessary $16,000 had been raised. Ronald Lee well knew that the first national preservation organization could not function indefinitely on letters that he had drafted for Grant. He also knew that setting up an office in Ford's Theatre or some other government building with a secretary who could handle correspondence would not be enough. Some kind of executive had to be included in the table of organization if the council was to become a working force in the preservation field. During the spring of 1948 Lee took advantage of his broad contacts in the Park Service to select an individual who possessed to a remarkable degree that mixture of zeal, diplomacy, and scholarly concern that would be necessary to launch the council and the National Trust.

Lee's candidate was Frederick L. Rath, Jr., the historian at the Home of Franklin D. Roosevelt National Historic Site. Rath had been a dedicated Park Service employee since 1937 (with the exception of the war years), and he had served at a number of historical areas along with a brief assignment in the Washington headquarters. He was a Dartmouth graduate and had done advanced work at Harvard. Rath had carefully maintained scholarly and professional contacts with fellow historians over the years.[85] Nevertheless, the suggestion that he might become the administrator of the first national clearinghouse on historic preservation temporarily stunned him. He confided in his diary for March 26, 1948, that his initial reaction to the flattering offer was negative. "I have loved this job [at Hyde Park] and I have been viewing the future with pleasure." He had seriously considered turning down any Park Service promotions in order to stay with superintendent George Palmer at the Roosevelt Home.[86] On the other hand, Rath, like so many of the Park Service historians, had a sincere love for the organization that had been intensified by working closely with Ronald Lee and the Washington office. Lee considered Rath the man best prepared to carry the gospel of the Park Service into the disorganized field of private preservation.[87]

On April 6 Rath reported to the Department of the Interior to confer with director Newton Drury, Waldo Leland (chairman of the Park Service Advisory Board), and Ronald Lee. Eventually David Finley also came to talk to the young historian about the great opportunity that lay before him as the first executive secretary of the National Council. The leaders of the council promised Rath that his job at Hyde Park would be waiting for him if the new position did not work out well.[88] A week later Rath returned to Washington to consider serving as "secretary" of the council for a period of six months, starting in the fall of 1948. As he left the meeting at the National Gallery, Rath must have known that Lee had set up the arrangement—and that it would go through if everyone agreed to it. By this time Rath had been able to think through the implications of the opportunity that had come to him, and his diary reveals a considerable degree of anticipation. He recorded: "A tremendous job and a great challenge. In it will be the fun of setting up something new, something for the good of the people and the country."[89] Here was the kind of spirit that the cause of preservation needed during the grim years after World War II—a person with a mission and a great capacity for work. Anyone who had been able to interpret the home of Franklin D. Roosevelt to the hundreds of thousands of devout tourists who had streamed in since 1946 was ready to wrestle with the problems involved in setting up the first offices of the National Council.

The historic preservation movement achieved some degree of permanence one morning in the middle of August 1948 when Frederick L. Rath, Jr., walked up three flights of stairs in old Ford's Theatre. Rath's office was furnished with cast-off pieces from the storerooms of the Department of the Interior, and his files consisted entirely of correspondence that had been carried on for more than a year by Ronald Lee. Rath quickly located a skilled and dedicated assistant in Betty Walsh from Cynthiana, Ky. He referred to their partnership as a miracle—a remarkable coincidence that made possible the start of the new central office.[90] No matter how humble the facilities might have been, the fact remains that for the first time in history a professional had been hired to coordinate all the varied activities of the preservation groups in the United States.

Just as the new executive secretary was preparing to move to Washington, an important figure decided to withdraw from the strenuous work of forming the National Trust. George McAneny was in poor health, and he probably wanted to concentrate his energies on the battle over Castle Clinton.[91] He left for his successors a list of proposals that showed what one of the founders had expected to accomplish through the new organization. McAneny believed that gifts of money and property should come to the trust and not to the National Park Service. He evidently shared David Finley's interest in finding ways to care for large estates that demanded more funding than private owners could hope to produce as heavy taxation and high-priced labor closed in on the old aristocracy.[92]

Finley and McAneny had been concerned with maintenance of

Ford's Theatre, Washington, D.C. (Photograph by Abbie Rowe, National Park Service)

large estates and Lee with preservation emergencies that the Park Service could not possibly manage. Frederick Rath had a somewhat broader view of the role of the National Council.

From the beginning we were thinking of ourselves as a clearinghouse to bring together as much information as possible. . . . I wanted a flow of information. I was faced with the matter of keeping up the Quarterly Report that Ronnie Lee had started in June of '48. And I needed information for that. But more than that, I always had the concept that these would be the greatest files in the country on the subject of preservation. The collection had to begin now, you see. And so here was this flow of material and, thus, of course you felt like a pioneer. You were building; you were constructing files; you were conducting experiments actually.[93]

Rath was well aware of the hundreds of requests that came to Lee's offices in the Branch of History. Rath wanted his organization to be even more than an information center—it was to be a screen for the Park Service.

Here I could begin to play a new role. I could begin to become . . . a shoulder to cry on. That is, the people to whom I was writing could come back to me; I could give them all of the time, in a sense, that they needed. A Park Service employee could not do that. . . . There was no other organization. And so almost immediately, not only for the big things like Oak Hill and Woodlawn. . . . I think [also] the files of the National Council must show that little places and little people with littler problems were beginning to come in, and Park Service couldn't take care of them. And again Park Service had a comfortable buffer. If it did come to Park Service, Ronnie Lee was able to say smoothly, "Well, why don't you get in touch with Fred Rath in the new National Council for Historic Sites and Buildings?" He didn't have to tell them that he was the secretary of that organization.[94]

The executive secretary of the National Council was both a professional historian and an idealist. First of all, Rath's contacts with the senior historians of the National Park Service who had come into the work during the depression gave him a reverence for their dedication that Horace Albright would have appreciated.[95] People such as Ronald Lee, Melvin Weig, and George Palmer had managed the national program of historic sites so competently that Rath partook of the zeal they generated. Rath's postwar baptism at the Home of Franklin D. Roosevelt taught him how to deal with vast crowds of sincere pilgrims who came to imbibe the spirit of a man and a place. His diary shows that he gave himself wholly to this challenging work. The same total commitment grew quickly with his new position at the National Council. Although he did not consider himself a powerful official in the late 1940s, Rath projected himself into a new role: "I became an important person. I was the executive secretary of the National Council for Historic Sites and Buildings, and both Betty Walsh and I wore a mantle and walked with a certain amount of pride."[96]

CONGRESSIONAL CHARTER

The council leaders had to put together a committee that could write a congressional charter for the National Trust. It was critical that the legislators authorize a board of trustees that would include high federal officials. U. S. Grant and Ronald Lee turned to H. Alexander Smith, Jr., a lawyer who was the son of a United States senator from New Jersey.[97] Smith possessed the interest, legal background, and vital political connections necessary to put through a charter for the new trust.[98] Lee provided Smith and the Committee on the Organization of the National Trust with a fair amount of relevant literature about the charter of the British National Trust and of a number of regional preservation groups in the United States.[99] When the committee met in Washington on September 3, the members had before them an agenda that included some knotty questions. How was the American Trust to be different from the British organization? How were the functions of the National Council to be differentiated from those of the trust? Was the trust to have any kind of special relationship with the National Park Service?[100]

David Finley worked closely with the committee. He hoped that for the time being the trust would stay out of scenic preservation and restrict itself to historic buildings. Finley believed that the council should continue to exist as a pressure group that drew its strength from the constituent organizations that had formed it; the trust would take on the property-management functions.[101] In the meantime Rath began to collect information on the operations of the British National Trust in order to assist the committee working under Smith.[102] Rath also took time to encourage the group in Dayton, Ohio, in its fight to save the old courthouse.[103] And he tried to get a public relations committee started for the council with Albert Kornfeld of *House and Garden* as the chairman.[104]

During October the National Council executive board prepared for the second annual meeting that was to take place the next month. The principal order of business turned out to be the presentation of the report of the Committee on the Organization of the National Trust. The board agreed that the trust had to be created; the Historic Sites Act of 1935 could not provide the kind of organizational model that would work as a stopgap. The new trust had to be chartered by an act of Congress, which would make the permanent nature of the organization hard to question. Everyone present at the board meeting agreed that the next logical step was an all-out effort to get a congressional charter within the next year.[105]

The center of the stage shifted in November 1948 from Ford's

Theatre to the National Gallery of Art, when the National Council held its annual meeting. The delegates who assembled on the morning of November 4 faced a very different situation from the previous year. The council was at last a functioning organization and not just an idea. There were many working committees whose reports at the meeting might well influence the group's future growth. Since the middle of August the council had been operating its own office; it was no longer a mere appendage of the National Park Service and Ronald Lee. And, most important of all, the delegates were going to have a chance to discuss the formation of yet another organization, the National Trust. Several different groups were prepared to define the goals of the trust.

The first order of business was a keynote address by Newton Drury that outlined what the Park Service could and could not do.[106] Drury complimented the historians of the Park Service for their role in bringing the council into existence. He admitted that the Department of the Interior already faced some great challenges that could strain the dedicated personnel working with its scenic and historical areas: river basin developments by the army engineers, greatly increased visitation in the parks, visual intrusions that came with real estate developments on the borders of historic sites—and the constant challenges involved in preserving the "spirit" of history in each of these places.[107] Drury knew that the country needed a "strong national, non-governmental organization that can rally together all of the forces of historic and cultural conservation." He acknowledged that the federal government could never carry the whole load, and he welcomed an awakening that would find its fullest expression in the National Council:

> Communities everywhere, I find as I travel through the United States, are more and more alive to the importance of preserving their old scenes, their old houses, old institutions, old ways of living and doing things, and they do this not because they are old or they are quaint or not even because they are beautiful, nor alone because they attract sightseers, although that, of course is a matter of considerable concern to the local chamber of commerce, but there is, I am sure, a deeper instinct which I believe is the reason why this National Council will grow and expand and succeed, and that has to do with the feeling that the people that have no regard for its past will have no future worth remembering; that only that community that preserved its landmarks has the sense of stability that comes with having roots in the past.[108]

In response to a question from General Grant, Drury went on to explain, on a case-by-case basis, the reasons why the National Park Service could not afford to take on any new responsibilities. It was clear that the leaders of the Park Service wanted the preservation needs of the United

States to be met by a proper blending of private and governmental agencies.

The next two speakers, David Finley and H. Alexander Smith, Jr., tried to explain the role of the National Trust. They both made bold statements about the influence that a congressionally chartered organization could have on the battle for preserving buildings and sites that could not be saved under the auspices of the Park Service. Both believed that the American National Trust would fulfill a function quite similar to that of the British Trust—the preservation of great houses that would continue to be used by their former owners.[109] Finley specifically referred to the new Woodlawn Plantation crusade of Armistead Rood and George Maurice Morris when he cited important homes that were in danger in the United States.[110] The director of the National Gallery recognized that the trust would have to set up criteria that would concentrate this preservation work on the most significant historic and architectural monuments. There should be a publicity campaign to convince the business community that historic preservation played a valid role in the economy; old buildings ought to remain as a functional part of an urban scene. Finley also warned the delegates that the National Council was fortunate to have a professional staff, considering the small size of the budget for operating the office in Ford's Theatre. The council would soon have to find a means of steady support for its staff functions. Finley concluded his talk by referring to the need for a reeducation of the American people at a time when "America and everything she stands for is under attack by ruthless, militant nations that do not believe in our American way of life or the institutions that produced the fabric we are trying to preserve."[111]

The formal presentation of the National Trust charter was Smith's responsibility. He began by building on Newton Drury's remarks about the limitations of the federal government as the chief agent of preservation in the United States. Smith pointed out that a number of important places, such as Oak Hill, needed to be saved, but they might never fit in well with the National Park System.[112] Then he got to the heart of the matter: The new trust must become a preservation organization with broad powers and financial resources that permitted it to respond to all kinds of emergencies. The trust should be able to rescue areas temporarily, with the understanding that suitable uses could be found for those buildings.[113]

The objective is preservation; the means to that end are legion—granted the necessary degree of imagination and flexibility on the part of the management of the Trust. In this connection, your committee is firm in its belief that acquisition per se should be the last resort. The Trust should not at any time seek to acquire properties. It should first exhaust every possible avenue short of acquisition. In appropriate cases, it would, for example, first attempt to find a sympathetic purchaser for a jeopardized property. Failing that, it would further, for example, then attempt to negotiate a restrictive arrangement with the owners to prevent the demolition or obliteration of the structure or site. It would attempt at all times to maintain in residence the owner and his family, so that the property may remain a living and not a dead example.[114]

With the charter of the National Trust before them, the delegates to the meeting immediately began to discuss questions involving temporary preservation of scenic sites up to 500 acres, size of landholdings, and the element of speed in emergencies. Obviously, they were hoping to create an organization that could move into emergency situations quickly, which the National Park Service had been unable to do.[115] Some people were disturbed about the restrictions that might be imposed on the definition of "historic" buildings, both from the standpoints of age and use. Delegates from the western part of the United States did not like the idea of ignoring buildings that might be less than fifty years old for consideration by the Park Service Advisory Board. Turpin Bannister of the Society of Architectural Historians argued for the inclusion of structures to illustrate important trends in industry and engineering.[116] Bannister's comments on industrial sites revealed that the preservation community was finally expanding its definition of the kinds of cultural and historical resources that should be set aside for the benefit of the public. It must have seemed especially heartening for some of these people to have a national forum for advocating such revolutionary ideas.

Grant attempted to devote most of the remaining meeting time to a series of informal reports from preservationists from all over the country. He began with George Maurice Morris, who told the group that the Woodlawn Public Foundation was the brainchild of Armistead Rood and that it was trying to raise a stupendous amount of money within a few months.[117] Laurence Fletcher reported on the work of the major preservation groups in New England, most notably Gore Place Society in Waltham, which had just paid off the large mortgage.[118]

The second day of the annual meeting included one scheduled talk by Kenneth Chorley and more remarks from the floor. Chorley was eager to take advantage of the difficult assignment Grant had given him, that of summarizing in twenty minutes the developments in historic preservation over the past twenty years. The president of Colonial Williamsburg did not shrink from the task. He bluntly stated that Williamsburg had become increasingly concerned about the interpretation of historic sites and less interested in the comparatively enjoyable process of restoring or reconstructing buildings of the past.[119] He went on to outline a possible program for the new National Trust. Based on his experience as a propagandist for preservation work, Chorley described the trust as a "Clearing House" for information. He hoped that it would also become an educational force in working with public officials at all levels of government. The public relations experts, for instance, could contribute a great deal to the preservation community by showing citizens how important it was to save and use old buildings.[120] After Chorley completed his brief summary, Louis Jones of the New York State Historical Association described the first Seminars in American Culture that had been held at Cooperstown during the previous summer. Jones announced that the 1949 seminars would deal with the "problems of restoring historic buildings."[121] Christopher Crittenden of North Carolina listed the projects that his state government had undertaken. At that point the delegates retired to the north portico of the National Gallery to watch President Harry Truman ride up Pennsylvania Avenue, following his electoral triumph of a few days before. During the remainder of the meeting delegates shared ideas on survey techniques, the reconstruction of missing buildings, preservation problems in the Midwest and Far West, and the new preservation organizations that were springing up in communities across the United States.[122]

Immediately following the annual meeting the executive board of the National Council met to plan the next major activities for the committees that had been set up to assist Frederick Rath and Betty Walsh. The priority items included approval of the budget for 1949, the effort to secure less cramped work areas in the Octagon House (1800) to replace the offices in Ford's Theatre as soon as the American Institute of Architects took over the building from the State Department, and the implementation of an informational campaign that would cover the country with the message of hope from the National Council.[123]

The council staff prepared to face its first full year of operation with a fair amount of unfinished business and a great many new challenges that were intensified by public recognition that a central office for historic preservation finally existed. The Avalon Foundation, the Mellon family philanthropy, expressed its willingness to help buy Oak Hill. A real estate office offered to sell to the National Council a fine early nineteenth-century house in the District of Columbia. And Rath heard from the Park Service staff about the work of Col. Maurice Fulton in restoring Lincoln, N.M. On top of all these requests for help and advice, the Washington staff of the council had to assist in the process of preparing the National Trust charter bill for submission to Congress. It was a big order.

WOODLAWN PLANTATION

That fall another significant preservation campaign had begun in the Washington, D.C., area, and it was closely tied to the movement to create the National Trust. The National Council offered its help, and eventually the trust took over the site as its first property. A group of prominent people, led by a young lawyer named Armistead Rood, had formed an organization that proposed to purchase Woodlawn (1800–1805, the Lewis estate near Mount Vernon) as a National Monument comparable to its neighbor. George Washington had given the estate to his foster daughter, Eleanor Parke Custis, and his nephew, Lawrence Lewis, who were married in 1799. People who came in contact with Rood during these months realized that he was consumed with the challenge of saving Woodlawn.[124] Rood's first and most important convert turned out to be a well-known Washington attorney, George Maurice Morris, owner of The Lindens, the eighteenth-century house that Walter Macomber had helped to move to Washington from Danvers, Mass., in the 1930s.[125]

Rood had set out to put together an organization in a matter of a week or so to head off the purchase of Woodlawn by a society of Belgian monks. He wrote letters to wealthy people all over the country who were known to have taken some interest in other preservation causes. In most instances Rood used a formula that had a certain degree of appeal: He mentioned Washington's connection with the house and then he slipped in the name of George Maurice Morris, noting that Woodlawn should be able to carry itself as a historical museum because of its nearness to Mount Vernon (which had had 791,000 paying visitors in 1947).[126] Rood knew that by early September his organization would have to make a more tempting bid on the property than the proposal the religious brotherhood had set forth. He succeeded in lining up as part of a Woodlawn Public Trust Committee Charles C. Wall, superintendent of Mount Vernon; Douglas Southall Freeman, the biographer of Washington; and David Finley.[127]

By the middle of September, Rood and Morris had formed the Woodlawn Public Foundation, and they asked for funds in hopes that the proprietor of Woodlawn would permit them to raise approximately $75,000 in cash before the end of the year.[128] One professional fund raiser sent Morris some astonishing proposals for the campaign, includ-

Woodlawn Plantation, Mount Vernon, Va., 1953. (Photograph by Abbie Rowe, National Park Service)

ing the sale of memorial cherry trees from the grounds of the estate. These saplings were supposed to serve as reminders of the honesty of George Washington because they would be taken from the original tree. As much as Rood and Morris wanted to raise money, this sort of approach did not appeal to them.[129]

Rood was one of the first preservationists to discover that the executive secretary of the new National Council was already operating out of an office in Ford's Theatre in Washington. Before Frederick Rath had a chance to catch his breath, he was in the clutches of a persistent advocate of preservation. Rood quickly convinced him that the Woodlawn Foundation should have a chance to work through the council for a few months to raise the necessary down payment that was due on January 3, 1949. Rath cautioned his visitor that use of the office space at council headquarters would have to be cleared with Ronald Lee of the National Park Service, the co-founder of the council and the man who had arranged for the new office in the first place.[130] Grant and David Finley went along with the idea, probably because the foundation could prove to be a good selling point for the council if the campaign for Woodlawn succeeded. Besides, there was room for them.[131] In the meantime, George Morris began to view with increasing concern the enormous fund-raising job that he and Armistead Rood had taken on.[132] Whether the movement succeeded or failed, Rath and the officers of the National Council were certain to learn a great deal about preservation campaigning in the next few months.

During the month or so that followed the annual meeting it became clearer than ever that the Mellon family, perhaps through the intervention of Finley, had entered the preservation field with a greater commitment than just the restoration and furnishing of Hampton. In the middle of November the Avalon Foundation announced that it would support the purchase of Oak Hill up to the amount of $331,000 if the council could take title to the property.[133] There were going to be some tricky negotiations, but the council had a much stronger bargaining position with the Mellon offer. At the same time Paul Mellon, through the Old Dominion Foundation, agreed to help the Woodlawn Public Foundation with a matching gift. The Woodlawn group had been floundering, even with the assistance of a public relations man. At the foundation's November 30 board meeting Rood reported that only a little more than $9,000 of the needed $80,000 had been raised by pledges and gifts.[134] The bombshell came on December 20, 1948, in the form of a letter from Mellon to Morris, following a short conversation between the latter and Mellon advisor Donald D. Shepard. Morris had not been afraid to ask the Mellon interests for help in raising the large sum of money needed for the down payment on Woodlawn. The Old Dominion Foundation offered to give the Public Foundation up to $100,000 if Morris and Rood could somehow raise about $33,000 in one year. That was a most effective tool in the hands of the foundations—the Mellons would give two dollars for every dollar collected elsewhere during 1949. It made wonderful publicity for the Woodlawn operation, because the traveling public could see that Mellon had a sincere interest in historic preservation. Woodlawn might be saved within the narrow span of time allotted to them.[135] No doubt some of the people associated with the board of the National Council for Historic Sites and Buildings began to wonder whether the officers of the Mellon philanthropies might even offer to endow the new National Trust. Nothing as important as the Avalon and Old Dominion gifts had come to the field of historic preservation since Henry Ford and John D. Rockefeller, Jr., had decided to invest in Greenfield Village and Colonial Williamsburg. David Finley seemed to be the crucial link in the new relationship that was opening up, but no one could be certain that the Mellons had switched their interests from the fine arts to historic buildings.

PUBLIC RELATIONS

By the fall of 1948 the National Council had already become all things to all people. Preservationists around the country had begun to look upon the fledgling office as the headquarters of an organization that had a large professional staff equipped to dispense information on any sticky question involving fund raising, restoration, or zoning. Others believed that the council had enough funds to cover any preservation emergency. At the same time Frederick Rath and Betty Walsh had to face the difficult job of working with all of these people while they tried to publish quarterly reports, locate new members, and dispense information to harried historians in remote parts of the United States. Rath, however, had reason to believe that the council was not really receiving the backing it deserved from the preservation field as a whole. "It wasn't as if we weren't trying. . . . And that slow growth, I think, is a perfect tip-off to the fact that damn few people were listening. The American public, even the organizations at work in this field presumably, were not ready for a national organization, didn't understand its potential. . . . I was a voice crying in the wilderness."[136]

There was a budgetary crisis in the offices of the National Council that reflected the indecision of the Board of Trustees and the general apathy of existing organizations. Shortly after the 1948 annual meeting General Grant hired a public relations expert from New York City, Ralph Wentworth, to assist in fund raising and general publicity.[137] The council files contain a proposed 1949 budget that called for $21,000 to run the headquarters, plus an additional $10,000 to send out an appeal to constituent organizations. The budget also alloted $25,000 for a national survey, $100,000 for a national registered landmarks program (which had never materialized with Park Service surveys), $300,000 for an endowment of the national headquarters, and $500,000 as a revolving fund to be used for preservation emergencies. Apparently Rath and Grant had anticipated the funding problems that were to plague the National Trust and the federal government in the 1950s and 1960s.

The challenge was in finding how to do all this at a time when most people did not fully grasp the kinds of changes that were taking place in the United States. *Antiques* magazine, a periodical that had been able to keep up with the historic house situation with increasing accuracy in the 1940s, devoted an editorial to the preservation cause in the January 1949 issue. The writer pointed out that the movement may have been national in scope, but it was not unified. The logical answer to this dilemma seemed to be the new National Council, which "should exert a vital influence in this country." *Antiques* expressed the hope that the council would help "determine what buildings all over the country should be preserved."[138] What a big order that was! Rath was indeed trying to find a way to assist the growing number of people who recognized that a national preservation headquarters did exist, but he was a long way from becoming the leader that could give firm direction to historical groups throughout the nation.

As the new year opened, the council was working at establishing its national image while helping to save Oak Hill (through a Mellon donation) and Woodlawn (through the use of office space and publicity).[139] Rath could not resist an opportunity to debate the role of the council, as he did with Howard Peckham, director of the Indiana State Historical Bureau. Peckham, along with some other officials in Indiana, had received a December mailing from the council inviting the state preservation agencies to join in the national effort. On February 2 he asked Rath if the new organization would drain money and talent away from Indiana and then spend it only for the preservation of Virginia shrines.[140] The executive secretary tried to explain how the National Council intended to supplement the efforts of state institutions. Rath bluntly stated that the time had come for some group to take a total view of the preservation crisis so that funds could be spent where they were most needed. He defended the people who had worked on the Committee on Standards and Surveys as selected specialists who would resist being taken in by merely emotional arguments regarding the value of historic sites in the East.[141] The debate became more pointed when Peckham stoutly defended states' rights in the field of historic buildings. He maintained that the loss of a few buildings of importance in Indiana could have a healthy effect on future preservation campaigns.[142] That was too much for Frederick Rath, who immediately sat down and composed a carefully reasoned reply. The National Council had worked hard to get nationally circulated magazines to push the subject of preservation, and the results had been gratifying. Would it not stand to reason that such extensive publicity would help the cause in Indiana? In addition to that function of the council, Rath pointed out that he had been giving advice to organizations in a number of states seeking professional help in preservation work. Then Rath described one of his major goals for the council offices: to mail out to inquirers technical "kits" that would outline different ways to approach both crisis situations and everyday administrative problems, and then supply the constituent organizations with help from a staff that could be sent anywhere in the United States.[143] At the request of Ronald Lee, Rath's long letter to Peckham never went out, but the exchange revealed how the first executive secretary viewed the role of the National Council.

One of these broad issues had already surfaced when Secretary of the Interior Julius Krug asked Grant if the council would want to participate in a survey that would carry on the classification process begun by the National Park Service in the 1930s.[144] The board of the council decided to pass the question of defining national historical significance along to the American Institute of Architects, and Grant immediately wrote the AIA that the National Council had put this item on its agenda.[145] The problem was a simple one—the organization was too small to take on an enormous job that other people believed should be its proper role in historic preservation.

At the February 18, 1949, board meeting the challenges became clearer. While the bill calling for the creation of the National Trust received final committee approval before it went to Congress, a number of tasks faced the council. The public relations program had to get under way with more publications and mailings to prospective donors. Rath proposed that he be permitted to take field trips to look into specific preservation situations. He believed that the intercession of the National Council would serve to acquaint the public with the importance of the organization. Armistead Rood appeared at the meeting to offer Woodlawn to the council at some time in the future, although the Woodlawn Public Foundation needed financial help at that moment.[146]

Early in March the first regular *Quarterly Report* of the National Council went out to the members. It carried a covering letter from Grant that served both as a president's report and as a warning to the field. The council had passed through its formative phase, Grant argued, but the accomplishments of the first year could not be repeated without substantial donations. It was clear that some method of funding the council offices had to be found. Most of the *Report* was devoted to the November annual meeting, but there were news items about the changes in the staff and some of the most significant activities of affiliated organizations. The members of the National Council could put down their copies of the first *Report* with a fair understanding of the problems involved in setting up the National Trust and with a good summary of the ideas that had been presented at the 1948 meeting. Condensations of all the important speeches appeared in a supplement to the *Report*.[147]

During the spring of 1949 the decisions made at the board meeting led the council further into the preservation field in a professional way. Ralph Wentworth undertook a massive mailing to individuals and organizations urging support of the council.[148] At the same time Grant agreed to have the staff represent the council at two educational programs that could enhance the public image of the organization. In one instance the executive secretary spoke at the Seminars in American Culture at Cooperstown, and in the other Betty Walsh participated in a seminar on preservation work given by the American University in Washington with the help of the National Park Service and Colonial Williamsburg.[149] The program for the preservation course, which lasted for two weeks in June 1949, showed how pervasive the influence of people such as Ronald Lee and Edward Alexander of the Williamsburg educational staff had become. The outline of the short course mirrored the Park Service's interest in research and documentation and Williamsburg's new concentration on interpretation.[150]

The second *Quarterly Report* of the National Council, which appeared in June, featured many brief news items about victories and losses all over the nation. Rath had obtained this information from a clipping service. On the first page of the *Report* was a laudatory editorial from the *New York Herald-Tribune* on the introduction of the National Trust bill in the House of Representatives.[151]

By the fall of 1949 both U. S. Grant III and Frederich Rath had concluded that some agreement should be made with the American Institute of Architects that would permit the National Council to have offices in the Octagon House. Grant wrote to the president of the AIA, outlining the needs of the council. He also showed that the group might well be able to pay its own way as a tenant in the Octagon and suggested that the presence of a preservation organization in the AIA headquarters would be a particularly suitable use for the old house.[152]

As delegates arrived in Williamsburg in October 1949 for the third annual meeting of the council, there were signs of steady progress, although some of the novelty of getting together for a national preservation convention had worn off. There was ample avidence that the hard work done by the small office staff in Ford's Theatre had already transformed the council into a genuine clearinghouse. Rath related in detail how he and Betty Walsh had corresponded with people in all forty-eight states

The Octagon, Washington, D.C. (Photograph by John T. Alexander)

in the previous year. He listed some of the personal contacts that had been especially helpful in saving old buildings. In some instances he had been able to put people in touch with the right professional service for restoration work; in other cases he gave technical advice to groups that could not afford to hire experts. Many of the contacts had been initiated because the office staff had made good use of the clipping service. In the first full year of operation (with only 235 individual members) the council sometimes volunteered its services to organizations that were unaware of the existence of a central office in Washington.[153] Alice Winchester of *Antiques* spoke about the growth of amateur, grass-roots interest in American history: "I have been extremely interested, in fact, to see how that public is growing constantly and what terrific enthusiasm there is among all kinds of people whom you wouldn't expect to be interested in old houses or historic restorations of any sort. I think there is not only a great actual interest but a great latent interest throughout the whole country, and it is just up to us to reach it."[154] She added that the council should eventually have an "encyclopedia" of information for historical groups. "I hope that the time will come when they can write to the headquarters of the National Council and find out exactly what to do with it [an old house], get all the pertinent information that anyone has dug up in any other part of the country."[155] Edwin O. Lewis gave a dinner address on the work in Philadelphia around the Independence Hall area, and he outlined the steps that had been taken to involve local, state, and federal governmental units.[156]

The second day closely resembled the final hours of the previous two annual meetings in Washington. The delegates wanted to share experiences from their particular areas, and the session quickly showed a lively cross section of the preservation movement. Rath later reported to Ronald Lee (who was at a UNESCO conference in Paris) that the meeting had gone as well as could be expected, although many people who had wanted to speak did not have a chance to share their stories. He also described to Lee a stormy meeting of the executive board in which Kenneth Chorley told his colleagues that it was time the National Council stopped operating on a shoestring. The officers, he said, must go out and seek funds from a broad segment of the preservation community. Rath concluded that Chorley's outburst had been sufficiently jarring to cause the board to approach fund raising in a much more systematic way in 1950.[157] At its November 30 meeting, the board decided to ask for aid from some of the larger foundations.[158]

The 1950 budget estimate indicated an obvious need for more workers for the National Council. Grant and Rath proposed an office staff of six that required a total of $40,000 to cover salaries, travel expenses, and field service activities for a year.[159] No doubt the initial work had been done well, although the response could have been much more encouraging. The passage of the bill creating the National Trust also added a note of permanence to the whole picture. The presence of federal officials on the board of the new organization appeared to insure support from various governmental agencies. But the problem that had haunted Rath and Betty Walsh from the beginning still remained: There were many people around the country who might support the council if they knew of its existence. There was no question about the zeal and eagerness of the staff in the Washington office. Day after day it answered requests for help and tried to inject some understanding of professionalism into a movement that had previously resisted any efforts toward centralization.

FUND RAISING

The most challenging preservation campaign that faced the National Council was the need to assist the Woodlawn Public Foundation in its struggle to pay off the large debt incurred in taking over the Nellie Custis home early in 1949. Armistead Rood continued to serve as secretary of the organization, and he and George Maurice Morris worked diligently to interest foundations and wealthy individuals in the Woodlawn proposition.[160] Unfortunately, Woodlawn did not possess the drawing power of its near neighbor, Mount Vernon. The professional fund raiser hired by the Public Foundation planned a variety of approaches that all seemed to backfire.[161] Rood approached several organizations, including the Masons and the Daughters of the American Revolution, but little came of these overtures.[162] Frederick Rath sincerely tried to guide Rood and his organization through the process of setting up Woodlawn as a museum—and Rath called on his own experience with the National Park Service. To begin with, he urged the Woodlawn Foundation to check with the major historic house museums already operating—Mount Vernon, Stratford, and Kenmore (in Fredericksburg). He urged Rood to set up two committees—one on planning that could take full advantage of professionals, such as engineers, historians, architects, and landscape architects, and a second one on furnishings. Rath also spent some time making specific recommendations about people who had proved to be helpful to other restorations. It is clear that he wanted to shake Rood out of his total commitment to raising a large amount of money in a short time, because Woodlawn was slated to open to the public that winter.[163]

But fund raising was certainly the principal concern of the Woodlawn Public Foundation with the approach of the February 22 ceremony that would mark the grand opening of the house. It desperately tried to get people to give during the final weeks in order to take maximum advantage of Paul Mellon's matching donation of two dollars for every one that came in from the general public.[164] In some ways Rood's accomplishment was notable; the foundation had nearly $80,000 in hand after only five months of campaigning. The trouble was that the foundation had agreed to pay $170,000 for the property.[165] Rood finally had to borrow the remaining $90,000 from a number of sources in order to complete the payment.[166]

Woodlawn had been saved, but there was still a large debt to be paid off, and the trustees were far from unanimous in their views on the future of the foundation. In May 1949 they voted to transform their campaign into a low-key membership drive. The office staff became largely volunteer and things moved along a little more smoothly.[167] However, none of the requests sent to the large foundations led to any substantial contributions. At least the major purchase had been negotiated and there was a close relationship with the National Council.[168] The major donations that came in were from private individuals contacted by Armistead Rood on the advice of Dean Suter of the Washington Cathedral.[169] The trustees appointed a new director for Woodlawn, Aubrey Marrs, who attempted to set up a national organization involving the use of local chapters.[170] The rest of the year seemed to be a time for regrouping and developing methods that might help the foundation acquire the funds necessary to collect the Mellon gift.[171] There was one brief effort to put Woodlawn under the control of the National Council, but that did not lead to any conclusive agreement. In the meantime General Grant and David Finley continued to serve on the board of the Woodlawn Foundation. Two years later the National Trust accepted Woodlawn as its first property.

The battle for Oak Hill had ended in an impasse by 1949 because owner Frank Littleton was not satisfied with the size of the donation proposed by the Mellon family. The National Park Service staff went to the trouble of getting President Truman to sign an executive order approving Oak Hill as a National Historic Site, so that if the owner were to lower his price the Department of the Interior might acquire the house in the same way it had taken over Hampton. But the November 1948 report of the Branch of History summarized the ending of the campaign:

Some of the best legal talent in the United States was supplied by those who offered the fund and they worked under great pressure for ten days to consummate this project which was so much in the public interest, but it proved impossible to deal on a reasonable basis either with the bankrupt owner of the estate or the contractor who had bid in the property at a court sale for $220,000. The court sale became final on December 3 and the property is now in the hands of the contractor. . . . Though disappointing in the final outcome, these events demonstrate how the National Council and the National Park Service may work together in the future for the public good.[172]

Oak Hill remained in private hands. Armistead Rood became convinced that the Mellon offer to help the Woodlawn Public Foundation had come immediately after Frank Littleton had decided not to work within the figures set by the Old Dominion Foundation.[173]

It was becoming increasingly clear that the council could offer only limited assistance in preservation emergencies as long as it could not own properties. In 1948 one Washington real estate broker offered to sell an old house (Woodley House, 1800) to the Woodlawn Public Foundation, which referred the letter to the National Council. But proposals of that type soon became rare; the National Trust would become the owner of any historic properties that were donated,[174] and the council could use its meager resources most effectively by trying to help other preservation organizations.[175]

INVOLVEMENT IN LOCAL PRESERVATION EFFORTS

Although the budget was inadequate and he was extremely busy, Frederick Rath hoped to intervene personally in a few carefully selected preservation efforts in order to establish the usefulness of the national organization. His first opportunity came when Clyde T. Franks of Laurens, S.C., asked the council for some advice on his restoration of a house called Rose Hill. Rath checked with architectural scholars in South Carolina about the merits of the house.[176] But he regretted that he could not spare the money to go to Laurens to look over the work.[177] Then Franks himself chose to pay for a visit from the executive secretary of the National Council. Fortunately, Rath was able to give him a positive report on the Rose Hill effort.[178]

He was doing a good job. . . . And he wanted advice on: was he doing it right? What should he do? How could he get the interest of the State? Well, I learned a lesson right there. The mere visit from Washington of someone like me with the title I had with the National Council for Historic Sites and Buildings—this in and of itself was an effective way to help, just that alone— which made you a little bit cautious upon occasion later. You had to know you were on pretty solid ground before you agreed to go visit something because just that visit might put the stamp of approval on it in the minds of a great many people, and sometimes you didn't want that.[179]

Before Rath had been able to think through a test for selecting the most promising preservation cases for his personal attention, he found himself deeply embroiled in the battle for a Connecticut hamlet called Hadlyme Ferry. The state highway department planned a new wharf, ferry boat, and road approach at Hadlyme that would have spoiled the setting of a small group of Federal houses that faced the Connecticut River. W. Langdon Kihn, an artist who lived in one of the buildings affected by the construction, tried to push through the state legislature a bill that would cancel the new work at Hadlyme. Kihn knew that he was up against a determined highway department and a philosophy that equated new construction with progress, so he tried to reach the National Council through Elmer Keith, a Connecticut antiquary who had a number of contacts in the preservation field.[180] It appeared that Kihn had a larger purpose in mind than merely saving a riverbank; he proposed that the council help him design a state agency that would have the power to stop highway developments in areas that possessed scenic and historical value.[181] He wanted the "National Trust [which did not yet exist] to bring its influence to bear upon the issue." Keith, too, urged that a man from the "National Trust" come to Hadlyme. "This would add an authoritative voice, at a critical time, to our local protests, that are likely to be discounted by the ruthless Highway Department."[182]

In those formative months Frederick Rath could not resist a challenge like this. The idea of going up from Washington to joust with a "ruthless Highway Department" must have been irresistible to a man who believed that he wore the mantle of the National Council for Historic Sites and Buildings. Whatever the merits of Langdon Kihn's case, he had beautifully timed his appeal to Washington. In mid-March 1949 Grant and Ronald Lee agreed to send the executive secretary to Hartford and Hadlyme Ferry to see what could be done to harmonize the interests of the state of Connecticut with those of the residents of the little river village.[183] Keith tried to galvanize local opinion for the visit—and Rath encountered a group of devoted followers when he arrived.[184]

The most important aspect of the journey to Connecticut proved to be Rath's intercession with the highway commissioner in Hartford. Apparently Rath took it upon himself to referee the skirmish instead of just taking up the cause of the Hadlyme residents. He stressed to highway commissioner J. Albert Hill that the state and the townspeople really had the same end in view. During his brief visit Rath helped to draft a substitute bill that would mitigate some of the worst visual effects of the new ferry boat.[185] But it was impossible to come up with a plan that pleased everybody.[186] Instead of making a second trip Rath deputized the new director of the Society for the Preservation of New England Antiquities, Bertram Little, to act as the council's emissary to Hartford. Rath gave Little a long account of the situation, including a proposed solution that would include state recognition of Hadlyme Ferry as a historic site that should not be substantially disturbed by highway development.[187] The local people managed to postpone a hearing until they could bring in United States Sen. Raymond Baldwin, who favored the preservation of Hadlyme Ferry.[188] The senator succeeded in drafting a bill that called for the designation of the town as a historic site but still permitted the boat to operate as long as the trees and road were not affected.[189] Kihn told Rath that the intervention of the National Council had been most helpful and that the new legislation might lead to the creation of some governmental body in Connecticut that could prevent future battles over historical areas.[190]

Rath did not choose to use the Hadlyme Ferry intervention as an example of a great victory. When he wrote a small article on the affair in the second *Quarterly Report* of the council, he concentrated on the lessons that had been learned:

Although action is still pending on the matter, several valid points can be made. First, the National Council can make its influence felt throughout the country effectively in just this sort of action. It was possible for the Council's representative to serve as a mediator between two opposed points of view. He could suggest on the basis of the experience of the whole membership of the Council a solution to the problem and could seek to make it work. But—and this is a most important point—because of lack of personnel and funds, the National Council was not able to follow through. The help that was given was limited, as it is in all similar cases. This is one of the greatest problems confronting the Council today. Until it is solved, until there is adequate trained personnel to cope with the amazing variety of problems that confront preservationists today, until there is money enough to meet emergencies and to follow through, the influence of your organization will necessarily be limited.[191]

Unfortunately Rath's pessimistic evaluation turned out to be a correct reading of the situation. The Connecticut Highway Department had already committed a good bit of money to surveying and planning; it had no intention of giving up its plans for putting in new ferry slips and a much larger boat. During July and August 1949, Langdon Kihn peppered the National Council with letters asking for support in appealing to Governor Bowles to keep the highway department from building the bigger ferry slips and permitting large trucks to use Hadlyme as a crossing.[192] Grant drafted a letter pointing out to the governor that the council had been sufficiently interested in the little community to send a representative to negotiate between the antagonists.[193] Still the juggernaut of progress moved on. By late August it was clear that a larger ferry boat would be used at Hadlyme, but there was some doubt about any new construction.[194] By October construction work on the ferry landing had begun, but the damage to the front yards and the overhanging trees had not been great. One thin shred of victory still remained: The governor had limited the work to the landing area and he had specified that big trucks could not come through Hadlyme.[195] Looking back from the vantage point of twenty years, Rath concluded that the lesson learned at Hadlyme Ferry was how "ruthless" departments of transportation could be.[196]

Rath's two principal journeys to support local preservation efforts had been generally helpful. At Rose Hill he was able to go to South Carolina to compliment an earnest preservationist who was already following a wise course of action. At Hadlyme Ferry the Connecticut commissioner of highways was obviously determined to carry through the improvements that had been surveyed; there was no reason to stand aside when only four homeowners were involved.

Rath must have discovered that he was wasting his potential power in those early days by going out in person to support small preservation battles. He decided that the National Council was probably a much more awesome force on the political and economic scene when it made its presence known through correspondence. A letter bearing the title "National Council for Historic Sites and Buildings" along with the signature of Maj. Gen. U. S. Grant III as president was surprisingly impressive. No one needed to know that the council really consisted of Frederick Rath and Betty Walsh in a walk-up office in Ford's Theatre. Rath's own expertise came across well in letters. He sensed what sorts of problems his correspondents faced and then showed that the council could recommend specific solutions when the issues were clearly defined. He also determined that the council would stay with a question until it had been resolved.

In a number of instances executive secretary Rath attempted to influence the development of worthwhile preservation projects by bringing professional people into contact with them. This kind of communication was an especially advantageous aspect of a central office located in Washington. For instance, when superintendent Charles Wall of Mount Vernon told Rath in May 1949 about a religious organization in Alexandria, Va., that wanted to restore the Old Presbyterian Meeting House (1774, 1836), Rath went to work to see what needed to be done.[197] Both the executive secretary and the president of the National Council decided that the meeting house was a project that deserved their close attention because the churchyard contained the grave of an unknown soldier of the American Revolution—no matter what the specific merits of the old building might be.[198] At that time Rath lived in nearby Arlington, so he could maintain close contact with the people concerned. He began by asking the corresponding secretary of the American Society of Landscape Architects if it would be possible to have a Washington landscape architect, Leon Zach, as the consultant for the churchyard restoration.[199] Zach soon gave some valuable advice to the fledgling preservation group in Alexandria.[200]

During the first full year of his administration Rath hoped to acquaint himself with the scope of the national preservation movement, so he depended heavily on a newspaper clipping service. One day he noted that the *Upper Darby News* of Upper Darby, Pa., carried an article about the recent purchase of a historic house by the local board of education. The idea of seeing an old structure destroyed by a civic organization devoted to the education of children bothered him, so Rath wrote the editor of the paper.[201] Within a week the National Council had a long letter from Freas B. Snyder, the town historian. Snyder explained all the problems involved with saving the Jonathan Evans Homestead (1693), which stood in the way of a proposed all-weather play area for the children of Upper Darby. The expenses involved in moving the house or taking it apart seemed to be beyond the reach of the people of the town.[202] At this point Rath moved into the situation in just the way he had expected the National Council to operate in the future. He urged Snyder to look into the work of another Pennsylvania school district that had made the restoration of an old house a functioning part of the vocational department of the local high school. He also cited a town in New York State that had restored an early house to serve as a community center. Having established the fact that the council was aware of the problems of local historical organizations throughout the East, Rath then paused to tell Snyder how the new national preservation headquarters operated:

You may wonder how we came to know about your problem. We subscribe to a clipping service. You may wonder also why we should take an interest in your problem. The enclosed pamphlet will tell you about the National Council for Historic Sites and Buildings. We are interested in the preservation of fine remains of our historic heritage wherever they may be. Because this is a young organization, the help that we can give is sometimes limited. But I assure you that we are interested. It may be, for example, that we can enlist the aid of other Pennsylvanians to assist you or give occasional technical advice that may be helpful. In any event, please let us know about any developments and do not hesitate to write me if you believe there is anything we can do.[203]

The Jonathan Evans case proved that Rath and his office had developed a certain amount of persistence. Freas Snyder wrote back that the house was doomed because the site was to be used by the board of education; but Rath did not simply give up and write a letter of sympathy.[204] Instead he urged Snyder to keep working up to the last minute. Although the house went down, the preservationists of Upper Darby realized they were not alone.

At times the National Park Service alerted Rath's office to situations where his advice might help to shoulder some of the load then carried by the staff historians and archaeologists. During 1948 and 1949 regional archaeologist Erik Reed asked Rath to assist Col. Maurice G. Fulton in Lincoln, N.M.[205] Fulton wanted to preserve his little cowtown—preferably under the auspices of the state of New Mexico. He hoped that the office of state historian in New Mexico could be recreated so that he could become custodian of the old Lincoln County Courthouse (1874). Fulton asked Rath how to force the state authorities to set up a commission to help save the entire town of Lincoln.[206] Rath promised that the National Council would be glad to give its "imprimatur" to the idea of a state historical commission if Fulton developed a "well-conceived line of action." Whatever power the council could muster would be directed toward the New Mexico legislature, but Rath and Grant had to be certain that Fulton knew what he was doing before they exerted pressure on the state government.[207] Soon Rath found in his mail a long account of the struggles the local historians had faced in trying to restore the courthouse and care for the old town. Fulton urged Rath to write the governor of New Mexico to back the historical commission proposal.[208] A few months later Fulton was able to thank the council for the encouragement he had received in setting up the Lincoln County Memorial Commission with a grant of $5,000 from the state for the first year of operation.[209]

859

Old Lincoln County Courthouse, Lincoln, N.M., after 1939. (Photograph by J. W. Hendron)

CORRESPONDENCE

The distribution of a quarterly newsletter—even to several hundred members—and the three annual meetings of the National Council helped to focus attention on the office in Ford's Theatre. Soon Grant and Frederick Rath had all the correspondence they could handle. There was abundant evidence that preservation-minded people needed encouragement, advice, and information on how old buildings had fared all around the country. Sometimes Grant sent out congratulatory letters to newspaper editors who had pushed important preservation causes in places like New York City and Dayton, Ohio.[210] When the secretary of the Onondaga Historical Association in Syracuse, N.Y., asked Rath for information on the historical work of city governments elsewhere, the executive secretary of the council fell back on his professional preparation in the National Park Service.[211] The news items that came to the council from the clipping service included stories that dealt with surveys, zoning laws, and other preservation techniques. In some instances Rath wrote to the people who were administering these programs in order to enrich his files for future reference.[212] At times either Rath or Grant asked preservation leaders to discuss the methods they had used to carry out their most successful campaigns.[213] Portions of these letters in copied form became part of the all-important background material that Rath used for technical kits to be sent to inquirers.[214] For the first time in the history of the preservation movement a formal master file came into being, a compendium of information about fund raising, legal problems, restoration work, the importance of research, and a host of other topics. There was no doubt about the depth of Rath's commitment to the services that could be performed by the National Council for Historic Sites and Buildings.

CHARTERING THE NATIONAL TRUST

The question of setting up a National Trust could not be ignored. Too many people had become convinced that a national preservation organization was the only answer for the many important properties coming on the market—properties that could not possibly be saved by local groups. The council had come into being to serve two vital purposes: the dissemination of information and the drafting of a charter for a property-owning organization. The council was an amalgamation of existing groups; the trust would be a new central focus for the preservation field and a property-owning entity. The second annual meeting of the National Council had officially endorsed the report of the Committee for the Organization of the National Trust, so H. Alexander Smith, Jr., and his colleagues went on drafting the bill that would go to Congress. A congressional charter would give the trust a quasi-public status (like the Smithsonian Institution), which would enable the trust to utilize tax advantages for its historic properties and report regularly to Congress.[215] On February 5, 1949, the committee met one more time at the National Gallery of Art to go over the trust bill before it was introduced in Congress. The discussion centered on the kinds of property that might come to the trust, the composition of the board of trustees, and the future relationship with the federal government.[216] The trust was intended to carry out the preservation purposes of the Historic Sites Act of 1935 by marshaling the resources of private historical organizations in the United States under federal auspices.

As soon as preservationists discovered that the National Trust bill was in Congress, requests started to come to the council for investigations of historic houses that needed to be saved. Frederick Rath had a standard response that he used through the summer of 1949: "No formal method of application for consideration has, as yet, been set up."[217] That statement was absolutely true, because the people working on the trust idea had been concentrating on wording a charter that would prove to be useful for many years. In February 1949 these same individuals turned their attention to the difficult job of getting the bill through the legislative process—an effort that consumed more than half a year. Under those conditions it was unthinkable to consider applications for new properties. During the summer a few women in Newport, R.I., proposed that the trust take over the Redwood Library, an important eighteenth-century public building designed by the colonial architect Peter Harrison.[218] Rath warned the Newport group that a Committee on Standards had been created within the National Council framework, and he sent along a copy of the committee's list of criteria for selecting buildings for preservation. The list, drawn up by professionals, was quite similar to the guidelines used by the National Park Service Advisory Board. At the same time Rath admitted that the new National Trust (which was before a Senate committee at the time) would have to set up a Committee on Selection. He advised the Newporters to draw up a dossier on the Redwood Library that could be used as soon as the trust came into existence.[219]

When the National Trust bill passed the House of Representatives, a *New York Times* editorial quoted several selections from one of David Finley's speeches on the trust. Then the *Times* referred to the new organization as a natural development that should succeed in helping Americans decide what to save. The trust would have the power to help private and public groups go about their work more effectively.[220] The principal proponent of the measure had proved to be Congressman J. Hardin Peterson of Florida. There was no leader in the Senate who would push the bill through at a time when there was a great backlog of pending legislation, so a number of preservationists began to put pressure on members of the Senate to report the bill to the floor.[221] The *New York Times* joined in the fight to get the bill out of the Senate committee by printing an editorial on September 8 that defined again the need for the trust. The *Times* could see no reason why the members of the committee would want to ignore such an important bill. After all, the trust would not cost the taxpayers anything, but it could help to rescue the "material symbols" of our culture which were in considerable danger.[222]

By October 17, 1949, the battle had been won. The bill cleared the Senate by unanimous consent and went to President Truman for his signature.[223] The editors of the *Times* congratulated the proponents of H.R. 5170 and looked forward to the preservation of an increasing number of historic sites in the next few years. However, the *Times* overdrew the role that the new organization would play in the 1950s. After showing that the federal government could not always move fast enough to save important buildings and after demonstrating that the patriotic and historical societies of the United States could not possibly save all the worthwhile structures that should be kept, the *Times* referred to the new trust as "a repository to which such buildings and areas can be deeded." The editorial became even more extravagant in its predictions: "And it is expected that it will also serve as a magnet to attract private contributions for the purchase of selected places of national interest."[224] Unfortunately, some people ignored the sober realities of the situation and assumed that a great and powerful preservation lobby had been created by the new law. The charter of the National Trust was an important single step forward, but it merely authorized the organizers to pool their existing resources. It did not create a fund, nor did it imply that the federal government would be a major force in backing the trust.

President Truman put his signature on the bill without much fanfare on October 26, and General Grant announced the creation of the National Trust for Historic Preservation on October 31, 1949.[225] On November 30, the executive board of the council discussed the composition of the trust's board of trustees in accordance with the terms of the new charter. In the initial discussions the idea arose of having the council absorbed by the trust. Everyone agreed that the difficulties involved in moving the internal government and membership of the council over to the trust were too complicated, so the council was put in the position of setting up the new trust. Several of the council's trustees believed that the trust should have a large board made up of famous people who would do little more than serve as window dressing. Others favored a smaller group of people who were known to be totally dedicated to the idea of a National Trust. The compromise solution seemed to reflect both schools of thought, and the National Council board set up a National Trust "interim executive officer" who happened to be Frederick L. Rath, Jr. In 1953 the council and the National Trust merged.[226]

Inevitably the public announcement of the creation of the National Trust led to a series of inquiries about the disposition of historic properties. Even before President Truman signed the bill U. S. Grant III received a letter from James G. Van Derpool of Columbia University asking if the new trust would be interested in taking over the Glen-Sanders Mansion at Scotia, N.Y.[227] Grant informed Van Derpool that the existing council could not acquire any old buildings, but it could recommend certain courses of action to the trust, which was in the process of coming into being.[228] As soon as the trust board began meeting, Grant asked the Sanders family in Scotia to indicate specifically "some plan for the eventual custody of your home for the benefit of the public." It was clear that Grant had set out to warn potential donors that endowments would have to accompany historic buildings given to the trust.[229] There were other proposals from private individuals who wanted to find out what kind of terms could be arranged for turning over properties to the new trust.[230] Grant told these people, too, that it would be necessary to find some means of endowing any buildings that came under the administrative control of the trust.[231]

Rath had a different view of the National Trust from the organization described in the *New York Times* as a "body of informed persons" that could act quickly in "emergencies." The trust, according to Rath, was to serve a function that the council could never have adequately covered:

> I felt it would be a court of last resort, the National Trust. Only if you could find no other solution to the problem, and then frequently (and again I say this for myself) you would not necessarily hold the property permanently. You would hold it because the critical emergency demanded that you do this for a period of time. And this was my concept of the role of the National Trust. And my disappointment was that it immediately became apparent that once a property was in the name of the National Trust, nothing in God's world was going to get it away from the Trust.[232]

(Only in the 1970s did it become possible for the National Trust to serve in the emergency role that Rath had sketched out in 1949. In 1974 it helped to save the Wainwright Building in St. Louis through the use of a purchase option. In that case the purpose of the option was clear: The trust bought time to help locate a suitable owner for this historic office building.)[233]

The preservation leaders who gathered in Washington in November 1949 to put together the board for the National Trust for Historic Preservation were well aware of the fact that the founding of the trust was a response to a great need. They also knew that the National Council, the National Park Service, and major professional organizations had been busy through the late 1940s trying to control the unplanned flow of progress all across the United States. The enemies of preservation had begun to emerge in the form of people who wanted to see Cold War America grow into a nation that set an example for the whole world—with broad suburban development, interstate highways, and a stress on consumer goods that would give an affluence for all to emulate. These people were not bent upon destruction for its own sake. They rarely viewed themselves as foes of preservationists, but they did want to see continual evidence of progress.

Frederick Rath knew full well that the mechanism already existed in 1949 to save the United States from obliterating its historic past. He also knew that the public did not consider preservation to be a particularly profitable activity. The individuals who were expected to support the National Trust and the National Council did not offer large enough donations to finance the preservation movement. Ronald Lee and the Park Service staff had unfulfilled hopes that through David Finley the Mellon family might take over where John D. Rockefeller, Jr., and Henry Ford had left off.[234] What the public at large did not yet fully realize was that significant amounts of money would have to go into preservation and restoration work in order to save the cultural heritage of America.

Two key ingredients that contributed to the great preservation victories of the succeeding decades were present in 1949: the major organizational framework that was to provide direction and the dedicated personnel who had the historical training and the administrative experience necessary to plan and execute new programs. The one missing element was the public awareness that Rath sought so eagerly during his early years with the National Council. A great many historic sites and buildings would need some form of protection even if they did not end up as historic house museums. The big challenge to the National Trust in the next two decades lay in the area of public relations. The men and women who would help to put through the Historic Preservation Act of 1966 were almost all in positions of responsibility either in the National Park Service or in the National Council for Historic Sites and Buildings when the National Trust received its charter from Congress. Nearly a century after Ann Pamela Cunningham first addressed her call to the ladies of the South to save Mount Vernon, the preservation movement had finally been able to bring itself together into an organization to coordinate all the different groups that had an interest in saving the visible reminders of America's past.

11

The Growth of Professionalism

WHEN John D. Rockefeller, Jr., told W. A. R. Goodwin to hire an architect to sketch out a plan for a fully restored Williamsburg in the fall of 1926, there was no professional in the United States who supervised restoration work on a regular basis. It was natural that Goodwin first turned to Thomas Tallmadge, a practicing architect who had written a well-known textbook on the history of architecture.[1] The administration of the preservation movement was still securely in the hands of dedicated amateurs who enjoyed renovating and exhibiting old buildings. Training programs did not exist for those who sought employment in restoration work. There had been no project in the United States large enough to give any architect or historian a full-time job, much less a planner, lawyer, archaeologist, or developer.

William Sumner Appleton of the Society for the Preservation of New England Antiquities came the closest to professional status, but he was an amateur living off a personal trust fund that freed him to donate all of his time to worthy causes. Appleton had not been trained as an architect, historian, or archaeologist. He simply came to understand buildings in his native New England through constant travel and frequent contacts with the small number of architects who had been engaged in restoration work. The same month that Rockefeller initiated a study of Williamsburg in 1926, Mabel Choate of Stockbridge, Mass., decided to move the Old Mission House (1739) from a ridge outside the town to the village center as a period restoration. She consulted a talented decorator, Henry Davis Sleeper (who was working at the time for Henry F. du Pont). Sleeper found some aspects of the building to be "peculiar" and he recommended that she ask Appleton to report on the structure. In her note of invitation she addressed Appleton as an expert: "I do not know whether you would be willing to do this professionally, but if you would not, perhaps you would let me show my appreciation of your kindness by making another contribution to your Society."[2] Mabel Choate had wisely turned to practically the only person in the nation who could have been called a restoration consultant. But the corresponding secretary of the SPNEA chose to retain his amateur status: "You ask whether I would make this examination of your house professionally. In reply let me say that I have never made any charge for inspecting an old house nor for helping anyone preserve one. I like to make a gift of my time as a trifling contribution to help public spirited owners in such work. My expenses will, I suppose, be so trifling that I can safely forget those too."[3] Appleton urged Miss Choate to contact the Rev. Donald Millar in New York City, another skilled antiquary who had studied the Mission House on his own a few months before. Within a comparatively short period of time she had managed to get some excellent advice from several of New England's architectural scholars for almost no payment. That sort of situation was not likely to occur again, because times were changing.

In the 1930s, only a decade after the moving of the Mission House and Goodwin's somewhat haphazard search for an architect for Williamsburg, the field of preservation became professional. Large depression-era projects soon required the employment of people who had specialized in different fields related to preservation, restoration, and interpretation. They had college degrees and often had done graduate work as a part of their professional preparation. Some of these professionals frankly sought employment that would carry them through the economic crisis; they were not initially motivated by a deep interest in historic buildings and the philosophical questions posed by the restoration process. However, they continued to be "students" of American culture because the spirit of intellectual inquiry persisted throughout the ranks of the restorers. These scholars worked with colleagues who had been trained in a number of disciplines, and in the larger restorations there were endless debates over each major decision. Because the federal programs focused on hiring personnel from professions that had traditionally included few if any women, the new generation of preserva-

Fiske Kimball. (National Archives)

tionists was overwhelmingly male. Those women who were paid professionals during this era were usually trained in the fields of history, architectural history, and museum studies.

A brief comparison of the careers of five individuals should serve to illustrate the remarkable transformation that occurred between 1926 and 1936: Fiske Kimball, Ronald F. Lee, Charles E. Peterson, Ned J. Burns, and Jean C. Harrington. Kimball, who was born in 1888, was about a generation older than the other four. By 1926 he was a recognized authority on architecture through the publication of two impressive books, *Thomas Jefferson, Architect* (1916) and *The Domestic Architecture of the American Colonies and of the Early Republic* (1922).[4] Kimball had taught architectural history at the University of Michigan and the University of Virginia. In 1926 he was the newly appointed director of the Pennsylvania Museum (later the Philadelphia Museum of Art) in Philadelphia. The sesquicentennial celebration that year made it possible for Kimball to supervise several restorations of eighteenth-century mansions in Fairmount Park for his museum.[5] There was reason to believe that he would continue to play a major role in the preservation movement through his publications and in his advisory capacity as architect for the restoration of Monticello for the Thomas Jefferson Memorial Foundation.[6] He was already chairman of the American Institute of Architects' Committee on Preservation of Historic Monuments and Scenic Beauties, and he had spoken at several AIA conventions about the responsibilities involved in taking on an architectural restoration.[7]

But where were the other four men in 1926? Ronald Lee was in his junior year at the University of Minnesota, majoring in economics.[8] Charles Peterson was a sophomore at the same school, majoring in architecture.[9] Jean Harrington had graduated from the University of Michigan two years before with a major in architecture. He had spent part of his senior year measuring old mission churches in New Mexico as a thesis project. After graduation Harrington had returned to the Southwest for awhile to see if he could practice architecture in a region he had grown to love. By 1926 he had worked for the New Mexico State Highway Department and a mining company and fully intended to pursue a career in architecture.[10] Ned Burns was the only one of the five who went into his chosen career without benefit of a college education. He had been a guard at the Staten Island Museum in New York City, but because he was a natural student he had quickly begun to work on related museum projects, including the preparation of displays. By 1926 he was at the American Museum of Natural History as a preparator with three years of experience following formal training at the New York School of Industrial Arts and the Art Students League.[11]

Within another ten years all five of these people found themselves in positions of considerable power and responsibility. Their training and their interests fitted into the historical needs of the United States during the Great Depression. Fiske Kimball was still director of the Pennsylvania Museum, but his influence on preservation and restoration had increased. He was not only the official architect for the restoration of Monticello (which would not begin for a couple of years), but he was also the restoration architect for Stratford Hall. And he was a member of two important advisory boards, one that met annually at Williamsburg and another that assembled at the Department of the Interior several times a year. Kimball was a dominant figure on the first of these.[12] His bluntness and bravado also characterized his performances on the other; from the first meeting of the Advisory Board on National Parks, Historic Sites, Buildings and Monuments, Kimball insisted that the National Park Service prepare a restoration policy for any sites under federal control.[13]

The career of Ronald Lee shows more clearly how quickly the federal programs had grown in such a short time. In 1933 Lee left graduate work at the University of Minnesota to take a position as a staff historian for the Civilian Conservation Corps at Shiloh Battlefield in Tennessee.[14] Only three years later he looked back over his Park Service record with some pride: "As Historian for the State Park Division of the National Park Service, from March 1935 to May 1936, I organized and gave technical direction to a Nation-wide program of research and preservation for state-owned historical areas. This program employed eighteen Associate, Assistant and Junior Historians in eight regional offices and resulted in historical-technical cooperation of the National Park Service on more than forty state historical projects, including several forts, two missions, two colonial iron furnaces, and several archeological sites."[15]

Charles Peterson was staff architect at the Jefferson National Expansion Memorial in St. Louis in 1936. He had already worked on the Colonial Parkway in Virginia and several restoration projects at Yorktown. His architectural training had been greatly enhanced by his contacts with the draftsmen who worked in nearby Williamsburg in the early 1930s. Peterson had served for a time as assistant chief of the eastern office of the National Park Service Branch of Plans and Design. He had consulted on several Park Service restorations in Morristown and had even taken out time to draw up the plans for the Historic American Buildings Survey.[16]

Jean Harrington was supervising the archaeological work at Jamestown as a part of the development of Colonial National Historical Park. He took the position while finishing his graduate work in archaeology at the University of Chicago. During the depression Harrington had found graduate training more rewarding than trying to make a living as a practicing architect.[17] At Jamestown he was in charge of an excavation that was destined to make the profession of historical archaeology a recognized branch of scholarly investigation. On top of that, Harrington was able to utilize a substantial number of CCC enrollees to carry on the work of uncovering Virginia's first capital.

After a few years with the Museum of the City of New York, Ned Burns became superintendent of field laboratories for the National Park Service with headquarters at Morristown National Historical Park in New Jersey. In 1936 he moved to Washington to become chief curator of the Interior Department Museum, but he still had substantial responsibilities for supervising the laboratory work in Morristown.[18]

Only a decade after 1926 these five men were involved in decision-making on a fairly high level in the federal government. It is true that

Fiske Kimball was merely a consultant, but people had to listen to him. After all, he was the elder statesman of the group at the age of forty-eight! But the other four were in positions of power and responsibility. They had many CCC laborers and staff consultants working with them. Each knew that he was helping to develop something that had never been tried before, and Harrington even believed that he was witnessing the birth of a new archaeological interest in the United States.

This unparalleled opportunity had come about because the depression had made it feasible for the federal and state governments to spend money on a scale undreamed of in 1926. Horace Albright and his successors in the National Park Service (particularly Verne Chatelain) were ambitious. They sketched out programs that were supposed to create a national system of historic sites, and it was obvious that historians, architects, archaeologists, and museum specialists would be needed to interpret these places to the visiting public.

Because federal recovery programs became an essential element in transforming the field of history, it can be said that most important developments in the growth of professionalism in preservation can be traced to the comparatively brief period of thirteen years from 1928 to the United States entry into war in 1941. The Williamsburg drafting room of 1928–29 became the first collaborative effort for professionals, but it was restricted almost entirely to architects. Large cutbacks in the architectural staff in 1933 meant that Williamsburg ceased to be a major research enterprise until about 1939, when Phase II of the restoration came into being.

From 1933 onward the National Park Service was the principal employer of the professionals who dedicated their careers to historic preservation. Most of these specialists began their work with the temporary CCC positions, but many of them found permanent Civil Service jobs in the regional offices or in Washington. The growth of the historical phase of the Park System meant that these comparatively young professionals had contacts with others who had training in complementary disciplines. There were debates, policy papers, and reports that required the collaboration of architects, historians, and archaeologists. Museum preparators depended on other professionals to supply authentic data for exhibits under consideration.

Three other organizations provided steady employment for a few architects and historians in either restoration or interpretation: the state governments of Illinois and Pennsylvania and the New York State Historical Association. The state architect's office in Springfield, Ill., included both Joseph Booton and Jerome Ray. Although these two men

Perry, Shaw, and Hepburn drafting room, Williamsburg, 1931. Left to right: *Richard A. Walker, David J. Hayes, Finlay F. Ferguson, Jr., George S. Campbell, Foster Townsend, Milton L. Grigg, J. Everette Fauber, Jr., Clyde F. Trudell* (standing, center), *Phoebus Jones, Singleton P. Moorehead, Joseph Kennedy, Thomas T. Waterman, Francis J. Duke, Albert Hoedtke, Washington Reed, A. Edwin Kendrew. (Colonial Williamsburg Foundation)*

spent considerable time in nonhistorical work, they became an effective team of restoration specialists in the late 1930s. They sometimes worked with outside consultants from the National Park Service, but usually they were on their own.[19] The creation of the office of state historian in Pennsylvania in 1937 brought S. K. Stevens into the preservation picture for a number of years. As with the Illinois staff, Stevens had many duties that did not relate directly to historic buildings, yet he worked hard on policy making and surveying the historical resources of his state.[20]

Stephen Clark's insistence on careful research at Cooperstown had a noticeable effect on the preservation movement. Between 1938 and 1949 the Farmers' Museum complex was administered by four remarkable people associated with the New York State Historical Association: Edward P. Alexander, Clifford Lord, Janet MacFarlane, and Louis C. Jones. The first two were trained historians who later went on to direct the State Historical Society of Wisconsin. Alexander also made a major contribution to the development of a program of interpretation at Williamsburg after World War II. Janet MacFarlane was a trained museum specialist who had studied under Arthur Parker in Rochester before coming to Cooperstown and who contributed to the museum's development through her emphasis on the "lived-in" look in the exhibition buildings.[21] She stayed on with the New York State Historical Association as curator after Louis Jones took over the directorship in 1946. Jones was a scholar and teacher of English who had specialized in folklore. His dynamic personality and his ability to work with the staff at Cooperstown made him a national figure in museum administration by the 1950s. He won the absolute confidence of Stephen Clark and was able to accomplish great things with the Farmers' Museum.[22]

No other private or governmental groups gave long-term employment to people who had been trained for preservation work. Many organizations employed professionals for relatively short periods of time, such as the Robert E. Lee Memorial Foundation, the Society for the Preservation of New England Antiquities, and Old Sturbridge Village. Budgetary limitations made it impossible for most institutions to retain a staff of researchers or architects in those years.

INVOLVEMENT OF PROFESSIONAL GROUPS

Although the depression created an unusual opportunity for those individuals who wanted to become skilled preservationists, graduate schools offering standard programs in history, architecture, and archaeology were not concerned with training people for preservation and restoration responsibilities that would come at Williamsburg and the National Park Service sites.

During the 1940s the Park Service historians began to wonder if the training of the graduate schools had been broad enough to enable them to handle all the different jobs they would encounter. Hans Huth, a German refugee who came over to study the National Park Service as a consultant in 1940, wrote on this theme several times. Huth told his new colleagues in the Department of the Interior that there was not enough specialization within the different professions represented on the Advisory Board and that the historians he had met in the field were not sufficiently object-oriented. Huth noted that these interpreters were especially weak in the areas of cultural history and the arts.[23] The regional supervisor of historic sites in Santa Fe, N.M., Aubrey Neasham, attacked the problem from a different angle in a paper he prepared in 1942 entitled "University Training for Park Personnel." Neasham seriously proposed that some large universities could prepare people for park work without adding any courses to the existing curricula. He believed that advisers could recommend a host of courses in diverse disciplines that would give students a greater understanding of the places they would have to interpret to the public. Neasham quite rightly asserted that the new program of training would "establish park employment upon a more professional basis."[24] The standard procedure at that time was preparation in a specific field of interest followed by an on-the-job "crash" course in park work.

Toward the end of the war the Advisory Board wrestled with the idea of using the "best brains in the country" as a task force to study the National Parks. The problem was that there had to be some source of funds to pay these highly qualified consultants.[25] Unfortunately, the small amounts of money voted to maintain the National Parks after World War II meant that no new interpretive or research services could be initiated. It was fine for the professionals to theorize about what they needed; it was another thing for Congress and the president to give the Department of the Interior the funds it requested.

Only two professional organizations in 1926 even paid lip service to the ideals of preservation: the American Institute of Architects and the American Historical Association. Both of these groups had committees that dealt with historic buildings; one—the architects—did make some efforts to improve restoration work from time to time. But the historians, with a few notable exceptions, were not interested in the preservation of buildings; their entire focus seemed to be on the protection and cataloging of documents.[26] The principal preservation goal of the AHA in the late 1920s probably was exemplified by the construction of the National Archives Building in Washington.

It was natural that architects would be interested in saving old buildings by the mid-1920s. Universally, their training had been based on a knowledge of the history of architecture. Like Jean Harrington, numberless young architects set out to record details from old buildings in many parts of the country. Park Service architect Stuart Barnette, writing in 1935, mentioned that during the 1920s he had carried on his own surveys of areas along the East Coast from the eastern shore of Maryland to Maine.[27] No doubt groups of architects had to work freely in the styles of the past because they were expected to produce both residential and commercial buildings in styles ranging from Collegiate Gothic to Georgian town houses.

American Institute of Architects

Interest in historic buildings by the American Institute of Architects extended to chapters in cities all over the country. The January 1926 issue of the AIA *Journal* included a brief letter from the Pittsburgh chapter, thanking members who had responded to an appeal for letters in support of the preservation of the Allegheny County Courthouse and Jail (1884–88) designed by Henry Hobson Richardson. The Pittsburgh architects had helped to win a stay of execution (largely because of a municipal election), but they warned their colleagues that the fate of the Richardson buildings had not yet been decided. A. Lawrence Kocher, editor of the *Architectural Record*, reported to the 1927 convention of the AIA as chairman of the Committee on Preservation of Historic Monuments and Scenery (formed 1914). He cited a surprising number of instances where local chapters of the Institute had been able to influence legislation or prevent serious alteration of important buildings by well-meaning owners.[28] It was clear that Kocher wanted his committee to be active, and he expected the chapters to respond to his calls for help. Kocher said in an article published in March 1928 that he wanted to be a clearinghouse for news of worthwhile preservation causes:

> Every Chapter is at present, in a sense, a local preservation society. The Committee representative is the active field agent of the Institute serving as the guardian of historic monuments, scenery and natural resources within his district.
>
> When cases that call for attention arise, the representative acts in a personal way or through the local chapter. The Institute Chairman also gives assistance by correspondence. The aid of the press is frequently called upon to arouse public opinion in behalf of preservation. It has been realized that it is easier to diagnose these evils than either to check or prevent them. We are continually confronted with the difficulty of arousing a public response.[29]

Each year during the late 1920s Kocher dutifully reported on the successful preservation work carried on by local chapters, sometimes through consultation and sometimes by bringing pressure to bear on governmental units.[30] Although Kocher was disturbed about the lack of coordination in the AIA, he could point to some accomplishments with understandable pride. John Gaw Meem of Santa Fe told the 1931 AIA convention that one individual architect could accomplish a great deal for the cause of preservation in certain sections of the United States if he joined together with public and private agencies that had similar in-

Entrance to Glessner House, Chicago. (Courtesy Chicago School of Architecture Foundation)

terests.[31] The Boston chapter had completed a chronological list of early buildings in Massachusetts and had attempted to control the proliferation of billboards. The Buffalo chapter had given some attention to the restoration of the "Castle" at Old Fort Niagara. The architects in Baltimore had helped to save some doorways and ironwork for the local art museum. The Central New York chapter reported that students at Cornell University had embarked on a survey of old buildings in the Finger

Lakes region under the direction of Albert C. Phelps. In New Orleans the AIA group had worked hard on gathering information on the architecture of the Vieux Carré in order to help the zoning commission. The Tennessee chapter had given advice to the Ladies' Hermitage Association on the restoration of two outbuildings at Andrew Jackson's home. In Chicago the AIA chapter campaigned for the preservation of the Water Tower on Michigan Avenue and the Fine Arts Building from the World's Fair of 1893. The Chicago group also announced that it had been given the deed to the Glessner House (1886) on Prairie Avenue; this important home, designed by H. H. Richardson, would serve as the chapter's headquarters. The AIA in San Francisco stood ready to cooperate with the new California State Park Commission in making up a list of buildings that should be preserved under the terms of the recent state bond issue.[32] While it is probable that Kocher overstated the claims made by some of the chapters, there is indisputable evidence that at least one national professional organization could muster some grass-roots support for preservation. The alert chairman of the Preservation Committee continued to support any chapters that fought the onrush of billboards, filling stations, and other harbingers of "progress" that severely damaged the American landscape.[33]

During the 1930s Leicester Holland of the Fine Arts Division of the Library of Congress took over as chairman of the AIA Committee on Preservation of Historic Buildings. Holland had been a professor of architecture at the University of Pennsylvania and at Vassar. Most of the committee reports he prepared dealt with issues that troubled the whole preservation field, so he did not concentrate heavily on the activities of the chapters. Holland was especially interested in three things: the creation of the Historic American Buildings Survey, the battle to keep museums from buying up old paneling and ironwork, and the encouragement of careful research for the restoration and reconstruction projects that were financed by federal emergency funds.[34] Holland did not object to the publication of articles that praised the "infinite taste and sensitiveness" of the Williamsburg restoration.[35] He was furious to find that Congress was considering a bill calling for a marble extension to the East Front of the United States Capitol, and he wrote a spirited defense of the old facade under the title "Wings over the Capitol."[36] A year later, in response to the Pennsbury reconstruction, Holland helped to push through a resolution at the national convention that condemned the use of federal funds for any restoration project that had not been "submitted for scholarly and scrupulous examination to the Advisory Board" or to the AIA Preservation Committee.[37]

After World War II Turpin Bannister, dean of the School of Archi-

Leicester B. Holland, 1933. (Photograph by Underwood and Underwood)

tecture and Arts at Alabama Polytechnic Institute in Auburn, assumed the chairmanship of the Committee on Preservation of Historic Buildings. He concentrated his energies on the difficult task of becoming a center for information on architectural landmarks that had been threatened in different parts of the country.[38] Bannister answered a great many questions that came to his committee, and he wrote a few letters in support of the preservation of some key buildings. He was not quite so vociferous as Leicester Holland, and his teaching duties at Rensselaer Polytechnic Institute and at Auburn meant that he was not in Washington, D.C., much of the time.[39] Holland had had the advantage of watching the federal programs operate from the capital in the 1930s.

The American Institute of Architects owned one historic property, The Octagon (1799) in Washington, D.C. Since 1900 the Institute had argued continually over the best way to restore and use the buildings on the property, and the inevitable result had been a compromise.[40] In 1948 the board of directors announced at the national convention in Salt Lake

City that $50,000 had been budgeted for a restoration that would bring back The Octagon "to its original form."[41] After half a century the architects had decided that the house would be most useful as a "shrine" instead of serving as a headquarters.

The fact that the vast majority of AIA members were practicing architects was something of a disadvantage for the cause of historic preservation. They were willing to push for noble causes from time to time during the prosperous 1920s, but in the 1930s the shrinking membership of the Institute forced the Preservation Committee to restrict itself to tabulating the results of the Historic American Buildings Survey. On the other hand, the existence of the chapter organization of the AIA meant that when Charles Peterson proposed the creation of the survey in November 1933, it was possible to have the administrative mechanism working nationwide within a matter of about three weeks.[42]

American Society of Architectural Historians

There were also architects who considered themselves primarily teachers. Fiske Kimball had been a professor until he took on the directorship of the museum in Philadelphia. Some of these academicians, like Henry-Russell Hitchcock of Wesleyan University in Connecticut, had been writing scholarly books on various phases of architectural history for a decade or more.[43] But they had no organizational focus, and neither the AIA nor the College Art Association gave them an adequate forum for exchanging ideas.

In the late 1930s Kenneth J. Conant of Harvard University sponsored some courses in art history at the Fogg Museum during the summer school sessions. In 1938 the students at one of these meetings proposed the creation of an association that would bring together all of the people interested in the study of architecture as an art form. Although nothing came of the idea at the time, these educators kept on coming to the Harvard Summer School, and they thoroughly enjoyed the tours that carried them into the Boston metropolitan area to discover architectural treasures of the late nineteenth and early twentieth century. Finally, on July 16, 1940, George Hanfmann of Harvard hosted a dinner meeting where Conant gave a talk on the history of the study of fine arts at Harvard University. Conant was pleased to report that there had been a great increase in student interest in the field of art history. Those present agreed that there should be more gatherings during the summer with weekend tours as a regular part of the agenda.[44] On July 31 the group organized formally as the American Society of Architectural Historians and elected Turpin Bannister president. He agreed to edit and distribute an experimental issue of a magazine for the new organization.[45]

The *Journal of the American Society of Architectural Historians* made its debut in January 1941 on twenty-six mimeographed pages. The Bannister family had produced the whole thing—including the mailing operation.[46] The journal included a short history of the formation of the society and a call to arms modestly labeled "Next Steps." Bannister reported that the working members of the organization wanted to return to another summer course at Harvard so that they could travel through interesting towns in Massachusetts. He believed that the group might also want to tour some other area that possessed architectural monuments, such as up-state New York. He suggested that the ASAH could help people in the academic world by fostering "new teaching techniques and aids." It might be possible to have a meeting where the members could share ideas on utilizing new machinery available for classroom use.[47] Bannister closed his appeal on a wistful note: "In addition to the twenty-five present members, this first issue of the JOURNAL is being mailed to about 175 others who are known to be interested in this field, or who are at least interested that such an organization should succeed."[48]

A shift toward the study of historic buildings could be detected among the ranks of those who looked on themselves as art historians. On January 31, 1941, a remarkable encounter occurred at the meeting of the College Art Association in Chicago. Henry-Russell Hitchcock chaired a session "in which problems common to preservation agencies as well as to colleges and universities might be discussed." He invited four representatives of the federal government to explain the National Park Service programs to the teachers of art and architecture: Leicester Holland of HABS, Charles Peterson of the Jefferson National Expansion Memorial, Dorr Yeager of the Western Museum Laboratory in Berkeley, Calif., and Hans Huth, special collaborator with the Park Service Branch of Historic Sites.[49] Hitchcock opened with a plea to find a way to save the great buildings designed by Louis Sullivan and H. H. Richardson. While he recognized that there was no immediate threat to these structures, the time had come to coordinate the activities of all the people who recognized the richness of America's architectural heritage. Unfortunately, the assembled dignitaries did not rise to Hitchcock's call, although they engaged in a useful exchange of ideas. The teachers were surprised to find out how broad and well organized the federal programs were, and Charles Peterson concluded that more had been taught in art history courses on American architecture than was currently offered in the architectural schools.[50] Those present agreed to pool information about their collections of photographs, and then Hitchcock invited as many as possible to continue the discussions at the time of the opening of the National Gallery in March 1941.

The subsequent meeting in Washington on March 18 at the Library of Congress was even more productive. Hitchcock was pleased to note the presence of Turpin Bannister (as president of the new American Society of Architectural Historians), Thomas Vint of the Park Service Branch of Plans and Design, and Charles Porter of the Branch of Historic Sites. In order to give everyone an understanding of the status of architectural preservation in the United States in 1941, the chairman asked Bannister and Vint to explain the programs fostered by the ASAH and the National Park Service, respectively. The summary notes on Bannister's presentation reveal quite a bit:

> A.S.A.H. was organized during the summer of 1940 among teachers and students of architectural history present at Harvard Summer School. Proposed to encourage contacts between all those working in or interested in architectural history, to encourage and aid in the dissemination of the results of research in architectural history, and to encourage the preservation of worthy architectural monuments of the past. Membership should be drawn from the staffs of professional schools of architecture and collegiate art departments, from practicing architects, from the governmental agencies dealing with the preservation of historic architectural monuments, and from interested laymen. The response to the initial issue of the Journal of the ASAH was most gratifying and assures the appearance of future numbers.[51]

The architects and art historians questioned Porter at some length on the way in which the Advisory Board of the Park Service chose to list sites that possessed national significance. The action of listing did not afford any federal protection to the sites selected, but no area could come into the Park System without approval from the board. Porter was fairly sure that in time the board would be willing to consider late nineteenth- and early twentieth-century buildings that possessed outstanding architectural qualifications. Bannister promised that the best thing he could do would be to "propagandize the idea of preservation," and he was true to his word.

The sixty pages of the second issue of the *Journal of the American Society of Architectural Historians* may well have been the most important publication on preservation in the United States up to the outbreak of World War II. All of the elements of the professionalism of the 1930s seemed to be represented: academics, architects, the National Park Service, planners, private preservation organizations, and even the enemy—in the person of Robert Moses![52] The journal opened with two detailed discussions of European preservation work by Hans Huth and Kenneth

Conant; Fiske Kimball contributed a short history of similar efforts in the United States. Newton Drury produced a brief account of the historical program of the National Park Service. William Sumner Appleton followed with a modest summary of the accomplishments of the SPNEA, and Helen McCormack described in some detail how the Charleston architectural survey she conducted had grown out of the report of Frederick Law Olmsted, Jr. Charles Peterson tried once more to sell his colleagues on the need for a museum of American architecture as a part of the Jefferson National Expansion Memorial. Carl Feiss, a professor of architecture and planning at Columbia University, traced the awakening of preservation sentiment in the older communities in the United States. A letter from Robert Moses recounted his opposition to the preservation of the Schenck Mansion in Brooklyn because the maintenance costs would have been far in excess of the value of the building to the community. And then came the most remarkable achievement of all: a twelve-page essay by Huth entitled "Preservationism: A Selected Bibliography."[53] But the July-October 1941 issue did not lead directly into an extended program of publications on preservation. Soon the *Journal* writers began to deal less with American preservation and more with construction styles, famous European and Latin American buildings, and tours.

Many individual architects had become historians long before the founding of the Society of Architectural Historians in 1940. Their interest in the buildings that represented the best work of the past can be traced through the many books and magazine articles that appeared throughout the 1920s and 1930s.[54] Three groups of people were writing: practicing architects who considered the study of old buildings a useful exercise, architects who supervised restoration work, and architectural historians who were teachers and critics. All of these scholars made important contributions to the literature on American buildings, and architectural historians in particular pioneered the field of biography in the 1930s. Antoinette Downing, of Providence, R.I., graduated from the University of Chicago and then studied under Norman Isham at the Rhode Island School of Design. She wrote the first major book on the eighteenth-century houses of the state, *Early Homes of Rhode Island* (1937), and became the central figure in the architectural surveys of Newport in 1947 and of Providence in 1959. She has continued prominence as a preservation leader.[55] A few authors who looked back on their publishing efforts in the depression era have concluded that these books stirred up some latent interest in the preservation of the historical evidence of the nation's growth. When Charles M. Stotz wrote a new introduction in 1966 for his 1936 book *The Early Architecture of Western Pennsylvania*, he concluded: "During the past thirty years [this book] . . . has helped to awaken in the public a lively interest in early buildings of our district. The book has been widely cited in historical and architectural works, often with reproductions of illustrations and excerpts from the text, and photographs and drawings from the records have been included in national exhibitions of early American architecture."[56]

Nonarchitectural Preservation Professions

The profession of architecture was uniquely ready to provide important skills needed for the preservation movement in the 1930s. By training and inclination a number of comparatively young architects became restoration scholars within the space of a few years. The Williamsburg restoration, the Historic American Buildings Survey, and the reports produced by the staff architects of the National Park Service proved that these people took advantage of the opportunity provided for them by the large-scale preservation programs financed by the Rockefellers and the federal government. But the administrators who worked with the best of these new restorationists knew that other professionals had to contribute to the total preservation picture, the historians and the archaeologists in particular.

Historians

Historians in the United States were ill-prepared, however, for the opportunities that opened up in the preservation field because their graduate training had been almost entirely based on the exploration of documents. The architects often had combined a certain amount of documentary research with the indispensable studies of the buildings themselves, but the historians in general tended to go the other way. No historians who were active in the United States in 1928 were known to be interested in architecture, so the staff that planned the work at Williamsburg did not bring in a historian as a part of the organization.

But administrators at Williamsburg knew that some kind of documentary research had to be done to back up the drawings prepared by the architects. On September 26, 1928, William G. Perry sent letters to seven large research libraries around the United States, asking if they had "documents, records, letters and other material relating to the Colonial period, to assist the architects in their work of restoration."[57] A week later the offices of Perry, Shaw, and Hepburn received a brief note from J. Franklin Jameson, one of the most noted research historians in the country. He told the Boston architects that there was nothing pertaining to eighteenth-century Williamsburg in the Division of Manuscripts at the Library of Congress (which he headed), but he had "caused to be inserted in the *American Historical Review*" a notice asking for assistance. He had even asked the editors of several other historical journals to print similar notices.[58] And that was the end of it.

Neither the august American Historical Association nor the readers of its *Journal* studied the history of the colonial period in a way that would have helped the young architects who were about to start drawing up plans for the reconstruction of an early town. In 1929 the council of the AHA did, however, set up a committee to look into the "accuracy and appropriateness of proposed inscriptions and monuments."[59]

There were a few historians who took a broader view of the past, and they referred to themselves as proponents of the "new history" that had been introduced early in the twentieth century. This reform movement sought to legitimize the study of all aspects of the life of ordinary people instead of concentrating on political and military figures.[60] In the late 1920s some of these scholars began to publish a multivolume work entitled *A History of American Life*. Dixon Ryan Fox and Arthur M. Schlesinger were the principal editors of these books, and they honestly attempted to offer students and teachers a survey of history that would treat every facet of life in the United States within certain chronological boundaries. One of the first books in the series was *The First Americans, 1607–1690*, written by Princeton professor Thomas Jefferson Wertenbaker. *The First Americans* appeared in 1927, and it might well have given the Williamsburg executives some idea of the kind of historical documentation that was available on seventeenth- and eighteenth-century buildings. Unlike many of his colleagues, Wertenbaker had a sincere interest in architecture as a means of understanding the life of the past. He devoted an entire chapter to colonial houses, and his footnotes show that he depended heavily on Fiske Kimball's books. Wertenbaker also used a number of primary sources from the seventeenth century as well as some standard works on the furnishings of New England homes.[61] In one passage he inspected a small village in Massachusetts through the eyes of a southerner. This viewpoint permitted him to give a straightforward picture of the crude frame houses that lined the streets of an agricultural community.[62] The book had only a few illustrations, and the descriptive accounts were too brief to help any research staff trying to bring back a colonial city to its original appearance.

In 1933 Arthur Schlesinger contributed a volume to the *American Life* series that covered the years from 1878 to 1898. He paused for eight pages to trace the development of architecture during those crucial years, listing only some of the most important architects and buildings in the Chicago area. Then he concluded his account with a few pages on the aesthetic triumph of the World's Columbian Exposition. Looking at the fair without the perspective of the architectural historian, Schlesinger judged it to be "both the visual evidence and the promise of a new stage in American civilization."[63] The books put out under the editorship of Fox and Schlesinger represented the most advanced historical thinking of the time on the subject of using buildings and townscapes as historical sources. But even these adventurous researchers did not grasp the demands that would be made on their profession as the New Deal work programs came into being. Trained historians did not really view the preservation and restoration of buildings as a part of their work; historians were supposed to teach and write.

The Williamsburg organization did not hire a trained historian until the late 1930s, when Hunter Farish replaced Harold Shurtleff. Before then, the necessary documentary research had been carried on by a staff trained in nonhistorical disciplines, including Helen Duprey Bullock, who went to Williamsburg in 1929 and stayed to become archivist with Shurtleff in the Department of Research and Record. She later joined the staff of the new National Trust and gave more than twenty years of her career to historic preservation through the advisory services and publications programs of that organization. Other examples include the Rev. Donald Millar, who spent the fall of 1928 in London looking up material for Perry, Shaw, and Hepburn, while Genevieve Dollfuss copied documents in the Paris archives.[64]

In a few isolated instances trained historians with particular research needs did come into preservation, but only in a restricted sense. Herbert A. Kellar, director of the McCormick Historical Association in Chicago, convinced Harold McCormick to restore the mill on the Virginia farm where the reaper had first been developed. Kellar went to Walnut Grove, Va., and spent part of 1938 and 1939 helping with the mill restoration. In a rare instance of historic-sites research, Kellar looked at pictures of old mills and visited a number of surviving examples in the Shenandoah Valley for his precedents. The Kellars returned to Chicago in 1938 with some bags of flour freshly ground in the McCormick Mill as evidence of their success in the restoration.[65] Kellar proposed the creation of "Living Agricultural Museums" in an address delivered at Monticello during the war.[66] He had not originated the idea (which had been discussed by the Park Service Advisory Board in the late 1930s), but he became a powerful advocate of living history. The remarkable aspect of this episode was the fact that Kellar was an academic historian.

Once the Institute of Early American History and Culture had been established in Williamsburg during World War II, one could safely assume that some historians would be tempted to research topics that touched on the activities of the preservation movement. Only one book in this vein came out before 1950, and that was Carl Bridenbaugh's *Peter Harrison, First American Architect*.[67] The preface makes it clear that the loss of Harrison's papers during the Revolution made it imperative for the historian to study contemporary accounts—and the surviving buildings themselves.[68] Bridenbaugh also acknowledged that he had depended largely on the advice and architectural library of A. Lawrence Kocher. One could almost say that the willing historian had been led into architectural subjects by the staff of Colonial Williamsburg.[69] In 1950 the restoration published Bridenbaugh's *Seat of Empire*, which put the colonial capital of Virginia in its political and social context.[70]

It would be unfair to claim that the staid and conservative American Historical Association was a monolith that had no splinter movements within its fold, but the only historians who could have propelled the association toward preservation activity were the nonacademic ones that concentrated on the study of local history. For many years librarians, editors, and administrators of historical societies who came to the AHA annual conventions met together for a session labeled the "Conference of State and Local Historical Societies."[71] In December 1939 the conference met for its usual round of reports, when "there was general discussion from the floor about revitalizing the Conference and concerning the desirability of creating a new organization, possibly separate from the American Historical Association."[72] One of the speakers at the meeting was S. K. Stevens of Pennsylvania, who told the delegates that local historical agencies needed better funding and a greater willingness to participate in programs with the public schools in their areas. He cited the work of the Pennsylvania Federation of Historical Societies as an example of promoting greater interest in local history throughout a whole state.[73]

Edward Alexander, who was then director of the New York State Historical Association, remembered the mood of the Conference of State and Local Historical Societies while it was part of the AHA: "It was a pretty weak thing, just a single meeting at the time of the AHA each year. In fact there was a strong move while I was chairman to do away with it. . . . The AAM [American Association of Museums] had been going for a long time, but it was fairly weak. . . . But the AAM was smallish; I would say maybe three hundred people at the meetings, and it was very nice. You knew everyone with that size. AHA wasn't much larger; they'd have maybe five hundred at a meeting, and it was great for me."[74]

The chairman of the 1939 meeting, Christopher Crittenden of the North Carolina Historical Commission, was empowered to appoint a policy committee of fifteen people who would explore the means for coordinating historical society work across the nation. In January 1940 he set up the committee, and it went to work on a report to be given at the 1940 session of the conference. The working group included several people who had some experience in historic preservation, such as Alexander and Stevens, but the members were obviously more interested in the work of state historical agencies of all kinds. Ronald Lee was the principal representative of the preservation community in the meetings, and there is some evidence that he had a reasonably important influence on the report that came out.[75]

The final break with the American Historical Association came at a meeting held in the assembly hall of the New-York Historical Society on December 27, 1940. Crittenden called upon Herbert Kellar to read the report of the Policy Committee, and the delegates sat back and listened to a carefully prepared list of the services that a new association could provide. Most of these activities centered on publications, conferences, and efforts to coordinate the activities of the member organizations. A careful study of the report shows that only two paragraphs out of twenty-six had anything to do with the preservation of old buildings. In one case Lee had managed to insert a statement about the need for greater exchanges of information between existing historical agencies and the National Park Service. Under the heading of "Clearing House" the Policy Committee declared: "*The restoration and preservation of historic sites and buildings*. As never before, the American people are waking up to the possibilities in this field, and there is much to be accomplished. The guidance and advice of the National Park Service, which has evolved valuable principles and techniques in meeting this problem, would be of value."[76] While the adoption of this "goal" constituted a ringing endorsement of the concept of historic preservation, it certainly did not commit the new organization to become the major agency for promoting such work. The Park Service was apparently supposed to share its expertise with any societies that chose to ask for it.

The assembled delegates decided to form the American Association for State and Local History as an entirely separate agency from the American Historical Association.[77] Edward Alexander remembered the objectives that he and his colleagues had in mind late in 1940: "It was largely historical-society centered. But of course anything that would strengthen the historical societies would help museums because most of them have museums. But it was really the other side more: publications, meetings, studying local history, and so on. We were more interested in that than strictly the museum or the preservation movement."[78] Ronald Lee and the other Park Service historians viewed the vote to create the AASLH as a positive step, but they, too, knew that the organization was not going to prove to be a strong support in the field of historic preservation. The professional contacts would be valuable, and Lee was always sensitive to the need for federal cooperation with scholarly groups.[79]

At the same time the Park Service historical staff was well aware of the fact that the vast majority of teaching historians in the United States had no interest in the work of the Branch of Historic Sites. Historians still had to climb an academic ladder in order to achieve success and recognition. The rungs of that ladder included the requirement to publish books and articles that showed an ability to locate and analyze primary source documents. Senior teaching positions at major universities went to the authors of historical monographs that opened up new interpretations of the past. Old buildings and the people who restored them were relegated in the *Harvard Guide to American History* to a section described as "Non-documentary sources."[80] Harold Shurtleff had insisted on the inclusion of some material on the subject of historical restorations back in the 1930s when he had had close contacts with people such as Samuel Eliot Morison of Harvard. Ronald Lee and Charles Porter knew that they had been involved in important historical work, but they were still sensitive to the fact that their decision to cast their lot with the federal government had put them outside the mainstream of their profession. Frederick Rath, one of the younger historians in the Park Service in the 1930s, encountered reminders of his second-class citizenship every time he went to professional meetings:

> I think I can personalize it by saying . . . that I lived under a rather dark cloud where my erstwhile colleagues at Harvard were concerned. This was not true of [Arthur M.] Schlesinger and [Frederick] Merk, who urged me . . . into [the] Park Service and said this was good. But some of the younger people who followed the path that led to the Holy Grail would look down their noses at me when I showed up at A.H.A. annual meetings. The common remark was, in a patronizing tone, "Well, Fred, what are you doing now?" . . . I wasn't on the academic trail, and it took many years before the attitude began to change; it was well into the '50s.[81]

Archaeologists

If historians who deserted the universities during the depression were considered second-class citizens in their professional groups, archaeologists who sifted the debris from colonial American historic sites were heretics. Their pioneer efforts did not really achieve any respectability until well after World War II. As with a number of the Park Service historians, the archaeologists who worked at Jamestown and Appomattox knew that they were thoroughly trained professionals who were exploring a new field of inquiry. But they had a long way to go in convincing their colleagues that artifacts from the basement of the McLean House were just as valuable as materials from the Mayan ruins of Central America or discoveries made in the Nile Valley. The sites connected with American history were too recent and too close to home to appeal to the imagination of the archaeological profession.

In 1942 Frank M. Setzler of the United States National Museum described the development of historical archaeology in the United States as one of the major scientific contributions in the 1930s, but only a few people were willing to recognize the accomplishments of the Park Service researchers.[82] Jean Harrington, who came to work at Jamestown, found that he was almost alone in his profession:

> One of the problems at that time was (and it went all through the '30s) that American archaeologists, working in the field of American archaeology, were not sympathetic to this [the Jamestown dig]. They said, "This is not our business; this is the business of historians. We are here to deal with prehistory. . . ." And they'd laugh; they kidded. I was kidded a lot, a joke. And I felt sensitive going to meetings with these people because I knew that they were looking down their nose at my activities dealing with something only a hundred, two hundred years old, particularly whenever I worked on something as recent as the Civil War. I think that's one reason that I took such an interest in Jamestown and Fort Raleigh; at least it pushed it back a little farther, and gave me a little more respectability.[83]

When Fiske Kimball insisted that the Williamsburg Restoration should take advantage of the advice of a competent archaeologist, the prejudice against colonial excavations must have been even stronger. It was essential that someone be hired, so the executives finally turned to an archaeological draftsman from the University of Pennsylvania, Prentice Duell. One of the members of the architectural staff recalled the curious challenge that faced a trained archaeologist who looked over the diggings at the Wren Building: Duell was

> just the man we needed on our Early American work! I believe his contract called for him to put in one week a year at Williamsburg to peer at the holes in the ground we were digging and inspect the Capitol and Palace foundations. He put up at the old Williamsburg Hotel. . . . Toward the end of the week a gal would be sent over from the typing pool and he would dictate his

Archaeological excavations at the site of the Governor's Palace, Williamsburg, ca. 1931. (Colonial Williamsburg Foundation)

report and we wouldn't see him again for another year. Whether or not his reports contributed anything to the work I wouldn't know as I never saw any of them. I don't see how they could have as he hadn't the foggiest idea what we were doing. Yet his name was big as life as one of our "consultants."[84]

Duell himself published a brief account of the Williamsburg excavations in the *Architectural Record* for January 1931. He showed how the staff had studied the brickwork on the Wren Building in an effort to understand how the structure had evolved over three centuries. He claimed that there had been a concerted effort to retain all of the important material from the dig, and many photographs remained to show the stages of the exploration. He could justly state that some of this evidence had helped the architectural staff in deciding what parts of the Wren Building to keep.[85] But the archaeologists at Williamsburg were always subsidiary to the architects. The excavations were supposed to reveal as much as possible about the foundations of long-lost buildings. Artifacts

Arthur A. Shurcliff, 1937. (Colonial Williamsburg Foundation)

that came out of the trenches had value only as long as they contributed to an understanding of the original use of each of the structures the architects wanted to rebuild.[86]

As had been the case with the field of history, most of the archaeologists were moving professionally in the direction of a pure science, a discipline that did not fit in well with the needs of historic preservation agencies. Jean Harrington was a lonely scholar at the University of Chicago because he declared openly that he was interested in archaeology as a "tool of history." One evening he discovered at a gathering of his fellow graduate students that he was the only person in the department who considered himself a historian![87] Virginia Sutton Harrington, his wife, joined him in her focus on archaeology as history. Serving as staff historian at Colonial National Historical Park in the 1930s, she interpreted the excavations at Jamestown to visitors. John Merriam, trained as a paleontologist, used his influence as president of the Carnegie Institution of Washington to start the St. Augustine survey in 1936.[88]

Landscape Architects

The profession of planning, which was new itself, did not contribute to historical programs, but a few landscape architects, especially Arthur A. Shurcliff and Frederick Law Olmsted, Jr., assisted in preservation programs as a logical outgrowth of the planning aspects of their profession. The California State Park Commission employed Olmsted to edit the survey of the state's park needs in 1928, and his report became the basis for the land-acquisitions policy of the 1930s.[89] Ten years later Olmsted went to Charleston on the urging of Robert N. S. Whitelaw to analyze the preservation problems of the Battery District. The Boston landscape architect recommended that his hosts begin an architectural survey that finally culminated in the publication of the successful book

This Is Charleston in 1944.[90] Shurcliff became famous through his work with Perry, Shaw, and Hepburn in the development of the Williamsburg gardens in the 1930s.[91] He also assisted Albert Wells in the layout of the first portions of Old Sturbridge Village before World War II.[92] Many younger landscape experts went into the CCC, because the New Deal projects often required knowledge of park planning. Some of them assisted in the restorations carried out under the auspices of the National Park Service, particularly in the Far West.[93]

Museum Specialists

It could be argued that the existing professional organizations and training programs made it easy for architects to go into restoration work, but the historians and archaeologists who chose to cast their lot with Williamsburg and the National Park Service committed a certain form of professional suicide. They knowingly abandoned the generally accepted paths to success in their fields in order to plunge into an unknown discipline. The challenges in the museum field were quite different. It was obvious that at some point the larger and more comprehensive preservation projects would require the services of curators, preparators, and artists who were skilled in planning and building exhibits. Museum specialists had one professional organization, the American Association of Museums, under the direction of Laurence Vail Coleman.

There were no training programs in museum studies that compared to the graduate instruction available to historians and archaeologists, and there were no schools for would-be curators that could offer a curriculum as comprehensive as that available in the schools of architecture. It required great imagination, perseverance, and dedication to enter museum work in the early 1930s. Ned Burns, as has been pointed out already, came into the profession by means of a tremendous amount of in-service experience, starting as a guard in the Staten Island Museum. Burns later had some formal training in art school, but his years at the American Museum of Natural History and the Museum of the City of New York constituted his real preparation for the National Park Service.[94] Janet MacFarlane, who was later to administer the collections of the New York State Historical Association in Cooperstown, began her career at the Rochester Museum of Arts and Sciences following graduation from college, as a volunteer worker under Arthur C. Parker. Within six months Parker offered her a full-time position in the museum, which permitted her to study and observe the approach of one of the most influential men in the whole field. Parker was writing *A Manual for History Museums* and editing a newsletter called the *Museologist* at the time.[95] The in-service training was certainly all-inclusive: "I was given a crash

Laurence Vail Coleman, ca. 1950. (Photograph by Underwood and Underwood; courtesy American Association of Museums)

course, assisting in every department for a period of months, then was made 'Assistant in History' to work with the culture history material, American. I put on dinners and teas for the museum a few times, as they had no women's association at the time, then was started on writing professional articles, under Dr. Parker's direction. Then the WPA came in and I was given several assistants, such as a man to hand-letter signs, a seamstress, secretarial help, etc. . . . Under Dr. Parker I was given some administrative training, verbally, as matters came up."[96]

While Janet MacFarlane was busy learning all the facets of the Rochester Museum, Ralph Lewis (who would later work with Ned Burns in the Park Service) was an undergraduate at the University of Rochester. He did some graduate work in entomology and then set out to look for a job in 1935. At that time Carl Russell, head of the Eastern Museum Division of the National Park Service, was trying to hire history majors with museum experience. Russell quickly found that such people did not exist. He eventually hired Lewis, in addition to a botanist from the University of Pittsburgh and an anthropologist from Harvard.[97] It could be said that people like Lewis had done just enough college work to be ready to learn how to be historical museum technicians. Another museum specialist was Helen McCormack, who studied with Albert Simons at the College of Charleston and served as director of the Valentine Museum in Richmond for ten years. This experience helped to prepare her for conducting Charleston's architectural survey in 1940 and 1941 and assembling an exhibit at the end of the survey.[98]

No one wanted more to create a sound set of professional standards for museum specialists than Laurence Vail Coleman, and he spent the better part of two decades writing books that were intended to be guides for museum administrators all over the country. Coleman happened to stumble onto the field of historic preservation as he tried to cover all aspects of museum operations:

> The list of open houses [in his 1933 book] came from correspondence and travel while I was preparing for the "Manual for Small Museums" and the "Handbook of American Museums" . . . and from intensified efforts of these and other kinds, such as combing thru state and local historical stuff, when I had focused on the matter of old houses and had set out in the field to find out what was what. Along the East Coast in the summer of 1932, [Lewis] Barrington and I found houses about the way ants find everything . . . by instinct. . . . As you know the concept of the house as an institution was new and not generally grasped in 1932, and however obvious the name "historic house museum" may seem now, I had to coin it to take the place of expressions such as "places like Mount Vernon, old houses open to the public, historical shrines, et al."[99]

In 1933 Coleman published *Historic House Museums*, a comprehensive study of the preservation movement at that time. It ranks in importance with the preservation issue of the *Journal of the American Society of Architectural Historians* in 1941. Coleman thoroughly applied all of the standard administrative challenges faced by museum directors to the organizations that were then exhibiting old houses. He tried to offer some thoughts on such all-important questions as philosophy, the use of professional personnel for restoration work, and the emerging science of interpretation. The book ended with a general directory of all the known preservation projects in the United States in 1933.[100] It is difficult to assess the influence of Coleman's work because he has continually been cited as an authority by people who have written about the background of the preservation movement. But this does not necessarily mean that the professional standards he sought in 1933 were accepted by the people who presumably took the time to read his book.

Lewis Barrington, Coleman's 1932 traveling companion, compiled a directory of 210 restorations that had been supported by the Daughters of the American Revolution. Barrington correctly described his 1941 volume as an "album" that was intended to inspire DAR chapters that might be considering the purchase and renovation of an old building. The author noted that one of the most impressive discoveries in his survey was the broad scope of the historical activities that characterized women's patriotic-hereditary organizations.[101]

If one concludes that the museum "profession" had not firmly drawn its borders in the 1930s, it might be possible to include museum directors and antiquaries within the fold. These people had made substantial contributions to preservation scholarship since the turn of the century, most notably through the career of George Francis Dow.[102] After all, Dow was the director of the SPNEA museum in Boston for nearly sixteen years. He carefully studied and labeled the thousands of objects that William Sumner Appleton had collected for the New England museum that was to be part of the Otis House complex in Boston. Dow's sudden death in 1936 was a great blow to Appleton, and he cast about for several years looking for a successor. In October 1938 he even wrote Laurence Coleman asking if the American Association of Museums might be able to help him locate a person who would do most of Dow's work for about half of Dow's salary. In spite of his inadequate budget Appleton really wanted "a first-class museum man."[103] But it turned out that during Appleton's tenure as corresponding secretary the SPNEA never did find that person. It was not just a matter of salary; the kind of curator that the society needed could find much more rewarding and steady employment in the National Park Service.

A few of the museum professionals wrote books that dealt with historic buildings and the interpretation of the past. In 1927 George Francis Dow produced an unusual work entitled *The Arts and Crafts in New England, 1704–1775*, which was made up of topical chapters containing quotations from notices and advertisements in the newspapers of the eighteenth century. For a number of years he put together a series in *Old-Time New England* that was called "Gleanings" from old newspapers, and it was inevitable that this material would someday become a book.[104] Dow's encyclopedic knowledge of most aspects of colonial life came into focus in his last work, *Everyday Life in the Massachusetts Bay Colony*, which was published in 1935 under the auspices of the SPNEA.[105] Neither of Dow's books was preservation oriented, but the two certainly embodied the kinds of research data that interpreters would eventually use in trying to furnish historic houses.

One of Sumner Appleton's friends, Russell Kettell, of Concord, Mass., brought out a large book, *Early American Rooms*, in 1936. Fresh from advising the Concord Antiquarian Society on the installation of its period rooms, Kettell chose to use twelve sample displays from East Coast museums representing every period through the Civil War. He provided his readers with clear pictures of the rooms, along with a text that filled in the historical background for each epoch illustrated.[106] The book was a useful device for interpreting period rooms.

The development of the Winterthur collection under the guidance of Henry Francis du Pont (discussed later in this chapter) provided employment for several people who were professionals—either as architects or as curators—including Charles O. Cornelius, Joseph Downs, Thomas T. Waterman, and Charles Montgomery.[107] These new, object-oriented historians dealt with all phases of early Americana. The increasing interest in antiques made it inevitable that a group of experts would begin to work in the field, and it was equally certain that these people would take some interest in historic preservation.

PROFESSIONALS AS CONSULTANTS IN RESTORATION PROJECTS

When the emergence of professionalism is viewed through preservation projects for building restoration or reconstruction, it is possible to isolate a series of factors that helped to turn administrators toward dependence on the people who had the training and skills to give expert advice. The first and most obvious decisive factor in the use of consultants was the goal of the individual or the group that made each project possible. Were these patrons deeply concerned about questions of historical accuracy? Henry Ford clearly did not trust academic historians who purported to tell the story of progress in this country, so he set out to illustrate America's growth through the medium of his museum and Greenfield Village. John D. Rockefeller, Jr., wanted his staff at Williamsburg to work for a thoroughness that could only be fully supported by the presence of a host of advisory boards. Kenneth Chorley, who worked closely with Rockefeller for many years, said that in the Williamsburg program the patron had wanted to strive for the "ideal," and if he did not accomplish it, he wanted to know what "he was deviating from."[108] Stephen Clark in Cooperstown had an innate sense of taste and correctness that led him to hire the best administrators that he could find in the historical profession. The Farmers' Museum became the educational force that it is through the constant process of discussion and evaluation. In the Department of the Interior it became quite clear to the staff of the Park Service that Harold Ickes wanted the most accurate restoration work that could be produced at that time. He did not care how long a project might take so long as he could refer to the final product as a sound recreation of the past.

The second major element in determining the degree to which professional people came into preservation work was the size of each program. If a local historical society with a relatively small budget chose to restore a headquarters house, it might call in an architect as an adviser. The architect was probably not particularly conversant with the historical period represented by the building and could not give much personal supervision to the construction work. But the restoration and interpretation of Colonial Williamsburg or the reconstruction of an entire California mission complex was an undertaking that commanded the talents of an army of architects, engineers, historians, archaeologists, landscape architects, curators, artists, ironworkers, and so on.

The third variable in the professional equation was speed. If the funding of a project was steady and the administrators were not in a hurry to see tangible results, the professionals had a better chance of influencing the labor force in the construction work. As long as Henry Ford was attempting to prepare the whole of Greenfield Village for the fiftieth anniversary of the development of the incandescent bulb on a particular day in October 1929, professional researchers would not have been useful. The Park Service staff always seemed to think in terms of setting up a work schedule and a master plan for the development of each program. Once those goals had been agreed on, it was possible to employ professional help on a regular basis.

A final factor was the availability of experts for specialized research. In 1929 the architectural staff working at Williamsburg under Kenneth Chorley found that it was going to have to make up working drawings for restorations that should have involved the talents of research historians and archaeologists. Because these experts were not available at that early date, the able young draftsmen took over the necessary research tasks themselves and performed them with the same skill that they used in measuring the plantation outbuildings they found in Tidewater Virginia. A few restoration projects were in such remote parts of the United States that professional people simply could not be brought in readily. The Robert E. Lee Memorial Foundation, for example, wanted to take full advantage of the services of Fiske Kimball and his assistant, Erling Pedersen; but the distance between Philadelphia and the Northern Neck of Virginia was great enough to keep the consulting architects away from the Stratford restoration a good deal of the time.

The depression had an enormous influence on the generation that finished its formal training between 1930 and 1936. These people expected to function in the academic world or in business, but in most instances they saw all of the generally accepted means of employment cut off. The desperation of the situation forced them to rethink their goals and in turn revolutionized the disorganized preservation movement. Charles Porter, fresh from a teaching position at the University of Virginia, joined a group of young historians who eagerly accepted positions in the emergency programs of the New Deal. "Most of the really qualified professional historians came in that same way. The Park Service got a better group of historians than it could ever have gotten again. Ordinarily all of us would have been teaching at some university or college, but the doors were all closed. We simply couldn't get a college job anywhere. Colleges were reducing their staffs; they weren't increasing

897

them."[109] The same economic pressures forced young architects to seek positions in state and federal offices. Jerome Ray, who had been working in the state architect's office in Springfield, Ill., noted the quality of his colleagues: "This was during the Depression, and we had a great number of competent men in the office because there was very little construction work going on and they couldn't find jobs elsewhere. We had a number of men graduates from the various universities—from Notre Dame, from MIT, from Illinois, from Princeton, from Pennsylvania, from Armour [Institute of Technology]."[110]

Williamsburg

Even before the stock market crash sent scores of young professionals into the National Park Service, the Williamsburg restoration had pioneered the concept of scholarly collaboration in the process of repairing and interpreting historic buildings. W. A. R. Goodwin, originator of the Williamsburg project, sought professional assistance for his 1926 restoration of the Wythe House, but he quickly discovered that there were not many people in the United States who were qualified to advise him—and who would journey to an obscure town in southern Virginia.[111] Goodwin corresponded briefly with William Sumner Appleton about some aspects of the physical restoration of the house.[112] R. T. Haines Halsey, director of the American Wing of the Metropolitan, offered some thoughts on lighting fixtures, and two architects, William G. Perry of Boston and Charles M. Robinson of the College of William and Mary, donated some time and thought to the project. Robinson designed a few of the most prominent elements of the restored Wythe House, including the neocolonial doorway.[113]

Once John D. Rockefeller, Jr., had authorized the preparation of preliminary drawings for the Williamsburg restoration, Goodwin knew that he would have to deal with experts, and he warned the architectural firm of Perry, Shaw, and Hepburn that "these studies should be made carefully, sympathetically, and thoroughly."[114] As soon as Rockefeller approved the preliminary plans, his desire for increased professional consultation became evident. He instructed Goodwin to get the opinion of "leading colonial architects and art critics."[115] Goodwin told Perry that the drawings for the Wren Building were fine, but they needed further corroboration. "I am authorized to ask you if you are willing to submit the tentative drawings, elevations, and perspectives, which you have drawn of the Christopher Wren Building, to certain consulting architects who are known to have specialized in Christopher Wren work. If so, I would like to take up with you the question of securing such consultation with a view of ultimately having the plans approved by a committee of the American Institute of Architects."[116] On November 19, 1927, Perry presented his drawings to a select committee in a New York hotel, and he received enthusiastic endorsement in writing from each of his colleagues, including Fiske Kimball.[117]

In the winter of 1928 the Rockefeller offices in New York began to insist that a qualified town planner be hired because some of the construction and demolition projects were certain to affect the development of Williamsburg. Kenneth Chorley had suggested several noted planners, such as Frederick Law Olmsted, Jr., but the Perry, Shaw, and Hepburn group proposed employing the landscape architect Arthur A. Shurtleff.[118]

At about the same time Goodwin urged Rockefeller to put together a committee to "direct the endeavor." In October, Rockefeller agreed to use a temporary advisory committee. This small working group was to include the president of the AIA and the chairman of the Institute's Committee on Preservation of Historic Buildings. Rockefeller and his associates accepted the idea that having this panel review Perry's plans would "prevent later criticism."[119] It was not easy to assemble the first Advisory Committee from all over the nation; it had to include some architects from the South who had good standing in the profession and understood the problems involved in the restoration.[120]

There is no question that the eight architects who met at the Wythe House in November 1928 represented the finest elements of professionalism in the world of architectural history. Three noted authors were there: Kimball, Kocher, and Thomas Tallmadge. Rounding out the committee were two well-qualified Virginians, Edmund Campbell of the University of Virginia and Finlay Ferguson, president of the Virginia chapter of the AIA; Milton Medary of Philadelphia, who came as a past president of the AIA; and two practicing architects from Baltimore and Boston, Robert E. Lee Taylor and Robert Bellows. In his official speech of welcome Goodwin said that John D. Rockefeller, Jr., "was most desirous that the work represent not the work of one mind, least of all his own, but the work of many minds."[121]

Through the winter of 1928–29 Arthur Woods, as president of the Williamsburg operation, held meetings with his senior staff advisers and grilled them on the major concepts of the restoration. For example, the minutes of a December 11 meeting reveal that Woods questioned Arthur Shurtleff's garden plans for the lots along Duke of Gloucester Street. Woods wanted to know why there had to be so many garden restorations in the center of the old town. The ensuing exchange shows that everyone was trying to understand as clearly as possible what the end goal of the project would be. Perry mentioned that Fiske Kimball had wanted to see at least two more professionals hired for the restoration as quickly as possible—a person to keep a careful record of all the information relating to the restoration of each individual building and an archaeologist who could study foundations, old brickwork, and other materials from the historical area.[122] The same day a group called the Antique Committee (which included Perry and Halsey) tried to decide which houses would eventually be exhibited to the public.[123]

There was continuing controversy over the usefulness of the different boards and committees that became a part of the Williamsburg operation, and this was particularly true of the Advisory Committee of Architects. This group met more often and cost more than any consultants hired by Goodwin. There are detailed minutes of every meeting between the first gathering in 1928 and the last one in 1948. William Perry believed that these scholars gave vitally important corroboration for each major decision, and they also provided a "code of principles" for the restoration process.[124] The men in the drafting room had no contact with these luminaries of the architectural world, so it was natural that the younger architects would conclude that the influence of the committee was negligible. One member of the drafting-room crew, Clyde Trudell, reasoned that the advisers "were sympathetic with the concept and intent of the project" or they never would have been chosen. Trudell also shrewdly guessed that these practicing architects did not fully recognize that the real scholarship at Williamsburg was fast developing within the group of young men working with Edwin Kendrew and Walter Macomber down in the drafting room: "After their meeting and a free meal, the Advisory Board was given a tour of the town and as, after one of their visitations, we never had to tear anything down and do it over, I can only assume they approved what we were doing! I can't recall any of them ever demeaning himself by visiting the drafting room!"[125] By the late 1930s Singleton Moorehead of the Williamsburg Architectural Department remembered the Advisory Committee as being "a little bit on the rubber stamp side."[126] However, after the first phase of the restoration process there was expertise in Williamsburg itself. The answer to the question of the usefulness of the blue-ribbon panel of architects may lie in the correspondence that went between Perry's office and individual members of the committee. During the first two years of the restoration Perry consulted with his colleagues about several difficult points that arose. Sometimes he used the committee to back him up when he needed support in battling either the Virginia State Art Commission or the Association for the Preservation of Virginia Antiquities.[127] In July 1929 John D. Rockefeller, Jr., was sufficiently impressed with the advice and support given by the executive

Advisory Committee of Architects, Mar. 28, 1940, on the front steps of the Wythe House, Williamsburg. Back row, left to right, *James L. Cogar, Arthur A. Shurcliff, William G. Perry, Andrew H. Hepburn, Thomas Mott Shaw, A. Edwin Kendrew, Singleton P. Moorehead, Washington Reed, Jr.;* middle row, *Susan Higginson Nash, W. Duncan Lee, Philip N. Stern, Merrill C. Lee, Vernon M. Geddy;* front row, *Robert P. Bellows, A. Lawrence Kocher, Edmund S. Campbell, Marcellus E. Wright, Fiske Kimball.* (Colonial Williamsburg Foundation)

committee of the Advisory Committee that he told Perry to hold up any decisions on general policy until the group had given its approval.[128] There is no doubt that the higher officials in Williamsburg referred to the restoration policy worked out by Perry and the architects' committee as the major guideline for the work done.[129] Kenneth Chorley checked with Perry every now and then to be sure that all major decisions on the houses had been referred to the committee. Chorley read the minutes of the meetings and knew full well what had transpired.[130] Whenever Perry and Macomber sent out a letter to the Advisory Committee members, the carefully worded replies showed that the consultants understood what their role was supposed to be.[131] The principal architects leaned quite heavily on the opinions of Fiske Kimball—in fact, Thomas Mott Shaw recommended that meetings of the committee be convened to fit Kimball's schedule ahead of all the others.[132]

Whether the Advisory Committee was a substantial help to the formulation of policy or merely window dressing, it is certain that a considerable amount of professional development took place in the drafting room under the watchful eye of Walter Macomber, the resident architect. The men liked Macomber, and yet some of them knew that he did not have an easy time trying to deal with his diverse crew of architects. Orin Bullock, who was at Williamsburg from the start, remembered that Macomber "had an unusually good eye for architectural detail, proportion and moulding profile. When confronted with engineering design such as a roof truss, he was lost."[133] Macomber loved to work with these draftsmen because they were so eager to learn: "With these young fellows coming out of college, I had no difficulty [assembling a staff]. I had more people apply. And they had to have a very special interest, and so I had to turn many of them away. And I'd try them and if they seemed to have some facility, well, then I'd develop them. And as I say this was one of my greatest enjoyments. A great group, really. We had very little dissension in the office."[134] The combination of the economic crisis and the exciting possibilities of historical research in a new field spurred them to work harder than ever. Everette Fauber remembered his motivation well: "I would say that we were a lot of young people, challenged by what we were doing and responding to this challenge and trying awfully hard to make a good impression on Bill Perry and on Walter Macomber and the principals because we prized our jobs, this being right in the middle of the Depression."[135]

When Perry, Shaw, and Hepburn hired Prentice Duell to supervise the archaeological work at the Wren Building in 1929, a new profession may have been born, but it was not off to a promising start.[136] Duell wanted to continue interpreting Williamsburg excavations on a piecemeal basis while he went to more spectacular digs in Italy and Egypt during 1930.[137] Dr. Goodwin was one of the first people to realize that the careless handling of artifacts from the excavations was getting to be a problem. He told Kenneth Chorley that he had gone by an open pit on the Coleman property one day in June 1930 and was horrified to see objects strewn around:

> There were a number of things which had been found piled up on the side of one of the trenches. But while I was standing there I saw a large number of pieces of china and earthenware thrown out upon the dirt pile and covered up by other dirt which was thrown out. In less than five minutes I picked up over a dozen pieces of china and glass, any one of which, under expert examination, might have helped to determine the nature and date of the building or buildings which stood on this foundation.
>
> This archaeological work is either not worth doing at all, or it is worth doing well, and I am perfectly sure from this observation and a number of

other observations which I have made that no special care is being taken in this matter.[138]

Chorley concluded that the situation was worse than Goodwin had described and that perhaps the problem was that the diggings were not under the overall direction of the architects or the landscape architects![139] Certainly no archaeologist was present—and all the explorations carried out in those years were intended to reveal either old garden paths and walls or the foundations of buildings that had disappeared.[140]

By 1931 almost all of the excavations were under the indirect supervision of the Department of Research and Record, which meant that Harold Shurtleff had to decide what to do with the materials brought in from the trenches that had been dug to find old foundations. With some backing from Fiske Kimball, Shurtleff told Perry, Shaw, and Hepburn that several problems had come up in the archaeological work. To begin with, the Boston office had decided to cut down the staff of archaeological draftsmen as the restoration began to wind down in 1933; but Shurtleff maintained that there were important sites all over Williamsburg that still required expert attention.[141] On top of that, Rutherfoord Goodwin had noted that there should be a proper exhibition of the most significant fragments uncovered during the previous three years. Young Goodwin (with some assistance from Kimball) asked for permission to transform the old courthouse into an archaeological museum.[142] Obviously the architects treated archaeology as a necessary adjunct to their work, but there was no one on the staff who had the proper training for the digging operations.

If the science of archaeology was unready to deal with the interpretation of the Williamsburg gardens and foundations, the profession of history was equally unready to assemble the documentation that could have contributed to the restoration of many of the eighteenth-century buildings in town. There were no historians in the nation in 1929 who had seriously considered the concept of utilizing historical areas as teaching aids for the visiting public. There was a curious assumption that was widely held in the Perry, Shaw, and Hepburn offices that any historian who might work at Williamsburg would carry out one of only two minimal functions: That person should either prepare studies that would aid the architects in drawing up restoration plans or spend considerable time attempting to record each major step in the reconstruction of the old town. Kenneth Chorley had the same limited view of the function of the historian at Williamsburg. This person would produce a "complete document which would be a record of the work done."[143] No one seemed to believe that historians should have a voice in the formulation of policy

Harold R. Shurtleff, ca. 1930–38. (Photograph by Bachrach; courtesy Colonial Williamsburg Foundation)

for the Williamsburg restoration—and probably historians themselves did not want the responsibility.

No one was appointed "historian" until the winter of 1930, and by that time many important decisions had already been made by people who were busy with new restoration projects. As a result there were inadequate records for most of the excavations that had been carried out. On top of that, the talented amateurs who had been doing research all over the world could not keep up with the demands of the architects for historical data on the buildings scheduled for restoration. So in 1930 William Perry located the architect Harold Shurtleff and brought him in to be director of research.[144]

A thirty-one-page interpretive booklet by Rutherfoord Goodwin gave the public its first detailed account of the organization of the Perry, Shaw, and Hepburn staff, as well as a description of the committees of experts. Here is one typical question in the book with its answer: "What provisions have been made to assure and preserve the accuracy of the work? The Department of Research and Record, a department within the architectural organization, was formed to search out all available evidence pertaining to the work of restoration and to prepare a written and photographic record of the work as it progresses, together with an explanation of the steps taken and the reasons therefor. The research campaign has extended into every possible source of information in America, England and France. It is still in progress."[145]

Harold Shurtleff quickly learned that his Department of Research and Record had been assigned an enormous task, but it had a small staff and no substantial backing from a committee of experts comparable to the Advisory Committee of Architects. Chorley proposed that they create a Committee of Research with W. A. R. Goodwin as chairman and Earl Swem of William and Mary as a key member.[146] While this was a creditable idea that never came to fruition, it also shows the limited function that Chorley expected the historians to serve. Shurtleff gradually came to realize that his office would have to be much more than an appendage to the architectural staff—and that he would have to get the assistance of a group of well-known historians to comment on the quality of historical material coming from Williamsburg. For example, in July 1930 he sketched out a film committee that could guarantee the accuracy of any movies that might be sent out. He also wanted a history committee to oversee the publications that Colonial Williamsburg would distribute.[147] Perry, too, believed that the Research Department needed some historical advisers, and he proposed the names of two Virginians who were known to have written in the area of colonial history.[148] Probably at this formative period Shurtleff did not yet understand that there really were no trained historians who could be assembled in Williamsburg to advise him on the research problems connected with restoration work. He had to develop the first research office in the nation on historic preservation entirely within the staff of the architectural office.[149]

All through 1932 Shurtleff prepared a series of reports that were intended to force Kenneth Chorley and his patron to think deeply about the kinds of historical material that would be needed for interpreting Williamsburg. These long reports always reminded Shurtleff's superiors that only good research could foster confidence on the part of visitors.[150] Shurtleff strongly held that a tie-in with the history department at William and Mary would hamper the work of the Research Department more than help it. He cited examples of research done at other universities where the purposes of the educational institution and the sponsoring organizations were distinctly different. It was possible, Shurtleff believed, that a new historical society might be the answer.[151] Using these arguments as his opening wedge, Shurtleff proposed a conference of historians to meet in Williamsburg in the fall of 1932.[152] Actually Rockefeller had accepted the idea of a conference already, and it only remained for Shurtleff to call the meeting.

The historians finally assembled in Williamsburg on October 21, 1932—and Shurtleff tried his best to take advantage of what appeared to be a unique opportunity. William Perry gave a fine speech that outlined the problems that would surface once the buildings had been restored. Could these structures on which so much time and talent had been expended speak for themselves? What should be their message?[153] All through the meeting the advice from the historians was repeated constantly: Publish more; put out popular books and learned texts showing Williamsburg's role in the economy and life of colonial Virginia.[154]

In January 1933 a subcommittee of the original historians' conference met in New York and drafted a brief report recommending the creation of a historical department that would have sole responsibility for all publications and the training of guides.[155] The administrative staff, however, did not respond with any great enthusiasm to the collective judgment of the historians.

The next two years marked a turning point in the professional emphasis at Colonial Williamsburg; the challenges shifted from the area of architectural research to interpretation. Dr. Goodwin and his son embarked on an ambitious program intended to train the hostesses in all the subtleties of the restoration organization.[156]

The collective research enterprise at Williamsburg, particularly in the years between 1928 and 1934, was a tremendous forward step in the area of professionalism. The omissions in historical and landscape research probably can be traced to the failings of historians, archaeologists, and landscape architects. These trained people were not prepared to work with a restored city because they had no background for understanding the buildings and sites to be found in Williamsburg. In sharp contrast, the architects were ready, and they did their job so well that they became the dominant force. John D. Rockefeller, Jr., was a perfectionist who doted on the superb work that his architectural staff turned out. It is no wonder that he did not seem quite so concerned about the publications that were issued by the staff; he had become thoroughly immersed in the detective work that led to the resurrection of the eighteenth-century buildings. The most important product of the Williamsburg experience was the group of workers who put in countless hours toiling at the tables in the drafting room and, on the weekends, measuring the vernacular buildings and great houses in Virginia. These architects set a standard that all large preservation organizations, as well as members of their own profession, had to emulate after 1933. Preservationists who have admired the Williamsburg project have had to find ways and means of operating within a limited budget while still carrying on creditable restoration work.

Stratford Hall

Almost certainly the Robert E. Lee Memorial Foundation wanted to emulate the procedures worked out by the Perry, Shaw, and Hepburn offices, but the foundation was a much smaller organization. The crusade to save Stratford Hall had been patterned in 1929 on the model of the Mount Vernon Ladies' Association of the Union. Mrs. Charles Lanier's emphasis on completing the purchase of the plantation left the long-term restoration planning in the hands of two other women, Ethel Armes and Mary Van Deventer. Neither of them was a professional restorationist, but Miss Armes was a writer who had a great interest in history. She had teamed up with May Lanier in the negotiations that led to the agreement to buy Stratford, and then she had convinced Mrs. Lanier and her close associates that the foundation needed a full-time historian who could also carry on the fund-raising effort. Mrs. Van Deventer knew quite a bit about the status of restoration work in the nation because she was the Tennessee vice-regent for Mount Vernon. Her experience with the oldest preservation project in the United States probably led to her selection as chairman of the Restoration Committee for the Lee Foundation. The awesome task of raising money had a positive delaying effect on restoration policy because the foundation simply could not spend any hard-earned dollars on Stratford beyond the most necessary repairs until the debt had been wiped out.

Ethel Armes told May Lanier in June 1928 that she hoped to assume the role for Stratford that Charles Hoppin had taken as historian of the Wakefield National Memorial Association.[157] On Mrs. Lanier's recommendation she conferred with a New York architect, William Lawrence Bottomley, who was deeply interested in the restoration problems posed by the Lee birthplace and really wanted to help.[158] He told the foundation officers that he had done some private restoration work in Virginia and had worked on garden plans with Arthur Shurtleff. He proudly described his approach to restoration work as "archaeological rather than architectural."[159] Bottomley volunteered to make a preliminary survey of the immediate repair work required at Stratford, carefully pointing out that he would donate his services.[160] Apparently Ethel Armes concluded that the Stratford restoration program could be carried out successfully if she did the historical research and Bottomley supervised the repairs on the house itself. What she did not count on was the forceful personality of Mary Van Deventer, who was soon to take over the chairmanship of the Restoration Committee.

The real headquarters of the Robert E. Lee Memorial Foundation in its earliest days was in Greenwich, Conn., where Ethel Armes had set up an office as the national executive director. She issued a "general outline" of the organization in April 1929, which announced that two surveys were already under way, one in historical documents and the other in architectural data.[161] However, she soon discovered that she was free to do all the historical research she wanted to do; the architectural side of the restoration was to have its base in Knoxville, Tenn., at the home of Mary Van Deventer.

Although a brief contact with Fiske Kimball in May 1929 impressed her, Mrs. Van Deventer turned to the Library of Congress for information on the building of Stratford Hall.[162] In June, Leicester Holland recommended that she look into Kimball's book on American architecture, which was "a mine of valuable information."[163] Holland's recommendation gave the new chairman of the house restoration enough courage to write to Kimball himself. She asked him if he had found any new information since the publication of his book in 1922, and she promised to keep his answers in strictest confidence. Imagine what her letter must have done for Kimball's ego: "If I have been too bold in my questions I hope you will pardon one who knows that she is utterly incapable of serving our Board as Chairman, unless you who are our Country's authorities will be generous enough to assist me."[164]

The answer to Mrs. Van Deventer's humble request proved that Kimball (in spite of his reputation for bombast) could be a diplomat. He sent a three-page letter full of restoration philosophy, followed by a few lines of praise for the foundation. Kimball added, "I still do this sort of thing professionally," but he enclosed a list of architects who had done restoration work all along the East Coast.[165] The message convinced Mary Van Deventer beyond any shade of doubt that the Robert E. Lee Memorial Foundation had located its architect by "divine guidance."[166] The ideal pattern for the Stratford restoration would be, in her words, hiring Kimball to work with a good contractor. For the next ten years she held doggedly to this view. Kimball was delighted to undertake the commission, and he promised to keep his charges well within the budget of the foundation.[167] It was a wise choice, and she never regretted her decision to employ the best architect available. Fiske Kimball may well have been the preeminent architectural scholar in the United States in 1930.[168] The Stratford organization could never have supported its own research and architectural staff, so Kimball's commission offered the only apparent road to excellence and authenticity.

By midsummer 1930 Mary Van Deventer and Ethel Armes had begun to disagree on restoration procedure. The Virginia Historic Garden Tour that year was formally dedicated to the restoration of the Stratford gardens, and the Garden Club chose Arthur A. Shurcliff (with his new name) to perform the task.[169] Miss Armes assumed that the hiring of Shurcliff meant that W. L. Bottomley could also be contracted to carry on the restoration, but after her correspondence with Fiske Kimball, Mrs. Van Deventer would not even consider using Bottomley.[170]

In the fall the Mabel Brady Garvan Institute of American Arts and Crafts at Yale University offered to support a research program for Stratford on the condition that no architect be appointed for the restoration at that time.[171] For an indeterminate period Ethel Armes would be free to work on a vast compilation of historical data on Stratford that could be utilized in restoring and furnishing the house and its dependencies.

In November she proposed a study program that would contribute to an understanding of the development of Stratford Hall. She carefully outlined all of the work that had been done and then sketched out a full "Stratford Survey" that was intended to cover all known sources.[172] The Garvan Institute assistance came at a most fortunate time and made possible the assembling of a considerable amount of documentary material on the Lees and the evolution of Stratford.

While documentary research moved ahead in the libraries of the East, archaeological explorations began to take shape in 1931 under the guidance of Arthur Shurcliff. The workmen assigned to the excavations had indeed uncovered "original architectural features of the immediate surroundings including walls, terraces, foundations and heretofore unknown and undiscovered outbuildings and garden structures."[173]

By late 1931 a real division began to appear in the ranks of those who claimed to be seeking an absolutely authentic restoration of Stratford. Ethel Armes, fresh from two years of research, was convinced that she knew more than anyone else about the evolution of the big house and its dependencies. She suspected Kimball's judgment on a number of questions as long as he appeared to ignore her reports and based his conclusions on structural evidence or his knowledge of Virginia building techniques of the eighteenth century. She persuaded the Research Committee of the foundation to form a committee of consulting architects who could review the correctness of Kimball's decisions.[174] In 1933 Miss Armes, whose background was in journalism, referred to herself in an article in *Antiques* as "a trained historian," so there was no doubt that she firmly believed she possessed the professional background to carry out the Stratford research program.[175] On the other hand Mary Van Deventer became more and more certain that her original decision to employ the finest architectural historian in America had been a correct one.[176] The disagreement with Ethel Armes was a deep one, but both preservationists were intensely interested in upholding historical truth. Throughout these debates Fiske Kimball kept his normally abrasive personality under remarkable control.

When the Garvan Institute checked over Miss Armes's research notes at the end of the first full year of work, there were some difficulties that had to be resolved. Dean Everett Meeks of the Yale School of Fine Arts and his assistants sent the Stratford material to one of the most distinguished historians at Yale, Ulrich B. Phillips, for his comments. Phillips admitted that he was impressed with Miss Armes's devotion and vigor, but he detected evidence of haste that would "not appear in the output of a trained historian." He decided that the useful research was nearly all done—a conclusion that Ethel Armes did not like at all.[177]

Meeks, acting on his own evaluation of the research report, told her that he and Francis Garvan (the philanthropist and collector who had donated the research funds) had concluded that the time had come to hire an architect and to start on the physical restoration of Stratford. Meeks complimented the researcher on her zeal and industry, but he admitted that he would have preferred that she concentrate more on material dealing specifically with the house and leave the detailed story of the Lee family for a later time.[178]

Then Meeks told Mrs. Van Deventer that he and Garvan had discussed the appointment of the restoration architect. Their first choice was W. Duncan Lee, a Virginian who had radically restored Carter's Grove for Mrs. Archibald McCrea about five years earlier. The Garvan Institute also would be happy with William Bottomley, Edmund Campbell (of the University of Virginia), or William G. Perry. In a vain attempt to change Mrs. Van Deventer's mind, Meeks admitted with some misgivings that Fiske Kimball was an eminent scholar: "However, Mr. Kimball is in Philadelphia, actively engaged with his museum, becoming more and more sympathetic with the modernistic movement in architecture and the other arts and also becoming involved in various organizations for public service. In other words, he is a busy man, at a distance from the proposed work. The work at Stratford will require continuous and meticulous attention to research and detail."[179]

The chairman of the Restoration Committee could not be convinced that there was any architect in the country who could contribute to the Stratford restoration the knowledge and understanding already shown by Kimball. She immediately wrote him about the decision the Robert E. Lee Memorial Foundation would have to make. She promised to recommend that the "restoration of Stratford shall be placed in your hands"—but she needed specific answers to questions that were certain to come up at the meeting. Could Kimball successfully supervise the project at such a distance? Would he be willing to work with the Richmond contractors Claiborne and Taylor?[180] Kimball readily answered that he was eager to undertake the work with the assistance of his colleague Erling Pedersen, an architect who had helped with the restoration of the Fairmount Park houses and several other commissions.[181] By May 1932 Kimball and Pedersen began to pore over the written material gathered by Ethel Armes, and they tried to get copies of the Shurcliff maps and archaeological reports from Morley Williams, who had taken over the landscape program for the Garden Club of Virginia.[182]

As the physical restoration of Stratford began to evolve in 1933, some of the directors of the Lee Foundation sounded a note of alarm. They believed that the delicate task of remaking the big house should not be in the hands of one person, especially an individual who appeared to be so sure of himself. Mrs. Emerson Newell of Connecticut proposed the use of several historical and architectural consultants as a means of checking on each major decision.[183] Thomas Waterman, one of the possible consultants, visited Stratford early in 1933 and found that most of his questions revolved around the work that had been done with the garden stairs under the direction of Arthur Shurcliff. He had no comments on Kimball's operations.[184]

It seemed that the conflict of interests was actually leading to a more authentic restoration. Dean Meeks proudly announced to the Research Committee in June 1933 that the AIA convention had just passed a resolution commending the Robert E. Lee Memorial Foundation for its preliminary research. The AIA went on record as favoring "the fact and the manner of the proposed restoration of Stratford, Virginia, and cites it to the country as an undertaking worthy of support and emulation."[185] Ethel Armes quickly put the wording of the AIA resolutions in the promotional literature as evidence that the "patriotic work" of the Stratford group was worthy of widespread support. The AIA action had been intended as a compliment to Meeks, Francis Garvan, and Miss Armes, but it is probable that Mrs. Van Deventer and Fiske Kimball also basked in the reflected glory.

When the Stratford restoration was under way, the "science" of studying the evolution of colonial architecture was still in its infancy. Undoubtedly some important alterations were made in the house in the 1930s that would be subject to review today in the light of the expertise that has been developed in the past quarter century. But in 1935 the Lee Foundation unconsciously stumbled onto a remarkable formula for the use of professional consultants: Find the most knowledgeable person in the country and then check on that individual constantly throughout the process of research and construction. The disagreements may have taken their toll on the people involved, but the constant debates served to keep the Restoration Committee and its hand-picked architect on their toes.

When one considers the difficulties inherent in studying a large eighteenth-century mansion in a remote part of Virginia and the limited budget that May Lanier and her allies had to cover the costs of restoration, it is a miracle that they did as well as they did. What saved the preservationists at Stratford was their unswerving dedication to the idea of professionalism (as it was then understood). Although they disagreed on the means to the end, all of them sincerely wanted to make the preservation of the Lee birthplace a labor of love and an exercise in sophisticated scholarship. As the AIA put it, their example was worthy of emulation.

Henry Francis du Pont in the 1960s. (Courtesy Henry Francis du Pont Winterthur Museum, Winterthur Estate Archives)

Henry Francis du Pont Winterthur Museum

While the Stratford and Williamsburg projects developed professional architectural skills in building preservation, it was Henry Francis du Pont's Winterthur furniture collection that developed the knowledge and skills for preservation of America's historic interiors and decorative arts. His steady support of a group of professionals helped to set a standard for restorations all over the nation.

Whether he realized it then or not, du Pont came into the field of collecting at just the right time in the mid-1920s. The magazine *Antiques* had already begun its notable career in 1922, demonstrating that a class of discriminating collectors had emerged in the United States. The American Wing of the Metropolitan Museum of Art had opened in New York City in the fall of 1924 at what was later referred to as the most "spectacular" museum event of the 1920s and 1930s.[186] Soon museums all over the country tried to imitate the work of the New Yorkers, and the issue of the removal of paneling from old houses became a factor in American historic preservation.[187] Du Pont's money, talent, and consuming zeal would transform his home Winterthur in Delaware into one of the great decorative arts museums in the world within a quarter of a century.

His fortune, as one of the younger members of the family that dominated the chemical and gunpowder industry, and his massive estate permitted him to become the dominant authority and patron in the field of the decorative arts at the same time that the Williamsburg Restoration and the Edison Institute were coming into being. By his own admission Henry du Pont was a born collector, and for his first forty years he visited the major museums of Europe as well as its great houses and received from these journeys a rare education in "colors and proportion," as he put it. But he eventually found the arts of his own country more interesting than those of other nations. "A visit to Mrs. Watson Webb's house in Shelburne, Vermont, in 1923 gave me, however, my first introduction to an early-American interior. Among other things, I was fascinated by the colors of a pine dresser filled with pink staffordshire plates. Seeing Harry Sleeper's house in Gloucester, Massachusetts, a few days later made me decide to build an American house at Southampton."[188]

Du Pont was impressed with the work done by the decorator Henry Davis Sleeper at Beauport on Eastern Point in Gloucester, Mass. Sleeper's home contained more than forty rooms filled with antiques and old paneling from Massachusetts and other parts of New England and New York. He entertained his guests with fascinating visual surprises throughout the house and an imaginative use of color and lighting.[189] Sleeper was indeed a major figure in the development of interior decoration, and he was an important influence on the evolution of Chestertown, a mansion that du Pont built on Long Island in the early 1920s. Du Pont consulted Sleeper on paint colors, woodwork, and fabrics, as well as lighting.[190] By the middle of 1927 the two men were seriously discussing the idea of setting up Chestertown House as a public museum, somewhat on the model of the Gardner Museum in Boston.[191]

But Henry du Pont's heart lay elsewhere; the family business had started along the banks of the Brandywine Creek just outside what is now Wilmington, Del. In 1924 Henry's sister, Louise du Pont Crowninshield, began to restore the family home at Montchanin, on the hill above the ruins of the old powder mills. Henry's interest in the area led him to make certain that the architects and landscape architects protected the powder mills as historic remains.[192] A few miles away was Henry's own ancestral home, Winterthur (1839), a large house that his father had remodeled early in the twentieth century. Henry inherited the Winterthur estate in December 1926 and almost immediately began to view it as his principal home.[193] Du Pont explained the shift in his residence this way: "When Chestertown House was almost finished I had occasion to buy another paneled room from Chestertown [Md.]. I realized it was too sophisticated for the other rooms in the Southampton house; so for the time being I stored it in my barn in Delaware. As time went on, I developed the plan of adding this and other rooms to Winterthur . . . in order to create a wing that would show America as it had been."[194]

The decision to add a wing to the Winterthur house and to install some period rooms on a grand scale was of fundamental importance for the preservation movement. Henry du Pont's search for woodwork constituted almost as much of a threat to would-be preservers as had Henry

Henry Francis du Pont Winterthur Museum, Del. (Courtesy Henry Francis du Pont Winterthur Museum)

Ford or the Metropolitan Museum's expeditions. But du Pont was much more sensitive in his work, and no significant confrontations ever resulted from his purchases. He made sure that his workers did not remove paneling from buildings that might be the objects of local preservation efforts. Sometime during 1928 he began to seek advice from Charles O. Cornelius, principal architect of the American Wing, and from Joseph Downs, curator of furniture at the Pennsylvania Museum in Philadelphia.[195] Du Pont also employed Henry Sleeper to advise him on fabrics, colors, and other decorative questions.[196] These contacts meant that du Pont had at his disposal the finest talent in the United States in the field of museum installation and the decorative arts.

There are clear stages in the evolution of the Winterthur collection that reflect du Pont's development toward a professional approach. From 1927 to 1931 he appears to have been busy constructing a comfortable home that would include old woodwork as its principal decorative feature. After that initial burst of activity he settled into a fourteen-year period marked by consolidation, enlargement, and refinement of the collection. Finally, after World War II he seems to have turned gradually to preparation for the opening of the Henry Francis du Pont Winterthur Museum in 1951. This last epoch was marked by great changes in the house, including the transformation of a number of service areas into exhibition spaces. Also during this period du Pont joined a few preservation organizations and started to catalog his collection.

The key to the changes in Henry du Pont's career was his relationship with Bertha Benkard, who was a friend of his sister, Louise Crowninshield. Mrs. Benkard was a collector and student of the decorative arts and a wealthy New Yorker who shared du Pont's insatiable desire to go to sales and to visit museums. She was willing to sit with him by the hour and plan revisions of the Winterthur collection.[197] She had a great influence on the Winterthur project during the 1930s, and her death in 1945 probably turned du Pont toward the final phase of preparation for a public museum; the enjoyment of hunting antiques had been replaced by the educational mission of a public institution.[198]

The first rooms purchased for the Winterthur Museum came largely through contacts with dealers, and these settings formed the nucleus of the great wing that du Pont hoped to build.[199] He selected Albert Ely Ives of Wilmington as the architect of his enlarged house, and the two of them drove around and inspected several of the rooms that were offered through the dealers.[200] By February 1928 a New York studio reported to du Pont that it had removed, measured, and stored substantial parts of four houses in Virginia and Maryland. From one house, Belle Isle (1760), from Litwalton, Va., du Pont had purchased a parlor, small hall, living room, hall, ceiling, stairs, second floor hall, dining room, bedroom, and kitchen. Late in February he made one of his most important purchases, an eighteenth-century house near Philadelphia called Port Royal, which provided an entrance hall and many exterior design features for the new Winterthur wing, including the doorway.

The correspondence between du Pont and Ives reveals that a number of conflicting considerations had to be harmonized in the floor plan of the new wing. Of course the new owner would have preferred to keep all rooms just as they were in the houses they came from, but this was impossible. As the creators of the American Wing had discovered a few years earlier, when one combines parts of different old houses in the same building, adjustments must be made in the dimensions of the rooms. In any case du Pont saw nothing wrong in 1928 with enlarging some rooms in order to put highboys between the windows.[201] The changes that Ives and Charles Cornelius made to fit in the old paneling point conclusively to du Pont's desire for a comfortable country home. Although the house was to be a showplace for his growing collection of eighteenth-century furnishings, there does not seem to be evidence of any particular interest in an eventual museum at that time.[202]

Even with all the professional advice he could command, Henry du Pont began to devote more of his own time, talent, and energy to the design of Winterthur. Henry Sleeper was unable to help at Winterthur in the way expected, and du Pont found himself the chief decorator of the new house, a role that kept him busy and happy. His goals began to firm up as he warned Sleeper that the curtains must be correct. "I am doing the house archaeologically and correctly, and I am paying the greatest attention even to the epoch of the fringes."[203] Du Pont had taken over the massive research job that would help him locate all the furniture, pictures, and rugs in the completed house. He was angry with Sleeper for leaving him with such a huge task, but it was really the thing that must have launched him into his remarkable career in the decorative arts.[204]

The words "archaeologically and correctly" suggest that du Pont had begun to think about a museum operation. In February 1930 he set up a Winterthur Corporation, although there was no hint about an opening date for the educational institution that would presumably emerge.[205] For several years the incorporation papers for the Winterthur organization hinted that either Charles Cornelius or Bertha Benkard might become curator of the collection.[206] Once the big house at Winterthur took final shape in 1931, Ives and Sleeper were no longer major influences on du Pont's career. Cornelius had had considerable experience working with the installation of old woodwork at the Metropolitan Museum in

Above, *Wentworth Room, from the Samuel Wentworth House, Ports-mouth, N.H., 1935*; below, *Montmorenci stair hall, Winterthur Museum.* *(Courtesy Henry Francis du Pont Winterthur Museum)*

the 1920s, and he had some knowledge of furniture. Mrs. Benkard had had very little architectural experience, but she knew furniture. Du Pont himself had begun to travel and do research on his own—and perhaps he really knew as much as Sleeper or any of the others in his circle of professional acquaintances. People from many academic backgrounds were attracted to the Winterthur collection in the early 1930s. During one weekend in 1932, for instance, du Pont entertained the principal administrators of the Yale School of Fine Arts.[207]

Although du Pont constantly repeated throughout the early 1930s that he had almost stopped collecting furniture and woodwork, he really was eager to add new items. In July 1931 he made a gentlemen's agreement with the New York collector Francis Garvan to avoid buying silver that would force Garvan to pay unnecessarily high prices. After declaring his intentions, du Pont admitted, "Of course, I might fall for some unusual piece of furniture that might turn up."[208] This escape clause also permitted him to add rooms that would fit into the existing house at Winterthur. For example, Mrs. Benkard spotted a fine set of rooms in a house at Lower Marlboro, Md., and he set a dealer to work looking into the purchase price.[209] This time du Pont's eagerness for the purchase almost ruined the whole transaction. He had to learn to keep in the background and avoid any appearance of affluence. The antiques dealer (du Pont used quite a number of them) found that the owner of the old paneling had sharply increased the price because of "the appearance . . . several weeks ago of a large expensive sedan driven by a liveried Chauffeur, the car bearing Delaware license plates and the passenger in this car requesting the owner to show him the old house."[210]

One era of professional association came to a close when Henry du Pont sent out two letters on November 7, 1932. The first was to Cornelius, who needed work at that time. Du Pont proposed that he be hired on a retainer to write an authoritative, room-by-room catalog of the Winterthur collection. Du Pont bluntly warned him that the work must be done within six months and went on to specify the kind of catalog that he needed—a sumptuous one. But Cornelius no longer possessed the temperament or the confidence necessary for advising a collector like du Pont, and even with some advance payments, the catalog was never completed.[211] The second letter went to the person who, along with Bertha Benkard, was to be the major influence at Winterthur for the next two decades—Thomas T. Waterman, one of the Perry, Shaw, and Hepburn draftsmen for the Williamsburg Restoration. Fiske Kimball, director of the Pennsylvania Museum, had recommended Waterman as the kind of person who could show du Pont and Mrs. Benkard the finest Virginia houses within a matter of a few days. Waterman, together with John Barrows, had produced a scholarly book on Virginia buildings, the only book to come from the first phase of the Williamsburg restoration.[212] In his letter to Waterman du Pont offered to bring his car and chauffeur for a four-day tour with his great friend Bertha Benkard.[213]

The most important aspect of the whirlwind journey was the remarkable friendship that developed with Thomas Waterman. The meeting had taken place at just the right time for both men; Waterman was about to leave Williamsburg and wanted to go to Europe for a year on a Guggenheim Fellowship. He had become something of an architectural scholar, thoroughly steeped in the research techniques developed in Williamsburg. Winterthur still seemed to du Pont to be much more of a home than a museum, but he was ready to move somewhat in the direction of a museum standard for the installation of his rooms. When the Walpole Society (an amiable group of well-traveled collectors) saw Winterthur for the first time in 1932, they were lavish in their praise.

We have seen restored houses, beautifully done. . . . Yet never have we seen so many old American rooms under one roof—the number seemed endless and we have serious doubts if any of us saw them all—possibly Mr. du Pont himself may sometimes forget a few of them. [His memory was amazing.] Nor could we imagine that there could be put into one house so many rooms so different, in size, period and character, in such way as to make it liveable—to make a home of it. Mr. du Pont had done it. Here are rooms that welcome the guest, furniture which seems glad to receive him. There is nothing of the museum in the air. We are not among the dead.[214]

Waterman fitted in well with the Benkard–du Pont combination. Within a matter of months all communications were on a first-name basis, and Waterman had sketched some changes for Bertha Benkard's own home. When Waterman left for Europe, du Pont followed his travels closely. He even sent money and encouraged the young architect to stay abroad longer.[215] There is a refreshing element of joy and frankness in the notes from du Pont to his Virginia guide. In his own way the great collector was becoming a scholar and a veteran traveler himself. In the summer of 1933, for instance, he visited Portsmouth, N.H., and then covered the Hudson Valley with Mrs. Benkard and Joseph Downs of the Metropolitan Museum. He was learning about New York Chippendale furniture and Dutch farmhouses, a liberal education indeed.[216]

Waterman was enough of a preservationist and scholar to be a little uneasy about his patron's individualistic approach to collecting interiors, but the glory of Winterthur had become an all-consuming goal for them both. Waterman wrote: "I must confess I feel a little sad and guilty when

I think of Montmorenci [a North Carolina house they had just stripped], but the stair hall should be glorious and I have reached the conclusion that any sacrifice is worth while to make Winterthur complete. It is so extraordinarily perfect otherwise, each time I see it I am amazed to think anyone could achieve so flawless a thing."[217] Du Pont comforted Waterman with the sage observation that very probably the house would have been burned or scattered "by bits in different houses all over the country."[218]

At this point Winterthur had become a cooperative enterprise involving du Pont, Waterman, and Mrs. Benkard. They agreed on all substantial matters and leaned heavily on each other. Bertha Benkard continued to be a source of ideas and inspiration, and it is impossible to estimate the degree to which her lasting friendship with du Pont influenced the development of Winterthur.[219] During the fall of 1935, for instance, du Pont pushed Waterman to prepare the plans for the stairway installation so that she could see them. Du Pont counted so much on her advice that he warned his architect that he would be "frantic" if she could not see the plans, a rare instance of emotion in the evolution of the collection.[220] Throughout that fall there was a brisk correspondence between du Pont and Waterman dealing with many interior changes in the big house, usually involving the addition of mantels and staircases—or the creation of new corners, new surprises for the visitor.[221]

A major project in the late 1930s was the installation of the woodwork from Morattico (1715) in Richmond County, Va. Here the influence of Waterman began to show more clearly than ever—and du Pont became increasingly grateful for the skill and knowledge of his helper.[222] Since 1929 some Morattico panels had been on display at Winterthur, but in 1938 it became possible to purchase more segments of woodwork from the house. The paneling was not cheap, but Waterman did a skillful job of measuring it and selecting the pieces that would fit into the assigned space. This time he prepared a series of "schemes" for the installation that varied with the tastes and interests of du Pont. It now became clear that Waterman's long-term goal was to talk Henry du Pont out of the idea of creating a beautiful home and into the track of restoration. In describing his "Scheme A" for the Morattico room, Waterman told his patron bluntly: "While I agree that the woodwork would look well as in Scheme A, it is an impossible arrangement archaeologically and now that you have the original woodwork I think your responsibility to rearrange it as it was is greater. . . . In Scheme C it is ideal and approximates the original more than any other would."[223] Waterman dared to tell the lord of Winterthur what his responsibility was and to persuade him to do a "literal restoration."[224] When the work was complete, Waterman produced a five-page detailed report on the steps he had taken to reassemble the Morattico paneling, in an effort to make Winterthur a museum. The next spring du Pont wrote his sister that he was delighted with the rooms because they were "just as practical for living purposes as before, and greatly improved from a museum point of view."[225]

Winterthur grew steadily, always in the direction of matching more paneling to the furniture already spread throughout the house. Du Pont purchased a room from a Connecticut dealer in 1935, but he complained bitterly when he learned that the paneling had been dismantled for shipment. His sense of authenticity had been violated, because he had hoped to move the room in sections, and had taken the trouble to send up a large truck for that purpose.[226] At times Waterman himself recommended the purchase of portions of buildings that were being demolished or altered.[227]

All of this growth was leading toward a museum at Winterthur. During the war years du Pont permitted people to tour the house on a limited basis for the first time. Charles Messer Stow, who announced the new policy through his column in the *New York Sun*, considered it a great privilege for the public because of the legendary quality of the collection.[228] The director of the National Gallery even asked du Pont to consider willing Winterthur to the Smithsonian. Du Pont probably was flattered by the offer but answered that his collection was already "provided for."[229]

At the end of the war the triumvirate broke up with the death of Bertha Benkard. Du Pont poured his abundant knowledge and energy into working harder than ever with Waterman in the project of turning the whole house into a museum. Waterman had been campaigning for several years to get his patron to turn a basement area into a street of shops where important collections could be displayed in the windows.[230] Waterman had sent along drawings of shop fronts he had seen in walking the streets of lower Manhattan.[231] Almost immediately du Pont had dealers searching for possible shop fronts.[232] Waterman also worked on a rearrangement of one Winterthur room so that the paneling would regain its original dimensions.[233] The changes that ensued in this massive program can be traced in a well-illustrated article by John A. H. Sweeney in the first *Winterthur Portfolio* entitled "The Evolution of Winterthur Rooms."[234] Joseph Downs, then in charge of the American Wing of the Metropolitan Museum, saw these changes and commented with real feeling to du Pont: "There is only one advantage of visiting you so seldom, namely, that your astonishing progress is so overwhelming after some absence. Never have I felt as I did this time, how perfect Winterthur has become. The Flock Room, the Port Royal Parlor, and the Empire Room seem to epitomize the quality of the whole."[235] Du Pont's sister, Louise Crowninshield, wrote him after touring the American Wing that, compared to Winterthur, the New York rooms looked "flat, stale and ill done."[236]

In 1948 and 1949 events moved even more swiftly toward the opening of the proposed museum. Thomas Waterman was seriously ill and could not work at his usual pace. The major changes that he had planned, however, were well under way. Now the problem of administration needed to be faced. The Winterthur Corporation had existed as a legal entity since 1930, but no single individual had emerged as the possible curator. Charles Cornelius, Bertha Benkard, and Henry Sleeper had died; Waterman was an architect and his own health was uncertain. So du Pont wisely decided to sign a contract with two of the most capable people he could find, Joseph Downs and Charles F. Montgomery. In return for a substantial income from du Pont, they both agreed on September 27, 1948, to pool their resources in 1949 and begin a massive catalog of the Winterthur collection. Once the catalog had been done— perhaps in five years or so—they stipulated that the museum should open, with Downs as curator.[237]

Downs's comprehensive study *American Furniture, Queen Anne and Chippendale Periods in the Henry Francis du Pont Winterthur Museum* was published in 1952. Du Pont and his wife moved out of the Winterthur house in January 1951 and settled into a nearby mansion that Waterman had helped to design during the final years of his life.[237] Du Pont's career as a collector and scholar was not over, but the opening of the museum under the direction of Downs must have been an important turning point.

In assessing Henry du Pont's influence on the preservation movement, his status as an arbiter of taste in the decorative arts needs no defense. Du Pont was not a destroyer, and he did not remove any paneling in the face of a genuine preservation effort. His preservationist leanings might account for the fact that he did not collect entire buildings in the same sense that Henry Ford did. Du Pont sometimes left a shell when he stripped the woodwork from a house, but he justified his actions on the grounds of imminent destruction. As early as 1929 he toyed with the idea of buying the Manigault gate lodge from the Pringle family in Charleston, only because he feared the building might go to ruin.[239] When Cornelius informed him that a room from Graeme Park (1721) near Horsham, Pa., might be sent to the Kansas City Museum, du Pont was horrified. Perhaps even by 1933 he had reached some conclusions on the appropriateness of removing woodwork from really important buildings.[240] At the same time he was not above looking for paneling if the building in question seemed to be in danger—or for sale. Cornelius had purchased a room from The Lindens (1754) in Danvers, Mass., for the Kansas City Museum.[241] Du Pont quickly contacted the dealer who owned The Lindens and went to see what was left.[242] He did not buy anything from that particular house, but the interest was clearly there. He considered acquiring some window frames from a seventeenth-century house discovered on Long Island by the Historic American Buildings Survey, but a local preservation effort quickly put a halt to that search.[243] In 1940 he also thought briefly of stripping Belle Grove (1856), an enormous Greek Revival mansion in Iberville Parish, La. This time he drew back because the owner would sell only the whole house, and the scale of the rooms would have forced du Pont to purchase more furniture.[244]

Any collector who traveled as widely as Henry du Pont soon came to be recognized as an authority on a host of subjects by professionally trained people in various fields. In his case the designation had some justification although he had no training in the decorative arts. The scope of his growing collection and his skill as a guide impressed preservation administrators. While he was in Williamsburg he volunteered his confidential judgment on the restoration of the Raleigh Tavern to Arthur Woods—and Woods listened.[245] From time to time du Pont freely advised restorations on such diverse topics as paint colors or lighting. The advice appears to have been given with the understanding that he would not be hurt if his correspondents chose to do things their own way.[246]

The size and quality of the Winterthur collection became legendary, and a host of important preservationists visited the mansion. They were guided through the rooms by the patron himself, and often they were his houseguests. It was a rare experience to sleep in one of the eighteenth-century bedrooms of the great house and have breakfast brought in.[247] Most of these visitors wrote effusive letters of thanks. Robert N. S. Whitelaw, director of the Carolina Art Association, declared that he had been more impressed by Winterthur than he had by any other collection. He believed it was "useless" for any museum to attempt to imitate du Pont's coverage of the American arts.[248] At one time Albert B. Wells and his brother, J. Cheney Wells, went through the collection with du Pont. They were working on Sturbridge Village and also were operating the Wells Historical Museum in Southbridge, Mass. Albert Wells could not find words to capture his evident feeling of awe: "I was about as tired as an individual can be when we left Wilmington, but I

Louise du Pont Crowninshield in the 1950s. (Courtesy Henry Francis du Pont Winterthur Museum, Winterthur Estate Archives)

had spent, I think, the grandest day in my life. . . . It's hard work for me to take people through and show them our antiques and what a different type of antique. I think one or two of your rooms are worth the whole of our collection put together."[249] These notes must have been a great source of satisfaction to du Pont, because he knew he was reaching the most selective audience in the country—antiques collectors.

Whatever the direct influence Henry du Pont may have had on the preservation movement, one must take into account the work of his sister. Louise Crowninshield, who was several years older than her brother, was surprisingly close to him in tastes and interests, although her world revolved more around Boston and Henry's centered on Winterthur and the Philadelphia–New York area. Mrs. Crowninshield was much more outgoing than her brother, which meant that she rose to positions of prominence in a number of organizations, ranging from preservation associations to musical and horticultural societies. She had been a steady supporter of the group that saved Kenmore in Fredericksburg, Va., and after the death of Josephine Rust she took over the Wakefield Memorial Association. She helped both the SPNEA and the National Park Service in furnishing the Richard Derby House in Salem, Mass., and she was one of the first trustees of the National Trust for Historic Preservation, serving as its vice chairman for several years. Her death in 1958 was a great loss in a number of areas in American culture—and the tributes that came forth in the form of permanent memorials are clear evidence of the respect that she won from her contemporaries.[250]

The du Pont preservation activities seem to fall into two clear groupings: his memberships in organization that preserved antiquities in Delaware and nearby Pennsylvania and societies that Louise Crowninshield had joined. Both of them were very close to Bertha Benkard. In

1934 Mr. and Mrs. Crowninshield donated a period room to the Museum of the City of New York in memory of Harry Benkard. Mrs. Benkard herself furnished the room with her best Duncan Phyfe pieces.[251] From 1937 onward du Pont was a member of the fledgling Delaware Society for the Preservation of Antiquities, and he and his sister contributed time and money to the campaign for the purchase and restoration of the Old Dutch House in New Castle, only a few miles from the Winterthur estate.[252]

But Henry du Pont kept his priorities. He was willing to give one thing to preservation organizations: advice, either on plantings or on the decorative arts. He did not expect to raise funds or to contribute labor from his Winterthur staff.[253] He explained his unwillingness to spread himself too thin as a "clear, cold, common sense point of view." His single-minded approach to the Winterthur collection demanded such attention; his sister could afford to consult on Kenmore, Wakefield, the Derby House, and many other New England and Virginia restorations.

Du Pont's concentration on his home did not preclude friendly contacts with other organizations when such correspondence might enhance Winterthur's authenticity. He had a brisk debate with William Sumner Appleton in 1938 over the correct brick pattern for seventeenth-century chimney backs.[254] Appleton used the correspondence as a chance to show du Pont that worthy structures in New England should remain on their *original* sites. Du Pont's response to Appleton is revealing: "I think it is much more interesting to preserve the old houses, but unfortunately as a rule they are so badly furnished it gives one rather a pang when one sees them. As this house may some day become a museum, every remaining resource I have must be devoted to finishing the work I have started here."[255]

It is difficult to place the career and personality of Henry Francis du Pont in the context of preservation history. He was a vital influence through the quality of his collection and the scholarship that he was able to bring together at Winterthur. The standard of authenticity that he worked to attain, particularly with Thomas Waterman and Joseph Downs, became an important example for the small group of people in the 1930s and 1940s who strove for absolute historical correctness. In his own life du Pont exhibited a selfless dedication to one controlling purpose. One who knew him well said that "he was always looking forward to what he was going to do tomorrow, or next year, never looked backwards."[256] Above all, he was a careful student of American life who gradually developed a sound critical sense. He traveled widely and kept on learning. He showed a desire to educate people who shared his interest in the decorative arts. Some would call this approach snobbish, and no doubt preservationists looked upon the Winterthur collection as something quite divorced from the life of the common person. But in his own way, whenever du Pont guided his guests through the wonders of Winterthur, he was an interpreter of the past. Where most museums had to concentrate on the education of the many, he could engage in the luxury of educating the few. Somewhere in the vast field of preservation there had to be one place where standards of scholarship meant more than visitor statistics. Through Henry du Pont's resources of money and patient study Winterthur became that place.

NATIONAL PARK SERVICE

The professionalism developed at Williamsburg and Stratford had been largely in the field of architecture and at Winterthur in the decorative arts; but it was the field of history that dominated the expansion of the historic-sites program of the National Park Service. The first professional employees of the Park Service at Colonial National Historical Park were historians, and the engineers, archaeologists, and architects had to contribute whatever they could to the development of a program to educate the public to United States history and national culture. The majority of historic sites administered by the Department of the Interior in 1933 were battlefields, forts, and Indian ruins. Horace Albright, as director of the National Park Service, saw these exhibition areas as educational tools, so it was natural for him to begin by hiring historians. There were only a few buildings in need of restoration at Yorktown, Gettysburg, and Morristown; the major challenge was describing to visitors the sufferings of the soldiers who had camped and fought on these battlegrounds. The first group of historians, which included Verne Chatelain, was greatly interested in planning and administration. Arno Cammerer (who succeeded Albright in 1933) was willing to let the historians decide policy matters in eastern parks, just as the archaeologists and naturalists had shaped the program in the West. Architectural research of the type carried on in Williamsburg was looked upon as an essential preliminary activity that made the task of teaching history somewhat easier. While the Williamsburg approach to architectural research had influenced the thinking of the professionals through the first half of the 1930s, it was the educational goals of the Park Service historians that dominated the last half of the depression decade.

The concentration on interpretation of America's past through sites and buildings developed naturally out of the experiences of the first staff historians at Yorktown in 1931. It was an amazing coincidence that just as the Williamsburg drafting room was reaching its peak of activity in the reconstruction of the Palace and the Capitol, only a few miles away on the York River a small group of National Park Service historians began to formulate policies that would eventually culminate in the passage of the Historic Sites Act of 1935 and the development of the powerful Branch of History in the late 1930s. The young historians who came to the Park Service in 1931 and 1933 almost without exception came directly out of graduate school or from their first teaching assignments. This situation was both an advantage and a disadvantage for the new park program. The new historians were teachable, but their outlook had been molded within the framework of graduate seminars emphasizing primary source documents rather than sites.

By the time the Yorktown Sesquicentennial had ended in the fall of 1931, the first historians began to realize that they were not well prepared for interpreting the battlefield to the hordes of visitors coming to Virginia to commemorate the ending of the Revolution. B. Floyd Flickinger, Elbert Cox, and others at Yorktown began to study the role of historians as interpreters of historic sites. In a 1931 memo Flickinger outlined two functions for these pioneer educators: They must offer popular and understandable history to the visitors, and they must also operate as "professionals" who work with technical problems. Flickinger went on to define the activities that might best be labeled "professional services." At Yorktown the historians had to put together a bibliography of major sources to be consulted in understanding the battlefield; they should publish articles in learned periodicals; they should investigate research problems posed by the development of the town, the parkway, and the battlefield park; they should form a local historical association to help finance the study of the Yorktown area and assemble a library that would provide a basis for their research. In addition the historians had to be aware of their "popular services," which included guide work, museum preparation, lectures, popular publications, and all forms of public contact.[257]

Verne Chatelain, the first chief historian, quickly decided that a complete professional reorientation had to take place. The Conference of National Park Executives in April 1932 gave him an opportunity to tell the superintendents of the western areas that it was time they offered a course in history to their visitors. Chatelain suggested that no park or monument "should be entirely free of historical activities."[258] A year later he became even more outspoken in a report to associate director Arthur Demaray: "I think that the historical work of the National Park Service is dependent upon the acquisition of an historical mind by those who control its administration, or at least upon their willingness to leave

the problem to the historically-minded."[259] That simple statement became Chatelain's goal for the next two years, and he saw it come to
fruition in the year that followed passage of the Historic Sites Act.

During the spring of 1934 the chief historian began to draft an outline for the Historic Sites Act, noting the program already proposed by
Gist Blair. Both plans included an advisory board to represent the views
of the American Historical Association to the secretary of the interior.[260]
Chatelain wanted to be sure that the new board would be composed of
"experts" and that the program of the Park Service would be administered by "expert historians." His viewpoint dominated the discussions
that accompanied drafting the act all through the fall.

In November the Park Service historical and archaeological superintendents held a conference in Washington to deal with the vital problems of restoration and historical administration. Chatelain admitted
that a considerable amount of experimentation still was needed in working out historical policies, but he was sure that the various professional
groups that had come together to develop the historical parks would
coordinate their activities.[261] The minutes of the meeting carry the distinct impression that the historians were the people who believed they
could unite the diverse interests within the Park Service staff, because
they had the larger view. Furthermore, Chatelain wanted to be sure that
the Park Service received suitable recognition for its new programs:

> He stated that the opportunities in the National Park Service for conducting
> research are many and urged upon the group serious consideration of fur-
> thering the research program. However, the keynote of our work must be
> "professional." We need to stand as authorities in our field and everyone
> should do his utmost to bring about that condition. We must show people
> the value of our work, in other words, we must "sell" the value of the pro-
> gram to those who do not now appreciate it. But in so doing, although we
> can secure much assistance from outside agencies, we cannot assume that
> universities, museums and other reseach groups can do *our* job. Our work
> must be given dignity and the proper importance and above all must be kept
> professionalized.[262]

By the winter of 1935 the tremendous growth of the New Deal
emergency programs had quickened the pace of activity in the Park Service offices. Chatelain and his assistants found that they could not keep
up with the administrative burden that seemed to increase daily as more
historians, architects, and archaeologists went out to supervise CCC
projects.[263] In this dizzy atmosphere of government spending and empire
building the chief historian tried one more time to define for director
Cammerer the functions of the Branch of History (as proposed in the

new act). He told Cammerer that several broad areas of activity were clearly the work of the historians: research of all kinds, educational work at all levels, administrative assistance for superintendents and the field staff, and the formulation of policies.[264] Whatever the judgment of the other professional groups might have been, the historians under Verne Chatelain stood ready to take over the major policymaking functions of the park areas in the eastern United States. No other group seemed as ready to assume the burden.

This onward rush toward a balanced program designed by and for historians culminated in the appointment of an Advisory Board for the secretary of the interior that was intended to serve the main interests of the historical areas in the Park System. John Merriam protested to Harold Ickes about the shift in the makeup of the advisory group from education to historical studies.[265] The old Educational Advisory Committee had been designed to support and advise the interpretive activities in the western parks, and the Historic Sites Act seemed to turn the Department of the Interior almost wholly toward the development of a new Park System in the East. Ickes promised that the new board would represent history, archaeology, architecture, and geography.[266] It would divide the study of historic sites into themes, making it possible for the first time to view the problems of interpretation on a national scale. Historians and administrators could talk about the relationships between *all* of the Civil War battlefields or they could sit down and discuss a number of mission sites throughout the western states. This kind of broad study would have been impossible before the 1930s.

Once historians could function under the mandate of the 1935 act, they took their responsibilities seriously, almost to the point of looking on themselves as guardians of the national culture. There were countless instances of concern over mistakes that had been made in marking and developing historical areas that had been part of the Park System in the years before the 1930s, not to speak of the interpretive methods used by the War Department in administering the battlefield parks before 1933. One example can convey the flavor of these formative years.[267] Alvin P. Stauffer was sent to the Lincoln Birthplace in Hodgenville, Ky., to survey the research needs of a historic site that had been under the control of the Park Service since 1916.[268] Stauffer was shocked to find that the so-called Lincoln cabin was probably not authentic and that the text of some of the tablets on the wall of the memorial temple that housed the legendary birthplace was in error. He insisted that something be done right away: "The reputation of the Park Service for accuracy and good workmanship is involved in these matters. For some years the Hodgenville inscriptions have been criticized by historians, some of whom also question the authenticity of the cabin. If such criticism continues to be ignored, the Service, and particularly the Branch of Historic Sites and Buildings, will appear indifferent to historical scholarship and will accordingly suffer in the eyes of historians."[269]

The responsibility for absolute fidelity to truth in all historical matters intensified greatly when Cammerer sent out a directive on June 20, 1938, calling for an orderly process of research to precede all fieldwork in restoring buildings and sites. Cammerer was most insistent that inaccuracies be eliminated, and he instituted an elaborate process of justification for each major decision.[270] The new supervisor of historic sites, Ronald Lee, wrote in 1939 that there must be careful interpretation "according to the best standards of modern American historical scholarship."[271]

Lee prepared several detailed statements of his duties that showed how widespread his professional interests had become. He could move freely through the fields of historical interpretation, surveys of proposed historic sites, research on specific areas, and relationships with learned societies and educational institutions. In spite of the tremendous demands made on him and his staff in Washington, Lee admitted that the ultimate professional reputation of the Park Service program would rest with the field historians who would put the theories into practice. "Theirs is the extremely important task of representing the Park Service with the public. In such capacity, they are ambassadors; and their intelligence, tact, skill and resourcefulness will be reflected in the reaction of the American public to the historical program of the National Park Service."[272]

As soon as the historians at Colonial National Historical Park came in contact with the tourists who flocked to Virginia in the early 1930s, there were discussions of the most effective ways for giving these learners a taste of the past. In March 1934, for instance, the staff at Yorktown reviewed the best kinds of museum exhibits, roadside displays, visitor contact stations, tours, lectures, and scientific materials that should be used.[273] Soon this line of investigation became the order of the day at every historical area. Staff historians had to prepare interpretive programs to cover every imaginable aspect of research, public contact, and museum work. They experimented as much as they dared, particularly while CCC enrollees were present at some of the sites as a large labor force. At Fort Pulaski, Ga., historian Rogers Young spent a good deal of time in the difficult process of selecting and training guides.[274] There was a supervisor of research and information in the person of Carl Russell in Washington, D.C. Although his training had been in administering the campfire programs and guide services offered in the western parks, Russell became deeply interested in history.[275]

In spite of the fact that historians tended to carry considerable weight in the area of policymaking, specialists in architecture, archaeology, museology, landscape architecture, and engineering had a chance to develop their talents and test them through contacts with their colleagues and the general public. Perhaps the most fruitful professional associations occurred at the regional offices, which were scattered from Richmond to San Francisco. The regional directors usually represented only one of the professional disciplines within the Park Service: They had to see to it that employee morale was high and that they provided "general administrative supervision to the history and archeology, architectural, landscape architectural, engineering, planning, and administrative staffs of the Regional Office."[276]

The people who worked out of the regional offices had broad responsibilities in the 1930s. No one had ever before looked on all the known historic sites within a large area from the standpoint of a trained architect or historian. Orin Bullock served for a while as regional architect in the Richmond office, which controlled an area from Maine to Louisiana along the coast and inland to Tennessee, Kentucky, and Ohio. He offered a brief account of his duties: "I actually visited the parks and reviewed all their building plans. Passing on plans meant in many cases that I contributed to the design. I sent back sketches and marked up blueprints and wrote long dissertations about what they ought to be doing, such as stop building 'round log' cabins used in the western mountains for park structures. I urged the use of the local historical idiom in architectural design of new structures; I tried to persuade them to preserve rather than rebuild."[277] Regional historian Aubrey Neasham realized that he had been given a unique opportunity.

It [Santa Fe] seemed to be a foreign country. And it was a great experience. My job basically at that time was connected with the Historic Sites Survey being conducted by the National Park Service historians and archaeologists, covering all the area between the Mississippi River and the western border of Arizona, which was a lot of territory. . . . There was considerable research involved, but it was more than that; it was a screening process, the location, the ownership, and the significance of sites to provide the federal government information as to which might be taken within the National Park Service or brought within the historic sites program.[278]

The regional office in Richmond was the place where the emphasis on historic preservation work was heaviest. Everyone assumed that there was more history in the older, settled areas of the East Coast, and a considerable amount of preservation money had been poured into the projects in Virginia in particular. It is not surprising that the staff in Richmond began to publish a magazine called the *Regional Review* in the summer of 1938. This periodical usually included from four to six articles representing each of the major disciplines found in the regional office. An article on the restoration of Derby Wharf would be balanced by an account of archaeology in the South and a description of a new national seashore.[279] At first the articles were brief and quite general in content. Each author strove to communicate clearly with his colleagues in other fields. By 1939 some of the essays had become significant discourses on National Park Service policy. The March 1939 issue included Ronald Lee's "Objectives and Policies of Historical Conservation." During the next two years there were articles by Carl Russell on the history of interpretive work in the National Parks and a defense of museums by Ned Burns.[280] The *Review* carried a copy of the official interpretive statement for Salem Maritime National Historic Site in hopes of stimulating "constructive discussion" in other park offices.[281]

Since the majority of park personnel ended up in the field offices at the historical areas, it is natural to expect that this same interdisciplinary communication should have worked its way down through the ranks. Frederick Rath, who served at a number of sites in the late 1930s, remembered his own first impression of the Park Service, fresh from graduate school at Harvard.

One of the things I take note of immediately is that it was not only historians coming into [the] Park Service (as professionals) but architects and landscape architects and archaeologists and perhaps others that we can think of—engineers and so forth. And what was important was the meeting and merging of a group of professional minds in the master plan concept. . . . I can't help but note that right away, starting at Morristown in 1937, I was caught in something that was rapidly professionalizing itself. . . . For example, there was an archaeological dig going on there at the time. Ned Burns, the chief of the Museum Laboratory of the National Park Service, I met for the first time there. . . . You had a historian like Elbert Cox as superintendent. You had a historian like Melvin Weig as the historian there, my boss at Morristown. And you were getting reports that were being put together by many people. For example, in the fall of 1938 they had me at work on a report on the Ford Mansion. . . . A person like Tom Waterman, the architect, was being called into consultation about this.[282]

The young experts who chose to remain with the National Park Service soon realized that they were in on the formation of something that was certain to grow in influence and effectiveness. A nationwide historical program had never been put together before, and it needed to be as broadly professional as possible. Each individual had much to do, whether the historical area included a large staff or a small one. Rath, for instance, found in 1940 when he took up his duties as historian at Vicksburg Battlefield that he had to compile a bibliography on the Vicksburg campaign while he was putting up outdoor displays, guiding visitors, and interviewing people who could supply him with eyewitness accounts of the crucial engagement of the Civil War in the West. Rath also wrote articles for the local newspapers and spoke on the Vicksburg radio station. At one point he even worked with a historical pageant.[283] It was a great experiment in the popularization of history by means of military sites.

The architects who were involved in the New Deal emergency programs were equally aware of the opportunity they had for influencing the discipline of architectural history. The ideal mechanism had been the Historic American Buildings Survey, which was only partly a product of the Park Service. When J. Thomas Schneider was preparing his *Report to the Secretary of the Interior*, he asked John P. O'Neill of the HABS office to summarize the development of his program. O'Neill offered a long memorandum that recounted the ways in which the survey work had trained and rehabilitated a needy group of architects.[284] But the most important recommendation to come from O'Neill was a proposal for the creation of a permanent "professional" field organization for HABS. He concluded that a central office for the architectural survey would be able to cooperate in a useful way with the new Historic Sites Survey that was about to get under way.[285] Obviously, he saw in the new Branch of Historic Sites a chance for architectural history to claim a foothold in park planning. Of course there was a Branch of Plans and Design in the Park Service already, but the people who worked under Thomas Vint had responsibilities that extended far beyond the study of old buildings.

During World War II Jean C. Harrington served as superintendent of Colonial National Historical Park, and this promotion put one of the major figures in historical archaeology into a position of power and influence. At the end of the war Harrington discovered that in June 1945 the American Council of Learned Societies and the Park Service had held a conference at Morristown on the utilization of objects and physical remains in the study of history. The response to this first interdisciplinary meeting encouraged him to sponsor an even more all-encompassing conference at Yorktown in the spring of 1946.[286] The Yorktown gathering became a means of initiating a group of academic historians and librari-

Historic American Buildings Survey veterans at Advisory Board meeting, 1961. Back row, left to right, *Charles E. Peterson, Worth Bailey, Charlee W. Lessig, Samuel Lapham, Jr., Richard W. E. Perrin;* front row, *Henry C. Forman, Earl Reed, William G. Perry, Thomas Vint, Virginia Daiker. (HABS)*

ans into the whole question of archaeological research. Waldo G. Leland of the American Council of Learned Societies hoped to introduce the academic researchers to the people who had been working for nearly ten years in the field of historical archaeology in the Virginia area.[287] The two-day meeting was divided evenly between consideration of the Jamestown excavations and a study of Edward Alexander's new program of interpretation at Williamsburg.[288] After so many years of encountering professional indifference, Harrington was heartened to hear some of the history professors say, "This has been a real education." Harrington was guarded in his optimism, however, when he surmised that the "benefits" of the Yorktown sessions would necessarily be long-range in character. He noted that the people from William and Mary and the Williamsburg staff seemed to be a little more interested in the program at Jamestown than they previously had been.[289] His analysis proved to be correct, because the professors sent in a number of comments on the need for more course offerings, including a serious study of physical objects as sources. At the same time there is little evidence that any of the people who attended the meeting put their preaching into practice right away.[290] Ronald Lee fervently hoped that there could be more such conferences to bring diverse disciplines together at particular historic sites so that each could contribute something from the standpoint of several lines of research.[291] It was a critical breakthrough for archaeology, but proper recognition of the achievements of the National Park Service research program did not come easily.

It would be fair to say that historical archaeology and architectural history did not really exist as professions in the late 1930s, so it is no wonder that they developed haltingly even within the sheltering arm of the Park Service emergency programs. In 1941 Charles Peterson told Turpin Bannister of the American Society of Architectural Historians that he had had a difficult time establishing his own role in the Park Service:

In spite of the fact that the National Park Service has been doing work with historic buildings for over ten years, the position in the bureau of the architectural historian is an anomalous one. The National Park Service has no professionals of that type maintained by a regular annual appropriation. This seems to be a reflection of the fact that the profession of archeologist in historic American architecture hardly exists as such. The same is not true of the archeologist of the American Indian, who has established his place definitely in our bureau, both on a full-time basis and on a loan basis from the Smithsonian and other institutions.

The support of the architectural historians in the National Park Service has been accomplished by all sorts of expedients. Mostly they are carried along on the budget of funds for regular architectural and landscape services allotted to what is called the Branch of Plans and Design. This has been possible under the emergency programs of the last eight years, but the future seems very uncertain.[292]

The most obvious way to gauge the growth and operation of the professional groups within the National Park Service is through specific preservation and restoration projects carried on in the field. Here one can see how the sheer size and staying power of the federal government had a tremendous impact on people trained in all the scholarly disciplines. The coming of the CCC in 1933 was a tremendous help in opening up opportunities for talented people who were willing to move out into areas of research that were not generally recognized.

The greatest contribution to the growth of professionalism came when the Park Service, using public works money available during the depression, began to carry out its own restoration and preservation projects on historic sites already within the Park System or areas in state parks. Here the field organization was peculiarly adapted to provide professional advice. The difficulties encountered by most park superintendents in getting funds for their construction projects meant that a great deal of useful time was consumed in conferences, research studies, and long reports to regional offices. These debates tended to have a positive effect on each of the programs that emerged because more and more highly qualified people participated in the decision-making process, and any plan that survived this rigorous process had considerable documentation and scholarly backing. Distance was no factor in the operation of the Park Service executive hierarchy. The vital element in getting an idea through the chain of command was patience and perseverance. If officials could satisfy the people at the regional office and in Washington, they could get the necessary money for almost any program.

Mission La Purisima Concepcion

Several veterans of the CCC administrative offices have referred to the reconstruction of Mission La Purisima Concepcion in Lompoc, Calif., as the most satisfactory historical project they encountered.[293] The idea of reconstructing the mission buildings in Santa Barbara County originated with a CCC inspector, Phillip Primm, who had visited the ruins in 1933. He discovered that some of the land that contained the most important buildings was already the property of the county and could easily be turned over to the state of California.[294] Newton Drury and Joseph Knowland of the California State Park Commission worked diligently to increase the size of the state reservation at La Purisima so that eventually the federal authorities could carry out a full restoration of the community.

In the summer of 1934 the CCC established a camp at Lompoc to clear the mission site of debris and conduct an archaeological investigation.[295] It was difficult to plan the long-term development of the site because these emergency programs were often funded on a three-month basis, and there was no certainty that a labor force would be available beyond the fall of 1935. Nevertheless, an impressive group of people assembled in front of the old columns of the residence building one day in early August to discuss future administration of the project. Those present were: Owen Coy of the California State Historical Commission; Arthur Woodward, curator of the Los Angeles County Museum; Ronald Adam, supervisor of Santa Barbara County; H. V. Johnson, the camp superintendent; Frank Dunne, county forester; W. C. Penfield, engineer for the County Planning Commission; Edward Rowe, landscape architect; Arthur Darsie, engineer; Fred Hageman, architect; and L. Deming

Mark Harrington, Arthur Woodward, and H. V. Smith examining artifacts from archaeological work at La Purisima Mission. (California Department of Parks and Recreation)

Tilton, director of planning for the county. Although they were doubtful about the final goals for the project, the people agreed to ask for the appointment of a trained "architect historian" to supervise any excavations. They also promised to try to find the necessary skilled labor to carry out some of the difficult construction tasks that would be required.[296]

Newton Drury and the other officials who worked with the California Division of Parks knew that the funding and administration of whatever happened at La Purisima would be federal but that eventually the state would receive the park under the provisions of the Emergency Conservation Work program. Drury set out to appoint a local advisory committee in the Santa Barbara area that could help to advise the State Park Commission on the best way to develop the Purisima site.[297] The members of the committee took their duties seriously and reported regularly to the Park Commission on the progress at Lompoc. The committee included an architect, a lawyer, an amateur historian, a planner, and an engineer.[298]

In May the Advisory Committee recommended the appointment of Fred Hageman as superintendent.[299] Although he did not become superintendent, Hageman did continue as architect for the restoration while several Park Service experts came in from time to time to advise him. One of the first things he received was a set of drawings of all the California mission buildings recorded by the Historic American Buildings Survey.[300] The Park Service regional historian for the CCC, Russell Ewing, inspected the mission site several times during the fall of 1935, made recommendations on construction techniques, and sent back long progress reports to his regional officer. Ewing's job was to conduct research on La Purisima in the principal California libraries in both printed and manuscript sources.[301]

Back in Washington, D.C., Ronald Lee, as historian for the State Park Emergency Conservation Work, read the reports coming from Ewing. Lee wanted to be sure that the people who administered the mission restoration had a clear understanding of their assignment. He had three concrete suggestions: (1) Read Laurence Coleman's books *Manual for Small Museums* and *Historic House Museums*; (2) make sure that all archaeological work was fully reported on; (3) request the state of California to buy up all the land that had contained the mission buildings.[302] Ewing outlined his role in the ECW program as that of an adviser and researcher. He had no control over the people at the camp, but he certainly could make his views known. By the fall of 1935 Hageman and his staff at the mission site could rest assured that they would never lack for good advice from either Washington or the regional office in San Francisco. And in the case of Ewing there was a promise of research notes from the sources that he had begun to explore in the Bancroft Library in Berkeley.[303]

Here the national scope of the Park Service operation made a profound contribution to a local restoration program. Ewing decided by December that he had exhausted all the available manuscripts on La Purisima; he would have to go to Spain or Mexico to carry on any further research in documents. However, he proposed that the regional office permit him to visit and study all the California missions that had been restored. "A knowledge of past mistakes in mission restoration would serve as a deterrent for the repetition of similar mistakes at La Purisima." His proposed study tour was intended to yield information on a host of important subjects, such as "mission furniture, hardware, gardens, walls and fences, decorations, and water systems."[304] The regional office even drew upon the experience of other CCC restorations at the time. In late 1935 Ewing contacted Erik Reed, the regional archaeologist in Texas who had supervised the investigations of Mission

Espiritu Santo near Goliad. Reed sent back a detailed account of his rules for field excavations as a guide for the staff at Lompoc.[305]

Regional officer Lawrence Merriam remarked several times that he was amazed to see how little friction there had been in planning the work at La Purisima, considering the number of people and the different administrative groups involved. It was remarkable that the staff at the site had been able to work smoothly with consultants from Los Angeles museums, the local advisory committee, the State Park Commission, the regional office in San Francisco, and the officials from the Washington headquarters of the National Park Service.[306]

As the restoration work at La Purisima progressed from one building to the next, more and more experts began to pay attention to the activities of the CCC company in Lompoc. After all, this project involved the only opportunity to recreate an entire mission community, and the progress made through 1936 led some authorities to believe that the task might be accomplished. Historians, architects, and ethnologists saw some factors at La Purisima that broke down the usual resistance to reconstruction: an unspoiled site with a large enough park to keep out visual intrusions, an adequately funded professional research staff that was enthusiastic about the project, a large labor force that was becoming increasingly expert in primitive construction methods, and the endless educational possibilities of the completed mission.[307] Rexford Newcomb of the College of Fine and Applied Arts at the University of Illinois stopped by to see the Purisima site in the summer of 1936. He had written a book on California mission architecture a decade earlier and had visited the spot several times. Newcomb told the chairman of the Advisory Committee that the work was "going forward in a highly commendable way" and that architect Hageman had shown a real understanding of the California mission style in his restoration of the missing portions of the buildings.[308] A few months later Mark Harrington, curator of the Southwest Museum in Los Angeles, published a glowing account of the Purisima program in an article in *Masterkey* entitled "The Right Kind of Restoration." Harrington argued that the rule for a good recreation was a simple one: adopt the building techniques of the past. He believed that the National Park Service had produced at Lompoc a "shining example" of this approach. And he was particularly impressed with Hageman and his sensitivity to the problems involved in the reconstruction.[309] The chemists of the National Bureau of Standards examined plaster chips excavated at the site and worked out the original formula for each paint color mixed by the Indians.[310] At the same time a local historian in Santa Barbara, Edith Webb, shared her research material on the community life of the mission Indian.[311] Many years later she published an authoritative book on the subject, *Indian Life at the Old Missions*. She was enormously pleased to see the way in which the CCC enrollees had been taught to use tools in the same way the Indians had utilized them.[312]

Russell Ewing left the CCC in 1937, and his replacement as regional historian, Olaf Hagen, was an experienced Park Service employee who had entered the federal service with Ronald Lee and the other graduate students from the University of Minnesota. Hagen picked up the work begun by Ewing and started to investigate the use of professional assistance from the Museum Division in the preparation of exhibits at La Purisima.[313]

In April 1939 Fred Hageman produced a voluminous illustrated report on the architectural restoration of La Purisima. Historian Hagen wrote the preface, in which he joined Mark Harrington in supporting the project as the right kind of restoration.[314] Hageman devoted two pages to a listing of the committees and individual experts who had helped him in the research. It was a testimonial to the spirit of the collaborative effort.

By 1939 the project was nearing another plateau, and a decision had to be made whether to continue the archaeological work and plan the reconstruction of more buildings. Ronald Lee, who had become chief historian of the Park Service by that time, expressed concern over the fact that some archaeological explorations had been carried out without enough expert supervision. Later on Lee visited La Purisima and gave it his general endorsement;[315] he could not resist the educational value of the site or the enthusiasm of the staff in California. During the next year Harrington personally supervised most of the digging and reported at length on what had been discovered.[316] During the latter half of 1940 artists from the Index of American Design began to decorate the interior of the reconstructed church, and the results seemed satisfactory to all concerned.[317] By that time Lee had begun to swing around to support the idea of total reconstruction of the complex of buildings. "It became evident that the restoration work at La Purisima had the confidence of eminent scholars who were anxious to see the restoration carried to completion. These men felt that adequate comparative and descriptive data were available to give genuine educational and interpretive value even to type restorations which might have to be resorted to in certain instances to make the projected restoration 100 per cent complete."[318]

H. V. Smith, superintendent of the Purisima project from 1937 until its completion, looked back over the history of the reconstruction in 1952 and came to his own conclusions on the success of the enterprise: (1) The architects had prepared the drawings on the site, so the excavations and ruins could be studied closely; (2) the highly trained regional historians had helped to make decisions when disagreements arose; (3) the regional office had provided money for the use of consultants in such diverse fields as archaeology, history, architecture, forestry, geology, engineering, landscape architecture, and historical administration; (4) the CCC officials had delegated authority to Smith as project superintendent, and they had freed him from needless paper work.[319]

Tumacacori National Monument

The development of the museum building at Tumacacori National Monument in Arizona illustrates the way in which the organizational peculiarities of the Park Service worked for the professionals. At San Jose Mission in San Antonio, Tex., the WPA had undertaken a total restoration of the church and the barracks. At La Purisima the CCC started to reconstruct the whole complex of buildings that once formed the mission community. At Tumacacori (which had been in the Park System since 1908) the staff decided to stabilize the church as a ruin and to pour its time and talents into the development of a museum that would tell the story of the mission chain founded by Father Kino in the seventeenth and eighteenth centuries. This approach reflected the expertise that could be found in the National Park Service staff by 1935.

The real father of the Tumacacori museum was Carl Russell, who was field naturalist for the western parks in 1933. That year he participated in a study of the Tumacacori situation and was led to sources in the Bancroft Library at Berkeley. A year later he employed Hero Rensch to compile a critical bibliography on the development of the Sonora mission chain with special emphasis on the chronology of Tumacacori. During the winter of 1934-35 Russell helped to set up a major archaeological investigation of the mission grounds under Paul Beaubien. The report of that dig was prepared by Arthur Woodward for the National Park Service in March. While the archaeologists worked on artifacts from the mission site, Russell and an assistant studied most of the surviving mission churches in northern Mexico and then prepared a preliminary exhibit plan for the proposed Tumacacori museum. Shortly after their return two Park Service engineers produced a detailed report on the stabilization of the Tumacacori ruins.[320] Obviously, Russell had been preparing his superiors for the recommendation that a major museum be located at Tumacacori.

The staff that interpreted the mission ruins to the public considered it important to have some exhibits that would place Tumacacori in its historical and cultural context. One 1934 report concluded that the visitor would need some help in looking at the old church: "The distinct

Tumacacori Mission National Monument, Ariz. (National Park Service)

impression should be left on his mind that the Tumacacori Mission is not just a curious thing to see; a thing to while away an idle hour, but that it was the loom upon which was spun some of the history of the Southwest and as such it is an intensely interesting place for all Americans to visit."[321]

When Russell first developed his exhibit plan for the museum, he submitted a draft to the staffs at Casa Grande National Monument (where another museum was to be located) and the division of education at Berkeley and to Verne Chatelain in Washington.[322] By 1935 Russell had concluded that the exhibit plan should cover the history of the construction of the mission buildings by means of either pictures or dioramas. The only way in which the earliest phase of the history of the site could be researched would be to send an architect and a photographer into the northernmost province of Mexico to study the other churches in the chain.[323] It took Russell six months to achieve his goal, but finally in early 1936 a party of six architects and museum specialists toured the Sonora missions to gather material for the displays at Tumacacori.[324] Russell had won the backing of Chatelain and Thomas Vint of the Branch of Plans and Design.[325] Olaf Hagen, the regional historian, supported the contention of the engineers that the Tumacacori church should be stabilized as a ruin because any real interior restoration would involve conjecture, not fact.[326] The field staff acquired exhibit plans from the Park Service museums at Morristown, Vicksburg, Shiloh, and Colonial in an effort to draft its own proposal in finished form.[327] Arthur Woodward, who was working as a consultant at La Purisima, finally wrote the exhibit plan, which called for a series of rooms that explained the position of Tumacacori in the development of southern Arizona.[328] In June, Russell submitted all of the relevant reports to the superintendent of southwestern monuments, Frank Pinckley. Russell conservatively concluded: "It is apparent to all of us concerned that adequate data is now at hand with which to make such restorations and repairs as are deemed necessary at Tumacacori and to proceed in following existing exhibit plans for the interpretation of the several phases of the story that should be presented by the museum method."[329]

Russell and his colleagues had done their homework well, and they understood the administrative operations of the National Park Service. Secretary Ickes released $50,000 of Public Works Administration funds for the construction and furnishing of the museum at Tumacacori in August 1936.[330]

Final success came on April 23, 1939, when Ickes and a host of distinguished guests went to Tumacacori to dedicate the completed museum.[331] Although the new building did not wholly satisfy the staff, which had its offices at the mission, there is no question that it had been provided with a remarkable interpretive tool for giving the visitor a greater understanding of the ruins of the church and the subsidiary buildings. The administrative machinery of the Department of the Interior had been slow in responding to the proposals for a new museum, but the delay had only worked to improve the quality of the studies that went into the preparation of the exhibit plan. Carl Russell and his fellow professionals had used the time-honored expedient of buttressing their proposals with every possible research tool available to them.

Salem Maritime National Historic Site

The regional staff organization of the Park Service permitted a kind of professional collaboration in restoration work that was not possible before the mid-1930s. In any number of instances after 1938 there could be as many as three or four reports dealing with one specific restoration question, produced by historians, architects, archaeologists, engineers, and landscape architects. Most of the time these experts agreed with each other on all major issues, and their separate research efforts only served to strengthen the arguments presented collectively. In a few instances they did engage in good-humored debates over tricky questions of restoration techniques.

The decision to put the fence in front of the Richard Derby House in Salem, Mass., on a granite base should serve as a good example of the process of professional debate as it was used in the National Park Service. During the late spring of 1938 assistant architect Stuart Barnette prepared drawings for the restoration of the Derby House. Once those plans were ready, Barnette submitted them to coordinating superintendent Elbert Cox in Morristown and acting superintendent (historian) Edwin Small in Salem.[332] Small and engineer Oscar Bray, after discussing several features of the proposed restoration, agreed that there might have to be some changes in the plans and asked Barnette to come to the Derby House to talk over the controversial issues. What finally occurred was a meeting that included two architects, a landscape architect, an engineer, and one or two historians. The principal issue was whether the Derby fence had rested on a stone base. Barnette argued that there was an eighteenth-century precedent in New England for such an installation, but Small maintained that there was no historical evidence for stonework under the Derby House fence. Those present agreed that an excavation would be necessary.[333]

Director Cammerer received an inconclusive report from Salem a month later, signed by Bray, Small, and Barnette, in which they agreed that there had been an adequate excavation and that the results had been

Derby House, with controversial fence, Salem. (National Park Service)

entirely neutral. The materials found in the trenches neither proved nor disproved the existence of a stone foundation.[334] Arthur Demaray, in his capacity as acting director of the Park Service, cut the knot and decided that the granite base should be used because it would act as a "buffer against traffic," although he saw no significant evidence on either side of the crucial question.[335] The most surprising aspect of this incident is the amount of time and talent expended on this seemingly inconsequential decision. But these people were serious scholars and they genuinely wanted their work to reflect the best research techniques of the day. It is equally noteworthy that by 1938 people from so many professional backgrounds could be assembled in Salem for a conference on the restoration of a few eighteenth-century houses.

Morristown National Historical Park

The keynote of the Morristown development was also interdisciplinary cooperation. The historians (who doubled as archaeologists) and the ar-

945

Back of the Ford Mansion, Morristown, after restoration. (National Park Service)

chitects worked together in attempting to cover every possible alternative course of action in dealing with the buildings that were at the old campground. There was a general willingness to explore all the possible sources of information—no matter what the results might be. With the 1939 restoration of the Ford House (1772) in Morristown, N.J., the experts worked on their reports independently, but they came to similar conclusions. The renovation had been precipitated by the construction of a museum and library behind the Ford House. With the larger exhibit area available the Washington Association of New Jersey could take its accumulation of treasures out of the old building. Superintendent Elbert Cox believed that the time had finally come to return the Washington headquarters to its 1780 appearance.[336]

The physical restoration of the house required the services of a diverse group of experts, some local and some from New York and Washington. For example, Cox had a staff of WPA researchers at Morristown going through all kinds of documentary evidence from English, American, and French sources on the situation in New Jersey during the Revolution. The research had included exact surveys of the military campground and the typing of several thousand pages of translations from the French letters.[337] The principal figure in the restoration planning was architect Thomas T. Waterman, who was working for Thomas Vint in the Branch of Plans and Design. As he began to study the evolution of the Ford House, Waterman concluded that all of the dormer windows needed to come off, because they were later than the period of maximum historical interest. In order to accomplish this task, Vint had to send a letter to director Cammerer that was countersigned by Ronald Lee for the Branch of Historic Sites.[338]

But that was as far as the historians in Washington would go. When Lee saw fourteen sheets of drawings for the Ford restoration, he reminded the director that there had been a policy statement in June 1938 that required full documentation for every step in the physical restoration of any "historic or prehistoric remains" in the Park System.[339] At this point Cox turned to his research historian, Melvin Weig, and asked him to prepare a report that would cover all the difficult issues from the available documents. As he put his report together, Weig was greatly relieved to discover that his material supported almost every change Waterman wanted to carry out.[340] Although it was somewhat after the fact, the report bore the awesome title "Documentary Justification for the Restoration of Washington's Headquarters." Weig's essay had only four pages of text, but it included seven pages of footnotes and illustrations.[341] Superintendent Cox exaggerated when he forwarded the document to Washington, claiming that Waterman had "carefully considered" the material in the report. Technically, he may have been correct in that Waterman could have consulted the same sources, but he certainly did not see the manuscript prepared by Weig until after the drawings had been completed.[342] A few weeks later Waterman prepared his own restoration report, which was based entirely on structural evidence.[343] Armed with both research documents, chief of planning Vint went to the Branch of Historic Sites and gathered the signatures of Charles Porter and Ronald Lee, thereby obeying the directive sent out by Cammerer.[344]

While the restoration work was in process, the Park Service engineer decided to insert extra beams in the ceilings of the dining room and library in order to handle the large number of visitors who might want to see the house during the peak tourist season.[345] Also at that time Waterman discovered that the principal stairway of the Ford House had been moved from its original location, and he wrote a two-page justification for changing the stairway to fit the evidence he had found on the walls of the first floor.[346] Melvin Weig inspected the building with Waterman and concurred in the decision to take out the later work.[347] But the report was not enough to fulfill the spirit of the Park Service policy on restoration. Porter, the chief skeptic of the Washington office, commended Waterman for "ably and logically" presenting his arguments, but Porter requested HABS photographs of the structural evidence used to locate the old stairway. He asserted that the report must include these photographs because once the restoration was complete the evidence would be obliterated.[348] It seems fair to conclude that the historians were not trying to be difficult; they wanted to be certain that future interpreters of the Morristown headquarters would know why the changes had been made.

As soon as the physical restoration came to a close, a new committee went to work on the furnishing plan. Alfred Hopkins of the Museum Branch prepared a report on the typical eighteenth-century assortment of furniture that would be required. And Weig looked carefully into documents that might show what had actually been in the house when the Ford family lived there.[349] Then the new superintendent, Herbert Kahler, called together a select group of experts to assist in finding the best available objects for the exhibition rooms. The committee included Mrs. Paul Moore, who had offered to donate the money for the furnishings, Bertha Benkard, Henry du Pont's close friend and adviser at Winterthur, and Joseph Downs of the Metropolitan Museum. It would have been difficult to assemble at that time a more astute circle of collectors than these people.[350] Over the period of a year the committee met several times to inspect the rooms and approve the paint colors and the draperies. Henry du Pont himself attended one meeting.[351] Hopkins worked closely with the advisers and attempted to follow their orders where he could. He complained to Ronald Lee that he found most historians had absolutely no understanding of the meaning and use of physical objects, a situation that he hoped would be corrected as more and more Park Service exhibition buildings opened to the public.[352]

Appomattox Court House

One of the last joint efforts before the outbreak of World War II came with the planning of the reconstruction of the McLean House at Appomattox Court House in Virginia. There had been a debate over the wisdom of carrying out any work at Appomattox, and this exchange delayed the preparation of research studies through 1939.[353]

When chief historian Ronald Lee finally capitulated to the Appomattox Association and agreed to the idea of a reconstruction in February 1940, he immediately set in motion a program that included the appointment of a research team that would consist of an architect, a historian, and an archaeologist.[354]

By June 1940 the whole staff of the Richmond office had begun to work on the Appomattox development. Architect Orin Bullock, landscape architect Walter Sheffield, associate engineer James Head, assistant historical technician Ralston Lattimore, and acting superintendent Hubert Gurney all surveyed the buildings in order to compile a list of priority projects. They found ten separate items that required study and research.[355] A month later a battery of Park Service executives met at the regional director's office to firm up the decisions made by the personnel in the field. They all agreed that the studies for the McLean House reconstruction must come first. That meant that the old plans had to be checked and purchased immediately. The superintendent promised that a documentary report on the house could be ready in three months.[356] The major professional staff members of the Richmond office became an official committee to establish the development plan for the whole townsite. Historian Ralph Happel produced a "McLean House Study" in December 1940. It was a thirty-eight-page introduction to the problems that would influence the reconstruction, and it became a prelude to the massive report that was ready a year later.[357]

Director Newton Drury received the final research results in March 1942. The *Collaborative Justification for Reconstruction of the McLean House at Appomattox*, by Ralph Happel (historian), Preston Holder (archaeologist), and Ray Julian (architect), was the first joint document of this kind ever prepared, and Arthur Kelly of the Archeological Division referred to it as "a model for future work of the character carried on at the McLean House site."[358] The *Justification* was mainly the work of the historian and the archaeologist, who were both in residence at Appomattox. The fact that the architect was in Richmond working under regional architect Al Higgins did not hinder the research, but it did mean that he reached many of his conclusions after reading the other two portions of the report. The architect changed the overall dimensions of the house slightly for structural reasons, and this alteration became something of a sore point in the Branch of History.[359] Fortunately, the three researchers got along well, and the resulting document can safely be described as a professional collaboration.[360] They obviously did not have the task of deciding *whether* the McLean House should rise again; they merely justified the operation from the standpoint of the available documentation.

With the completion of the Appomattox research the Park Service staff believed that it had reached a peak of professional competence never before equaled. Herbert Kahler, acting supervisor of historic sites, wrote: "The documented study or collaborative justification accompanying Plan App. 2010 is certainly the most complete and scholarly work yet undertaken by this Service in connection with a restoration project. The method is sound and strict adherence to this procedure will place the National Park Service in a position of complete security with regard to the McLean House project."[361] Unfortunately the *Justification* proved to be the last major research effort of the Park Service for a number of years because of the war emergency, and the years following the war were equally discouraging for the professionals who had engaged in so many exciting research ventures all through the late 1930s.

POSTWAR PROFESSIONAL EFFORTS

Perhaps it could be argued that the lack of support for historical scholarship in the 1940s ultimately led to the creation of the National Council for Historic Sites and Buildings and the National Trust. Ronald Lee, who played a key role in setting up the first national preservation organization, acknowledged that many professional groups were interested in saving buildings. The problem was that the postwar situation seemed to demand "that something be done to try to mobilize sentiment and opinion in the field of preservation."[362] As soon as Frederick Rath took over the administration of the National Council, he realized that he would have to act as a buffer for the National Park Service, which was under pressure from private preservation organizations and local governments to provide money and advice. The professionals in the federal service found that they had little time for the kinds of research they had done before the war.[363] The understaffed Branch of Historic Sites had to concentrate its energies on developing and interpreting sites already in the Park System.

Training programs for people involved in preservation projects began to develop. Lee, as usual, was deeply interested in professional cooperation. In May 1948 he chaired a session at the annual convention of the American Association of Museums and brought in Bertram K. Little of the Society for the Preservation of New England Antiquities to deliver a paper to aid people in the process of selecting houses for preservation.[364] During the summer of 1949 Little directed a short course on preservation at the Seminars in American Culture at Cooperstown. He invited experts, such as architect Edwin Brumbaugh of Pennsylvania, to give the amateurs an idea of the professional viewpoint on restoration.[365] The people who attended the seminar certainly represented the preservation field on the local level. Little estimated that they were "officers or

Helen Duprey Bullock teaching a course entitled "The American Frugal Housewife" in 1955 Seminar on American Culture, Cooperstown. (Courtesy New York State Historical Association, Cooperstown)

leaders of small and medium-sized historical societies and museums . . . , members of the staff of some larger state or regional organizations, and a few just intelligent laymen and women generally interested in Americana."[366] The new director of the SPNEA exposed his students to a series of lectures and discussions that centered on the problems involved in research through the medium of architectural and archaeological analysis. Brumbaugh and Nina Fletcher Little gave the participants some understanding of their experiences in restoration work in Pennsylvania and Massachusetts. Considering the limitations of the two-week format, Bertram Little had crammed a good deal of information into his short course. It was a reasonably professional presentation that should have awakened the students to the responsibilities that came along with the administration of historic buildings.[367]

Ronald Lee also hoped to use a short course as a means of focusing some of the professional expertise of the National Park Service into one place for a few weeks. He planned a summer "Institute in the Preservation and Interpretation of Historic Sites and Buildings" that ran for three weeks in June 1949 at the Department of the Interior and at Colonial Williamsburg. It was particularly fitting that this first formal course offering in historic preservation work should bring together the staff experts of the two largest organizations in the field. The summer institute included three main features: morning lectures by the historians, archaeologists, museum specialists, and architects of the National Park Service; visits to the major historic sites and museums in the Washington area; and individual research on preassigned projects. Lee himself taught several sessions dealing with the history and philosophy of preservation. Frederick Rath came over from the National Council to lecture on the organizations that were involved in preservation work.[368] During the final week of the program the whole group moved to Williamsburg, where the emphasis changed to the fields of architectural restoration and furniture selection. Edward Alexander and his staff gave a description of the new orientation program.[369] This brief coordinated effort achieved its main purpose when some of the students saw that the problems involved in preserving, restoring, and interpreting old buildings were much more complex than they appeared to be.[370] It is probable that another goal was realized as well—the students must have gained a healthy respect for the professionals who had come together to devote themselves to the new and exciting challenge of researching all the diverse fields that contributed to an understanding of the past through historic buildings.

The summer institute was a symbol of the maturity of the preservation movement, and it appropriately ended in Williamsburg, where the first group of professionals had gathered twenty-one years before to begin the study of Virginia's colonial architecture. In 1949 their successors were prepared to lead the preservation field into the challenging decade of the 1950s.

I 2

New Restoration Techniques Emerge

THE MAJOR DILEMMA of restoration theory, resolved in varying ways by preservationists in the 1920s and '30s, was expressed in 1940 by Aubrey Neasham, who drew on his National Park Service experience in the Southwest:

> The argument is put forth by some that the visiting public goes to an historic site to get as full a picture as possible. From that standpoint, many consider it necessary to restore and to reconstruct the historic setting in full. What results is an illusion. The illusion not only affects those who see it today, but also those who will see it in the future, even to the extent that what we have reconstructed and restored may be called the work of our predecessors. Such reconstruction and restoration is not only artificial and unreal, but scientifically unsound. No matter what we do, we cannot supply in exact detail or spirit that which was done before us.[1]

The history of this dilemma can be found in nineteenth-century Europe in the opposing restoration theories of John Ruskin in England and Eugène Viollet-le-Duc in France. Charles W. Porter III, who came into the Washington office of the Branch of Historic Sites shortly after the passage of the Historic Sites Act, was a careful student of European concepts of repair and restoration and of the ideas of John Ruskin and the English antirestorationists. (Ruskin described restoration as "total destruction" because modern workmen cannot recapture the spirit of the past.) Porter had studied in France and had inspected the restored walls at Carcassonne and the Roman buildings at Nîmes. He could read French and he had carefully gone over the deliberations of the 1933 Athens conference on restoration practice, which concluded that restoration should be avoided unless the building was in a serious state of decay.[2] He immediately recognized the philosophical debt that the Williamsburg project owed to Viollet-le-Duc. The French architect believed that he could restore buildings to a state of completeness they might never have had in the past.[3] The idea of restoring an entire complex of buildings to one general period may well have originated in America in the imagination of W. A. R. Goodwin, but it had been attempted elsewhere. In addition to Porter, Ronald Lee, who was chief historian of the National Park Service in 1938, began to study the ideas and achievements of the two major British organizations, the Society for the Protection of Ancient Buildings and the National Trust for Places of Historic Interest or Natural Beauty.[4]

In Neasham's defense of the Ruskinian antirestorationist principle he was to reflect the increasingly scholarly philosophy of the Park Service on the subject. This conservative approach is best exemplified by the Park Service policy statement, probably authored by Fiske Kimball, that is perhaps the most important single pronouncement on the subject of restoration that came out of the 1930s: "Better preserve than repair, better repair than restore, better restore than construct."[5] After 1935, in particular, the discovery of inaccuracies in the reconstructed Washington Birthplace at Wakefield led to increasing resistance to reconstructions throughout the Park System. Lee and his staff opposed any restoration work that could not be justified by structural, documentary, or archaeological evidence.

Opposing the antireconstruction approach, first espoused in the United States by William Sumner Appleton and the Society for the Preservation of New England Antiquities, was the romanticized view of the Williamsburg Restoration. Although the studies at Williamsburg set a new standard for research efforts and literally began the profession of restoration architecture, John D. Rockefeller, Jr., admitted to Dr. Goodwin from their first meetings that it was the beauty and charm of the old city that appealed to him. Rockefeller rarely wrote or spoke on the subject, but his view of the colonial town has inevitably colored the development of restoration philosophy in the United States. As William G. Perry was to write, "Only through architecture could the picture be recreated." While the picture was to be as authentic as possible, nonetheless it was the creation of that picture and its educational and inspirational value for the American public that was more significant than the architecture itself.

The most important developments in restoration thought came mainly during the 1930s, when the money, labor, and professionals were available at one time. Although statements on preservation ideals were published during these busy years, the buildings themselves became the real testament; the research and supervision given to the larger projects were much more influential than the production of books and articles. A visit to a restored Williamsburg also was many times more powerful for most people than reading an article by Goodwin in the *National Geographic*.

From the beginning of his career with the SPNEA, Appleton used the pages of *Old-Time New England* as a forum to preach the gospel of repair versus restoration or reconstruction. He was absolutely wedded to whatever evidence he found in an old building. Near the end of a long article on the renovation of the Claflin-Richards House (1662) in Wenham, Mass., Appleton noted with regret that mistakes had been made in the restoration because occasionally the structural details had been ignored. At that point he paused to issue an eloquent warning to all people who might choose to refurbish early New England buildings: "The evidence on which restoration is based should not be destroyed in the course of the work, but should be carefully preserved as a voucher for the accuracy of this work."[6]

In 1931 Norman Isham, a New England architect who had long experience in restoration work, called for the "scientific idea" to come to the front in museum installations.[7] His Rhode Island humor might have cheered a wider readership than the exclusive Walpole Society he was addressing, for Isham admitted at the end of his message that a first-rate museum restoration would be a triumph in "the gentle art of faking." In this case he used the term *faking* in a constructive sense.

The first full-length statement on restoration came from Laurence Vail Coleman in his 1933 book, *Historic House Museums*. Coleman was a rank outsider to the field of architecture, but he was striving for a greater degree of professionalism in the presentation of museum exhibits. The fifth chapter of his book took up the challenges involved in physical restoration. He listed some principles that every museum administrator and board member could follow: Hire an architect who is experienced in working with old buildings; give that individual a clear definition of the purposes of the restoration; be patient enough to do the necessary research in preparation for any construction or modification; and, finally, leave a full and complete report on all the evidence used to arrive

Archaeological excavations at the site of the Raleigh Tavern, Williamsburg, 1929. (Colonial Williamsburg Foundation)

at the major decisions.[8] Coleman believed that the scientific spirit was essential, so he incorporated a quotation to this effect from Fiske Kimball's letter to Mary Van Deventer at Stratford.[9] Kimball's comments achieved wide circulation among preservation administrators because he dealt frankly with the important question of artistic preference versus historical truth.[10] *Historic House Museums* included an annotated bibliography of works on old houses in different parts of the country. Coleman urged his readers to utilize his booklist as a logical starting point in the search for an experienced consultant on restoration projects.[11]

The cause of scientific restoration received a great boost with the first published results of the Williamsburg restoration. William Perry's "Notes on the Architecture," which appeared in the December 1935 issue of the *Architectural Record*, was a summary of the scholarly discussions that had highlighted the Williamsburg experience. Perry employed his gift for understatement when he admitted that tremendous problems had been involved in the study of Virginia architecture. The draftsmen had begun to do their studies by means of books, measured drawings from magazines, and visits to older buildings in the Tidewater area. He described the challenges involved in carrying out both archaeological and documentary research, and then he typified the spirit of the drafting room in well-chosen words:

> The problem [architectural research] confronting the fortunate architects in 1927 was made up of all these things and many more. The trouble was that at the time neither they nor any one else had a full realization of them.
>
> There was little known precedent; there was no precedent in this country for a reconstruction or restoration of such scope and magnitude; there was no precedent for the reconstruction of a large group of buildings which were to represent the appearance of a complete town at a given period—and thereby hangs the tale of years of effort, conference and adjustment so to balance all considerations that the result, with its inevitable inconsistencies of coexistence and the like, would present a convincing and attractive appearance.
>
> There were no architects, draftsmen, craftsmen and mechanics trained to put their unerring hands to the delicate task of so constructing each mass and detail at the first attempt that there would be no necessity to demolish and to try again.
>
> It was evident that investigation and training must precede restoration and that careful choice of associates and assistants must precede both.[12]

Several other statements ruled out "fakery" in the use of old materials for reconstruction or in conscious efforts to "antique" new work.[13] Thoughtful architects who read the Perry article must have realized how great the responsibilities would be whenever they undertook restoration work in the future.

Two years after the initial publicity on the Williamsburg restoration, W. A. R. Goodwin prepared an article for the *National Geographic* that started with a brief statement by John D. Rockefeller, Jr. Both men emphasized the inspirational goals of the project, and Goodwin stressed the importance of "authenticity" in presenting Williamsburg to the visitor. He had unbounded faith in the research efforts of 1928 and 1929, boasting that "every possible source of documentary evidence" in Europe and America had been located and utilized.[14]

At least one historian took time during the 1930s to deal with the philosophical problems of restoration. Aubrey Neasham, then regional historian in the National Park Service, centered his attention on the master-plan concept as it applied to Monterey, Calif. In the *Pacific Historical Review* for June 1939 he outlined for his colleagues the way in which he had helped to draw up a plan for keeping the city of Monterey a "living community" with historical values. He argued that the population of the peninsula area included a great many "historians, writers, artists, nature lovers, educators, scientists, business men, workers, home-makers, sportsmen, people of wealth, and world travelers." How could the town ever become a dead historical exhibition? Although the final preservation plan was still under study, Neasham believed that Monterey could prove to be an example in formulating the principles of preservation through cooperation between historians and other cultural groups.[15]

Herbert Clairborne, who had helped to restore Stratford and a number of other houses in Virginia and Maryland, offered a brief statement on restoration in the 1951 *Notebook* of the Walpole Society. Clairborne theorized that the "guiding light of any restoration is the purpose for which it is to be used." Under the title "Philosophy of Restoration" the Virginian reasoned that at least four variables could significantly alter the direction of a project: Was the building in question (1) a memorial to a person, (2) a symbol of a cultural development, (3) the setting for an important event, or (4) an old house that was to be made over into a comfortable residence? Once these questions had been answered, the success or failure of the restoration depended wholly on the "sympathetic and understanding mind" of the person in charge.[16]

The proponents of renovation found a vigorous champion in architect W. Duncan Lee. In 1933 Lee described, under the title "The Renascence of Carter's Grove," his extensive alteration of a major Virginia mansion. Lee disarmed his purist critics by placing his philosophical cards on the table in the first paragraphs:

I started to head this "The Restoration of Carter's Grove," but I feel that the word "restoration" has been stretched far out of shape and I don't want to start an argument right at the beginning. An old building can be and should be faithfully restored, and left at that, if it is to be used for museum purposes solely, but if a person buys an old house, pays a lot of money for it, and intends to use it as a year-round home, he is not going to be satisfied to take his bath in a tin foot-tub and go to bed with a candle in one hand and a warming-pan in the other just for archaeological reasons.

So the job has got to be a "restoration-plus," and the plus is a great big part, like the plus in those cost-plus contracts. What is there must be brought back to its original condition. What has been destroyed must be replaced in keeping, and the whole preserved for the future. This we may call "restoration." When enlargements are absolutely necessary, a precedent of the period should be found and followed, and while this cannot be truthfully called a restoration as applying to this building, it is still a restoration of a condition of the time as shown by other examples.[17]

Lee proceeded to show how he had added wings to the house while he extended the roofline upward to accommodate bedrooms in the attic. He boasted that he had added modern conveniences with a minimum of disruption to the "original work." In fact, Lee believed that the atmosphere of the house had been retained.[18]

WILLIAMSBURG RESTORATION THEORY

There is really only one way to understand the theories worked out by the preservationists of 1926-49, and that is a case-by-case analysis of their projects. Fortunately the people who carried out the Williamsburg restoration sensed their unique mission, and they left an adequate record of their deliberations.

Two of the people most concerned about the philosophical questions posed by the restoration of the old city were W. A. R. Goodwin and his son Rutherfoord. Kenneth Chorley noted the unique influence of the person who had initially inspired the restoration: "Dr. Goodwin had a very fertile imagination. He had a very daring mind. He could get on a horse and ride off in all directions at the same time, and he had a terrific amount of nerve. He, not having the responsibility of financing Williamsburg and directing it, so to speak, as Mr. Rockefeller really did during those early days, had much more time to sit around and let his very fertile mind work. The result was that he could foresee the great

Sketch of brickmaking for restoration at Williamsburg, 1933. (Drawing by Thomas Mott Shaw, Colonial Williamsburg Foundation)

educational potentiality of Williamsburg."[19] William Perry quickly discovered that Goodwin was really interested in total reconstruction of the city and saw how the skills of the architects could contribute to the inspiration: "He was living within the atmosphere of the original setting of events. He could visualize the preservation of the many original buildings still extant and, further, the recreation of the important buildings that had been lost by fire or by demolition. His approach was intellectual; it was most important that such was the case. The architectural

960

concept was inherent but by no means controlling in his mind but he saw at once that only through architecture could the picture be recreated."[20]

At first Goodwin was so caught up in the idea of saving all of Williamsburg for its inspirational value that he had remarkably little interest in authentic restoration. The *Baltimore Sun* made fun of him editorially in November 1924 by suggesting that he wanted to put wax figures of the founding fathers in the reconstructed Capitol.[21] Goodwin replied that he *did* favor the installation of bronze and marble figures as well as a series of portraits of Virginia notables![22]

In the summer of 1928 Goodwin admitted to Arthur Woods that after a few months of watching the restoration he realized that the research was absolutely essential and would require more time than anyone had expected. The contractors should not push the architects into preparing working drawings when vital documentary and archaeological information still needed to be put into usable form.[23] By February 1929 Goodwin completely accepted the viewpoint of the Advisory Committee of Architects when he told Woods that the "essence" of the restoration *"must be fidelity to an ideal, rather than fidelity to a time schedule."* The contractors must wait. He realized that if the experts in the fields of history, architecture, art, and archaeology were going to contribute to the planning process, it was going to take time.[24] Goodwin also agreed that it was important to retain every possible remnant of old Williamsburg, even at some extra expense.[25] In a few cases he sent letters to Perry that offered specific comments on restoration work in progress, but he realized that the architectural staff in Virginia was quickly building up enough expertise to answer almost any question he might raise.[26] For example, Goodwin tried to get the architects to install rough-hewn beams in the rooms of restored houses—not realizing that the draftsmen had discovered that the Williamsburg homes of the eighteenth century simply did not have exposed framing in the formal rooms. He gently campaigned for the inclusion of log outbuildings, an idea that Harold Shurtleff quickly killed because there was no evidence for that kind of construction in Williamsburg.[27]

Everyone who worked with William Archer Rutherfoord Goodwin has said in one way or another that his thinking was always ahead of the ideas fostered by other people at Williamsburg. Essentially working as a dreamer and a futurist, Goodwin began as early as the spring of 1930 to be deeply concerned about the need to advertise and interpret the exhibition area.[28] He saw sooner than anyone else that scholars all over the nation would soon be looking to the architectural staff for restoration precedents. He warned Woods that Williamsburg should be prepared to greet visitors who would come to study it "critically and realistically."[29] In 1933, just as John D. Rockefeller, Jr., was thinking about closing down the restoration program, Goodwin proposed to Kenneth Chorley that the large houses that faced the Market Square and the Palace Green be restored in order to give visitors an understanding of the life of the upper middle class in the colonial capital.[30] He could never resist the inclination to push for the kind of project that would fully achieve his ideal.

The restorers of Williamsburg realized that they were not going to be alone in planning their giant project. Perry decided to meet Fiske Kimball and A. Lawrence Kocher in the fall of 1927 in order to get their viewpoints. Kocher was willing to defer totally to the ideas of Kimball, so Perry went to Lemon Hill mansion in Philadelphia to talk to the famous architectural historian. Kimball told Perry that the drawings for the restoration of the Wren Building at the College of William and Mary had to be as simple as possible, no matter what the "Wren tradition" might appear to dictate. Perry reported to Goodwin that several New York architects had been favorably impressed with the relative excellence of the design of the restored Wren Building, whereas Kimball and Kocher had stressed the importance of adhering to known Virginia precedents in surviving eighteenth-century structures. It must have been a real education for the Boston architect to hear both sides of the restoration question—beauty versus authenticity.[31]

The year 1928 was an important philosophical turning point in the restoration process for Perry, Shaw, and Hepburn. When they prepared the first drawings to be presented to Rockefeller and his associates, the shift toward authenticity had begun. Orin Bullock, one of the younger architects on the staff, remembered this change in emphasis:

Ideas of academic restoration were almost unknown when Perry, Shaw and Hepburn were employed. They went to Williamsburg, looked it over and prepared a set of sketches done in the currently popular garden-city manner—beautiful, lovely drawings, an artist's conception, not carefully supported by historical or other research. But we all very soon realized that we had an academic and not a design problem. I think it's this contribution that Williamsburg has made to preservation more than anything else—that one doesn't design when preserving or restoring. Nothing should be reproduced which has not been based or proved by a proper precedent.[32]

Perry himself faced two great challenges in the fall when he acted as spokesman for his partners. He had to prepare a report to the officers of the Williamsburg Holding Corporation that gave a clear definition of the scope of the work. Soon afterward he chaired the first meeting of the

Advisory Committee of Architects. In both cases Perry had to present philosophical statements that could serve as guidelines for the enormous enterprise that was about to transform Williamsburg.

In the report submitted on September 21, Perry defined "restoration" in a new way, showing how his thinking had evolved through two years of research and discussion. He acknowledged that a strict "restoration" of Williamsburg to the year 1780 would mean the omission of some important buildings that would otherwise present a full picture of the city's contributions to history. So he proposed a new long-range goal: "A composite representation of the original forms of a number of buildings and areas known or believed to have existed in Williamsburg between the years 1699 and 1840." Perry believed that adhering to his definition would permit visitors to trace the architectural development of the community; any voids in the composition could be filled by moving in old houses from nearby communities or by designing faithful reproductions of most of the buildings that had disappeared.[33] As Rockefeller's vision of a totally restored city came into focus, the architectural staff had done enough research to know that no eighteenth-century structures from nearby communities could equal a series of carefully executed reconstructions.

Perry's long association with the Williamsburg project was summarized in 1946 in a "General Statement" in which he attempted to word a definition of "reconstruction" that described the goals of the staff in the 1930s: "A reconstruction or representation of the original building in a form best suited to the purposes to which it is to be put and embodying all of the embellishments that one hopes that it originally possessed."[34] This approach permitted the architects to work toward some degree of authenticity while preparing drawings of buildings that could be useful in the future as dwellings or shops. In time Perry, Shaw, and Hepburn found that they were so adept at working in the style of Tidewater Virginia that they became "proxies" for the builders of a bygone era. It was a responsibility they all took seriously.[35]

A statement of the fundamental purpose of the whole project had been proposed by Fiske Kimball at the 1928 Advisory Committee meeting. He wanted to know whether it was simply an effort to preserve the old buildings or whether Goodwin and the Rockefeller organization intended to oversee the reconstruction of an entire city "in such a way as to show the whole Colonial economy." Goodwin replied that he thought the restoration should present a picture that would be "representative" of the past even if it was not a total reproduction.[36] Lawrence Kocher seized on this admission to push his purist views on restoration practice. He hoped that any new materials used in the buildings would be clearly marked as belonging to the twentieth century, as had been the case in England.[37] Perry sidestepped the issue skillfully by pointing out that private homes would obviously include features that had been added over the years for the convenience of the families that had lived there. The Architects' Committee urged Perry and the Rockefeller staff to retain all buildings up to at least 1840 if they had any elements of the classical tradition left in them (although Williamsburg ceased to have historical significance after the government moved to Richmond in 1780). It was assumed that post–Greek Revival structures would mar the ideal picture of an eighteenth-century city.[38]

At the end of the two-day session Kimball and his associates drafted a set of twenty resolutions that provided the Williamsburg staff with a set of guidelines embodying an essentially conservative philosophy of restoration practice. Nearly half of the proposals dealt with the retention of every possible scrap of colonial brickwork or wood in the buildings. Kimball attempted to commit Perry, Shaw, and Hepburn to a binding agreement that would prohibit the predominance of new work in a fully restored Williamsburg, but when Perry finally prepared a decalogue for the project this point was conspicuously missing. The revised guidelines included a pledge that wherever possible old buildings would be preserved on their original sites, even if they were not in the restored area. Perry carefully differentiated between preservation and "restoration," which to him was really reconstruction. He also noted that restoration work should be much slower than ordinary construction and he commended the use of old materials for repairs if they were properly marked.[39] The Advisory Committee even went so far as to urge that no well-known colonial doorways or important features should be copied in the restoration. It was quite enough to prepare designs that had the same general character as the features found in other Virginia houses, but it was another matter if Williamsburg were to become a museum of carefully contrived borrowings.[40]

In December, Perry went to New York City to face Arthur Woods and some of the Rockefeller confidants who would be working on the Williamsburg restoration. The minutes of the Architects' Committee became the focal point of the discussions because Woods was anxious to know how Perry had fared in his encounter with the handpicked experts. The representatives of Todd and Brown, the contractors, were present at the New York meeting, and they bristled at the thought of spending extra money to save every possible fragment of eighteenth-century work. Woods listened to the arguments from both sides, although he believed Rockefeller would prefer to preserve rather than reconstruct.

Woods concluded that even if the retention of some old timbers involved the expenditure of a few thousand dollars, it should be done.[41]

Within a comparatively short period it had been possible to work out a general policy for the restoration of the principal buildings in Williamsburg. During the spring of 1929 the Perry, Shaw, and Hepburn office issued several revised statements on the work to be done, but the principles did not change. It was clear that the architectural experts had insisted on keeping as much original eighteenth- and early nineteenth-century material as possible, and it was equally obvious that Rockefeller was willing to cover this additional expense.[42] By 1930 there was a general working procedure that included a series of consultations starting with Rockefeller himself and going down through the research office to the architects and the archaeological crew.[43] Perry understood what he was supposed to do, and he was prepared to do battle with the contractors if their natural inclination to rush the project interfered with maintaining the guidelines that had been enshrined in the minutes of the meetings in New York and Williamsburg.

But it is impossible to understand the restoration philosophy that emerged at Williamsburg between 1928 and 1934 simply by consulting the statements of purpose and the guidelines issued by Perry, Shaw, and Hepburn. One must turn to the story of the building operations and the initial decisions that were made in the effort to move toward the goal of historical authenticity.

Wren Building

The logical place to start is the Wren Building of the College of William and Mary, the first large operation planned in the restoration scheme. Many of the people who worked on the Wren Building referred to it as the "training school" for what followed.[44] No one learned more than William Perry, and once he found evidence for some particular feature in the old structure, he held courageously and persistently to the cause of historical truth.

In his 1946 "General Statement" Perry admitted that his initial presentation drawings of the Wren Building had been somewhat similar to the authentic form, but he and his partners had included "a door frame of undisguised 'Westover' type" on the main entrance. Fiske Kimball and Lawrence Kocher insisted that the architects study the structure carefully and restore the doorway correctly.[45] In November 1927 Perry received a letter from Kimball offering one important guideline for the restoration process: "Exhaust first every vestige of evidence as to what the old was actually like."[46] That is exactly what the architects tried conscientiously to do. They began with a most important document, a daguerreotype showing the east front of the Wren Building shortly before the fire of 1859. They realized that this photograph substantially represented the 1710 reconstruction of the college after a fire had destroyed most of the original edifice.

Even before the Advisory Committee of Architects met, some crucial decisions had to be made so that the contractors could begin work. The old walls of the main college building had withstood at least three fires (which had weakened them), and the top story of the 1710 facade had been removed in the nineteenth century. Ancient brickwork would have to be reproduced for a full-scale restoration. At first Perry and the contractors tried to buy old brick from the surrounding area, but they soon found that it was impossible to find enough. The staff in Williamsburg was delighted to learn that a few experiments with the local clay had led to a rediscovery of the secret of making eighteenth-century bricks![47]

In June 1928 the indomitable Perry encountered one of the greatest challenges of his Williamsburg career, although it was not immediately apparent. He discovered that because the Wren Building was the property of the Commonwealth of Virginia, the Art Commission would have to approve all of the designs. This turn of events meant that Perry had to deal with the chairman of that august group, Edmund S. Campbell of the University of Virginia.[48] Campbell was in the peculiar position of sitting on both the Art Commission and the newly constituted Advisory Committee. He could easily have found himself in the dual role of helping Perry to develop the ideas that would eventually win the approval of the commission that he administered.[49]

An impasse developed for nearly six months while Perry, Shaw, and Hepburn argued with the Art Commission of Virginia. On December 10, 1928, Campbell made it clear to the Boston architects that he believed the entrance portico added in 1710 was undignified, and a return to the 1699 appearance (based on a crude eighteenth-century sketch) was the answer. He also noted that his committee would insist on revising the first-floor plan (for reasons no one really understood) and would want a larger cupola.[50] Perry gallantly promised to study the whole situation to see if a middle ground existed, but he could find no room for real compromise. Underneath the surface of this conflict was a much more important issue: the depth of the commitment of the Williamsburg restoration program to historical accuracy.

The net result of the long delay and the interminable correspondence that flowed between Charlottesville and Boston during 1929 was positive, but one that was not readily apparent to the protagonists. The

Wren Building, Williamsburg, daguerreotype ca. 1859. (Photographic copy, Colonial Williamsburg Foundation; reproduced by permission of the College of William and Mary)

more William Perry and his partners studied the criticisms of the Art Commission, the more convinced they became that the plans as prepared were indeed the best answer. Perry had a strong case: He had the nineteenth-century photograph, a painting from the eighteenth century, and the evidence uncovered on the old brick walls themselves. Campbell made a move that could have been his trump card—he set out in a vain effort to locate Wren's original plan for the building. The nineteenth-century photograph simply would not satisfy him.[51]

The Art Commission delivered its full report in December 1928, and it listed three principal objections to the Perry, Shaw, and Hepburn design: (1) The entrance pavilion was ugly and poorly proportioned; (2) the cupola should be larger in order to be in scale with more recent buildings at William and Mary; (3) the interior stairways were incorrectly placed according to "Wren" precedent.[52] Eventually Perry won his battle for the 1732 design because he had the weight of historical and archaeological evidence on his side, and he had wisely permitted a long and thoughtful discussion of the issue. He stood firm, in spite of threats from Campbell and despite warnings from the contractors to Rockefeller that the delay was costing a great deal of money.

The Wren Building debate became a major testing ground for the subcommittee of the Advisory Committee of Architects, and Perry used his distinguished colleagues with great skill. He consulted closely with Fiske Kimball, Milton Medary, Robert P. Bellows, and Robert E. Lee Taylor. Medary, for instance, gave a strong argument for putting in the brick entrance pavilion added in 1705. He noted that the seventeenth-century facade had existed only two or three years before it was partly destroyed by fire, whereas the building that Perry wanted to display "was occupied by the college during the 150 years of its influence on American history."[53] Kimball supported Medary's arguments by urging that no "surviving feature" should be changed. Kimball even went so far as to admit that the connection with Sir Christopher Wren was tenuous at best, and so comparisons with the major works of the great English architect were irrelevant for a colonial building.[54]

In January 1929 Perry met with the Art Commission and the officials of the college in Gov. Harry Byrd's office in Richmond. Perry thought that he had won an important point when those present appeared to accept the 1732 building as the principal focus for the restoration. The commission, however, still refused to agree to the narrow brick entrance pavilion that appeared in the surviving pictures. At this point Perry's dependence on historical research and his growing conviction that Rockefeller wanted the restoration to be accurate became stronger than his sense of artistic taste. Campbell never fully succeeded

Courtyard excavations, Wren Building, Williamsburg, ca. 1929. (Colonial Williamsburg Foundation)

in making the same jump. A passage from a letter Perry sent to Arthur Woods shows how difficult it was for a trained architect to give himself wholly to the cause of an archaeologically correct restoration: "A restoration of the building of 1732 requires accurate restoration of every part regardless of its architectural quality or divergent opinions as to the same. We believe that the central entrance and cupola should be as shown. The College and the Art Commission do not like the entrance architecturally any better than we do and request restudy with a view to improving the appearance of the building. We agree that something better could be invented but we have stated that the invention would defeat the purpose of the restoration."[55] Perry had one more powerful argument. The excavations at the Wren Building had revealed that the foundations of the 1710 brick pavilion still existed up to the level of the water table. The entrance was an addition, but the bricks appeared to be quite similar to those in the 1695 foundations. In a letter to an unconvinced member of the Advisory Committee Perry revealed how Andrew

Hepburn cleverly pushed Campbell into the philosophical position of a vandal:

> We believe the Art Commission to be inconsistent but very seriously concerned in procuring the best possible result. "Hep" saw Campbell in New York the other day and discussed this matter with him. His statement to Campbell that we cannot assume the responsibility of demolishing brickwork of such an early date, since we feel certain that it antedated 1732 (the date of the restoration) and his enquiry as to whether Campbell would personally sanction the demolition of this old work, caused Campbell to remark that the matter should be very seriously considered before any demolition is done.[56]

By March Perry had become so convinced of the rightness of his stand on retaining the entrance pavilion to the Wren Building that he secretly admitted to Kimball that the steelwork for the new entrance had already been ordered.[57] The partners in Boston were prepared to debate the issue as long as the Art Commission wanted to, but there would be no retreat on the essential question of a correct restoration insofar as the available evidence could be interpreted.

In June, Woods took the final plans for the building to Governor Byrd, who decided in favor of Perry, Shaw, and Hepburn.[58] Byrd had become so distressed at the delay that he was prepared to fire the whole Art Commission![59]

A more difficult decision had to be made with regard to the restoration of the west side of the Wren Building. The pictorial material available for planning the elevations of the courtyard was not as trustworthy as the daguerreotype that had decided the principal features on the front of the building. The architects depended heavily on the existing brick walls, but there was evidence of considerable damage from the fires.[60] Andrew Hepburn, who was the principal designer for the firm, admitted to Walter Macomber in the Williamsburg office that there was much conjecture in the preliminary designs for the west side: "We have gone over the West elevation from every angle and believe this is the best thing to be done. Remember that the little girl's drawing [mid-nineteenth century] has nothing to do with the elevation we are trying to restore. The original elevation was modified completely some time before 1820 and there is no record of what it was except old brick work which remains at the ends of the piazza. Starting with this information we have worked out these windows as best we can."[61]

Campbell objected to the design as it had been prepared in Boston. He thought the arrangement of the windows was not a good one, although he had no record as to what the original plan may have been.[62]

The architects were concerned because the new delay was holding up the process of framing the Wren Building in steel (to support the ancient brick walls). But in that instance Campbell's intransigence saved the Rockefeller organization money, because the most important research discovery of the entire restoration process was only a couple of months away.

On December 24, 1929, Perry, Shaw, and Hepburn received a telegram from W. A. R. Goodwin in Williamsburg telling of Mary Goodwin's finding in England of the copper plate that showed both sides of the main building of the college.[63] Several curious hipped gables appeared on the roofline. Perry asked Arthur Woods to authorize the money necessary to make the rear roof conform to the picture on the Bodleian plate.[64] Speaking for Rockefeller, Woods agreed to the necessary changes (which cost about $20,000) as long as the advisory architects concurred.[65]

The Wren Building continued to be a training ground for the architectural staff. Hepburn corresponded with Fiske Kimball in an effort to get an expert opinion on many involved restoration questions: the best wood for the chapel, the placement of doors, the most logical number of window panes for the east front of the building.[66] Thanks to the historical references drawn together by Earl Swem in 1928 and to the archaeological notes of Prentice Duell, by 1931 the architects had a complete set of reports to guide them through their deliberations. The research data covered every major phase of the college restoration project—architecture, archaeology, history, and structural engineering.[67] At one point nearly every person in the drafting room had something to do with the drawings that had to be prepared for the contractors.[68] There were compromises, but in general the staff learned to put aside its own artistic preferences in order to present all of the features that were known to have been present in 1732. The letters and reports show a certain degree of excitement as it moved from one discovery to another. The whole staff, from the three partners down, found itself becoming thoroughly imbued with the spirit of the eighteenth-century builders.

Restoring Houses

The treatment of the houses of Williamsburg turned out to be as much of a challenge as the restoration and reconstruction of the public buildings. Although it had been Goodwin's dream to restore the entire city to its appearance in the colonial period, it was clear that many of the houses would not be used as exhibits. Some would have to be rebuilt, and those that lacked the elements of "classical tradition" might be removed. Decisions on questions of restoration, reconstruction, and demolition did

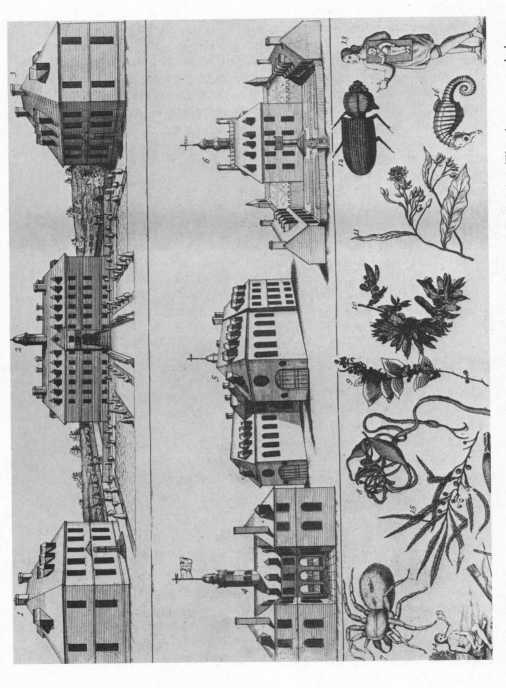

Copperplate engraving of Williamsburg, found in the Bodleian Library, Oxford University. The plate was made between 1732 and 1747. Top panel, the Brafferton building, the main building, and the President's House of the College of William and Mary; center panel, the Capitol, the rear of the main building of the College of William and Mary, and the front of the Governor's Palace; bottom panel, flora and fauna of Virginia. (Colonial Williamsburg Foundation)

Wren Building of the College of William and Mary, Williamsburg. (Colonial Williamsburg Foundation)

not invite easy or categorical answers; it was a case of weighing all the factors, such as cost if all original material was to be saved, historical authenticity based on a long process of research, and the future use of each house.

The Rockefeller staff decided that the Ludwell-Paradise House (1757) on Duke of Gloucester Street would eventually become an exhibition building. However, the interior finish of the house presented a dilemma. There was evidence in the walls that there probably had been woodwork, but almost none of the original paneling had survived.[69] The first meeting of the Advisory Committee explored the controversial issue of using old paneling from other houses in Virginia. Some of those present wanted to be sure that the Perry, Shaw, and Hepburn firm would not become known as a group of looters that moved freely through the Old Dominion buying up rooms from old buildings.[70] In this case William Perry had already been offered some fine paneling by dealers who suspected that the restoration would need it, and Arthur Woods had authorized the purchase.[71]

When Walter Macomber prepared to restore the Ludwell-Paradise House in the spring of 1930, he encountered directly the historical and ethical question of using the old woodwork. Fiske Kimball said that he was "very dubious" about the process unless he could be absolutely certain that the house had originally been paneled. He favored leaving the interior with plastered walls because a number of eighteenth-century houses had been finished off in that way.[72] Macomber reasoned that the two rooms he had purchased fitted into the house "remarkably well." The only problem seemed to be that the fireplace openings in the paneling did not fit the larger openings in the Paradise rooms. Macomber asked if it were better to desecrate the house itself or to cut into the woodwork.[73] Robert Bellows favored changing the fireplaces to fit the old woodwork and using the remaining fireplaces of the Paradise House as evidence for whatever had been there.[74] Kenneth Chorley wanted to be sure that Kimball approved the proposed changes, and soon a letter from the Philadelphia Museum director helped to reassure the Williamsburg staff. If there was clear evidence of blocking in the walls for paneling, then Kimball agreed to the installation of the rooms Macomber had purchased.[75] There was a more disturbing note from Lawrence Kocher in New York: "It is my understanding that the Paradise House will be one of a group of restored houses in Williamsburg. As such, the interior should necessarily be the original interior or a reproduction of the original. To bring in paneling and fireplaces from other houses would be to change the actual appearance of the old Paradise House. This is a strict interpretation of what I consider a desirable restoration."[76] Kocher suggested that the paneling, if ever used again, could be labeled carefully as coming from some other site.[77] Macomber did install the old woodwork even if it violated the "pure" spirit of a restoration. He believed that a house museum required a formal backdrop for antique furnishings.[78] The fireplaces were altered and the Williamsburg staff has continued to acknowledge the presence of woodwork from Petersburg, Va., in the Paradise House.[79]

The restoration of important old houses that were not intended to be open to tourists but were to be maintained as private residences posed just as many problems as the work on the Ludwell-Paradise House. The research that was done on the St. George Tucker House, for example, revealed a multitude of difficult decisions that would have to be made because the building had been changed in so many ways over a century and a half. To begin with, the Tucker House contained substantial portions of an earlier house that had faced the Palace Green until 1788.[80] This smaller building probably was associated with the family that operated the first theater in Williamsburg. But by 1930 the Tucker-Coleman House had been extended in several directions and had been raised to a two-and-a-half-story structure.

In February 1929 the Perry, Shaw, and Hepburn offices stated that as a matter of policy the houses that were to be used as private homes would be subject to detailed exterior restoration, but "it would not be necessary to touch the interiors."[81] Shortly after this pronouncement the Williamsburg organization purchased a life interest in the St. George Tucker House from George Coleman, and the agreement specified that the house would be made livable for the Coleman family.[82]

This acquisition gave Andrew Hepburn an opportunity to warn Chorley and the Rockefeller staff:

> It seems to me that a decision in regard to the first point [a complete interior restoration] is one of policy and is still undecided. If the construction is in such sound condition that the interior does not have to be ripped out, we have no objection to making only necessary repairs. In making such repairs, however, should substantial changes in interior finish be necessary, we would make them in accordance with the character of the original building. (You of course, understand that we would prefer to restore the interior as well as the exterior of this building.)[83]

Chorley decided that the most logical procedure would be for the architects to do the necessary research and then submit two sets of plans and cost estimates, one specifying only repairs to the inside of the house and the other calling for a complete restoration.[84] The alternatives were estimated at $38,000 for the exterior restoration with general repairs for the interior and $41,000 for the complete restoration. Hepburn considered the house to be one of "great importance" and suggested that the larger figure would provide results that would be amply justified in the future.[85] Chorley agreed with the architect's recommendations and authorized the restoration of the house at the then impressive figure of $41,120.[86]

The Coleman family moved out and watched with a mixture of relief and horror as the contractors took their house apart board by board. Mrs. Coleman and her husband went abroad for some of the time, but they attempted to cooperate with the staff in every way possible while the work was going on. She noted in her diary: "Besides the strain of emptying the old house, we had a nerve-wracking time discussing plans with the architects. We lived in a waste of blue prints which we were supposed to study and approve. We felt positively panicky, lest we should indicate approval of some point which we had completely failed to grasp."[87]

The placement of the outbuildings on the Coleman property seemed to be another great challenge. By 1930 there was a two-story Greek Revival office somewhat in front of the house that everyone thought should be somewhere else in the yard. Ultimately the little building was cut down to one story and moved to the site of a garden building discovered by Arthur Shurcliff's excavators.[88] Mrs. Coleman found Shurcliff to be an "alarming" person. He appeared to be a "terribly enthusiastic man" who wanted to tear up every vestige of the Coleman garden in order to put in plants that he knew had been used in Virginia in the eighteenth century, including a tremendous amount of old boxwood.[89]

There was a postscript to the St. George Tucker restoration program that came up a few months after the Colemans took over their refurbished home in 1931. Perry told Chorley that the placement of the outbuildings had forced the restoration staff to make a fundamental decision about the appearance of two of Williamsburg's principal open spaces, the Market Square (which included the St. George Tucker House) and the Palace Green (which went along the west side of the Tucker-Coleman garden). At that point in the planning the architects believed that the first theater would be reconstructed on the side of the green, so it seemed logical also to rebuild the home of William Levingston, who had operated the theater. The foundations had been discovered in the garden of the Tucker House. Another possibility was to install the reconstructed coach house and other outbuildings that had surrounded the St. George Tucker House at the end of the eighteenth century. But the Levingston House still existed; it had been moved in the 1780s and was the center portion of the Tucker House! In both cases Perry noted that groups of buildings would be set up that had never existed together at a given time. The reconstructed Levingston House would complete the picture of the Palace Green, but it would be an anachronism because the Tucker home was a later structure. On the other hand, the Tucker coach house had never faced the Green while the original Palace was still standing. Perry concluded: "Thus if, as we maintain, the importance historically of the appearance of the Palace Green is greater than that of any of its component parts, we must abandon the tempting proposal to reestablish the Tucker-Coleman domain, with its . . . outbuildings."[90] The advisory architects agreed with Perry's reasoning and urged the rebuilding of the Levingston House and outbuildings.[91] Hepburn and Perry showed that they had developed a clear sense of the picture that Goodwin and Rockefeller had in mind, and they wanted to construct that complete ensemble if at all possible. Finally they reconstructed the Levingston kitchen and left the Tucker House group on the Market Square.

The achievement of the picture of an eighteenth-century city was not a simple matter, and the Maupin House on Duke of Gloucester Street illustrates another facet of the agony of decision making, that of compatible styles. The Advisory Committee of Architects had decided at its first meeting that all buildings in Williamsburg displaying elements of the "classical tradition" should be retained even if they had been constructed later than the general 1780 cutoff date for the restoration.[92] When Perry drafted the first report to the Williamsburg Holding Corporation he stated, "It is an obvious assumption that it is not contemplated that such buildings as the . . . Maupin and other fine houses of the Early Republic Period shall be destroyed."[93]

In the late 1920s the Holding Corporation purchased the Maupin House subject to a life tenancy. Under the provisions of the agreement, architects could restore the house but they could not remove it. The home was situated directly across from Bruton Parish Church and could be seen from the Palace Green. Its prevailing style was Greek Revival, and the best research that could be done at the time led the architects to conclude that the structure dated from the late 1840s. In the summer of 1930 Walter Macomber requested permission to make some repairs to the building, but Chorley urged that everyone consider carefully the whole question of keeping the house in the restored area.

It was decided to proceed with the working drawings on this building on the following basis: The Greek exterior and interior trim of this building is obviously part of the original building and may definitely determine the period

Maupin House, Williamsburg, razed 1930. (Colonial Williamsburg Foundation)

of the building as early 1800. The thought has been that it would serve as a comparison between the Colonial and this period, and in spite of the fact that this building has been recommended for partial restoration, it is possible that at some later date it may be decided it does not fit the picture and as it occupies such an important position it may seem necessary to remove it and possibly a colonial building replace it.[94]

The issues were now out in the open. In this case the architects and administrators had to face the possibility of destruction—for the purpose of preservation. It appeared to those in Williamsburg in 1930 that only three alternatives existed with the Maupin House: Leave it alone as a good example of Greek Revival; tear it down and construct a colonial house on a foundation that had been located in the yard; or attempt to "restore" it by means of adding some eighteenth-century details to the windows and cornice. There was no discussion of moving the house. Goodwin strongly favored the last choice because the building occupied such an important location in town. Hepburn said that he saw the reasoning behind Goodwin's desire to colonialize the house, but he feared the long-term consequences of such a step: "It is my belief that if the basis of the restoration is to be a picturesque background, there is danger of an unreal, and what I should call a 'movie' atmosphere, which would not be nearly as desirable as a restoration which showed in its architectural reconstruction the various fashions as they came along, eliminating only those things which are bad."[95]

The architects on the Advisory Committee leaned toward Hepburn's preservationist view. Fiske Kimball, for instance, could not believe that the Maupin House "could ever be really inharmonious with colonial Williamsburg or injure the setting of Bruton Church."[96] However, most of the consultants admitted that the presence of the Greek Revival building in the heart of the Georgian city made them uneasy.

In spite of all the earnest pleading from the architectural authorities, the Maupin House did disappear in 1931. This remarkable case of destruction can only be explained as evidence of the growing power and influence of the staff in Williamsburg. Walter Macomber, as resident architect, complained to Perry, Shaw, and Hepburn that he could not countenance the presence of an unrestored mid-nineteenth-century house in the center of town. After all, said Macomber, buildings of the same era had been torn down in other parts of Williamsburg as a step toward the restoration of the whole city. Macomber also pointed out that the advisory group was evenly divided between those who strongly urged retention of the house and those who mildly supported its preservation.[97] The minutes for the committee meeting of December 9, 1931, state that the Maupin House had been replaced by a new building on the old foundations. The life tenants had been persuaded that they could live just as comfortably in a new house as they had in the old one.[98] It is difficult to say what really happened, but there is good reason to believe that Perry and Macomber decided that the achievement of the total picture of the eighteenth-century street was much more important than the preservation of a late Greek Revival house. The somewhat indefinite stand taken by the advisory architects had freed the staff in Williamsburg to make the final decision.

Goodwin occasionally let his desire to achieve a harmonious eighteenth-century atmosphere get the best of his preservationist sentiments. As the instigator of the restoration he was deeply committed to the concept of a whole picture, and this was especially true when it came to the Palace Green. He told William Perry in 1930:

The Green and its environment, viewed from the point of view of the Palace or from the point of view of a person walking from the Palace towards the Duke of Gloucester Street, would be harmonious except for the Neale [now called Geddy] House [1730s] and the Greek form of the Maupin House. . . . I raise the question, therefore, as to whether the importance of creating on the Palace Green, which is the center of the Restoration endeavor, a picture which would be as completely harmonious as possible of the early Palace Green period, does not call for a re-study of this problem from the historic and artistic point of view. . . . My own feeling is that the opportunity of doing this in the light of what now exists, in the light of known dates of other structures which do not exist, would justify the ultimate removal of the Neale House and the Maupin House from the picture, unless these two buildings could be restored so that they would be brought into harmony with the unique historic environment in which they will stand.

I especially feel this with reference to the Neale House, where there is distinct evidence of early foundations, and I am wondering if we would not, in the light of this fact, be justified in using as much of the present structure of the Neale House as may be required in the reconstruction of a Colonial house which would be of the appearance of a house which would have been built on the foundations of 1705.[99]

In this memorandum Goodwin violated some of the central guidelines of the restoration program. He was fully prepared to tear down a pre-Revolutionary house in order to erect a brick building across from Bruton Church. Any number of times Goodwin stalked into Walter Macomber's office and attempted to get the architectural staff to make studies of the building that might have been there at one time.[100] When Perry received Goodwin's long letter about the historical and artistic aspect of the Palace Green, he made a pencil notation on the last page, under the doctor's signature: "I think the doctor is wrong—my idea of reconstructed Williamsburg is not a town which is homogeneous, but a town which has remained *unspoiled*. This in a sense was the attitude of the consulting architects who passed upon this point."[101] Perry then composed an answer to Goodwin, which was a characteristic example of the Bostonian's soundly reasoned prose. The Neale House, he argued, would "justify" itself once the landscaping and fencing had been put in. Perry maintained that it would be a great mistake to move a house of "known colonial derivation" and replace it with a reconstruction that would have to be based on scanty evidence. At the same time he admitted to Goodwin that the Maupin House, which was not even on the old property line, might have to go. After all that house was "palpably modern" compared to the Neale House.[102] In this case Perry's desire to keep the town "unspoiled" carried the day, and the Neale House was saved.

There were other instances where neither Perry nor Shurtleff could save old buildings that the senior administrators considered expendable. In the fall of 1934 Kenneth Chorley decided that a small dwelling called the Craig House should be torn down. It was deteriorated, and the property was outside the restored portion of Williamsburg. Nevertheless, Shurtleff, looking at the situation from the vantage point of the research office, concluded that the house of a working family should be preserved. The Craig House had a somewhat unusual floor plan that gave it some architectural interest.[103] Perry asked Chorley to sell the property if the Williamsburg organization was determined to remove it. "If the house must be destroyed, would it not be better that it be destroyed by another owner than the Restoration?"[104] Eventually it was demolished at Chorley's request because the senior staff concluded that there was not enough antique material left in the house to warrant a restoration.[105]

At the beginning of the restoration program Goodwin proposed that old buildings from the countryside around Williamsburg be brought in and placed on the old foundations that existed all over the city. He offered to send his son Rutherfoord out into the Tidewater to locate these relics and to purchase them for a nominal sum.[106] When Dr. Goodwin brought forth this proposal in May 1928, no one on the architectural or administrative staff up to that time had given any thought to the probable consequences of introducing other houses into the restored area, so the Rockefeller offices authorized the purchase of a small brick home in Tabb, Va. Macomber soon began to put pressure on Perry, Shaw, and Hepburn to help find a suitable location for the Tabb House.[107] Thomas Shaw had a suggestion, but he admitted that the house could not be moved in until the whole staff had decided whether to reconstruct the building that had originally occupied that site.[108] For two years Macomber and Harold Shurtleff debated the merits of various locations throughout Williamsburg, but there always seemed to be historical problems that made them unsure about the appropriateness of each proposal for placing the Tabb House. Helen Bullock of the Research Department, for example, favored the site of a tavern near the Capitol. Shurtleff's lukewarm support of her idea illustrates the complexities of the situation: "The justification for putting the Tabb House up there, in case digging showed no indication of the character of the building, whether brick or wood, would be that our records do not disclose the fact as to whether the Blue Bell was built of brick or wood, and therefore we might be entitled to recommend the place as a site for the

Tabb House. The fact that we know the thing was a tavern and that the Tabb House was a residence would have no bearing on the subject, because we know that a great many houses were converted into taverns."[109] Ultimately the restoration took the Tabb House down and used portions of it for repair work in different parts of Williamsburg. As can be seen from Shurtleff's reasoning, it was almost impossible to introduce a building onto an existing foundation once research had established the size, use, and construction of the structure that had disappeared.

Landscape Restoration

The architects quickly discovered that Arthur A. Shurcliff, the landscape architect, operated as an independent entity within the restoration scheme. He did his own excavating and visited sample gardens in the South and in England.[110] Perry found that Shurcliff shared the "forward-looking zeal" that motivated the restorers in other departments.[111] But the research staff found that it was almost impossible to get him to change his mind once he had studied the layout for a particular garden.[112] Harold Shurtleff had grave reservations about some of Shurcliff's plans for the more elaborate gardens in town.

The difference between the approach to landscape restoration and the work of Macomber's staff can be traced through the evolution of one design in the Governor's Palace park, the maze. Shurcliff had declared in his initial report, drafted in September 1928, that "pretty close adherence to historic precedent will be necessary in laying out the gardens."[113] It should be noted that such a vague phrase as "pretty close" does not appear in the reports of the architectural department. In October 1934 Shurcliff was putting the finishing touches on the garden area north of the Governor's Palace, and he proposed to Kenneth Chorley that a maze would be "appropriate" as a feature in front of the mount. Shurcliff did not claim that there ever had been a maze in Williamsburg, but he did point out that the proposed addition would be inexpensive to install and easy to maintain. He referred to the popular maze at Hampton Court in England as a logical precedent.[114]

The wily landscape architect then sent a long letter to Perry, Shaw, and Hepburn summarizing his arguments for the new garden arrangement. The justification did not read like one of Harold Shurtleff's tightly reasoned research reports: "I think the authenticity of mazes in England at our period is a more important matter for us to consider than mazes in Virginia at that time. In our Palace work it has been necessary to look to England constantly because the Virginia data had either perished or was doubtful. Under these circumstances we have not hesitated to copy English designs."[115] Shurcliff added that he had found references to

The Maze, Governor's Palace garden, Williamsburg, 1970. (Colonial Williamsburg Foundation)

983

mazes in literary sources that dealt with the colonial South. But the bulk of the five-page report consisted of artistic and economic arguments for the inclusion of the maze.

Apparently Chorley was amused by the whole idea, and he told Perry, Shaw, and Hepburn that he did not care whether there was a maze. He just wanted to be sure that if there was to be one on the Palace grounds, it should be planted right away.[116] Perry told Shurcliff politely that the maze sounded like a pleasant idea, but it simply had to be accounted a low priority in the budget for the Palace grounds. After all, Perry admitted, the architects had given up all thoughts of reconstructing the Palace stable because they had been unable to find archaeological evidence for the building. Perry agreed that the maze would be attractive to visitors, but he concluded that any such planting should be postponed until there was "definite information" on the subject.[117] Shurcliff immediately appealed to Chorley's sense of urgency. He told the president of Colonial Williamsburg that the winter of 1935 was the logical time to plant the maze and it would certainly be one of the cheapest additions to the gardens.[118] Perry washed his hands of the matter by telling Chorley that the architects did not think they were competent to express an opinion on the decision.[119] Armed with this partial capitulation, Shurcliff immediately prepared to stake out the plan of the maze. He was certain that Chorley would quickly agree to the idea.[120]

In the Williamsburg research office, Shurtleff thundered away about the plan. He wrote Andrew Hepburn that he had just told Chorley that there were at least seven "unauthentic items" about to be added to the gardens—and one of these was the maze. Shurtleff was deeply concerned about the long-term effect these questionable additions would have on Williamsburg's reputation:

> Inasmuch as our records will presumably remain open to architectural students, and antiquarians, it seems to me that it is only a question of time before somebody puts a stick of dynamite under us on the strength of the above record. A recent editorial in the New Leader [a newspaper] spoke of the fact that the town had been "idealized" (in other words the town is not as it was in the 18th century) and it is only a short step, on the strength of this accepted fact, from the New Leader's kind interpretation of the thing to a hostile, and critical, and embarrassing version of the same thing from some ill-disposed person.[121]

Shurtleff told Chorley in no uncertain terms that there was absolutely no record of a maze at the Palace.[122] Apparently Shurtleff's arguments could not match the economic and artistic appeal that characterized

Shurcliff's reports: The maze was begun, and it has remained a popular aspect of the Palace grounds.

The maze interlude is helpful in understanding the development of the philosophy of restoration at Williamsburg because it illustrates how far the architectural staff had come in its thinking with regard to historical accuracy, compared to the thinking of the administrators and the other professional groups associated with the enterprise. William Perry had learned at the beginning of the restoration process that John D. Rockefeller, Jr., and his lieutenants had expected the architects to utilize all the known avenues for research. They were supposed to adhere as closely as possible to historical truth. The draftsmen and the partners in Boston had become skilled architectural historians (at least in one limited field) by the end of the first phase of the restoration. It was no wonder that they were concerned about any landscape development that did not meet the exacting standards they had worked out for their own construction projects.

Second Phase Restorations

As the first phase of the Williamsburg program drew to a close in 1934, both the techniques and the philosophy of restoration had emerged in recognizable form. The real test of the persistence of the scholarly spirit of the restoration came with the decision to begin a new series of construction projects in 1938. Several of the veterans of the Perry, Shaw, and Hepburn crew came back to assist in positions of greater responsibility.[123]

One of the most elaborate operations in this second program was the restoration of the George Wythe House and its array of outbuildings. In 1928 the advisory architects had told Arthur Woods that they did not care for the rehabilitation that Goodwin had supervised the year before.[124] Ten years later, in the spring of 1938, the Williamsburg veterans finally had their first chance to redo an earlier restoration.[125] Goodwin, who was still alive, offered to turn over all his notes on the work he had done in the 1920s, together with a long description of his interior renovations.[126]

The massive series of reports, studies, and collaborative investigations of the Wythe House exemplify the cool efficiency that pervaded the drafting room in the late 1930s. The same people were at work, but they had the confidence and the knowledge that had come with a decade of experience. At the beginning of the second phase of the restoration, A. Edwin Kendrew prepared a three-page "Check List for Restoring a Building," which outlined in considerable detail every step to follow in

George Wythe House and outbuildings, Williamsburg. (Colonial Williamsburg Foundation)

preparing a structure for a physical restoration. Included were eight different kinds of documentary and archaeological research reports that had to be made for the Architectural Department.[127] The first report that came in from the crew that excavated the yard of the Wythe House displayed the same degree of competence that marked Kendrew's plan of operation. Even when the archaeologist could not identify the use of an outbuilding, he offered a few possible answers and left the final decision up to the architects.[128] In January 1940 Rutherfoord Goodwin requested a complete architectural report on the Wythe House so that he could immediately start to train the hostesses who would show the building to visitors. He realized that a detailed document would insure better interpretation in the future, and he knew that by 1940 the staff had learned how to organize and present the necessary information.[129]

It is clear that the staff members at Williamsburg looked upon themselves as students of eighteenth-century architecture just as much as they had in the early 1930s. But they knew how to read the evidence much more effectively. They had understandable pride in the expertise they had developed through research, and they continued to show considerable respect for every scrap of surviving colonial work in the buildings that were to be restored. Unfortunately, many of the people who doubted the authenticity of the Williamsburg restoration did not realize how much research and careful consideration went into each step in the process of painting the picture of eighteenth-century life. Nor did they appreciate the degree to which the staff in Virginia tried to respond to Rockefeller's perfectionism. From the first meetings with Goodwin, Rockefeller admitted that it was the beauty and charm of the old city that appealed to him, and this information was never forgotten by the architectural staff.

GREENFIELD VILLAGE

Suppose that John D. Rockefeller, Jr., could have invited Thomas Jefferson to inspect the College of William and Mary, and suppose that the retired faculty of William and Mary had advised the Williamsburg staff on the restoration of the college buildings. That is the kind of personal contact that motivated Henry Ford in his incredible attempt to honor his great friend Thomas Edison. At the same time that Walter Macomber was opening up the architects' office in Williamsburg in 1928, in Dearborn, Mich., Henry Ford decided to undertake a total reconstruction of a complex of buildings from Edison's Menlo Park laboratories in New Jersey. The project is an anomaly in the development of restoration techniques because Ford was foresighted enough to reconstruct a site of recent historical importance, with ample documentation available. As discussed in chapter 2, however, his other reconstructions at Greenfield Village did not approach the Menlo Park project in authenticity, and he primarily viewed the museum complex as an educational institution "wherein young boys can be taught the history and development of American manufacture."[130]

Ford himself set out to make all the crucial decisions about the project from start to finish, and he certainly was no authority on the intricacies of the restoration process. Obviously he was a powerful person who could command the services of a great many people—but money alone could not purchase historical truth. To begin with, only two of the original Menlo Park structures were still standing, and one of them had been moved by the General Electric Company to another location. The equipment for the laboratories had been widely scattered in the fifty years since Edison had worked at Menlo Park; some of it was at the Edison offices in West Orange, and other important material was with the Edison Pioneers in New York. Ford had no architect on his staff, and his trusted assistant, Edward Cutler, had really been trained as an artist.[131] Finally, there was a specific deadline for the completion of the Menlo Park exhibit. On October 21, 1929 (the fiftieth anniversary of the event), Ford intended to have Edison reenact the lighting of the first commercially successful bulb, in the reconstructed laboratory. How could a group of workmen who had little professional direction operate under a deadline and produce anything that could be historically accurate?

The extraordinary success of the project can be attributed to a number of special factors: The restoration was intended to show the Menlo Park setting in the late 1870s, and the laboratories had been photographed quite thoroughly at that time; some older men who had worked for Edison freely shared their recollections with Ford's staff—and one of them came to live at Dearborn to reassemble the equipment for the interior of the main building; Edison and his family cooperated completely with Ford because they realized that he was serious about his plan to memorialize the career of the inventor. One final element must be taken into account, and that was the zeal and imagination of Henry Ford. Ford had worked with machinery all of his life, and he fully understood the atmosphere that would be required to produce a busy laboratory. Every item in the Menlo Park exhibit had to be in working order.

For an entire year Ford and his staff became historical researchers, delving deeply into primary source documents in the broadest sense of that term. As soon as the property at Menlo Park had been purchased,

Henry Ford and Thomas Edison at the foundations of the Menlo Park laboratory, N.J. (Courtesy Ford Archives, Dearborn, Mich.)

Ford took Edison, along with some of the Edison Pioneers, to survey the foundations. Francis Jehl, who was there, witnessed a remarkable scene:

> While I was still in New York City I was requested by Mr. Ford to accompany him to Menlo Park where with some of his men he was making excavations. I was surprised to notice that he himself did not hesitate to take up a pick or shovel and help. It was during one of these diggings that he found the pieces of our old mortar which he cemented together and later, when Edison visited the Old Laboratory in 1929, surprised him by presenting it to him. . . .
>
> Still more was done, for Mr. Ford had heard that the old laboratory had been dismantled by farmers and others and that the timber had been used in building barns and sheds as well as for other purposes. Some had collected and saved the wood in large quantities, thinking it would, no doubt, bring its price in the future. He started a hunt that would have made G-men proud, and the country around Menlo Park was combed for miles. He found what he was looking for. Yes—he managed to salvage nearly all the timber of the old laboratory, together with the doors and most of the window stiles. . . . Wherever the timber was located, it was either replaced or new barns, sheds, coops, doors and stiles were substituted.[132]

Civil engineers went out to measure all the foundations at the Menlo Park site so that when Ed Cutler received the carloads of bricks from New Jersey he could place the footings for the buildings in the right order.[133] The Edison Pioneers dutifully traced the later career of the old organ that had stood on the second floor of the laboratory—only to find that it had disappeared. But Ford purchased an identical instrument made by the same company.[134] He sent agents to New York and New Jersey to buy up as much old Edison machinery as they could locate, especially early phonographs and related objects.[135] During the winter of 1928–29 Jehl and a group of Edison Pioneers sat down in New York and drew up furnishing plans that documented each floor of the major Edison buildings. As proof of authenticity, the sketches contained the signatures of the veterans.[136] Some of Ford's assistants wrote to factories that had manufactured the equipment Edison had used in the 1870s and 1880s to see if there might still be extra machinery available.[137] In furnishing the Sarah Jordan Boardinghouse across the street from the Edison complex, Ford made sure that he got some original furniture from Jordan descendants and the correct type of wiring for the electric lights. The prime importance of the boardinghouse was the fact that it was the first dwelling to be illuminated by incandescent electric bulbs.[138] One embarrassed member of the Edison staff offered Ford some washroom equipment that the inventor had used, and the material was soon on its way to Dearborn.[139] Another Edison Pioneer went out to Menlo Park and picked off some clippings from the rose bush that had stood by the laboratory.[140]

By May 1929 the pace of the operation had quickened, and the center of activity shifted to Dearborn. Ford asked Jehl to move to the Detroit area to assist in the placement of the equipment.[141] The laboratory complex was soon back in its original setting. Seven boxcar loads of red clay from the New Jersey site had been spread out, along with Edison's trash pit. Ford sent Edison pictures of the restoration as it moved along and even asked him to practice a few chords on an organ before coming to the Golden Jubilee so that he could play on the instrument Ford had purchased for the laboratory.[142]

Perhaps the real secret of the successful Menlo Park restoration was in the fact that Henry Ford was preparing for an event that could never have been attempted in Williamsburg. He wanted to have the original owners reoccupy the reconstructed buildings. The culmination for Ford was the day that Thomas Edison came to Dearborn in the fall of 1929 and stepped back into his own past. Francis Jehl was there to greet his old boss, and he recorded the event:

Edison's eyes now began to scintillate, for ahead of him he saw—no, his eyes did not belie him—his Menlo Park laboratory, all so real as though time had swung back for a half century. When Mr. Ford led him through the picket gate by the office building his gaze was centered on the ground— could it be—yes, it was the real red Jersey clay. Looking up, he saw me standing on the laboratory porch. Waving his hand he cried out: "Hello, Francis," and I hastened toward him. We entered the old shrine, and the enraptured thrill that he experienced admits of no description. Yet when we had ascended the stairs to the second story he simply stood there for a few moments in dumbfounded amazement; his lips quivering seemed to ejaculate a prolonged silent—"Aaa—hhh—!"

When he had recovered, he walked around; checking some of the chemicals in the bottles, and, finding everything in order and genuine, he passed on and gazed affectionately on the instruments and apparatus with which he had worked. There they were—it seemed hardly possible—all in order and everything as it was in 1879.[143]

The placement of the buildings and trees was so exact that Edison soon forgot he was in Michigan. A few days after the Golden Jubilee, while still at Dearborn, Edison mentioned in a conversation with Jehl that he had once employed a carpenter from Metuchen, and at that instant Edison absent-mindedly pointed in the direction of that city—as if he had been back in Menlo Park![144]

Although the American people could admire the way in which the auto manufacturer had paid tribute to his friend Edison, there was reason to believe that no other restoration of such magnitude could be carried out at that time. The Greenfield Village development was unique, and its influence grew principally through the comments of the thousands of people who visited the buildings. There was no public relations staff to spread the ideas of Henry Ford to other restoration projects. A few reporters did interview Ford with the intention of getting at the essence of his philosophy, and they usually turned in stories that dealt with his ideas on education.[145] Comments from people such as Charles Peterson and William Perry show that professionals who visited Greenfield Village found the whole arrangement so puzzling that they could not discuss Ford's restoration techniques.[146]

STRATFORD HALL

The situation was quite different with Fiske Kimball's restoration of Stratford Hall in Westmoreland County, Va., which provided guidelines for much future restoration work. The people who founded the Robert E. Lee Memorial Foundation wanted to repair the birthplace of the great Confederate general in the most reverent and scholarly manner possible. Mary Van Deventer, chairman of the Restoration Committee, feared that an imaginative renovation of the house would be a disaster. In March 1929 she told May Lanier, president of the foundation, that it was absolutely essential to hire real experts:

> I think architects are pretty poisonous. They do not care a hoot whether the results of their work and plans is to make an old thing exactly like it was, they want their own ideas set forth, and their ideas may or may not conform to facts. If I was in charge nobody would even drive a nail on the whole premises until it had been decided after investigation that a nail had been in that place when the house was first built. That is one of the things your Foundation is for. To do research work and find out what is to be done to put the place in its original form, and that will be a large part of the pleasure in the future that comes from holding it. . . . An architectural restoration simply won't do. That is what they are doing at Wakefield, of which they have no original plans or even a sketch of the property, and when they claim it is a *restoration* with a view of making believe that it is a replica of the original, well I won't say what it is, for by a miracle they may hit on Wash-

ington's Wakefield, but the chances are about a million to one against it. So I think architectural restorations are anathema.[147]

Mrs. Lanier quickly assured her friend in Tennessee that the two architects she had talked to were genuine "scholars—experts—archaeologists." One of these men was Edward Donn, who had already prepared the drawings for the conjectural reconstruction of Wakefield.[148]

William Lawrence Bottomley, the New York architect who volunteered to supervise the immediate repair of Stratford, urged the foundation to undertake a "scientific survey" of the building. He proposed that every structural feature of the house and outbuildings be recorded at once.[149] In the winter of 1930 Bottomley ordered the work crew to store a number of stone fragments of balusters in the old kitchen.[150] He theorized that the discovery of these remains made it likely that the exterior stairway on the great house was a later addition and that there may have been no interior stairways in the eighteenth century.

When Fiske Kimball was selected to supervise an authentic restoration of Stratford, he chose to reward Mrs. Van Deventer's admiration with an essay on restoration, in which he revealed his innermost thoughts on the proper treatment of old buildings.

In such a precious building the dominant thought, no doubt, should be *preservation*—and the greatest conservatism should be exercised as to changing anything, even if this is believed to be changing it back the way it is supposed formerly to have been. More harm has perhaps been done to historic buildings by ill-judged "restoration" than by neglect, and such damage is really irreparable. In a building with a long history, where certain minor changes have been made from time to time, there is an interest in these traces of centuries which would be lost in an attempt to "purify" the style by making it all once more of the first period of its building—replacing what is, after all, now of respectable age by what is merely new. I think that there would be general agreement that at least any work which preserves the classical tradition, even down to the time of the Confederate war, should be undisturbed.

An even greater danger is that, in any work which is undertaken, our modern preferences in artistic matters be indulged, when really we should follow the evidence as to how things *were*, whether *we* would have made them that way or not. Thus if the evidence is that certain interior finish was painted from the start, we should not leave it unpainted just because "It seems a shame to cover up such beautiful grain"; or, if we find a certain original color, change it because *we* don't like it, and pretend it must have faded! . . . You will readily realize from all this . . . that preserving and restoring an old house is quite a different thing from designing a new one, and takes quite different qualities in an architect—not imagination, but historical knowledge; not originality, but self-abnegation.[151]

This extraordinarily conservative statement became a watchword for administrators and public officials all over the country in the years that followed. Laurence Vail Coleman quoted it in his book *Historic House Museums*, and twenty years later the Kimball letter was circulating in the offices of the National Park Service in mimeographed form.[152] Kimball carved out a most challenging role for himself at Stratford, considering the fact that he was going to have to be in Philadelphia most of the time the restoration work would be going on.

Mary Van Deventer never swerved from her original inclination toward Kimball. Once Kimball had been hired, he studied the garden plans that were based on the excavations of Arthur Shurcliff and Morley Williams for the Garden Club of Virginia. Kimball began to analyze insurance policy notations, inventories of estates, and other documents that might assist him in getting a picture of how the rooms in Stratford were used at different times.[153] He decided to start two projects right away: roofing the house with a permanent material and preparing an extensive report on the restoration.[154]

By October 1932 he was able to send to the foundation headquarters a statement on the restoration procedure entitled "Stratford Yesterday and Tomorrow." He included his preliminary conclusions on the way in which the house had been constructed and offered his theory on the original room arrangement. Much of this part of the report had been based on his inspection of the mansion itself.[155] He commented that there was evidence that the original south staircase had been "much handsomer than the present one," in view of the fact that so many ornate stone balusters had survived in fragmentary form.[156] He included a five-page essay on the development of restoration philosophy in France and Britain in the nineteenth century. Kimball refused to put himself in the camp of the restorationists who chose to follow the French model and return a structure to a certain date. He also declined to stick with English precedent and retain every possible vestige of old work: "If we chose to be consistent with 1810 we should have to rebuild, by guess, the north porch of 1805, and leave the awkward stairs of that year which so much injure the old beauty of Stratford. Too strict adherence to the doctrine of preservation would condemn us to keep every makeshift replacement of the period of dilapidation. We must follow, instead of an exact consistency a wise opportunism, keeping in mind both authenticity and beauty."[157] Kimball revealed that he had already made two important judgments about the future of the restoration program in these

Stratford Hall before restoration, 1932. (National Park Service)

few sentences. The south stairway (which was more than 100 years old) marred the "old beauty of Stratford," and the additions put on after 1810 belonged to the "period of dilapidation." These aesthetic pronouncements did not reflect the same philosophy that he had enunciated in the famous 1930 letter, where he proposed to keep any old work that retained elements of the classical tradition.

The first major repair job at Stratford involved shoring up the wall of the old kitchen. Kimball was proud to note that he had been able to introduce new brickwork so skillfully that no one could tell where the original portion of the wall joined with the new work.[158] He spent hours exploring the house as the contractors took up old floors to check on the timbering, and he "read" the woodwork in an effort to detect the different changes that had been made in the nineteenth century.[159] He cheerfully accepted the discoveries of General Cheatham, the resident superintendent, and admitted that the general had indeed located evidence for the original stairway arrangement.[160]

By the time Kimball had reported on his first year of restoration activity in the fall of 1933, he had come to the conclusion that there had been only one small interior stairway in Stratford before 1805. He also proposed to repair three rooms that had been redecorated by Robert E. Lee's father in the early nineteenth century.[161] This suggestion fitted in well with the idea of respecting all later additions that adhered to a classical standard. In fact, he attempted to head off a movement on the part of one of the directors to remove some 1805 woodwork in order to carry a room back to the early eighteenth century. Kimball told her in several different ways that he had no evidence for the design of the earlier paneling.[162] He warned Mrs. Van Deventer that the foundation had a difficult choice: "Do we want 1805-old, or do we want 1740-new?"[163] In the hallway outside the room where Robert E. Lee was born Kimball ordered that some nineteenth-century partitions be retained because they were part of the ensemble that existed at the time of Lee's birth.[164]

During the summer of 1934 Kimball and his assistant Erling Pedersen discovered some evidence for large brick stairways at the east and west ends of the house. The problem was that the profile of the former stairway did not give substantial clues as to the design of the railing.[165] Kimball wrote on one drawing sent to Pedersen, "God only knows how the parapet and coping went."[166]

The next summer Kimball embarked on the most controversial of all the projects in the restoration program. He proposed the construction of a set of stairs on the south side of the mansion that conformed to the evidence deduced from the stone balusters that had been found all over the front lawn. He was certain that he had studied the foundations of the nineteenth-century stairway enough to tell how the masonry had been constructed originally.[167] Cheatham did some excavating on his own and came up with a different theory on the foundations, but this time Kimball did not listen.[168] During the fall the old stairway was removed, and the contractors began to install a larger set of steps that supported new stone balusters.

When the directors of the foundation first looked at the addition, there was considerable consternation. Mrs. Van Deventer reported to Kimball that she considered the stone stairs to be "a master piece of architectural effort," but she had to admit that about half of her fellow board members did not agree with her. Some of them refused to believe that there had been conclusive archaeological evidence for such a massive set of steps.[169] In addition, Kimball had forwarded a set of drawings for an equally large brick stairway to go at the east end of the mansion, and he had not followed proper procedure in checking with the different committees.[170]

Stratford Hall after restoration.

Throughout the storm Fiske Kimball patiently stuck to his guns. He studied the garden walls and the stone balusters that had been dug up—and concluded again that the south stairs had been placed there in the eighteenth century just as he had restored them.[171] By 1941 the essential exterior work had been done, including four large stairways leading up to the second floor of the house.[172]

When one surveys the story of the first Stratford restoration, one realizes that it would be unfair to say that Kimball did not live up to the guidelines he proposed for sound architectural practice. He violated some of the conservative methods described in his 1930 letter because he definitely disliked some of the changes made to the house in 1805. But the 1932 report on Stratford did become the policy statement for Kimball's work; it was to be a compromise between the retention of the old and the removal of additions that detracted from the historical and architectural picture (this was sometimes a question of personal taste). The whole process was a heavy responsibility for a man who was administer-

997

ing a major art museum, and it was probably Kimball's great knowledge and extreme self-confidence that carried him through the period when the foundation board seriously considered replacing him. He left a fairly clear record of all of his decisions, and he never failed to listen patiently to his critics as the work progressed. Kimball was a true scholar, and he could look back on his work at Stratford in 1941 with a great sense of satisfaction.[173] If the Robert E. Lee Memorial Foundation had carried out the restoration in more recent times, it is possible that it might have come to some different conclusions. Neverthless, Kimball undoubtedly made a considerable contribution to restoration scholarship while he helped to revive the home of the Lees.

WILLIAM SUMNER APPLETON'S RESTORATION THEORIES

Other experts had developed their own theories on restoration by the 1930s, most notably William Sumner Appleton of the Society for the Preservation of New England Antiquities. His far-flung real estate empire demanded so much of his time and skill by the late 1920s that Appleton never really engaged in the full supervision of a major project after the Abraham Browne House in Watertown, Mass., in 1919.[174] But he continued to dictate long letters to anyone who asked for his advice on subjects pertaining to preservation. His correspondence shows that while he had a fair amount of respect for architects who had done restorations (many of whom were his friends), there was no substitute for looking at the evidence in the building under consideration. At times Appleton believed that a thoroughgoing renovation was needed (particularly with seventeenth-century buildings), and in other instances he urged his correspondents to settle for minimal repairs.

Because Appleton often summered on the island of Nantucket, he took personal interest in the restoration of the Jethro Coffin House (1686). In 1925 he outlined in a six-page letter a complete program for the local historical society if it sincerely wanted to return the little building to its original appearance. Near the end of the essay he urged the Nantucket people to take a great many pictures of the house while the repairs were in progress so that visitors could study these photographs in later years. In many ways Appleton showed he was an elitist when it came to restoration: "Eighty per cent of the visitors will probably care nothing about this, but their opinions will be of no interest whatsoever to the Historical Society and to notable antiquarians. It is the opinion of the other 20% that counts, and most of all the smallest group of that 20%, those who know the subjects thoroughly and will look to this house for instruction and inspection for further work in New England."[175]

In 1930 Appleton engaged in a protracted and good-humored debate on restoration philosophy with an architect in Mendham, N.J., named William W. Cordingley. The subject that started the fuss was a brief note from Cordingley to Appleton's assistant, George Francis Dow, regarding the upcoming restoration of the Old Ship Meeting House (1681) in Hingham, Mass. Appleton had printed a favorable article on the Hingham project in *Old-Time New England*, and he was sincerely interested in trying to work with the architects who had begun to remove the ceiling that covered the famous seventeenth-century framing.[176] Cordingley warned Dow: "I am sorry they are bringing Hingham Meeting House up to date—that is a date it never was in such condition before. The old building had an accumulated serenity worth a whole lot of exposed beams—far more than they show—and any one could get into the attic to see. Another generation will talk about us if we are not careful, as people do about the English Cathedral restorers!"[177] Once he had seen Cordingley's letter, Appleton was intrigued with the supposition that he might be listed with James Wyatt and other radical restorers of the previous century. Appleton admitted that the SPNEA might have taken more pictures of its own restoration work as a matter of historical record, but he thought the project at Hingham was both sensible and conservative.[178] The New Jersey architect replied that many restorers either thought too much about their own personal convenience or they concerned themselves completely with aesthetic considerations to the exclusion of historical truth. Cordingley even hinted that Appleton had been guilty of the first error in working on the Browne House.[179]

The intimation that Appleton had been willing to compromise his prize restoration for convenience was enough to bring forth a five-page letter. With the Hingham restoration Appleton stoutly maintained that the congregation needed to use the building, so it could not be put back exactly the way it was. But when he looked back to the Browne House work done in 1919, he pointed out how many unfortunate changes had been made on the little building because W. W. Cordingley, acting as an architectural adviser, had thought the modifications would make the living quarters more serviceable. Appleton admitted that he had made some compromises in his own recent restoration of the Richard Jackson House in Portsmouth, N.H., where conjectural seventeenth-century casement windows had been installed. But the recent SPNEA work in Newbury, Mass., he maintained, would stand the test of time:

The more I work on these old houses the more I feel that the less of W. S. Appleton I put into them the better it is. I am perfectly certain that 999 restorers out of 1000 working on the Tristram Coffin, Jr. house at Newbury would have made all sorts of changes that I didn't make. In fact I am positive that William W. Cordingley would have done something to the front door that I left, just what no one on earth would be able to say, but nevertheless I left there a perfectly good classic porch and door of about 1850. On opening this you are faced with the staircase built not in 1651 but at the time that the chimney and stairs were altered, perhaps twenty or thirty years later, whereas the doors from the entry into the rooms on each side are of goodness only knows what dates, and so it goes throughout the house. It shows the process of evolution during 280 years and it seemed to me that it should be continued to show this process which was of infinitely more interest than a restoration of the old appearance of any part of the building would have been.[180]

But there were instances later in his career when Appleton chose to abandon the preservationist theory. Over the protests of Robert P. Bellows of the Williamsburg Advisory Board, Appleton and Frank Chouteau Brown restored the front of the Emerson-Howard House in Ipswich, Mass., to two different centuries. Appleton could rarely resist putting in a reproduction when he found an opening for a casement window, and in this case he succumbed. In a letter to a descendant of the Emersons he boasted that the two-part facade would prove to be "one of the most attractive" in New England.[181]

Sometimes the secretary of the SPNEA supported the decisions of his colleagues in restoration practice. For example, Appleton continually encouraged J. Fred Kelly of New Haven through the difficult renovation of the Whitman House in Farmington. Kelly was completely dependent on one patron for the money to do the work, although the building was to serve the needs of a local historical society. Appleton first found out the approach Kelly wanted to take in the restoration, and then he turned around and wrote to the man who was sponsoring the operation. Appleton did not hesitate to tell him that Kelly was "one of the very best outstanding antiquarian architects in the country."[182] Curiously enough, the patron had decided not to hire Appleton to supervise the work at the Whitman House because on a previous visit the Bostonian had proposed stripping the building down to its frame in order to fix the chimney and put on new clapboards with casement windows. All the distraught philanthropist could say was, "Why, that man Appleton wanted me to tear the whole house to pieces!"[183] Apparently there was just as much con-

Howard House, Ipswich, Mass. (Photograph by Samuel Chamberlain, SPNEA)

cern over contrasting approaches to restoration in New England as there had been in Virginia.

Private organizations that did not employ architects and other professional help occasionally had to wrestle with difficult restoration decisions on their own. One unusual example of this approach shows how involved an apparently simple repair job could become. In 1930 the First Church of Christ, Scientist, in Boston purchased the house on Broad Street in Lynn where Mary Baker Eddy had completed the first edition of the Christian Science textbook in 1875.[184] The principal restoration challenge centered on the little attic room where Mrs. Eddy had worked on her manuscript. The church authorities knew that there was a widespread conviction among Christian Scientists who made the pilgrimage to Lynn that Mrs. Eddy had written *Science and Health* sitting in a chair under a small skylight.[185] This idea was based on a drawing in one of her books of poems that depicted her at work in a room similar to the one in Lynn. The directors of the church decided to "duplicate" the illustration.[186] However, the picture showed no other source of light in the room except the skylight, and the house in Lynn had a back window on the top floor along with the skylight. The church officers debated whether the window might have been a twentieth-century addition or whether the artist had taken liberties with the facts.[187] The people who were going to interpret the house to visitors finally reasoned that the published biographies of Mary Baker Eddy did not prove conclusively that the back window was an intrusion, so it remained.[188] It is hard to imagine a more questionable source for a furnishing plan than an illustration in a book of poems, but the Christian Science board of directors was well aware of the degree to which this picture had implanted itself on the memories of church members, and Mrs. Eddy herself had assisted the artist. The entire discussion had been restricted to people who worked for the church, not to an architect or decorator. The result of this consultation was a restoration that reflected a compromise between the room shown in the book of poems and the physical arrangement of the house as it stood in 1930.

STATE RESTORATION POLICIES

Whenever restoration projects continued for a considerable time, there were almost always heated debates over doubtful points in historical accuracy. The state agencies that supervised the larger work programs of the 1930s had to develop policies on historic sites. This was especially true with the states of Illinois and California, where professional staffs worked over a number of years on several different kinds of projects.

In Illinois the philosophy of Joseph Booton in the state architect's office prevailed during the years that he was chief draftsman. Booton and his assistant, Jerome Ray, were not dogmatic in their adherence to one particular approach to restoration and reconstruction, but they did develop a keen sense of history and an appreciation for the "picture" of the past. Ray noted that he and his boss often sought outside advice: "We always tried in the case of historic restoration projects to have a, shall I say, restoration or authenticity committee . . . to sit down with us and review our findings so that we got an outside point of view on it. Sometimes you get so close to a project yourself you can't see it as a whole. You have to get back and look at it from afar to get the proper perspective."[189]

In 1937 a controversy with a respected colleague forced Booton to spell out his goals for a reconstruction. Henry Pond, a local historian in

Petersburg, Ill., sought to develop at New Salem State Park a village-industries program using the money and material that had been earmarked for the reconstruction of the first Berry-Lincoln store.[190] Robert Kingery of the Chicago Regional Planning Association (and former director of the Department of Public Works and Buildings) sided with the stand taken by Pond. Booton quickly realized that a local committee was working with Kingery to turn the Berry-Lincoln site into an archaeological exhibit. That threat was real enough to impel Booton to state his theories on reconstruction as they applied to the log village he had helped to recreate in the early 1930s. Booton warned that an exposed excavation would conflict with the policy of reproducing the whole town "to the last detail with absolute authenticity." He proposed that no effort be made to furnish the store (as there was another Berry-Lincoln store already open to the public). Then Booton summarized his reasons for preferring the reconstruction:

This [rebuilding the store] will accomplish the following:
(1) Keep our usual practice of authenticity.
(2) Avoid a "park" feature in the village.
(3) Add a cabin in the gap between the two surveys.
(4) Use up the material for the purpose, thereby pushing the final completion just that much closer.
(5) Explain the excavations and how they looked *when first opened*.
(6) Will not require additional furniture or supplies.
(7) Complete a link in the *Lincoln Chain of Cabins*—i.e. those Lincoln had direct contact with.
(Since this village is a memorial to Lincoln this cabin is *very* important since he actually traded here and a certain portion of his time was spent here.)[191]

Kingery, with equal fervency, presented his arguments for omitting the building. He noted that a number of other sites in the New Salem plan had been omitted because they did not have a high priority. Kingery gave a different definition to the term "authenticity":

How much more interesting and how much more authentically correct will it be to retain the present depression, have the bottom drained and sodded, have the fragments of foundation just exactly as they were found, connected together and possibly reinforced to prevent their injury by vandals, leave the sides practically vertical or sloped and sodded as may seem appropriate, keeping it clean, of course, retain the foundation for the chimney and cornerstones where they were found and be able to answer one question which is most often asked namely, "How do you know about all this?" . . . Our usual practice of authenticity might be bettered by retaining this excavation and fragments of foundation. Who knows but that the building was burned or that it was taken down and moved elsewhere and merely a hole in the ground left shortly after it was vacated as a store or as a residence. In that case, might not our restoration of the excavation be the most authentic?[192]

From all indications Booton read this disquisition and then decided to stick to his own policy. He had the ultimate power to carry out the reconstruction if he wanted to, and yet he continued to debate with Kingery. In fact, he went to Chicago from Springfield to try to convince his former chief that the completion of the village scene at New Salem was the most important consideration.[193] In a follow-up letter Booton offered two more compelling arguments: The foundations would be extremely difficult to maintain as an exhibit from the standpoints of drainage and vandalism; on top of that, the public clearly wanted to have a building. The CCC guides at New Salem had taken the trouble to ask a number of visitors about their reaction to the open hole on the site of the Berry-Lincoln store. The statistics were impressive: 976 favored the reconstruction, while only 302 preferred the kind of archaeological exhibit Kingery proposed. Booton readily admitted that there should be educational features in the park, but like Rockefeller and Goodwin in Williamsburg, he was convinced that the Berry-Lincoln site was too near the center of New Salem to be anything but a visual intrusion if it served as an archaeological exhibit.[194] In his usual friendly way Booton closed off the discussion.

In California there was no architectural staff to work on restoration projects, but Newton Drury, acquisitions officer for the State Park Commission, tried to draft a policy for the historic sites under state administration. On August 27, 1937, the commission adopted a seven-point statement that Drury had prepared.[195] It included a comment on preservation that proved Drury was leaning in the direction of the Ruskin ideal: "Recognizing that the original and genuine has more meaning historically than a replica, no matter how skillfully finished, emphasis is to be placed upon protection and preservation, rather than upon restoration [reconstruction]. All modification of historical sites and structures, as they now exist, should be undertaken only after specific authorization of the Commission, based upon the best available expert advice."[196] The commission also immediately approved a set of "recommendations" that were intended to put the new policies into effect for each of the properties in the state system. The commissioners agreed to defer any state intervention on policy matters at La Purisma until the National Park Service and the CCC had finished the reconstruction.[197]

In most other projects Drury's reluctance to destroy old work was re-flected in the emphasis on repairs rather than replacement.

NATIONAL PARK SERVICE POLICIES

The federal government tended to become the most important single agency in the field of restoration simply because of the size of its program and the quality of the professional staff. As soon as the CCC moved into state and federal park areas with historians, architects, archaeologists, and landscape architects, there was certain to be debates on the best way to recreate the atmosphere of earlier epochs. Park Service executives looked on the historic sites they administered as educational tools. Visitors would see each area as it appeared at the moment of its greatest historical importance.

The historians and administrators who began to thrash out a National Park Service policy on historic restorations in the mid-1930s already had the example of Colonial Williamsburg, with its architectural emphasis. They attempted to move beyond the focus of a single community restored to a particular time. Verne Chatelain, in a 1933 report to associate director Arthur Demaray, scorned the idea of acquiring typical "archeological or architectural remains of different periods" if that put the Park Service in the same position as the local historical societies that had already begun to do this work. The new chief historian wanted a broad historical program that took into account the most important trends throughout the nation's history. He asserted that the historian is a "philosopher" because he works with causes and effects in an analytical fashion. In the Park Service frame of reference the historians had to hold to the larger picture—the development of American nationhood.[198]

When Dr. Goodwin heard that the Society of Colonial Wars was pushing for a national historic-sites program, he added his own twist to the idea. The next step, argued the creator of the Williamsburg restoration, was to fashion a "national policy and programme" that could greatly enrich the life of all Americans.[199] And that was exactly the role the Park Service staff had begun to assign to itself.

Even before passage of the Historic Sites Act, historians in particular became aware of the fact that they were going to be setting standards for restoration work all over the country and that restoration had to be part of a larger interpretive process.[200] The planning sessions that preceded the writing of the Historic Sites Act provided a forum for professional people from different parts of the Park System to contribute their ideas on the concept of restoration. The Group Conference of Historical and Archeological Superintendents held in Washington in November 1934 was one such meeting. Harold Bryant, who represented the educational end of the Park Service program, expressed his concern over the way in which the emergency labor force available to the Park Service had suddenly facilitated large restoration projects:

> Dr. Bryant says that the idea of time is an important element in history and he is opposed to general restoration of an area for it takes away from the historical atmosphere. Mr. Chatelain agreed with this. Dr. Bryant opposed a complete restoration in military and historical areas. Some should be left in a more or less "fallen-down" condition to show the changes in time.
>
> Mr. Flickinger suggested a policy of "type" or "sample" restoration.
>
> Dr. Bryant mentioned a statement made by Dr. Merriam of the Educational Advisory Board that we are ruining historical areas by too much restoration.
>
> Mr. Flickinger suggested the term "restoration" as compared with "reconstruction" as perhaps not expressing just what the group has in mind.
>
> Mr. Demaray said that if he understood things correctly, our policy should be one of partial restoration. For example, Fort Pulaski is a place where some restoration should be done, but not a complete restoration. Our old policy has been the practical view of making certain restorations, but also keeping the physical remains as nearly as possible the same so that people can see them, as we have found them. This has been our only policy up to the present time and is more or less definite. Mr. Demaray believed that Wakefield is purely a restoration or as nearly one as anything which we have done. On the other hand, he said that the Moore House is a "reconstruction" rather than a "restoration."
>
> Mr. Flickinger stated that he felt what Mr. Spalding [of Fredericksburg Battlefield Park] wanted was a definite policy outlined to present to visitors when they come into an area.[201]

These new Park Service officials were sensitive to the fact that they were operating in an era of experimentation, and they yearned for clear policy guidelines. It would take another two and a half years for these ideas to appear in the form of an official statement from the director of the Park Service, but the search for historical truth continued unabated.

When Secretary of the Interior Harold Ickes testified in behalf of the Historic Sites Act in 1935, he suggested that the proposed Advisory Board would provide the "specialized knowledge and experience" needed to devise federal policy on preservation and restoration.[202] W. A. R. Goodwin warned the legislators that the times demanded that the government of the United States take a role in preservation-policy planning. The American people, said Goodwin, were becoming "history-minded." They were coming into Williamsburg by the thousands. Now it was time for the federal government to pick up where John D. Rockefeller, Jr., had left off.[203]

Passage of the Historic Sites Act intensified pressure on the Department of the Interior. Ronald Lee warned assistant director Conrad Wirth that "if we do not carry this program to the States soon they will bombard us with requests for statements of our attitudes and place us in a position where we are simply defending ourselves rather than carrying the program to them."[204] Ickes said essentially the same thing in February 1936 when he greeted his first Advisory Board, and he empowered the experts to make their own policies.[205] Within a few hours the board members discovered that they were deeply involved in preservation planning for the whole country. There had to be some set of standards if the federal government were to grant money to state and local governments. The board concluded that there should be a "central agency such as the National Park Service, to pass on plans for the excavation, restoration and reconstruction of sites."[206]

During 1935 and 1936 Chatelain and Lee continued to hire historians for all kinds of supervisory and survey assignments. These men often came directly from graduate training into positions of considerable responsibility. They sometimes had to advise on restoration work at historic sites that were developed under the Emergency Conservation Work—and the uneven quality of the projects they inspected often produced a rude awakening. The more experienced Park Service historians, who had been on the job only a few years, were more concerned about the status of the national preservation movement as federal money became available. It is fairly surprising today to find an essay on restoration theory buried in a 1936 report by regional historian Olaf Hagen on the development of Tumacacori Mission National Monument. He claimed that the National Park Service would have to develop principles and policies in its restoration work in order to serve as a "model" for other organizations. Hagen reasoned that it would be utterly foolish and dishonest to restore the interior of the mission ruin when there was no dependable evidence to tell the restorers what had been there originally.

The proposed restoration of altars, pulpit, and choir loft are neither justifiable nor possible. These details of the interior of the building are not necessary to its preservation. Furthermore, as Mr. Tovrea's report shows, the information necessary for the restoration is not available. His recommendations are based on what he terms "substantial and logical proof" and on "the very best and latest guesses." The other Kino missions studied were found to be "radically different" from each other, and San Ignacio only is "probably" like Tumacacori. To permit the piecemeal reconstruction proposed under the guise of "restoration" would be tolerating architectural and artistic license comparable to the doctoring of documents. The results would not present the visitor with an accurate picture of what these details were originally, but what they were believed to be by certain individuals in 1936.[207]

Hagen pointed out that he had never seen a restoration where the atmosphere of the past had been achieved by the addition of details by modern restorers. He argued that at Mission San Diego de Alcala in California and Mission San Jose in San Antonio, Texas, capable architects had supervised the work, but both of these projects had failed to recapture the indefinable quality a visitor found in a church that was still in use. Hagen detected an "atmospheric effect" at Mission San Xavier del Bac in Tucson, Ariz., where the Indians have worshipped continuously since the eighteenth century. At Tumacacori this same feeling of authenticity could be retained as long as the Park Service determined to do nothing more than to stabilize the old church as a ruin. The only repairs Hagen could countenance were minimal changes required to keep the building from deteriorating. His logic, of course, was intended to support the construction of the interpretive museum as a means of developing the mission site.[208]

From the first meeting in the winter of 1936 it was obvious that Fiske Kimball was going to be a major influence on the Park Service Advisory Board although Clark Wissler of the American Museum of Natural History and Hermon C. Bumpus also played important roles. Charles Porter described Kimball's role:

I think he is the man mainly responsible for the original Advisory Board restoration policy. He almost certainly was, because he was the only man competent in that group to speak on the subject, and he had done a great deal of restoration work himself. He was thoroughly versed in the history of restoration policy and practice from Viollet-le-Duc's time to the present. I have always had great respect for him. He made enemies readily; some of the members of the Board hated him, but he again could carry conviction because of his sheer bulk (he was a big man physically) and his intense conviction in what he was saying. He just bulldozed his way along. I'm sure when our restoration policy came up, it was basically his work and that he put it over almost single-handedly.[209]

Whether Kimball's influence was the principal driving force or not, four important policy statements regarding restoration came out of the

Park Service between 1936 and 1938, and in all probability the historical staff initially drafted these statements. The first of these concerned restoration and archaeological projects funded by the Works Progress Administration. After August 1936 all programs that involved historical areas had to have the approval of the regional officers of the National Park Service. This directive did not guarantee that historians and architects in the regional offices would have the chance to review each proposal, but it certainly helped to prevent some ill-considered reconstructions.[210]

At the Advisory Board meeting in March 1937, the question of a restoration policy for battlefield areas came up. Acting assistant director Branch Spalding, who was an expert in battlefield interpretation, produced a policy draft that the board accepted unanimously. The discussion that followed showed that Richard Lieber and some others preferred not to remove the memorials that had been erected by the veterans' and patriotic associations. The only work sanctioned by the new policy involved clearing out vegetation that hampered the visitor's understanding of the progress of each battle. The board acknowledged that some "structures, earthworks, plant growth, etc." might be added, but the park staff would have to be aware of the "artificial element" these changes might introduce.[211] The board also noted that there had been some recent controversy over the restoration work done at Valley Forge by the commission that administered the area for Pennsylvania. Superintendent Elbert Cox of Morristown received a vote of confidence from the experts when he explained that the campground at Jockey Hollow in New Jersey included a few log buildings that were meant to serve as "sample" restorations. "Col. Lieber expressed the view that sample restoration is much more commendable than the 'pious fraud' of substituting a reproduction of the original without indicating its lack of authenticity."[212]

The debate over the battlefield developments was only the prelude to the drafting of the overall restoration policy that emerged from the May 1937 meeting of the board. That statement has remained a basic document for the National Park Service. Kimball's own experience with such diverse projects as Monticello, the Fairmount Park houses, Williamsburg, and Stratford came into play in wording the preamble to this all-inclusive policy:

> The motives governing these activities are several, often conflicting: aesthetic, archaeological and scientific, and educational. Each has its values and disadvantages.
>
> Educational motives often suggest complete re-constitution, as in their

heyday, of vanished, ruinous or remodelled buildings and remains. This has often been regarded as requiring removal of subsequent additions, and has involved incidental destruction of much archaeological and historical evidence, as well as of aesthetic values arising from age and picturesqueness.

The demands of scholarship for the preservation of every vestige of architectural and archaeological evidence—desirable in itself—might, if rigidly satisfied, leave the monument in conditions which give the public little idea of its major historical aspect or importance.

In aesthetic regards, the claims of unity or original form or intention, of variety of style in successive periods of building and remodeling, and of present beauty of texture and weathering may not always be wholly compatible.

In attempting to reconcile these claims and motives, the ultimate guide must be the tact and judgment of the men in charge.[213]

The board chose to append some observations to the policy as a guideline for Park Service personnel. In general these directions urged caution, deliberation, respect for old work, sublimation of individual preferences for certain styles, and a refusal to antique new material introduced into any structure.[214] Fiske Kimball, if he was indeed the principal author, had helped to define a standard that was intended to keep restorers from going to extremes. The only possible way to avoid excessive dependence on one line of reasoning was the "tact and judgment" of the person in charge. It was a large order, and Kimball must have believed with all his heart that he and his colleagues were equal to the challenge.

The controversies generated by the Pennsbury reconstruction and the discoveries at Wakefield eventually culminated in one last memorandum from director Arno Cammerer in the summer of 1938. He required people stationed in Washington and in the field offices to submit to the Park Service headquarters all archaeological and historical data used in preparing plans before starting any restoration work. Near the end of the directive Cammerer summarized the goal of the new policy: "The Service should be capable of instantly proving the authenticity of its work."[215]

The professional staff of the National Park Service had locked itself into a series of guidelines that should have given each historian and architect an increased respect for caution and deliberation. At times it seemed as if the emphasis on careful restoration bordered on religious devotion to authenticity. When park people looked at other restoration work, they tended to become somewhat critical and smug. An unsigned article that appeared in *Park and Recreation Structures* in 1938 and received wide circulation in the Park Service offices stated that "the curse of most historical restorations, reconstructions, or re-creations is an almost irresistible urge to gild the lily."[216]

Richard Lieber may well have been the author of the article mentioned because he was pushing the Park Service staff toward specific restoration programs that had never been tried before. Lieber was glad that some efforts were being made to visualize history. His sense of "intellectual honesty" had been insulted by "excrescences in restorative treatment" at Williamsburg and Dearborn. He could never agree to what had happened at Wakefield. He noted that Theodore Roosevelt had denounced "nature fakers," and now it seemed America was about to be taken over by history fakers. "Whatever is done by the Federal government, if it be done at all, must be scrupulously objective. As many facts as we can gather, but strictly no 'prettification,' let alone convenient white washing in the execution."[217]

In the fall of 1938 the new chief historian, Ronald Lee, delivered a paper before the Southern Historical Association in New Orleans on the objectives and policies of historic conservation. He told the group that the federal government had come into the preservation field because there was evidence of "new social conditions" that required the development of historical exhibits. Lee followed the trail already marked out by Laurence Vail Coleman when he cited the great increase in the use of automobiles and buses. Seven and a half million people had visited the historic sites and monuments administered by the Department of the Interior during the year 1938 alone. Lee's principal solution to this challenge was more cooperation: "The historic sites act and its corrolaries undoubtedly confer broad powers on the federal government, but these powers can be implemented effectively only through public and professional support. The confidence, aid and sympathy of the influential, learned and scientific societies concerned with history and archeology, with architecture and art, provide an indispensable stimulus to any federal program, and constitute the first assurance of its growth and the best guarantee of protection for its standards."[218] Lee's talk clearly showed that the Branch of Historic Sites hoped to set a scholarly standard in the quality of its restoration and interpretation activities, but that goal could be reached only if the whole preservation community began to work together. Lee was not far from the idea of forming a national trust in the years just before World War II.

Lee was not alone. Aubrey Neasham, the historian in the regional office in Santa Fe, prepared a number of thought-provoking essays on the future of historic-sites programs in the United States. In the winter of 1940 he wrote a brief paper for the Region III *Quarterly* entitled "Save the Ruins!" The archaeologists and historians in the Southwest had discussed the question of ruins stabilization for many years, so it was natural that Neasham could produce a carefully reasoned defense of John Ruskin's ideas on restoration. He began by suggesting that the preservation of ruins would not present a true picture of a historic site. But he quickly added that, as an alternative, reconstruction was worse.[219] He envisaged alternatives to radical reconstruction, including good museum exhibits such as the dioramas recently installed at Tumacacori.

During the late 1930s Neasham had been introduced to the writings of Ruskin by Newton Drury.[220] Once Drury became director of the National Park Service in the summer of 1940, there was even greater resistance to reconstruction projects than there had been under Arno Cammerer. Drury maintained, "I felt that even a fragment of the real thing was far more significant historically than a reproduction."[221] In 1948 Drury came across a copy of Fiske Kimball's famous 1930 letter on restoration, which he forwarded to his brother in California. Drury admitted that he had always agreed with the conservative principles set forth by Kimball: "You will perhaps remember my protest against the 'restoration' of the Chalet originally erected by Governor Vallejo in the fifties and subsequently demolished and recreated by the W.P.A. in 1935 or thereabouts. Friend Knowland remarked that 'the visitor would never know the difference' and I remarked that 'that makes it all the worse.'"[222]

By the end of World War II the scholarly approach introduced under Cammerer and extended under Drury was the rule in the National Park Service. The Branch of History held to the idea that it was impossible to erect too many safeguards against misguided restoration. Charles Porter handled most of the correspondence with organizations that requested advice on the management of historic sites, and he usually sent out copies of the Advisory Board's restoration policy along with Cammerer's directive regarding the need for research before actual construction work. For example, the state archivist of Colorado asked the Park Service in 1945 for some guidelines to use in planning a restoration of Fort Garland. Porter immediately drafted a three-page essay on the problems involved and included references to some substantial War Department collections in the National Archives. At the beginning of his letter Porter listed five steps that he believed would insure "authentic restoration":

> 1. The preparation of an orientation report, which should contain all basic historical data available, such as descriptions, photographs, and plans, placed in chronological order so that structural changes made at various times can be detected.

2. A careful archeological investigation of each building site and area immediately around it, to determine the original outline of each structure and to uncover artifacts useful for museum purposes.

3. The study of the above data (1. and 2.) jointly by an historian, archeologist, and architect to bring together all the data relative to this particular site.

4. Collection of data on related structures of the same historical period and type. At this point, a decision should be reached as to whether the evidence is sufficiently complete to make an accurate restoration possible. If the decision is in the affirmative, the next step is:

5. Preparation of restoration plans, each detail of which should be carefully documented against the historical and archeological evidence. The documentation of the plans may disclose gaps in the evidence which will have further direct bearing on the decision to restore or not to restore.[223]

These detailed instructions contained one final element in the development of restoration philosophy that probably could have occurred only in the offices of the National Park Service. Porter proposed that the people in Colorado delay the decision to restore their fort until *after* the research had been done. The evidence available from the surviving buildings and from documentary and archaeological sources should be the principal factor in deciding whether a restoration should ever take place. The Branch of History seriously considered nonrestoration as an important alternative—a luxury smaller preservation organizations could not afford. It would have been foolhardy for private groups to raise money to save buildings they did not intend to restore. It must be granted that this act of historical forbearance would have been a hard choice to accept, but the key element in the equation had to be accuracy. If the proposed restoration or reconstruction appeared to be conjectural, the Park Service officials reasoned that there should be only a research report and nothing more.

Colonial National Monument

The challenge at Yorktown, Va., was one of selecting the restoration policy that would most contribute to an understanding of the social, economic, and military history of the little riverport. About all outgoing superintendent William Robinson could recommend in 1933 was that the government should purchase more of the battlefield area and then put back the old road plan. In this way visitors could drive to the various headquarters and campgrounds present in 1781.[224]

After the CCC arrived in 1933 the staff at Colonial National Monument had to plan projects that would keep a large number of laborers busy. One of the first operations was the reconstruction of the Swan Tavern with its outbuildings. The new superintendent, B. Floyd Flickinger, returned a set of plans for the tavern stable without his approval to architect Charles Peterson with a typical historian's complaint:

The more we get into restoration and reconstruction work, the more I am convinced that we have not evolved a satisfactory working policy for this very exacting and specialized type of work. It is very embarrassing to one in an administrative position such as mine to have suddenly thrust before me a complete set of plans and drawings for a particular project. Personally, I feel that in every instance where you propose to restore or reconstruct any one of our Colonial buildings according to plans which you have evolved and prepared, you should submit a memorandum explaining why certain details were incorporated in plan.[225]

Peterson was surprised to have such a request when the plans for the Swan Tavern group had been under way for more than a year. He explained to Flickinger that the precedents were clear: "The general size of the building is based upon the insurance records and the actual remains of the foundation which were excavated some time ago. The architectural study evolved was, generally speaking, taken from the Botetourt Hotel stable (now destroyed), the barns at Stratford, Four Mile Tree, and Claremont Manor."[226] As far as the architects were concerned, Peterson had quite enough precedent for the stable designs. There is a distinct possibility that he and his assistants were much more sure of themselves than were the historians.

In his preface to a twenty-five-page report on the history of the Moore House Peterson showed that he had been troubled by some of the questions raised by another scholarly restoration:

Curiously enough architects agree that the most interesting ancient buildings are those which have not been tampered with by other architects. In a good piece of restoration work the new parts are so skillfully blended with the old that it is difficult or impossible to separate them. The antiquarian is thus unable to give most carefully restored structures a complete and intelligent examination. The architect who planned and supervised the work had all the details in the back of his mind at the time. In a relatively few years most of the factual matter was lost or forgotten.

It is my opinion that any architect who undertakes the responsibility of working over a fine old building should feel obligated to prepare a detailed report of his findings for the information of those who will come to study it in future years.[227]

There were restoration challenges in the Jamestown segment of Colonial that could not be treated in the same manner. For example, archaeologist H. Summerfield Day asked Flickinger to choose one of three plans for the final disposition of the ruins of the eighteenth-century Ambler House. In a carefully worded memorandum Day tried to weigh the possible advantages of (1) tearing down the ruins to the foundation, (2) bracing the old brick walls, or (3) reconstructing the building by using the walls and window openings as the nucleus of a Georgian house that could serve as a museum. Day did not seem to favor any one of the plans over the others. The demolition of the brickwork above ground would remove the only "discordant element" in the primitive setting of Jamestown. The stabilized ruin would be a logical place to tell the story of the Virginia capital as it declined in the years following the construction of Williamsburg. The restored house would help to orient visitors and could serve as a storage place for the artifacts that came out of the excavations.[228] The staff finally decided to stabilize the old walls.

The two major restoration reports that came out of Yorktown show that the main decisions had been made by the architectural staff according to procedures developed elsewhere. There seemed to be an assumption that a historically minded architect was competent to do all of the different kinds of research necessary to understand the evolution of an old building. Clyde Trudell had studied the domestic architecture of the Tidewater area for three years as a Williamsburg architect before he came to work for the National Park Service. In stark contrast, the historians and the archaeologists were not prepared to contribute much to these early restorations.

Morristown National Historical Park

The approach to the restoration problems in Morristown was distinctly different because nearly all of the discussions centered on three simple issues: Should the Revolutionary huts be reconstructed in the Jockey Hollow camp area? Should the Tempe Wick House be restored as a museum? Should the Guerin House be restored as a residence for park personnel? Just as the people in Morristown were preparing to dedicate the National Historical Park in June 1933, director Horace Albright announced a policy decision about the old campground in a letter drafted by Verne Chatelain:

We do not expect to make a wholesale restoration of cabins on the sites . . . [where] they once existed but we do hope to locate a few cabins here and there to serve as indications where military units once camped thereby enabling the visitor more easily to imagine the campground of the Revolution. Archeological remains will be left as far as possible in an unmodified condi-

Reconstructed officers' hut, Jockey Hollow, Morristown. (Photograph by Theodore C. Sowers and Kenneth Absalon, National Park Service)

tion. The National Park Service holds to the theory that our duty is to preserve rather than to restore artificially since restoration is apt to destroy the
source materials with which future generations have as much right to work
as we have ourselves.[229]

It was a remarkably eloquent defense of sample reconstruction for such
an early date, and the conservative note introduced by Albright continued to characterize the Morristown philosophy.

From 1934 until 1939 the administrator in charge of the Morristown
operation was Elbert Cox, one of the original historians at Yorktown in
1931. He was a slow and deliberate planner, so the erratic pace of the
work at Jockey Hollow must have fitted easily into his cautious approach
to decision making.[230]

The architectural decisions for the Morristown project were made
in an entirely different manner from the staff conferences held at Yorktown in 1933 and 1934. The abrasive relationship between architects
and the superintendent at Yorktown had disrupted communications
with Washington on many significant issues. Two architects at Park Service headquarters, Charles Peterson and Thomas Waterman, and one in
Morristown, Dan Jensen, conferred with Cox constantly throughout the
period. The custom carpentry and handwork that were required for
both the Guerin and Wick House restorations also slowed down the
pace.[231] Finally, the staff historian at Morristown took a great interest in
the basic documentary research for these projects.[232]

The first important question that had to be settled in 1934 was the
ultimate development of the Jockey Hollow area. Peterson surveyed the
buildings and the woodland that had just come into the Park System
and concluded that the Guerin and Wick houses should be used as staff
residences, and therefore the architectural staff would not have to make
the detailed study necessary for a full interior restoration.[233] Peterson
argued with the historians in Washington and New Jersey over the question of turning the Wick House into an exhibit. He claimed that almost
no significant interior elements of either house had survived. It would
make more sense to restore some other nearby homes that still contained
pre-Revolutionary woodwork.[234] But the historians countered with two
facts that made the restoration of the interior of the Wick House inevitable: It had been the headquarters of an important general on Washington's staff, and there was a popular legend connected with the house that
involved a girl who hid her horse from the British troops.[235]

The architects held firmly to the idea that there was so little information about the original interior of the Guerin House that it could not
be restored for exhibition purposes.[236] This argument stood up well in

the next two years, and it established a principle that Peterson probably wanted to use in other Park Service projects: The actual amount of surviving original material in a building should be a crucial factor in deciding whether to carry out a restoration. There was nothing more abhorrent to the architects who had worked with the Williamsburg program than a "conjectural restoration."

Vernon Setser, the historian, made an equally important contribution at Morristown by pushing hard for exploratory excavations in the yards of both of the houses. He admitted that there would be some element of amateurism because there was no staff archaeologist, but Setser could not imagine ignoring the vital information that was certain to come from an analysis of hardware, glass, and other artifacts that usually ended up in eighteenth-century dumps.[237] He completed a brief documentary report on the Guerin House that centered on the information gained from interviews with descendants of the original owner of the house. And he too concluded that there was no point in executing an interior restoration on the two farmhouses at Jockey Hollow, especially where there was little evidence to support such an expensive treatment of the Guerin House.[238]

The early projects in Morristown reflect a transition between the structural methods and goals perfected at Williamsburg and the heavy emphasis on documentary research that pervaded the Park Service restorations of the later 1930s. Thomas Waterman and Charles Peterson had both lived in Williamsburg, and Waterman had participated in some of the debates that preceded the reconstruction of the Palace and the Capitol. The Morristown restorers broadened their horizons into furniture studies, reports on the ownership of each tract of land, and historical and archaeological data. The slow pace of the program gave the historians and amateur archaeologists time enough to prepare statements for the architects to look over *before* beginning the designs for the restored buildings. Although Waterman produced a report on his restoration of the Tempe Wick House, before the preparation of the working drawings he read the papers from the historical staff covering the lifestyle of the families who had lived at Jockey Hollow. This research had not been planned, but it certainly helped to insure greater authenticity in the restoration. No administrator in Washington issued an order that directed all of the Morristown staff to concentrate on historical accuracy. There was no prearranged sequence of research priorities. The people who participated in the work came to their conclusions naturally and deliberately. Considering the fact that the restoration project for the first two houses ended in 1937 (only nine years after Williamsburg's first major effort), that was a considerable step forward in the effort to turn restoration work into a science.

Mission La Purisima Concepcion

The historical and architectural problems encountered in the development of Mission La Purisima Concepcion in Lompoc, Calif., illustrate the evolution of restoration philosophy through the whole of the late 1930s, but there were unique features about the work at La Purisima that contributed to the success of the endeavor. By the summer of 1934, when the CCC company arrived, nearly all of the mission site had become state property. There was one substantial ruin (the residence building); the rest of the buildings had disappeared. Once the residence began to take form again, a snowball effect made it increasingly difficult to halt the reconstruction program. The town of Lompoc was several miles away, and no major road or commercial development threatened the site. Because the CCC had been brought in to develop a historical monument for the state of California, there was a four-level hierarchy of consulting boards responsible for monitoring the decision-making process, and as a result there were significant differences of opinion as to how far the work should go in reproducing the original community. So many administrators and consultants were connected with the program at La Purisima that nearly all shades of contemporary restoration theory were represented. Newton Drury, for instance, preferred to concentrate on the preservation of the ruins and continuation of the archaeological investigations. He was acting as acquisitions officer for the State Park Commission, and he certainly did not want to see the Division of Parks saddled with a difficult maintenance and interpretive problem in the years to come. At the opposite extreme was the principal architect, Fred Hageman, who became consumed with a desire to see the whole mission community rise again from the dust of the valley at Lompoc. Several Park Service historians took a middle ground, hoping to offer the public something in the form of carefully reconstructed buildings, while mixing these recreations with museum exhibits and stabilized portions of the original foundations exposed by the excavations.

One of the most vociferous proponents of a complete mission reconstruction as an educational exhibit was Owen C. Coy of the California State Historical Commission. Coy favored rebuilding the whole community, including workshops, granaries, and the water system. The professional staff discussed his proposition and then reached a set of conclusions that reflected a certain degree of interest in the broad plan. The first step would be a complete archaeological survey of the site under a trained architect. Following the excavations, "a decision should be reached as to the extent and character of the restoration work to be undertaken."[239] It is clear that the experts did not rule out a complete reconstruction, but they wanted to have some dependable evidence available for the research staff before making a final decision.

During the first six months most of the archaeological work was performed on the site of the residence because the only sizable ruins above ground were at that point. Charles Wing, the engineer who inspected CCC camps, concluded in January 1935 that any construction project that came out of this dig would have to be planned in increments small enough to conform to the funding periods for CCC work.[240] Once the excavations on the first set of foundations were finished, a steady pressure began to build up for a reconstruction.

Another advocate of the recreation of La Purisima was a Park Service architect, Herbert Maier, who was serving as a district officer for the Emergency Conservation Work, which put federal money into state projects. He admitted that the concept of rebuilding the community with hand labor appealed to him "very strongly." Maier estimated that it would be impossible to stabilize the ruins of the residence building against both earthquake and rain damage and still retain anything of real historical interest. Nor could he accept the idea of restoring a portion of the building as a sample reconstruction. Maier then provided patriotic arguments to support the expansion of the work:

> Now let us consider the possibility of completely restoring the main building as well as the possibility of restoring the entire Mission settlement. Personally, I do not believe there is any project more suitable to conservation work than is the restoration and preservation of the remains of a past culture especially in a part of our Country which has had only one really "Golden Age"—that of the Mission Padres. I am a Native Son and can fully appreciate this. I know that most Native Sons feel that the "Days of '49" was the Golden Age of California—but they are wrong. The Mission days were the days of contentment for which we hopelessly hope the future holds a return. To contribute toward preserving the spirit of this era is one of the finest things we can do.[241]

Maier argued that the decision to maintain the old adobe walls would mean keeping a feature that was "depressing and unattractive to all but archeologists." Even Newton Drury (who was normally inclined toward caution) found Maier's enthusiasm hard to resist.[242]

An advisory committee on policy planning went to work at once and proposed a course of action that was neither conservative nor radical as far as a complete reconstruction of the mission community was concerned. Instead, the group "strongly urged" the immediate rebuilding of the residence because the ruins would not survive another winter in their exposed state. It also requested that the office, museum, and other park functions be included in this new structure and that the CCC camp buildings be moved out of the mission garden area so that excavations could be made throughout the park.[243] In March the State Park Commission unanimously accepted the program outlined in the report.[244]

The complicated mechanism of the ECW required that a regional historian visit historical and archaeological projects regularly. This requirement brought another important individual into the Purisima picture, Russell C. Ewing, the historian of Region VIII and a trained researcher who was well aware of the current European theories on restoration. With this broad background it was natural for Ewing to recommend that all reconstruction planning stop with the completion of the residence building. He admitted that Hageman and the CCC staff were doing an excellent job in attempting to imitate the construction methods used by the Indians, but Ewing argued that the remaining old foundations possessed "great historic and archeological significance in their present state." Apparently the idea of housing the park superintendent in the reconstructed residence seriously violated Ewing's concept of a restoration. Moreover, the most important justification for putting museum and residence facilities in the building was a negative one: There was no conclusive evidence on its furnishing.[245] The museum and the public toilets should be put somewhere else, Ewing argued, so that visitors could look over the large adobe building as a true recreation of the mission period.[246] He also warned his superiors in San Francisco that, although the park had no master plan, there already were proposals for putting in a garden. He doubted that the Franciscans ever had developed an elaborate landscape setting.[247] He was sharply critical of several aspects of the work that he inspected, especially whenever he thought the work depended on conjecture instead of positive knowledge. He protested against poorly recorded archaeological explorations that tended to undermine what little was left of the old church.[248]

In its preliminary report to the State Park Commission in the fall of 1935, the Purisima Advisory Committee noted that Owen Coy had initially stressed the "educational opportunity" presented by a reconstructed mission community. "He pictured the similarity between the young CCC workers and the Indian neophytes who originally built the structure, and showed that they might work in much the same manner." This approach would certainly mean that the reconstruction program would have some educational value for the relief workers who joined the CCC. The committee carried the educational argument further by stating a possible guiding principle for the development of the park: "the preservation of the atmosphere of an authentic mission community in its natural setting." The Santa Barbara leaders further proposed that the federal government reconstruct every building at La Purisima that could be reproduced authentically from the evidence available, so long as each unit could be put to some present-day use.[249] With these goals in mind the committee called for immediate planning for a reconstruction of the long building next to the residence and for the replanting of a mission garden.[250] The commission accepted the idea of completing the residence, but it held back from approving the grandiose plan for rebuilding the whole mission complex.[251]

Despite the philosophical differences there was evidence of cooperation. Ewing and architect Hageman, for example, made a long tour of almost all the existing California missions to study furnishings and structural details relevant to planning the residence building at La Purisima. They inspected painted walls and different kinds of plaster, hardware, and other nineteenth-century artifacts.[252] Following the example of other missions, Ewing even encouraged the architect to use the old methods of plastering, although it seemed to Hageman that "his reputation as an architect is at stake."[253] Ewing tried desperately to prevent the erection of a garden wall that he firmly believed had never been part of the Purisima plans. He used every kind of professional argument he could find in his stand for authenticity:

> Historians and archaeologists agree that historic and archaeological structures and sites are documents. Langlois, Bernheim, and Bury, leading authorities on historical methods, maintain that physical remains are just as important source materials as are original written records. This, too, is the stand taken by the distinguished members of the Advisory Board of the Branch of Historic Sites and Buildings, National Park Service. Therefore, historic sites and structures warrant the same consideration and interpretation as would be given to written materials; and the source materials for the history of La Purisima fall in both these categories.
>
> The historian of this office does not take the view that the work at La Purisima should be in the nature of a type restoration. The history of the Mission is its own, and not the history of any one of several other California missions.[254]

The latter half of 1936 marked a crucial turning point in the approach to the project at La Purisima. As long as the CCC camp had been able to restrict its activities to the archaeological work and the construction of the residence building, it was possible for the proponents of total reconstruction and the advocates of preservation of the archaeological evidence to work in harmony. Finally the residence building was almost complete, and the decision to close down the camp was at hand. There was really only one way to keep this operation going—reconstruct more of the principal mission buildings.

By the end of the second year the major decision-making groups had lined up in their respective philosophical camps. The staff at the mission site and the Advisory Committee in Santa Barbara still favored reconstruction of all of the buildings; the State Park Commission was undecided about the future; and the Washington headquarters of the National Park Service and the regional office in San Francisco generally favored stopping the work with the one main restoration. It might be said that architect Hageman ably represented the reconstructionist group and historian Ewing provided the strongest arguments for preservation of the ruins. Before the decision was made each group turned to experts for advice. Newton Drury, the influential acquisitions officer of the State Park Commission, was a dedicated antirestorationist. Usually he did not hesitate to recommend the preservation of every possible vestige of original material, but this time he was not sure which way to turn.[255] He asked Ewing to prepare a statement on preservation philosophy that might be utilized in arriving at a decision on the future development of La Purisima.[256]

The regional historian wrote a four-page essay entitled "The Treatment of Historic Structures" that showed a broad understanding of European preservation. He neatly divided the major authorities into three camps: "There are several schools of thought upon the subject of the treatment of historic monuments. One of these believes in complete restoration, the other in total preservation. A third stands midway between these two extremes. This latter group maintains that by compromise between complete restoration and total preservation the best solution to the problem is reached. Those who would compromise, however, are more often in accord with the general philosophy of preservationists than with the stand enunciated by the restorationists."[257] The footnotes proved that Ewing had read the French documents on the Athens Conference of 1933 as well as some British and Spanish works on preservation and restoration. He argued that the "general policy" of the National Park Service had been to accept sample restoration. "That is, by restoring a part of a structure, or a part of a group of structures, the unimaginative members of society will be better able to grasp what the original was like."[258] He noted that the success of a sample restoration depended on how much information was available on the appearance of the original. Ewing could support the reconstruction of the residence building because most of the walls had survived and there were a number of clear nineteenth- and twentieth-century photographs of the building as it gradually fell into ruin. He could not agree to the reconstruction of the church or the shops and quarters building because the evidence of their original appearance was so unsatisfactory.

Rexford Newcomb of the University of Illinois also summarized the two major theories on restoration in much the same terms used by Ewing, but he came to distinctly different conclusions:

> In the past I have held mixed feelings about both procedures. I have seen the first method [preservation] followed with the result that in time what was left has gone on to cureless ruin. Under the second procedure [restoration] I have observed, upon occasion, historic relics so inaccurately "restored" as to destroy the whole original intent and spirit of them.
>
> At Purisima I was considerably encouraged to see the second method being carried out in what I felt was workmanlike and archaeologically accurate manner. . . . I came away with the matter pretty well settled in my own mind that Purisima could be made a splendid museum in which all the phases of mission administration could be made available to the public.[259]

Obviously Newcomb favored reconstruction of the remaining mission buildings, although he had grave reservations about the proposed garden.

A week after winning Newcomb's support, Hageman received an educator's evaluation from Father Thomas Plassmann of St. Bonaventure College in New York.

> I have visited excavation and restoration work in the far east and in other lands and I must say that I have hardly ever found such fine appreciation, such expert workmanship and such a wholesome sense of proportion as I discovered among the men under your charge at that Mission. . . . There is a big difference between showing the remnants of history and showing the history revivified as it really was. For this reason your efforts will be crowned with a two-fold success: the promotion of historic research and the re-awakening of an interest in the past.[260]

On November 14, 1936, obviously moved by the quality of the work done under Hageman, the State Park Commission unanimously approved carrying "the restoration of La Purisima to completion."[261] Russell Ewing then warned the director of the National Park Service that it would be wise to think through the implications of this new construction program. He complained that there was not much good information on the church and the shops and quarters building, and these structures had not existed together at any one time, because the chapel just decorated by the Federal Arts Project in the reconstructed residence had originally replaced the church which had fallen into ruin. Ewing accepted the fact that he had been overruled in the reconstruction dispute, but he wanted to make it clear that he was ready to achieve a successful "completion" of the whole project:

> La Purisima, then, is to provide a working basis for the development of a typical California Mission community. As such, many functions of the mission must not be overlooked. The mission was not only a religious institution; it played quite as prominent a part in social, economic and political affairs. A true picture of what such institutions really were would call for the restoration of all the mission structures which were connected with these many phases of activity. I should, therefore, not care to see the reconstruction stop with the erection of the workshops and church. The buildings intimately associated with Indian life should by all means be rebuilt, as should all other structures for which there is authentic evidence, either written or archaeological. This should logically result in the appearance of the following features: Indian dwellings, infirmary, *monjerio*, monastery, church, cemetery, tallow vats, water and irrigation systems, gardens and orchards, *matanza*, storehouses, workshops and quarters for the mission guards.[262]

When the request to continue the Purisima restoration reached the desk of associate director Arthur Demaray of the National Park Service, he quickly realized that an important decision was at hand. Demaray was enough of a student of departmental politics to do his historical homework. He asked Herbert E. Bolton of the University of California (and the Park Service Advisory Board) to go to Lompoc with Ewing and look over the project—past, present, and future.[263]

Ronald Lee, chief historian and an opponent of reconstruction, forwarded some penetrating questions to the San Francisco regional office to serve as an agenda for Bolton's visit to La Purisima. He wanted Bolton particularly to decide whether approval of the church reconstruction would violate the stand just taken by the Advisory Board. Lee also questioned whether total reconstruction of the mission community would be the best way to carry out an interpretive program:

> The development now in contemplation for La Purisima has been justified chiefly on grounds of its educational value. This raises the question of the educational value of a restored structure compared with a museum display of excavated artifacts. It is our view that the historic object itself, even if only a fragment of the original structure, properly displayed, frequently has far greater educational value than a complete replica or restoration. It is easy to overlook the great educational value of the excavated artifacts themselves, and to use them simply to secure evidence for a restoration. We are under

the impression that the real objects found at La Purisima have been somewhat neglected in favor of an over-emphasis on the conjectural restoration of the church and garden.[264]

Lee also wanted more documentary material to support the construction plans forwarded to the Park Service offices.

If the antireconstructionists had been pinning their hopes on Bolton's report, they were sadly mistaken. He was captivated by the work already accomplished at La Purisima, and the possible reconstruction of an entire mission complex as a teaching device excited him as a historian. Bolton probably perceived that this was the only chance left in the country to show the visitor how much more there had been to the typical mission community than just a church edifice surrounded by some Indian huts. He also detected in the plans a real opportunity for California to offer a display that would equal or surpass New Salem and Williamsburg. And then Bolton brought up two arguments that seemed to make further reconstruction a certainty: "To stop now with only the monastery restored would give as distorted a notion as that given in other places with only the church in evidence. The foundations of the work buildings are plain, and I think it will be possible to reproduce them faithfully. The same is true of the church, the cemetery walls, and the dwellings of the neophytes. The water system is surprisingly complete in its original form, and with very little reconstruction it will be possible to have it in actual operation."[265] In fact, Bolton added, it was "too late" to debate preservation versus reconstruction. The archaeological work on the church had sufficiently weakened the old foundations to make them useless for display purposes. The rebuilding of the residence had been something of a commitment. Bolton closed his letter with an admission that even Russell Ewing and Newton Drury had reluctantly joined the ranks of the restorers. "Both Mr. Drury and Dr. Ewing agree with me now that it is too late to proceed on that basis [preservation]." The only alternative in 1937 was a National Park Service pledge to make La Purisima the most authentic project of its type in the country.[266]

Immediately Hageman and Ewing sent reports to Washington that covered all the architectural and documentary sources consulted for the church drawings. Hageman, in particular, stated that he had leaned heavily on survey data from the other California missions for his ideas. And he had carefully studied the surviving portions of the residence and the foundations of the church.[267]

The decision to proceed with the church reconstruction was inevitable, and many factors contributed to the capitulation of Ewing and his fellow preservationists in the Park Service. Anyone who went to Lompoc to see the construction program was immediately impressed with the authenticity of the mission site. There were almost no visual intrusions to spoil the picture of a rural valley settlement of the 1820s. The CCC enrollees were obviously having a wonderful time recreating the buildings with thousands of handmade adobe bricks and roof tiles manufactured in a manner reminiscent of the nineteenth century.[268] A close inspection of the initial reconstruction showed that architect Hageman had indeed worked hard to preserve almost all of the surviving elements of the building, including the stone buttresses and half of the original columns along the front. Of course, the experts who looked over the residence in 1937 were looking at the best-documented building in the whole group. It did seem natural to assume that the rest of the structures would be built just as carefully.

Ewing left the position of regional historian, and Olaf Hagen, his replacement, was not quite so firmly opposed to the mission reconstruction program. Hagen's reports tended to be freer of editorial comments on preservation philosophy, mainly because many of the most important decisions had already been made when he took over. He quickly decided that his principal assignment was to be in the area of museum development. The master plan for the mission still called for the installation of a museum exhibit in the restored residence building, but Hagen noticed that the consultants had assumed that each of the major reconstructions would be furnished with items that illustrated the various occupations and social groupings within the mission community.[269]

Drury asked the architect to provide him with a statement of the probable ultimate goals for the reconstruction program, and Hageman prepared a spirited defense of the total revival of the life of the 1820s at La Purisima.

There are the restored buildings, with their fittings and furniture, of course. There are also the industries, such as weaving, leather work, soap and tallow making, carpentering, blacksmithing and so on. There is the garden, with its fountains and pools and collection of old historic trees and shrubs. Then, there is the famous pear orchard, a little way up the valley, whose location, size, and appearance we know. The rather elaborate water system, with its dams, lakes, flumes, aqueducts, etc., is a splendid thing; well worth study. An important feature of this area was the old "Camino Real," the highroad of California, passing through the very center of the Mission.[270]

In order to recreate this scene, Hageman could see no alternative to restoring "the authentic appearance of the Mission valley." That would entail the purchase of some additional property and the construction of

Group of CCC enrollees working on beams in front of the Monastery building, La Purisima Mission, 1938. (California Department of Parks and Recreation)

adobe buildings on every foundation uncovered by the archaeological staff.[271]

The superintendent of the southern district of the California State Park System did not share Hageman's enthusiasm for the total picture. Guy Fleming knew that he would eventually have to find people to administer the new state park, and that prospect made him exceptionally cautious:

> The development and restoration program will require firm guidance, if it is to be kept within the means of reasonable administration and maintenance. The program at the present time is governed by idealists who are carried away with the romanticism of a complete restoration of a presupposed Mission settlement. This is without regard to the cost of future administration and maintenance. We must come down to earth in this matter and force the development to take a sound course which can be economically administered. It is my recommendation that the restoration construction program be restricted to the complete restoration of the Monastery building, the church, the workshops and the fountains and cisterns in the forecourt. The site of all other buildings and institutions connected with the mission settlement should be located and suitably marked with appropriate historical markers. Instead of burdening the visitor to the Mission with a wearisome journey through a series of empty reconstructed buildings (which will be very difficult to administer and maintain), let him wander over the area and with the aid of a map and a historical sketch reconstruct in his imagination the pattern and activities of this old mission establishment.[272]

Fleming also sharply criticized the mission garden as "an extremely doubtful restoration." The ultimate plan as presented by Hageman would require a minimum of six people for maintenance and interpretive services, and the California park budget could not stand such an expense. Fleming's strongest arguments were based on the impression the reconstructed buildings would leave with the uninformed visitors. But the Purisima Advisory Committee, instead of accepting the idea of holding the construction program to three large structures, recommended the addition of more buildings to complete the picture of the mission complex.[273]

The realists and the idealists held a conference at La Purisima in August 1938 to try to hammer out an agreement. Pearl Chase of the Advisory Committee and Fleming both urged that caution be exercised in planning for more reconstructions, and they argued that it would be much cheaper for the state if the custodian and the museum were both housed in parts of the residence.[274] Consultants Arthur Woodward and

Mark Harrington took the opposite view, as reported by park historian Aubrey Neasham. They proposed that a separate museum building be constructed near the entrance to the park area and that the custodian be given a house on the ridge above the valley. The reconstructionists had a bold new solution for the problem of staffing the mission in the future: "There is a possibility that, with the aid of the County of Santa Barbara, one or two families of Indians or Mexicans may be placed in the restored Indian quarters of the mission. In that case, they will be available as help for maintenance. If properly guided, they may assume some of the old mission life; and they may develop some craft work, which would add to their earnings and the mission atmosphere."[275]

In clear language the California park commissioners went on record in September in favor of completing the three large buildings already under construction. They also agreed to the fabrication of "proper period furniture" and a partial restoration of the water system. But there the authorization stopped. Instead of asking for federal funds for additional construction, they chose to request money to hire and train the personnel who would interpret the restored mission.[276]

In March 1939 Fred Hageman asked the State Park Commission to define the limits of the construction program for the next few years. The commissioners then reversed their stand on one key issue—they agreed to the reconstruction of three neophyte (Indian) dwellings near the county road. The reason for this about-face was not difficult to understand; Hageman had offered to design at least one of the new buildings to serve as a museum or visitor service building.[277] The real decision had to be made in Washington.

While the debate over the neophyte barracks was intensifying, Harrington took on the position of consultant to the reconstruction program. He went up to Lompoc nearly every weekend from Los Angeles and divided his time between drawing up authoritative furnishing plans and supervising the excavations of the foundations of the remaining portions of the Purisima complex. The furnishing plans were intended for the CCC workers who had been assigned the job of reproducing the mission furniture.[278]

At the same time, the officials at the Park Service headquarters became increasingly suspicious of the proposals from the Purisima consultants because these documents lacked references to source material as precedents for the construction details. This concern was understandable because the available evidence for the exterior appearance of the proposed neophyte dwellings was thin. Olaf Hagen reported to the regional director that Woodward, Harrington, and Hageman were depending almost entirely on archaeological information for these buildings. The dimensions and the general floor plans were plainly evident, but the placement of windows and doors had to be based on surveys of "somewhat similar" structures at other mission sites.[279] In a letter to the regional director Harrington stated that the foundations, combined with old photographs of ruins and his knowledge of similar buildings elsewhere, made it possible to erect these structures in "typical form." Harrington believed that the overriding issue was not the exact authenticity of the proposed reconstructions: "We have at La Purisima a unique opportunity to present to the public a complete view of a California Mission as a going concern and to stop now, so near our goal, would be most unfortunate. The reconstruction of the remaining buildings would be a minor task compared to what has already been accomplished."[280]

What had happened by the fall of 1939 was that the proponents of the total mission reconstruction had retreated to a final philosophical position: Although there was not much information about the rest of the buildings, the achievement of the whole picture was so worthwhile that construction should go on. It could be said that there were three stages to the planning: first was the residence building, where there had been excellent archaeological and pictorial data; then came the church, the shops, and quarters, where only the foundations remained and the pictorial documentation was reasonably good; and finally there were the Indian dwellings, where almost no early drawings existed. Each time the advocates of reconstruction wanted to further their cause, they proudly referred to what had already been accomplished.[281]

Over the summer of 1939 landscape architect Edward Rowe had worked on planning the garden. Arthur Demaray and Ronald Lee must have been alarmed by the report when they read about Rowe's precedents:

> The design of the garden and plant material used today at Mission La Purisima Concepcion is in no sense a reproduction of the original surroundings of the mission at the time of its occupation by the Franciscan Order.
>
> The Fathers were then busy with missionary work, the cultivation of crops and the raising of livestock. These duties left little time for garden development. . . . The area directly in front of the major buildings and adjacent to them was probably a bare, dusty space in which were the fountains, basins, a reservoir and a few trees. . . . For purely historical reasons, the bare dusty area is the best treatment, but it will be of little interest to the majority of the visitors who come today. The historically-minded minority will question the present treatment. It is probable that if the missions had continued, some attempt would have been made to improve the amenities of the surroundings. The gardens as now designed and planted are perhaps

what might have happened under the authority and guidance of a mission padre interested in plants.[282]

Harrington had one further argument in support of the project that injected a new perspective. He had spent nearly two years attempting to turn the park into a "living museum." Even Guy Fleming of the California Division of Parks admitted that La Purisima might be developed and interpreted in this fashion.[283] At one point Harrington seriously proposed that he be assigned an "apartment" in the shops and quarters building which he could visit from time to time and to which he could contribute articles that he found in Mexico and the Southwest that might relate to the life of the mission community.[284] Woodward agreed to the idea of having Indian or Mexican families live in the mission buildings. He suggested that they could plant crops that were known to have been common there in the 1840s. They could also make cloth, manufacture leather objects, make pottery, candles, hand-forged nails, and even furniture. Woodward pointed out that all of these crafts could be found at different locations in California, particularly on Olvera Street in Los Angeles. "At La Purisima the activity would be concentrated on a proper setting and could be regulated and given the necessary guidance to make them historically correct."[285]

The crafts-program proposal seemed to be the final step in the drive to make the Purisima site resemble an actual mission community. Hagen suddenly became interested in the idea during the summer of 1941. He quoted several long reports that included descriptions of the interpretive activities at Williamsburg, at New Salem in Illinois, and in the Swedish outdoor museums with their concentration on folk life through dances, music, and games. Hagen argued that the "permanent value" of the project would be greatly increased with the reintroduction of mission arts and crafts. As a Park Service staff member, Hagen was well aware of the practical problems that stood in the way of such an elaborate interpretive device. He proposed the creation of an Arts and Crafts Advisory Board to help choose the laborers who would work at the mission, and then to assist in the marketing of the products that would be manufactured there. He also realized that the introduction of family groups in the exhibition area would mean a great change in the sanitary arrangements and the work areas already constructed.[286] And he warned Harrington that there would have to be a salary budget for trained people to carry on permanent craft exhibits because the county relief rolls might soon dwindle (as they did) and temporary workers would disappear.[287]

But the "living museum" aspect of the mission was doomed from the start. To begin with, almost every preservation organization that

went heavily into a crafts program had difficulty in keeping steady workers. Modern artisans refused to work in the design patterns of another
era. No one would agree to live at La Purisima because of its remoteness
and meager visitation.[288] Once more Fleming criticized the plans of the
idealists. He accepted the principle that there could be a subsidized
crafts program in a state park, but he insisted that some special organization be formed to oversee the details of such an operation.[289]

The scope of the building program and the steady federal funding
meant that the Purisima development would inevitably engender debates. Over a period of six years the CCC invested more than $400,000
in labor and materials for the mission complex.[290] At the end of it all
there was a solid accomplishment, and the few visitors who found their
way to Lompoc in the early years of World War II came upon something
surprisingly close to Mark Harrington and Arthur Woodward's dream of
a complete California mission community. When the park was finally
dedicated in December 1941 no one seemed to have noticed that the
relief workers had taken almost as long to rebuild La Purisima as the
Indians had to construct it in the nineteenth century.

When the first CCC camp was established in 1934 at Lompoc, the
National Park Service was just preparing to draft the Historic Sites Act.
By the time the reconstructed mission community had opened for visitors, the historic sites program of the New Deal had already changed
the face of preservation. The Park Service had an Advisory Board and
a restoration policy. The National Survey of Historic Sites and Buildings had started. The Department of the Interior had moved from an
era of relatively unplanned expansion to a period of emphasis on scholarship in the restoration process.

Hopewell Village

In the final years of the Park Service historical program before World
War II there were a number of policy statements as well as arguments
among the experts who had to plan for the restoration of buildings under
the jurisdiction of the Department of the Interior. The effort to draft a
set of guiding principles for Hopewell Village National Historic Site in
Pennsylvania illustrates the number of issues that could be debated by
a group of Park Service professionals who already subscribed to the restoration policy adopted by the Advisory Board in 1937. The Hopewell
question arose in the spring of 1940 and remained somewhat unresolved
as late as 1942, when war priorities temporarily ended all hopes of carrying out any restoration of the small iron-making community.

The exchange began in April 1940, when two historians, an archaeologist, and the superintendent of the National Historic Site drafted a

La Purísima Mission fully restored. (California Department of Parks and Recreation)

preliminary set of "Guiding Principles" for future development of the area. The first article called for restoration of the community as of 1880, when the furnace closed. "Assuming, for purposes of illustration, that separate portions of the Big House were built in 1790, 1821, and 1868, this would mean the restoration of those portions as, respectively, of those dates."[291] The second article in the list called for the reconstruction of any features once part of the village. These were to be developed as of the "period of their earliest known existence." All interiors at Hopewell were to be restored to the same period as the exteriors. The restoration and reconstruction projects had to be preceded by a series of reports that covered all the relevant data in the fields of history, archaeology, architecture, and "antiquarian features. This formulation of principles is based upon the fact that many important existing features in Hopewell Village are of later date than others, and that, in consequence, the confining of the restoration-reconstruction program within too limited a period would necessitate their elimination. . . . To avoid difficulty in future as to what *is* the restoration-reconstruction policy for Hopewell, it is believed that consideration should be given at once to the proposal outlined above."[292]

Within the space of four months superintendent Lemuel Garrison submitted a modified policy for Hopewell. He had talked at some length with archaeologist John C. F. Motz, and they both detected a tone of inflexibility in their initial draft. They discovered that the best roofing material for the blacksmith shop would be old tile from buildings in the neighborhood. The handmade tile would be authentic, but it would represent the earliest period of use. Garrison also pointed out that some of the crucial buildings associated with the iron-making process had disappeared and would have to be reconstructed if the village was to become a "complete" functioning exhibit; visitors would need to see these structures if they were to follow the iron-making process.[293] Most of these buildings were reconstructed in the 1950s. Historian Melvin Weig, who had helped to draw up the original document, agreed that there would have to be some reconstruction, but he suggested that the heading "guiding principles" should be understood to imply flexibility.[294]

After a pause for the winter of 1940–41, the debate started up again over one sticky issue: the correct date for the restoration. Garrison, together with Motz and Alfred Hopkins, the furnishings expert, drew up a statement that eloquently defended 1870 as the best possible point of concentration. With a late nineteenth-century stopping point it would be possible to retain the vast majority of the existing buildings in the community with a minimum of repairs. The furnace machinery in operation in 1870 closely resembled the apparatus in use a century earlier.

The furnishings representing the years 1840–60 would not be expensive to obtain, when compared to the then more popular antiques of the period before 1800. Most important of all, the post–Civil War date would present "the optimum opportunity for showing Hopewell as an ever-changing, growing community."[295] The regional chief of planning accepted the 1870 cutoff date because it seemed to him that a "golden age" could be established that would minimize the temptation to take some building back to an earlier era. The eighteenth-century village could be shown through the use of pictures and dioramas.[296] Regional historian Roy Appleman took exception to the whole proposal. As the original discoverer of Hopewell Village in the mid-1930s, Appleman stoutly maintained that the "golden age" had been around the year 1800. He thought that most of the restoration and reconstruction planning should be geared toward presenting the site as a colonial iron-making town.[297]

During the spring of 1942 senior engineer Edmund Preece, as requested, prepared a plan for the stabilization of the existing buildings at Hopewell for the duration of World War II. He went over the correspondence and the reports prepared by the staff at the village but could not find in all of the research material any guidelines for the final development of the area. His question was a simple one: Should the stabilization take into account the need to save every bit of surviving old material, or could the engineers have some freedom in repairing buildings that had serious structural defects caused by age and negligence?[298] The regional director in Richmond finally settled the dispute by ordering a policy of stabilization with no attempt at restoration of any kind.[299] It would be many years before the Park Service budget would permit any reconstructions.

The complex problems that baffled the Park Service professionals at Hopewell Village had also come up at a number of other places where restorations were planned and executed. The difference was that in 1940 the National Park Service staff had completely hemmed itself in with restrictions that favored total preservation of original elements wherever possible. At Hopewell one group wanted to keep as many of the nineteenth-century features as possible, because that would be cheaper and there would be considerably less destruction and reconstruction. Appleman, however, raised the equally important question of interpretation and held to the idea that the village had achieved its greatest importance in the years following the Revolution. Fortunately, the dilemma could not be worked out for several years, so the staff at the site had time to pin down the historical basis for a restoration that would center on the long history of iron-making in rural Pennsylvania. The final result has been a village that illustrates all the major developments at Hopewell, including the later nineteenth century.

Jefferson National Expansion Memorial

The restoration of the Manuel Lisa Warehouse at the Jefferson National Expansion Memorial in St. Louis was one of the Park Service's last projects before the war broke out, and the philosophical discussions that attended this renovation were just as intense as those at Hopewell. Charles E. Peterson was in charge of the work, and he eventually wrote a detailed report on the Old Rock House, which was published in 1948 in the *Bulletin of the Missouri Historical Society*. Peterson admitted that there were "many problems" involved because of a "multitude of physical changes" to the little building over the years. For example, he had detected five different types of stonework while he was making his architectural reconnaissance.[300] Once he was convinced that he was dealing with a remnant of an important building, Peterson had made some basic decisions about the restoration:

> Unfortunately, so much of the original materials had been lost through the years that it was doubtful that more than twenty percent was present and suitable for use in restoration, even taking the greatest care to preserve all old bits. This was a low percentage, but the remarkable history of the building justified retaining what remained and this, in turn, required the restoration of the missing parts. The fact that architecturally the building is very simple made the problem easier.
>
> Several alternatives were possible in planning for restoration, among which was that of leaving the building in its 1939 condition and simply repairing it. But the number of incongruous changes in its appearance, especially those of the last seventy years, made this seem undesirable.
>
> After some discussion it was decided to restore the warehouse to its earliest period—that is, as it existed when first built by Lisa. While less was known about the building at that time, it was the period of greatest historical interest.[301]

Portions of the building had been recorded by artists and photographers over the years, and Peterson had consulted these pictorial sources. He had followed two guiding principles in the actual construction work, even with unskilled labor from the relief rolls: (1) He had utilized every fragment judged to be a part of the original Rock House; (2) wherever possible the workmen had used the tools and construction methods common in the early 1800s (even mixing a homemade paint).[302]

The most important philosophical statement to come out of the St.

Louis restoration was a paper prepared by Edmund Preece in September 1941, "A Discussion concerning the Relation of Historical Restoration and Structural Design." As an engineer Preece chose not to debate the validity of the restoration process itself. He focused on the problems that would arise through imitating the materials and methods of the workmen of the nineteenth century. "Because of the limitations inherent in the period of their construction, many of the historical structures incorporate either inadequate materials or incompetent design."[303] Using the Manuel Lisa Warehouse as an example, Preece concluded that if Peterson's workmen used exactly the right kind of lumber and prepared it with the authentic tools, they would be constructing a building that would be difficult to maintain and, in fact, would become a fire hazard that might collapse within a few years. Preece believed that it was inconsistent for the architect to admit that there were many doubtful points about the original appearance of the warehouse while he chose to use absolutely nothing but "authentic" materials. Preece was understandably concerned about the fact that modern technology had made it possible to give the Rock House a longer life without sacrificing its appearance as a historic landmark.[304] The question did not lend itself to an easy solution, and the restoration was well under way when he raised his objections. Undoubtedly Peterson went on to complete the project in the way he had intended. The fact remains that all of the historians, architects, and engineers who had any responsibility for the Rock House renovation knew full well what the philosophical implications of that work would be. They knew that the chief justification for the project had been the antiquity of the building and its connection with one of the most important figures in the evolution of the fur trade. Working from that basis, it was not hard to strip the warehouse of all of its later additions and concentrate on the construction techniques of a century earlier.

Park Service Influence

The National Park Service's deliberative scholarly approach to restoration policy did not have much effect on state and municipal programs. Most attempts to influence public officials outside the federal government did not succeed unless funds came with the advice. During the late 1930s state and local preservation work usually involved the use of federal money through such agencies as the Works Progress Administration and the National Youth Administration. Until 1939 or 1940 these projects were planned and carried out without much interference from the staff of the Park Service.

The historical restorations instituted in Pennsylvania became particularly annoying to the Branch of History because the federal government seemed to lack the ability to slow down the restorers, who operated under semi-independent commissions. In 1936, for example, one of the architects who worked for the WPA office in Philadelphia asked for data on the reconstructed Revolutionary huts at Morristown, N.J. The Valley Forge Park Commission had decided to carry out a full-scale restoration of the Continental Army winter camp, and it was essential for the architects to investigate the work already done by the National Park Service in a related area.[305] The historians in the Washington office and at Morristown told the Pennsylvanians in every way possible that there was no point in reconstructing a large number of log buildings at Valley Forge.

In at least one spectacular instance the Park Service found a public official who steadfastly refused to take advantage of its professional services. When Mayor Maury Maverick of San Antonio, Tex., began to renovate the group of buildings known as La Villita, he had his own theories on the purpose of the restoration. It was to be a "place for the living, and those not yet born."[306] He hired a talented local architect, O'Neill Ford, to plan the project, and Maverick chose to concentrate on the development of the Villita area as a center for international understanding. Ford quickly realized that he had considerable freedom in working on the buildings: "Maury didn't have any special ideas about restoration except that he had good ideas about the significance of the whole place—for the use of the town and to document history. He didn't interfere too much with the actual work. He didn't know anything about it. What the heck! He wasn't an architect, and he wasn't strictly a historian. He was a political historian and a great one, and so he didn't interfere too much there."[307] When director Cammerer suggested that Maverick hire a historian with some archaeological training, the colorful Texan complained to the undersecretary of the interior: "All he suggests is I hire a lot of people. My idea was that this project was interesting enough for the Federal Government to send somebody here. . . . I am not going to hire a bunch of archeologists which would be very expensive and then have the Park Service 'supervise' it, because I feel sure it will be a waste of money."[308] Maverick's goal of a restoration that would appeal to the "living" obviously did not require the services of a group of professional scholars sent from Washington or Santa Fe.[309]

Whether the National Park Service officials ever admitted it or not, they were largely ignored by the mass of preservation organizations throughout the country. People were willing to accept federal money and the labor force provided by the CCC, but the scholarly guidelines for restoration practice worked out by the Advisory Board did not fit the philosophy adhered to by most amateur historians and antiquaries. Park Service personnel rarely engaged in the difficult task of raising money to preserve sites. The fact that a building or site had been saved was much more important to most preservationists than worrying about how much of the structure had survived. The protection of the urban landscape was more important than the correctness of shutters or window sashes. Visitors were more interested in hearing about the events and people who were associated with historic house museums than they were in knowing how many reports had been prepared on the physical restoration of the buildings. With the notable exceptions of Colonial Williamsburg, the Robert E. Lee Memorial Foundation, and a few state governments, no organization had the time or the money to devote to real research in preparation for restoration work. This meant that by 1941 the engineers, architects, historians, and archaeologists of the National Park Service were talking mainly to themselves. They could point with pride to their accurate restorations and reconstructions, knowing well how many years of study and discussion had gone into them. Their great challenge was finding a way to get the rest of the country to awaken to the need for some standards.

Ronald F. Lee, the chief historian, tried to meet this obligation by helping to found a national preservation organization in the fall of 1946. In a speech before the American Association for State and Local History, Lee urged his fellow professionals to come together to share their ideas in a national forum.[310] He was deeply concerned about the inability of the preservation movement to unite in the face of the tremendous postwar building boom, but he also wanted to extend the influence of the small group of people who had worked so diligently to treat historic places as documents. Lee considered that the sites and buildings under his care were the "source materials" of American history. Structures that had been radically restored lost their documentary value. Very few preservationists had begun to talk about adaptive uses for restorations that could never be museums; that development came in the 1950s.[311]

The minutes of the Informal Conference Preliminary to the Organization of a National Council on Historic Sites and Buildings in February 1947 show clearly that the assembled delegates wanted to have a national clearinghouse on preservation and restoration. Discussions centered on the nature of the emergency that the preservation movement faced, but there was ample evidence in the minutes that many of the people at the meeting also wanted to talk about the problems involved in restoration work.

Many interests and organizations can be drawn upon to bring about more effective preservation of the physical sources of American history. Several national and regional organizations, including the principal professional associations of historians, architects, archeologists, museologists, and planners count the preservation of historic sites as among their important interests. The Federal Government through the National Park Service is already extensively engaged in activities for the preservation of historic sites and a number of state governments now have or plan to establish commissions for this purpose. Several hundred state and local historical organizations as well as numerous patriotic societies are directly or indirectly interested in the preservation, marking and exhibit of historic places. A growing body of basic data for an understanding of the problem is provided in the records of the Historic American Buildings Survey, the Historic Sites Survey, and the Federal Writers' project. Experience of the past 20 years at Colonial Williamsburg, St. Augustine, in the National Park System and elsewhere has thrown some light on the techniques of preservation, stabilization and restoration.[312]

The only way to bring about "effective preservation" of the historical resources of the whole country would be through the educational work of a new national organization. And that is just what Ronald Lee set out to achieve with the founding of the National Council.[313]

In the fall of 1948 Kenneth Chorley addressed the second annual meeting of the National Council on "Historical Preservation—Issues and Problems." After he had listed the lessons that had been learned from the Williamsburg restoration, Chorley launched into a discourse on his hopes for the National Council. He fully expected that the council (and eventually the National Trust) would play a major role in awakening public officials and the American people to the need for preserving physical evidences of the past. In that effort to proclaim the "necessity" of saving historic sites, the council also had to influence the preservation field itself. "I am greatly in favor of having the National Council become a clearing house for information regarding historic sites and buildings, of disseminating advice on preservation and restoration, of supplying data regarding techniques, becoming a repository of information, publications, et cetera, relating to this field."[314]

The men and women who had helped to found the National Council could sit back in the comfortable seats of the auditorium of the National Gallery with a great sense of assurance. Kenneth Chorley, with his prestige and power, had called for a national clearinghouse. In the years to come the preservation community would finally have an opportunity to pause and study what it had been doing. The deeper questions relating to restoration and preservation theory could be ignored so long as the movement remained splintered. But once there was a national headquarters, people all over the United States would have to find ways to shoulder the responsibility of using their historic buildings as cultural resources that deserved respect and preservation.

13

Preservation Theory Comes of Age

THE DEPRESSION YEARS marked a turning point for the preservation movement as historical activity moved—for a brief period—into the mainstream of American life. During the 1920s the Rockefeller and Ford programs had begun to change the scale of preservation work, but it was the economic crisis of the 1930s that led the whole nation to re-evaluate its heritage, and in particular to focus the energy of the architectural profession on saving the vestiges of America's past. World War II and the Cold War era brought reduced national attention and spending for preservation, a fact that dictated the need to weld an organization that could meet the challenges of the future.

Henry-Russell Hitchcock clearly saw this trend toward increased preservation activity in 1968 when he looked back on the atmosphere that surrounded the publication of his book *Rhode Island Architecture* in 1939. "It is widely recognized today that one of the side effects of the Depression was the discovery (or rediscovery) of the American scene. This was especially evident in the field of painting, but there was also apparent a new interest both by scholars and by the general public in the earlier architecture of America—not only in the Colonial and so-called Federal periods of the two centuries before 1830, but also in American architecture of the mid and even late nineteenth century."[1]

Community pride led urban preservationists to move from education into political action and financial innovation. The aroused citizens of Charleston, San Antonio, and New Orleans came to look on their old buildings as symbols of a noteworthy past and as usable elements in the urban scene. In the 1930s there was not much interest in saving commercial buildings; most people favored neighborhoods where eighteenth-century houses were the predominant element. Eventually love for their cities transcended the barriers of their taste and carried them into preservation of the whole urban scene through use of zoning, legislation, surveys, planning, and adaptive use. The principal goal was the maintenance of a setting where structures of all types could be given uses that would be compatible with a historic district.

The people who preserved and restored historic buildings before the 1950s were usually too busy to sit down and think about or write out a rationale for their projects. Most of their work had practically no enunciated philosophical underpinning because the preservation movement then operated almost entirely by instinct. The continual effort to save endangered landmarks drained too much time and energy. On the other hand, one should not say that the preservationists of the past had no philosophy. They usually stated their objectives, not in words, but in bricks and mortar. Only a few individuals, who were really just interested observers, commented in any meaningful way about the deeper questions involved in preservation activity.

A few of these critics attempted to find ways to broaden the scope of the movement, which had been rooted strongly in the field of patriotic education; many of the programs instituted at Williamsburg, Greenfield Village, and throughout the National Park System had this same goal. If education of the mass of Americans was to be the basis for saving buildings, it was crucial for preservationists to broaden their definition of history beyond the narrow confines of patriotism. The scale of the federal assistance offered to state park systems and the surveys carried out by historians and architects during the depression helped a great deal to give the study of history a new dimension. Buildings that illustrated the life of ordinary people in preindustrial America received attention, particularly in architectural surveys like the Historic American Buildings Survey. Concepts of beauty did not change so quickly, however, and the preservation movement rarely united to save important structures from the late Victorian period. The America of the New Deal had little to learn from the monuments of the Gilded Age.

The staff of the National Park Service attempted to educate travelers by means of buildings, battlefields, and museums that illustrated many themes in American history. The historians who administered most of the areas that came into the National Park System looked on their responsibilities as educational, but even the widened definition of historical studies current in the 1930s did not include the study of the evolution of American architectural forms. The Park Service generally preferred original buildings to studied reconstructions, but it was often pushed into large projects by pressure groups and congressional appropriations. Local historical associations insisted on federal ownership of the homes of the famous and well-to-do, while architects and historians were eager to have the everyday life of the past illustrated.

BROADENING VIEWS

As usual, architects and architectural historians remained predominant among the preservation observers. Henry-Russell Hitchcock attempted to broaden the tastes of the preservation community with a brief article entitled "Destruction" in the December 1928 *Architectural Record*. He warned that the best work of the nineteenth century was in great danger, while the classical buildings of the eighteenth century usually received reverent attention. He urged his colleagues to "weigh the destruction of nineteenth-century buildings with equal care and more aesthetic delicacy."[2] A decade later Hitchcock made the same plea at a meeting of historians and architects held at the National Gallery. He wanted to know why pre-Revolutionary buildings had been saved "without regard to essential architectural merit," and yet the great monuments of the late nineteenth century were still being destroyed.[3] While Hitchcock was asking for preservation of the Victorian portions of Harvard Yard, H. I. Brock of the *New York Times* angrily denounced the cultural leaders of New York City who had permitted Stanford White's Madison Square Garden (1883–90) to come down.[4]

The prevailing attitude toward Victorian architecture is illustrated by a humorous quotation from a 1932 congressional debate over the Old State, War, and Navy Building (1871–88) in Washington, D.C. Sen. Reed Smoot referred to the structure as a "monstrosity." "I never saw so many gimcracks and spizzerinktums put upon any other building I ever saw in this world." Sen. George Norris unsuccessfully attempted to elicit a definition of "spizzerinktum" and then announced to his colleagues that, whatever they were, he favored them—and the culture that had produced them! Soon other legislators joined Norris in his defense of the florid decoration of the Grant era.[5] Later that same year William S. Rusk defended late nineteenth-century architecture in a long article in *Art and Archaeology* that bore the heading "What Price Progress?" He noted with real regret the demolition of the old Boston Art Museum on Copley Square, especially because the building had been "the master-

State, War, and Navy Building, Washington, D. C. (Photograph by Ronald Comedy, HABS; Library of Congress)

Old Museum of Fine Arts, Boston. (SPNEA)

piece of Victorian Gothic in America." Rusk went on to show how the remarkable architectural ensemble of mansions along New York's Fifth Avenue had been torn down to make way for offices and apartments, while Philadelphians, as well, were ripping down portions of Rittenhouse Square. Rusk asked if the economic gain had really made up for the civic loss in any of these cases.[6]

Some of the most perceptive preservation critics were outsiders who had not saved any buildings. When Laurence Vail Coleman wrote *Historic House Museums* in 1933, he had just returned from a long journey that had taken him to a number of restorations throughout America. While he unhesitatingly referred to the maintenance of the monuments of the past as a "duty," he was sorry to admit that most buildings he visited had been selected for preservation almost by accident.[7] Coleman linked the rise of the historic house museum with the growing popularity of the automobile. He noted that the Rockefeller decision to restore the whole of Williamsburg was a "convincing finale." "The historic house movement seeks not to *use* but to *know*—to *understand* American houses of the past. This is not a revival but an awakening; its result is education. It is an advance on the modern frontier of ideas which has more and more engaged our energies since the old frontier of land was closed in 1890."[8] So Laurence Coleman tied the burgeoning preservation field to the frontier thesis of Frederick Jackson Turner. The idea that the study of visible reminders of the past was a sign of national maturity seemed to typify the optimism of the 1930s.

Some organizations, such as the National Park Service, envisaged a national chain of sites that would illustrate themes in American history. The Department of the Interior already had some battlefields and Indian ruins that could be united through a carefully planned system of museums and visitor centers. Urban preservationists preferred to save any grouping of buildings that constituted an oasis of beauty and stability in neighborhoods that might be threatened by commercialism. And leaders such as Maury Maverick hoped to memorialize a cultural heritage through exhibits, such as La Villita in San Antonio.

But most people who saved historic buildings still thought their projects were shrines—places that had been made sacred by associations with events or with important figures in the past. As late as 1946 Clay Lancaster, an architectural historian, regarded the attitude toward historic landmarks pessimistically when he wrote the following comments for *Antiques*:

The United States, for the most part, still refuses to take its heritage seriously. The American architectural shrine is, generally speaking, scarcely beyond the adolescent stage. Our country has come so far that it recognizes, with numerous proddings from private and disinterested individuals, that certain buildings such as those at Williamsburg, Mount Vernon, Monticello, and a few other places, should be preserved. This vague, hit-or-miss attitude has not matured to the point where it can bear to take into account a great many houses of almost equal architectural importance that are still unknown.[9]

In general, the restoration theory and patriotic education ideas evolved at Williamsburg dominated the first half of the 1930s. The broader view of a National Historic Sites program, preservation of varied architectural traditions, and the conservative restoration philosophy taken by the National Park Service staff in the late 1930s greatly influenced the preservation field after the passage of the Historic Sites Act in 1935; but there were no substantial changes in restoration practice or additions to the ranks of the professionals who supervised this work in the 1940s.

PUBLICATIONS ADVANCE PRESERVATION THEORY

The development of preservation theory and the major issues it raised can be traced through the many books and magazine articles that appeared throughout the 1920s and 1930s. In his *Bibliography of Early American Architecture* Frank Roos, Jr., of Ohio State University in 1943 assessed the growing interest in early American buildings by a simple mathematical process—he counted the number of books on the subject published during two-year periods from 1900 to 1939. His comments document the change. At the turn of the century he could locate only 21 titles, but by 1920 that total had risen to 126. In 1939 there were 202. Roos concluded that the depression had held back these publications, but since 1935 the interest sparked by the Williamsburg restoration had made the public more receptive to works on colonial and post-Revolutionary buildings.[10] Roos correctly predicted that there would be a decided drop in the number of monographs appearing after 1940 as the war turned the attention of Americans toward national survival. In his introduction to the *Bibliography* he outlined for younger scholars the most serious omissions in geographical, biographical, and stylistic research. He praised the handful of authors who had already explored documentary sources (which was often a weakness with architectural historians), and then he described the most challenging research projects of all: sociological and critical accounts that placed architecture in its cultural context. Roos singled out John Coolidge's recently published *Mill and Mansion* as an example of the kind of work that was needed. The Coolidge book discussed in considerable detail the city plan, industrial development, and residential architecture of Lowell, Mass.[11] Roos warned his readers: "It is time now to study further some of the many factors that influenced plans and elevations, such as religious and national habits and backgrounds, laws, geographic distribution of materials, and climate. . . . Studies could profitably be made, too, of early evidences of factors common in architecture today, such as functionalism, or American ingenuity."[12]

Early preservation writings appeared primarily in periodicals. The *Architectural Record*, particularly under the editorship of A. Lawrence Kocher, published a great deal of material on this subject. For example, Richard F. Bach of the Avery Library at Columbia University produced a bibliography, "Early American Architecture and the Allied Arts," that ran intermittently in the *Record* from 1915 through 1928. Bach was confident that the vast pictorial and documentary record of American architecture available in books and magazines had influenced the preservation movement: "The result has been most beneficial. Many buildings have been preserved or restored; as have also many lesser items of furniture and other portable objects. With great knowledge of the things themselves, methods of preservation and restoration—the bugbear of the archaeologist—have also improved. That alone is a prodigious gain. Museums and private collectors have been busy assembling material of Early American provenience; the American Wing at the Metropolitan Museum has had a record breaking attendance."[13]

One of the principal centers for collectors was the magazine *Antiques*, which from 1938 on under the editorship of Alice Winchester included more and more articles dealing with the contribution of architects and curators to the preservation movement. Miss Winchester found ways to praise private owners who had worked hard to restore old homes. In 1949 Frederick Rath of the new National Council for Historic Sites and Buildings could say: "Alice became a figure in this [preservation] almost immediately and became in my estimation a very important figure because she latched onto this and began to plug it consistently."[14]

Even during the war years, when the interest in historic buildings seemed to die down in the midst of the national crisis, *Antiques* steadily increased its coverage of preservation and restoration work. When the magazine celebrated its twentieth anniversary in January 1942, Charles Messer Stow of the *New York Sun* contributed a helpful and provocative article on the growing interest in early American life, placing *Antiques* in its pivotal role as an interpreter of the rising tide of antiquarianism.[15] In

Alice Winchester ca. 1950. (Photograph by Kate Swift)

1946 Miss Winchester included a stirring article by Clay Lancaster entitled "Save Boscobel!" Lancaster denounced the tendency in the United States to spend money for the repair of art treasures abroad while ignoring a cultural monument of the American Classical Revival.[16]

By mid-century Alice Winchester had decided that the preservation movement was a serious phenomenon that required constant coverage in *Antiques*. The most spectacular recognition came in the July 1950 issue, which was wholly devoted to the preservation movement, starting with a symposium on the principles of historic restoration. The editorial showed that the creation of the National Council and the National Trust was a vital step, but the existence of a central headquarters meant only that the problems of the preservation field had been focused in one place. *Antiques* magazine intended to show its readers what those problems were and what the leading authorities thought the solutions might be.[17]

Perhaps the greatest service performed by architects for the preservation movement can be found in the books published between 1926 and 1950. No doubt research into the development of preservation organizations throughout the United States in the 1940s and 1950s would show that these reference books became weapons in the hands of dedicated amateurs who needed to prove conclusively that they were trying to save the most representative buildings from the past.

By the late 1930s the results of this research effort were spectacular. When Charles M. Stotz published his remarkable survey, *The Early Architecture of Western Pennsylvania*, in 1936, he commented in the foreword: "The Survey was not primarily intended to encourage a revival of building in the old manner. But for those interested in perpetuating local building traditions, this book will for the first time furnish authentic source material. Also, it is hoped, efforts toward the preservation and restoration of our more noteworthy structures may be stimulated."[18]

The major books produced by practicing architects were labors of love, often put together for some specific purpose. These works rarely dealt with buildings later than 1830 and usually centered on specific regions or towns that had been "discovered" by the authors. The eclecticism of the 1920s gave writers a breadth of taste that has probably not been equaled since that decade.

For example, Philip B. Wallace, in collaboration with William Allen Dunn, brought out three large picture books on various aspects of the architecture of the greater Philadelphia area. One study covered ironwork; the other two took up houses and churches. There was no text, but all three volumes included measured drawings that would be useful to architects who might want to copy details for their own work.[19] These books were planned to be large and expensive, probably on the assumption that they would appeal to practicing architects. Eleanor Raymond, another Philadelphia architect, published *Early Domestic Architecture of Pennsylvania* in 1931. Her account evidently was intended to cover rural buildings that had been missed in the Wallace surveys, but the format was the same—measured drawings and large photographs in a treatise prepared for a limited public.[20]

John Mead Howells, who was a successful designer of skyscrapers and other large buildings, took a great deal of his own time in the late 1920s assembling documentary pictures of principal structures of the colonial period that had disappeared. This catalog was published in 1931 as *Lost Examples of Colonial Architecture*. As was often the case with works on architectural history in those years, Fiske Kimball wrote an introduction in which he deplored the lack of governmental preservation activity in the United States.[21] The original edition of *Lost Examples* gives the student of colonial and Federal architecture an unparalleled opportunity to look at large photographs of representative private and public buildings that had never been touched by a restorer. It was a great accomplishment that was not surpassed for several decades. Howells's later books on Portsmouth, N.H., and Newburyport, Mass., did not include preservation appeals; he simply hoped that the richness of architectural detail presented in his books would focus attention on possible losses. In the Portsmouth book, for instance, he described a fine frame house of the eighteenth century in this way: "It is to be regretted that the position of this splendid house, directly on the busy corner of a through route for motor traffic, is a danger to its being preserved indefinitely."[22] His analysis proved to be correct, because the building was torn down in the 1960s.

The Historic American Buildings Survey had a beneficial influence on preservation thinking because the unemployed architects chose to record structures of all types—residential, commercial, cultural, and governmental. Surveyors sought buildings that had been used by ordinary people, not merely the noble homes of the eighteenth century.

The economic dislocation that came with the depression not only helped to create HABS: it also led directly to a number of smaller cooperative efforts to record historic buildings. In New York City the Architects' Emergency Committee under William Lawrence Bottomley published two large volumes entitled *Great Georgian Houses of America* in 1933 and 1937. Private subscribers agreed to purchase a number of these books in an effort to support unemployed draftsmen who went out to photograph and measure some of the larger homes of the last half of the eighteenth century. As an unemployment project the enterprise was a success. Bottomley boasted in the preface to the second volume that 110 men had been hired to work on the books between 1932 and 1937. All of the money collected had gone directly into publishing and mailing the two volumes.[23]

During World War II a decorator, Deering Davis, teamed with a historian, Stephen Dorsey, and a St. Louis architect, Ralph Cole Hall, to produce two architectural surveys of old towns in the Washington, D.C., area. The first of these books, *Georgetown Houses of the Federal Period*, appeared in 1944. In their introduction the authors called upon the presidents of all the private preservation and patriotic organizations in the United States to band together into "a great National Association" that would have the power to force Congress to create a system of national monuments in private ownership. Apparently these three men, marooned in Washington during the war, had begun to perceive the need for a National Trust and a National Register.[24] Shortly after the war they produced a second work, *Alexandria Houses*, which also began with a brief preservation appeal: "The most destructive of all wars has come and gone and our own old buildings are now a tragically larger share of the architectural heritage of mankind. So it is of more than national importance now that we preserve and restore what we have, and it was to that end that we undertook this book and its predecessor on Georgetown."[25] Almost instinctively these architects described the shift in preservation sentiment in postwar America. During the prosperous 1920s the challenges had come from the rush of a nation bent upon realizing the good life through the automobile. The threats came from highways, filling stations, and commercial strips that were developed to serve the newly liberated American public. The hard times of the 1930s reversed much of this expansion, and preservationists found themselves briefly free from large construction programs. Historic sites would help to reinforce a return to basic values, the ideals that had built a nation. With the return of peacetime prosperity in 1945 the authors of *Alexandria Houses* probably realized that their fellow citizens had once again turned onto the road of "progress." The preservation movement would have to fight for its life.

BOOKS BY RESTORATION ARCHITECTS

Although it may seem artificial to divide a profession into groups, the deepest analysis of cultural trends came with books published during the 1930s and 1940s by architects who had supervised major restorations. A few of them considered themselves to be primarily restoration experts, so their ideas were drawn from experience. The studies were more than just preservation tracts; they were research reports that gave restorers documentary evidence gained during years of patient examination of historic buildings. While it is impossible to cover all of these works, it would be unfair not to single out some of the more significant monographs prepared by the people who became the first generation of scholar-architects.

The Walpole Society published Norman M. Isham's *Early American Houses* in 1928. Probably no more than fifty copies were printed, but the people who worked with New England restorations of the seventeenth century knew the book well. Isham had written monographs on Rhode Island and Connecticut buildings in the 1890s, and over the years he had made a great many sketches of details he had discovered in the framing of the buildings he was restoring. Antoinette Downing, who was to produce a book of her own in 1938 under the title *Early Homes of Rhode Island*, heard Isham lecture at the Rhode Island School of Design: "He started off his 17th-century section saying that to understand the house you must understand the structure because the structure *is* the house. We analyzed the framing, the foundation, everything that would make a structure stand up, the box frame, added in the decoration—the vertical boarding."[26] In *Early American Houses* Isham correctly assumed that his scholarly readers were already interested in seventeenth-century buildings and simply wanted to know more about them through photographs, detailed drawings, and a carefully constructed text. The same spirit of historical inquiry pervaded the final pages of his next book, *In Praise of Antiquaries*, published three years later. He told his colleagues to set a "scientific" standard for all future restorers.[27]

Although the Williamsburg restoration did not issue any published reports or studies in its early years, a few books could be called by-products of the Williamsburg drafting room. The first of these was by

Thomas T. Waterman and John Barrows, *Domestic Colonial Architecture of Tidewater Virginia* (1932), a catalog of fifteen of the largest and best-known Virginia houses of the seventeenth and eighteenth centuries. The format permitted enormous measured drawings of the facades, along with a number of good photographs.[28]

Waterman's greatest book was *The Mansions of Virginia*, which proved to be one of the most detailed and possibly one of the most controversial architectural monographs up to that time. Waterman covered many more houses in the 1945 work than he and Barrows had treated in 1932, and the later volume propounded some theories that had not been mentioned in the first. The only measured drawings in the *Mansions* book were small comparative floor plans, but the text included detailed architectural descriptions of every building that Waterman had seen. The author also grouped the mansions according to a series of known master builders, although the evidence for many of his attributions was mainly stylistic. In his postscript he showed a decided reluctance to locate or to use documentary sources; however, he did not hestitate to draw conclusions based on English precedents and a few scraps of information that he had picked up about Virginia architects. Waterman ended the book with an essay on restoration practice as it had developed at Williamsburg.[29]

Two other books by architects can be said to have originated in the research files at Williamsburg: Harold Shurtleff's *Log Cabin Myth* and A. Lawrence Kocher and Howard Dearstyne's *Colonial Williamsburg: Its Buildings and Gardens*. The Shurtleff book was published posthumously under the editorship of Samuel Eliot Morison at Harvard. During his years in Virginia, Shurtleff had become annoyed at references in basic American history books to the log cabins of the first settlers at Jamestown and Plymouth. He knew of some articles in *Old-Time New England* on the origin of log houses in America that showed these structures were not a common building type for the first English settlers.[30] He was also aware that some reconstruction, such as the trading post at Aptucxet, Mass., and George Francis Dow's Pioneer Village, in Salem, correctly displayed seventeenth-century buildings with post-and-lintel construction, not as the log cabins of popular myth. Whatever the motivation may have been, both Shurtleff and his editor greatly enjoyed showing that many historians and architects (who should have known better) were still telling their readers and pupils that the log cabin was a typical seventeenth-century English building.[31] The Kocher and Dearstyne book, which appeared in 1949, represented the first effort by architects to explain the Williamsburg restoration process in any detailed way since William G. Perry's 1935 article in the *Architectural Record*. During World

War II Kocher had joined the architectural staff in Williamsburg to serve as an editor. He studied all of the reports of the restoration and reconstruction work done in the 1930s and tried to give these diverse documents a certain amount of continuity. *Colonial Williamsburg* covered each aspect of the process, including gardens and furnishings, and it presented clear documentary illustrations that showed the reader how major decisions had been made when the buildings were restored or reconstructed.[32] It is regrettable that the men (other than Waterman) who worked so hard over the years to understand the buildings of Tidewater Virginia were too busy to publish their findings.

One architect who worked at Jamestown under the National Park Service, Henry Chandlee Forman, compiled a considerable amount of material on his work. His first book, *The Early Manor and Plantation Houses of Maryland*, came out in 1934. It was a pioneer effort in architectural research that included pictures Forman had taken in parts of Maryland that most of his colleagues considered too remote for travel. Over the years the book has become increasingly valuable because Forman carefully recorded obscure manor houses that have since been torn down.[33] His second major book, produced in 1938, caused a stir within the staff of Colonial National Historical Park.[34] In *Jamestown and St. Mary's, Buried Cities of Romance* Forman described the curious relationships that existed between the first two English towns in the South. Both of them had become archaeological sites by the 1930s (although St. Marys City was still functioning as a community), and Forman told in considerable detail how the skills of the archaeologists and the architects had been used to study and explain these two settlements.[35] The Jamestown book represented the kind of research report that the scholarly community had been expecting from Colonial Williamsburg and the National Park Service; but no such published documents were forthcoming from those organizations until the 1950s, and consequently Forman's study remained the only major source on the subject.

Although Charles E. Peterson wrote no books during these years, he attempted to record the work that had been done by the architects of the National Park Service, including submitting a report in 1935 to the Park Service on the Yorktown restorations and writing an *Antiques* magazine article on Jamestown in May 1936.[36] Later, when he was in St. Louis, Peterson published some articles on his researches in the Mississippi Valley that were almost book length, such as a report on his restoration of the ill-fated Manuel Lisa Warehouse (the Old Rock House). He used all of the research techniques that he had learned at Williamsburg to produce a model paper, listing precedents for nearly every important decision he had made in 1941.[37] Peterson's use of structural and documentary evidence was easily as good as any of the material published in the major periodicals of the day.

One other active restoration architect produced a book during these years, and it was the first detailed documentary report on a historical project available to the public. Joseph Booton, working for the Division of Architecture and Engineering for the state of Illinois, wrote the *Record of the Restoration of New Salem* and published it in July 1934. This eighty-eight-page monograph covered every imaginable topic on the reconstruction of the log cabin village that had been so closely associated with the life of Lincoln. Booton was a history-minded civil servant who hoped to satisfy his future critics with carefully reasoned arguments that explained each of the decisions made in rebuilding New Salem.[38]

Although the architects who supervised the restorations that flourished during the depression years often found time to include some of their conclusions in books and articles, these publications gave only a faint impression of the total picture. Most of the best scholarly work had to be recorded in notebooks, daily journals, or in unpublished reports that eventually found their way into the files of different government departments.

BOOKS BY TEACHERS AND ART HISTORIANS

Another band of architectural scholars who published can best be grouped under the general heading of teachers and art historians, most of whom were connected with colleges and universities. Fortunately for the cause of historic preservation these people wrote a considerable number of worthwhile books, particularly in the 1930s. They tended to concentrate on types of research that had not been covered by the rest of the architectural profession, and because they were able to travel more they often treated broader and more theoretical subjects than their colleagues in the drafting rooms.

First and foremost in this group of historian-architects was Henry-Russell Hitchcock, who wrote a book on Frank Lloyd Wright in 1928, at a time when the American architect was considered to be outside the mainstream of world developments.[39] Although he published some important works on modern architecture and on Victorian styles, Hitchcock also had an influence on the preservation movement through his valiant efforts to broaden the horizons of the literate public, who had tended to believe that buildings later than 1830 did not possess enough historical or architectural interest to be preserved.[40] For example, Hitchcock's 1936 monograph *The Architecture of H. H. Richardson and His Times* opened up for many readers the story of a whole new world of American architectural development in the later nineteenth century.[41] Lewis Mumford's *The Brown Decades* (1931) prepared the way for Hitchcock's revisionism. In a series of lectures first delivered in 1929 Mumford had denounced America's neglect of the works of Louis Sullivan and H. H. Richardson. He noted that Richardson had given post–Civil War society an entirely new language in architecture, but the people of the 1920s were busy tearing it down![42] "In reality the monuments of the nineteenth century have too few loyal supporters to defend them," Hitchcock lamented in the *Architectural Record* in December 1928. "Destruction is not only conscience-stricken but is accepted as even righteous."[43]

These critics were tragically prophetic. In the Richardson book Hitchcock blasted away at a commercial society that could destroy the magnificent Marshall Field Warehouse (1885–87) in Chicago without a whimper. It would appear that this passage from the 1936 study is almost the only protest uttered over the demolition of the masonry building that greatly influenced the work of Sullivan and several other architects:

> The building was destroyed a few years ago to make room for an outdoor parking garage. It was really sacrificed to the urban congestion the skyscraper has created. It is futile to suggest that this building should have been preserved and all the blocks around torn down to display one of the greatest monuments of architecture in America. The first skyscrapers, the Home Insurance and the Tacoma, have been torn down as well. These three monuments, historically among the most interesting buildings in America, should have made Chicago a center of pilgrimage for all who are interested in architecture. The money and the effort that might have saved them was poured instead into the temporary structures of an ironical "Century of Progress" exposition. Pointless piety has preserved of the Marshall Field Wholesale Store only the carved capitals, things absolutely without value or interest in this period of Richardson's career.[44]

One might ask who the architectural pilgrims would have been in 1930. Would anyone have led a battle to save the giant stone warehouse? Hitchcock was relieved to report in 1961, when he wrote a new preface to his book, that there was "a growing consciousness of the intrinsic value of fine nineteenth-century buildings."[45] But it had taken at least twenty-five years to develop that awareness.

Certainly a scholar with such broad interests could not pause to fight only for the preservation of Richardson buildings. In 1938 Henry-Russell Hitchcock put together an exhibit at the Rhode Island School of Design that covered every aspect of the architecture of one small state.

Marshall Field Wholesale Warehouse, Chicago, razed 1930. (Chicago Historical Society)

This narrow geographical format permitted Hitchcock to include mills, small villages, the mansions of Newport, and even the buildings of the twentieth century. The catalog contained judgments that were obviously intended to give the public a wider view of the mission of historic preservation: "Together with the mills and mill villages, from which much of the wealth that here flowed so copiously was derived—it is a pity the Lippitt Castle is no longer extant to be illustrated beside the Lippitt Mills—these houses constitute the obverse and reverse of the New England medal of architecture in the nineteenth century. We should study both sides of the medal, not only with our eyes but with our minds, in order that we may grasp the story of American architecture in its fullest meaning."[46]

Another architectural historian, Hugh Morrison, followed along the path Hitchcock had explored in the 1920s by doing a considerable amount of research on Louis Sullivan. In 1935 he published a remarkably complete and thoughtful biography of Sullivan that discussed both the works and the writings of the man who had done so much for the cause of modern architecture. Although Morrison incorrectly assumed that Sullivan's greatest buildings were safe for the foreseeable future, he did pause in his description of the Auditorium Building (1887–89) in Chicago to argue superbly for its preservation:

> The Auditorium was the chief monument upon which the later success of Adler & Sullivan was built. In point of cost, it was the largest building enterprise in the city of Chicago at that time, and ten times greater than any previous commission of the firm. As an engineering achievement it was outstanding, being the heaviest structure yet carried on floating foundations, and embodying extremely ingenious solutions of many other complex problems of planning, construction, and mechanical equipment. Its historical importance as a turning-point in Sullivan's style and as a great institution in the civic life of Chicago, not to speak of its architectural excellence, make it a building which should be preserved to future generations as one of the great monuments of American architecture.[47]

No group of Park Service historians and architects could have put together a more complete and authoritative justification for the preservation of a national landmark at that time. Few people in 1935, though, would have considered Morrison's strong statement enough reason for keeping such a large building in the downtown section of a growing city. After World War II Morrison's arguments might have had some influence on the decision to preserve the Auditorium. Roosevelt University purchased the building and gradually adapted many of the former hotel service areas to new uses for an educational institution.[48]

Auditorium Building, Chicago. (Photograph by Ralph Line; courtesy Commission on Chicago Historical and Architectural Landmarks)

In 1940 George Kubler of Yale University published *The Religious Architecture of New Mexico*, a classic that has been reprinted in more recent years. In an extraordinarily thorough way Kubler analyzed the religious buildings as to climate, materials, Indian building techniques, Spanish society and religion, and a host of historical trends. Charts and illustrations helped to make a complex subject understandable.[49]

During the late 1930s Columbia University became a center for architectural historians who clustered around Talbot F. Hamlin. Between 1939 and 1944 this group produced three books that were intended to increase public appreciation for nineteenth-century styles through the medium of biography and cultural analysis. The first of these publications was Everard Upjohn's life of his great-grandfather, Richard Upjohn, the designer of Trinity Church in New York City and one of the founding members of the American Institute of Architects.[50] Kenneth Conant wrote a brief foreword in which he claimed that a book on the father of the American Gothic Revival would stir preservationists:

> My sincere hope is that Everard Upjohn's sympathetic account of his great forebear's work will call to the attention of many the significance which it has as a part of our national heritage. There has already been a heavy toll of the buildings in which the architectural history of the last century was written—sometimes the result of catastrophe; but far too often a building which was a part of our common artistic birthright has been swept away just for dollars, perhaps with no consciousness of the loss inflicted. The remedy is a wider knowledge of the works of our great creative spirits and a fuller appreciation of the gifts which they have left behind them for the commonwealth of art-lovers everywhere.[51]

In 1943 Roger Hale Newton of the Columbia University circle published *Town and Davis, Architects*. Newton became the most outspoken defender of American Victorian buildings of all types; and telling the story of the firm of Town and Davis gave him a chance to provide aesthetic and philosophical arguments for preserving the principal monuments of each of the major revivals of the nineteenth century.[52]

The last book to come from the New York group was Talbot Hamlin's own compendium, *Greek Revival Architecture in America*, published in 1944. The subject was so vast that Hamlin had consumed the better part of a decade in travel in his efforts to compare the various regional interpretations of classical architecture.[53] Apparently Hamlin concluded that there was no need to reorient the tastes of his fellow Americans with respect to the venerable buildings of the Greek Revival; it had never completely gone out of favor. Instead he devoted two chapters to the early history and development of the idea of the Classical Revival.[54]

Hamlin admitted that his book constituted an introduction to a subject that could keep scholars busy for many years, but he believed that the time had come to describe the movement that led to a truly American form of architecture.

Between the publication of Thomas Waterman's *Mansions of Virginia* in 1945 and the founding of the National Trust in 1949, no major new works on architectural history appeared. There were a few regional studies on midwestern and southern themes, but the research begun in the 1930s had spent itself during the war years. The next generation of scholars did not generally complete its books until the 1950s, beginning with Agnes A. Gilchrist's life of William Strickland.[55]

Only a few standard textbooks on the evolution of American architecture were available to undergraduates, principally one by Fiske Kimball, *American Architecture* (1928), and another by Thomas Tallmadge, *Story of Architecture in America*. In the 1936 edition of his book Tallmadge chose to end the story of modern America with some account of the Williamsburg restoration. He enjoyed "ending our story almost exactly where we began it" by taking his readers back to Tidewater Virginia. He recounted his 1926 visits with W. A. R. Goodwin when the idea of the restoration still seemed to be visionary.[56] Tallmadge let the magic of the restoration process create a mood: "It is the peculiar triumph of Williamsburg that after you have been there awhile you become one with the place and the old time and that it is the modern world that is unreal: an unpleasant, incomprehensible dream that you had last night in your four-poster."[57] Tallmadge was hoping that the good planning and collaborative scholarship represented by the experiment in Williamsburg might transform America into a better place. He clearly considered historic preservation to be the wave of the future.

Even some Europeans became more outspoken than Americans about the need for preservation in the United States. Sigfried Giedion, a Swiss scholar, strongly supported the idea of converting the doomed buildings on the site of the Jefferson National Expansion Memorial to museums, but he was too late to stop the clearance. He also condemned the Chicago business community in a footnote in his book *Space, Time and Architecture* (1941) for allowing the Home Insurance Building to be torn down in 1929 when it "was still sound."[58]

COMING OF AGE

The preservation movement in 1950 was ready for another period of expansion, but this was not immediately apparent. The opening of

Hampton National Historic Site seemed to foreshadow a federal interest in architectural history, but the dedication of the reconstructed McLean House at Appomattox the same year pointed back to the emphasis on historical shrines. Critics who bemoaned the limited perspective of most preservers and restorers were outside the active field of historic-sites management. The National Survey of Historic Sites and Buildings and the activities of the Advisory Board of the Secretary of the Interior had initiated the National Register of Historic Places. When historians reported to the board on the qualifications of various sites throughout the nation, they were evaluating buildings that were not typical house museums. By the end of the depression the professional staff in the Department of the Interior was searching for some method of saving the historical landscape rather than a few isolated sites, and this culminated in the founding of the National Trust for Historic Preservation. The generation of leaders that created the historic districts of the 1930s and 1940s pioneered techniques that would be put to good use during the 1950s. From Charleston to Newport local historians had experimented with zoning, architectural surveys, parking plans, adaptive uses, and foundations that could purchase and renovate useful structures. Large historic districts became an accepted feature of urban life. People found eighteenth- and nineteenth-century neighborhoods good places to live. Would-be preservers were no longer looked on as obstructionists; they could convince their fellow citizens that saving old buildings was a form of progress.

Afterword

by the National Trust for Historic Preservation

PRESERVATION COMES OF AGE is an apt title for a history of the youthful years of the preservation movement, an era that began in 1926 and culminated in the formation of the National Trust for Historic Preservation in 1949. The coming of age of preservation brought growth and, as in any maturation process, development of self-awareness and the skills and knowledge necessary to function productively. During this period, especially in the depression years, Americans generally developed their own self-awareness as never before; this national consciousness of the value of their cultural and architectural heritage in turn helped nurture preservation's growth.

The period covered by this book was a time of firsts, the fruits of which the preservation movement is seeing today. The first preservation zoning ordinance, passed in Charleston, S.C., in 1931, was the forerunner of hundreds of zoning ordinances that now protect historic neighborhoods in cities and towns all across the United States. When the Louisiana constitution was amended in 1936 to create the Vieux Carré Commission in New Orleans, a legal precedent was set for the establishment of commissions in most major cities today and the initiation of a body of case law that affirms regulation of environmental and aesthetic qualities as being within the public welfare. Early preservation campaigns, such as that for Stratford Hall, were the first of thousands of national, state, and local efforts to save important historic and architectural landmarks. Today there are more than 1,500 National Historic Landmarks and more than 20,000 properties of national, state, and local significance listed in the National Register of Historic Places, including more than 1,000 districts. From its first few visitors to Colonial National Historical Park in Yorktown, Va., in the 1930s, the National Park Service has expanded to become a major source for the enjoyment and education of the American public and the protection of significant sites. The first state survey of historic sites, conducted by Frederick Law Olmsted, Jr., in California in 1928, was the prototype of surveys now conducted in all states of the union. And when Henry-Russell Hitchcock argued for preservation of the then unpopular Victorian architecture in the 1930s, little did he know that in the 1970s Americans would acquire Victorian buildings with as much eagerness as they once did colonial structures.

Preservation came of age during this period, in particular, by developing new skills required by new demands. Much of this book is devoted to describing these skills: organizational and fund-raising techniques; professional preservation disciplines, especially in the field of architectural restoration; theories and techniques for restoring old buildings; and new area-preservation tools, such as surveys, historic-district zoning, and legislation. These last techniques, developed by urban preservationists to save and revive their cities and neighborhoods, are in the forefront today as preservation tools, but at the time they were considered innovative. Their initiation represented another expansion of preservation beyond a focus only on individual buildings to consideration of broad community values and needs in solving common social problems. It is in this context that preservation came of age and has taken its place as a necessary and respected social goal.

Writing in 1965, Helen Duprey Bullock, National Trust historian and archivist, conjectured, "When the second volume of 'Presence of the Past—A History of the Preservation Movement in the United States after Williamsburg' is written, it may more appropriately be titled 'Presence of the Remains—Or the History of Destruction after 1926!'" Fortunately, that is not the title of this book. While destruction has indeed been widespread, it is through use of the tools developed during preservation's youth and through the efforts of preservationists around the nation that many more losses have been avoided.

Today the preservation movement in the United States is far-ranging, covering a diversity of issues and approaches. The National Trust for Historic Preservation, whose founding is described in chapter 10 of this book, has now served for three decades as the national organization responsible for encouraging public participation in preservation. A private, nonprofit organization supported by both private and public funds, the National Trust provides leadership for the various activities and interests of preservationists in the United States, works closely with fed-

eral preservation agencies and programs, provides advice and encouragement for local and state efforts, and acts as an information clearinghouse
between public bodies and private groups. The National Trust seeks to
educate the American public about preservation through the news me-
dia, films, books, and its publications, including *Preservation News*, its
monthly newspaper, and *Historic Preservation*, its bimonthly magazine.
The National Trust owns historic properties and administers them as
centers for preservation activity in their communities. A wide range of
advisory services is available from the Trust, as are funding programs
for consultants, educational programs, conferences, and local revolving
funds. Six regional offices bring preservation resources closer to local
and state needs in all areas of the country.

As the National Trust has always been aware, its strength and purpose lie in the needs of its members—the numerous professionals, organizations, and interested citizens who are working to save America's cultural and architectural heritage. A survey of preservation in the United
States at the beginning of the 1980s shows an exciting and expanding
breadth of activity.

Since passage of the National Historic Preservation Act in 1966,
federal and state involvement in preservation has increased enormously.
The act provided for expansion of the National Register of Historic
Places—the official list of districts, sites, buildings, structures, and objects of national, state, and local significance maintained by the U.S.
Department of the Interior. It also established the Advisory Council on
Historic Preservation to provide vigilance over federal actions that adversely affect historic properties in the National Register. To develop
statewide preservation plans and surveys and acquire and restore historic properties with matching federal funding authorized under the act,
historic preservation offices have been created in every state and territory. Despite this activity, it is estimated that the states have identified
less than 25 percent of the potential places with cultural significance;
identification of such properties in federal ownership or control is less
than 10 percent complete. At the current rate of selection, twenty-eight
more years will be required to list extant resources in the National Register, not including sites with newly recognized significance. In 1977,
for example, the Interior Department was able to provide only $17.5
million in matching grant assistance to the states and the National Trust
in the face of identified needs totaling $340 million.

Clearly, more is needed. As a special task force on national heritage
policy concluded in 1977, "The Federal Government has a fundamental
responsibility to provide leadership in the identification and protection
of culturally significant places. In the first place, that government has

been the source of much that has adversely affected the cultural environment. More important, it is the only vehicle which can provide a comprehensive framework for state, local and private conservation efforts."

To help fulfill this responsibility, a new National Heritage program was proposed by President Carter in 1978. This renewed federal effort, directed by the Department of the Interior, is designed to provide a comprehensive program for the protection of natural and cultural resources through parallel but coordinated programs, recognizing not only the similarities but the differences between the two types of resources. Preservationists have already joined hands with conservationists at various levels to find common solutions to their interrelated goals of creating a more livable total environment. Under the new program a comprehensive inventory of national heritage resources, both natural and cultural, has the potential to identify 70 percent of such resources within five years. Collections and objects, arts and skills, and folklife and contemporary cultures also would be brought under the umbrella of the program, bringing full circle efforts to identify and preserve the most valuable of America's cultural and natural resources. Funding levels and protective mechanisms also would be increased with the new program.

But federal involvement in preservation now reaches far beyond its traditional place in the Interior Department and its programs that originated during the Great Depression, such as the Historic American Buildings Survey, now joined by a Historic American Engineering Record. Directories published by the Trust in 1974 and 1976 showed that there were some 250 programs in 50 agencies, ranging from the significant support programs of the U.S. Department of Housing and Urban Development and the National Endowment for the Arts to those of the Farmers Home Administration, the Small Business Administration, Federal Home Loan Bank Board, and Amtrak.

In addition to these government programs, a wide range of private national preservation groups has developed, many focusing on specific architectural interests, such as the Victorian Society in America, Friends of Cast-Iron Architecture, and the Society for Industrial Archeology. Through UNESCO, the International Council of Monuments and Sites and the International Centre for Conservation, U.S. preservationists are exchanging information with preservationists in other countries. An increasing number of private statewide organizations coordinate the efforts of preservationists in their states and work for preservation legislation. On the local level, most major cities have landmarks or historic district commissions where not too long ago, during the years covered in this book, there were only a handful; more than 500 of these local government commissions administer a variety of historic district and landmarks ordinances through regulations protecting historic areas and individual buildings. These boards, as well as the even more numerous citywide and neighborhood preservation groups and public planning and community development agencies, conduct education programs to awaken interest in the value of the built environment; many develop specific plans for recycling buildings for new uses, showing how downtown commercial areas can be revitalized and residential neighborhoods can be stabilized.

Neighborhood conservation has now become a major focus of the preservation movement, as community groups and city agencies work to make available low-interest loans for rehabilitation by homeowners, to promote a neighborhood commitment and resident pride, and to formulate protective ordinances and guidelines to assist residents in maintaining their neighborhood's architectural integrity or special character. The Department of Housing and Urban Development's Community Development Block Grants (federal funds administered by local governments) are being used to improve basic services to old neighborhoods, to give the unemployed jobs restoring old houses, and to aid preservation efforts in numerous other innovative ways determined by each local community. Instead of focusing on selected historic buildings, conservation of entire areas has become a major objective, in the belief that without background buildings the integrity of the entire neighborhood is lost. "Our people need a sense of place," neighborhood advocate Msgr. Geno Baroni has said, "a particular place in which something has [happened] or continues to happen, which serves to elicit multiple and varied responses. And for many communities, neighborhoods can and should be such a place."

Downtown merchants, as they work to maintain their businesses in the face of the suburbanization of American shoppers, are beginning to join together to revitalize urban commercial areas. The Main Street Project of the National Trust, initiated in 1977, undertook the revitalization of the main streets of three small midwestern cities as a model for many more, by working with the communities to focus on the architectural uniqueness of the area, restoring original facades, and promoting appropriate signs and other amenities as a means to economic revitalization.

Planning has become an essential part of historic preservation, and vice versa. From the comprehensive preservation plans required of each state historic preservation office by the federal government, to a city planning office's development of a historic waterfront area, to a community design center's plan for adaptive use of old commercial office buildings as housing for the elderly, planners are helping to analyze the resources that are available and the choices that must be made to produce

Above, *Main Street, Madison, Ind. (Photograph by Balthazar Korab);*
below, *removal of Main Street sign covering historic facade, Madison, during filming of a National Trust film on Main Street revitalization. (Photograph by John Beckman)*

a better living environment. Preservation plans are increasingly integrated with, and seen as essential to, comprehensive area planning.

Legal tools for preservation that have gained acceptance in the past few decades include zoning, landmarks designation and historic district ordinances, aesthetic and environmental quality regulations, protective easements—and, as necessary—lawsuits. Justice William O. Douglas helped establish the "right of cities to be beautiful" in 1954 (*Berman* vs. *Parker*) by stating that "the concept of the public welfare is broad and inclusive. . . . It is within the power of the legislature to determine that the community should be beautiful as well as healthy, spacious as well as clean, well-balanced as well as carefully patrolled." Courts since then have continued to uphold the constitutionality of zoning and landmarks designation.

While most of the efforts described in this book focus on America's European heritage, the diversity of the American heritage is stressed by today's preservationists. They promote maintaining the integrity of urban ethnic neighborhoods; identification and preservation of sites related to the history of blacks, Hispanics, women, and native Americans; appreciation of our maritime tradition; and the cultural contribution of vernacular and industrial architectural forms, including such disparate ones as Lucy the Margate Elephant in New Jersey, Gas Works Park in Seattle, and workers' housing in Galveston. Especially as a result of Bicentennial efforts in 1976, communities across the country are publishing surveys of local architecture and oral histories of aged residents. The technical skills for research and documenting buildings and areas have improved substantially, including photogrammetric recording of buildings and historical archaeology techniques.

Increasingly, the general public is recognizing that preservation is also economically advantageous. As building materials and labor costs skyrocket and as the public becomes more conscious of the energy efficiency of many old buildings and the waste of resources involved in destroying them, more developers and architects are renovating old buildings for continued or new uses. Local, state, and federal programs assist developers by underwriting mortgages and providing direct matching grants-in-aid or tax write-offs. The Tax Reform Act of 1976 included provisions favorable to the preservation and rehabilitation of historic commercial and income-producing structures, including the disallowance of tax deductions for razing certified historic structures and allowance for accelerated depreciation of expenses incurred in restoring such buildings. Local preservation groups have initiated revolving funds through which they purchase old buildings and restore them and resell

Gas Works Park, Seattle. (Photograph by Carleton Knight III, National Trust for Historic Preservation)

them, frequently for a profit and often with an easement or covenant guaranteeing preservation of their exteriors or sites.

In the field of restoration, major technical advances were made in the 1970s, including special plastics to duplicate previously "irreplaceable" missing architectural details, X-ray photography to examine original construction, and sophisticated analysis of paint composition of old buildings. As individual rehabilitation efforts have become increasingly popular, catalogs of products and services useful to those restoring their homes have become available to the public, as have rehabilitation guidelines to help individuals without professional expertise maintain standards of architectural integrity. Changes in building codes to regulate more fairly safety standards in old buildings are making renovation and continued use more feasible.

Adaptive use, or recycling, of old buildings is a common approach to preservation today, as real estate investors have come to realize the economic advantages of reusing old buildings, and preservationists have accepted that the number of historic house museums society can support is limited. Recycled buildings include a wide range of types: railroad stations, schools, churches, theaters, courthouses, office buildings, factories and warehouses, hotels, and even locomotive shops. *Old & New Architecture: Design Relationship*, a book based on a 1977 conference cosponsored by the National Trust and Washington, D.C., chapters of the American Institute of Architects and the Society of Architectural Historians, explores such topics as designing new buildings to fit sympathetically into a streetscape, design review boards for neighborhoods, and new additions to old buildings.

Educational opportunities are expanding as preservation work becomes an increasingly professional field, with graduate degrees available at universities throughout the United States and courses offered at countless more. Specialized internships, work-study programs, conferences, and workshops are available to equip preservationists with the skills they need in the variety of disciplines now considered integral to preservation. These include not only architecture, archaeology, history, and museum studies, whose professional development is discussed in this book, but also the legal, planning, landscape architecture, journalism, community organizing, public relations, real estate, finance, and business professions.

Preservation publications programs are flourishing in many cities and towns, as well as in national publishing programs such as that of the Preservation Press of the National Trust and the American Association for State and Local History. Audiovisual resources are being used to further the preservation cause. The National Trust in 1977 produced the film *A Place in Time* to introduce general audiences to preservation.

Although the preservation movement today is so wide-ranging that it could never be covered in one volume, or even two, a supplement to one section of this book may be of interest to readers. *The History of the National Trust for Historic Preservation, 1963–1973* by Elizabeth D. Mulloy (Preservation Press, 1976) presents the evolution of the National Trust from the founding of the predecessor National Council for Historic Sites and Buildings in 1947 through passage of the National Historic Preservation Act in 1966 and the growth of the Trust and its programs, federal efforts, and related preservation activities. Charles Hosmer's first book, *Presence of the Past: A History of the Preservation Movement in the United States before Williamsburg*, is a vital companion to *Preservation Comes of Age*. As Winston Churchill said, "The farther backward you can look the farther forward you are likely to see." With that goal in mind, the National Trust has committed itself to recording preservation's own past—through publication of the history of its earlier years, by providing publishing assistance with Professor Hosmer's first history of the American preservation movement, and by copublishing this second work in that history.

Preservationists today must be aware that preservationists twenty or thirty years from now will look back and also see "firsts" like those recorded in this book. Unlike human beings, the preservation movement, now that it has come of age, is not likely ever to become "old," for our built environment will always be with us, and its protection and maintenance will always be our concern. As new buildings are constructed, some will become the landmarks of the future, continuing the preservation cycle.

"Culturally significant places, though tangible and fixed, are fragile resources," said a task force that recently studied the future of preservation in the United States.

If unrecognized and unprotected, they are subject to deterioration, indiscriminate alteration and destruction. Such diminishment of a heritage means not only the loss of usable resources but also the degradation of the intangible cultural values they represent.

Culturally significant places may be the victims of neglect. More often they have suffered in the path of America's drive to build and instinct to replace. Today there is a growing conviction that the preservation of such places may be accommodated in the continuing process of technological and industrial changes—indeed, that conservation will flourish and inform that process while helping to provide cultural continuity and to sustain the environmental and intangible qualities of American life.

With recognition and protection of the built environment now established as public policy and with many tools and resources available to preserve that heritage, our task is the continuing one of enriching the quality of life of future generations. It was with that hope that the early preservationists labored. And in appreciating their legacy today we can commit ourselves to leaving an even fuller legacy for the future.

NOTES

BIBLIOGRAPHY

CHRONOLOGY

INDEX

ACWF	Archives, Colonial Williamsburg Foundation
AHA	American Historical Association
Bancroft	Bancroft Library, University of California at Berkeley
CA	California State Archives
Cal.	California, Division of Beaches and Parks
Cal. Parks	California, Department of Parks and Recreation
CH	Court House (Appomattox)
CH	Custom House (Philadelphia)
CIW	Carnegie Institution of Washington
CS	San Antonio Conservation Society
CSC	Civic Services Committee
CSMB	Conservation Society Minutes Book
CWF	Colonial Williamsburg Foundation
FA	Ford Archives
FAC	Fine Arts Commission
GWB	George Washington Birthplace
Harpers Ferry	Archives of the National Park Service at Harpers Ferry Center
HCF	Historic Charleston Foundation
HFML	Henry Ford Museum Library
HFMR	Registrar's File, Henry Ford Museum
HV	Hopewell Village
IA	Indiana Archives
IC	Illinois Department of Conservation
INHP	Independence National Historical Park
Int.	U.S. Department of the Interior
ISHL	Illinois State Historical Library
JNEM	Jefferson National Expansion Memorial
LC	Library of Congress
LMF	Robert E. Lee Memorial Foundation
MHAA	Monterey History and Art Association
NA	National Archives
NC	National Council for Historic Sites and Buildings
NHP	National Historical Park
NHS	National Historic Site
NM	National Monument
NPS	National Park Service
NT	National Trust
NYSHA	New York State Historical Association
OSV	Old Sturbridge Village
OTNE	*Old-Time New England*
PA	Pennsylvania Archives
PHC	Pennsylvania Historical Commission
PHMC	Pennsylvania Historical and Museum Commission
PS&H	Perry, Shaw, and Hepburn
PSC	Preservation Society of Charleston
PSNC	Preservation Society of Newport County
Reg. Off.	Registrar's Office
RG	Record Group
SCHS	South Carolina Historical Society
SHP	State Historic Park
SMNHS	Salem Maritime National Historic Site
SPC	State Park Commission
SPNEA	Society for the Preservation of New England Antiquities
SPOD	Society for Preservation of Old Dwelling Houses of Charleston
UCSB	University of California at Santa Barbara
VCC	Vieux Carré Commission
WEA	Winterthur Estate Archives
Wint.	Henry Francis du Pont Winterthur Museum
WNMA	Wakefield National Memorial Association

NOTES

Introduction

1. John Braeman, Robert H. Bremner, and David Brody, eds., *Change and Continuity in Twentieth-Century America: The 1920s* (Columbus, Ohio, 1968).

2. Charles B. Hosmer, Jr., *Presence of the Past: A History of the Preservation Movement in the United States before Williamsburg* (New York, 1965), 41–62, 153–92.

3. U.S. Department of Commerce, Bureau of the Census, *Historical Statistics of the United States, Colonial Times to 1970* (Washington, D.C., 1975), 396.

4. Ibid., 716.

5. Ibid., 170.

6. President's Research Committee on Social Trends, *Recent Social Trends in the United States* (New York, 1934), xxvi–xxvii.

7. Ibid., 1002–3.

8. Ibid., 921.

9. Alice G. B. Lockwood, "Problems and Responsibilities of Restoration," *Old-Time New England*, No. 90 (Oct. 1937), 49.

10. Stanley Coben and Lorman Ratner, eds., *The Development of an American Culture* (Englewood Cliffs, N.J., 1970), 196–97.

11. Alfred Haworth Jones, *Roosevelt's Image Makers* (Port Washington, N.Y., 1974), 8.

12. Hosmer, *Presence of the Past*, 23.

Chapter 1: *The Williamsburg Restoration*

1. W. A. R. Goodwin, *Bruton Parish Church Restored and Its Historic Environment* (Petersburg, Va., 1907), 13.

2. Ibid., 33.

3. Ibid.

4. Parke Rouse, Jr., *Cows on the Campus: Williamsburg in Bygone Days* (Richmond, 1973), 116.

5. Elizabeth Hayes, "The Background and Beginnings of the Restoration of Colonial Williamsburg, Virginia, 1933," 10, Archives, Colonial Williamsburg Foundation (ACWF).

6. W. A. R. Goodwin to Barclay, Mar. 15, 1931, quoted ibid., 16.

7. T. Rutherfoord Goodwin, "The Williamsburg Restoration, Its Conception," 1, ACWF.

8. W. A. R. Goodwin to Edsel Ford, June 13, 1924, quoted in Hayes, "Background," 20–21.

9. H. M. Cordell to W. A. R. Goodwin, July 1, 1924, quoted ibid., 22.

10. W. A. R. Goodwin to William Ford, July 24, 1924, Restoration, Its Conception, W. A. R. Goodwin Files, ACWF.

11. W. A. R. Goodwin to J. Stewart Bryan, Sept. 9, 1924, ibid.

12. *Baltimore Sun*, Nov. 4, 1924.

13. W. A. R. Goodwin to editor, *Baltimore Sun*, Nov. 11, 1924, Goodwin Files.

14. W. A. R. Goodwin, "Notes on Wythe House," Mar. 16, 1938, quoted in "George Wythe House," Sept. 1, 1938, 36, Architectural Reference Library, Colonial Williamsburg Foundation (CWF).

15. Oral history interview with William G. Perry, Aug. 14, 1956, 48–49, CWF.

16. Hayes, "Background," 34–35; *New York Times*, Mar. 29, 1926.

17. Hayes, "Background," 34–35.

18. Interview with William G. Perry, July 17, 1970.

19. W. A. R. Goodwin to William Mitchell, Apr. 15, 1926, Goodwin Files.

20. Hayes, "Background," 35–38.

21. Ibid., 42–44.

22. John D. Rockefeller, Jr., "The Genesis of the Williamsburg Restoration," *National Geographic Magazine*, 71 (Apr. 1937), 401.

23. Hayes, "Background," 46.

24. W. A. R. Goodwin to J. D. Rockefeller, Jr., Nov. 29, 1926, quoted ibid., 47–50.

25. J. D. Rockefeller, Jr., to W. A. R. Goodwin, two letters, Nov. 29, 1926, quoted ibid., 51–55.

26. Hayes, "Background," 59–60.

27. W. A. R. Goodwin to Perry, Jan. 3, 1927, quoted ibid., 63–64.

28. W. A. R. Goodwin to J. D. Rockefeller, Jr., Jan. 11, 1927, quoted ibid., 66–68.

29. Interview with Perry.

30. W. A. R. Goodwin, Address delivered Feb. 15, 1935, 7, ACWF.

31. Interview with Walter M. Macomber, July 8, 1972.

32. W. A. R. Goodwin to J. D. Rockefeller, Jr., Jan. 19, 1927, quoted in Hayes, "Background," 70–71.

33. Interviews with Milton Grigg, Sept. 15, 1972, Macomber, and Perry.

34. W. A. R. Goodwin to Perry, Jan. 28, 1927, quoted in Hayes, "Background," 72–73.

35. Interview with Perry.

36. Hayes, "Background," 80.

37. Ibid., 80–82.

38. Ibid., 82–84.

39. W. A. R. Goodwin to Perry, May 23, 1927, quoted ibid., 86–87.

40. Hayes, "Background," 92–99.

41. J. D. Rockefeller, Jr., to Goodwin, Sept. 19, 1927, quoted ibid., 110–13.

42. Hayes, "Background," 115–23.

43. Ibid., 135–39.

44. J. D. Rockefeller, Jr., "Genesis," 401.

45. Hayes, "Background," 139–51.

46. Ibid., 158.

47. J. D. Rockefeller, Jr., to Arthur Woods, Nov. 30, 1927, quoted ibid., 161–62.

48. J. D. Rockefeller, Jr., to W. A. R. Goodwin, Nov. 29, 1927, quoted ibid., 163.

49. W. A. R. Goodwin to J. A. C. Chandler, Dec. 3, 1927, quoted ibid., 164–66.

50. W. A. R. Goodwin to Perry, Dec. 3, 1927, quoted ibid., 167–69.

51. W. A. R. Goodwin to J. D. Rockefeller, Jr., Dec. 12, 1927, quoted ibid., 172–74.

52. *New York Times*, Jan. 8, 1928.

53. W. A. R. Goodwin to Woods, Jan. 9, 1928, quoted in Hayes, "Background," 188–90.

54. Resolution of Board of Visitors of College of William and Mary, Feb. 14, 1928, quoted ibid., 197.

55. Hayes, "Background," 199–202.

56. Ibid., 205–6.

57. W. A. R. Goodwin to J. D. Rockefeller, Jr., Feb. 11, 1928, Goodwin Files.

58. Charles B. Hosmer, Jr., *Presence of the Past: A History of the Preservation Movement in the United States before Williamsburg* (New York, 1965), 208–10.

59. Interviews with Perry and Macomber.

60. John D. R. Platt, "The Historian and Historic Preservation," Paper for the American Historical Association Annual Meeting, Dec. 28, 1963, Independence National Historical Park.

61. Interview with J. C. Harrington, May 18, 1970.

62. Perry to W. A. R. Goodwin, Jan. 30, 1928, Administration—Architects and Engineers, ACWF.

63. Kenneth Chorley to Woods, Feb. 24, 1928, ibid.

64. Chorley to Woods, Jan. 26, 1928, ibid.

65. Hayes, "Background," 208–9.

66. Ibid., 221–22.

67. Ibid., 224–27; Perry, Memo, Apr. 3, 1928, Buildings General, 1928–1930, Perry, Shaw, and Hepburn Files (PS&H), ACWF.

68. Hayes, "Background," 229; interview with Macomber.

69. Hayes, "Background," 215.

70. Interviews with Perry, Finlay F. Ferguson, July 1, 1973, Macomber, and Orin M. Bullock, July 28, 1970.

71. Hayes, "Background," 242–52.

72. *New York Times*, June 13, 1928.

73. Hayes, "Background," 265–73.

74. Ibid., 275–85.

75. W. A. R. Goodwin to Woods, July 19, 1928, Procedure—Restoration, Goodwin Files.

76. Interviews with Perry and Macomber.

77. Perry to Library of Congress, Sept. 26, 1928, and J. Franklin Jameson to Perry, Shaw, and Hepburn, Oct. 2, 1928, Historical Data, PS&H.

78. F. C. Beech to Perry, Sept. 17, 1928, and Donald Millar to Perry, Oct. 24, 1928, ibid.

79. W. A. R. Goodwin to Woods, Aug. 6, 1928, Administration—Architects and Engineers, ACWF.

80. Minutes of conference held at Williamsburg, Va., on Oct. 2–5, 1928, Reports of Meetings Monthly, PS&H.

81. Interview with Perry.

82. Perry, Shaw, and Hepburn to Prentice Duell, Sept. 11, 1929, Buildings—Wren–Prentice Duell, 1929–1930, PS&H.

83. Interviews with Bullock, J. Everette Fauber, Jr., Sept. 12, 1972, Ferguson, Grigg, Macomber, Perry, and Clyde E. Trudell, Aug. 3, 1971.

84. Robert P. Bellows, Edmund S. Campbell, Finlay F. Ferguson, Fiske Kimball, A. Lawrence Kocher, Milton B. Medary, Thomas E. Tallmadge, and Robert E. Lee Taylor.

85. Interview with Macomber.

86. Report on meeting of Advisory Committee of Architects invited to Williamsburg to confer upon the various policies touching the Restoration, Nov. 25–26, 1928, Advisory Committee of Architects, ACWF.

87. Proceedings of Williamsburg Conference Meeting, Dec. 11, 1928, 15, 55–70, 75–78, Conferences—Minutes and Reports, ACWF.

88. Perry to W. A. R. Goodwin, Feb. 9, 1929, Buildings—Wren–Prentice Duell, 1929–1930, PS&H; Prentice Duell, "The Excavations at Williamsburg," *Architectural Record*, 69 (Jan. 1931), 16–17.

89. Interview with Perry.

90. Perry to Edmund S. Campbell, Dec. 12, 1928, Campbell to Perry, Shaw, and Hepburn, Dec. 17, 1928, Art Commission of Commonwealth of Virginia, Report, Dec. 24, 1928, M. B. Medary to Perry, Shaw, and Hepburn, Jan. 3, 1929, and Perry to Woods, Jan. 10, 1929, Buildings—Wren, Art Commission, Advisory Committee, PS&H.

91. W. A. R. Goodwin, "Report and Recommendations," Feb. 4, 1929, 7, Restoration, Its Conception, Goodwin Files.

92. John Garland Pollard to W. A. R. Goodwin, Aug. 8, 1928, Block 8–Building 11, ACWF.

93. Perry to Woods, Mar. 8, 1929, Policy and Procedure, PS&H.

94. W. A. R. Goodwin to Woods, Apr. 9, 1930, ibid.

95. Thomas T. Waterman to Perry, Shaw, and Hepburn, Oct. 11, 1928, and Waterman to A. H. Hepburn, Feb. 26, 1929, Block 8—Building 11, PS&H.

96. E. G. Swem to W. A. R. Goodwin, May 31, 1929, Block 8—Building 11, ACWF.

97. W. A. R. Goodwin to Perry, Apr. 10, 1929, Research General, PS&H.

98. W. A. R. Goodwin to Perry, May 18, 1929, ibid.

99. Mary Goodwin to W. A. R. Goodwin, Oct. 16, 1929, Research—Mary Goodwin, PS&H.

100. Perry to Chandler, Oct. 7, 1929, Buildings—Wren, PS&H.

101. W. A. R. Goodwin to Perry (Telegram), Dec. 23, 1929, Copperplate, PS&H.

102. Perry to W. A. R. Goodwin (Telegram), Dec. 24, 1929, ibid.

103. Perry to Hepburn, Jan. 13, 1930, ibid.

104. Chorley, Memo, Jan. 21, 1930, Rolfe House–Jail–Powder Horn, ACWF.

105. Interview with Helen D. Bullock, July 29, 1970.

106. Chorley to Hepburn, Aug. 21, 1929, Research—General, ACWF.

107. Perry to Woods, Mar. 29, 1930, and Perry to Harold R. Shurtleff, Mar. 29, 1930, Research—Shurtleff, Goodwin Files.

108. W. A. R. Goodwin to Perry, Apr. 8, 1930. ibid.

109. Perry to Shurtleff, Mar. 29, 1930, ibid.

110. Interview with Fauber.

111. Hepburn, Memo of a meeting, July 16, 1930, Reports of Meetings, 1930, PS&H.

112. Shurtleff to Hepburn, July 25, 1930, Research—General, ACWF.

113. W. A. R. Goodwin to Chorley, Apr. 9, 1930, Guide Service, ACWF.

114. W. A. R. Goodwin to Chorley, Dec. 5, 1930, Research—General, ACWF.

115. Shurtleff to Perry, Dec. 18, 1930, ibid.

116. Shurtleff to Perry, Shaw, and Hepburn, Jan. 15, 1931, ibid.

117. "Matters of policy and decisions which were arrived at during Mr. Rockefeller's visit to Williamsburg, Jan. 19–21, 1931," Conferences—Minutes and Reports, ACWF.

118. Shurtleff to Perry, Feb. 17, 1931, Advisory Committee, PS&H.

119. W. A. R. Goodwin to Chorley, Feb. 20, 1931, Research—General, ACWF.

120. T. Rutherfoord Goodwin, *A Brief History of the Guide Book to James-town, Williamsburg, and Yorktown* (Richmond, 1930).

121. [T. Rutherfoord Goodwin], *The Williamsburg Restoration* (Williamsburg, 1931); T. R. Goodwin to Chorley, Apr. 1, 1931, Guide Service, ACWF.

122. T. R. Goodwin to Mrs. William Hard, Sept. 2, 1931, Block 8—Building 11, ACWF.

123. "Matters Discussed with Mr. Rockefeller," Feb. 3, 1932, Reports of Meetings, PS&H.

124. Shurtleff to Chorley, May 28, 1932, Research—General, PS&H.

125. Shurtleff to Chorley, June 1, 1932, Research—Excavated Materials, ibid.

126. Shurtleff to Chorley, June 1, 1932, Research—Conference of Historians, ACWF.

127. W. A. R. Goodwin to Shurtleff, June 14, 1932, ibid.

128. Shurtleff to James Truslow Adams, June 20, 1932, ibid.

129. "Proceedings at meetings of historians," Oct. 21, 1932, 20–21, Advisory Committee of Historians, ACWF.

130. Ibid., 37.

131. Ibid., 58.

132. "Final Report of Sub-Committee of Historians' Conference," Jan. 28, 1933, Research—Conference of Historians, ACWF.

133. Shurtleff to H. I. Brock, Dec. 14, 1933, ibid.

134. Meeting of Advisory Committee of Architects, Oct. 27–28, 1932, 36, Advisory Committee of Architects, PS&H.

135. Bela Norton to Chorley, Jan. 3, 1933, Guide Service, ACWF.

136. Kathryn I. Bowen to Chorley, Oct. 4, 1932, and R. T. Haines Halsey to Vernon Geddy, Oct. 4, 1932, Museum visits, ACWF.

137. "First Meeting of the Committee on Education," Jan. 12, 1934, Hostess Training, ACWF.

138. "Second Meeting of the Committee on Education," Jan. 25, 1934, ibid., 1–4.

139. Ibid., 5.

140. "Summary of the Recommendations and Opinions of the Committee on Education," Jan. 29, 1934, Hostess Training, ACWF.

141. T. R. Goodwin, Memo, Feb. 9, 1934, ibid.

142. T. R. Goodwin to Chorley, Mar. 2, 1934, ibid.

143. *New York Times*, Feb. 25, 1934.

144. W. A. R. Goodwin to J. D. Rockefeller III, Mar. 3, 1934, Restoration, Its Conception—Rockefeller, John D., Goodwin Files.

145. Staff memo to Chorley, May 22, 1934, Procedure—Restoration, ACWF.

146. Harold R. Shurtleff, *The Log Cabin Myth* (Gloucester, Mass., 1967); Oral history interview with Perry, 88–89, ACWF.

147. Oral history interview with Singleton P. Moorehead, 1957, 100–101, CWF.

148. Interview with Perry.

149. Interview with Fauber.

150. Ferguson to author, May 31, 1973.

151. Interview with Trudell.

152. Oral history interview with Moorehead, 40–41, CWF.

153. W. A. R. Goodwin to Woods, Oct. 11, 1930, Reports—Goodwin, W. A. R., ACWF.

154. Interview with Perry.

155. Memo of meeting held at 9:15 A.M., Dec. 15, 1931, Conferences—Minutes and Reports, ACWF.

156. "Matters Discussed with Mr. Rockefeller," Feb. 3, 1932, Reports of Meetings, ACWF.

157. W. A. R. Goodwin to Perry, Mar. 2, 1932, Policy and Procedure, PS&H.

158. Perry to W. A. R. Goodwin, Mar. 7, 1932, ibid.

159. Hepburn, Memo of meeting, Jan. 16, 1933, Reports of meetings, ibid.

160. W. A. R. Goodwin to Chorley, May 8, 1933, Procedure—Restoration, ACWF.

161. Interview with Perry.

162. Chorley to Perry, Shaw, and Hepburn, Aug. 15, 1933, Administration—Architects and Engineers, ACWF.

163. H. I. Brock, "Virginia's Colonial Capital Emerges," *New York Times Magazine*, Sept. 17, 1933, 9, 14.

164. W. A. R. Goodwin to Woods, Nov. 7, 1933, Procedure—Restoration, ACWF.

165. W. A. R. Goodwin to J. D. Rockefeller III, Mar. 3, 1934, Restoration, Its Conception, Rockefeller, John D., Goodwin Files.

166. Horace M. Albright to Rockefeller, May 3, 1934, Procedure—Restoration, ACWF.

167. Chorley to Perry, Shaw, and Hepburn, Aug. 24, 1934, Administration—Architects and Engineers, ACWF.

168. Interview with Perry.

169. J. D. Rockefeller, Jr., to Henry Ford, Feb. 7, 1935, Dearborn, Mich., PS&H.

170. Minutes of meeting of Advisory Committee of Architects, Apr. 9, 1935, 9, Advisory Committee of Architects, ACWF.

171. Harold R. Shurtleff and Helen D. Bullock, Report, Aug. 12, 1935, Research—General, ACWF.

172. Shurtleff to Chorley, Oct. 24, 1935, ibid.; Shurtleff to T. R. Goodwin, Sept. 15, 1936, Goodwin—Personal, ACWF.

173. Shurtleff to Chorley, Jan. 20, 1937, Goodwin, Rutherfoord, ACWF.

174. Interview with Minor Wine Thomas, July 13, 1970.

175. Minutes of meeting of Craft Advisory Committee, Apr. 27, 1937, Crafts-Advisory Committee, ACWF.

176. A. E. Kendrew to Chorley, May 15, 1937, Architectural, ACWF.

177. Oral history interview with Moorehead, 350–53, ACWF.

178. Shurtleff to Chorley, Dec. 7, 1936, Research—General, ACWF; Shurtleff to Perry, July 9, 1937, Research Department, PS&H.

179. Interview with Thomas.

180. Parke Rouse, Jr., "Seer of Williamsburg," *New York Times Magazine*, Sept. 7, 1941, 16–17, 24–25.

181. Interview with Thomas, oral history interview with Kenneth Chorley, July 23, 1956, 181, CWF.

182. Oral history interview with Moorehead, 91–92, CWF.

183. Interview with Perry.

184. Kendrew to Research Department, Feb. 1, 1938, Research, ACWF.

185. Kendrew, "Report of Proposed Ultimate Restoration Work, Williamsburg, Virginia," Reports, ACWF.

186. Kendrew to Chorley, May 3, 1939, and Kendrew to James Knight, May 24, 1939, Architectural, ACWF.

187. Interview with Thomas.

188. Kendrew to Chorley, July 22, 1939, Architectural, ACWF.

189. Interview with Ferguson.

190. Moorehead and George S. Campbell, "Architectural Report, George Wythe House," March 26, 1940, Architectural Research Library, ACWF.

191. Helen D. Bullock, *The Williamsburg Art of Cookery* (Williamsburg, 1938).

192. Interviews with Edward P. Alexander, May 28, 1970, and Thomas.

193. *Newport News Daily Press*, Oct. 25, 1938.

194. *Richmond Times-Dispatch*, Nov. 6, 1938.

195. *Boston Evening Transcript*, Dec. 12, 1938.

196. "The Restoration of Colonial Williamsburg in Virginia," *Architectural Record*, 78 (Dec. 1935), 356–414; W. A. R. Goodwin, "The Restoration of Colonial Williamsburg," *National Geographic Magazine*, 71 (Apr. 1937), 402–43; "Colonial Williamsburg, Virginia," *House and Garden*, 72 (Nov. 1937), 37–80.

197. T. R. Goodwin to Norton, Jan. 13, 1938, Edison Institute, ACWF.

198. John Marshall, "Some Educational Possibilities of the Williamsburg Restoration," Oct. 18, 1939, Educational Program, ACWF.

199. Norton to Chorley, Nov. 14, 1939, Hunter D. Farish to Chorley, Nov. 18, 1939, and James Cogar to Chorley, Dec. 8, 1939, ibid.

200. T. R. Goodwin to Chorley, Jan. 25, 1940, ibid.

201. T. R. Goodwin to Chorley, Apr. 12, 1941, ibid.

202. Chorley to J. D. Rockefeller III, July 18, 1941, ibid.

203. Chorley to Louis B. Wright, Dec. 11, 1941, and Chorley to Rockefeller, Jan. 13, 1942, ibid.

204. Goodwin to Committee on Education, Nov. 25, 1941, Corporate Matters, Colonial Williamsburg, Committee on Education, ACWF.

205. Minutes of meeting of Committee of Colonial Williamsburg, Dec. 1, 1941, ibid.

206. John E. Pomfret to Chorley, Sept. 11, 1943, Institute of Early American Culture, ACWF.

207. Press Release, Jan. 8, 1944, ibid.

208. Executive Order No. 26, Feb. 1944, Oral History Chronology, ACWF; interview with Thomas.

209. T. R. Goodwin, "Agenda for the Committee on Interpretation," Nov. 9, 1944, Corporate Matters, Colonial Williamsburg, Committee on Interpretation, ACWF.

210. Interview with Thomas.

211. Interview with Alexander. See also chapter 3.

212. Interview with Thomas.

213. Meeting of Orientation Subcommittee of Colonial Williamsburg Planning Committee, May 29, 1946, Colonial Williamsburg Planning Committee, ACWF.

214. Kendrew to J. D. Rockefeller III, July 9, 1946, ibid.

215. Harland Bartholomew and Associates, "A Plan for the Development of the Visitor Facilities of Colonial Williamsburg," June 1948, Architectural Research Library, CWF.

216. *New York Times*, Jan. 25, 1949; Interview with Thomas.

217. W. A. R. Goodwin to Chorley, Oct. 21, 1929, Moore House, ACWF.

218. Perry to Mrs. Robert M. Reese, Mar. 28, 1930, Historical Data—Deeds, Wills, PS&H.

219. Shurtleff to Ethel Armes, Aug. 7, 1931, Research—General, ACWF.

220. Louis La Beaume to Macomber, Oct. 13, 1931, Research—General, PS&H.

221. Bryan Conrad to Shurtleff, Jan. 9, 1932, Research—General, ACWF; William E. Carson to Chorley, Jan. 31, 1933, Restoration—Outside Points, ibid.

222. Macomber to Carson, Mar. 20, 1933, General Correspondence, ibid.

223. Nancy L. Pope to Cogar, Sept. 6, 1933, Museum Visits, ibid.

224. Thomas E. Tallmadge to Perry, Dec. 8, 1933, Advisory Committee, PS&H.

225. William K. Doty to W. A. R. Goodwin, July 11, 1934, and W. A. R. Goodwin to Doty, July 14, 1934, Restorations other than Williamsburg, Goodwin Files.

226. Shurtleff to Chorley, Oct. 6, 1934, Research—General, ACWF.

227. H. Jermain Slocum to W. A. R. Goodwin, Oct. 29, 1934, and W. A. R. Goodwin to Slocum, Nov. 2, 1934, Restorations other than Williamsburg, Goodwin Files.

228. A. E. Demaray to Geddy, Apr. 20, 1935, National Parks, ACWF.

229. Chorley to Mrs. J. E. Hunter, Oct. 3, 1938, Restorations—Fort Hill, ACWF.

230. Philip D. Laird to Chorley, Jan. 4, 1940, Restorations—New Castle, ACWF.

231. Hepburn to Chorley, Jan. 19, 1940, ibid.

232. D. M. Bates, "Notes on Talk Thursday Evening, 21, March, 1940," ibid.

233. Laird to Bates, Apr. 2, 1940, ibid.

234. Laird to Chorley, Apr. 6, 1940, ibid.

235. Hepburn to Laird, Apr. 9, 1940, ibid.

236. Laird to Hepburn, Apr. 23, 1940, ibid.

237. Chorley to Laird, May 3, 1940, ibid.

238. Chorley to Bates, May 27, 1946, ibid.

239. Chorley to Bates, Oct. 26, 1946, ibid.; contract between Bates and Perry, Shaw, and Hepburn, Nov. 13, 1946, ibid.

240. Chorley to Bates, Dec. 3, 1946, ibid.

241. For other examples of Kenneth Chorley's efforts to assist urban preservation groups, see chapter 5.

242. Allston Boyer to Chorley, Sept. 27, 1946, Restorations, ACWF.

243. *New York Times*, Feb. 11, 1940.

244. Ibid., Feb. 15, 1940.

245. J. D. Rockefeller, Jr., to Chorley, Mar. 26, 1940, Philipse Castle Restoration, ACWF.

246. Ferguson, Memo, Apr. 15, 1940, ibid.

247. Kendrew to Chorley, June 20, 1940, ibid.

248. *New York Times*, Apr. 27, 1941.

249. Cogar to Chorley, Feb. 10, 1942, Philipse Castle Restoration, ACWF.

250. T. R. Goodwin to Chorley, Aug. 5, 1942, ibid.

251. Moorehead to Chorley, Sept. 3, 1942, ibid.; interview with Thomas.

252. Chorley to J. D. Rockefeller, Jr., Aug. 10, 1943, Philipse Castle Restoration, ACWF.

253. Moorehead, Memo, Dec. 17, 1945, Sunnyside, ACWF.

254. A. Lawrence Kocher to Hugh Grant Rowell, July 5, 1946, Sunnyside-Tarrytown, ACWF.

255. Chorley to Rowell, Oct. 23, 1947, Philipse Castle Restoration, ACWF.

256. Thomas to author, May 24, 1971.

257. Interview with Perry.

258. Interview with Thomas.

259. Oral history interview with Chorley, 141, CWF.

Chapter 2: *The Outdoor Museums*

1. William Greenleaf, *From These Beginnings: The Early Philanthropies of Henry and Edsel Ford, 1911–1936* (Detroit, 1964), 107.

2. Oral history interviews with Edward J. Cutler, May 1951, 138, Roy Schumann, May 1951, 7, and E. G. Liebold, Oct.-Dec. 1951, 901, Ford Archives (FA).

3. Charles E. Peterson, memorandum, Nov. 10, 1936, 1936–37–P, Historic American Buildings Survey Files, Princeton Photographs, Library of Congress; interview with Charles E. Peterson, Feb. 9, 1970.

4. Charles E. Peterson, memorandum, Nov. 10, 1936, 1936–37–P, Historic American Buildings Survey Files, Princeton Photographs, Library of Congress.

5. George Wells to J. F. Gregory, Mar. 15, 1937, Archives, Old Sturbridge Village (OSV).

6. C. Malcolm Watkins, "Notes on visit to Edison Institute and Greenfield Village, August 17, 1938," OSV.

7. Kenneth Chorley, Notes on visit to Greenfield Village, June 1944, Greenfield Village, Archives of the Colonial Williamsburg Foundation (ACWF).

8. Ibid.

9. *Edison Institute of Technology* (Dearborn, Mich., 1929), 14.

10. Ibid., 27.

11. *New York Times*, Oct. 18, 1929.

12. Ibid., Jan. 10, 1934.

13. Oral history interview with Cutler, 168–69, FA.

14. "General Information—Edison Institute Staff," July 12, 1934, Accession 285, Box 1602, FA; oral history interview with William A. Simonds, June 3, 1961, 19, Henry Ford Museum Library (HFML).

15. S. J. Woolf, "Mr. Ford Shows His Museum," *New York Times Magazine*, Jan. 12, 1936, 3.

16. Ibid.

17. Ibid., 20.

18. Greenleaf, *From These Beginnings*, 71–111.

19. "Ford's Platform Out: 'No Place like Home,'" *Literary Digest*, 78 (July 14, 1923) 36–38; Margaret Ford Ruddiman, "Memories of My Brother Henry Ford," *Michigan History*, 37 (Sept. 1953), 239–40.

20. Oral history interview with Cutler, May 17, 1956 (Ford Homestead), 8–9, HFML.

21. Oral history interviews with Fred L. Black, Mar. 10, 1951, 42–44, and W. J. Cameron, June, 1952, 95, FA; with Cutler, Oct. 27, 1955 (Gardner), 11, HFML.

22. Oral history interview with Liebold, 890, FA.

23. Oral history interview with Cutler, May, 1951, 135–36, FA.

24. Greenleaf, *From These Beginnings*, 147.

25. Interview with E. Florence Addison, Oct. 24, 1969.

26. William W. Taylor, "Report for week ending May 10th 1924," Oral History—W. W. Taylor, HFML.

27. Taylor, reports of May 5 and 6, 1924, and Feb. 13, 1928, ibid.

28. Quoted in "Ford's Platform Out," 36.

29. Greenleaf, *From These Beginnings*, 76.

30. William T. Gregory to Liebold, Dec. 19, 1923, Accession 292, Box 35, FA.

31. Clipping from Clinton, Mich., paper, Sept. 17, 1927, Archives of Greenfield Village (Clinton Inn), HFML.

32. *New York Times*, Mar. 26, 1926.

33. Oral history interview with Cutler, May 17, 1956 (Ford Homestead), 8, HFML.

34. Oral history interviews with Cutler, May 1951, 18, FA, and June 2, 1955 (Job Beginnings), 14–15, HFML.

35. Oral history interview with Cutler, June 2, 1955 (Job Beginnings), 15–16, HFML.

36. *Detroit News*, Oct. 9, 1927.

37. Francis Jehl, *Menlo Park Reminiscences*, 3 vols. (Dearborn, Mich., 1941), III, 1121–31.

38. Liebold to Thomas A. Edison, Mar. 28, 1928, Accession 104 addenda, Box 6, FA.

39. Jehl, *Menlo Park Reminiscences*, III, 1130.

40. Oral history interview with Cutler, May, 1951, 19–21, FA.

41. Samuel Crowther, "Henry Ford's Village of Yesterday," *Ladies' Home Journal*, 45 (Sept. 1928), 10.

42. Ibid., 118.

43. Oral history interview with Cutler, 29, 37–40, 77, FA.

44. Ibid., May 17, 1956 (Ford Homestead), 7, HFML.

45. Ibid., May 1951, 138–40, 143, FA.

46. James A. Humberstone to H. I. Brock, July 8, 1929, Archives—Correspondence, HFML.

47. H. F. Morton, *Strange Commissions for Henry Ford* (York, England, 1934), 21.

48. Ibid., 21–22.

49. Frank Campsall to Sir Percival Perry, Feb. 4, 1929, Cotswold Cottage, Registrar's File, Henry Ford Museum (HFMR).

50. Campsall to Perry, July 6, 1929, ibid.

51. Morton to Campsall, Oct. 21, 1929, Bennett Shop, HFMR.

52. Taylor, report for July 15, 1929, Oral History—W. W. Taylor, HFML.

53. Priscilla D. Bassett to William Sumner Appleton, Nov. 18, 1929, N.H.—Sandown Meeting House, Files of the Society for the Preservation of New England Antiquities (SPNEA).

54. Oral history interview with Charles Voorhess, April-June 1951, 167–68, FA.

55. *Detroit News*, Mar. 29, 1929.

56. *New York Times*, Nov. 25, 1929.

57. Clipping, ca. Sept. 10, 1929, Logan County Courthouse, HFMR.

58. *Lincoln Evening Courier*, Aug. 19, 1929, Archives—Greenfield Village, Logan County Courthouse, HFML.

59. Ibid., Aug. 21–22, 1929.

60. Ibid., Sept. 3, 1929.

61. Cameron to Lawrence B. Stringer, Aug. 22, 1929, quoted ibid., Aug. 26, 1929.

62. *Lincoln Evening Courier*, Sept. 3, 1929.

63. Ibid., Sept. 5–6, 1929.

64. Ibid., Sept. 7, 1929; oral history interviews with Cutler, May 1951, 40, FA, and Sept. 29, 1955, Oral History—Logan County Courthouse, 1, HFML.

65. *Lincoln Evening Courier*, Sept. 11, 1929.

66. Ibid., Sept. 12, 1929.

67. Ibid., Sept. 13, 1929. A replica was constructed on the original site in 1953.

68. Ibid., Sept. 17, 1929; oral history interview with Cutler, Sept. 29, 1955, Oral History—Logan County Courthouse, 14–15, HFML.

69. *Lincoln Evening Courier*, Oct. 21, 1929.

70. Jehl, *Menlo Park Reminiscences*, III, 1137–40.

71. Ibid., 1152.

72. Mrs. Emerson R. Newell to Mrs. Robert L. Messimer, Feb. 14, 1930, B2–6a/92, Archives of Robert E. Lee Memorial Foundation (LMF).

73. Campsall to Mrs. Charles Lanier, Dec. 23, 1929, Accession 292, Box 36, FA.

74. Campsall to Lanier, Jan. 11, 1930, ibid.

75. Newell to Messimer, Feb. 14, 1930, B2–6a/92, LMF.

76. Ethel Armes to Campsall, Feb. 8, 1930, Accession 292, Box 36, FA.

77. Lanier to Campsall, Mar. 12, 1930, ibid.

78. Memo on Stratford, no date (ca. May 1930), ibid.

79. Campsall to Lanier, May 23, 1930, ibid.

80. Campsall to Lanier, Aug. 30, 1932, Accession 285, Box 2341, FA.

81. The rescue of Stratford Hall is discussed in chapter 4.

82. Oral history interview with J. F. Gregory, June 7, 1951, 45–47, FA.

83. Harold L. Ickes to Henry Ford, Mar. 16, 1935, Accession 285, Box 1785, FA.

84. Campsall to Gregory, Mar. 25, 1935, ibid.; clipping, ca. Mar. 1935, ibid.

85. Ford to Ickes, Mar. 27, 1935, ibid.

86. Ickes to Ford, Apr. 8, 1935, and Ickes to Thomas Gamble, Apr. 8, 1935, ibid.

87. Kenneth Metcalf, memo on conversation with Stark Hickey, Mar. 4, 1964, Archives—Greenfield Village, Cape Cod Windmill, HFML.

88. Hickey to Campsall, Oct. 4, 1935, Cape Cod Windmill, HFMR.

89. J. F. Syme to Ford, Nov. 10, 1935, ibid.

90. *New York Times*, Nov. 13, 1935.

91. Ibid., Nov. 16, 1935.

92. Campsall to Syme (telegram), Nov. 14, 1935, Cape Cod Windmill, HFMR.

93. Oral history interview with Cutler, May 1951, 76, FA.

94. *New York Times*, Nov. 17, 1935.

95. Humberstone to Charles W. Lyons, Oct. 25, 1935, Buildings Considered, HFML.

96. Charles B. Hosmer, Jr., *Presence of the Past: A History of the Preservation Movement in the United States before Williamsburg* (New York, 1965), 223; Israel Sack to Humberstone, Oct. 29, 1935, Buildings Considered, HFML.

97. R. T. Haines Halsey to Edsel Ford (telegram), July 29, 1936, Webster House, HFML.

98. *New York Times*, Sept. 11, 1936.

99. Oral history interviews with Cutler, Dec. 15, 1955 (Wright Cycle Shop), 18–20, and Jan. 19, 1956 (Wright Home), 23, HFML; *Detroit News*, July 3, 1936.

100. Orville Wright to Henry Ford, Jan. 28, 1936 (Wright Cycle Shop), HFML.

101. Oral history interviews with Liebold, 926, FA, and Cutler, Dec. 15, 1955 (Wright Cycle Shop), 19–20, HFML; *Detroit News*, July 3–4, 1936; *New York Times*, July 4, 1936.

102. Oral history interviews with Liebold, 926, FA, and Cutler, Dec. 15, 1955 (Wright Cycle Shop), 19–20, HFML.

103. Oral history interview with Liebold, 926, FA.

104. *Lynn Evening Item*, Nov. 4, 1941; Addison to author, May 16, 1974.

105. Interview with Addison; Appleton to M. Louise Hawkes, Nov. 11, 1941, Mass.—Saugus Ironworks House, SPNEA.

106. Leverett Saltonstall to Henry Ford, Dec. 13, 1941, ibid.

107. Campsall to Saltonstall, Dec. 22, 1941, ibid.

108. F. E. Searle To Essex County Selectmen's Association, Dec. 15, 1941, ibid.

109. Searle to Appleton, Sept. 30, 1942, ibid.

110. Appleton to Walter R. Ingalls, June 20, 1944, ibid.

111. Cutler to A. E. Kendrew, Oct. 12, 1945, Cutler, E. J., ACWF.

112. Vernon M. Geddy to Chorley, June 27, 1947, Greenfield Village, ACWF.

113. Oral history interview with H. S. Ablewhite, May, 1951, 77–81, 84, FA; H. R. Waddell to Bela Norton, June 15, 1948, Accession 285, Box 2936, FA.

114. Oral history interview with Ablewhite, 77–81, 84, FA.

115. Interviews with Edward P. Alexander, May 28, 1970, Louis C. Jones, Aug. 5, 1969, and Clifford L. Lord, Nov. 5, 1969.

116. Paul S. Kerr to author, Aug. 26, 1970; Louis C. Jones, *Cooperstown* (Cooperstown, N.Y., 1949), 53.

117. Kerr to author, Aug. 26, 1970.

118. Stephen C. Clark to Dixon Ryan Fox, Aug. 25, 1938, New York State Historical Association (NYSHA); Hosmer, *Presence of the Past*, 277–78.

119. Fox to Horace A. Moses, Sept. 29, 1938, NYSHA.

120. Interview with Alexander.

121. Clark to Fox, Aug. 25, 1938, NYSHA.
122. Fox to Clark, Sept. 14, 1938, NYSHA.
123. Fox to Moses, Sept. 29, 1938, Moses to Fox, Oct. 6, 1938, and Fox to Moses, Oct. 11, 1938, NYSHA.
124. Clark to Fox, late Sept., 1938, NYSHA.
125. Fox to Alexander, Apr. 10, 1939, and Clark to Alexander, Apr. 18, 1939, NYSHA.
126. Interview with Alexander.
127. Ibid.; interview with George P. Campbell, Aug. 5, 1970.
128. Interview with Lord.
129. Ibid.
130. Kerr to author, Aug. 26, 1970.
131. Interview with Lord.
132. Lord to Fox, Nov. 25, 1941, NYSHA.
133. Clark to Fox, Nov. 26, 1941, NYSHA.
134. Lord to Fox, Dec. 2, 1941, NYSHA.
135. Interview with Jones.
136. Interview with Lord.
137. Janet MacFarlane Cooley to author, Aug. 20, 1970.
138. Lord to Fox, Jan. 23, 1942, NYSHA.
139. Fox to Alexander, July 6, 1942, NYSHA.
140. Kerr to author, Aug. 26, 1970.
141. Ibid.; interview with Campbell.
142. Interview with Lord.
143. Owen C. Becker to Lord, July 9, 1943, and Becker to Mrs. Al Munro, Aug. 10, 1943, NYSHA.
144. Interview with Cooley, July 8, 1970.
145. Ibid.
146. Ibid.
147. Lord to Fox, Feb. 10, 1944, NYSHA.
148. Clark to Fox, Dec. 19, 1944, NYSHA.
149. Interview with Cooley.
150. Interview with Campbell; Minutes of Trustees' Meeting of NYSHA, June 30, 1945, NYSHA.
151. Interview with Cooley.
152. Interview with Jones.
153. Interview with Cooley.
154. Interview with Jones.
155. Janet MacFarlane to Lord, Oct. 7, 1946, NYSHA.
156. Becker to Clark, Apr. 17, 1948, NYSHA.
157. MacFarlane, Guidelines to accompany Albert Kaupe report, ca. Nov. 1949, NYSHA.
158. Jones to Ned J. Burns, Jan. 19, 1950, NYSHA.
159. Becker to MacFarlane, June 5, 1946, NYSHA.
160. Alexander to MacFarlane, May 24, 1948, NYSHA.

161. Burns to MacFarlane, May 4, 1948, and MacFarlane to Reinhold Pusch, Nov. 22, 1948, NYSHA.

162. *History Notes* (n.d.), Village Crossroads Law Office, ca. 1950, NYSHA.

163. MacFarlane to Becker, June 6, 1946, NYSHA.

164. MacFarlane to Becker, Oct. 18, 1946, NYSHA.

165. MacFarlane, Guidelines to accompany Kaupe report, ca. Nov. 1949, NYSHA.

166. Louis C. Jones, Director's Report, 1949, The Farmers' Museum, July 8, 1949, NYSHA.

167. MacFarlane to Lord, Oct. 7, 1946, NYSHA.

168. Doris Wood, "Old Sturbridge Village: A Chronicle," 1959, 1–2, Library, OSV.

169. Albert B. Wells to Henry F. du Pont, Oct. 21, 1947, Wells Historical Museum, Winterthur Estate Archives, Henry Francis du Pont Winterthur Museum (Wint.).

170. Interview with C. Malcolm Watkins, July 6, 1970.

171. Interview with Ruth D. Wells, July 18, 1969.

172. Ibid.

173. Interview with Watkins; A. B. Wells to du Pont, Oct. 21, 1947, Wells Historical Museum, Winterthur Estate Archives, (Wint.).

174. Interview with Watkins.

175. A. B. Wells to Margaret Shurcliff, Dec. 2, 1948, OSV.

176. Ibid.; Wood, "Chronicle," 5–6, OSV.

177. Wells to Shurcliff, Dec. 2, 1948, OSV.

178. Chorley to George B. Wells, July 17, 1936, OSV.

179. A. B. Wells to Shurcliff, Dec. 2, 1948, OSV.

180. Interview with Watkins.

181. G. B. Wells to Gregory, Mar. 15, 1937, OSV.

182. Wood, "Chronicle," 13, OSV; A. B. Wells to G. B. Wells, May 20, 1937, OSV.

183. William B. Goodwin to A. B. Wells, Sept. 30, 1938, and Wells to Goodwin, Oct. 24, 1938, OSV.

184. Watkins to Wells, Aug. 14, 1939, OSV.

185. Floyd L. Thoms to J. Cheney Wells, Jan. 22, 1940, OSV.

186. A. B. Wells to Austin Cheney, July 12, 1935, OSV.

187. Wood, "Chronicle," 11–12, OSV.

188. Ibid., 17.

189. Ibid., 18–19.

190. Ibid., 19–20.

191. Interview with Watkins; A. B. Wells to Shurcliff, Dec. 20, 1948, OSV.

192. Wells to Shurcliff, Dec. 20, 1948, OSV.

193. Ibid.

194. A. B. Wells, *Old Quinebaug Village* (1941), quoted in Wood, "Chronicle," 20–21, OSV.

195. Ibid., 22.

196. Ibid., 23.

197. Ibid., 25.

198. Interview with Watkins.

199. Wood, "Chronicle," 27–28, OSV.

200. A. B. Wells to Watkins, July 5, 1945, OSV.

201. Wells to Watkins, Aug. 17, 1945, OSV.

202. Interviews with Ruth Wells and Watkins.

203. Interview with Wells.

204. Ibid.

205. Wood, "Chronicle," 32–33, OSV.

206. Ibid., 35.

207. Interview with Wells.

208. Wood, "Chronicle," 75, OSV.

209. Interview with Wells.

210. A. B. Wells to George H. Watson, Jan. 29, 1946, OSV.

211. Interview with Ruth Wells.

212. J. C. Wells to A. B. Wells, Mar. 1, 1946, OSV.

213. Minutes of special meeting at Old Sturbridge Village, Oct. 24, 1946, OSV; "Old Sturbridge Village Policies," Oct. 15, 1946, OSV.

214. Interview with Ruth Wells.

215. Wells to Miss Green and Baptist Church Members, Dec. 2, 1946, OSV.

216. Interview with Wells.

217. Russell H. Kettell to Wells, Dec. 13, 1948, OSV.

218. J. C. Wells to Ruth Wells, Dec. 17, 1948, OSV.

219. Ruth Wells to Trustees of Old Sturbridge Village, Nov. 4, 1948, OSV.

220. "Policies," Dec. 1, 1947, OSV.

221. G. B. Wells to Edwin F. Dakin, Dec. 5, 1947, OSV.

222. Wells, Memo, Jan. 16, 1948, OSV.

223. Interview with Ruth Wells.

224. Ruth Wells, "Progress Report, Market Analysis and Craft Program Survey," Dec. 1948, OSV.

225. William Barrett and Dakin, memorandum, Aug. 25, 1949, OSV.

226. Jones, "Preliminary Report on Old Sturbridge Village," Aug. 1949, OSV.

227. Ruth Wells to Lord, Nov. 3, 1949, OSV.

228. Amelia F. Miller, *The Reverend Jonathan Ashley House* (Deerfield, Mass., 1962), 109–11.

229. Roger Bowen, "The Light Falls Where the Light Fell," *Yankee*, 31 (Sept. 1967), 135–36.

230. Frank L. Boyden to Appleton, Nov. 12, 1923, Mass.—Deerfield, SPNEA.

231. Boyden to Appleton, Apr. 22, 1924, Mass.—Deerfield, Ephriam Williams House, SPNEA.

232. Hosmer, *Presence of the Past*, 34–35.

233. Appleton to Boyden, Apr. 24, 1924, Mass.—Deerfield, Ephriam Williams House, SPNEA.

234. Hosmer, *Presence of the Past*, 33–34.

235. Gertrude Porter Ashley, *Memories of Old Deerfield* (Deerfield, Mass., 1934), 25–34.

236. Interview with Helen and Henry Flynt, Aug. 1, 1969.

237. Ibid.

238. Ibid.

239. Bowen, "The Light Falls," 135.

240. Henry Flynt to author, Feb. 11, 1970.

241. Interview with FIynts.

242. Ibid.

243. Ibid.

244. Ibid.

245. Miller, *Ashley House*, 76.

246. Ibid., 86–87.

247. *New York Times*, Sept. 26, 1949.

248. Interview with Flynts.

249. Carl Cutler to Appleton, Dec. 29, 1941, Marine Historical Association, SPNEA.

250. Marine Historical Assn., *Bulletin of Information*, No. 31, May 1, 1945.

251. Cutler to Arthur B. Lisle, Aug. 7, 1946, Marine Historical Assn., SPNEA.

252. Marine Historical Assn., letter to members, June 30, 1948.

253. Charles R. Strickland, "The First Permanent Dwellings at Plimoth Plantation," *Old-Time New England*, 40 (Jan. 1950), 163–69; Resolution of the Board of Governors of Plimoth Plantation, Nov. 26, 1949, Files of the Branch of History, U.S. Department of the Interior.

254. Arthur G. Pyle to Ruth Wells, Oct. 17, 1949, OSV.

255. Henry Hornblower II to Ronald F. Lee, Sept. 30, 1948, Files of Branch of History, U.S. Dept. of Interior.

256. Clark to Jones, June 1, 1949, NYSHA.

Chapter 3: *The New England Scene*

1. Charles B. Hosmer, Jr., *Presence of the Past: A History of the Preservation Movement in the United States before Williamsburg* (New York, 1965), 237–59, 284–87.

2. Edith G. Wendell to William Sumner Appleton, Sept. 9, 1931, N.H.—Portsmouth, Warner House, Files of the Society for the Preservation of New England Antiquities (SPNEA).

3. Appleton to Mrs. Wallis D. Walker, Aug. 12, 1935, ibid.

4. Appleton to Lucy S. Walker, Sept. 12, 1932, ibid.

5. Appleton to Mrs. Henry Vaughn, Aug. 3, 1933, ibid.

6. Appleton to Joseph E. Chandler, June 17, 1936, ibid.

7. Appleton, "Corresponding Secretary's Report," *Old-Time New England (OTNE)*, No. 73 (July 1933), 17–21.

8. Ibid., 31–33.

9. Interview with E. Florence Addison, Oct. 24, 1969.

10. Appleton, "Report," *OTNE*, No. 122 (Oct. 1945), 42–48.

11. Ibid., No. 130 (Oct. 1947), 35–49.

12. Interview with E. F. Addison and Bertram K. Little, Feb. 5, 1960.

13. Appleton, "Report," *OTNE*, No. 89 (July 1937), 21–23.

14. Ibid., 23–26.

15. Ibid., No. 96 (Apr. 1939), 149.

16. Ibid., No. 105 (July 1941), 28–29.

17. Ibid., No. 112 (Apr. 1943), 70–73, and No. 122 (Oct. 1945), 30, 41–42, 48.

18. Ibid., No. 130 (Oct. 1947), 52.

19. William G. Perry to author, Aug. 18, 1970.

20. Interview with Addison.

21. Interview with Little, Oct. 30, 1969.

22. Interview with Addison.

23. Charles B. Hosmer, Jr., "George Francis Dow," in Clifford Lord, ed., *Keepers of the Past* (Chapel Hill, N.C., 1965), 157–66.

24. Interview with Addison.

25. George Francis Dow, *Every Day Life in the Massachusetts Bay Colony* (Boston, 1935).

26. Appleton to George Dudley Seymour, June 10, 1936, Geo. D. Seymour, SPNEA.

27. Interviews with Addison and Little.

28. Interview with Addison.

29. Ibid.

30. Ibid.; interview with Little.

31. Interview with Philip Dana Orcutt, Oct. 31, 1969.

32. Interviews with Addison and Little.

33. Appleton to Arthur B. Lisle, Sept. 2, 1939, Arthur B. Lisle, SPNEA.

34. Interview with Addison.

35. Appleton to Edith Rantoul, Nov. 10, 1926, Mass.—Salem, Richard Derby, SPNEA.

36. William A. Pew to Appleton, Mar. 9, 1927, Richard Derby, SPNEA.

37. Appleton to Margaret F. Browne, Nov. 6, 1939, Mass.—Gloucester, White-Ellery House, SPNEA.

38. Appleton to William C. Endicott, June 7, 1927, Richard Derby, SPNEA.

39. SPNEA to William D. Chappell, July 2, 1927, ibid.

40. Dow, Memo to Appleton, June 25, 1928, ibid.

41. Appleton to Mrs. Francis B. Crowninshield, May 9, 1929, and Crowninshield to Appleton, July 31, 1929, ibid.

42. Harlan P. Kelsey to Endicott, Apr. 30, 1935, Mass.—Salem, Derby Wharf, SPNEA.

43. Appleton to Endicott, ca. Aug. 14, 1935, Salem Maritime National Historic Site (SMNHS), 0–36 General, Records of National Park Service (NPS). National Archives (NA), Record Group (RG) 79.

44. Appleton to Charles K. Bolton, Dec. 26, 1935, Richard Derby, SPNEA.

45. Appleton to Kelsey, Feb. 24, 1936, SMNHS, 0–36 General, Records of NPS, NA, RG 79.

46. Kelsey to Arno B. Cammerer, Feb. 26, 1936, ibid.

47. Appleton to Henry P. Benson, June 16, 1936, Richard Derby, SPNEA.

48. Appleton to Mrs. Carl A. Mead, Feb. 27, 1941, N.H.—Portsmouth, Wentworth-Gardner, SPNEA; Appleton, "Report," *OTNE*, No. 105 (July 1941), 17.

49. Interview with Little.

50. Appleton to Heloise Meyer, Dec. 31, 1928, Tufts, SPNEA; Appleton, Memo, Jan. 16, 1929, ibid.

51. *OTNE*, No. 58 (Oct. 1929), 95–96.

52. Appleton, "Report," *OTNE*, No. 73 (July 1933), 22–23.

53. Ibid., 22; James W. Spring, "The Coffin House in Newbury, Massachusetts, and Those Who Have Made It Their Home," *OTNE*, No. 57 (July 1929), 28–29.

54. Appleton to Arthur S. Dewing, Dec. 12, 1934, and Stephen B. Luce to William R. Harvey, Feb. 11, 1936, Maudsley, SPNEA.

55. Appleton to Mrs. M. K. Estabrook, Dec. 20, 1935, ibid.

56. Appleton to Luce, Mar. 5, 1936, ibid.

57. Maud Lyman Stevens to Appleton, Mar. 24, 1936, and clipping, ibid.

58. Appleton to Mrs. Harold Brown, Apr. 6, 1936, ibid.

59. Printed letter sent out from Newport, R.I., Aug. 15, 1936, ibid.; Appleton to Mrs. Draper Tuckerman, Aug. 6, 1936, ibid.

60. Interview with William King Covell, Nov. 3, 1969.

61. Fiske Kimball to Appleton, July 19, 1937, Woodbridge-Short, SPNEA; interview with Erling H. Pedersen, Sept. 14, 1972.

62. Appleton, "Report," *OTNE*, No. 96 (Apr. 1939), 127–28.

63. *OTNE*, No. 111 (Jan. 1943), 44.

64. Appleton, "Notes concerning Mr. Henry Davis Sleeper's House at Eastern Point, Gloucester, Mass.," Oct. 28, 1934, Beauport, SPNEA.

65. Appleton to Margaret Curtis, Aug. 8, 1935, ibid.

66. Appleton to Mrs. Charles E. F. McCann, Oct. 7, 1936, ibid.

67. Appleton, "Notes on Harry Sleeper's Estate," Feb. 18, 1937, ibid.

68. Appleton to Mrs. Willis Betts, Oct. 17, 1939, ibid.
69. Edward S. Gremse to Appleton, Apr. 8, 1940, ibid.
70. Hosmer, *Presence of the Past*, 222–31.
71. H. E. Winlock to Appleton, Apr. 6, 1933, Wentworth-Gardner, SPNEA.
72. Appleton to Vaughn, May 12, 1933, ibid.
73. Appleton to Mrs. Winslow Pierce, May 9, 1933, ibid.
74. Appleton to Dewing, July 31, 1933, Tobias Lear, SPNEA.
75. W. C. Hobart to Appleton, May 18, 1935, ibid.
76. Appleton to John Mead Howells, Apr. 10, 1936, Wentworth-Gardner, SPNEA.
77. Appleton to Dewing, July 16, 1937, Tobias Lear, SPNEA.
78. Dewing to Appleton, Oct. 22, 1937, ibid.
79. Howells to Appleton, Nov. 5, 1937, Wentworth-Gardner, SPNEA.
80. Winlock to Appleton, Apr. 5, 1938, ibid.
81. Howells to Appleton, Oct. 6, 1938, ibid.
82. Appleton to Elizabeth Perkins, Nov. 16, 1938, and Appleton to Robert Marvin, June 2, 1938, ibid.
83. Appleton to Howells, Nov. 2, 1939, ibid.
84. Howells, "Memorandum on the Wentworth-Gardner House, Portsmouth," Nov. 3, 1939, ibid.
85. Dewing to Appleton, Oct. 16, 1939, Tobias Lear, SPNEA; William M. Ivins, Jr., to Appleton, Nov. 21, 1939, Wentworth-Gardner, SPNEA.
86. Appleton to Carl A. Mead, Feb. 27, 1941, N.H.—Portsmouth, Wentworth-Gardner, SPNEA.
87. Appleton, "Report," *OTNE*, No. 100 (Apr. 1940), 137.
88. Ibid., No. 73 (July 1933), 27–28; Appleton to John Nicholas Brown, Dec. 3, 1936, R.I.—East Greenwich, Weaver-Howland House, SPNEA.
89. Appleton to Lisle, Apr. 30, 1940, ibid.
90. Orcutt to author, Mar. 8, 1976.
91. Appleton to Boylston Beal, Oct. 29, 1931, Mass.—Boston, Charter Street, Vernon Court, SPNEA.
92. Hollis French to Appleton, July 8, 1931, ibid.
93. Appleton to French, June 22, 1931, ibid.
94. Appleton to Norman Isham, Aug. 1, 1931, ibid.
95. Appleton to Meyer, Nov. 18, 1931, ibid.
96. Appleton to Bolton, Jan. 30, 1931, Mass.—Boston, Clough-Langdon, SPNEA.
97. Appleton to Arthur A. Shurcliff, June 8, 1933, ibid.
98. J. Lovell Little to Appleton, July 31, 1933, ibid.
99. Appleton to the Rev. Francis Webster, Mar. 14, 1936, ibid.
100. Appleton to Robert S. Chase, Aug. 14, 1946, ibid.
101. Appleton to Chase, Aug. 16, 1946, ibid.
102. Appleton to Edward D. Noyes, July 21, 1933, Maine—Portland, Morse-Libby, SPNEA.
103. Appleton to Walter G. Davis, Oct. 10, 1935, ibid.

104. Davis to Appleton, Oct. 16, 1935, and Davis to Appleton, Feb. 17, 1936, ibid.

105. Appleton to Davis, May 14, 1936, ibid.

106. Appleton to Endicott, Aug. 11, 1936, William C. Endicott, SPNEA.

107. Davis to Appleton, Nov. 9, 1936, Maine—Portland, Morse-Libby, SPNEA.

108. Appleton to Davis, Nov. 13, 1937, ibid.

109. Appleton to Margaret H. Jewell, May 17, 1938, ibid.

110. Davis to Appleton, Aug. 16, 1938, ibid.

111. John Howard Stevens to Appleton, Aug. 15, 1940, ibid.

112. Appleton, "Notes on the Morse-Libby House," Aug. 18, 1940, ibid.

113. Appleton to Jewell, Aug. 20, 1940, ibid.

114. Appleton to Stevens, Oct. 7, 1940, ibid.

115. Appleton to Harry B. Ayer, Jan. 3, 1941, ibid.

116. William H. Holmes to Appleton, Apr. 7, 1941, ibid.

117. Holmes to Appleton, Apr. 21, 1941, ibid.

118. Holmes to Appleton, Sept. 17, 1941, ibid.

119. Holmes to Appleton, July 21, 1941, ibid.

120. Roger Hale Newton, letter in *Portland Press-Herald*, Sept. 19, 1941.

121. Holmes to Appleton, Oct. 23, 1941, Maine—Portland, Morse-Libby, SPNEA.

122. Holmes to Appleton, June 25, 1943, and Appleton to Newton, June 26, 1943, Roger Newton, ibid.

123. Addison to Clara Holmes, Jan. 7, 1948, Maine—Portland, Morse-Libby, SPNEA; W. H. Holmes to Appleton, Apr. 21, 1941, ibid.

124. Helen B. L. Patterson and Orcutt, "Report on Sewall's Bridge," Nov. 8, 1933, Maine—York, Sewall's Bridge, SPNEA.

125. Appleton to William Tudor Gardner, July 17, 1933, ibid.

126. Ege Sawtelle to Mrs. J. Fremont Hill, July 27, 1933, and Frank C. Deering to Appleton, Aug. 1, 1933, ibid.

127. Patterson and Orcutt, "Report," Nov. 8, 1933, ibid.; Patterson and Orcutt, "The Saving of Sewall's Bridge," *OTNE*, No. 75 (Jan. 1934), 100–103.

128. Perkins to Appleton, July 11, 1933, Maine—York, Sewall's Bridge, SPNEA.

129. Petition to the Maine State Highway Commission, July 19, 1933, ibid.

130. Patterson and Orcutt, "Report," Nov. 8, 1933, ibid.

131. Perkins to Appleton, Aug. 26, 1933, ibid.

132. Patterson and Orcutt, "Report," Nov. 8, 1933, ibid.; interview with Orcutt; Patterson and Orcutt, "Saving of Sewall's Bridge," 102.

133. Patterson and Orcutt, "Report," Nov. 8, 1933, Maine—York, Sewall's Bridge, SPNEA.

134. Ibid.

135. Orcutt to author, Mar. 8, 1976.

136. Interview with Orcutt.

137. See chapter 4 for the story of Gore Place.

138. Appleton to Laurence B. Fletcher, Mar. 2, 1939, Mass.—Concord, Old Manse, SPNEA.

139. Fletcher to Appleton, Apr. 8, 1939, ibid.

140. Fletcher, printed letter, Mar. 29, 1939, ibid.

141. Fletcher, printed letter, summer 1939, ibid.

142. Fletcher to Appleton, ca. July 18, 1939, Trustees of Reservations, SPNEA.

143. Fletcher to SPNEA, Nov. 3, 1939, Mass.—Concord, Old Manse, SPNEA.

144. Appleton to Lisle, Nov. 27, 1940, Arthur B. Lisle, SPNEA.

145. Fletcher to Appleton, June 14, 1943, Trustees of Reservations, SPNEA.

146. Interview with Edwin W. Small, Aug. 2, 1961.

147. Helen Storrow to Appleton, July 3, 1927, Mass.—West Brookfield, Gilbert House, SPNEA.

148. Appleton to Storrow, Feb. 11, 1944, Mass.—West Springfield, Storrowton, SPNEA.

149. Appleton to Storrow, July 1, 1927, Mass.—West Brookfield, Gilbert House, SPNEA.

150. Storrow to Appleton, July 3, 1927, ibid.

151. Appleton to Chandler, July 19, 1927, ibid.

152. Chandler to Appleton, Dec. 31, 1928, Joseph Chandler, SPNEA.

153. Storrow to Appleton, Oct. 29, 1928, Arts and Crafts—Pottery, Mrs. Storrow, SPNEA.

154. Appleton to Newton C. Brainard, Sept. 24, 1929, Mass.—West Springfield, Storrowton, SPNEA.

155. Appleton to Mrs. Oscar P. Tabor, Jr., Nov. 25, 1941, N.H.—Webster, Old Meeting House, SPNEA.

156. Appleton to Donald Tuttle, May 2, 1941, ibid.

157. Appleton to Small, July 3, 1941, ibid.

158. Frank Chouteau Brown to Appleton, July 18, 1941, ibid.

159. Appleton to Tabor, July 30, 1941, ibid.

160. Appleton to Tabor, Sept. 2, 1941, ibid.

161. Appleton to Tabor, Sept. 19, 1941, ibid.

162. Tabor to Appleton, June 6, 1942, ibid.

163. Appleton to Mabel Choate, Oct. 26, 1926, Appleton to Choate, Nov. 4, 1926, and Choate to Appleton, Nov. 8, 1926, Mass.—Stockbridge, Mission House, SPNEA.

164. Appleton to Endicott, June 26, 1933, Mass.—Danvers, Lindens, SPNEA.

165. Appleton to Mrs. Endicott Peabody, June 27, 1933, ibid.

166. John Hill Morgan to Appleton, Sept. 7, 1934, ibid.

167. Charles O. Cornelius to Henry F. du Pont, June 6, 1933, Registrar's Office, Henry Francis du Pont Winterthur Museum.

168. Appleton to Morgan, Aug. 31, 1934, Mass.—Danvers, Lindens, SPNEA.

169. Interview with Mrs. George Maurice Morris, Aug. 22, 1972.

170. Appleton to Thomas T. Waterman, Sept. 14, 1934, Mass.—Danvers, Lindens, SPNEA.

171. Ibid.

172. Appleton to Mrs. Frederic W. Wallace, Sept. 19, 1934, Mass.—Danvers, Lindens, ibid.

173. Appleton to Fletcher, Dec. 4, 5, 1935, Laurence Fletcher, SPNEA.

174. Hosmer, *Presence of the Past*, 111–13.

175. Appleton to Richard T. Crane, Jr., Aug. 31, 1927, Mass.—Ipswich, Whipple, SPNEA. (This letter was probably not sent.)

176. Appleton to Kimball, Sept. 6, 1927, ibid.

177. Appleton, Petition addressed to President and Directors of Ipswich Historical Society, ca. Sept. 1927, ibid.

178. Appleton to Harriet Condon, Nov. 3, 1927, ibid.

179. Appleton to Mrs. T. Franklin Waters, Nov. 10, 1927, ibid.

180. Appleton to A. Warren Stearns, Mar. 18, 1932, Mass.—Billerica, Mrs. Ward's House, SPNEA.

181. Percival Hall Lombard, "The Aptucxet Trading Post," *OTNE*, No. 72 (Apr. 1933), 160–64.

182. Lombard to Appleton, Dec. 6, 1928, Bourne Historical Society, SPNEA; Lombard, "Aptucxet Trading Post," 162.

183. Lombard, "Aptucxet," 159–74; Lombard, "The First Trading Post of the Plymouth Colony," *OTNE*, No. 50 (Oct. 1927), 70–86.

184. Appleton to Lombard, Sept. 10, 1929, Mass.—Bourne, Trading Post, SPNEA.

185. Lombard to Appleton, Sept. 13, 1929, ibid.

186. Everett B. Mero to Appleton, Feb. 18, 1928, Mass. Bay Tercentenary, Inc., SPNEA.

187. Appleton to A. R. Rogers, Feb. 12, 1930, ibid.

188. Appleton to James M. Curley, Oct. 3, 1930, and Appleton to Henry I. Harriman, Dec. 3, 1929, Boston Tercentenary Commission, SPNEA.

189. Appleton to John F. Fitzgerald, Mar. 15, 1930, ibid.

190. Fitzgerald to Appleton, Apr. 14, 1930, and F. C. Brown to Appleton, Apr. 15, 1930, ibid.

191. Appleton to Curley, Oct. 3, 1930, ibid.

192. Dow, "The Colonial Village Built at Salem, Massachusetts, in the Spring of 1930," *OTNE*, No. 65 (July 1931), 3–14.

193. [George Francis Dow], *A Reference Guide to Salem, 1630* (Salem, Mass., 1935).

194. *Boston Globe*, Feb. 18, 1940; John M. Bullard to Appleton, Mar. 25, 1941, Whaling Ship "Morgan," SPNEA.

195. Appleton to Carl C. Cutler, Nov. 17, 1941, Marine Historical Assn., SPNEA.

196. Appleton to C. Lester Ames, Nov. 23, 1941, Maine—Bridgeton, Narrow Gauge R.R., SPNEA.

197. Appleton to Mrs. Jason Westerfield, Mar. 5, 1943, Maine—Damariscotta, Old cannon, SPNEA.

198. Appleton to George J. Bates, July 8, 1929, Mass.—Salem, Market, SPNEA.

199. Appleton to Waldon Fawcett, Sept. 9, 1937, Mass.—Nantucket, Publicity, SPNEA.

200. Appleton to Fletcher, Sept. 23, 1939, Trustees of Reservations, SPNEA.

201. George Coffing Warner to Appleton, Mar. 17, 18, 1932, George Coffing Warner, SPNEA.

202. Warner to Appleton, July 8, 1933, ibid.

203. Warner to Appleton, Jan. 11, 1936, ibid.

204. "Preliminary Announcement, Connecticut Association (Inc.)," ca. Jan. 1933, ibid.

205. J. Frederick Kelly to Appleton, Jan. 17, 1936, J. Fred Kelly, SPNEA.

206. Appleton to Warner, Jan. 20, 1936, George Coffing Warner, SPNEA.

207. Ibid.

208. Warner, mimeographed letter, June 6, 1936, George Coffing Warner, SPNEA.

209. Appleton to Seymour, June 10, 1936, George D. Seymour, SPNEA.

210. *Quarterly News-Letter of the Antiquarian and Landmarks Society, Inc., of Connecticut*, 1 (June 1937), 2–3.

211. Ibid. (Nov. 1937), 1, 5.

212. Appleton to Mrs. Oakes Ames Spalding, Oct. 28, 1937, George Coffing Warner, SPNEA.

213. Appleton, "Report," *OTNE*, No. 100 (Apr. 1940), 138, and No. 105 (July 1941), 26.

214. John P. Brown to Lisle, July 14, 1944, Arthur B. Lisle, SPNEA. The story of preservation in Newport is covered in chapter 5.

215. Robert P. Bellows to Appleton, May, 1928, Boston Society of Architects, SPNEA.

216. Leicester B. Holland to Appleton, Aug. 18, 1930, Congressional Library, SPNEA.

217. Appleton to Holland, Aug. 21, 1930, ibid.

218. Holland to Appleton, Sept. 3, 1930, ibid.

219. Millard B. Gulick to Appleton, May 23, 1932, Boston Emergency Planning and Research Bureau, SPNEA.

220. G. H. Edgell to Appleton, June 1, 1932, ibid.; Appleton to Richard H. Dana, June 11, 1932, R. H. Dana, SPNEA.

221. Appleton to Edsel Ford, Aug. 5, 1932, Boston Emergency Planning and Research Bureau, SPNEA. (This was probably not sent.)

222. William V. Dixey to Appleton, Sept. 14, 1932, ibid.

223. William S. Parker to Appleton, Sept. 20, 1932, ibid.

224. Dana to Appleton, May 27, 1932; and Appleton to Dana, Jan. 24, 1933, R. H. Dana, SPNEA.

225. F. C. Brown to Appleton, Dec. 18, 1933, HABS, SPNEA.

226. Appleton to Harold Davis, Dec. 26, 1933, Conn.—CWA, SPNEA.

227. Davis to Appleton, Jan. 3, 1934, ibid.

228. Stevens to Appleton, Jan. 24, 1934, Maine (N.H. and Vt.)—CWA, SPNEA.

229. Appleton to Brown, Sept. 17, 1934, HABS, SPNEA.

230. Ibid.; 1934 appeal for funds, SPNEA.

231. Appleton to Davis, Mar. 20, 1934, Conn.—CWA, SPNEA.

232. Appleton to Allen French, Feb. 8, 1936, Mass.—Concord, Antiquarian Society, SPNEA.

233. J. Thomas Schneider to SPNEA, Dec. 13, 1934, U.S. Dept. of Interior, Parks and Shrines, SPNEA.

234. Appleton to Schneider, Dec. 17, 1934, ibid.

235. Interview with Small; Appleton, memo, Aug. 8, 1935, WPA, SPNEA.

236. Appleton to Small, Aug., 1935, ibid.

237. Appleton to SPNEA membership, Nov., 1935, U.S. Dept. of Interior, NPS, SPNEA.

238. Small to Appleton, Jan. 11, 1936, ibid.

239. Appleton to Edward Forbes, May 5, 1937, Mass.—Plymouth, Winslow House, SPNEA.

240. Small to author, Aug. 8, 1961; interview with Little.

241. Franklin D. Roosevelt to Harold L. Ickes, Jan. 2, 1942, Proposed NHS Mass—0—36, Records of NPS, NA, RG 79.

242. Appleton to Mrs. Charles S. Hamlin, Mar. 20, 1942, Maine—Kittery, Proposed NHS, SPNEA.

243. Appleton to Ronald F. Lee, Apr. 14, 1947, Headquarters File (Org), Society for the Preservation of New England Antiquities, National Trust.

244. Appleton to Lee, Apr. 25, 1947 (mailed Oct. 6, 1947), National Council, Miscellaneous Correspondence, National Trust.

245. Lee to Appleton, Oct. 16, 1947, ibid.

246. Appleton, "Report," OTNE, No. 130 (Oct. 1947), 52.

247. Appleton to Seymour, June 10, 1936, George D. Seymour, SPNEA.

248. Appleton, "Report," OTNE, No. 105 (July 1941), 24–25.

249. F. C. Brown to Appleton, June 7, 1940, N.Y.—Cutchogue, Horton House, SPNEA.

250. Appleton to Fletcher, Sept. 23, 1939, Trustees of Reservations, SPNEA.

251. Bertram K. Little, "Report of the Corresponding Secretary," OTNE, No. 134 (Oct. 1948), 52–53.

252. Ibid., 58.

253. Little to author, Feb. 23, 1970.

254. Interview with Little.

255. Little to author, Feb. 23, 1970.

256. Little, "Selection of Historic New England Houses for Preservation," talk at meeting of American Association of Museums, May 28, 1948, Files of Branch of History, U.S. Department of Interior.

257. Lee to Newton B. Drury, Oct. 22, 1948, attached to Little, "Selection."

258. U.S. Grant III to Little, July 2, 1948, National Trust, SPNEA.

259. Little, "Report," *OTNE*, No. 138 (Oct. 1949), 156.

260. Little to G. Edwin Brumbaugh, Mar. 27, 1949, NYSHA Seminars (1949), SPNEA.

Chapter 4: *Preservation Organizations*

1. Charles B. Hosmer, Jr., *Presence of the Past: A History of the Preservation Movement in the United States before Williamsburg* (New York, 1965), 59–60, 65–72, 131–52, 237–59.

2. Harrison Howell Dodge, *Mount Vernon, Its Owner and Its Story* (Philadelphia, 1932), 169–83; Elswyth Thane, *Mount Vernon: The Legacy* (Philadelphia, 1967).

3. Thane, *Mount Vernon*, 29–32.

4. Ibid., 123.

5. Ibid., 147.

6. Hosmer, *Presence of the Past*, 180–82.

7. *Walpole Society Notebook, 1926* (N.p., privately printed, 1926), 20.

8. Theodore Fred Kuper to author, Sept. 11, 1970.

9. Ibid.

10. *New York Times*, July 25, 1927.

11. Ibid., Aug. 17, 1927.

12. Stuart G. Gibboney to William Sumner Appleton, June 2, 1928, Va.–Monticello, Society for the Preservation of New England Antiquities (SPNEA).

13. Appleton to Kuper, Dec. 26, 1928, Theodore Fred Kuper, SPNEA.

14. Fiske Kimball to Appleton, Oct. 26, 1928, Va.–Monticello, SPNEA.

15. Walter Rendell Storey, "Monticello, Now a Shrine, Mirrors a Bygone Age," *New York Times Magazine*, Oct. 28, 1928, 14, 23.

16. *New York Times*, July 12, 1929.

17. *Editor and Publisher, the Fourth Estate*, Oct. 24, 1931, 5–6, 56, 57.

18. *New York Times*, Aug. 8, 1932.

19. *Monticello* (New York, 1931), brochure.

20. Kuper to author, Sept. 11, 1970.

21. Verne E. Chatelain to Horace M. Albright, Feb. 25, 1932, Proposed National Monument (NM), Mt. Vernon 0–35, Records of the National Park Service (NPS), National Archives (NA), Record Group (RG) 79; *Washington Star*, Apr. 5, 1932.

22. Chatelain to Albright, Nov. 1, 1932, Proposed National Historic Site (NHS), Monticello 0–36, Records of NPS, NA, RG 79.

23. William E. Carson to Harold L. Ickes, June 22, 1933, ibid.

24. Kuper to author, Sept. 11, 1970.

25. Interview with Milton Grigg, Sept. 15, 1972; *New York Times*, Apr. 10, 1938; *Richmond Times-Dispatch*, Jan. 8, 1938.

26. *New York Times*, Feb. 27, 1941.

27. Ickes to James L. Fieser, May 5, 1943, Proposed NHS, Monticello 0–36, Records of NPS, NA, RG 79.

28. Franklin D. Roosevelt to Ickes, Sept. 23, 1944, ibid.

29. Francis S. Ronalds to Newton B. Drury, Apr. 6, 1945, and Kimball to Drury, Aug. 12, 1946, ibid.

30. John C. Fitzpatrick, ed., *Some Historic Houses* (New York, 1939), 10–13.

31. Ibid.

32. Lewis Barrington, *Historic Restorations of the Daughters of the American Revolution* (New York, 1941).

33. Laurence Vail Coleman to author, July 22, 1965.

34. Hosmer, *Presence of the Past*, 131–38.

35. Mrs. John H. Kinzie, *Wau-bun, the "Early Day" in the North-West* (Chicago, 1932).

36. Louise Phelps Kellogg, "The Old Indian Agency House Association," *Wisconsin Magazine of History*, 22 (Mar. 1939), 282–83.

37. See chapter 1 for Henry Ford's visit to Stratford.

38. Kate Cabell Cox, "Colonial Dames of America in Virginia," Report, 1916, Robert E. Lee Memorial Foundation Archives (LMF).

39. Ethel Armes, *Stratford Hall, the Great House of the Lees* (Richmond, 1936), 443.

40. H. Latane Lewis to Armes, Oct. 3, 1928, B2–3/233, Armes, Research and Restoration, LMF.

41. Armes to Mrs. Charles Lanier, May 24, 1928, A2–2a/Appendix, LMF.

42. Lanier, "Story of the Purchase of Stratford," dictated Jan. 16, 1946, A2–2a/Appendix, LMF.

43. Ibid.

44. Armes to Lewis, June 15, 1928, B2–3/233, Armes, Research and Restoration, LMF.

45. Ibid., June 19, 1928.

46. Ibid.

47. Ibid.

48. *New York Times*, Sept. 23, 1928.

49. "Report of the Committee on Origin, October, 1935–Momentous Minutes," 9, LMF; Lanier to Hilton H. Railey, Dec. 7, 1928, H2–2a/Appendix, Binder, History LMF (UDC), 1928–29, LMF.

50. Mrs. Frank H. Griffin, "Story of the Establishment of the Robert E. Lee Memorial Foundation," May 4, 1963 (mimeographed), 2, LMF; Ethel Armes, *Stratford on the Potomac* (Greenwich, Conn., 1928).

51. Lanier to Armes, Nov. 15, 1928, and Lewis to Armes, Nov. 19, 1928, A2–29/Appendix, Binder, History LMF (UDC) 1928–29, LMF.

52. Lanier to Armes, Nov. 15, 1928, ibid.

53. "Report of Mrs. Charles D. Lanier," Nov. 28, 1928, 1–2, A2–2a/ Appendix, Binder, History LMF (UDC), 1928–29, LMF.

54. "Tentative Proposition for the Purchase of Stratford Hall," (UDC Convention, 1928), A2–2a/Appendix, LMF.

55. "Report of Mrs. Charles D. Lanier," Nov. 28, 1928, 1–2, A2–2a/ Appendix, Binder, History LMF (UDC), 1928–29, LMF.

56. Ibid.

57. Horace Van Deventer to Lanier, Nov. 29, 1928, 1–2, A2–2a/Appendix, Binder, History LMF (UDC), 1928–29, LMF.

58. "Report of Mrs. Charles D. Lanier," 6, ibid.

59. Lanier, "Story of the Purchase of Stratford," A2–2a/Appendix.

60. Railey to Lanier, Dec. 6, 1928, A2–2a/Appendix, Binder, History LMF (UDC), 1928–29, LMF.

61. Lanier to Railey, Dec. 7, 1928, ibid.

62. Lanier, "Story of the Purchase of Stratford," A2–2a/Appendix.

63. Armes, *Stratford on the Potomac*, 42.

64. Lanier to Van Deventer, Feb. 14, 1929, B2–6a/3, LMF.

65. Griffin, "Story of the Establishment of the Robert E. Lee Memorial Foundation," 3.

66. Lanier to Van Deventer, Feb. 14, 1929, B2–6a/3, LMF.

67. *New York Times*, Mar. 24, 1929.

68. Lanier to Van Deventer, Feb. 25, 1929, B2–6a/3, LMF.

69. Van Deventer to Lanier, Mar. 2, 1929, ibid.

70. Lanier to Van Deventer, Mar. 7, 1929, ibid.

71. "Minutes of Informal Meeting of Board of Directors, LMF," Apr. 30, 1929, A2–2a/Appendix, Binder, History LMF (UDC), 1929–, LMF.

72. Armes, "Outline General Organization Form of the Robert E. Lee Memorial Foundation," Apr. 1929, ibid.

73. Mrs. Emerson R. Newell to Lanier, July 16, 1929, ibid.

74. Lanier, "Story of the Purchase of Stratford," A2–2a/Appendix.

75. Newell to Lanier, Oct. 1, 1954, A2–2a/Appendix, Binder, History LMF (UDC), 1929–, LMF.

76. *New York Times*, Nov. 23, 1929.

77. [Armes], *Stratford-on-Potomac*, LMF.

78. Armes, "Twelve Reasons Why Stratford Should Become a National Shrine," LMF.

79. "State Directors Send Enthusiastic Messages to Officials of Robert E. Lee Memorial Foundation," LMF.

80. Mrs. Horace Van Deventer to Kimball, July 1, 1930, B2–6a/46, LMF; Kimball to Van Deventer, July 15, 1930, B2–6a/46, Restoration Committee, LMF.

81. *New York Times*, Apr. 26, 1931.

82. Ibid., Jan. 31, 1932.

83. Griffin, "Story of the Establishment of the Robert E. Lee Memorial Foundation," 6.

84. Mrs. George Gordon Battle, form letter, Feb. 6, 1932, A2–1a/499, LMF.

85. Lanier to Kimball, Mar. 13, 1933, B2–5a/Lanier I, LMF.

86. Helen Knox to Mrs. William C. Bruce, June 16, 1933, A2–1a/500, LMF.

87. Lanier to Mrs. Robert W. Bingham, July 21, 1933, ibid.

88. "The Dedication of Stratford Depends on You!" LMF.

89. Jessie Ball duPont to Lanier, June 7, 1935, B2–6a/2, LMF.

90. *New York Times*, Nov. 24, 1934; Knox to Mrs. William E. Massey, Oct. 1, 1935, A2–2a/Appendix, Binder, History LMF (UDC), 1929–, LMF.

91. Douglas Southall Freeman, "The Cornerstones of Stratford," address, Oct. 12, 1935, 4–5, LMF.

92. *New York Times*, Oct. 13, 1935.

93. Armes, "Outline of Tentative Development Plans for Stratford Hall," ca. 1930, A2–2a/145, LFM.

94. Armes, "Stratford on the Potomac," *Antiques*, 23 (May 1933), 175–77.

95. Armes, *Stratford Hall, the Great House of the Lees*, 477–93.

96. For an account of the Stratford restoration, see chapters 11 and 12.

97. Appleton to Charles H. Metz, Feb. 23, 1921, Mass.–Waltham, Gore Place, SPNEA; Appleton to Chairman of House Committee, Waltham Country Club, Feb. 10, 1923, ibid.

98. Interview with Philip Dana Orcutt, Oct. 31, 1969.

99. Bradford Williams to Laurence B. Fletcher, May 24, 1935, Mass.–Waltham, Gore Place, SPNEA.

100. Interview with Orcutt.

101. Williams to Fletcher, May 24, 1935, Mass.—Waltham, Gore Place, SPNEA.

102. Interview with Bertram K. Little, Oct. 30, 1969.

103. Notes on a meeting held at the Harrison Gray Otis House on Thursday, May 10, 1935, Mass.–Waltham, Gore Place, SPNEA.

104. Williams to Fletcher, May 24, 1935, ibid.

105. Williams to Joseph Lee, May 18, 1935, ibid.

106. "To All Friends of Old Houses in Massachusetts," June 8, 1935, ibid.

107. Appleton to Richard C. Cabot, May 22, 1935, and Appleton to Mira Pitman, July 29, 1935, ibid.

108. Frank Chouteau Brown to Appleton, May 13, 1935, ibid.

109. "To All Friends of Old Houses in Massachusetts," ibid.

110. Appleton to Albert Bushnell Hart, June 14, 1935, ibid.

111. Interview with Orcutt; Orcutt to author, Mar. 8, 1976.

112. "Report on Gore Place," ca. 1941, Mass.—Waltham, Gore Place, SPNEA.

113. Ronald F. Lee to Regional Director, Region One, July 23, 1947, Proposed NHS (Mass.), 0–36, Records of NPS, NA, RG 79; Helen B. L. Patterson to Newton Drury, Aug. 15, 1947, ibid.

114. *Octagon, a Journal of the American Institute of Architects*, 2 (Aug. 1930), 13.

115. *Proceedings of the 64th Annual Convention of the AIA, April 14–16, 1931* (Washington, D.C., 1931), 114–15.

116. Interview with Erling H. Pedersen, Sept. 14, 1972; George B. Tatum, *Philadelphia Georgian* (Middletown, Conn., 1976), 27–28.

117. Philadelphia Society for the Preservation of Landmarks, leaflet, ca. 1954.

118. Charles S. Penhallow, Jr., to Appleton, Mar. 31, 1931, N.H.—Portsmouth, Warner House, SPNEA.

119. Interview with Orcutt; Warner House Association, Inc., leaflet, fall of 1931, Warner House, Portsmouth, N.H.

120. Mrs. Barrett Wendell to Appleton, Sept. 9, 1931, N.H.—Portsmouth, Warner House, SPNEA.

121. Minutes of Warner House Assn., Sept. 16, 1931, Warner House.

122. Ibid., Sept. 30, 1931.

123. Ibid., Oct. 21, 1931.

124. Lucy S. Walker to Appleton, Aug. 24, 1932, N.H.—Portsmouth, Warner House, SPNEA.

125. Appleton to Walker, Sept. 12, 1932, Appleton to Mrs. Henry Vaughn, Aug. 3, 1933, and Appleton to Joseph E. Chandler, June 17, 1936, ibid.

126. Appleton to Wendell, Oct. 26, 1937, File Box, Warner House.

127. Helen Worden Erskine, *Out of This World* (New York, 1953), 161–63, 170–77.

128. Ibid., 170–72; George Chapman to Appleton, Jan. 28, 1935, and Chapman to Appleton, Feb. 5, 1935, N.Y.–N.Y., Seabury-Tredwell House, SPNEA.

129. Chapman to Appleton, Jan. 28, 1935, ibid.

130. Chapman to Appleton, Feb. 5, 1935, ibid.

131. Chapman to Appleton, June 21, 1935, ibid.

132. Appleton to Chapman, June 23, 1935, ibid.

133. Chapman to Appleton, Dec. 11, 1935, ibid.

134. *New York Times*, May 3, 1936.

135. Talbot Hamlin to Appleton, July 17, 1936, Columbia University, SPNEA.

136. Chapman to Appleton, Jan. 31, 1938, N.Y.–N.Y., Seabury-Tredwell House, SPNEA.

137. Historic Landmark Society, "The Story of the Old Merchant's

House," leaflet, ca. 1939, ibid.; Chapman to Appleton, two letters dated Nov. 27, 1939, ibid.

138. Chapman to Appleton, Jan. 12, 1942, ibid.

139. Chapman to Appleton, Jan. 15, 1942, with summary sheet, ibid.

140. Appleton to Chapman, Feb. 4, 1942, and Appleton to Francis T. P. Plimpton, Mar. 19, 1942, ibid.

141. Appleton to Plimpton, Apr. 13, 1942, ibid.

142. *New York Times*, Apr. 16, 1951.

143. *The Campbell House, a Romantic Survival of Early St. Louis* (St. Louis, 1960), 2.

144. Interview with Irving Dilliard, Dec. 28, 1972.

145. *St. Louis Post-Dispatch*, Feb. 17, 1941.

146. Ibid., Feb. 13, 1941.

147. Interviews with John Albury Bryan, Aug. 25, 1969, Charles E. Peterson, Feb. 9, 1970, and Dilliard.

148. Interview with Charles van Ravenswaay, July 9, 1973.

149. Interviews with van Ravenswaay and Dilliard.

150. Interviews with Peterson, Dilliard, and van Ravenswaay.

151. *St. Louis Post-Dispatch*, Feb. 14, 1941.

152. Interview with Dilliard; *St. Louis Post-Dispatch*, Mar. 9, 1941, and Feb. 19, 1941.

153. Interviews with Dilliard and van Ravenswaay.

154. Interviews with Dilliard and van Ravenswaay.

155. *St. Louis Post-Dispatch*, Mar. 9, 1941.

156. Ibid., Feb. 18, 1941.

157. Ibid.

158. Interview with Bryan; *St. Louis Post-Dispatch*, Mar. 9, 1941.

159. *St. Louis Post-Dispatch*, Feb. 21, 1941.

160. Ibid., Feb. 22 and 23, 1941.

161. Ibid., Feb. 24, 1941.

162. Ibid., Feb. 25, 1941.

163. Ibid.

164. Ibid.

165. Ibid., Feb. 27 and 28, 1941.

166. Ibid., Mar. 29 and 30, 1941.

167. Ibid., Apr. 12, 1941.

168. Ibid., Apr. 27, 1941.

169. Ibid., May 16, 1941.

170. Ibid., June 2, 1941.

171. Ibid., Nov. 23, 1941.

172. Ibid., Apr. 10, 1942; interview with Bryan.

173. Jesse P. Henry, address, Feb. 6, 1943, quoted in *The Campbell House*, 10; Dec. 9, 1944 edition of *Campbell House* booklet.

174. Ibid.

175. *St. Louis Post-Dispatch*, Sept. 24, 1942.

176. Interview with Bryan.

177. *St. Louis Post-Dispatch*, Feb. 21, 1946.

178. Hosmer, *Presence of the Past*, 65–68.

179. See chapter 1.

180. Interview with Walter M. Macomber, July 8, 1972.

181. Interviews with J. C. Harrington, May 18, 1970, and Elbert Cox, May 9, 1970.

182. Leaflet, Thomas Rolfe Branch, Association for the Preservation of Virginia Antiquities, ca. June 1935, APVA, SPNEA.

183. Interview with Mary Wingfield Scott, Aug. 8, 1972.

184. Thomas T. Waterman to Appleton, ca. Jan. 1936, T. T. Waterman, SPNEA.

185. Hosmer, *Presence of the Past*, 253–55.

186. Arthur B. Bibbins to Appleton, Nov. 8, 1931, and leaflet, Society for the Preservation of Maryland Antiquities, SPNEA.

187. Ibid.

188. Bibbins to Appleton, Mar. 16, 1932, SPMA, SPNEA.

189. Bibbins to Appleton, Dec. 5, 1935, ibid.

190. Philip M. Wagner to Appleton, Jan. 29, 1940, ibid.

191. Robert Garrett to Appleton, Feb. 19, 1946, ibid.; Lee to Drury, Mar. 12, 1947, Hampton, Files of the Branch of History, U.S. Dept. of Interior.

192. Garrett, speech, Apr. 30, 1949, quoted in *National Council for Historic Sites and Buildings Quarterly Report*, 2 (Mar. 1950), supplement, 1–2.

193. Lee to Garrett, Mar. 12, 1947, and Lee to Drury, Mar. 12, 1947, Hampton, Files of Branch of History, U.S. Dept. of Interior.

194. For a detailed discussion of the negotiations see chapter 9.

195. Christopher C. Crittenden to Lee, Nov. 21, 1938, and enclosures, Proposed NHS, North Carolina, 0–36, Records of NPS, NA, RG 79; Mrs. C. A. Gosney to Appleton, July 13, 1939, North Carolina Society for the Preservation of Antiquities, SPNEA.

196. Joseph H. Pratt to Lee, Jan. 15, 1941, Proposed NHS, North Carolina, 0–36, Records of NPS, NA, RG 79.

197. Gosney to Appleton, Jan. 29 and Feb. 4, 1941, N.C. Society for Preservation of Antiquities, SPNEA.

198. Ibid.

199. Howard C. Sherwood to Appleton, Nov. 3, 1947, N.Y.–Setauket, Sherwood (SPLIA), SPNEA.

200. Interview with Ward Melville, Nov. 14, 1969.

201. *Newsletter, the Society for the Preservation of Long Island Antiquities*, 1 (Feb. 1957), 1.

202. Interview with James J. Morrison, June 12, 1971.

203. Interviews with Harnett T. Kane, June 12, 1971; Martha G. Robinson, June 11, 1971; and Samuel Wilson, Jr., June 9, 1971.

Chapter 5: *Historic Communities Awaken*

1. Richard Hofstadter, *The Age of Reform* (New York, 1960), 288–89; Henry Nash Smith, *Virgin Land* (New York, 1957), 123–44, 201–10.

2. C. Vann Woodward, *The Burden of Southern History* (New York, 1960), 6.

3. Ibid., 12, 24.

4. Alice R. Huger Smith and D. E. Huger Smith, *The Dwelling Houses of Charleston, South Carolina* (Philadelphia, 1917), 375.

5. Susan Pringle Frost to *Charleston News and Courier*, 1941, quoted in *Preservation Progress*, 16 (Jan. 1971), 2, 6.

6. Interview with Alston Deas, June 26, 1972.

7. Frost, letter of invitation, Apr. 12, 1920, Manigault House—My Family's Efforts to save it, Files of Mrs. Charles Anderson, Charleston, S.C.

8. Minutes of Society for Preservation of Old Dwelling Houses of Charleston (SPOD), Apr. 21, 1920, Box—Frost, SPOD, Preservation Society of Charleston (PSC).

9. Estimate of expenses, ca. 1932, Manigault House—My Family's Efforts to save it, Anderson file, Charleston.

10. Minutes of SPOD, Feb. 14, 1925, Box—Frost, SPOD, PSC.

11. Ibid., May 15, 1925.

12. Ibid., June 3, 1925.

13. George Garner, "An American City Which Should Be Preserved," *Manufacturers' Record*, May 20, 1926.

14. Albert Simons and Samuel Lapham, Jr., *Charleston, South Carolina* (New York, 1927).

15. Clipping, undated, Architectural Significance, Historic Charleston Foundation (HCF).

16. Samuel G. Stoney to William Sumner Appleton, Mar. 21 and Apr. 3, 1929, Preservations Miscellaneous, Society for the Preservation of New England Antiquities (SPNEA).

17. Charles B. Hosmer, Jr., *Presence of the Past: A History of the Preservation Movement in the United States before Williamsburg* (New York, 1965), 252–53.

18. Appleton to Stoney, Mar. 26, 1929, Preservations Misc., SPNEA.

19. *Year Book, 1929, City of Charleston, South Carolina* (Charleston, 1929), 320–21.

20. Minutes of City Planning and Zoning Commission, May 21, 1929, Zoning Commission, Charleston City Archives (CCA).

21. *Year Book, 1929, Charleston*, 294–95.

22. Interviews with Albert Simons, June 22, 1972, and Deas; *Charleston News and Courier*, Sept. 21, 1929.

23. Interview with Deas; *Year Book, 1929, Charleston*, 306–7.

24. *Year Book, 1929, Charleston*, 314–19.

25. Minutes of City Planning and Zoning Commission, Mar. 31, 1930, Zoning Commission, CCA.

26. Ibid., 10.

27. *Year Book, 1930, City of Charleston, South Carolina* (Charleston, 1930), 447; interview with Deas.

28. Minutes of Special Committee on Zoning, July 3, 1930, All Committees except Ways and Means, CCA; *Year Book, 1930, Charleston*, 482–83.

29. *Year Book, 1930, Charleston*, 487–88.

30. Ibid., 498–99.

31. "Mayor Stoney's Annual Review," ibid., xxi, 308.

32. *Year Book, 1931, City of Charleston, South Carolina* (Charleston, 1931), 649–51.

33. Simons to Horace W. Peaslee, July 8, 1931, Simons—Committee for Safeguarding Charleston Architecture, HCF.

34. *Year Book, 1931, Charleston*, 696–97.

35. *Rules and Regulations of Board of Adjustment under the Zoning Ordinance of the City of Charleston* (Charleston, 1931), 20–21.

36. Simons to Thomas R. Waring, Sept. 3, 15, 23, Oct. 8, 1932, Simons—Board of Architectural Review, South Carolina Historical Society (SCHS).

37. Simons to Leicester B. Holland, Dec. 17, 1931, Simons—Manigault House, HCF.

38. Waring to Simons, Sept. 7, 1932, Simons—Board of Architectural Review, 1931–43, SCHS.

39. Simons to Waring, Oct. 8, 1932, ibid.

40. Simons to William Emerson, Nov. 5, 1932, Simons—Plantation Houses, William Emerson, SCHS.

41. Simons to Delos Smith, Aug. 10, 1933, Simons–Board of Architectural Review, 1931–43, SCHS.

42. Mrs. Thomas J. Mauldin to Simons, May 27, 1935, Simons–HABS Collaborator at Large, HCF.

43. James J. Morrison to Simons, May 26, 1939, Simons–Board of Architectural Review, 1931–43, SCHS.

44. Simons to Morrison, May 29, 1939, ibid.

45. Sophie G. Friedman to Charleston Chamber of Commerce, Aug. 3, 1939, PSC.

46. Helen McCormack to Mary Wingfield Scott, May 14, 1942, Personal Correspondence, McCormack, HCF.

47. Smith to Simons, Dec. 7, 1946, Simons, 1945–48, City Planning and Zoning Commission, SCHS.

48. Simons to Mrs. William Emerson, Apr. 28, 1928, Simons papers, Mrs. William Emerson, Heyward House Fund, SCHS.

49. W. Emerson to Simons, Apr. 5, 1928, Simons papers, Plantation Houses, William Emerson, SCHS.

50. Mrs. Emerson to Simons, Apr. 23, 1928, Simons papers, Mrs. William Emerson, Heyward House Fund, SCHS.

51. Simons to Mrs. Emerson, Apr. 28, 1928, ibid.

52. *Charleston News and Courier*, May 11, 1928.

53. Ibid., May 13, 1928.

54. Laura Bragg to Mrs. Emerson, May 22, 1928, Simons papers, Mrs. William Emerson, Heyward House Fund, SCHS.

55. Simons to Deas, May 26, 1928, and Simons to Emerson, May 28, 1928, ibid.

56. W. Emerson to Simons, June 5, 1928, Simons papers, Plantation Houses, William Emerson, SCHS.

57. Leaflet on Heyward-Washington House, early 1929.

58. Simons to Emerson, Mar. 12, 1929, Simons papers, Plantation Houses, William Emerson, SCHS.

59. Clipping, May 1, 1929, on Heyward-Washington House, Scrapbook, PSC.

60. Mrs. Emerson to Simons, Aug. 27, 1930, Simons—Committee for Safeguarding Charleston Architecture, HCF.

61. Simons to Mrs. Emerson, Sept. 2, 1930, ibid.

62. Simons to Robert D. Kohn, Oct. 20, 1930, ibid.

63. *Octagon*, 4 (May 1931), 20.

64. Simons to Holland, Sept. 27, 1932, Simons—Preservation of Historic Buildings, Holland, HCF.

65. Holland to Simons, Oct. 28, 1932, ibid.; Holland, "Colonial Interiors as Museum Trophies," *Octagon*, 4 (Nov. 1932), 6–7.

66. Fiske Kimball to Simons, Nov. 23, 1932, Simons—Preservation of Historic Buildings, Holland, HCF.

67. Simons to Kimball, Nov. 26, 1932, ibid.

68. *Charleston Evening Post*, Feb. 18, 1933.

69. Simons to Holland, Feb. 23, 1933, Simons—Preservation of Historic Buildings, Holland, HCF.

70. Holland to Simons, Feb. 25, 1933, ibid.

71. Simons to Kohn, Oct. 23, 1930, Simons—Committee for Safeguarding Charleston Architecture, HCF.

72. Simons to Kohn, Dec, 3, 1930, ibid.

73. Simons to Mrs. Emerson, Feb. 2, 1931, ibid.; Simons to author, March 26, 1973.

74. Interview with E. Milby Burton, June 27, 1972; H. I. Brock, "Charleston Has Preserved," *New York Times Magazine*, Nov. 1, 1931, 12–13, 21; Elizabeth W. Frothingham to Simons, Oct. 24, 1931, Simons—Mrs. William Emerson, Heyward House Fund, SCHS.

75. Simons to Mrs. Emerson, Sept. 28, 1931, Simons—Mrs. William Emerson, Heyward House Fund, SCHS.

76. Simons to Mrs. Emerson, Feb. 27, 1932, ibid.

77. Simons to Kohn, Mar. 27, 1931, Simons—Committee for Safeguarding Charleston Architecture, HCF.

78. Minutes of SPOD, May 6, 1930, Box—Frost SPOD, PSC.

79. *Charleston News and Courier*, Feb. 25, 1931.

80. Simons to George W. Bacon, Apr. 15, 23, 1931, Simons—Manigault House, HCF.

81. Ibid.

82. Interview with Burton; Burton to Simons, Oct. 21, 1937, Simons—Manigault House, HCF.

83. Frost, letter, *Charleston News and Courier*, Apr. 8, 1932.

84. Minutes of SPOD, Apr. 7, 1932, Box—Frost SPOD, PSC.

85. Ernest G. Pringle to G. Corner Fenhagen, Apr. 16, 1932, Anderson file, Charleston.

86. Ibid.

87. Fenhagen to Kohn, Apr. 20, 1932, Anderson file, Charleston; *Charleston News and Courier*, Apr. 10, 1932.

88. Minutes of SPOD, May 5, 1932, Box–Frost SPOD, PSC.

89. Ibid., June 3, 1932.

90. Victor Morawetz to Burton, Nov. 1, 1932, Burton—SPOD, PSC.

91. Mrs. Francis B. Crowninshield to Burton, Nov. 29, 1932, ibid.

92. Burton to Mrs. Crowninshield, Dec. 9, 1932, ibid.

93. Interview with Burton.

94. *Charleston News and Courier*, May 5, 1933.

95. Burton to Burnet R. Maybank, Oct. 16, 1933, Simons—Mrs. William Emerson, Heyward House Fund, SCHS.

96. Interview with Simons.

97. Interview with Burton.

98. Interview with Simons.

99. *Charleston Evening Post*, Dec. 11, 1933.

100. Simons to Holland, Dec. 15, 1936, Files of HABS, Library of Congress.

101. Ralston Lattimore to Branch Spalding, Oct. 7, 1937, Proposed National Historic Site (NHS), South Carolina, 0–36, Records of the National Park Service (NPS), National Archives (NA), Record Group (RG) 79.

102. Finlay F. Ferguson, Jr., to Simons, Dec. 18, 1934, Simons—Historic Centers, Charleston, HCF.

103. Simons to Maybank, Nov. 29, 1934, ibid.

104. Interview with Simons.

105. Ibid.

106. *Charleston News and Courier*, ca. Feb., 1935.

107. Ibid., May 6, 10, 1935.

108. John Mead Howells to Arno B. Cammerer, Apr. 18, 1935, Proposed NHS, South Carolina, 0–36, Records of NPS, NA, RG 79.

109. *Charleston Evening Post*, Feb. 5, 1937.

110. *New York Times*, Oct. 1, 1938.

111. Lattimore to Cammerer, Oct. 7, 1938, Proposed NHS, South Carolina, 0–36, Records of NPS, NA, RG 79.

112. Ronald F. Lee to Roy E. Appleman, Dec. 7, 1938, ibid.

113. Simons to Elbert Peets, Sept. 30, 1941, Simons—City Plan for Charleston, 1939–42, SCHS.

114. Robert N. S. Whitelaw to Thomas A. Stone, Mar. 20, 1939, Simons—Carolina Art Association, 1936–42, Whitelaw, Robert N. S., SCHS.

115. Ibid.

116. Simons to Mrs. Emerson, Jan. 20, 1938, Simons—Plantation Houses, William Emerson, SCHS.

117. Whitelaw to Frederick P. Keppel, Nov. 30, 1939, City Plan, Director's Correspondence, 1939–42, HCF.

118. Whitelaw, open letter, Jan. 13, 1937, printed.

119. Whitelaw to Keppel, Nov. 30, 1939, City Plan, Director's Correspondence, 1939–42, HCF.

120. *Charleston News and Courier*, Dec. 10, 1939.

121. Whitelaw to Howells, Dec. 11, 1939, Simons—City Plan for Charleston, 1939–42, SCHS.

122. Frederick Law Olmsted to W. Emerson, Dec. 13, 1939, ibid.

123. Howells to Keppel, Dec. 15, 1939, ibid.

124. Olmsted to Whitelaw, Dec. 15, 1939, ibid.

125. Whitelaw to Olmsted, Dec. 20, 1939, ibid.

126. Keppel to Whitelaw, Dec. 27, 1939, ibid.

127. Interview with R. N. S. Whitelaw, June 22, 1972.

128. Whitelaw to Olmsted, Jan 8, 1940, Simons—City Plan for Charleston, 1939–42, SCHS.

129. Minutes of informal meeting, Jan. 22, 1940, ibid.

130. Kohn to Simons, Feb. 1, 1940, ibid.

131. Simons to Kohn, Feb. 8, 1940, ibid.

132. Olmsted, report, Feb., 1940, 5B and 6B, ibid.

133. Ibid., 6C.

134. Ibid., 4D.

135. Whitelaw, memo to committee members, Mar. 1, 1940, Simons—City Plan for Charleston, 1939–42, SCHS.

136. Simons to Whitelaw, Mar. 20, 1940, ibid.

137. *Charleston News and Courier*, Nov. 9, 1940.

138. Interview with Helen McCormack, June 9, 1972.

139. Ibid.

140. McCormack to Simons, Mar. 4, 1941, and Simons to McCormack, Mar. 11, 1941, Simons—City Plan for Charleston, 1939–42, SCHS.

141. McCormack to Howells, Aug. 21, 1941, Correspondence with Committees, HCF.

142. McCormack, Report of Charleston Regional Planning Committee, June 20, 1941, Olmsted Report, HCF.

143. McCormack to T. Rutherfoord Goodwin, Apr. 15, 1941, Correspondence with Museums, HCF.

144. Vernon Geddy to McCormack, May 19, 1941, ibid.

145. Pearl Chase to McCormack, Aug. 18, 1941, Correspondence Pending, HCF.

146. McCormack to Charles W. Porter III, Aug. 29, 1941, and Porter to McCormack, Sept. 11, 1941, Proposed NHS, South Carolina 0–36, Records of NPS, NA, RG 79.

147. McCormack to Vieux Carré Commission, Nov. 6, 1941, Correspondence, Planning Association, HCF.

148. Chester H. Wicker to McCormack, Dec. 3, 1941, ibid.

149. McCormack to Whitelaw, Oct. 1941, Personal Correspondence, McCormack, HCF.

150. McCormack, "An Architectural Inventory for Charleston," *Journal of the American Society of Architectural Historians*, 1 (July–Oct. 1941), 21–23.

151. Whitelaw, "Review of the Work of the Charleston Regional Planning Committee," Dec. 4, 1941, Olmsted Report, HCF.

152. Minutes of Civic Arts Committee, Jan. 30, 1942, Civic Services Committee (CSC), HCF.

153. Interview with McCormack.

154. Whitelaw, "Request to the Rockefeller Foundation from the Carolina Art Association," Feb. 11, 1942, Simons—City Plan for Charleston, 1939–42, SCHS.

155. McCormack, "This Is Charleston," *Journal of the American Society of Architectural Historians*, 2 (Jan. 1942), 37–38.

156. *Charleston News and Courier*, Apr. 16, 1942.

157. Interview with McCormack.

158. Minutes of CSC, May 19, 1942, Simons—City Plan for Charleston, 1939–42, SCHS.

159. Minutes of CSC, June 1, 1942, Minutes, CSC, HCF.

160. McCormack, "This Is Charleston," original recommendations, ca. June 1942, 24, 38, HCF.

161. Frederick Bigger to Simons, May 30, 1942, and Simons to Bigger, June 4, 1942, Simons—City Plan for Charleston, 1939–42, SCHS.

162. Interview with Whitelaw; Minutes of CSC, Sept. 28, 1942, Minutes, CSC, HCF.

163. *Charleston News and Courier*, Oct. 6, 1942; Minutes of Organization Meeting of National Council for Historic Sites and Buildings, Oct. 21, 1947, 201, National Trust.

164. Simons to Harold A. Mouzon, Oct. 8, 1942, CSC, Wagner file, HCF.

165. Minutes of CSC, Dec. 15, 1942, Minutes, CSC, HCF.

166. Ibid.

167. Ibid.

168. *Charleston Evening Post*, May 26, 1943.

169. Whitelaw to George W. Simons, Jr., Sept. 30, 1943, Civic Services, Simons, George W. (Personal), HCF.

170. Whitelaw to Simons, Jan. 24, 1944, ibid.

171. Simons to Whitelaw, Mar. 11, 1944, ibid.

172. Minutes of CSC, Dec. 17, 1943, Minutes, CSC, HCF.

173. Whitelaw to Simons, Jan. 24, 1944, Civic Services, Simons, George W. (Personal), HCF.

174. Minutes of CSC, Aug. 1, 1944, Minutes, CSC, HCF.

175. Samuel Gaillard Stoney, *This Is Charleston* (Charleston, 1944), 55, 57.

176. Interview with Whitelaw.

177. Ibid.; Gerald Bath to Kenneth Chorley, Mar. 31, 1945, Lectures and speeches, 1945, Archives of Colonial Williamsburg Foundation (ACWF).

178. Minutes of CSC, Apr. 17, 1945, Minutes, CSC, HCF.

179. Chorley to Whitelaw, Jan. 9, 1945, Lectures and speeches, Charleston, ACWF.

180. Bath to Chorley, Mar. 19, 1945, ibid.

181. Kenneth Chorley, *The Challenge to Charleston* (Charleston, 1945).

182. Minutes of CSC, Apr. 17, 1945, Minutes, CSC, HCF.

183. Ibid., Jan. 30, 1945.

184. Ibid., Mar. 16, 1945.

185. Ibid., June 28, 1945.

186. Ibid., July 12, 1945; "Planning in Charleston," June 28, 1945, Minutes, CSC, HCF.

187. Condensed minutes of meeting of City Council, Nov. 13, 1945, ibid.

188. Minutes of CSC, Jan. 4, 1946, ibid.; Minutes of Organization Meeting of National Council, Oct. 21, 1947, 201, National Trust.

189. Whitelaw, memo to CSC, Jan. 28, 1946, Minutes, CSC, HCF.

190. Minutes of CSC, Feb. 6, 1946, ibid.

191. Ibid., July 30, 1946.

192. Whitelaw to Homer Pace, Dec. 2, 1946, CSC, correspondence and memos to members, HCF.

193. Ibid.

194. Interview with Burton.

195. Minutes of SPOD, May 17, 1929, Box—Frost, SPOD, PSC.

196. Kate Hammond Price to Joseph W. Welch, Dec. 8, 1933, box (Burton, SPOD), PSC; *Charleston News and Courier*, Jan. 5, 1934.

197. William Means, open letter to members, Mar. 27, 1940, Means papers, PSC.

198. Interview with Whitelaw.

199. Whitelaw, report to CSC, Dec. 12, 1946, Simons—HCF, 1946–55, SCHS.

200. Interview with Whitelaw.

201. Whitelaw, report to CSC, Dec. 12, 1946, Simons—HCF, 1946–55, SCHS.

202. Proposed constitution for HCF, Dec. 17, 1946, ibid.

203. Minutes of CSC, Dec. 19, 1946, Minutes Book, HCF.

204. *Charleston News and Courier*, Dec. 30, 1946.

205. Whitelaw to Chorley, Jan. 2, 1947, Restorations, Charleston, S.C., 1947, CWF.

206. Minutes of CSC, Feb. 14, 1947, Minutes Book, HCF.

207. Carolina Art Association Report, Feb. 28, 1947, Simons—History Early Charleston Architecture, SCHS.
208. Clipping, Mar. 15, 1947, ibid.
209. Minutes of HCF Incorporating Committee, Apr. 9, 1947, Minutes, CSC, HCF.
210. Minutes of Committee to Consider Arrangement of Tours of Old Houses, Apr. 15, 1947, Minutes Book, HCF.
211. Henry P. Staats, Suggestions for Future Tours, Apr. 23, 1948, ibid.
212. C. Bissell Jenkins, President's Report, May 19, 1948, ibid.
213. Minutes of HCF, June 4, 1948, ibid.
214. Ibid., Mar. 8, 1949.
215. Burton to Jenkins, Apr. 1, 1948, Minutes Book, HCF.
216. Frances Edmunds, Annual Report of Tours Director, June 1949, ibid.
217. *Charleston News and Courier*, Apr. 17, 1928.
218. Stoney to A. Simons, July 14, 1928, Simons—Plantation Houses, Stoney-Waring, etc., SCHS.
219. Marcus M. Marks, letter, *New York Times*, Feb. 9, 1930.
220. Undated clipping, ca. 1935, Preservation Society Scrapbook, PSC.
221. Charles J. Rhoads, in *Charleston News and Courier*, late Feb. 1947.
222. Interview with Simons.
223. Interview with McCormack.
224. Interview with Whitelaw.
225. Interview with Mrs. Jules Fontaine, June 29, 1971.
226. Clifford L. Lord, ed., *Keepers of the Past* (Chapel Hill, N.C., 1965), 203–14.
227. Speech by Rena Maverick Green, Founders' Day, Mar. 22, 1962, transcript at San Antonio Conservation Society (CS).
228. Minutes of CS, Mar. 22, 1924, Conservation Society Minutes Book (CSMB) I.
229. Ibid., Apr. 19, 1924; interview with Mrs. Walter P. Webb, June 28, 1971.
230. Interview with Webb; Richard B. Henderson, *Maury Maverick, a Political Biography* (Austin, 1970), 94, 199–201.
231. Minutes of CS, June 7, 1924, CSMB I.
232. Ibid., June 14, 1924.
233. Ibid., June 21, 1924.
234. Ibid., July 5, 1924.
235. [Emily Edwards], *Conservation in San Antonio since 1924* (San Antonio, 1970), 10.
236. Interview with Emily Edwards, June 24, 1971; Minutes of CS, Aug. 23, 1924, CSMB I.
237. Minutes of CS, Oct. 4, 1924, and Jan. 10, 1925, CSMB I.
238. Ibid., May 2, Oct. 3, 1925.
239. Interview with Edwards; [Edwards], *Conservation*, 10–11.
240. Interview with Edwards.

241. Speech by Edwards, June 1968, transcript at CS.

242. Interview with Edwards.

243. [Edwards], *Conservation*, 11.

244. Ibid.; clippings in Early Conservation Scrapbook, CS.

245. Clippings in Early Conservation Scrapbook, CS.

246. Clipping in Early Conservation Scrapbook, CS.

247. 1931 clipping, ibid.

248. Minutes of CS, Nov. 24, 1930, CSMB I.

249. Speech by Mrs. Lane Taylor, June 1968, transcript at CS.

250. Minutes of CS, Nov. 24, 1931, CSMB I.

251. *San Antonio Express*, Mar. 13, 1932.

252. Interview with Fontaine.

253. Interview with Ethel Harris, June 24, 1971; [Edwards], *Conservation*, 11; Elizabeth O. Graham to E. A. Baugh, Aug. 5, 1935, San Jose Mission, File 1, CS.

254. Minutes of CS, Nov. 23, 1933, CSMB I.

255. Ibid., May 9, 1934.

256. Graham to Baugh, Aug. 5, 1935, San Jose Mission, File 1, CS.

257. Maury Maverick to Conrad L. Wirth, Jan. 14, 1935, San Jose Mission, Records of NPS, NA, RG 79; Henderson, *Maverick*, 94.

258. Maverick to Harold L. Ickes, Jan. 23, 1935, San Jose Mission, Records of NPS, NA, RG 79.

259. Verne E. Chatelain to Cammerer, Jan. 30, 1935, and Cammerer to Ickes (Hermann Kahn), Jan. 31, 1935, Files of Branch of History, U.S. Dept. of Interior (Int.).

260. Henderson, *Maverick*, 94; *Congressional Record*, 74 Cong., 1 Sess., 12737 (Aug. 8, 1935).

261. Maverick to Ickes, July 31, 1936, San Jose Mission, Records of NPS, NA, RG 79.

262. Minutes of CS, Jan. 4, 1936, CSMB I.

263. Ibid., Jan. 27, 1938.

264. Henderson, *Maverick*, 199–201.

265. Interview with Webb.

266. Ibid.; *San Antonio Light*, July 18, 1939.

267. *San Antonio Light*, July 18, 1939.

268. Minutes of CS, Aug. 17, 1939, CSMB I.

269. Ibid., Sept. 28, 1939.

270. Interview with Webb; *The Restoration of La Villita* (National Youth Administration, Nov. 1939), 4.

271. Interview with O'Neill Ford, June 29, 1971.

272. Ibid.

273. Ibid.

274. Webb, speech, Mar. 21, 1968, transcript at CS.

275. The Villita Ordinance, OI–355, Oct. 12, 1939, City of San Antonio.

276. Ibid.
277. *Restoration of La Villita*, 5–6.
278. Maverick to Ickes, Oct. 27, 1939, Proposed NHS, Texas, 0–36, Records of NPS, NA, RG 79.
279. Ickes (Neasham, Porter) to Maverick, Nov. 16, 1939, ibid.
280. Maverick to Alvin Wirtz, Jan. 15, 1940, ibid.
281. Maverick to Wirtz (telegram), Jan. 10, 1941, ibid.
282. Maverick to Oscar L. Chapman, Jan. 20, 1941, ibid.
283. Hillory A. Tolson to Herbert E. Kahler, Aug. 10, 1944, ibid.
284. Ickes (Porter) to Maverick, Mar. 1, 1945, ibid.
285. Maverick to Ickes, Mar. 13, 1945, ibid.
286. Cammerer to M. S. Carriga, Mar. 9, 1940, Files of Branch of History, Int.; George C. Gibbons to Wirth, Mar. 14, 1940, and John R. White to Cammerer, July 30, 1940, San Jose Mission, Records of NPS, NA, RG 79.
287. A. E. Demaray to Ickes, June 24, 1940, Files of Branch of History, Int.
288. Interview with V. Aubrey Neasham, July 26, 1971; Wirtz to Newton B. Drury, Aug. 21, 1940, San Jose Mission, Records of NPS, NA, RG 79.
289. White to Cammerer, July 30, 1940, ibid.
290. Interview with Harris; R. Tillotson to Drury, Dec. 5, 1940, Files of Branch of History, Int.
291. Frank D. Quinn to Wirtz, Oct. 19, 1940, San Jose Mission, Records of NPS, NA, RG 79.
292. *San Jose Mission, State and National Historic Site*, Leaflet, Texas Parks and Wildlife Dept.
293. Minutes of CS, Dec. 19, 1940, CSMB I.
294. Ibid., Jan. 23, 1941.
295. Ibid., Oct. 22, 1942, CSMB II.
296. *San Antonio Light*, July 12, 1945.
297. Minutes of CS, Feb. 25, 1947, CSMB II.
298. Interview with Mary Harral, June 29, 1971.
299. Collective letter to National Park Service, Jan. 28, 1942, and Lee to Garrett P. Robertson, Feb. 23, 1942, Proposed NHS, Texas, 0–36, Records of NPS, NA, RG 79.
300. Minutes of CS, Oct. 28, 1938, CSMB I.
301. Ibid., May 3, 1949, CSMB II.
302. Interview with Edwards.
303. Letter to mayor of San Antonio and resolution, Oct. 27, 1949, CSMB II.
304. Interview with Elsa Watson, June 29, 1971.
305. Neasham, special report on 18th and 19th century Spanish sites, Mar. 1941, 13, Files of Branch of History, Int.
306. Sherwood Anderson to Maverick, Jan. 6, 1940, quoted in Howard Mumford Jones, ed., *Letters of Sherwood Anderson* (Boston, 1953), 456.

307. Interview with Richard Koch, June 8, 1971.

308. Interview with Allison Owen, ca. 1939–40, Interviews, Files of Vieux Carré Commission (VCC).

309. Koch to author, Sept. 23, 1963.

310. Ibid.

311. Clipping, ca. 1920–21, Collection of Ted Liuzza.

312. Vieux Carré *News*, Nov. 7, 1925.

313. Ross E. Breazeale to T. S. Walmsley, Feb. 1, 1926, and to Arthur J. O'Keffe, Sept. 10, 1926, Official Vertical File, Louisiana Division, Vieux Carré Improvement (VCI), New Orleans Public Library (NOPL).

314. Arnold Genthe, *Impressions of Old New Orleans* (New York, 1926), 32–33.

315. Theodore A. Walters to Bertrand F. Cahn, Dec. 10, 1926, Official Vertical File, VCI.

316. Walters to William Sumner Appleton, Apr. 1, 1929, Vieux Carré Assn., SPNEA.

317. Clipping, Oct. 10, 1929, Official Vertical File, VCI.

318. Ibid., Oct. 2, 1929.

319. Interview with Walter Loubat, ca. 1939–40, Interviews, Files of VCC.

320. *New York Times*, Jan. 17, 1932.

321. Interview with Samuel Wilson, Jr., June 9, 1971; *New Orleans Times-Picayune*, Jan. 25, 1937.

322. Vieux Carré Ordinance, Constitution of 1921, Section 22 A, as added by Act 139 of 1936.

323. Interview with Harnett Kane, June 12, 1971.

324. Interview with William Boizelle, June 8, 1971.

325. Interview with Koch.

326. Interviews with James J. Morrison, and Kane, June 12, 1971.

327. Stanley C. Arthur to Robert S. Maestri, Aug. 20, 1937, Official Vertical File, Mayor's Correspondence, Maestri Report, Aug. 1937, NOPL.

328. Minutes of VCC, Aug. 4, 1937, VCC, Minutes Book I.

329. Ibid.

330. *New Orleans Item*, Aug. 5, 1937.

331. Ibid., Oct. 24, 1937.

332. John S. Kendall, "Old New Orleans Houses," *Louisiana Historical Quarterly*, 17 (Oct. 1934), 704–5; William R. Hogan to Cammerer, Oct. 12, 1937, Proposed NHS, Louisiana, 0–36, Records of NPS, NA, RG 79.

333. *New York Times*, Dec. 19, 1937; Herbert Maier to Cammerer (telegram), Feb. 1, 1938, Proposed NHS, Louisiana, 0–36, Records of NPS, NA, RG 79.

334. Demaray to Carl P. Russell, May 13, 1938, ibid.

335. Pearl Chase to Demaray, May 1938, ibid.

336. Interviews with Kane and Morrison; Charter of Vieux Carré Prop-

erty Owners' Assn., Inc., June 6, 1938, Vieux Carré Property Owners' Assn., VCC.

337. Interview with Morrison.

338. Interview with Kane.

339. Boizelle to Graham Rushton, July 16, 1938, Proposed NHS, Louisiana, 0-36, Records of NPS, NA, RG 79.

340. Appleman to Cammerer, Aug. 25, 1938, ibid.

341. Appleman to regional director, Sept. 28, 1938, ibid.

342. Ibid.

343. Boizelle to Lee, Nov. 29, 1938, Proposed NHS, Louisiana, 0-36, Records of NPS, NA, RG 79.

344. *New Orleans Item*, Jan. 9, 1939.

345. *New Orleans Times-Picayune*, Jan. 11, 1939.

346. *New Orleans Item*, Jan. 12, 1939.

347. Interviews with Kane and Morrison.

348. *New Orleans Times-Picayune*, Jan. 15, 1939.

349. *New Orleans Item*, Feb. 1, 1939.

350. Ibid.

351. Minutes of VCC, Mar. 10, 1939, VCC, Minutes Book I.

352. Undated clipping, ca. Mar. 1939, VCC scrapbooks.

353. *New Orleans Item*, Mar. 28, 1939.

354. Minutes of VCC, Aug. 13, 1939, VCC, Minutes Book I.

355. *New Orleans Times-Picayune*, Apr. 2, 1939.

356. Ibid., June 17, 1939.

357. Clipping, ca. June 30, 1939, VCC scrapbooks.

358. *New Orleans States*, July 5, 1939.

359. Ibid., Aug. 3, 1939; *New Orleans Tribune*, Aug. 4, 1939.

360. *New Orleans Item*, June 12 and 17, 1939.

361. Undated clipping, ca. Sept. 1939, VCC scrapbooks.

362. Minutes of VCC Architectural Committee, Oct. 5, 1939, Notebook, VCC.

363. Ibid.

364. Ibid., Nov. 21, 1939.

365. Ibid., Feb. 9, 1940.

366. Ibid., Oct. 8, 1940; Minutes of VCC, Feb. 26, 1940, VCC, Minutes Book I.

367. Minutes of VCC Architectural Comm., Dec. 19, 1940, Notebook, VCC.

368. Ibid., Mar. 4, 1941.

369. Clipping, Oct. 31, 1941, VCC scrapbooks.

370. Minutes of VCC, Nov. 4, 1941, VCC, Minutes Book I.

371. Ibid., Feb. 24, 1942.

372. Undated clipping, ca. 1942, VCC scrapbooks.

373. Minutes of VCC, Mar. 12, 1946, VCC, Minutes Book I.

374. Ibid., June 25, 1946; clipping, Mar. 20, 1946, VCC scrapbooks.

375. Morrison, letter in clipping, Mar. 25, 1946, ibid.

376. Minutes of VCC, June 25, 1946, VCC, Minutes Book I.

377. Ibid., Jan. 11, 1949.

378. Paul H. Maloney to Walter Cook Keenan, Dec. 3, 1945, National Parks—1948, VCC.

379. R. B. Roessle to F. Edward Hebert, Jan. 31, 1946, ibid.

380. Keenan to Russell B. Long, July 26, 1949, and draft of act, ibid.

381. Long to Keenan, Aug. 3, 1949, ibid.

382. *New Orleans Item*, Nov. 19, 1937.

383. Ibid., Aug. 4, 1939.

384. Interview with Ted Liuzza, June 12, 1971.

385. Ibid.

386. Kane, quoted in *New Orleans Times-Picayune*, May 13, 1974.

387. Interview with Kane.

388. Interviews with Martha G. Robinson, June 11, 1971, Samuel Wilson, Jr., June 9, 1971, and Kane.

389. Susan Williams Massie and Frances Archer Christian, eds., *Descriptive Guide Book of Virginia's Old Gardens* (Richmond, 1929).

390. *Some Gardens and Mansions of Maryland* (Baltimore, 1930).

391. Harnett T. Kane, *Natchez on the Mississippi* (New York, 1947), 334.

392. Note by Mrs. Balfour Miller, in scrapbook in her possession.

393. Mrs. G. P. Bullis, "Background on Origin of Natchez Pilgrimage," ca. 1947, Mrs. Balfour Miller scrapbook.

394. Mrs. Balfour Miller, *Natchez of Long Ago* (Natchez, 1938), 24–26.

395. *Natchez Democrat*, Mar. 21, 1931.

396. Miller, address of welcome, Mar. 20, 1931, text in Miller scrapbook.

397. Miller, *Natchez*, 29–30.

398. Ibid., 30.

399. Ibid., 33.

400. Ibid., 38–48; two clippings from *Natchez Democrat*, ca. Mar. 1932, Miller scrapbook.

401. Miller, *Natchez*, 49, 51; Bullis, "Background."

402. *Arkansas Gazette*, Apr. 19, 1932.

403. Miller, *Natchez*, 51.

404. Clippings from *Natchez Democrat*, ca. Sept. 1932, Miller scrapbook.

405. *Meridian* (Miss.) *Star*, quoted ibid.; Miller, *Natchez*, 64.

406. Miller, *Natchez*, 64.

407. Bullis, "Background."

408. Ibid.

409. *State-Times*, Aug. 7, 1941.

410. Bullis, "Background"; Kane, *Natchez*, 344–48.

411. Kane, *Natchez*, 344–48.

412. Sophie G. Friedman to Charleston Chamber of Commerce, Aug. 3, 1939, Means papers, PSC; *Natchez Democrat*, Aug. 17, 1939; Friedman to

Means, Aug. 18, 1939, Means papers, PSC; Ronald W. Miller, "Historic Preservation in Natchez, Mississippi," *Antiques*, 111 (Mar. 1977), 538–45.

413. *Evolution of the Oldest House* (Tallahassee, 1962).

414. Interviews with Verne E. Chatelain, Sept. 17, 1971, Herbert E. Kahler, June 19, 1970, and Albert Manucy, Nov. 11, 1972.

415. Interview with Manucy.

416. Kahler to Cammerer, Oct. 10, 1936, Proposed NHS, Florida, 0–36, Records of NPS, NA, RG 79.

417. Interviews with Chatelain and Manucy.

418. Walter B. Fraser to Chatelain, June 24, 1936, and Kahler to Cammerer, July 24, 1936, Proposed NHS, Florida, 0–36, Records of NPS, NA, RG 79.

419. Harry Slattery to Fraser, July 28, 1936, ibid.

420. Fraser to Chatelain, Aug. 20, 1936, ibid.

421. Ibid., Sept. 19, 1936.

422. Kahler to Spalding, Oct. 10, 1936, ibid.

423. Minutes of meeting of National Committee for the Preservation and Restoration of St. Augustine, Florida, Oct. 26, 1936, St. Augustine, Carnegie Institution of Washington (CIW).

424. Ibid.

425. John C. Merriam to A. V. Kidder, Oct. 31, 1936, St. Augustine, CIW.

426. Merriam to C. B. Reynolds, Nov. 12, 1936, ibid.

427. Chatelain to Merriam, Nov. 18, 1936, ibid.

428. Interviews with Chatelain, Sept. 9, 1961, and Sept. 17, 1971.

429. Interview with Manucy; Report of Sub-Committee No. 1 Dealing with the Fact Finding Survey of Historical Materials Pertaining to St. Augustine, Fla., Mar. 1937, Proposed NHS, Florida, 0–36, Records of NPS, NA, RG 79.

430. Fraser to Merriam, Nov. 19, 1936, St. Augustine, CIW.

431. Merriam to Fraser, Dec. 5, 1936, ibid.

432. Rogers Johnson to Merriam, Dec. 21, 1936, ibid.

433. Fraser to Cammerer, Jan. 7, 1937, ibid.

434. Report of Sub-Committee No. 1, Mar. 1937, 6, and Kahler to Cammerer, Mar. 4, 1937, Proposed NHS, Florida, 0–36, Records of NPS, NA, RG 79.

435. Report of Sub-Committee No. 2 of National Committee for the Survey and the Development of the Historical Resources of St. Augustine, Fla., Mar. 1937, 5, ibid.

436. Kahler to Spalding and Lee, Mar. 9, 1937, ibid.

437. Cammerer to H. C. Bryant and Spalding, Mar. 17, 1937, ibid.

438. *St. Augustine Record*, June 9, 1937.

439. Drury to Merriam, Dec. 10, 1937, Proposed NHS, Florida, 0–36, Records of NPS, NA, RG 79.

440. Kahler to Cammerer, June 28, 1937, ibid.

441. Drury to Merriam, Dec. 10, 1937, ibid.

442. Esther C. Webb to Merriam, Feb. 7, 1937, St. Augustine Program, Miscellaneous Correspondence, 1939, CIW.

443. Minutes of Board of Trustees of Llambias House, May 23, 1944, St. Augustine Historical Program, CIW.

444. Ibid.

445. Scott M. Loftin to Chorley, Nov. 19, 1946, Restorations—St. Augustine, 1946–47, ACWF.

446. Waldo G. Leland and William E. Lingelbach to Vannevar Bush, Dec. 3, 1938, and memo from W. M. Gilbert on conversation with Chatelain, Oct. 31, 1939, St. Augustine Program, 1940, CIW.

447. Kahler to Cammerer, Mar. 27, 1939, Proposed NHS, Florida, 0–36, Records of NPS, NA, RG 79.

448. Minutes of meeting of St. Augustine Restoration and Preservation Association, Oct. 31, 1939, St. Augustine Program, 1940, CIW; Gilbert, memo of conference with John Pickering, Nov. 11, 1939, St. Augustine Historical Program, CIW.

449. *Carnegie Institution of Washington Year Book No. 38, 1938–39* (Washington, D.C., 1939), 357–58.

450. Bush to Leland, Mar. 8, 1940, St. Augustine Program, 1940, CIW.

451. Lee, memo, Dec. 21, 1940, Proposed NHS, Florida, 0–36, Records of NPS, NA, RG 79.

452. Interview with Manucy.

453. Fraser to Chorley, Sept. 23, 1946, Restorations—St. Augustine, 1946–47, ACWF.

454. *St. Augustine Record*, Feb. 28, 1947.

455. Chorley To Fraser, Sept. 26, 1946, Restorations—St. Augustine, ACWF.

456. *St. Augustine Record*, Feb. 28, 1947.

457. Chorley to David R. Dunham, Mar. 17, 1947, Restorations—St. Augustine, ACWF.

458. Neasham, "Jewels of the Spanish Crown," June 1940, 2, Collection of V. Aubrey Neasham.

459. Jacob H. Morrison, *Historic Preservation Law* (New Orleans, 1957), 83.

460. Joseph R. Knowland, *California, a Landmark History* (Oakland, 1941), 89–94, 124–28.

461. Interview with Mrs. Mayo Hayes O'Donnell, Aug. 6, 1971; Allen Griffin to author, Oct. 13, 1971.

462. Interview with O'Donnell; "First Annual Report of the Board of Directors of the Monterey History and Art Association, Limited," Jan. 18, 1932, Minutes of Membership, Monterey History and Art Assn. (MHAA).

463. "Fifth Annual Report," Jan. 20, 1936, ibid.

464. "First Annual Report," ibid.

465. *Monterey Peninsula Herald*, Nov. 8, 1930.

466. "Second Annual Report," Jan. 16, 1933, Minutes of Membership, MHAA.

467. "Third Annual Report," Jan. 15, 1934, ibid.

468. "Fourth Annual Report," Jan. 21, 1935, ibid.

469. "Fifth Annual Report," ibid.

470. R. G. Church to State of California, Feb. 12, 1937, Monterey State Historic Park (SHP), General Correspondence 1, 419.0 – 455, California, Division of Beaches and Parks (Cal.).

471. Drury to Church, Mar. 6, 1937, ibid.

472. Interview with Neasham; Knowland to Cammerer, Apr. 7, 1938, Proposed NHS, Monterey, 0 – 36, Records of NPS, NA, RG 79.

473. Knowland to secretary of treasury, Mar. 15, 1937, Monterey SHP, see Old Custom House, General Corr. 1, 419.0 – 455, Cal.

474. Albert E. Carter to Knowland, Apr. 5, 1937, ibid.

475. Drury to Cammerer, Apr. 10, 1937, and Frank A. Kittredge to Cammerer, Mar. 19, 1938, Proposed NHS, Monterey, 0 – 36, Records of NPS, NA, RG 79.

476. Drury to Knowland, May 13, 1937, Monterey SHP, see Old Custom House, General Corr. 1, 419.0 – 455, Cal.

477. Ibid., July 14, 1937; interview with Newton B. Drury, July 28, 1971.

478. Carmel Martin and Clyde Dorsey to John C. Merriam, Oct. 1, 1937, Monterey SHP, see Old Custom House, General Corr. 1, 419.0 – 455, Cal.

479. Drury to Merriam, Dec. 10, 1937, Proposed NHS, Florida, Records of NPS, NA, RG 79; Drury to Mrs. J. E. Butterfield, Oct. 11, 1937, Mrs. Butterfield, California State Archives (CA).

480. Drury to Knowland, Oct. 29, 1937, Monterey SHP, see Old Custom House, General Corr. 2, 419.0 – 455, Cal.

481. Martin to Drury, Nov. 19, 1937, ibid.

482. Drury to Martin, Nov. 27, 1937, ibid.

483. Drury to Knowland, Dec. 1, 1937, Joseph R. Knowland, CA.

484. Drury to Griffin, Dec. 11, 1937, Monterey SHP, see Old Custom House, General Corr. 2, 419.0 – 455, Cal.

485. Howard D. Severance, "Notes Pertaining to the Waterfront Development of Monterey," ca. 1944, Severance File, Bancroft Library, University of California at Berkeley (Bancroft); Knowland, *California*, 89 – 90.

486. Emerson Knight to Roger S. Fitch, Jan. 31, 1938, Custom House, MHAA.

487. Knight, "Preliminary Report concerning Master Plan for Historic Monterey, California," Feb. 11, 1938, Monterey SHP, see Old Custom House, General Corr. 2, 419.0 – 455, Cal.

488. Griffin to author, Oct. 13, 1971; Knowland to C. J. Peoples, Feb. 14, 1938, and Griffin to Drury, Feb. 25, 1938, Monterey SHP, see Old Custom House, General Corr. 2, 419.0 – 455, Cal.

489. Drury to Severance, Apr. 11, 1938, Severance File, Bancroft.

490. *Monterey Peninsula Herald*, July 6, 1938.

491. Knight, "Memorandum on Planning Progress toward Preservation of Historic Monterey," July 6, 1938, Interpretive Services, Cal.

492. Neasham, "Historic Monterey to Be Preserved," Sept. 1938, Neasham Collection.

493. Knight, "A Master Plan for the Historic City of Monterey," Address to MHAA, Sept. 12, 1938, Interpretive Services, Cal.

494. Knight, *Master Plan of the City of Monterey* (Monterey, Calif., 1939).

495. Neasham, "The Preservation of Historic Monterey," *Pacific Historical Review*, 8 (June 1939), 215–24.

496. Resolution 38 36 C.S., Monterey City Council, Aug. 15, 1939, Monterey SHP, see Old Custom House, General Corr. 3, 419.0–455, Cal.

497. Dorsey to Cammerer, May 16, 1940, Proposed NHS, Monterey, 0–36, Records of NPS, NA, RG 79.

498. "Monterey Zoning Ordinance," City of Monterey, No. 528 C.S., adopted Sept. 24, 1940, Files of Branch of History, Int.

499. Olaf T. Hagen to regional director, May 15, 1941, Proposed NHS, Monterey, 0–36, Records of NPS, NA, RG 79; Minutes of MHAA, Oct. 2, 1941, Minutes of Board of Directors, 1940–49, MHAA.

500. Drury to Ickes, Dec. 11, 1941, Proposed NHS, Monterey, 0–36, Records of NPS, NA, RG 79.

501. Minutes of Board of MHAA, Aug. 7, 1939, Minutes of Board of Directors, 1935–40, MHAA.

502. Ibid., Mar. 14, 1940.

503. Neasham to Hagen, Feb. 8, 1940, Proposed NHS, Monterey, 0–36, Records of NPS, NA, RG 79.

504. Minutes of Board of MHAA, Apr. 2, 1945, Minutes of Board of Directors, 1940–49, MHAA; Griffin to author, Oct. 13, 1971.

505. Martin to J. H. Covington, Jan. 23, 1946, Monterey SHP, First Theater, General Corr., 419.0–455, Cal.

506. F. J. Honey to John A. Hennessey, Jan. 6, 1948, ibid.

507. Neasham to Lee, Apr. 21, 1948, and Lee to Neasham, May 24, 1948, Geographic File, Monterey, Calif., National Trust (NT).

508. Stoney to A. Simons, July 14, 1928, Simons—Plantation Houses, Stoney-Waring etc., SCHS.

509. Hosmer, *Presence of the Past*, 222.

510. Stephen Decatur to Howells, Oct. 29, 1934, Proposed NHS, Portsmouth, 0–36, Records of NPS, NA, RG 79; Edwin W. Small to author, July 21, 1970.

511. Decatur to Howells, Oct. 29, 1934, Proposed NHS, Portsmouth, 0–36, Records of NPS, NA, RG 79.

512. Demaray to Ickes, Nov. 13, 1934, ibid.

513. [Decatur?], "Restoration and Housing Project for Portsmouth, New Hampshire," ca. Nov. 1934, ibid.

514. Howells to Charles E. Peterson, Nov. 15, 1934, ibid.

515. Horatio B. Hackett to administrator, Federal Emergency Administration of Public Works, Nov. 21, 1934, ibid.

516. Howells to Cammerer, April 4, 6, 1935, ibid.

517. Howells to Appleton, Apr. 7, 1936, Wentworth-Gardner, SPNEA.

518. Donald Corley, "Report on Restoration and Housing Project, Portsmouth, New Hampshire," Aug. 31, 1936, and Corley to Small, Sept. 10, 1936, Files of Branch of History, Int.

519. Howells to Charles Moore, Jan. 7, 1937, Portsmouth Rehabilitation Project, Fine Arts Commission, NA, RG 66; Howells to Franklin D. Roosevelt, Jan. 18, 1937, Proposed NHS, Portsmouth, 0–36, Records of NPS, NA, RG 79.

520. Spalding to Small, Feb. 10, 1937, Salem Maritime National Historic Site, 0–36, General, Records of NPS, NA, RG 79.

521. Small to Spalding, Feb. 15, 1937, Proposed NHS, Portsmouth, 0–36, Records of NPS, NA, RG 79.

522. Chester Garst Mayo, *John Mayo of Roxbury, Massachusetts, 1630–1688* (Huntington, Vt., 1965), 217; Mayo to author, Aug. 28, 1974.

523. Small to Spalding, Feb. 15, 1937, Proposed NHS, Portsmouth, 0–36, Records of NPS, NA, RG 79.

524. Mayo, memorandum for Historical Restoration Committee, Feb. 16, 1937, Mayo papers, author's collection.

525. Stuart M. Barnette to Spalding, Mar. 2, 1937, Proposed NHS, Portsmouth, 0–36, Records of NPS, NA, RG 79.

526. Howells to Mayo, July 23, 1937, Mayo papers.

527. Wendell to Appleton, June 27, 1937, Mrs. Barrett Wendell, SPNEA.

528. Mayo, Historical Restoration Committee, report of chairman to members, July 28, 1937, Mayo papers.

529. Undated report, Mayo papers.

530. Mayo to author, Aug. 28, 1974.

531. Portsmouth survey sheets, Mayo papers.

532. Minutes of meeting of Historical Restoration Comm., Nov. 19, 1937, Mayo papers.

533. Mayo to Cammerer, Dec. 14, 1937, ibid.

534. Demaray to Mayo, Dec. 20, 1937, ibid.

535. Small to Cammerer, Jan. 24, 1938, Proposed NHS, Portsmouth, 0–36, Records of NPS, NA, RG 79.

536. Mayo to Eugene W. Clark, Jan. 24, 1938, Mayo papers.

537. Fred Englehardt to Mayo, Feb. 4, 1938, ibid.

538. Harlan Little to Mayo, Feb. 15, 1938, ibid.; *Christian Science Monitor*, Dec. 14, 1937.

539. Mayo to Little, Feb. 23, 1938, Mayo papers.

540. Kennard E. Goldsmith to Mayo, Mar. 2, 1938, ibid.

541. Mayo to Arthur I. Harriman, Apr. 6, 1938, ibid.

542. Clark to Mayo, May 27, 1938, ibid.

543. Mayo to Robert R. Mullen, July 15, 1938, ibid.

544. *Christian Science Monitor*, July 30, 1938.

545. Mayo to Dorothy M. Vaughn, Aug. 8, 1938, Mayo papers.

546. Clark, report on survey of historical sites and buildings, Oct. 7, 1938, ibid.

547. Mayo to Charles M. Dale, Oct. 17, 1938, ibid.

548. Mayo, *John Mayo*, 218.

549. Clark, report on survey, Mar. 1, 1939, Mayo papers.

550. Clark to Mayo, Mar. 6, 1939, ibid.

551. Howells to Mayo, Mar. 17, 1939, ibid.

552. Clark to Mayo, Nov. 8, 1939, ibid.

553. Mayo to Clark, Nov. 10, 1939, ibid.

554. Mimeographed invitation to exhibition in Portsmouth and Mayo to Clark, May 22, 1940, ibid.

555. Appleton to Mrs. Louis Lawrence Green, July 16, 1940, Wentworth-Gardner, SPNEA.

556. Appleton to Mrs. Charles S. Hamlin, Mar. 20, 1942, Maine—Kittery, Proposed NHS, SPNEA.

557. Howells to Roosevelt, Feb. 8, 1944, Proposed NHS, Portsmouth, 0–36, Records of NPS, NA, RG 79.

558. Tolson (Porter) to Howells, Feb. 26, 1944, ibid.

559. Hosmer, *Presence of the Past*, 269–70.

560. *Walpole Society Notebook, 1942* (N.p., privately printed, 1943), 15–25.

561. W. A. R. Goodwin to Arthur Woods, May 2, 28, 1928, W. A. R. Goodwin Files, Furnishings—Halsey, ACWF.

562. *New York Times*, Feb. 12, 1928.

563. "St. John's College Upholds American Traditions," *DAR Magazine*, 57 (Oct. 1928), 611–12.

564. R. T. Haines Halsey, "Annapolis Homes," Navy Women's Lecture, 1932, Halsey research notes, Joseph Downs Manuscript Collection, Henry Francis du Pont Winterthur Museum.

565. Brock, "The Rebirth of Old Southern Mansions," *New York Times Magazine*, May 18, 1930, 12–13, 21.

566. Rosamond Randall Beirne and Edith Rossiter Bevan, *The Hammond-Harwood House and Its Owners* (Annapolis, 1941), 64–65.

567. *New York Times*, Jan. 19, 1936.

568. D. F. Sellers to Cammerer, Dec. 13, 1937, Proposed NHS, Misc. Maryland, 0–36, Records of NPS, NA, RG 79; St. Clair Wright, "Historic Preservation in Annapolis," *Antiques*, 111 (Jan. 1977), 152–56.

569. Mrs. Harry R. Slack, Jr., report on Hammond-Harwood House, Inc., Mar. 21, 1939, Hammond-Harwood House Assn. (HHHA).

570. Slack to Stringfellow Barr, Mar. 14, 1938, and Slack to Mrs. Miles White, Mar. 19, 1938, ibid.

571. Minutes of Hammond-Harwood House meeting, Oct. 12, 1938, ibid.

572. Beirne to Slack, Dec. 1, 1938, ibid.

573. Minutes of HHHA, Feb. 14, 1939, ibid.

574. Ibid., Mar. 28, 1939.

575. Albert D. Graham to Barr, May 1, 1939, HHHA.

576. Hammond-Harwood House Committee Report, Nov. 1939, and Minutes of HHHA, Nov. 22, 1939, ibid.

577. Minutes of HHHA, Nov. 22, 1939, ibid.

578. Beirne to Appleton, Nov. 22, 1940, Hammond-Harwood House, SPNEA.

579. Beirne to David Jenkins, Feb. 2, 1940, HHHA.

580. White to Appleton (form letter), Feb. 15, 1940, Hammond-Harwood House, SPNEA.

581. Appleton to White, Feb. 19, 1940, ibid.

582. Minutes of HHHA, Mar. 22, May 24, 1940, HHHA.

583. Ibid., June 13, 1940

584. Ibid., July 2, 1940.

585. Appleton to Beirne, Nov. 15, 1940, Hammond-Harwood House, SPNEA.

586. Beirne to Appleton, Nov. 22, 1940, ibid.

587. Tolson (Porter) to James W. Rader, July 11, 1945, and Rader to regional director, July 23, 1945, Proposed National Monument (NM), Maryland, 0–35, Records of NPS, NA, RG 79.

588. Beirne to Rader, July 22, 1945, ibid.

589. Polly Pommer Slayton to Marguerite Allen, Feb. 27, 1947, Restorations, 1946–47, ACWF.

590. Interview with Mary Wingfield Scott, Aug. 8, 1972.

591. Scott, "A.P.V.A. Tries to Save Old Richmond," *Journal of the American Society of Architectural Historians*, 3 (Oct. 1943), 26–28.

592. Ibid.

593. Ibid., 26–27.

594. Interview with Scott.

595. Ibid.; Scott, "A.P.V.A," 27.

596. Mary Wingfield Scott, *Houses of Old Richmond* (Richmond, 1941), 313.

597. *Old Richmond News*, 1 (Jan. 1944).

598. Ibid., 1 (Sept. 1944).

599. Ibid., 2 (Apr. 1945).

600. Ibid., 1 (Apr. 1944).

601. Ibid., 4 (Feb. 1947) and 5 (Jan. 1948).

602. Ibid., 5 (Oct. 1948).

603. Ibid., 6 (Oct. 1949).

604. Ibid., 4 (Apr. 1947).

605. Interview with Scott.

606. Ibid.; McCormack to author, June 11, 1972.

607. Interview with Ronald F. Lee, June 29, 1970.

608. Henry Hornblower II to Kelly, Aug. 21, 1941, Proposed NM, Mass., 0–35, Records of NPS, NA, RG 79.

609. Kelly to Hornblower, Sept. 10, 1941, ibid.

610. Robert W. Ludden to Collins, Oct. 21, 1941, SMNHS, 857, Travel, ibid.

611. Interview with Mrs. George Henry Warren, July 16, 1970.

612. Interview with William King Covell, Nov. 3, 1969.

613. Appleton to John Nicholas Brown, Feb. 9, 1945, R.I.—Newport, Hunter House, SPNEA.

614. Covell to Appleton, Sept. 1, 1942, and Apr. 11, 1943, ibid.

615. Appleton to Herbert E. Macauley, July 23, 1943, R.I.—Newport, Quaker Meeting House, SPNEA.

616. Interviews with Warren and Covell.

617. John P. Brown to Elmer Keith, Aug. 15, 1944, R.I.—Newport, Hunter House, SPNEA.

618. Brown to Appleton, Feb. 18, 1945, ibid.

619. Covell to Appleton, July 19, 1945, ibid.

620. Interview with Warren.

621. Interviews with Warren and Covell; Minutes of Executive Committee of the Preservation Society of Newport County (PSNC), Sept. 9, 1946, PSNC.

622. Minutes of First Meeting of Incorporators, Aug. 9, 1945, PSNC.

623. Minutes of First Meeting of PSNC, Aug. 20, 1945, PSNC.

624. Ibid., Sept. 11, 1945, and Minutes of Executive Comm., Sept. 25, 1945, PSNC.

625. Minutes of PSNC, May 1, 1946, PSNC.

626. Minutes of Executive Comm., July 11, 1946, PSNC.

627. Interview with Warren; *Providence Journal*, Sept. 27, 1946.

628. Minutes of Executive Comm., Sept. 28, 1946, PSNC.

629. Warren, "Notes on Conversation with Kenneth Chorley," Oct. 10, 1946, Kenneth Chorley File, PSNC.

630. Minutes of Executive Comm., Oct. 17, Nov. 23, 30, 1946, PSNC.

631. Interview with Warren.

632. Chorley, *"Only Tomorrow"* (Newport, R.I., 1947), 15–17.

633. Minutes of Executive Comm., Mar. 26, Apr. 25, and May 13, 1947, PSNC.

634. Interview with Antoinette Downing, Oct. 4, 1974.

635. Ibid.

636. Minutes of Executive Comm., Apr. 25, 1947, PSNC; interview with Warren.

637. Interview with Warren.

638. Warren to Bath, Oct. 17, 1947, Gerald Bath File, PSNC.

639. Minutes of National Trust Annual Meeting, Oct. 21, 1947, 155, NT.

640. Interview with Warren.

641. Demaray to Barnette, June 25, 1946, Proposed NHS, Misc., 0–36, Records of NPS, NA, RG 79.

642. Interview with Lee, June 29, 1970.

643. Barnette, report to Thomas Vint, July 24, 1946, Proposed NHS, Misc., 0–36, Records of NPS, NA, RG 79.

644. Appleton to Warren, Aug. 19, 1947, and Warren to Appleton, Sept. 2, 1947, R.I.—Newport, Breakers, SPNEA.

645. Interview with Warren.

646. *New York Times*, June 11, 1948.

647. Interview with Warren.

648. Minutes of Executive Comm., June 10, 1948, PSNC.

649. Francis S. Ronalds to regional director, June 17, 1948, Morristown, 871 Associations and Clubs, Records of NPS, NA, RG 79.

650. Interview with Warren.

651. Lee to Wirth, Dec. 3, 1948, Proposed NHS, Misc., 0–36, Records of NPS, NA, RG 79.

652. Exhibit "C," Minutes Book II, Sept. 30, 1948, PSNC.

653. Ibid.

654. Minutes of Executive Comm., July 22, 1948, PSNC.

655. Annual Meeting Minutes, Sept. 24, 1948, PSNC.

656. Interview with Warren; *Newport Gazette*, No. 24 (Oct. 1965).

657. Philip H. Wootton, Jr., to Warren, Oct. 20, 1949, *Life Magazine*, PSNC.

648. Elmer Keith report, Jan. 11, 1948, Newport Historical Society, SPNEA.

659. Interview with Warren.

660. Interview with Covell.

661. F. Clinton Knight to Ickes, Proposed NHS, Virginia, 0–36, Records of NPS, NA, RG 79; interview with Milton Grigg, Sept. 15, 1972; Gay Montague Moore, *Seaport in Virginia* (Charlottesville, 1949), 99.

662. Hall Crews, "Old Salem, North Carolina," *Monograph Series*, 15 (1929), 36; Frances Griffin, *Old Salem: An Adventure in Historic Preservation* (Winston-Salem, N.C., 1970), 5.

663. Paul S. Delaney to author, Aug. 6, 1973; Griffin, *Old Salem*, 5.

664. *Alexandria Gazette*, Feb. 14, 1946.

665. Ibid., July 24, 1946.

666. Ibid., Feb. 14, 1946.

667. Alexandria City Council *Proceedings*, Vol. 33, 434, City of Alexandria.

668. Interview with Paul L. Delaney, Aug. 25, 1972.

669. *Alexandria Gazette*, July 24, 1946.

670. Ibid., May 15, 1946; interview with Delaney.

671. Mrs. Robert M. Reese, speech at Organization Meeting of the National Council for Historic Sites and Buildings, Oct. 21, 1947, 146–51, NT.

672. Griffin, *Old Salem*, 6–7.

673. Ibid., 7–9.

674. Ibid., 10–11.

675. H. S. Cody to city engineer, Alexandria, Va., Dec. 4, 1947, Proposed NHS, North Carolina, 0–36, Records of NPS, NA, RG 79.

676. Griffin, *Old Salem*, 5.

677. Ibid., 14.

678. Ibid., 15–19.

679. Ibid., 18–19.

680. Ibid., 18–23.

681. Odie B. Faulk, *Tombstone, Myth and Reality* (New York, 1972), 200.

682. *Tombstone Epitaph*, Oct. 15, 1929.

683. John P. Clum, *Helldorado, 1879–1929* (Tombstone, Ariz., 1930), 1.

684. Faulk, *Tombstone*, 201–3.

685. Ibid., 203–5.

686. *Tucson Star*, May 2, 1933.

687. Walter H. Cole to Cammerer, Jan. 24, 1934, Proposed NM, Tombstone, 0–35, Records of NPS, NA, RG 79.

688. Cole to Wirth, Feb. 17, 1934, ibid.

689. Demaray to Cole, Mar. 15, 1934, ibid.

690. William R. Hogan, preliminary report on Tombstone, Ariz., Oct. 1936, Neasham Collection.

691. Cole to Demaray, Jan. 5, 23, 1937, Proposed NM, Tombstone, 0–35, Records of NPS, NA, RG 79.

692. Maier to Lee, Mar. 15, 1937, and Spalding (Lee) to Maier, Mar. 23, 1937, ibid.

693. Milton McCohn to Cammerer, June 11, 1940, ibid.

694. Neasham, Special Report on the Proposed National Historic Site of Tombstone, Ariz., May, 1941, 4, Neasham Collection.

695. Ibid., 5–7.

696. *Tombstone Epitaph*, Sept. 15, 1949.

697. Ibid., Oct. 13, 1949.

698. Ibid.

699. Ibid., Oct. 27, 1949.

700. Ibid., Nov. 3, 1949.

701. Ibid., Nov. 24, 1949.

702. Ibid., Dec. 29, 1949.

703. Caroline Bancroft, *Gulch of Gold: History of Central City* (N.p., 1958), 334–38.

704. Ibid., 340.

705. *New York Times*, June 18, 1933.

706. *Denver Post*, Aug. 6, 1933.

707. *Rocky Mountain News*, July 14, 1935.

708. Ibid., June 24, 1945.

709. Benjamin P. Draper to author, Aug. 30, 1974.

710. Draper, "A Town Reborn in Colorado," *Antiques*, 55 (Jan. 1949), 39.

711. Draper to author, Aug. 30, 1974.

712. *Antiques*, 58 (July 1950), 42.

Chapter 6: *State Preservation Programs*

1. Charles B. Hosmer, Jr., *Presence of the Past: A History of the Preservation Movement in the United States before Williamsburg* (New York, 1965), 93–101.

2. Ibid., 93–100.

3. Alexander C. Flick, "Suggestions for a State Policy Relating to Historic and Scientific Reservations," *New York State Museum Bulletin 284* (24th Report of the Director), 69.

4. Ibid.

5. Ibid., 69–71.

6. John J. Vrooman, "Preservationism in New York State," *Journal of American Society of Architectural Historians*, 4 (Apr. 1944), 37.

7. State of New York, *Interim Report of the Joint Legislative Committee to Study Historic Sites*, Legislative Document 73 (Feb. 28, 1950), (Albany, 1950), 13–14.

8. Ibid., 17.

9. Ibid., 21.

10. Ibid., 25.

11. Laurence Vail Coleman, *Historic House Museums* (Washington, D.C., 1933), 30.

12. *New York Times*, Feb. 10, 1944.

13. Claude H. Hultzen, Sr., "Restoration of Old Fort Niagara," *New York History*, 18 (Oct. 1937), 386–87.

14. Ibid., 389.

15. Ibid., 391–92.

16. *Proceedings of Historical and Archaeological Superintendents Held in Connection with National Park Service Superintendents' Conference*, Nov. 23–24, 1934, 426, Colonial, Special File, 0–13, General Conference, History, Records of National Park Service (NPS), National Archives (NA), Record Group (RG) 79.

17. State of New York, *Interim Report*, 34

18. *New York Times*, July 26, 1931.

19. Interview with Herbert Evison, July 21, 1973.

20. Robert Allen Frederick, "Colonel Richard Leiber, Conservationist and Park Builder: The Indiana Years," Diss., Indiana, 1960, 106–7, 143; Emma Lieber, *Richard Lieber* (Indianapolis, 1947), 102.

21. Interview with Paul V. Brown, Nov. 9, 1974.

22. Frederick, "Col. Lieber," 192–93.

23. Charles G. Sauers, "Notes on Colonel Richard Lieber," July 12, 1955, Lieber papers, Lilly Library, Indiana Univ.

24. Interview with Brown.

25. Frederick, "Col. Lieber," 106–7.

26. Interview with Charles W. Porter III, Apr. 20, 1970.

27. Richard Lieber, "Address to the Indiana Pioneers," Dec. 1, 1919, Senator Guthrie, Indiana Archives (IA).

28. "Historic and Picturesque Spots in Indiana" (1919–21), Capt. Sauers Personal, Asst. to Director, 1919–21, IA.

29. Lieber Diary, June 20, 1931, Lieber papers.

30. Ibid., Aug. 16–18, 1938.

31. Ibid., Nov. 23, 1924.

32. Frederick, "Col. Lieber," 245; *Madison* (Ind.) *Herald*, June 8, 1926.

33. Lieber Diary, Sept. 21, 1926; *Madison Leader*, Aug. 18, 1926.

34. *Indianapolis News*, Oct. 9, 1926.

35. Frederick, "Col. Lieber," 252–53.

36. Ibid., 253–56; *Bedford* (Ind.) *Mail*, Aug. 11, 1926.

37. *Indianapolis North Side News*, Dec. 23, 1926.

38. McKim C. Copeland, report, March 8, 1929, Conservation Department RG, Memorials General, IA.

39. *Corydon Republican*, May 9, 1929.

40. Brown to Copeland, Aug. 9, 1929, Clifty Falls Park, 1929–30, IA.

41. Lieber Diary, Aug. 22, 1929.

42. Christopher B. Coleman, "Restoration of the Capitol at Corydon," *Indiana Magazine of History*, 30 (Sept. 1934), 258.

43. E. Y. Guernsey, *Spring Mill State Park* (Indianapolis, 1931), 8.

44. Interview with Brown.

45. Undated clipping, Lieber Diary, Sept. 8, 1927.

46. Lieber to Guernsey, Oct. 10, 1927, Woods, Donaldson, Spring Mill Park, 1927–1928, IA.

47. Guernsey, *Spring Mill*, 8.

48. H. H. Wessel to Lieber, Nov. 23, 1927, Woods, Donaldson, Spring Mill Park, 1927–1928, IA.

49. Richard E. Bishop to Lieber, Nov. 18, 1927, ibid.

50. Brown to Guernsey, July 24, 1928, Guernsey, E. Y., Proposed State Parks, Spring Mill, 1928, IA.

51. Lieber to president, West Baden Springs Hotel, Aug. 1, 1928, Woods, Donaldson, Spring Mill Park, 1927–1928, IA.

52. Guernsey to Brown, Aug. 6, 1928, Guernsey, E. Y., Proposed State Parks, Spring Mill, 1928, IA.

53. Guernsey to Lieber, ca. Aug. 7, 1928, ibid.

54. Ibid., ca. late Aug. 1928.

55. Guernsey to Sauers, ca. Sept. 1, 1928, ibid.

56. Lieber to Harry C. Trexler, Sept. 20, 1928, Woods, Donaldson, Spring Mill Park, 1927–1928, IA.

57. Guernsey to Brown, Sept. 21, Nov. 29, 1928, Guernsey, E. Y., Proposed State Parks, Spring Mill, 1928, IA.

58. Guernsey to Lieber, Sept. 28, 1928, ibid.

59. Lieber to Guernsey, Sept. 28, 1928, ibid.

60. Brown to Sauers, ca. Oct. 1928, Paul V. Brown, IA.

61. Guernsey to Brown, Nov. 1, 1928, Guernsey, E. Y., Proposed State Parks, Spring Mill, 1928, IA.

62. J. K. Lilly to Guernsey, Nov. 6, 1928, ibid.

63. Lieber to George Sargent, Jan. 2, 1929, Spring Mill State Park, 1929, IA.

64. [Guernsey], "The Story of an Indiana Pioneer Village, Spring Mill," ca. Mar. 1929, Spring Mill State Park, General, IA.

65. Lieber to William H. Weitknecht, Apr. 29, 1929, ibid.

66. Guernsey, "Spring Mill Village," *Indiana History Bulletin*, 7 (Apr. 1930), 189.

67. Guernsey to Brown, Dec. 17, 1930, Charles G. Sauers, IA.

68. Guernsey, "Report of Activities during the Month of December, 1931," Conservation Dept. RG, E. Y. Guernsey, 1931, IA.

69. Guernsey, "A Suggested Program for Spring Mill," Dec. 27, 1931, ibid.

70. E. P. Lacey, Report for Mar. 1931, Conservation Dept. RG, Ed. P. Lacey, Custodian, Spring Mill Park, IA; Brown to Guernsey, June 30, 1931, Conservation Dept. RG, E. Y. Guernsey, 1931, IA.

71. Denzil Doggett, "The Story of the 'Spring Mill' Water Wheel," *Indiana Magazine of History*, 28 (June 1932), 84–87.

72. John C. Diggs to Lieber, Jan. 3, 1933, and Diggs to Brown, Jan. 7, 1933, Conservation Dept. RG, Memos Jan.–Apr. 1933, IA.

73. Frederick, "Col. Lieber," 333–41.

74. Interviews with Brown and Evison.

75. Interviews with V. Aubrey Neasham, July 26, 1971, Porter, and Evison; Interview with Paul V. Brown and Herbert Evison, Oct. 10, 1962, Archives of NPS.

76. Myron L. Rees to Fred Ryan, May 17, 1934, Conservation Dept. RG, Spring Mill State Park, 1934, Custodian, IA.

77. Zach Sanderson, "Trip to Bedford, Mitchell, and Spring Mill Park, July 13, 1942," Conservation Dept. RG, Sanderson, Z. C., Research on Spring Mill, IA.

78. Andrew H. Hepburn, "Resurrection of a Village," *Saturday Evening Post*, June 12, 1943, 59.

79. Evison to regional director, Aug. 12, 1944, Appomattox—Master Plan, Records of NPS, NA, RG 79.

80. Interview with Evison.

81. *Corydon Republican*, May 9, 1929.

82. Brown to Lieber, Apr. 28, 1932, memos from division chiefs, Jan.-June, 1932, IA.

83. Newton B. Drury to Lieber, Feb. 21, 1927, State Parks General, IA.

84. Harlow Lindley to Lieber, Nov. 19, 1929, Lanier Home, IA.

85. *Louisville Times*, May 29, 1931.

86. Helen Elliott, "New Harmony," *Indiana History Bulletin*, 17 (Feb. 1940), 109–17.

87. Lieber to Robert Kingery, Dec. 30, 1930, Robert Kingery, 1930 Correspondence, IA.

88. "A System of State Parks for the State of Illinois," Dec. 1930, 18–23, ibid.

89. Lieber to Kingery, Dec. 30, 1930, ibid.

90. Paul Angle to author, Jan. 17, 1973.

91. Thomas B. Littlewood, *Horner of Illinois* (Evanston, 1969), 89.

92. Ibid., 7.

93. "The Lincoln Memorial Commission," Nov. 13, 1933, Lincoln Memorial Commission, Henry Horner Papers, Illinois State Historical Library (ISHL).

94. Henry Horner to Louis L. Emmerson, Nov. 15, 1932, George H. Luker, Superintendent of Parks, Henry Horner Papers, ISHL.

95. Thomas M. Pitkin to author, Aug. 1, 1974; interviews with Joseph F. Booton, Apr. 17, 1971, and Jerome V. Ray, July 12, 1971.

96. Pitkin to author, Aug. 1, 1974.

97. Logan Hay, report, June 20, 1935, State of Illinois, *Journal of the Senate* (59th General Assembly, Jan. 9–June 29, 1935), 1325–27.

98. Thomas P. Reep, *Lincoln at New Salem* (Petersburg, Ill., 1927); Booton interview with Reep, Oct. 18, 1934, New Salem Misc., Division of Parks and Memorials, Illinois Dept. of Conservation (IC).

99. Reep, *Lincoln*, 140.

100. Booton to author, Nov. 17, 1974.

101. Joseph F. Booton, *Record of the Restoration of New Salem* (Springfield, Ill., 1934), 13.

102. Ibid., 15.

103. Interviews with Booton and Ray.

104. Interview with Booton; Angle to author, Jan. 17, 1973.

105. C. W. Macardell to Reep, Sept. 23, 1932, Reep Correspondence, Lincoln's New Salem, Div. of Parks and Memorials, IC; Booton to Mrs. Josephine Craven Chandler, Sept. 29, 1932, Josephine Chandler, Lincoln's New Salem, Div. of Parks and Memorials, IC.

106. C. Herrick Hammond to Henry H. Kohn, Oct. 15, 1932, New Salem—1930s research, Lincoln's New Salem, Div. of Parks and Memorials, IC.

107. Booton, *Record*.

108. Robert B. Atwood, "The Town That Was a School to Lincoln," *New York Times Magazine*, Feb. 12, 1933, 10–11, 17.

109. Booton interview with Reep.

110. Booton to Angle, Dec. 13, 1934, New Salem Research, Div. of Parks and Memorials, IC.

111. Robert I. McKeague to H. H. Cleaveland, July 31, 1930, Grant's Home, Galena, Land Acquisition, Div. of Parks and Memorials, IC.

112. Booton, "Pierre Menard's Home," *Bulletin of the Illinois Society of Architects*, 26 (Nov. 1941), 8.

113. Joseph F. Booton and George M. Nedved, *Record of Restoration, Third State House, Vandalia, Illinois* (Springfield, 1945), 44–45.

114. Ibid., 45.

115. Interview with Booton.

116. Interviews with Josephine and Mary Burtschi, Dec. 29, 1972, Ray, and Booton.

117. Angle to Kingery, Dec. 11, 1933, Fort Chartres, Booton Material, Lincoln's New Salem, Div. of Parks and Memorials, IC.

118. Interview with Booton.

119. Interview with Ray.

120. Booton to Hultzen, Jan. 31, 1934, Fort Chartres, Booton Material, Lincoln's New Salem, Div. of Parks and Memorials, IC.

121. Angle to author, Mar. 14, 1973; interview with Ray.

122. Angle to author, Jan. 17, 1973.

123. Interview with Booton.

124. Booton to George H. Luker, Apr. 13, 1939, Vandalia State House, Lincoln's New Salem, Div. of Parks and Memorials, IC.

125. *21st Annual Report of the Division of Waterways, July 1, 1937, to June 30, 1938*, 37–38; Ronald F. Lee, "State Parks: Cooperation with the National Park Service," Mar. 16, 1936, Files of Branch of History, U.S. Department of the Interior (Int.).

126. Interviews with Booton and Ray.

127. Booton to William Ryan, Mar. 7, 1940, Metamora Court House, Booton Old Material, Lincoln's New Salem, Div. of Parks and Memorials, IC.

128. Lee, "State Parks"; Fern N. Pond to Kingery, July 16, 1937, and Kingery to Charles P. Casey, July 19, 1937, Pond papers, ISHL.

129. R. N. Johnson to Booton, Dec. 5, 1938, Carding Mill, Booton Material, Lincoln's New Salem, Div. of Parks and Memorials, IC.

130. Booton to Johnson, Dec. 7, 1938, ibid.

131. Booton, "Preliminary Report of the Research for the Carding Mill—New Salem State Park," May 1, 1940, ibid.

132. Booton to Henry Ford, Jan. 31, 1941, ibid.

133. Interviews with Booton and Ray; Booton to McWilliams and Whittiker, Feb. 21, 1941, Carding Mill, Booton Material, Lincoln's New Salem, Div. of Parks and Memorials, IC; Booton, "New Salem Carding Mill," *Bulletin of the Illinois Society of Architects*, 26 (Feb.-Mar. 1942), 8.

134. Booton to Ray, Jan. 30, 1943, Fort Chartres, Booton Material, Lincoln's New Salem, Div. of Parks and Memorials, IC; Booton and Nedved, *Record of Restoration*, v.

135. Coleman to Booton, Mar. 25, 1944, Vandalia State House, Lincoln's New Salem, Div. of Parks and Memorials, IC.

136. Booton to Margaret C. Norton, Jan. 22, 1946, Bishop Hill Church, Old Correspondence, Div. of Parks and Memorials, IC.

137. Booton to George Williams, Sept. 25, 1947, ibid.

138. Booton to author, June 21, 1971.

139. Williams to Hammond, May 1, 1943, Market House—Galena, Land Acquisition, Div. of Parks and Memorials, IC.

140. Williams to I. L. Gamber, Mar. 12, 1947, and Dwight H. Green to Walter A. Rosenfield, Oct. 6, 1948, ibid.

141. Earl H. Reed to Green, May 14, 1947, Market House—Galena, Restoration, Div. of Parks and Memorials, IC; John W. Jenkins to Green, May 19, 1947, and John W. Chapman to Rosenfield, June 4, 1947, Market House—Galena, Land Acquisition, Div. of Parks and Memorials, IC.

142. Reed to Rosenfield, July 10, 1947, Market House—Galena, Restoration, Div. of Parks and Memorials, IC.

143. Interview with Booton.

144. *Bulletin of Illinois Society of Architects* (1934), clipping, HABS Files, Library of Congress.

145. *Biographical Sketch of Joseph Charles Burtschi* (Vandalia, Ill., 1962), 3.

146. Interview with Ray.

147. Booton to author, Oct. 22, 1975.

148. Hosmer, *Presence of the Past*, 125–29.

149. Interview with Neasham.

150. Interview with Newton B. Drury, July 28, 1971.

151. Drury to Lieber, Feb. 21, 1927, State Parks General, IA.

152. Frederick Law Olmsted to William E. Colby, Aug. 25, 1928, Reports, California State Archives (CA).

153. Frederick Law Olmsted, *Report of the State Park Survey of California* (Sacramento, 1929).

154. Ibid., 10.

155. Aubrey Drury, "Historic Sites in California," Aug. 25, 1928, Interpretive Services, Division of Beaches and Parks, Dept. of Parks and Recreation, California (Cal. Parks).

156. Ibid., 4.

157. Ibid., 60.

158. Olmsted, *Report*, 53.

159. Ibid., 66.

160. Ibid.

161. *Statutes of California* (Sacramento, 1931), 320.

162. State Park Commission (SPC) Minutes, Aug. 17, 1931, 161, Cal. Parks.

163. Frank McKee to John H. Covington, Dec. 29, 1934, Historical Landmarks, Division of Parks, 1936, No. 7, CA.

164. "Plan for a Statewide Survey of Historic Sites and Landmarks in California," Apr. 30, 1935, ibid.

165. Interview with Drury.

166. Ibid.

167. Interview with Horace M. Albright, Dec. 2, 1969; Horace M. Albright, *Origins of National Park Service Administration of Historic Sites* (Philadelphia, 1971), 10.

168. Olmsted to William E. Metzger, Nov. 7, 1928, Columbia State Historic Park (SHP), General Correspondence, 419.0–307, no. 1, Cal. Parks.

169. Olmsted to Frank Dondero, Nov. 24, 1928, ibid.

170. "Plan for a Statewide Survey," Apr. 30, 1935, Historical Landmarks, Div. of Parks, 1936, No. 7, CA.

171. Hero E. Rensch, Report on Project S3-F2–27, Research on the Old Mining Town of Columbia, Apr. 30, 1935, Columbia SHP, Gen. Corr., 419.0–307, No. 1, Cal. Parks.

172. Joseph R. Knowland, *California, a Landmark History* (Oakland, 1941), 197.

173. Gerald H. Bath to Kenneth Chorley, Apr. 1946, Restoration, Columbia, Calif., 1946–47, Archives of Colonial Williamsburg Foundation (ACWF).

174. Rensch, Report on the Proposed Field Study at Columbia, Nov. 5, 1934, Francis W. Wilson, The Columbia Historical Project, Feb. 28, 1935, and Rensch, Research on the Old Mining Town of Columbia, April 30, 1935, Columbia SHP, Gen. Corr., 419.0–307, No. 1, Cal. Parks.

175. Mrs. James Ellis Tucker to California SPC, Sept. 14, 1933, ibid.; SPC Minutes, Nov. 11, 1933, II, 111, Cal. Parks.

176. Rheta L. Zimmermann to California SPC, Nov. 4, 1933, Columbia SHP, Gen. Corr., 419.0–307, No. 1, Cal. Parks.

177. Drury to W. A. R. Goodwin, Dec. 4, 1933, ibid.

178. Drury, title page on Columbia, Jan. 15, 1934, ibid.

179. Drury to Zimmermann, Feb. 1, 1934, ibid.

180. Zimmermann to Colby, Mar. 29, 1934, ibid.

181. Drury to Zimmermann, July 3, 1934, ibid.

182. Neil Cunningham to Dept. of Natural Resources, Apr. 4, 1934, ibid.

183. Drury to Zimmermann, July 3, 1934, ibid.

184. Drury to Zimmermann, Sept. 4, 1934, ibid.

185. SPC Minutes, Jan. 23, 1936, 218, Cal. Parks.

186. Drury to Mrs. J. E. Butterfield, Apr. 4, 1936, Mrs. Butterfield, CA; Drury to Fred C. Tatton, Apr. 22, 1936, Columbia SHP, Gen. Corr., 419.0–307, No. 1, Cal. Parks.

187. SPC Minutes, Sept. 24, 1937, 52, Cal. Parks.

188. Ibid., Sept. 23, 1938, 52.

189. Ibid., Mar. 15–17, 1941, 54.

190. *Watsonville Register*, Sept. 23, 1931, Folder No. 165, Interpretive Services, Cal Parks.

191. SPC Minutes, Apr. 27, 1931, I, 119–20, Cal. Parks.

192. Morrow and Emerson Knight, "A Report on the Proposed San Juan Bautista Plaza State Monument," May, 1931, Interpretive Services, Folder No. 179, Cal. Parks.

193. Ibid., 3.

194. Clipping, Oct. 1, 1935, No. 5 Reports, Statements, etc., Div. of Parks, 1935, CA.

195. SPC Minutes, Jan. 3, 1933, II, 55, Cal. Parks.

196. Drury to W. I. Hawkins, Feb. 2, 1933, San Juan Bautista SHP, Gen. Corr., 419.0–411, No. 1, Cal. Parks.

197. Drury to Mrs. Edmund N. Brown, Sept. 17, 1935, ibid.

198. Clipping, Oct. 1, 1935, No. 5 Reports, Statements, etc., Div. of Parks, 1935, CA.

199. Honoria Toumey to SPC, Dec. 29, 1928, and General Vallejo Memorial Association to Colby, Aug. 22, 1931, Sonoma SHP (Vallejo Home), Gen. Corr., 419.0–243, Cal. Parks.

200. SPC Minutes, Dec. 29, 1931, I, 195, Cal. Parks.

201. John H. Wood to SPC, Dec. 2, 1931, Cal. Parks.

202. W. F. Chipman to SPC, May 11, 1933, ibid.

203. Knowland, *California*, 165.

204. Christine Sterling, *Olvera Street, Its History and Restoration* (Los Angeles, 1947), 10.

205. Ibid., 14.

206. Ibid., 14–18.

207. Ibid., 20.

208. *San Antonio Light*, July 18, 1939.

209. Ed Ainsworth, *Recuerdos de la Calle Olvera: Memories in the City of Dreams, a Tribute to Harry Chandler* (Los Angeles, 1959); interview with Drury.

210. Edwin J. Symmes, "The Building of Fort Tejon," Sept. 24, 1932, No. 142 Misc. Material on Fort Tejon State Historical Monument, Interpretive Services, Cal. Parks.

211. SPC Minutes, Sept. 24, 1937, 53, Cal. Parks.

212. John R. White, report, Jan. 3, 1941, Fort Tejon SHP, Gen. Corr., 419.0–517, Cal. Parks; Knowland, *California*, 96; Clarence Cullimore, *Old Adobes of Forgotten Fort Tejon* (Bakersfield, 1941), 77–78.

213. Grant Towle to Charles B. Wing, Apr. 18, 1930, Monterey SHP, see Old Custom House, Gen. Corr., 419.0–455, No. 1, Cal. Parks.

214. Albert E. Carter to Knowland, Apr. 5, 1937, ibid.

215. Drury to Arno B. Cammerer, Apr. 10, 1937, ibid.

216. *California Conservationist*, 3 (Sept. 1938), 4.

217. Drury to John C. Porter, Sept. 6, 1938, Monterey SHP, Casa de Oro, Gen. Corr., 419.0–455, Cal. Parks.

218. Roger S. Fitch to Covington, Apr. 12, 1941, Monterey SHP, Stevenson House, Gen. Corr., 419.0–455, Cal. Parks.

219. Interview with Neasham.

220. Interview with Philip T. Primm, Aug. 21, 1971.

221. Ibid.

222. Ibid.

223. Clipping, Aug. 5, 1934, Pearl Chase File, University of California at Santa Barbara (UCSB); interview with Primm, Mar. 1, 1974.

224. Meeting at La Purisima, Aug. 8, 1934, quoted in Fred C. Hageman, *An Architectural Study of the Mission La Purisima Concepcion, January, 1935 to April, 1938* (typed report), 152, Interpretive Services, Cal. Parks.

225. SPC Minutes, Sept. 14, 1934, II, 169, Cal. Parks.

226. Herbert Maier, report to district officer, Jan. 1935, No. 6 ECW Camps, Park Division, 1935, CA.

227. Drury to Pearl Chase, Jan. 25, 1935, and Colby to Chase, Mar. 11, 1935, Pearl Chase File, UCSB.

228. SPC Minutes, Mar. 28, 1935, II, 178, Cal. Parks.

229. Ibid., Sept. 28, 1935, II, 202.

230. Ibid., Nov. 9, 1935, II, 213.

231. Colby to Harold L. Ickes, Nov. 22, 1935, Colby, CA.

232. SPC Minutes, Nov. 14, 1936, 264, Cal. Parks.

233. Hageman to Drury, Mar. 18, 1938, Newton Drury, La Purisima, Records of NPS, NA, RG 79.

234. Wallace Penfield to SPC, Aug. 2, 1938, Pearl Chase File, UCSB.

235. A. E. Henning to Penfield, Sept. 20, 1938, quoted in SPC Minutes, Sept. 23, 1938, 109, Cal. Parks.

236. SPC Minutes, Mar. 4, 1939, 140, Cal. Parks.

237. Ibid., June 27–28, 1940, 7–8.

238. Ibid., Mar. 15–17, 1941, 54.

239. Chase, Old Mission Days letter, Nov. 1941, Proposed NHS, California, 0–36, Records of NPS, NA, RG 79; interview with Pearl Chase, Aug. 8, 1971.

240. Drury to Brown, July 5, 1932, Mrs. Brown, CA.

241. SPC Minutes, Sept. 28, 1935, II, 207, Cal. Parks.

242. Ibid., May 28, 1937, 27, and July 30, 1937, 39.

243. Ibid.

244. Ibid., Dec. 10, 1937, 64.

245. [Rensch], "Plan for a Statewide Survey of Historic Sites and Landmarks in California," Apr. 30, 1935, Historical Landmarks, Div. of Parks, 1935, No. 7, CA.

246. Interview with Neasham.

247. McKee to George D. Nordenholt, Oct. 24, 1935, Historical Landmarks, Div. of Parks, 1935, No. 7, CA.

248. Interview with Neasham.

249. SPC Minutes, Dec. 29, 1931, I, 198, Cal. Parks.

250. Ibid., Aug. 27, 1937, 42.

251. Ibid., 43–44.

252. Interviews with Drury and Neasham.

253. SPC Minutes, June 18–19, 1943, 9, Cal. Parks.

254. Ibid., Oct. 21, 1944, 67.

255. James Mussatti to Warren T. Hannum, Oct. 5, 1944, Historical Landmarks, Beaches and Parks, No. 7, CA.

256. Sallie R. Thaler to Covington, Nov. 29, 1944, ibid.

257. George H. Schrader to Dewitt Nelson, Nov. 21, 1944, No. 3 Misc., Beaches and Parks, 1944, CA.

258. Senate Bill No. 1256, passed California Senate, June 16, 1945.

259. Undated news release, "First California Public School Acquired for Columbia State Park," Proposed NHS, California, 0–36, Records of NPS, NA, RG 79.

260. Elizabeth Gray Potter, "Columbia—'Gem of the Southern Mines,'" *California Historical Society Quarterly*, 24 (Sept. 1945), 267–70.

261. California SPC, policy statement, fall, 1945, Columbia SHP, Gen. Corr., 419.0–307, No. 1, Cal. Parks.

262. News release, Dec. 3, 1945, ibid.

263. Ibid., Jan. 30, 1946.

264. SPC Minutes, Feb. 1, 2, 1946, 3–4, Cal. Parks.

265. Ibid., June 13, 1946, 4.

266. Ibid., Sept. 20–21, 1946, 193.

267. Senate Bill No. 32, Jan. 9, 1947.

268. John A. Hennessey to Ada Rehm Koppitz, Jan. 21, 1947, Columbia SHP, Gen. Corr., 419.0–307, No. 2, Cal. Parks.

269. W. Stanley Pearce to James E. McConnell, Dec. 5, 1946, Columbia SHP, Appraisals, 419.0–307, Cal. Parks.

270. Hannum to Chorley, Apr. 9, 1947, Restorations, Columbia, Calif., 1946–47, ACWF.

271. Chorley to Hannum, Apr. 17, 1947, ibid.

272. Chorley to McConnell, July 2, 1947, ibid.

273. Camille G. Cavalier to Chorley, July 6, 1947, and Chorley assistant to McConnell, Aug. 4, 1947, ibid.

274. Drury to Lee, Aug. 5, 1947, Proposed NHS, California, 0–36, Records of NPS, NA, RG 79; SPC Minutes, Aug. 15, 1947, 17, Cal. Parks.

275. Interview with Neasham.

276. Dorr G. Yeager, "A Study of Museum Possibilities, Columbia State Park, California," Feb. 9, 1948, Interpretive Services, Folder No. 132, Cal. Parks.

277. SPC Minutes, Sept. 17, 1948, 3–5, Cal. Parks.

278. Neasham, "Columbia Historic State Park, Historical Summary and Recommendations," Oct. 1, 1948, Columbia Report, Cal. Parks.

279. SPC Minutes, Nov. 18, 1949, 30, Cal. Parks.

280. "Columbia Historic State Park, Report on Acquisition Expenditures as of October 1, 1949," Columbia Reports, CA.

281. SPC Minutes, June 29, 1945, 112, Cal. Parks.

282. Ibid., Nov. 18, 1949, 8.

283. Phil T. Hanna, memorandum on registration and marking, Nov. 1, Dec. 16, 1948, Historical Monuments, Beaches and Parks—1949, No. 8, CA.

284. Miles D. Allen, "Chronological Sequence of Events Pertaining to Acquisition of Proposed Amestoy State Park," Jan. 20, 1949, Los Encinos SHP, Gen. Corr., 419.0–546, Cal. Parks.

285. Henning to Mrs. J. Earl Stewart, May 24, 1949, ibid.

286. [Sylvester K. Stevens], "A Plan for Historic Preservation," 1970, 4, Pennsylvania Historical and Museum Commission (PHMC), Harrisburg.

287. Act of July 25, 1913, quoted in Donald H. Kent, "Pennsylvania Historical Commission Manual," Sept. 29, 1941, 8, Pennsylvania Archives (PA).

288. Ibid., 50–53.

289. Ibid., 121.

290. Ibid., 122–23.

291. Ibid., 6.

292. Transcript from Charles M. Stotz, Nov. 10, 1975.

293. Roy F. Nichols, *The Pennsylvania Historical and Museum Commission, a History* (Harrisburg, 1967), 12; interview with Sylvester K. Stevens, July 26, 1973.

294. Ross Pier Wright to Hiram H. Shenk, May 13, 1932, Historical Commission, Shenk, Ex. Secretary, General Correspondence, 1929–33, Ross P. Wright, RG 13, PA; Wright to Frank W. Melvin, Mar. 28, 1936, Hist. Comm., Cadzow, A&A, Gen. Corr., 1934–36, Ross P. Wright, RG 13, PA.

295. Wright to Melvin, Apr. 15, 1936, Hist. Comm., Cadzow, A&A, Gen. Corr., Ross P. Wright, RG 13, PA.

296. Nichols, *Commission*, 12; Kent, "Manual," 6.

297. Kent, "Manual," 141–42.

298. Ibid., 128–132.

299. Ibid., 81–82.

300. Ibid., 127.

301. G. Edwin Brumbaugh, "Report, John Morton Homestead, Prospect Park, Pennsylvania," July 8, 1947, Morton Homestead, History, PHMC.

302. Pennsylvania Historical Commission (PHC) Minutes, Oct. 28, 1935, Hist. Comm., Administration File, Minutes (1934–36), RG 13, PA.

303. Wright to John S. Fisher, May 4, 1939, Hist. Comm., Cadzow, A&A, Gen. Corr., 1939, Ross P. Wright, RG 13, PA.

304. Melvin to Stevens, Nov. 25, 1940, Hist. Comm., Adm. File, Stevens, Historians, Reports, 1940, RG 13, PA.

305. Wright to Fisher, May 4, 1939, Hist. Comm., Cadzow, A&A, Gen. Corr., 1939, Ross P. Wright, RG 13, PA.

306. Wright to Melvin, Mar. 28, 1936, ibid., 1934–36.

307. Melvin to Wright, Apr. 16, 1936, ibid.

308. PHC Minutes, Sept. 28, 1936.

309. Interview with Stevens.

310. Ibid.

311. Ibid.

312. Charles Henry Moon to Fisher, Feb. 8, 1928, Hist. Comm., Shenk, Ex. Secy., Gen. Corr., 1928–33, M, RG 13, PA.

313. Shenk to Joseph R. Grundy, Apr. 10, 1928, ibid., 1927–33, G; interview with Stevens.

314. PHC Minutes, June 15, 1934.

315. Albert C. Myers, *William Penn, a Radio Address*, Oct. 24, 1934, Bulletin No. 3, PHC (Harrisburg, 1934).

316. PHC Minutes, Jan. 7, 1935.

317. Ibid., Oct. 28, 1935.

318. Ibid., May 11, 1936.

319. Melvin, "The Romance of the Pennsbury Manor Restoration," *Pennsylvania History*, 7 (July 1940), 142–48.

320. Interview with Stevens.

321. PHC Minutes, May 20, 1932 (1932–33).

322. Donald A. Cadzow to Wright, July 14, 1932, Hist. Comm., Cadzow, A&A, Gen. Corr., 1932–33, Ross P. Wright, RG 13, PA.

323. PHC Minutes, June 24, 1932.

324. Cadzow to Wright, July 25, 1932, Hist. Comm., Cadzow, A&A, Gen. Corr., 1932–33, Ross P. Wright, RG 13, PA.

325. Cadzow, address to Welcome Society, May 26, 1934, Hist. Comm., Cadzow, A&A, Gen. Corr., 1934–36, Welcome Society and other addresses, RG 13, PA.

326. PHC Minutes, May 26, 1933; Grundy to James N. Rule, Hist. Comm., Shenk, Ex. Secy, Gen. Corr., 1929–33, G, RG 13, PA.

327. Cadzow to Rule, June 25, 1933, Hist. Comm., Keeny, Acting Ex. Secy., Gen. Corr., 1933–34, Cadzow, RG 13, PA.

328. Harold R. Shurtleff to Cadzow, Oct. 27, 1933, Hist. Comm., Cadzow, A&A, Gen. Corr., 1933, S, RG 13, PA.

329. PHC Minutes, Sept. 26, 1933.

330. Ibid., Jan. 24, 1934 (1934–36).

331. Leicester B. Holland to Myers, Mar. 16, 1934, Hist. Comm., Stevens, Historian, Gen. Corr., Pennsbury Manor, 1941, leaflet, RG 13, PA.

332. Cadzow, address to Welcome Society.

333. Martha J. Bring to R. Brognard Okie, Aug. 27, 1936, and Cadzow to Okie, Nov. 20, 1936, Hist. Comm., Cadzow, A&A, Gen. Corr., 1932–39, O, RG 13, PA.

334. Charles J. Dutton, Bring, and Cadzow to Melvin, May 26, 1937, Hist. Comm., Cadzow, A&A, Gen. Corr., 1937, Frank W. Melvin, RG 13, PA.

335. Cadzow to M. Atherton Leach, June 16, 1937, Hist. Comm., Cadzow, A&A, Gen. Corr., 1936–39, M. Atherton Leach, RG 13, PA.

336. B. F. Fackenthal to Cadzow, June 26, 1937, ibid., 1937, F.

337. Cadzow to Mrs. Fred C. Eaton, Oct. 26, 1937, ibid., 1937–8, E.

338. Melvin, "Romance of Pennsbury," 151.

339. Melvin to Cadzow, Mar. 3, 1938, Hist. Comm., Cadzow, A&A, Gen. Corr., 1938, Frank W. Melvin, RG 13, PA.

340. Carl A. Ziegler to Holland, Mar. 2, 1938, Proposed National Historic Site (NHS), Pennsylvania, 0–36, Records of NPS, NA, RG 79.

341. Holland to Maurice F. X. Donahue, Mar. 2, 1938, ibid.

342. Fiske Kimball to John Rankin, Apr. 13, 1938, ibid.

343. Resolution adopted at 70th Convention of the American Institute of Architects, *Octagon*, 10 (May 1938), 27.

344. *Philadelphia Evening Public Ledger*, Apr. 21, 1938.

345. Melvin to Okie, Aug. 5, 1938, Hist. Comm., Cadzow, A&A, Gen. Corr., 1938, Frank W. Melvin, RG 13, PA.

346. Melvin to Leach, Dec. 15, 1938, Hist. Comm., Philadelphia Office, Frank Melvin, Chairman, L, RG 13, PA.

347. Arthur E. Demaray to Ickes, June 8, 1938, Proposed NHS, Pennsylvania, 0–36, Records of NPS, NA, RG 79.

348. H. A. Gray to Demaray, Sept. 6, 1938, ibid.

349. John P. O'Neill to Lee, Oct. 16, 1938, ibid.

350. Ickes to Melvin, Apr. 27, 1939, ibid.

351. Interview with Ronald F. Lee, July 29, 1970.

352. PHC Minutes, May 13, 1938 (1937–39); Melvin to Leach, Aug. 5, 1938, Hist. Comm., Philadelphia Office, Melvin, Chairman, L, RG 13, PA.

353. Demaray to Gray, Nov. 16, 1938, Proposed NHS, Pennsylvania, 0–36, Records of NPS, NA, RG 79.

354. Stotz, "Threshold of the Golden Kingdom: The Village of Economy and Its Restoration," *Winterthur Portfolio 8* (Charlottesville, Va., 1973), 140–41; PHC Minutes, Jan. 26, 1938.

355. Transcript from Stotz.

356. Melvin to Leach, Aug. 26, 1938, Hist. Comm., Philadelphia Office, Melvin, Chairman, L, RG 13, PA.

357. *Pennsylvania Education Bulletin*, 6 (Jan. 1939), 18.

358. PHC Minutes, Jan. 6, 1939.

359. Margaret Lindsay to Gregg Neel, May 9, 1940, Hist. Comm., Cadzow, Ex. Secy., Gen. Corr., Margaret Lindsay, Supervisor, Economy Museum Project, RG 13, PA.

360. PHC Minutes, Nov. 1–2, 1940 (1940).

361. Transcript from Stotz.

362. PHC Minutes, Mar. 4, 1940; Charles M. and Edward Stotz, Jr., "Report on the Restoration of Old Economy," Dec. 18, 1941, Old Economy, Physical, PHMC.

363. Stotz, "Report on October Meeting," Oct. 9, 1942, appended to PHC Minutes, Oct. 30, 1942 (1942).

364. Karl J. R. Arndt, *George Rapp's Successors and Material Heirs, 1847–1916* (Cranbury, N.J., 1971), 354–61.

365. PHC Minutes, Dec. 20, 1943 (1943).

366. Stotz, "Threshold," 141.

367. *New York Times*, Aug. 15, 1937.

368. Cadzow to Wright, Mar. 12, 1941, Hist. Comm., Cadzow, Ex. Secy., Gen. Corr., Jan.-Mar. 1941, Ross P. Wright, RG 13, PA.

369. PHC Minutes, Apr. 9, 1941 (1941).

370. Eugene Doll to Stevens, Sept. 18, 1941, Hist. Comm., Stevens, Historian, Gen. Corr., 1939–41, D, RG 13, PA; Doll, "Architectural Notes on the Ephrata Cloister," Oct. 1941, Ephrata Cloister, History, PHMC.

371. Brumbaugh, "Ephrata Kloster, Preliminary Report," Oct. 1, 1941, Ephrata Cloister, History, PHMC.

372. PHC Minutes, Oct. 6, 1941.

373. Wright to Cadzow, Oct. 28, 1941, Hist. Comm., Cadzow, Ex. Secy., Gen. Corr., Aug.-Dec. 1941, Ross P. Wright, RG 13, PA.

374. Wright to Cadzow, Mar. 3, 1942, ibid., 1942.

375. Brumbaugh, "Medieval Construction at Ephrata," *Antiques*, 46 (July 1944), 18–20.

376. Brumbaugh to Cadzow, Apr. 21, 1945, Ephrata Cloister, Misc., PHMC.

377. Ibid.

378. PHMC Minutes, Apr. 1, 1948, Hist. and Mus. Comm., Adm. File, Minutes, 1948, RG 13, PA.

379. Ibid., Mar. 3, 1949.

380. Marjorie P. Wendell to Cadzow, Mar. 15, 1939, Hist. Comm., Cadzow, A&A, Gen. Corr., 1939, W, RG 13, PA; interview with Stevens.

381. E. Kaye Hunter to Cadzow, Apr. 10, 1939, Hist. Comm., Cadzow, A&A, WPA, Gen. Corr., G.H.I., RG 13, PA.

382. Act of Aug. 5, 1941, quoted in Kent, "Manual," 90–92.

383. PHMC Minutes, July 10, 1947 (1947).

384. Melvin to Leach, May 18, 1939, Hist. Comm., Cadzow, A&A, Gen. Corr., 1936–39, M. Atherton Leach, RG 13, PA; Stevens, in *Pennsylvania Public Education Bulletin*, 6 (Jan. 1939), 17.

385. Interview with Stevens; Neel to George Bloom, Mar. 26, 1943, Hist. Comm., Cadzow, Ex. Secy., Gen. Corr., 1942–43, Gregg Neel, RG 13, PA.

386. Cadzow to Arthur Woodward, May 22, 1933, Hist. Comm., Cadzow, A&A, Gen. Corr., 1933–34, W, RG 13, PA; Cadzow to J. C. Harrington, Jan. 5, 1937, ibid., 1936–37, H.

387. Interview with Stevens.

388. Ibid.

389. Cadzow to Melvin, Sept. 6, 1938, Hist. Comm., Cadzow, A&A, Gen. Corr., 1938, Frank W. Melvin, RG 13, PA.

390. Ibid.

391. Ibid., Mar. 2, 1938.

392. Cadzow to Charles J. Biddle, July 2, 1948, Hist. and Mus. Comm., Cadzow, Ex. Dir., Gen. Corr., 1947–48, Charles J. Biddle, RG 13, PA.

393. Cadzow to John Haudenshild, July 28, 1939, Hist. Comm., Cadzow, A&A, Gen. Corr., 1938–39, H, RG 13, PA.

394. Interview with Stevens.

395. Wright to Cadzow, Mar. 25, 1940, Hist. Comm., Cadzow, Ex. Secy, Gen. Corr., Jan.–Apr. 1940, Ross P. Wright, RG 13, PA.

396. Transcript from Stotz.

397. PHC Minutes, July 15, 1940 (1940).

398. Ibid., Dec. 7, 1942 (1942–43), Commission Staff.

399. Stevens to Committee on Historical Policy and Program, Dec. 7, 1938, Hist. Comm., Cadzow, A&A, Gen. Corr., 1938–39, Committee on Hist. Policy and Program, RG 13, PA.

400. Ibid.

401. PHC Minutes, Jan. 6, 1939 (1937–39).

402. *Pennsylvania Public Education Bulletin*, 6 (Jan. 1939), 17–18.

403. Committee on Hist. Policy and Program Minutes, Feb. 13, 1939, Hist. Comm., Cadzow, A&A, Gen. Corr., 1938–39, Comm. on Hist. Policy and Program, RG 13, PA.

404. Stevens to Wright, Jan. 7, 1941, Hist. Comm., Stevens, Historian, Gen. Corr., 1941, Ross P. Wright, RG 13, PA.

405. Stevens, "Considerations Governing Property Acquisitions," approved Mar. 14, 1941, Hist. Comm., Adm. Files, Minutes, 1941, RG 13, PA.

406. PHC Minutes, May 16, 1941 (1941).

407. Herbert D. Vegel to Stevens, Sept. 3, 1941, Hist. Comm., Stevens, Historian, Gen. Corr., 1941–43, Somerfield Bridge, RG 13, PA.

408. Stevens to PHC, Dec. 20, 1943, Hist. Comm., Cadzow, Ex. Secy, Gen. Corr., 1939–43, S, RG 13, PA.

409. Minutes of the Pennsylvania Committee on the Conservation of Cultural Resources, May 8, 1942, Hist. Comm., Stevens, Historian, Gen. Corr., 1941–42, Pa. Comm. on Conservation of Cultural Resources, RG 13, PA; interview with Stevens; Stevens to Edwin O. Lewis, Aug. 12, 1942, Hist. Comm., Stevens, Historian, Gen. Corr., Independence Hall Assn., President, 1942–43, RG 13, PA.

410. Comm. on Historical Restoration Minutes, June 20, 1944, Hist. Comm., Cadzow, Ex. Secy. Gen. Corr., 1944–45, Post-War Planning Comm., RG 13, PA.

411. Ibid., July 18, 1944, memos to Dr. Haas.

412. Ibid., Aug. 14, 1944.

413. Nichols, *Commission*, 24.

414. Interview with Stevens.

415. Ibid.

416. Senate Concurrent Resolution, May 27, 1947, Serial No. 124, Hist. and Mus. Comm., Stevens, Historian, Gen. Corr., 1947–51, Joint State Government Commission, RG 13, PA.

417. List of Criteria for Selection of Historical Sites and Buildings, Oct. 1947, ibid.

418. Stevens, form letter to Historical Societies, Oct. 31, 1947, ibid.

419. Cooperative arrangements with PHMC, Oct. 1947, ibid.

420. Melvin to Stevens, Nov. 6, 1947, Hist. and Mus. Comm., Stevens, Historian, Gen. Corr., 1945–49, M, RG 13, PA.

421. Stevens to Wright, Aug. 31, 1948, Hist. and Mus. Comm., Stevens, Historian, Corresp., 1945–50, Ross P. Wright, RG 13, PA.

422. Minutes of Annual Meeting of National Council for Historic Sites and Buildings, Nov. 5, 1948, 60–63, National Trust.

423. Oberlaender Trust to Cadzow, Nov. 1, 1949, Hist. and Mus. Comm., Adm. File, Minutes, 1949, RG 13, PA.

424. PHMC Minutes, Oct. 7, 1948 (1948).

425. Stevens, "Pennsylvania Historical and Museum Commission," *Historic Preservation*, 18 (Nov.-Dec. 1966), 266.

426. *Antiques*, 49 (Jan. 1946), 64; interview with Richard Lawwill, Aug. 12, 1976.

427. Merrill Denison to George McAneny, Oct. 1944, Files of Branch of History, Int.

428. Interview with Clifford L. Lord, Nov. 5, 1969.

429. Coleman, *Historic House Museums*, 31–32.

Chapter 7: *The Federal Government Enters the Field of Historic Preservation, 1926–35*

1. Susan Massie, *Descriptive Guide Book*, inside cover.

2. Horace M. Albright, *Origins of National Park Service Administration of Historic Sites* (Philadelphia, 1971), 9–10.

3. Charles B. Hosmer, Jr., *Presence of the Past: A History of the Preservation Movement in the United States before Williamsburg* (New York, 1965), 64–65.

4. Ibid., 73–74.

5. George J. Olszewski, "House Where Lincoln Died: Furnishing Study," Apr. 15, 1967, 32, 35, Files of Branch of History, U.S. Department of the Interior (Int.).

6. Hosmer, *Presence of the Past*, 145.

7. Gloria Peterson, "An Administrative History of Abraham Lincoln Birthplace National Historic Site," Sept. 20, 1968, 38–39, Division of History, Int.

8. Ronald F. Lee, *Family Tree of the National Park System* (Philadelphia, 1972), 9–20.

9. John D. McDermott, "An Outline of the Development of a National Policy for Historic Preservation," Mar. 1966, 22, Int.

10. Ibid., 23.

11. Ibid., 24.

12. Interview with Roy E. Appleman, Feb. 10, 1971, Archives of National Park Service at Harpers Ferry Center (Harpers Ferry).

13. U.S. Congress, House of Representatives, Committee on Military Affairs, *Commemoration of Certain Military Historic Events, and for Other Purposes*, Report to accompany HR 11489, May 19, 1930 (Washington, D.C., 1930).

14. Ibid., 2–5.

15. Albright, *Origins*, 8.

16. Interview with Appleman, Harpers Ferry.

17. U.S. Cong., House of Rep., Comm. on Library, *Restoration of the Lee Mansion in the Arlington National Cemetery*, Report to accompany H.J. Res. 264, June 3, 1924 (Washington, D.C., 1924).

18. Interview with Louis C. Cramton, Sept. 10, 1962, Harpers Ferry.

19. Ibid.

20. U.S. Cong., Jt. Comm. on Library, *Restoration of Lee Mansion*, on H.J. Res. 264 (Washington, D.C., 1925), 2.

21. Ibid., 2–6.

22. U.S. Cong., H.J. Res. 264, 68th Cong., 2nd Sess., approved Mar. 4, 1925.

23. Report to Quartermaster General, ca. Apr. 18, 1929, Custis-Lee Mansion, Va.

24. Ibid.

25. L. H. Bash to quartermaster supply officer, May 29, 1929, Custis-Lee Mansion, Va.

26. B. F. Cheatham to Mrs. Mark Henderson, Jan. 16, 1930, ibid.

27. Murray Nelligan, "Drawing Room Mantels," Oct. 21, 1952, ibid.

28. *Antiques*, 27 (Jan. 1935), 26–27.

29. Ronald F. Lee, *The Antiquities Act of 1906* (Washington, D.C., 1970), 117.

30. Ibid., 86.

31. Ricardo Torres-Reyes, *Mesa Verde National Park: An Administrative History* (Washington, D.C., 1970), 122, 185, 195, 197.

32. Lee, *Antiquities Act*, 114.

33. Albright to Robert S. Yard, Dec. 20, 1928, quoted in Donald C. Swain, *Wilderness Defender: Horace M. Albright and Conservation* (Chicago, 1970), 181–82.

34. Albright, *Origins*, 2.

35. Interview with Horace M. Albright, Dec. 2, 1969.

36. Ibid.

37. Albright, *Origins*, 4.

38. Ibid., 5.

39. Swain, *Wilderness Defender*, 197–99; interview with Albright.

40. Albright, *Origins*, 6; U.S. Cong., *Joint Resolution to Create a Joint Committee on the Reorganization of the Administrative Branch of Government*, on S.J. Res. 282, Jan. 1924 (Washington, D.C., 1924), 126.

41. Albright, *Origins*, 8–9.

42. Charles Moore to Josephine Rust, Dec. 15, 1927, Wakefield National

Memorial Association (WNMA), Records of Fine Arts Commission (FAC), National Archives (NA), Record Group (RG) 66.

43. Charles E. Hatch, Jr., *Chapters in the History of Popes Creek Plantation* (Washington, D.C., 1968), 109–11.

44. Ibid., 117–18.

45. Ibid., 130–31.

46. Minutes, June 11, 1923, "Wakefield, A Chronological History of the Restoration of the Birthplace of George Washington," WNMA, Cammerer Scrapbook I, Records of FAC, NA, RG 66.

47. Ibid.

48. Moore to James A. O'Connor, June 11, 1925, WNMA, General, Records of FAC, NA, RG 66.

49. O'Connor to Moore, June 15, 1925, ibid.

50. Moore to Lyon G. Tyler, Nov. 10, 1926, WNMA, Business Matters, Records of FAC, NA, RG 66.

51. Hatch, *Chapters*, 140.

52. Charles A. Hoppin to Rust, Jan. 1, 1927, WNMA, Legal, Records of FAC, NA, RG 66.

53. Interview with Albert Erb, July 31, 1970.

54. Edward W. Donn to Rust, July 16, 1927, WNMA, Correspondence Architect, Records of FAC, NA, RG 66.

55. Interview with Erb.

56. Donn to Rust, Aug. 15, 1927, WNMA, Corr. Arch., Records of FAC, NA, RG 66.

57. Moore to Rust, Nov. 7, 1927, WNMA, Gen., Records of FAC, NA, RG 66.

58. Donn to Rust, Nov. 19, 1927, WNMA, Corr. Arch., Records of FAC, NA, RG 66.

59. Moore to Rust, Dec. 15, 1927, WNMA, Gen., Records of FAC, NA, RG 66.

60. Rust to secretary of war, Dec. 22, 1927, ibid.

61. Dwight F. Davis to Rust, Jan. 31, 1926, ibid.

62. "Concrete Proposals by the Wakefield National Memorial Association to the United States Commission for the Celebration of the Two Hundredth Anniversary of the Birth of George Washington," 1927, WNMA, Bicentennial Comm., Records of FAC, NA, RG 66.

63. Fiske Kimball to Moore, Feb. 23, 1928, WNMA, Gen., Records of FAC, NA, RG 66.

64. Hoppin to Rust, Nov. 23, 1928, WNMA, Legal, Records of FAC, NA, RG 66.

65. Kenneth Chorley to Rust, Jan. 11, 1929, ibid.; *New York Times*, Feb. 18, 1929.

66. Moore's draft of a letter, Feb. 2, 1929, WNMA, Gen., Records of FAC, NA, RG 66.

67. *New York Times*, Mar. 8, 1929.

68. Moore to Frederick Law Olmsted, Mar. 5, 1929, WNMA, Gen., Records of FAC, NA, RG 66.

69. Olmsted to Moore, Mar. 18, 1929, WNMA, Fine Arts Comm., Records of FAC, NA, RG 66.

70. Moore to Chorley, Apr. 12, 1929, ibid.

71. Brehon Somervell to Rust, Apr. 13, 1929, George Washington Birthplace (GWB), 620—Buildings, Records of National Park Service (NPS), NA, RG 79.

72. S. O. Bland to Rust, Sept. 12, 1929, WNMA, Gen., Records of FAC, NA, RG 66.

73. Albright to author, Dec. 24, 1970.

74. Rust to John D. Rockefeller, Jr., Dec. 28, 1929, WNMA, Gen., Records of FAC, NA, RG 66.

75. W. A. R. Goodwin to Rust, Dec. 31, 1929, WNMA, History, Records of FAC, NA, RG 66.

76. Hoppin, "How the Size and Character of Washington's Birthplace Were Ascertained," *Tyler's Quarterly Historical and Genealogical Magazine*, 11 (Jan. 1930), 146–62; Hatch, *Chapters*, 142–43.

77. Cramton to Moore, Jan. 3, 1930, WNMA, Gen., Records of FAC, NA, RG 66.

78. Cramton to Rust, Jan. 17, 1930, WNMA, Legislative, Records of FAC, NA, RG 66.

79. S. 1784, 71st Cong., approved Jan. 23, 1930.

80. Patrick J. Hurley to Ray L. Wilbur, Feb. 28, 1930, GWB, 607—Jurisdiction, Records of NPS, NA, RG 79; interview with Albright.

81. Albright to Rust, Jan. 24, 1930, WNMA, Interior Dept., Misc., Records of FAC, NA, RG 66.

82. Albright, Memo, Mar. 10, 1930, GWB, 620—Buildings, Records of NPS, NA, RG 79.

83. Minutes of meeting of WNMA, Apr. 12, 1930, WNMA, Gen., Records of FAC, NA, RG 66.

84. Somervell to Albright, Apr. 21, 1930, GWB, 620—Buildings, Records of NPS, NA, RG 79.

85. Rust to Chorley, May 2, 1930, and Chorley to Rust, May 19, 1930, WNMA, J. D. Rockefeller, Records of FAC, NA, RG 66.

86. Albright to William E. Carson, May 8, 1930, WNMA, Int. Dept., Misc., Records of FAC, NA, RG 66; Edmund S. Campbell to Donn, June 3, 1930, ibid.

87. Chorley to A. E. Demaray, June 10, 1930, GWB, 620—Buildings, Records of NPS, NA, RG 79.

88. Oliver G. Taylor to Rust, June 19, 1930, WNMA, Int. Dept., Misc., Records of FAC, NA, RG 66.

89. Robert Kingery to Demaray, July 3, 1930, GWB, 620—Buildings, Records of NPS, NA, RG 79.

90. Arno B. Cammerer to Taylor, July 17, 1930, ibid.

91. Taylor, report of work for Sept. 1930, WNMA, NPS Reports, Records of FAC, NA, RG 66.

92. Donn, "Wakefield Foundations Uncovered in Oct., 1930," WNMA, Gen., Records of FAC, NA, RG 66.

93. Hatch, *Chapters*, 156.

94. Wat T. Mayo to Rust, Oct. 8, 1930, WNMA, Virginia—Mayo, Records of FAC, NA, RG 66.

95. Rust to Mayo, Oct. 16, 1930, WNMA, Rust Corr., Records of FAC, NA, RG 66.

96. Mayo to Rust, Oct. 17, 1930, WNMA, Va.—Mayo, Records of FAC, NA, RG 66.

97. Taylor to Albright, Oct. 14, 1930, GWB, 207–002.3 Monthly Reports, Records of NPS, NA, RG 79.

98. Albright to Rust, Oct. 22, 1930, WNMA, Corr. FAC, Records of FAC, NA, RG 66.

99. Hoppin to Donn, Oct. 24, 1930, GWB National Monument (NM), 101—History and Legislation, Records of NPS, NA, RG 79.

100. Albright to Cammerer, Oct. 25, 1930, GWBNM, 620—Buildings, Records of NPS, NA, RG 79.

101. Rust and Moore, memo explaining excavations, late Oct. 1930, WNMA, Taylor Corr., Records of FAC, NA, RG 66.

102. Charles E. Peterson to Albright, Oct. 8, 1930, GWBNM, 611—Garden, Records of NPS, NA, RG 79.

103. V. Roswell Ludgate to Albright, Nov. 17, 1930, ibid.

104. Demaray to Albright, Nov. 18, 1930, GWBNM, 620—Buildings, Records of NPS, NA, RG 79.

105. Taylor to Albright, Nov. 20, 1930, ibid.

106. Peterson to Albright, Nov. 21, 1930, ibid.

107. Cammerer to Albright, Nov. 20, 1930, ibid.

108. Rust to Mrs. Anthony W. Cook, Nov. 24, 1930, WNMA, Oregon, Records of FAC, NA, RG 66.

109. "Wakefield National Memorial Association, Inc.," Leaflet, WNMA, Gen., Records of FAC, NA, RG 66.

110. Moore to Frederick Keppel, Dec. 3, 1930, ibid.; Rust to Cook, Feb. 26, 1931, and May 22, 1931, WNMA, Oregon, Records of FAC, NA, RG 66.

111. Ludgate to Albright, Dec. 6, 1930, GWBNM, 620—Buildings, Records of NPS, NA, RG 79.

112. Hoppin, "Was Washington Born in a Cabin?" *Antiques*, 19 (Feb. 1931), 98–101.

113. Henry Woodhouse, "Where Was Washington Born?" *Liberty Magazine*, Feb. 25, 1933, 35.

114. Hoppin to WNMA, Mar. 18, 1931, WNMA, Caemmerer [*sic*] Scrapbook II, Records of FAC, NA, RG 66.

115. Isabelle F. Story, memo, Apr. 4, 1933, GWBNM, Publicity—Woodhouse, Records of NPS, NA, RG 79.

116. Verne E. Chatelain, memo, ca. Apr. 1933, ibid.

117. Hoppin to Albright, ca. Apr. 6, 1931, WNMA, *New York Times*, Records of FAC, NA, RG 66.

118. Rust to Albright, Apr. 7, 1931, ibid.

119. Edwin P. Conquest to Mrs. J. Allison Hodges, Feb. 9, 1931, WNMA, Va., Records of FAC, NA, RG 66.

120. Donn to Albright, Apr. 13, 1931, GWBNM, 101—History and Legislation, Records of NPS, NA, RG 79.

121. Albright to Rust, Apr. 17, 1931, WNMA, Mrs. Rust Corr., Records of FAC, NA, RG 66.

122. Peterson to Albright, Apr. 27, 1931, GWBNM, 611—Garden, Records of NPS, NA, RG 79.

123. Special meeting of WNMA, June 22, 1931, WNMA, Misc., Records of FAC, NA, RG 66.

124. Moore to WNMA, July 16, 1931, WNMA, Publicity, Records of FAC, NA, RG 66.

125. Hodge to Moore, July 21, 1931, WNMA, Corr., Records of FAC, NA, RG 66.

126. Minutes of WNMA, Nov. 30, 1931, WNMA, Gen., Records of FAC, NA, RG 66.

127. Hoppin to Moore, Oct. 28, 1931, ibid.

128. Plaque for Washington Birthplace, WNMA, Reports—Golden Book, Records of FAC, NA, RG 66.

129. Hoppin to Albright, Jan. 29, 1932, WNMA, Gen., Records of FAC, NA, RG 66.

130. Albright, "Progress of the Wakefield Restoration," *Civic Comment*, 37 (Jan.-Feb. 1932), 10–11.

131. Demaray to Philip R. Hough, Jan. 28, 1933, GWBNM, Records of NPS, NA, RG 79.

132. Moore to Albright, Mar. 3, 1932, WNMA, Gen., Records of FAC, NA, RG 66.

133. Hoppin to Wilbur, Sept. 7, 1932, GWBNM, 608—Memorials, Records of NPS, NA, RG 79.

134. Peterson to Taylor, Apr. 15, 1932, GWBNM, 620—Buildings, Records of NPS, NA, RG 79.

135. Taylor to Chatelain, Nov. 1, 1932, GWBNM, 101—Hist. and Legis., Records of NPS, NA, RG 79.

136. Hough to Albright, Mar. 17, 1933, GWBNM, WNMA, Records of NPS, NA, RG 79.

137. Albright (Chatelain) to Caroline Worthington, Apr. 1933, GWBNM, Buildings Gen., Records of NPS, NA, RG 79.

138. Swain, *Wilderness Defender*, 155–56; Albright, *Origins*, 13.

139. Chorley to Goodwin, Mar. 25, 1929, Colonial and Chorley, Goodwin Files, Archives of Colonial Williamsburg Foundation (ACWF); Albright to Chorley, Mar. 27, 1929, quoted in Chatelain, "Origins of the Colonial National

Monument Idea," Jan. 1933, Colonial National Historical Park (NHP), Files of Branch of History, Int.

140. Albright, *Origins*, 13.

141. Interview with Charles E. Peterson, Feb. 9, 1970.

142. Albright to H. J. Eckenrode, Jan. 15, 1933, Colonial NHP, History and Development, Files of Branch of History, Int.

143. Carson to Albright, Mar. 20, 1929, Colonial NHP, 120—Legislation, Records of NPS, NA, RG 79.

144. Albright, *Origins*, 10.

145. *New York Times*, July 30, 1928.

146. Albright to Chorley, Mar. 27, 1929, quoted in Chatelain, "Origins."

147. Albright to Wilbur, Mar. 27, 1929, Colonial NHP, General History, Records of NPS, NA, RG 79.

148. Albright, *Origins*, 14.

149. Ibid.

150. Interview with Horace M. Albright, Dec. 2, 1969.

151. Albright to George Moskey, Dec. 19, 1929, Colonial NHP, 120—Legislation, Records of NPS, NA, RG 79

152. Moskey to Albright, Dec. 27, 1929, ibid.

153. Albright, *Origins*, 10.

154. Interview with Louis C. Cramton, Oct. 20, 1957, Colonial Williamsburg Foundation (CWF).

155. Mrs. J. Taylor Ellyson to Cramton, Feb. 20, 1930, Colonial NHP, 120—Legislation, Records of NPS, NA, RG 79.

156. U.S. Cong., House of Rep., Comm. on Public Lands, *Creating the Colonial National Monument: Hearings on H.R. 8424* (Washington, D.C., 1930), 70–78.

157. Interview with Cramton, CWF.

158. *Richmond News Leader*, Apr. 9, 1930; Cramton to Albright, Apr. 12, 1930, Colonial NHP, 857—Travel, Records of NPS, NA, RG 79.

159. *Richmond Times-Dispatch*, Apr. 9, 1930.

160. U.S. Cong., House Comm. on Public Lands, *Creating Colonial*, 46–48; interview with Cramton, CWF.

161. U.S. Cong., House Comm. on Public Lands, *Creating Colonial*, 10–11.

162. Ibid., 12–15.

163. Ibid., 18, 24.

164. Ibid., 22.

165. Ibid., 26.

166. Ibid., 85.

167. Ibid., 45–46.

168. Albright, *Origins*, 16.

169. Albright to Demaray, June 20, 1930, Colonial, 120—Legislation, Records of NPS, NA, RG 79.

170. Demaray, Taylor, and Herbert Brooks to Albright, July 19, 1930, Colonial, 204.020—Inspections, Records of NPS, NA, RG 79.

171. Eckenrode, memo, July 20, 1930, ibid.

172. Interview with Peterson (Feb. 9, 1970); interview with Charles E. Peterson, Jan. 31, 1971, Harpers Ferry.

173. Interview with Peterson (Feb. 9, 1970); Peterson to Eckenrode, Sept. 20, 1930, Colonial, History General, Records of NPS, NA, RG 79.

174. Cramton to Albright, Nov. 6, 1930, Colonial, 832—Sesquicentennial, Records of NPS, NA, RG 79.

175. Peterson to Albright, Nov. 27, 1930, Colonial, 620—Moore House, Records of NPS, NA, RG 79.

176. Demaray to Peterson, Feb. 2, 1931, ibid.

177. Albright to Chorley, Jan. 9, 1931, ibid.

178. Chorley to Albright, Jan. 10, 1931, ibid.

179. Chorley to Albright, Jan. 22, 1931, ibid.

180. Cammerer to Moskey, May 22, 1931, and Albright to Cammerer, Demaray, and Moskey, June 15, 1931, ibid.

181. Peterson to Albright, Jan. 28, 1931, and May 29, 1931, Colonial, 620—Restoration, Records of NPS, NA, RG 79.

182. Albright to Chorley, Dec. 10, 1930, Colonial, 601—Lands, Records of NPS, NA, RG 79.

183. *Newport News Daily Press*, Jan. 4, 1931.

184. *New York Times*, July 5, 1931.

185. Interview with Elbert Cox, May 9, 1970.

186. Demaray to Eckenrode, Dec. 1, 1930, Colonial, 840—Educational Activities, Records of NPS, NA, RG 79.

187. William M. Robinson to Demaray, Mar. 30, 1931, GWBNHP, 857—Travel, Records of NPS, NA, RG 79; Peterson to H. C. Bryant, April 10, 1931, Colonial NM, 857—Travel, Records of NPS, NA, RG 79.

188. Interview with Cox.

189. Demaray to Robinson, June 25, 1931, Colonial NHP, 201–006—Administration, Records of NPS, NA, RG 79.

190. Taylor to J. Luther Kibler, Colonial NHP, History Gen., Records of NPS, NA, RG 79; Peterson to Albright, May 29, 1931, Colonial NHP, 620—Restoration, Records of NPS, NA, RG 79.

191. Press release, July 14, 1931, Colonial NHP, 501.03—Press Releases, Records of NPS, NA, RG 79.

192. Peterson to Robinson, July 28, 1931, Colonial NHP, History Gen., Records of NPS, NA, RG 79.

193. Interview with Cox.

194. Press Release, Aug. 25, 1931, Colonial NHP, 840—Educational Activities, Records of NPS, NA, RG 79.

195. B. Floyd Flickinger to Robinson, Aug. 30, 1931, ibid.

196. Demaray to Robinson, Sept. 3, 1931, ibid.

197. *New York Times*, Oct. 17, 1931.

198. Ibid., Oct. 25, 1931.

199. Interview with Cox.

200. Ibid.

201. Interview with Albright; Carson to Albright, June 18, 1932, Colonial NHP, 610—Private Holdings, Barney, Records of NPS, NA, RG 79; Albright to Munger, June 3, 1933, Colonial NHP, Land Holdings, Barney, Records of NPS, NA, RG 79.

202. Interview with Cox.

203. Robinson to Demaray, Oct. 26, 1931, Colonial NHP, History Gen., Records of NPS, NA, RG 79.

204. Demaray to Robinson, Oct. 29, 1931, ibid.

205. Chatelain to Albright, Oct. 30, 1931, ibid.

206. Flickinger to Robinson, Nov. 19, 1931, Colonial NHP, 1—Conferences, Records of NPS, NA, RG 79.

207. Peterson to Albright, Nov. 7, 1931, Colonial NHP, 620—Moore House, Records of NPS, NA, RG 79.

208. Chatelain to Albright, Nov. 28, 1931, Colonial NHP, 1—Conferences, Records of NPS, NA, RG 79.

209. Interviews with Peterson, Feb. 9, 1970, Albright, and Cox.

210. Robinson to Albright, Dec. 4, 1931, Colonial NHP, 1—Conferences, Records of NPS, NA, RG 79.

211. Albright to Robinson, Dec. 3, 1931, ibid.

212. Peterson to Robinson, Dec. 15, 1931, Colonial NHP, 620—Moore House, Records of NPS, NA, RG 79; Peterson, Memo, Jan. 22, 1932, ibid.

213. Chatelain, "Origins."

214. Robinson to Albright, June 17, 1932, Colonial NHP, 101—Gen. History, Records of NPS, NA, RG 79.

215. Cramton to Eckenrode, Nov. 28, 1932, ibid.

216. Chatelain to Albright, Mar. 15, 1932, Colonial NHP, 840—Educational Activities, Records of NPS, NA, RG 79.

217. Demaray to Albright, Mar. 16, 1932, ibid.

218. Peterson to Robinson, Apr. 19, 1932, Colonial NHP, 620—Swan Tavern, Records of NPS, NA, RG 79.

219. Robinson to Albright, May 20, 1932, ibid.; interview with Peterson, Feb. 9, 1970.

220. Peterson to Robinson, June 4 and July 23, 1932, Colonial NHP, 620—Moore House, Records of NPS, NA, RG 79.

221. Albright to Chorley, June 8, 1932, and Albright to Goodwin, Oct. 13, 1932, Colonial NHP, 832—Sesquicentennial, Records of NPS, NA, RG 79.

222. Albright to Cammerer and Demaray, July 25, 1932, Colonial NHP, 620—Moore House, Records of NPS, NA, RG 79.

223. Demaray to Albright, July 26, 1932, Colonial NHP, 201.006—Administration, Records of NPS, NA, RG 79.

224. Demaray to Albright, Nov. 15, 1932, Colonial NHP, 832—Sesquicentennial, Records of NPS, NA, RG 79.

225. Peterson to Thomas Vint, Dec. 16, 1932, Colonial NHP, 201—Administration, Records of NPS, NA, RG 79.

226. Interview with Albright.

227. Albright to Robinson, May 18, 1933, Colonial NHP, 620—Swan Tavern, Records of NPS, NA, RG 79.

228. Interview with Cox.

229. Robinson, outline of development, Colonial NM, July 12, 1933, 24, Colonial NHP, development outline, Records of NPS, NA, RG 79.

230. Ibid., 43.

231. Ibid., 211.

232. Demaray to Flickinger, Aug. 2, 1933, and Flickinger to Demaray, Aug. 22, 1933, Colonial NHP, 620—Moore House, Records of NPS, NA, RG 79.

233. Albright, *Origins*, 15–16.

234. Interview with Albright.

235. Albright to author, Jan. 14, 1976.

236. Interview with Albright.

237. Interview with Charles W. Porter III, Apr. 20, 1970.

238. Chatelain, "Recollections of National Park Service Days, 1931 to 1936," author's collection.

239. Interview with Verne E. Chatelain, Sept. 9, 1961; interview with Harold C. Bryant, Oct. 25, 1962, Harpers Ferry.

240. Interviews with Roy E. Appleman, Apr. 15, 1970, and Chatelain.

241. Interviews with Melvin J. Weig, Aug. 1974, and Chatelain.

242. Interviews with George A. Palmer, May 20, 1976, and Chatelain.

243. Interview with Ronald F. Lee, June 29, 1970.

244. Interview with Peterson, Feb. 9, 1970.

245. Interview with Cox.

246. Interview with Peterson, Jan. 31, 1971, Harpers Ferry.

247. Interview with Peterson, Feb. 9, 1970.

248. Chatelain, "Recollections."

249. Interview with Albright.

250. Chatelain, "Recollections."

251. Ibid.

252. Albright to Wilbur, June 17, 1930, Proposed NM, Milburn Home, Buffalo, 0–35, Records of NPS, NA, RG 79.

253. Sol Bloom, *Our Heritage* (New York, 1944), 9–12, 56–200; U.S. George Washington Bicentennial Commission, *News Releases Relating to the Life and Time of George Washington* (Washington, D.C., 1932).

254. Albright, *Origins*, 16.

255. H. C. Bumpus to Albright, Dec. 7, 1931, and Albright to Bumpus, Dec. 8, 1931, General History File, 101, Records of NPS, NA, RG 79.

256. Albright to M. R. Cross, Mar. 31, 1931, and Lloyd W. Smith to Albright, Dec. 31, 1931, Morristown NHP, 101—General, Records of NPS, NA, RG 79.

257. Albright to Cross, Mar. 31, 1931, Morristown NHP, 101—General, Records of NPS, NA, RG 79.

258. *New York Times*, Apr. 12, 1933.

259. U.S. Cong., House Comm. on Public Lands, *Creating the Morristown National Historical Park*, Hearings on H.R. 14302 (Washington, D.C., 1933), 4.

260. Douglas Southall Freeman, *Young Washington* (New York, 1966), 262.

261. U.S. Cong., House Comm. on Public Lands, *Morristown*, 4.

262. Ibid.

263. Smith to Albright, Dec. 31, 1931, Morristown NHP, 101—Gen., Records of NPS, NA, RG 79.

264. Albright to Smith, Jan. 6, 1932, ibid.

265. Chatelain to Albright, Apr. 16, 1932, Morristown NHP, Files of Branch of History, Int.

266. Waldo G. Leland to Albright, Mar. 30, 1932, Morristown NHP, 101—Gen., Records of NPS, NA, RG 79.

267. Leland to Albright, Apr. 25, 1932, ibid.

268. Cammerer to Albright, Apr. 20, 1932, ibid.

269. Interview with Albright.

270. Cammerer to Bryant and Chatelain, Apr. 2, 1932, Morristown NHP, 101—Gen., Records of NPS, NA, RG 79.

271. Chatelain, memo, June 27, 1932, ibid.; Edmund C. Burnett to Chatelain, June 23, 1932, Morristown NHP, Files of Branch of History, Int.

272. Interviews with Cox and Weig.

273. Interview with Chatelain.

274. Clyde Potts to Albright, Oct. 6, 1932, Morristown NHP, 101—Gen., Records of NPS, NA, RG 79.

275. A. Harry Moore to Albright, Oct. 24, 1932, Morristown NHP, Files of Branch of History, Int.

276. Chatelain to Conrad L. Wirth, Nov. 3, 1932, Morristown NHP, 101—Gen., Records of NPS, NA, RG 79.

277. Cramton to Chatelain, Nov. 30, 1932, Morristown NHP, H.R. 14302, S 5469, Records of NPS, NA, RG 79.

278. Potts to Albright, Dec. 5, 1932, ibid.

279. Cramton to Albright, Dec. 5, 1932, Morristown NHP, Files of Branch of History, Int.

280. Potts to Albright, Dec. 30, 1932, Morristown NHP, H.R. 14302, S 5469, Records of NPS, NA, RG 79.

281. Chatelain to Potts, Jan. 14, 1933, ibid.; interview with Albright.

282. Interview with Albright.

283. Chatelain to Potts, Jan. 20, 1933, Morristown NHP, H.R. 14302, S 5469, Records of NPS, NA, RG 79.

284. Albright to Wilbur, Jan. 21, 1933, Morristown NHP, Files of Branch of History, Int.

285. U.S. Cong., House Comm. on Public Lands, *Morristown*, 6–7.

286. Ibid., 14.

287. Ibid., 16–19.

288. Ibid., 24.

289. Chatelain to Albright, Jan. 28, 1933, Morristown NHP, H.R. 14302, S 5469, Records of NPS, NA, RG 79.

290. Chatelain to Albright, Feb. 6, 1933, ibid.

291. Cammerer to Smith, Feb. 24, 1933, ibid.

292. *New York Times*, Mar. 1, 1933.

293. Potts to Chatelain, Mar. 16, 1933, Morristown NHP, 101—Gen., Records of NPS, NA, RG 79.

294. Potts to Albright, Mar. 27, 1933, ibid.

295. Albright to Potts, Mar. 31, 1933, ibid.; interview with Cox.

296. Albright to Harold L. Ickes, Apr. 4, 1933, Morristown NHP, 101—Gen., Records of NPS, NA, RG 79.

297. *New York Times*, July 5, 1933.

298. Interview with Albright.

299. Peterson to Albright, Jan. 15, 1932, Proposed NM, Red Hill, 0–35, Records of NPS, NA, RG 79.

300. Goodwin to Albright, Jan. 23, 1932, ibid.

301. Chatelain to Moskey, Mar. 11, 1932, ibid.; Albright to Wilbur, Mar. 25, 1932, ibid.

302. Dakota Best Brown to Albright, Apr. 1932, Proposed NHS, Washington Town House, Alexandria, 0–36, Records of NPS, NA, RG 79.

303. Chatelain to Albright, May 7, 1932, ibid.

304. Albright to Rockefeller, May 12, 1932, ibid.

305. Chatelain to Albright, Feb. 25, 1932, Proposed NM, Mount Vernon, 0–35, Records of NPS, NA, RG 79.

306. Albright to A. T. Treadway, Mar. 28, 1932, ibid.

307. *Washington Star*, Apr. 5, 1932.

308. *Washington Post*, Apr. 7, 8, 1932.

309. *Washington Star*, Apr. 19, 1932.

310. John Garland Pollard to Wilbur, Apr. 30, 1932, Proposed NM, Mount Vernon, 0–35, Records of NPS, NA, RG 79.

311. Caroline L. Livermore to Wilbur, Feb. 10, 1932, Proposed NM, Stratford, 0–35, Records of NPS, NA, RG 79.

312. Wilbur to Livermore, Mar. 1, 1932, ibid.

313. Chatelain to Albright, Oct. 1932, Proposed NM, Dogue Run Mill, Va., 0–35, Records of NPS, NA, RG 79.

314. Chatelain, memo, Oct. 20, 1932, ibid.

315. Albright, *Origins*, 12–13.

316. Minutes of 12th Conference of National Park Executives, Hot Springs, Ark., April 3–8, 1932, 59–60, Files of Branch of History, Int.

317. Ibid., 61.

318. Wirth, Roger W. Toll, and Chatelain to Albright, Dec. 12, 1932, Files of Branch of History, Int.

319. Chatelain to Demaray, Apr. 21, 1933, General History Branch File, History Branch, Activities, Functions, Organization, Files of Branch of History, Int.

320. Swain, *Wilderness Defender*, 219–20.

321. Ibid., 206–15.

322. Albright to Chorley, May 19, 1933, Horace M. Albright, Kenneth Chorley, Records of NPS, NA, RG 79.

323. Albright, *Origins*, 17.

324. Ibid., 20–21.

325. Harold L. Ickes, *The Secret Diary of Harold L. Ickes: The First Thousand Days, 1933–1936* (New York, 1954), 18–19.

326. Albright to all superintendents and monument custodians, Aug. 9, 1933, Files of Branch of History, Int.

327. Ibid.; Swain, *Wilderness Defender*, 231.

328. Swain, *Wilderness Defender*, 223–24.

329. Interview with Albright.

330. Interview with Chatelain.

331. Ibid.; interview with Peterson, Feb. 9, 1970.

332. Interview with Herbert E. Kahler, Jan. 6, 1971, Harpers Ferry.

333. Interview with Ronald F. Lee, Aug. 17, 1962.

334. Ibid.

335. Interview with Ronald F. Lee, Feb. 1, 1971, Harpers Ferry.

336. Interview with Kahler.

337. Ellen M. Bagby to Cammerer, Jan. 23, 1934, Colonial NHP, Land Holdings—Barney, Records of NPS, NA, RG 79.

338. Interview with Chatelain.

339. Interview with Peterson (Feb. 9, 1970).

340. Malcolm Gardner to Flickinger, Mar. 16, 1934, Colonial NHP, Reports, Records of NPS, NA, RG 79.

341. Ibid.

342. Ibid.

343. Flickinger to Cammerer, Aug. 22, 1933, Colonial NHP, 620—Moore House, Records of NPS, NA, RG 79.

344. Peterson, memo, Aug. 30, 1933, ibid.

345. Flickinger to Demaray, Sept. 27, 1933, Colonial NHP, 620–051—Post Offices, Records of NPS, NA, RG 79.

346. Chatelain and Frank Kittredge, report on Morristown NHP, May 20, 1933, Morristown NHP, Records of NPS, NA, RG 79.

347. Albright (Chatelain) to Fred A. Crane, June 21, 1933, Morristown NHP, 101—Gen., Records of NPS, NA, RG 79.

348. Interview with Cox.

349. Chatelain to Vernon G. Setser, Aug. 24, 1933, Morristown NHP, 101—Gen., Records of NPS, NA, RG 79.

350. Chatelain to Potts, Oct. 10, 1933, ibid.

351. Cammerer (Chatelain) to Ickes, Dec. 9, 1933, Morristown NHP, 618—Public Works, Records of NPS, NA, RG 79.

352. Flickinger to Cammerer, Oct. 7, 26, 1933, Colonial NHP, 620—Hall of Patriots, Records of NPS, NA, RG 79.

353. Flickinger to Cammerer, Oct. 20, 1933, Colonial NHP, 620—Moore House, Records of NPS, NA, RG 79.

354. Flickinger to Cammerer, Nov. 2, 1933, Colonial NHP, 620—Swan Tavern, Records of NPS, NA, RG 79.

355. Peterson to W. W. McCollum, Jan. 11, 1934, Morristown NHP, 620—Guerin and Wick Houses, Records of NPS, NA, RG 79.

356. Flickinger to Cammerer, Nov. 3, 1933, Colonial NHP, 620.051—Post Office, Records of NPS, NA, RG 79.

357. Interview with Cox.

358. Cox to Chatelain, Dec. 30, 1933, Colonial NHP, 620—Swan Tavern, Records of NPS, NA, RG 79.

359. Interview with Peterson, Feb. 9, 1970.

360. Peterson to Flickinger, Feb. 20, 1934, Colonial NHP, 620—Reynolds House, Records of NPS, NA, RG 79.

361. Flickinger to Peterson, Feb. 22, 1934, ibid.

362. Demaray to Flickinger, Aug. 7, 1934, and Flickinger to Demaray, Aug. 10, 1934, ibid.

363. Flickinger to Peterson, Sept. 11, 1934, ibid.

364. Interview with Peterson, Feb. 9, 1970.

365. Flickinger to Peterson, Mar. 17, 1934, Colonial NHP, 620—Swan Tavern, Records of NPS, NA, RG 79.

366. Peterson to Flickinger, Mar. 21, 1934, ibid.

367. Interview with Cox.

368. Flickinger to Peterson, Apr. 4, 1934, Colonial NHP, 620—Buildings Gen., Records of NPS, NA, RG 79.

369. Peterson to Setser, Jan. 19, 1934, Morristown NHP, 620—Guerin and Wick Houses, Records of NPS, NA, RG 79.

370. Grace J. Vogt to Cammerer, Feb. 5, 1934, ibid.

371. *Pencil Points*, 15 (Apr. 1934), 15–16; Setser to Chatelain, Apr. 16, 1934, Morristown NHP, 620–036—Hospitals, Records of NPS, NA, RG 79.

372. Chatelain to Setser, May 24, 1934, Morristown NHP, 620—Guerin and Wick Houses, Records of NPS, NA, RG 79.

373. Interview with Cox; Setser, memo to Chatelain, July 12, 1934, Morristown NHP, Files of Branch of History, Int.

374. Demaray to Cammerer, Mar. 3, 1934, Colonial NHP, Land Holdings, Barney, Records of NPS, NA, RG 79.

375. H. Summerfield Day, Alonzo W. Pond, and Walter S. Flickinger, memo on archaeology at Jamestown, Dec. 15, 1934, Colonial NHP, Files of Branch of History, Int.

376. B. F. Flickinger to Chatelain, Nov. 26, 1934, Colonial NHP, 833—Exhibits Gen., Records of NPS, NA, RG 79.

377. Interview with J. C. and Virginia Harrington, May 18, 1970.

378. A. E. Booth, report, Jan. 7, 1935, Colonial NHP, 885.01—Reports, ECW, Records of NPS, NA, RG 79; Chatelain to Demaray, Feb. 7, 1935, Colonial NHP, 740.02—Archeology, Records of NPS, NA, RG 79.

379. Booth, reports, Apr. 11, Sept. 30, 1935, Colonial NHP, 885.01—Reports, ECW, Records of NPS, NA, RG 79.

380. Ibid., Apr. 11, 1935.

381. B. F. Flickinger to Cammerer, Apr. 29, 1935, Colonial NHP, Buildings Gen., Records of NPS, NA, RG 79.

382. Cammerer to Ickes, Dec. 27, 1935, Colonial NHP, 620—Moore House, Records of NPS, NA, RG 79.

383. Edmund S. Campbell to Cammerer, report, Aug. 20, 1935, ibid.

384. Cammerer to Demaray, Sept. 13, 1935, Colonial NHP, Buildings Gen., Records of NPS, NA, RG 79; Cammerer to Ickes, Dec. 27, 1935, Colonial NHP, 620—Moore House, Records of NPS, NA, RG 79.

385. Edgar G. Fisher to Cammerer, telegram, Apr. 30, 1935, Morristown NHP, 620—Guerin and Wick Houses, Records of NPS, NA, RG 79.

386. Interview with Peterson, Feb. 9, 1970; Gardner and R. Taylor Hoskins to Flickinger, Mar. 9, 1934, Colonial NHP, 840—Educational Activities, Records of NPS, NA, RG 79.

387. Gardner et al. to Flickinger, memo, Apr. 3, 1934, Colonial NHP, Historical Report, Records of NPS, NA, RG 79.

388. Interview with Harringtons.

389. Flickinger to Cammerer, Nov. 7, 1934, Colonial NHP, 620—Buildings, Lightfoot House, Records of NPS, NA, RG 79.

390. Cammerer to Flickinger, Nov. 14, 1934, ibid.

391. Vint to Cammerer, Nov. 3, 1934, Colonial NHP, 620—Moore House, Records of NPS, NA, RG 79.

392. Interviews with Peterson, Feb. 9, 1970, and Weig.

393. Interview with Weig.

394. Interview with Clyde F. Trudell, Aug. 3, 1971.

395. Peterson to Ernest A. Connally, Dec. 9, 1974, copy in author's possession.

396. Leicester B. Holland, "Pictorial Archives of Early American Architecture," *Journal of the American Institute of Architects* (AIA), 2 (June 1930), 7–8.

397. Interview with Peterson, Feb. 9, 1970.

398. Ibid.

399. Peterson to Cammerer, Nov. 13, 1933, reprinted in *Journal of the Society of Architectural Historians* (SAH), 16 (Oct. 1957), 29–31; Peterson, "HABS in and out of Philadelphia," in Richard J. Webster, *Philadelphia Preserved* (Philadelphia, 1976), xxviii-xxxiv.

400. Williamsburg Advisory Comm. to Peterson, telegram, Nov. 16, 1933, Colonial NHP, 620—Restoration, Records of NPS, NA, RG 79.

401. *Journal of the Society of Architectural Historians*, 16 (Oct. 1957), 31.

402. Ibid., 30.

403. Horace Peaslee to Cammerer, Nov. 21, 1933, 1933–35 P, Leicester Holland File, Princeton Photographs Division, Library of Congress (LC).

404. Thomas E. O'Donnell, "Illinois Architecture," *Transactions of the Illinois State Historical Society*, 17th Meeting, May 6–8, 1926, 75–79.

405. Sidney E. Martin, "A Survey of 'Old Philadelphia,'" *Journal of the American Institute of Architects*, 4 (June 1932), 14–15.

406. "A Vote on Historic Buildings," *Journal of the American Institute of Architects*, 5 (Feb. 1933), 15–16.

407. Minutes of Advisory Comm. of Architects, Nov. 16, 1933 (verbatim), Advisory Comm., Minutes of Meetings, 1932–33, Perry, Shaw, and Hepburn Files, ACWF.

408. Ibid.

409. Kimball to William G. Perry, Nov. 22, 1933, 1933–36 P, Holland File, LC.

410. Thomas E. Tallmadge to Perry, Nov. 22, 1933, ibid.

411. W. Duncan Lee to Perry, Nov. 22, 1933, ibid.

412. Robert P. Bellows to Perry, Nov. 23, 1933, ibid.

413. Campbell to Perry, Nov. 24, 1933, ibid.

414. Holland to Frank C. Baldwin, Nov. 25, 1933, Reports and Committee Work, Holland File, LC.

415. Holland to Willard Northrup, Dec. 8, 1933, 1933–36 N, Holland File, LC.

416. *Charleston Evening Post*, Dec. 11, 1933.

417. HABS Circular No. 1, Dec. 12, 1933, Holland File, LC; Albert Simons, "HABS," Feb. 1, 1934, Preservation Society Box (Burton, SPOD), Preservation Society, Charleston, S.C.

418. Simons, "HABS."

419. E. Walter Burkhardt to Holland, Dec. 8, 1933, Holland File, LC.

420. HABS Circular No. 1.

421. Jamieson Parker, "Historic American Buildings Survey," *Oregon Historical Quarterly*, 35 (Mar. 1934), 33.

422. Holland to Walter Hall, Dec. 20, 1933, 1933–36 H, Holland File, LC.

423. Frank Chouteau Brown to William S. Appleton, Dec. 18, 1933, HABS, Society for the Preservation of New England Antiquities (SPNEA).

424. Interview with Richard Koch, June 8, 1971.

425. Interview with Finlay F. Ferguson, July 1, 1973.

426. Kimball to Helen Knox, Dec. 19, 1933, A2–1a/128, Robert E. Lee Memorial Foundation.

427. Earl H. Reed, Jr., to Holland, Dec. 21, 1933, 1933–36 R, Holland File, LC.

428. DeLisle Stewart to Holland, Dec. 23, 1933, 1933–36 C, Holland File, LC.

429. Holland to Stewart, Jan. 30, 1934, ibid.

430. Tallmadge to Perry, Dec. 26, 1933, Advisory Comm., Perry, Shaw, and Hepburn File, ACWF.

431. Perry to Tallmadge, Jan. 3, 1933, ibid.

432. HABS Bulletin No. 10, Jan. 11, 1933, HABS-HQ, Holland File, LC.

433. Holland to Northrup, Jan. 31, 1934, 1933–36 N, Holland File, LC.

434. Burkhardt to Holland, Feb. 1, 1934, 1933–36 B, Holland File, LC.

435. Alexander Carl Guth, "HABS," *Pencil Points*, 15 (June 1934), 271–72.

436. Parker, "HABS," 35.

437. HABS Bulletin No. 24, Feb. 23, 1934.

438. Holland, Harlean James, and Leland to Ickes, Mar. 9, 1934, 1933–36 I, Holland File, LC.

439. Ickes to Holland, Mar. 30, 1934, ibid.

440. Memorandum of agreement between NPS, AIA, and LC, July 23, 1934, File on Agreements, Holland File, LC.

441. Holland to H. I. Brock, Aug. 1, 1934, Reports and Comm. Work, Holland File, LC.

442. "H.A.B.S. Redivivus," *Journal of the American Institute of Architects*, 6 (Nov. 1934), 15–16.

443. Perry to Vint, Oct. 22, 1934, Perry, Shaw, and Hepburn File, Architects' Relief, 1933, CWF.

444. Holland to H. Daland Chandler, Jan. 22, 1935, 1933–36 C, Holland File, LC.

445. Holland to Ernest J. Russell, May 15, 1935, Reports and Comm. Work, Holland File, LC.

446. *Journal of the American Institute of Architects*, 67 (Mar. 1977), 12.

447. Peterson, "Thirty Years of HABS," *Journal of the American Institute of Architects*, 40 (Nov. 1963), 84.

448. Appleton to Brown, Sept. 17, 1934, HABS, SPNEA.

449. Brown to Appleton, Sept. 21, 1934, ibid.

450. Holland et al. to Ickes, Mar. 9, 1934, 1933–36 I, Holland File, LC.

451. *New York Times*, May 13, 1934.

452. I. T. Frary to Vint, Feb. 26, 1934, 1933–36 F, Holland File, LC.

453. Brown to Appleton, Feb. 21, 1935, HABS, SPNEA.

454. Demaray (R. F. Lee) to Fiorello LaGuardia, Nov. 11, 1936, Proposed NHS, New York, 0–36, Records of NPS, NA, RG 79.

455. LaGuardia to Demaray, Dec. 2, 1936, ibid.

456. Press release, Nov. 15, 1936, Dept. of Interior, Buildings Considered, Henry Ford Museum Library.

457. Thomas T. Waterman to John P. O'Neill, Dec. 18, 1936, Proposed NHS, New York, 0–36, Records of NPS, NA, RG 79.

458. Weig to Cammerer, Jan. 4, 1937, ibid.

459. S. F. Voorhees to Franklin D. Roosevelt, Mar. 26, 1937, and Weig to Appleman, Apr. 12, 1937, ibid.

460. Kimball to Demaray, Apr. 18, 1937, ibid.

461. Brown, "'The Old House' at Cutchogue, Long Island, New York," *Old-Time New England*, 31 (July 1940), 11–12.

462. Ibid., 21; clipping, ca. May 1938, Winterthur Museum Archives, Old Houses and Museums, Winterthur, Del.

463. Brown, list of buildings saved and destroyed, Aug. 24, 1936, 1936–37 B, Holland File, LC.

464. A. Lammert to Holland, Aug. 25, 1934, 1933–36 L, Holland File, LC.

465. Gail Seale to LC, July 20, 1937, 1937–38 F, Holland File, LC.

466. Harriet M. Skogh to LC, July 14, 1937, 1937–38 I, Holland File, LC.

467. Joseph H. Booton to LC, May 6, 1938, ibid.

468. John Mead Howells to Holland, Dec. 29, 1937, 1937–38 H, Holland File, LC.

469. John P. O'Neill, ed., *Historic American Buildings Survey* (Washington, D.C., 1938), 245–64.

470. *New York Times*, May 8, 1938.

471. Interview with Chatelain.

472. Ibid.

473. Interview with Albright.

474. Swain, *Wilderness Defender*, 221.

475. Ibid., 222; interview with Albright.

476. Interview with Chatelain.

477. Swain, "Harold Ickes, Horace Albright, and the Hundred Days: A Study in Conservation Administration," *Pacific Historical Review*, 34 (Nov. 1965), 456.

478. Albright, *Origins*, 21; U.S. Cong., House Comm. on Public Lands, *Preservation of Historic American Sites, Buildings, Objects, and Antiquities of National Significance*, Hearings on H.R. 6670 and H.R. 6734 (Washington, D.C., 1935), 12.

479. Interview with Albright.

480. Roosevelt to Gist Blair, Nov. 10, 1933, Rufus Poole File on Historic Sites Act, Files of Branch of History, Int.

481. Ibid.

482. Blair to Roosevelt, Mar. 7, 1934, Poole File, Int.

483. Roosevelt to Ickes, Mar. 10, 1934, ibid.

484. Goodwin to D. M. Bates, Mar. 23, 1934, quoted in General Society of Colonial Wars, *Minutes of the 47th General Council Meeting, April 7, 1934* (Philadelphia, 1934), 12–14.

485. Ibid., 15.

486. Statement of principles, Dec. 18, 1933, National Parks, 1932–36, ACWF.

487. Ickes (Chatelain) to Louis M. Howe, ca. May 14, 1934, ibid.

488. "Criticism of Two Plans," ca. May 14, 1934, ibid.

489. Chatelain to Chorley, May 14, 1934, ibid.

490. Interview with Albright.

491. Harold R. Shurtleff to Chorley, Oct. 6, 1934, Research, General, 1934, ACWF.

492. Interview with J. Thomas Schneider, Sept. 15, 1961.

493. E. K. Burlew to Demaray, Sept. 10, 1934, General Files 12–0, Records of NPS, NA, RG 79.

494. Ickes to Nathan Margold, Sept. 28, 1934, Poole File, Int.

495. Interview with Chatelain, Sept. 9, 1961.

496. Ibid.

497. Ibid.

498. Ibid.

499. Flickinger to Chatelain, Oct. 8, 1934, Activities, Functions and Organization, Gen. Section, Files of Branch of History, Int.

500. Group Conference of Historical and Archeological Superintendents, Nov. 23–24, 1934, 425–433, Colonial NHP, Special File, 01.3 Gen. Conference—History, Records of NPS, NA, RG 79.

501. Ibid., 434.

502. Ibid., 439.

503. Interview with Schneider.

504. Schneider to Appleton, Dec. 13, 1934, U.S. Dept. of Interior, Parks and Shrines, SPNEA.

505. Appleton to Schneider, Dec. 17, 1934, ibid.

506. Carson to Ickes, Dec. 31, 1934, Poole File, Int.

507. Schneider to Ickes, Jan. 25, 1935, Secy. of Interior, Legislation 12–33, NA, RG 48.

508. Burlew to Daniel W. Bell, Jan. 21, 1935, ibid.

509. Chatelain to Cammerer, Feb. 20, 1935, Activities, Functions and Org., Gen. Section, Files of Branch of History, Int.

510. Bryant to Bureau of Budget, Sept. 28, 1933, Cammerer to Public Works Administration, Oct. 31, 1933, and Cammerer to H. M. Kleinknecht, Jan. 30, 1934, Proposed NM, McKinley Homestead, 0–35, Records of NPS, NA, RG 79.

511. Chatelain to Demaray, Oct. 30, 1933, ibid.

512. Demaray to J. Hardin Peterson, Mar. 7, 1935, Proposed NM, Misc., 0–35, Records of NPS, NA, RG 79.

513. McDermott, "An Outline," 36–38.

514. Interview with Chatelain, Sept. 9, 1961.

515. Interview with Lee, June 29, 1970.

516. Richard B. Henderson, *Maury Maverick, a Political Biography* (Austin, 1970), 94.

517. U.S. Cong., House Comm. on Public Lands, *Preservation of Historic American Sites*, 18–25.

518. Ibid., 1–4.

519. Ibid., 5.

520. Ibid., 7.

521. Ibid., 8–13.

522. Ibid., 13–14.

523. Ibid., 14–15.

524. Ibid., 16.

525. Ibid., 17.

526. Ibid., 18–28.

527. Ibid., 31–32.

528. Ibid., 41–42.

529. Ibid., 47–55.

530. Ibid., 53.

531. Ibid., 56–57.

532. Ibid., 57–59.

533. Demaray to Vernon Geddy, Apr. 20, 1935, National Parks, 1932–36, ACWF.

534. General Society of Colonial Wars, *Minutes of the 48th General Council Meeting, May 17, 18, 1935* (Philadelphia, 1935), 26–28.

535. Ickes, *Secret Diary*, I, 385.

536. McDermott, "An Outline," 40.

537. Schneider to Ickes, July 27, 1935, Gen. Files, 12–33, Records of NPS, NA, RG 79.

538. Interview with Schneider.

539. Swain, *Wilderness Defender*, 244–47.

540. Interview with Lee, Aug. 17, 1962.

Chapter 8: *The National Park Service and the New Deal, 1935–41*

1. J. Thomas Schneider, *Report to the Secretary of the Interior on the Preservation of Historic Sites and Buildings* (Washington, D.C., 1935), 142–43.

2. Ibid., 20.

3. Conrad L. Wirth, memo on historic sites legislation, Sept. 30, 1935, Files of Branch of History, Dept. of Interior (Int.)

4. Interview with Ronald F. Lee, Aug. 17, 1962.

5. "Regulations Effective under the Historic Sites Act of August 21, 1935," Files of Branch of History, Int.

6. Interview with Charles E. Peterson, Feb. 9, 1970.

7. Interview with Lee.

8. Ibid.

9. Interview with Ronald F. Lee, Feb. 1, 1971, Archives of National Park Service at Harpers Ferry (Harpers Ferry); interviews with Roy E. Appleman, Apr. 15, 1970, and Thomas M. Pitkin, Dec. 19, 1974.

10. Lee to Civil Service Commission, Oct. 14, 1936, Lee Papers, Harpers Ferry.

11. Interview with J. C. and Virginia Harrington, May 18, 1970.

12. Interview with Appleman.

13. Interview with Herbert E. Kahler, June 19, 1970.

14. Interview with V. Aubrey Neasham, July 26, 1971.

15. Interview with Pitkin.

16. Lee to author, Feb. 18, 1971.

17. Lee, covering letter, Mar. 16, 1936, with Notebook "State Parks Co-operation with the National Park Service," Files of Branch of History, Int.

18. *New York Times*, June 9, 1935.

19. Lee, covering letter.

20. Ibid.

21. Ibid.

22. Ibid.

23. Interview with Kahler.

24. Interview with Charles W. Porter III, Apr. 20, 1970.

25. Group Conference of Historical and Archeological Superintendents, Nov. 23–24, 1934, 433, Colonial National Historical Park (NHP), Special File, 01.3—General Conference History, Records of National Park Service (NPS), National Archives (NA), Record Group (RG) 79.

26. Harold L. Ickes to Henry Ford, Mar. 16, 1935, Acc. 285, Box 1785, Ford Archives, Dearborn, Mich.; A. E. Demaray to Ickes, Mar. 9, 1935, Proposed National Historic Site (NHS), Misc. 0–36, Records of NPS, NA, RG 79.

27. See chapter 2.

28. Edward C. H. Bagley to Ickes, June 24, 1935, Proposed NHS, Misc. 0–36, Records of NPS, NA, RG 79.

29. Arno B. Cammerer to Bagley, July 6, 1935, ibid.

30. John C. Merriam to Cammerer, June 25, 1935, Proposed National Monument (NM), Misc. 0–35, Records of NPS, NA, RG 79.

31. Cammerer to Harold C. Bryant and Wirth, July 2, 1935, ibid.

32. John A. Bryan to Harry Slattery, Aug. 17, 1935, Proposed NHS, Misc. 0–36, Records of NPS, NA, RG 79.

33. Wirth to Regional Officer, Aug. 28, 1935, ibid.

34. Verne E. Chatelain to B. Floyd Flickinger, June 13, 1934, Colonial NHP, History and Legislation, Records of NPS, NA, RG 79.

35. Interview with Edwin W. Small, Aug. 2, 1961.

36. William S. Appleton, Memo, Aug. 8, 1935, WPA, Society for the Preservation of New England Antiquities (SPNEA).

37. Appleton to Small, ca. Aug. 1935, ibid.

38. Small to Appleton, Nov. 15, 1935, U.S. Dept. of Interior, SPNEA.

39. Appleton, letter to members, Nov. 1935, ibid.

40. Small to Appleton, Jan. 11, 1935, ibid.

41. John P. O'Neill to Schneider, Aug. 26, 1935, and attached sheets, Schneider Report, Leicester Holland File, Princeton Photographs Division, Library of Congress (LC).

42. Peterson to Schneider, Aug. 30, 1935, ibid.

43. Stuart M. Barnette to Peterson, Sept. 17, 1935, ibid.

44. Ibid.

45. Letters from Barnette, Charles S. Grossman, Henry C. Forman, Clyde F. Trudell, A. A. Davis, Cornelius Howry, F. D. Nichols, Thomas T. Waterman, O'Neill, Fred P. Parris, William M. Haussmann, Walter G. Peter, Jr., to Peterson, Sept. 17–21, 1935, Holland File, LC.

46. Chatelain, "Archeological and Historic Sites," *American Planning and Civic Annual* (Washington, D.C., 1936), 39–43.

47. Interview with Verne E. Chatelain, Sept. 17, 1971.

48. Ickes to Cammerer, June 11, 1936, General File 12–33, Records of NPS, NA, RG 79.

49. Cammerer to Ickes, July 7, 1936, ibid.

50. "Statement Regarding the Activities in Historical Research of the Branch of Historic Sites and Buildings," ca. July 1936, ibid.

51. Appleman to Lee, Apr. 10, 1936, Hopewell NHS, General 101, Records of NPS, NA, RG 79.

52. Interview with Appleman.

53. Interview with Ronald F. Lee, June 29, 1970.

54. Lee to regional historians, July 16, 1937, Proposed NHS, Misc. 0–36, Records of NPS, NA, RG 79.

55. Charles P. Russell to Cammerer, Jan. 6, 1938, ibid.

56. Statement on historic sites survey, for Bureau of Budget, Nov. 17, 1938, in notebook on Historic Sites and Buildings, Files of Branch of History, Int.

57. Warren K. Moorehead to Ickes, Dec. 21, 1935, Proposed NHS, Misc. 0–36, Records of NPS, NA, RG 79.

58. Supplementary statement on historic sites and buildings, for Bureau of Budget, Nov. 29, 1939, Files of Branch of History, Int.

59. Interview with Pitkin.

60. Neasham, "Jewels of the Spanish Crown," June 1940, in the possession of Neasham.

61. Neasham, "Special Report on 18th and 19th Century Spanish Sites," Mar. 1941, Files of Branch of History, Int.

62. Merriam to Ickes, July 1, 1935, Historic Sites Act, Files of Branch of History, Int.

63. Ickes to Merriam, July 15, 1935, ibid.

64. Minutes of Advisory Board on National Parks, Historic Sites, Buildings and Monuments, Feb. 13–14, 1936, 2, Int.

65. Ibid., 6.

66. Ibid., 9.

67. Ibid., March 26, 1937, 12.

68. Ibid; interviews with Kahler, Neasham, and Porter.

69. Minutes of Advisory Board, Mar. 26, 1937, 12.

70. Interviews with Paul V. Brown, Nov. 9, 1974, and Neasham.

71. Richard Lieber to Demaray, May 25, 1937, Proposed NHS, Misc. 0–36, Records of NPS, NA, RG 79.

72. Lieber to Cammerer, May 25, 1937, ibid.

73. Herbert A. Kellar, "An Early American Gristmill," *Westerners Brand Book* (Chicago Corral), 6 (Mar. 1949), 1–8.

74. Cammerer to Demaray, Wirth, and Branch Spalding, Jan. 10, 1938, Proposed NHS, Misc. 0–36, Records of NPS, NA, RG 79.

75. Interview with Porter.

76. Minutes of Advisory Board, Oct. 28, 1937, 2–3.

77. Fiske Kimball to Hillory A. Tolson, Oct. 7, 1938, Proposed NHS, Missouri, 0–36, Records of NPS, NA, RG 79.

78. Minutes of Advisory Board, Aug. 15–18, 1938.

79. Interview with Porter.

80. Interview with Lee, Aug. 17, 1962.

81. Interview with Porter.

82. Minutes of Advisory Board, Nov. 30–Dec. 2, 1938, 9.

83. Ibid., Nov. 7, 1939, 3.

84. Ibid., 12; Lieber Diary, Nov. 9, 1939, Lilly Library, Bloomington, Ind.

85. Lieber Diary.

86. Interview with Chatelain. For a contrasting view of the events, see Donald Swain, *Wilderness Defender: Horace M. Albright and Conservation* (Chicago, 1970), 249–50.

87. Interview with Chatelain.

88. Interviews with Elbert Cox, May 9, 1970, and Porter.

89. Interviews with Cox and Porter.

90. Swain, *Wilderness Defender*, 249–50; reminiscences of Horace M. Albright, 1962, 565–67, Oral History Research Office, Columbia Univ.

91. Interview with Porter.

92. Ibid.; interview with Ronald F. Lee, Feb. 1, 1971, Harpers Ferry.

93. Interview with Lee, Feb. 1, 1971, Harpers Ferry.

94. Interview with Porter.

95. Interview with Appleman.

96. Interview with Lee, June 29, 1970.

97. Interview with Kahler.

98. Interviews with Appleman and Neasham.

99. [Lee], "Organization and Functions, Branch of Historic Sites and Buildings," ca. 1940, History Branch, Function Report, Files of Branch of History, Int.

100. Interview with Lee, June 29, 1970; Hans Huth, "Observations concerning the Conservation of Monuments in Europe and America" (Washington, D.C., 1940).

101. Huth, "Observations," 10–14.

102. Charles Moore to Mrs. Charles Worthington, Mar. 6, 1935, Wakefield National Memorial Assn. (WNMA), General, Records of Fine Arts Commission (FAC), NA, RG 66.

103. Barnette and Oscar F. Northington, Jr., to Cammerer, June 23, 1936, George Washington Birthplace (GWB) NM, Archeology, Records of NPS, NA, RG 79.

104. H. Summerfield Day, "Report on Committee Inspection of the Archeological Project at George Washington's Birthplace, N.M." Nov. 10, 1936, ibid.

105. Interview with Appleman.

106. Porter, marginal comment on Lee to Newton B. Drury, May 29, 1941, GWBNM, Administration, Records of NPS, NA, RG 79.

107. Philip R. Hough to regional director, Sept. 30, 1941, GWBNM, Conferences—Gen., Records of NPS, NA, RG 79.

108. *Washington Post*, Oct. 26, 1941.

109. Louise Crowninshield to Drury, Nov. 1, 1941, GWBNM, Archeology, Records of NPS, NA, RG 79.

110. Lee to Demaray, Nov. 5, 1941, ibid.

111. Drury to Crowninshield, Nov. 21, 1941, GWBNM, Files of Branch of History, Int.

112. David Rodnick, "Orientation Report on the George Washington Birthplace National Monument," Oct. 17, 1941, 95–99.

113. Ibid., 63.

114. Edmund F. Preece to Branch of Historic Sites, Dec. 17, 1941, GWBNM, Files of Branch of History, Int.; Arthur R. Kelly to Drury, Dec. 30, 1941, ibid.; Appleman to Regional Office, Jan. 5, 1942, GWBNM, Reports Gen., Records of NPS, NA, RG 79.

115. Lee to Drury, Dec. 20, 1941, GWBNM, Reports Gen., Records of NPS, NA, RG 79.

116. Kimball to Lee, Dec. 18, 1941, ibid.

117. Drury to Ickes, Jan. 20, 1942, GWBNM, Files of Branch of History, Int.

118. Hough to Drury, Jan. 7, 1942, GWBNM, Reports Gen., Records of NPS, NA, RG 79.

119. Drury to Lee, Nov. 3, 1941, GWBNM, Archeology, Records of NPS, NA, RG 79; interview with Kahler.

120. Interview with Porter.

121. "Report of First Meeting in the Office of the Superintendent, Colonial National Monument," Mar. 6, 1936, Colonial NHP, Master Plan, Records of NPS, NA, RG 79.

122. A. E. Booth, "Concrete Reproductions," Apr. 21, 1936, Colonial NHP, 885.01—Reports, ECW, Records of NPS, NA, RG 79.

123. Edward M. Riley, "The History of the Development of Colonial National Monument," Apr. 30, 1936, Colonial NHP, History Gen., Records of NPS, NA, RG 79.

124. Peterson, "Some Recent Discoveries at Jamestown," *Antiques*, 29 (May 1936), 192–94.

125. H. R. 5722, 74th Congress, *To Provide for the Addition or Additions of Certain Lands to the Colonial National Monument in the State of Virginia*, approved June 5, 1936.

126. Tolson to E. K. Burlew, June 22, 1936, Colonial NHP, Jamestown investigation, Records of NPS, NA, RG 79.

127. J. C. Harrington, "Job Discussion," Nov. 27, 1936, Colonial NHP, 620–046—Museums, Records of NPS, NA, RG 79.

128. Harrington to Flickinger, Feb. 16, 1937, Colonial NHP, History Gen., Records of NPS, NA, RG 79.

129. Mrs. Julian G. Goodhue to Spalding, Mar. 15, 1937, Colonial NHP, 620—Moore House, Records of NPS, NA, RG 79.

130. Spalding to Demaray, Mar. 20, 1937, ibid.

131. Cammerer to Flickinger, Apr. 17, 1937, ibid.

132. Flickinger to Cammerer, Mar. 22, 1938, ibid.

133. Interview with Roy E. Appleman, Feb. 10, 1971, Harpers Ferry.

134. Ibid.; interview with Harringtons.

135. Interview with Cox.

136. Interview with Pitkin.

137. Appleman to regional director, Aug. 20, 1938, Colonial NHP, 620—Lightfoot House, Records of NPS, NA, RG 79.

138. Harold W. Sorrill to Flickinger, Jan. 27, 1939, Colonial NHP, Buildings Gen., Records of NPS, NA, RG 79.

139. Flickinger to Cammerer, Jan. 30, 1939, ibid.

140. Herbert Evison to Cammerer, Feb. 9, 1939, Colonial NHP, 620—Lightfoot House, Records of NPS, NA, RG 79; interview with Harringtons.

141. Cox to Cammerer, Jan. 31, 1939, and J. C. Harrington to Cox, March 16, 1939, Colonial NHP, Jamestown, Files of Branch of History, Int.

142. Kimball to Lee, Mar. 30, May 22, 1939, Colonial NHP, 870–1–APVA, Records of NPS, NA, RG 79.

143. Kimball to Lee, May 22, 1939, ibid.; interviews with Cox and Harringtons.

144. Interview with Harringtons.

145. Demaray to Ellen H. Smith, Feb. 21, 1940, Colonial NHP, Jamestown, Files of Branch of History, Int.

146. Lee to Demaray, Sept. 23, 1940, Colonial NHP, 870–1–APVA, Records of NPS, NA, RG 79.

147. Albert H. Good, "Architectural Report on the Old Town of Yorktown," Apr. 15, 1940, Colonial NHP, Yorktown Architecture, Files of Branch of History, Int.; Cox to Drury, Dec. 9, 1940, Colonial NHP, 840—Educational Activities, Records of NPS, NA, RG 79.

148. Good, "Architectural Report."

149. Thor Borresen, "A Thesis on Restoration of Field Fortifications," Aug. 21, 1941, Colonial NHP, Files of Branch of History, Int.

150. Interview with Melvin J. Weig, Aug. 1974.

151. Interview with Cox.

152. Interview with Weig.

153. Ibid.

154. Ibid.

155. Ibid.

156. Ibid.

157. Interviews with Weig and Cox.

158. Interview with Cox.

159. Cox to Peterson, Oct. 26, 1935, Morristown NHP, 620—Guerin and Wick Houses, Records of NPS, NA, RG 79.

160. Thomas Vint to Cox, Oct. 30, 1935, ibid.

161. Clyde Potts to Demaray, Nov. 15, 1935, and Cox to Cammerer, Nov. 27, 1935, Morristown NHP, 620—Fenner House, Records of NPS, NA, RG 79.

162. Chatelain to Cox, Mar. 10, 1936, ibid.

163. Chatelain to Demaray, Dec. 7, 1935, ibid.; Waterman to Vint, Dec. 24, 1935, ibid.

164. Vernon G. Setser and Lloyd W. Biebigheiser, "Report on the Furnishing of the Wick House," May 1936, Morristown NHP, 620—Wick House, Records of NPS, NA, RG 79.

165. Cox to Vint, May 18, 1936, Morristown NHP, 620—Guerin and Wick Houses, Records of NPS, NA, RG 79.

166. *Morristown Daily Record*, Aug. 6, 1936.

167. Borresen, "Fort Nonsense's Historical Record," Aug. 1936, Morristown NHP, Files of Branch of History, Int.

168. Cox to Cammerer, Nov. 25, 1936, Morristown NHP, 620—Guerin and Wick Houses, Records of NPS, NA, RG 79.

169. Cox to Cammerer, Jan. 15, 1937, and Cox to Vint, Oct. 11, 1937, ibid.

170. Cox, Report on dedications, Jan. 25, 1937, ibid.; Cox to Cammerer, Feb. 11, 1938, Morristown NHP, 833.05—Museums, Records of NPS, NA, RG 79.

171. Cox, "Policy Governing the Furnishings of Washington's Headquarters," May 18, 1938, Morristown NHP, 620—Guerin and Wick Houses, Records of NPS, NA, RG 79.

172. Lee to Cammerer, Jan. 21, 1939, Morristown NHP, 620—Buildings Gen., Records of NPS, NA, RG 79.

173. Ibid.

174. Weig, "Documentary Justification for the Restoration of Washington's Headquarters," Feb. 2, 1939, ibid.

175. Waterman, "Architectural Justification for the Restoration of Washington's Headquarters," Feb. 25, 1939, Files of Branch of History, Int.

176. Waterman, "Justification for the Reconstruction of the Main Stair, Washington's Headquarters," May 1939, Morristown NHP, 620—Buildings Gen., Records of NPS, NA, RG 79.

177. Interview with Porter.

178. *Biographical Directory of the American Congress, 1774–1971* (Washington, D.C., 1971), 952.

179. Eula May Burke to Ickes, Oct. 26, 1933, and Joel L. Flood to Cammerer, Feb. 3, 1934, Appomattox Courthouse (CH) NHP, Gen., Records of NPS, NA, RG 79.

180. Burke to Ickes, Oct. 26, 1933, ibid.

181. Moore to L. H. Bash, Oct. 6, 1931, ibid.

182. Ibid.

183. Bash to Moore, Oct. 7, 1931, Appomattox CHNHP, Gen., Records of NPS, NA, RG 79.

184. *Pencil Points*, 13 (Apr. 1932), 279–81.

185. Moore to Bash, Oct. 13, 1932, Appomattox CH Memorial, Records of FAC, NA, RG 66.

186. Patrick J. Hurley to Moore, Nov. 17, 1932, ibid.

187. U.S. Cong., House Comm. on Public Lands, *Creating the Morristown National Historical Park*, Hearings on H.R. 14302 (Washington, D.C., 1933), 24.

188. Interview with Horace M. Albright, Dec. 2, 1969.

189. Interview with Chatelain.

190. *New York Times*, Mar. 4, 1934.

191. Flood to Cammerer, July 5, 1935, Appomattox CHNHP, Gen., Records of NPS, NA, RG 79.

192. Press release, Aug. 29, 1935, ibid.

193. Demaray to Douglas S. Freeman, Nov. 21, 1935, ibid.

194. J. P. Andrews to Cammerer, June 27, 1936, and Spalding to Andrews, Nov. 3, 1936, ibid.

195. P. C. Hubard to Cammerer, Jan. 20, 1937, ibid.

196. Porter, supplementary report on Appomattox CH, Va., July 21, 1937, Files of Branch of History, Int.

197. Ralph Happel, report, Sept. 1940, in possession of Happel; J. Edgar Hoover to Drury, Sept. 20, 1940, Files of Branch of History, Int.

198. Porter, supp. report.

199. Lee (Porter) to William G. Carnes, Oct. 22, 1938, Appomattox CHNHP, Gen., Records of NPS, NA, RG 79.

200. Spalding to Cammerer, Sept. 5, 1939, ibid.

201. Francis S. Ronalds (Porter) to Spalding, Sept. 13, 1939, ibid.

202. Cammerer to Flood, Nov. 17, 1939, and Demaray to Flood, Dec. 29, 1939, ibid.

203. Vint and Lee to Cammerer, Jan. 12, 1940, ibid.

204. Interview with Porter.

205. Lee to Cammerer, Feb. 29, 1940, Appomattox CHNHP, Gen., Records of NPS, NA, RG 79.

206. Appleman, memo, July 29, 1940, Appomattox CHNHP, Reports, Records of NPS, NA, RG 79.

207. Ned Burns to Russell, Oct. 16, 1940, Appomattox CHNHP, Conferences, Records of NPS, NA, RG 79.

208. Happel, "McLean House Study," Dec. 1940, Files of Branch of History, Int.

209. Happel, Preston Holder, and Ray Julian, "Collaborative Justification for Reconstruction of the McLean House at Appomattox," Mar. 18, 1942, ibid.; interview with Appleman.

210. Demaray to Hubert Gurney, Oct. 22, 1941, Appomattox CHNHP, McLean House, Records of NPS, NA, RG 79.

211. Appleman, memorandum, July 29, 1940, Appomattox CHNHP, Reports, Records of NPS, NA, RG 79.

212. Interview with Peterson.

213. Paul Simpson McElroy, *The Story of the Gateway Arch* (St. Louis, 1968), 4–5.

214. Dickson Terry, "A Monument to Thirty Years of Patience, Perseverance, and Determination," *Cherry Diamond* (Sept. 1964), 26–27.

215. Ibid., 31.

216. Merrill D. Peterson, *The Jefferson Image in the American Mind* (New York, 1962), 420–30.

217. Public Resolution No. 32, 73d Congress, S.J. Res. 93, Approved June 15, 1934.

218. Minutes of meeting of U.S. Territorial Expansion Memorial Commission (TEMC), Dec. 19, 1934, 5, Files of Branch of History, Int.

219. Ibid., 4–5.

220. *Thomas Jefferson and the Pioneers to Whom We Owe Our National Expansion* (St. Louis, ca. 1934), drawing by LeBaume.

221. Minutes of TEMC, Dec. 19, 1934, 8.

222. Ibid., 10.

223. Ibid., 12–13.

224. Ibid., 14–15.

225. Ibid., 30–31.

226. Ibid., Feb. 1, 1935, 60.

227. Ibid., 63.

228. *St. Louis Globe-Democrat*, Feb. 8, 1935.

229. *Thomas Jefferson and the Pioneers*.

230. Terry, "Monument," 33.

231. John L. Nagle, "Report on United States Territorial Expansion Memorial at St. Louis," Aug. 20, 1935, Jefferson National Expansion Memorial (JNEM), 0–35 Proposed, Records of NPS, NA, RG 79.

232. Newspaper advertisement, ca. Aug. 1935.

233. *St. Louis Globe-Democrat*, ca. Aug. 1935.

234. Luther Ely Smith to Cammerer, telegram, Sept. 10, 1935, JNEM, 0–35 Proposed, Records of NPS, NA, RG 79.

235. Memo on JNEM, mid-Sept. 1935, ibid.; Terry, "Monument," 33–34.

236. Cammerer (Nagle) to Ickes, Nov. 15, 1935, JNEM, 0–35 Proposed, Records of NPS, NA, RG 79.

237. *St. Louis Globe-Democrat*, June 8–9, 1964.

238. Ibid.; Paul W. Ward, "Washington Weekly," *Nation* (Mar. 4, 1936), 267–68.

239. Harold L. Ickes, *The Secret Diary of Harold L. Ickes: The First Thousand Days, 1933–1936* (New York, 1954), I, 489.

240. Ickes to Franklin D. Roosevelt, Dec. 20, 1935, Files of Branch of History, Int.

241. Executive Order, Dec. 21, 1935; Alvin Stauffer and Pitkin, "Historical Problems Raised by the Executive Order Authorizing the Jefferson National Expansion Memorial, St. Louis," Apr. 1939, Files of Branch of History, Int.

242. Executive Order, Dec. 21, 1935.

243. *Christian Science Monitor*, Dec. 23, 1935; Terry, "Monument," 35–37.

244. Terry, "Monument," 35–37; *St. Louis Post-Dispatch*, Jan. 28, 1936; interview with Irving Dilliard, Dec. 28, 1972.

245. Demaray to Ickes, Nov. 17, 1937, JNEM, 0–35 Gen., Records of NPS, NA, RG 79.

246. Terry, "Monument," 37.

247. *St. Louis Globe-Democrat*, Jan. 21, 1936.

248. Interviews with Kahler and Peterson.

249. Demaray to Burlew, Feb. 19, 1936, JNEM, 0–35 Proposed, Records of NPS, NA, RG 79.

250. Ward, "Washington Weekly," 267–68.

251. Interview with Peterson.

252. Interviews with John A. Bryan, Aug. 25, 1969, and Peterson.

253. Interview with Peterson.

254. Interviews with Charles van Ravenswaay, July 9, 1973, Peterson, and Dilliard.

255. Peterson to Vint, July 16, 1936, JNEM, 0–35 Gen., Records of NPS, NA, RG 79.

256. Peterson to Demaray, July 13, 1936, ibid.

257. Peterson to Albright, Aug. 3, 1936, ibid.

258. Peterson, "A Museum of American Architecture," Aug. 13, 1936, ibid.; Peterson, "A Museum of American Architecture," *Journal of American Institute of Architects*, 8 (Nov. 1936), 3–7.

259. Peterson to Demaray, Sept. 29, 1936, Peterson to Nagle, Oct. 1, 1936 and May 11, 1937, and Nagle to Demaray, May 12, 1937, JNEM, 0–35 Gen., Records of NPS, NA, RG 79.

260. Interview with Ralph H. Lewis, Dec. 16, 1969.

261. Interviews with Lewis and Pitkin; Burns to Peterson, Feb. 11, 1937, JNEM, 0–35 Gen., Records of NPS, NA, RG 79.

262. Interview with Pitkin.

263. *St. Louis Post-Dispatch*, Mar. 30, 1937.

264. Ibid., Oct. 8, 1937.

265. Ibid., July 28, 1937.

266. Ibid., July 29, 1937.

267. Bryant and Burns to Nagle, July 30, 1937, JNEM, 0–35 Gen., Records of NPS, NA, RG 79.

268. Cammerer to Burlew, Jan. 5, 1938, ibid.

269. John C. Ewers to Burns, Feb. 19, 1938, JNEM, 833.05 Museums, Records of NPS, NA, RG 79; interview with Pitkin.

270. Pitkin to Nagle, Mar. 14, 1938, Files of Branch of History, Int.

271. Ibid., March 24, 1938.

272. Interview with Pitkin.

273. Pitkin, "Suggestions for the Participation of the Branch of Historic Sites and Buildings in the Development of the Jefferson National Expansion Memorial," Aug. 7, 1937, Files of Branch of History, Int.

274. Chatelain to Demaray, Aug. 12, 1936, JNEM, 0–35 Gen., Records of NPS, NA, RG 79.

275. Hermon C. Bumpus, Herbert E. Bolton, and Archibald McCrea to Cammerer, Sept. 2, 1937, and McCrea to Cammerer, Sept. 8, 1937, ibid.

276. Minutes of Advisory Board, Oct. 28–29, 1937, ibid.

277. Interview with Dilliard.

278. Demaray to Ickes, May 11, 1938, Files of Branch of History, Int.

279. "The Nature of the Jefferson National Expansion Memorial," draft, Jan. 24, 1939, and covering letter from Daniel Fahey, Pitkin, and Peterson to Nagle, Jan. 25, 1939, ibid.

280. Lee to Demaray, Mar. 1, 1939, ibid.

281. Nagle, memo, May 6, 1939, JNEM, 0–35 Gen., Records of NPS, NA, RG 79.

282. Terry, "Monument," 39.

283. *Kansas City Star*, Oct. 28, 1939.

284. Sigfried Giedion, *Space, Time and Architecture* (Cambridge, 1967), 201.

285. Lee to Demaray, Nov. 4, 1939, Files of Branch of History, Int.

286. Harry Slattery to Bernard F. Dickmann, July 31, 1937, JNEM, 0–35 Gen., Records of NPS, NA, RG 79.

287. Nagle to Cammerer, Aug. 25, 1937, ibid.

288. Nagle to Cammerer, Oct. 1, 1937, JNEM, 833.05 Museum, Records of NPS, NA, RG 79.

289. Pitkin, Peterson, and Fahey to Nagle, Nov. 30, 1937, JNEM, 0–35 Gen., Records of NPS, NA, RG 79.

290. George A. Moskey to Cammerer, Feb. 24, 1938, ibid.

291. Cammerer to Ickes, Mar. 1, 1938, ibid.

292. Dickmann to Cammerer, Apr. 26, 1938, ibid.

293. Nagle to Cammerer, Sept. 8, 1939, JNEM, 620 Courthouse, Records of NPS, NA, RG 79.

294. Burlew to Advisory Board, Nov. 8, 1939, JNEM, 0–35 Gen., Records of NPS, NA, RG 79.

295. Bumpus to Burlew, Nov. 10, 1939, Files of Branch of History, Int.

296. Minutes of Advisory Board, Nov. 8, 1939, 11, ibid.

297. Waldo G. Leland to Ickes, Feb. 14, 1939, JNEM, 0–35 Gen., Records of NPS, NA, RG 79.

298. Ickes to Roosevelt, Nov. 10, 1939, Files of Branch of History, Int.

299. Nagle to Cammerer, Nov. 13, 1939, JNEM, 0–35 Gen., Records of NPS, NA, RG 79.

300. Demaray to Ickes, Nov. 24, 1939, Files of Branch of History, Int.

301. A. J. Wirtz (Lee) to Dickmann, Jan. 23, 1940, JNEM, 620 Courthouse, Records of NPS, NA, RG 79.

302. Interview with van Ravenswaay.

303. Ickes to Roosevelt, Mar. 4, 1940, Files of Branch of History, Int.

304. Demaray to regional director, Nov. 8, 1940, JNEM, 620 Courthouse, Records of NPS, NA, RG 79.

305. Lewis, "Temporary Museum Outline," Feb. 11, 1941, JNEM, 618 WPA, Records of NPS, NA, RG 79.

306. Peterson to Julian Spotts, Mar. 3, 1941, JNEM, 620 Courthouse, Records of NPS, NA, RG 79.

307. Spotts to Drury, Mar. 4, 1941, ibid.

308. Kahler to Drury, Mar. 14, 1941, and Vint to Drury, Mar. 17, 1941, Files of Branch of History, Int.

309. Henry E. Rice, Jr., "Results of Exploratory Work at the Old Rock House," Sept. 7, 1940, JNEM, 620 Rock House, Records of NPS, NA, RG 79.

310. Burns to Nagle, Sept. 19, 1940, JNEM, 620 Buildings, Records of NPS, NA, RG 79.

311. Lee to Nagle, Sept, 19, 1940, Files of Branch of History, Int.

312. Peterson and Bryan, "Recommendations concerning the National-Scott's Hotel and a Sketch of Its History," Aug. 1937, JNEM, 0–35 Gen., Records of NPS, NA, RG 79.

313. McCune Gill to Dickmann, Nov. 9, 1939, JNEM, 620 Buildings, Records of NPS, NA, RG 79.

314. Nagle to Gill, Nov. 17, 1939, ibid.

315. Interview with van Ravenswaay.

316. Fahey to Cammerer, Nov. 14, 1939, JNEM, 620 Buildings, Records of NPS, NA, RG 79.

317. Nagle to Cammerer, Aug. 3, 1940, JNEM, 01 Conferences, Records of NPS, NA, RG 79.

318. Peterson to Nagle, Aug. 9, 1940, JNEM, 620 Custom House, Records of NPS, NA, RG 79.

319. Nagle, memo, Aug. 14, 1940, Files of Branch of History, Int.

320. Peterson to Nagle, Nov. 20, 1940, JNEM, 620 Custom House, Records of NPS, NA, RG 79.

321. Spotts to Drury, Nov. 20, 1940, ibid.

322. Drury to Demaray, Dec. 13, 1940, ibid.

323. Perry T. Rathbone to Spotts, Jan. 17, 1941, ibid.

324. *St. Louis Post-Dispatch*, Jan. 24, 1941.

325. Lee to Drury, Feb. 4, 1941, Files of Branch of History, Int.

326. Peterson to Spotts, June 23, 1941, JNEM, 620 Buildings Gen., Records of NPS, NA, RG 79.

327. Demaray (Porter) to Spotts, July 7, 1941, Files of Branch of History, Int.

328. *Salem Maritime National Historic Site*, leaflet, Int., 1940.

329. Henry W. Belknap, "Derby Wharf Preservation Fund," Oct. 15, 1928, and Belknap to Appleton, Oct. 22, 1928, Mass.—Salem, Derby Wharf, SPNEA; Harlan P. Kelsey to Cammerer, Mar. 11, 1935, Salem Maritime (SM) NHS, 0–36 Gen., Records of NPS, NA, RG 79; Chatelain, "Derby Wharf National Historic Site," Jan. 29, 1936, Files of Branch of History, Int.

330. Small to author, July 20, 1970; Kelsey to Albright, Jan. 5, 1931, Colonial NHP, 204.020 Inspections, Records of NPS, NA, RG 79.

331. Small to author, July 20, 1970.

332. Kelsey, "Can Salem Live on Its Past?" speech to the Club, Feb. 5, 1935, SMNHS, 0–36 Gen., Records of NPS, NA, RG 79.

333. Kelsey to Cammerer, Mar. 11, 1935, ibid.

334. Cammerer to Kelsey, Mar. 26, 1935, ibid.

335. Kelsey to Cammerer, Mar. 28, 1935, ibid.

336. A. Piatt Andrew to Kelsey, Apr. 8, 1935, ibid.

337. Chatelain to Cammerer, Apr. 16, 1935, and Chatelain to Demaray, Apr. 22, 1935, ibid.

338. Demaray to Cammerer, Apr. 18, 1935, ibid.

339. Cammerer to Chatelain, Apr. 20, 1935, ibid.

340. Cammerer to Andrew, Apr. 23, 1935, ibid.

341. Cammerer to Kelsey, Aug. 15, 1935, ibid.

342. Kelsey to William C. Endicott, Apr. 30, 1935, Mass.—Salem, Derby Wharf, SPNEA.

343. Demaray to George J. Bates, May 20, 1935, SMNHS, 0–36 Gen., Records of NPS, NA, RG 79.

344. Appleton to Endicott, Aug. 14, 1935, ibid.

345. Kelsey to Oliver G. Taylor, Sept. 14, 1935, ibid.

346. Kelsey to Vint, Oct. 10, 1935, ibid.

347. Chatelain to Cammerer, Oct. 31, 1935, ibid.

348. Small to author, July 20, 1970.

349. Mass., House Bill No. 142, Jan. 1936, Richard Derby, SPNEA.

350. Cammerer to Ickes, Dec. 5, 1935, SMNHS, 0–36 Gen., Records of NPS, NA, RG 79.

351. Kelsey to Appleton, Dec. 27, 1935, Richard Derby, SPNEA.

352. Appleton to Endicott, Dec. 28, 1935, ibid.

353. Crowninshield to Appleton, Jan. 11, 1936, ibid.

354. Chatelain, "Derby Wharf."

355. Kelsey to Appleton, Feb. 26, 1936, Mass.—Salem, Derby Wharf, SPNEA.

356. Appleton to Henry P. Benson, June 16, 1936, Richard Derby, SPNEA.

357. Stephen B. Gibbons to Ickes, June 27, 1936, Files of Branch of History, Int.

358. Small to Chatelain, July 1, 1936, ibid.

359. Small to Chatelain, July 22, 1936, and Taylor and Dudley C. Bayliss to Cammerer, July 23, 1936, ibid.

360. Kelsey to Cammerer, Aug. 5, 1936, SMNHS, 0–36 Gen., Records of NPS, NA, RG 79.

361. Donald Corley to Small, Sept. 10, 1936, and Oscar S. Bray to J. H. Peterson, Sept. 22, 1936, Files of Branch of History, Int.

362. Small, report, Nov. 6, 1936, SMNHS, 0–36 Gen., Records of NPS, NA, RG 79.

363. Lee to Cammerer, Jan. 18, 1937, Files of Branch of History, Int.

364. Cox to Vint, Apr. 12, 1937, and Barnette to Spalding and Vint, July 15, 1937, ibid.

365. Cammerer to Bates, Aug. 10, 1937, ibid.

366. Barnette to Spalding, Aug. 25, 1937, ibid.

367. Small to Cox, Aug. 27, 1937, SMNHS, 0–36 Gen., Records of NPS, NA, RG 79.

368. Small to Cammerer, Jan. 31, 1938, ibid.

369. Cox to Cammerer, Feb. 3, 1938, Files of Branch of History, Int.

370. Small to Cammerer, Nov. 1, 1938, SMNHS, 0–36 Gen., Records of NPS, NA, RG 79.

371. Small to Cox, Dec. 1, 1938, Files of Branch of History, Int.

372. Frank Chouteau Brown to Barnette, Dec. 6, 1939, SMNHS, 620 Buildings Gen., Records of NPS, NA, RG 79.

373. Small to Cammerer, June 21, 1940, ibid.

374. Cammerer to Ickes, Dec. 5, 1935, SMNHS, 0–36 Gen., Records of NPS, NA, RG 79.

375. Small to author, July 20, 1970.

376. Small to Appleton, Nov. 11, 1937, U.S. Dept. of Interior, National Park Service, SPNEA.

377. Small to Bates, Nov. 15, 1938, Proposed NHS, Morgan 0–36, Records of NPS, NA, RG 79.

378. Small to author, July 20, 1970.

379. Small to Kahler, Oct. 31, 1939, SMNHS, 833 Exhibits, Records of NPS, NA, RG 79.

380. Kelsey to John R. White, Jan. 14, 1942, SMNHS, 0–36 Gen., Records of NPS, NA, RG 79.

381. Small to author, July 20, 1970.

382. Interview with E. Florence Addison, Oct. 24, 1969.

383. Interview with Lee, June 29, 1970.

384. Lee, "Inspection Report on French Creek Submarginal Land Project," May 29, 1935, Hopewell Village (HV) NHS, 101, Records of NPS, NA, RG 79.

385. Ibid.

386. Appleman to Melvin B. Borgeson, Aug. 12, 1935, HVNHS, 101, Records of NPS, NA, RG 79.

387. Interview with Appleman, Apr. 15, 1970.

388. Appleman, "Proposed Restoration Plan for Old Iron Making Village, French Creek Project," Jan. 15, 1936, Files of Branch of History, Int.

389. Ibid.

390. Lee to Wirth and Chatelain, Jan. 23, 1936, HVNHS, 101, Records of NPS, NA, RG 79.

391. Appleman to Lee, May 13, 1936, ibid.

392. Interview with Weig.

393. Jackson Kemper to Arthur C. Sylvester, Nov. 19, 1936, HVNHS, 101, Records of NPS, NA, RG 79.

394. Kemper to Sylvester, Dec. 16, 1936, ibid.

395. Demaray to Ickes, Feb. 17, 1937, ibid.

396. Spalding (Appleman) to Cammerer, Dec. 22, 1937, ibid.

397. Lee to Demaray, Sept. 14, 1938, ibid.

398. Appleman to regional director, Apr. 12, 1938, and Weig to Cox, May 3, 1938, ibid.

399. Interview with Weig; Borresen, "Report on Visit to Hopewell Village National Historic Site," Oct. 15–17, 1940, HVNHS, 740.02 Archeology, Records of NPS, NA, RG 79.

400. Appleman to regional director, Mar. 18, 1939, HVNHS, 101, Records of NPS, NA, RG 79.

401. Weig, Borresen, John C. F. Motz, and Lemuel A. Garrison to regional director, Apr. 11, 1940, ibid.; interview with Weig.

402. Cammerer to Ickes, Jan. 13, 1936, Proposed NHS, Misc. 0–36, Records of NPS, NA, RG 79.

403. Park W. T. Loy to Chatelain, Feb. 28, 1936, John J. Cornwell to Wirth, Mar. 10, 1936, and mimeographed letter on Harpers Ferry, Mar. 9, 1936, Proposed NHS, Harpers Ferry, 0–36, Records of NPS, NA, RG 79.

404. Clipping, Feb. 18, 1937, ibid.

405. Ibid.

406. Lee to Wirth, Aug. 4, 1937, Proposed NHS, Harpers Ferry, 0–36, Records of NPS, NA, RG 79.

407. *Baltimore Sun*, Feb. 18, 1938, ibid.

408. Henry T. McDonald to Lee, July 22, 1938, ibid.

409. Appleman to Lee, Sept. 19, 1938, ibid.

410. Demaray to Jennings Randolph, Oct. 12, 1938, ibid.

411. White to Randolph, Aug. 4, 1939, ibid.

412. Wirtz to Morris Sheppard, Sept. 27, 1940, ibid.

413. Interview with Merrill J. Mattes, Sept. 14, 1962, Harpers Ferry.

414. J. G. Masters to Chatelain, Mar. 4, 1932, Ft. Laramie, Gen., Records of NPS, NA, RG 79.

415. *Wyoming State Tribune*, Sept. 14, 1932.

416. George E. Brimmer to Albright, Sept. 17, 1932, Ft. Laramie, Gen., Records of NPS, NA, RG 79.

417. Masters to Chatelain, Feb. 1, 1935, and H. J. Dollinger to Chatelain, Feb. 2, 1935, ibid.

418. Dollinger to Chatelain, Feb. 14, May 6, 31, 1935, ibid.

419. C. M. Gates, report, July 8, 13, 1935, Ft. Laramie, Reports, Records of NPS, NA, RG 79.

420. Gates to Regional Office, July 27, 1935, ibid.; *New York Times*, Sept. 27, 1936.

421. H. H. Schwartz to Demaray, Jan. 22, 1937, Ft. Laramie, Gen., Records of NPS, NA, RG 79.

422. Donald B. Alexander to Demaray, Feb. 1, 1937, ibid.

423. Interview with Brown.

424. Alexander to Demaray, Feb. 6, 1937, Ft. Laramie, Gen., Records of NPS, NA, RG 79.

425. Demaray to Alexander, radiogram, Feb. 4, 1937, ibid.

426. Edward A. Hummel, Feb. 18, 1937, ibid.

427. Olaf T. Hagen to Spalding, Mar. 11, 1937, ibid.

428. Dan Greenburg to Cammerer, Mar. 29, 1937, ibid.

429. Cammerer to Ickes, July 24, 1937, ibid.

430. Hummel to Cammerer, June 11, 1937, Proposed NM, Wyoming, 0–35, Records of NPS, NA, RG 79.

431. Greenburg to Cammerer, Dec. 14, 1938, ibid.

432. Demaray to Greenburg, Dec. 30, 1938, ibid.

433. Minutes of Advisory Board, Mar. 26, 1937, appendix, Files of Branch of History, Int.

434. Lee to Spalding, Jan. 5, 1938, Ft. Laramie NHS, Gen., Records of NPS, NA, RG 79.

435. Brown to Cammerer, Jan. 17, 1938, ibid.

436. Hummel, memo, May 15, 1938, ibid.

437. Thomas E. Whitecraft to Cammerer, June 24, 1938, ibid.

438. G. Hubert Smith, report, Aug. 22–Sept. 29, 1938, ibid.

439. Lee to Cammerer, Mar. 27, 1939, ibid.

440. Wilfred G. Hill, report, June 29–30, 1941, Ft. Laramie NHS, Reports, Records of NPS, NA, RG 79.

441. Interview with Neasham.

442. Tolson to acting regional director, Nov. 21, 1939, and Cammerer to John J. Dempsey, Dec. 15, 1939, Proposed NM, Ft. Union, 0–35, Records of NPS, NA, RG 79.

443. Tolson to regional director, Oct. 23, 1940, ibid.

444. E. B. Wheeler to Tolson, Nov. 26, 1940, and Feb. 19, 1941, ibid.

445. Tolson to author, Oct. 4, 1971.

446. Ethel S. Swanstrom to Ickes, Apr. 18, 1935, Proposed NM, Misc., 0–35, Records of NPS, NA, RG 79.

447. Jesse S. Douglas, report on Fort Simcoe, Aug. 12, 1935, ibid.

448. Interview with Lee, June 29, 1970.

449. Swanstrom to Cammerer, Jan. 9, 1937, Proposed NM, Ft. Simcoe, 0–35, Records of NPS, NA, RG 79.

450. William Zimmerman to Cammerer, June 13, 1938, ibid.

451. Lee to regional director, Sept. 13, 1938, ibid.

452. Hagen, report to regional director, Oct. 4, 1938, ibid.

453. Frank Kittredge to Swanstrom, Mar. 8, 1940, ibid.

454. Hagen to M. A. Johnson, Mar. 5, 1941, ibid.

455. James MacGregor Burns, *Roosevelt: The Soldier of Freedom* (New York, 1970), 199–200; *New York Times*, Feb. 6, 1940.

456. *New York Times*, Feb. 6, 1940.

457. White to Ickes, Oct. 4, 1939, Vanderbilt Mansion (VM) NHS, 0–36, Records of NPS, NA, RG 79.

458. Interview with Lee, June 29, 1970.

459. White to Ickes, Oct. 4, 1939, VMNHS, 0–36, Records of NPS, NA, RG 79.

460. Cammerer to Ickes, Oct. 5, 1939, ibid.

461. F. L. Cook and Ronalds to Cammerer, Oct. 24, 1939, ibid.

462. Roosevelt to Daisy Van Alen, Nov. 1, 1939, ibid.

463. Roosevelt to Ickes, Nov. 9, 1939, ibid.

464. William G. Murphy to Ronalds, Oct. 31, 1939, ibid.

465. Minutes of Advisory Board, Nov. 7, 1939, 6–7.

466. Roosevelt to Van Alen, Nov. 14, 1939, VMNHS, 0–36, Records of NPS, NA, RG 79.

467. Ickes to Van Alen, Nov. 17, 1939, ibid.

468. Roosevelt to Van Alen, Nov. 17, 1939, ibid.

469. Roosevelt to Ickes, May 17, 1939, Proposed NM, Ft. Union, 0–35, Records of NPS, NA, RG 79.

470. Ickes to Murphy, Nov. 28, 1939, VMNHS, 0–36, Records of NPS, NA, RG 79.

471. Lee and Cook to Cammerer, Dec. 4, 1939, ibid.

472. *New York Times*, Aug. 17, 1940.

473. Cammerer to Ickes, Mar. 6, 1940, VMNHS, 0–35, Records of NPS, NA, RG 79.

474. Cammerer to Ickes, Apr. 6, 1940, VM, Secy. of Int., NA, RG 48.

475. Roosevelt to Ickes, May 3, 1940, ibid.

476. Roosevelt to Ickes, May 13, 1940, ibid.

477. Ickes to Roosevelt, May 14, 1940, ibid.

478. Alfred F. Hopkins to Lewis, June 25, 1940, VMNHS, Records of NPS, NA, RG 79.

479. Weig, report on official travel, July 16–Aug. 22, 1940, VMNHS, 207 Reports, Records of NPS, NA, RG 79.

480. Interview with Weig.

481. Ibid.; Burns, *Roosevelt*, 199.

482. Burlew to Demaray, July 2, 1940, VMNHS, 0–36, Records of NPS, NA, RG 79; H. K. Roberts to Cammerer, July 26, 1940, ibid.

483. Roosevelt to Burlew, Aug. 12, 1940, Secy. of Int., 12–42 VM, NA, RG 48.

484. Interview with Weig.

485. Weig, report on official travel.

486. Drury to Ickes, Dec. 9, 1940, Secy. of Int., 12–42 VM, NA, RG 48.

487. "You Can't Give Them Away," *Saturday Evening Post*, Nov. 30, 1940, 39.

488. Ickes to R. D. W. Connor, July 14, 1941, Home of Franklin D. Roosevelt, NHS, 0–36, Records of NPS, NA, RG 79.

489. Minutes of Advisory Board, Oct. 28, 1937, 4–5, and Nov. 7, 1939, 6.

490. Demaray (Lee) to Frederic A. Delano, Nov. 27, 1937, Proposed NHS, DC, 0–36, Records of NPS, NA, RG 79.

491. Myrta Ethel Cawood to Bumpus, Dec. 28, 1937, ibid.; B. Houston McCeney to Mrs. Truxton Beale, Jan. 7, 1938, Beale Papers, National Trust (NT).

492. W. A. R. Goodwin to Roosevelt, May 30, 1938, Proposed NHS, DC, 0–36, Records of NPS, NA, RG 79.

493. Kimball to Advisory Board, Jan. 1938, ibid.

494. Ronalds to Cammerer, May 4, 1938, Proposed NHS, Blair House, 0–36, Records of NPS, NA, RG 79.

495. *Washington Times-Herald*, May 5, 1938.

496. Beale to Ickes, May 6, 1938, Proposed NHS, DC, 0–36, Records of NPS, NA, RG 79.

497. Robert W. Bliss to Cammerer, June 7, 1938, ibid.

498. Memo to Waggaman about Decatur House, ca. July 1938, ibid.

499. Melvin C. Hazen to Harold D. Smith, June 13, 1939, and Burlew to Beale, Dec. 8, 1939, ibid.

500. Beale to Edith Nourse Rogers, June 11, 1941, Beale Papers, NT.

501. Roosevelt to Gist Blair, Nov. 10, 1933, Rufus Poole File on Historic Sites Act, Files of Branch of History, Int.

502. Interview with Lee, June 29, 1970.

503. Percy Blair to Ickes, May 7, 20, 1942, Proposed NHS, Blair House, 0–36, Records of NPS, NA, RG 79.

504. Ickes to Roosevelt, June 5, 1942, ibid.

505. Roosevelt to Ickes, Aug. 28, 1942, ibid.

506. Roosevelt to Cordell Hull, Aug. 28, 1942, ibid.

507. Peterson to Vint, Mar. 9, 1940, Proposed NM, Uncle Sam Plantation, 0–35, Records of NPS, NA, RG 79.

508. Vint to Cammerer, Mar. 11, 1940, ibid.

509. Cammerer to Robert G. Lovett, telegram, Mar. 12, 1940, ibid.

510. W. F. Tompkins to Cammerer, telegram, Mar. 13, 1940, ibid.

511. Minutes of Advisory Board, Oct. 28, 1937, 3.

512. Hermann Hagedorn to Ickes, Oct. 6, 1941, Files of Branch of History, Int.

513. Ickes to Hagedorn, Dec. 27, 1941, ibid.

514. Hagedorn to Ickes, Jan. 5, 1942, Proposed NHS, New York, 0–36, Records of NPS, NA, RG 79.

515. *Burlington* (Vt.) *Daily News*, Oct. 3, 1935.

516. Lorenzo F. Hagglund, *A Page from the Past* (Lake George, N.Y., 1949), 30.

517. Hagglund, "The Continental Gondola *Philadelphia*," U.S. Naval Institute *Proceedings*, 65 (1936), 665–69.

518. Roosevelt to Ickes, Sept. 15, 1937, Proposed NHS, "Philadelphia" Sloop, 0–36, Records of NPS, NA, RG 79.

519. Ickes to Cammerer, Sept. 20, 1937, ibid.

520. Spalding to Cox, Oct. 7, 1937, Salem Maritime NHS, 0–36, Gen., Records of NPS, NA, RG 79.

521. Cox to Cammerer, Oct. 22, 1937, Proposed NHS, "Phila." Sloop, 0–36, Records of NPS, NA, RG 79.

522. Minutes of Advisory Board, Oct. 28, 1937, 6.

523. Small to Cox, Oct. 22, 1937, Proposed NHS, "Phila." Sloop, 0–36, Records of NPS, NA, RG 79.

524. Cox to Cammerer, Dec. 14, 1937, ibid.

525. Demaray to Ickes, Dec. 29, 1937, ibid.

526. Cox to Cammerer, Mar. 3, 1938, ibid.

527. Curtis B. Norris, "The Gundalow of Valcour Bay," *Yankee* (Sept. 1966), 164–65.

528. Interview with Lee, June 29, 1970.

529. Maury Maverick to Wirth, Jan. 14, 1935. San Jose Mission (SJM) NHS, Records of NPS, NA, RG 79.

530. Evison to Maverick, Jan. 15, 1935, ibid.

531. Maverick to Ickes, Jan. 23, 1935, ibid.

532. Chatelain to Cammerer, Jan. 30, 1935, ibid.

533. Maverick to Ickes, Feb. 25, 1935, ibid.

534. *Congressional Record*, 74th Cong., 1 Sess., 12737 (Aug. 8, 1935).

535. Maverick to Albright, June 28, 1935, SA-JO, Harpers Ferry.

536. Ibid., July 10, 1935.

537. Maverick to Chatelain, Sept. 17, 1935, SJM, Files of Branch of History, Int.

538. Hagen to Chatelain, Sept. 19, 1935, ibid.

539. Maverick to Ickes, Sept. 20, 1935, SJMNHS, Records of NPS, NA, RG 79.

540. Herbert Maier to Evison, Sept. 21, 1935, SJM, Files of Branch of History, Int.

541. George Nason to Maier, Sept. 25, 1935, ibid.

542. Demaray to Maverick, Sept. 26, 1935, ibid.

543. Lee to Wirth and Chatelain, Sept. 30, 1935, ibid.

544. Clipping from San Antonio newspaper, Oct. 22, 1935, ibid.

545. Lee, "Report on Proposed Relationship of the National Park Service to San Jose Mission," Nov. 14, 1935, ibid.

546. Maverick to Demaray, Oct. 2, 1935, ibid.

547. Demaray to Ickes, Dec. 31, 1935, ibid.

548. Maier to Chatelain, Apr. 28, 1936, ibid.

549. Maverick to Ickes, telegram, July 7, 1936, SJMNHS, Records of NPS, NA, RG 79.

550. Advisory Board minutes, May 8, 1936, quoted in Ickes to Maverick, July 13, 1936, ibid.

551. Maverick to Ickes, July 31, 1936, ibid.

552. *San Antonio Light*, Aug. 9, 1936.

553. T. A. Walters to Maverick, Aug. 13, 1936, Files of Branch of History, Int.

554. William R. Hogan to Maier, Aug. 25, 1936, Proposed NHS, Texas, 0–36, Records of NPS, NA, RG 79.

555. See chapter 6.

556. Lee, "Report on Historical Significance of Old Main Building, Knox College, Galesburg, Illinois," Dec. 5, 1935, Proposed NHS, Old Main, 0–36, Records of NPS, NA, RG 79.

557. Demaray to Ickes, June 4, 1936, ibid.

558. Cammerer to Ickes, Mar. 2, 1937, ibid.

559. Donald B. Littrell to Regional Office, Mar. 20, 1936, and Pitkin, "Report of Inspection of Old Main," Mar. 21, 1937, ibid.

560. Ibid.

561. Carter Davidson to Demaray, Apr. 12, 1937, Proposed NHS, Old Main, 0–36, Records of NPS, NA, RG 79.

562. Interview with Lee, June 29, 1970.

563. Lee, "Report on Old Main."

564. Ruth Rose Richardson to James W. Mott, Feb. 20, 1936, Proposed NHS, Oregon, 0–36, Records of NPS, NA, RG 79.

565. Burt Brown Barker to Ickes, Mar. 21, 1936, ibid.

566. Hagen to Chatelain, Apr. 26, 1936, ibid.

567. Creed C. Hammond to Ickes, May 14, 1936, Eva Emery Dye to Ickes, May 16, 1936, and Charles H. Martin to Ickes, May 20, 1936, ibid.

568. Demaray to McCrea, May 11, 1937, ibid.

569. Mott to McCrea, May 29, 1937, ibid.

570. S. Tripp to Cammerer, July 14, 1937, ibid.

571. Minutes of Advisory Board, Oct. 28, 1937, 4.

572. O'Neill to Lee, Dec. 6, 1938, Proposed NHS, Oregon, 0–36, Records of NPS, NA, RG 79.

573. *McLoughlin House National Historic Site*, leaflet, 1966.

574. Ralston B. Lattimore to regional director, Oct. 30, 1939, Proposed NHS, Owens-Thomas House, 0–36, Records of NPS, NA, RG 79.

575. Minutes of Advisory Board, Nov. 7, 1939, 12.

576. Lee to Edmund H. Abrahams, Nov. 17, 1939, Proposed NHS, Owens-Thomas House, 0–36, Records of NPS, NA, RG 79.

577. Lattimore to Cammerer, Nov. 27, 1939, ibid.

578. Ickes to Roosevelt, Dec. 22, 1939, ibid.

579. Roosevelt to Ickes, Apr. 4, 1940, ibid.

580. Lattimore, report on Owens-Thomas House, May 1, 1940, ibid.

581. Kelly to Demaray, Oct. 13, 1939, Proposed NHS, New Mexico, 0–36, Records of NPS, NA, RG 79.

582. Tolson to Sophia Aberle, Nov. 28, 1939, ibid.

583. Aberle to Jesse Nusbaum, Aug. 31, 1940, ibid.

584. Erik Reed to regional director, Sept. 11, 1941, ibid.

585. Hobart S. Cooper to Daniel T. Blaney, June 22, 1936, Proposed NHS, Tennessee, 0–36, Records of NPS, NA, RG 79.

586. Cooper to Chatelain, Sept. 4, 1936, ibid.

587. C. L. Johnson to Spalding, Sept. 25, 1936, ibid.

588. Appleman to Lee, Oct. 13, 1936, ibid.

589. Johnson to Spalding, Oct. 21, 1936, ibid.

590. Appleman to Cammerer, Mar. 11, 1938, ibid.

591. Cammerer to G. E. Texter, Apr. 8, 1938, ibid.

592. Fred Manley to Earle Draper, May 31, 1938, ibid.

593. Kelly to W. T. N. Lewis, Mar. 31, Apr. 6, 1939, ibid.

594. Father Mark to Isabella Greenway, May 6, 1934, Proposed NM, San Xavier Mission, 0–35, Records of NPS, NA, RG 79.

595. Greenway to Cammerer, Feb. 13, 1935, ibid.

596. Herman Kahn, report on San Xavier del Bac, ca. Dec. 1934, ibid.

597. Slattery to Henry F. Ashurst, Nov. 30, 1937, ibid.

598. J. H. Haile to Mark, Jan. 20, 1938, ibid.

599. Cammerer to Bumpus, Feb. 10, 1938, ibid.

600. Bolton to Bumpus, Feb. 28, 1938, ibid.

601. Kimball to Bumpus, Mar. 12, 1938, ibid.

602. Lieber to Bumpus, Mar. 15, 1938, ibid.

603. Cammerer (Lee) to Ickes, Mar. 29, 1938, ibid.

604. L. Cabot Briggs to Neasham, May 11, 1941, ibid.

605. George W. Chambers to Neasham, July 17, 1941, ibid.

606. Demaray to Briggs, Oct. 20, 1941, ibid.

607. Briggs to Demaray, Oct. 22, 1941, ibid.

608. Drury to Briggs, Nov. 3, 1941, ibid.

609. Briggs to Drury, Nov. 7, 1941, ibid.

610. Tripp to Drury, Aug. 2, 1941, ibid.

611. Preece to Nusbaum, Jan. 17, 1942, ibid.

612. *Arizona Daily Star* (Tucson), July 5, 1942.

613. Chambers to author, Oct. 17, 1970.

614. Interview with Lee, June 29, 1970.

615. Charles B. Hosmer, Jr., *Presence of the Past: A History of the Preservation Movement in the United States before Williamsburg* (New York, 1965), 30–31.

616. *Philadelphia Evening Ledger*, Jan. 17, 1935.

617. Demaray to George E. Nitzche, Feb. 23, 1935, Files of Branch of History, Int.

618. Lee to Nagle, Feb. 6, 1939, ibid.

619. Ibid.

620. Lee to Struthers Burt, Feb. 9, 1939, Files of Branch of History, Int.

621. Burt to Lee, ca. Feb. 1939, ibid.

622. Demaray to Kimball, Dec. 13, 1940, ibid.

623. Kimball to Demaray, Dec. 19, 1940, Proposed NM, Misc. 0–35, Records of NPS, NA, RG 79.

624. Wirtz, to E. E. Lamberton, Mar. 5, 1941, ibid.

625. Lee, Memorandum, Apr. 23, 1941, Files of Branch of History, Int.

626. Lee to Howard W. Murphey, June 3, 1941, ibid.

627. Lee to Drury, June 7, 1941, ibid.

628. Lee to Bernard Samuel, Dec. 12, 1941, ibid.

629. Demaray to William E. Carson, Mar. 20, 1936, Proposed NM, Carpenters Hall, 0–35, Records of NPS, NA, RG 79.

630. Chatelain to Cammerer, Apr. 9, 1936, ibid.

631. Kimball to Cammerer, telegram, Jan. 21, 1938, Files of Branch of History, Int.

632. Minutes of a meeting, Jan. 24, 1938, Historical Commission, Philadelphia Office, Melvin Chairman, Cadzow, RG 13, Pennsylvania Archives.

633. Spalding to Cammerer, Jan. 24, 1938, Old Philadelphia Custom House (CH) NHS, Gen., Records of NPS, NA, RG 79.

634. Lee to Spalding, Jan. 24, 1938, ibid.

635. Ickes (Lee) to Christian J. Peoples, Feb. 2, 1938, ibid.

636. Alvin P. Stauffer, "The Old Custom House in Philadelphia," Feb. 14, 1938, Files of Branch of History, Int.

637. Lee to Cammerer, Feb. 18, 1938, Old Phila. CHNHS, Gen., Records of NPS, NA, RG 79.

638. Cammerer to Ickes, Mar. 15, 1938, ibid.

639. Demaray to Bolton, telegram, Mar. 25, 1938, ibid.

640. Barnette, "An Architectural History and Evaluation of the Second Bank of the United States," ca. Mar. 1938, Files of Branch of History, Int.

641. Cammerer (Lee) to Kimball, Apr. 18, 1938, Old Phila. CHNHS, Gen., Records of NPS, NA, RG 79.

642. Wilbur K. Thomas to Cammerer, Apr. 26, 1938, ibid.

643. H. E. Joilinz to Ickes, Sept. 19, 1938, ibid.

644. Thomas to Demaray, Nov. 7, 1938, ibid.

645. Cammerer to acting secy. of int., Nov. 30, 1938, and Demaray to under secy., Dec. 21, 1938, ibid.

646. Slattery to Peoples, Jan. 13, 1939, Files of Branch of History, Int.

647. Interview with Lee, June 29, 1970.

648. Charles E. Beury to Burlew, Feb. 17, 1939, Old Phila. CHNHS, Gen., Records of NPS, NA, RG 79.

649. Charles A. Ford to Burlew, Feb. 17, 1939, ibid.

650. Kimball to Cammerer, Mar. 16, 1939, ibid.

651. Demaray, memorandum for the files, Mar. 28, 1939, Files of Branch of History, Int.

652. Peoples to Ickes, May 8, 1939, Old Phila. CHNHS, Records of NPS, NA, RG 79.

653. Lee to Demaray, May 27, 1939, Files of Branch of History, Int.

654. Barnette to Vint, May 20, 1939, ibid.

655. Dick Sutton to Vint, June 21, 1939, ibid.

656. Press release, July 18, 1939, Old Phila. CHNHS, Gen., Records of NPS, NA, RG 79.

657. Beury to Ickes, July 29, 1939, ibid.

658. Thomas to Ickes, Aug. 9, 1939, Files of Branch of History, Int.

659. Virginius Dabney to Ickes, Aug. 12, 1939, Old Phila. CHNHS, Gen., Records of NPS, NA, RG 79.

660. Lee to Cammerer, Sept. 20, 1939, ibid.

661. Cammerer to Ickes, Sept. 2, 1939, Files of Branch of History, Int.

662. Wirth to Demaray, Nov. 2, 1939, ibid.

663. Demaray to Thomas, Nov. 9, 1939, ibid.

664. Memorandum of agreement between Int. and Carl Schurz Memorial Foundation, Dec. 18, 1939, ibid.

665. Thomas to Burns, Oct. 30, 1940, Old Phila. CHNHS, Gen., Records of NPS, NA, RG 79.

666. Thomas to Demaray, Dec. 26, 1940, ibid.

667. Drury (Lee) to Thomas, Dec. 6, 1941, ibid.

668. Robert Caro, *The Power Broker* (New York, 1974), 654.

669. Interview with Lee, June 29, 1970.

670. Minutes of Pre-organization Meeting, Sept. 28, 1939, Federal Hall Memorial Associates, Notebook, Files of Branch of History, Int.

671. Ibid.

672. Interview with Lee, June 29, 1970; *The Memorial Meeting in Honor of George McAneny*, Dec. 10, 1953 (New York, 1953), 15–17; Minutes of Board, Federal Hall Memorial Associates, Feb. 8, 1940, Fed. Hall Mem. Assoc., Notebook, Files of Branch of History, Int.

673. Interview with Neasham.

Chapter 9: *The Federal Program and the War Years, 1941–49*

1. Franklin D. Roosevelt to Harold L. Ickes, Mar. 28, 1942, Proposed National Historic Site (NHS), St. Francis Xavier, 0–36, Records of National Park Service (NPS), National Archives (NA), Record Group (RG) 79.

2. Ibid.

3. Robert Shankland, *Steve Mather of the National Parks* (New York, 1954), 306–7; Melvin J. Weig to author, Jan. 8, 1975; interviews with Roy E. Appleman, Apr. 15, 1970, and Newton B. Drury, July 28, 1971.

4. Charles W. Porter III, ed., "National Park Service War Work," 1946, 44–45, Files of Branch of History, Dept. of Interior (Int.)

5. Ronald F. Lee to Charles E. Peterson, Apr. 14, 1970, copy in author's possession.

6. Interview with Charles W. Porter III, Apr. 20, 1970.

7. Interviews with Herbert E. Kahler, June 19, 1970, Drury, and Porter.

8. Minutes of Advisory Board, May 22–23, 1942, quoted in Porter, "War Work," 45.

9. Interview with Drury.

10. Interview with Ronald F. Lee, June 29, 1970.

11. Interview with Drury.

12. Interview with Drury and Herbert Evison, 1965, "The National Park Service and the Civilian Conservation Corps," Regional Oral History Office, Univ. of Calif., Berkeley.

13. Interview with Porter.

14. Porter, "War Work," 29–30.

15. Ibid., 30–35.

16. Lee to Drury, June 4, 1947, Files of Branch of History, Int.

17. Ibid.

18. Elbert Cox to Stanley Pargellis, Apr. 24, 1946, Colonial National Historical Park (NHP), Special File, 1 Conferences, Records of NPS, NA, RG 79; interviews with J. C. and Virginia Harrington, May 18, 1970, and Mar. 15, 1971, Archives of NPS at Harpers Ferry Center (Harpers Ferry).

19. Porter to Drury, July 13, 1945, Files of Branch of History, Int.

20. Kenneth Chorley to Schuyler Otis Bland, June 3, 1948, Colonial NHP, Development Outline, Records of NPS, NA, RG 79.

21. Drury to Bland, July 19, 1948, ibid.

22. A. R. Kelly, memo for Drury, Aug. 3, 1944, Salem Maritime (SM) NHS, 207.02–3, Superintendent's Reports, Records of NPS, NA, RG 79; Edwin W. Small to author, July 20, 1970.

23. Ned J. Burns to regional director, Dec. 20, 1945, Files of Branch of History, Int.

24. Thomas J. Allen to Drury, Mar. 22, 1946, SMNHS, 833.05 Museums, Records of NPS, NA, RG 79.

25. Hillory A. Tolson to regional director, July 7, 1948, SMNHS, 901 Privileges, Records of NPS, NA, RG 79.

26. Small to author July 20, 1970.

27. Kahler, Sept. 27, 1944, Ft. Laramie National Monument (NM), Master Plan, Records of NPS, NA, RG 79.

28. Priority list of research projects at Fort Laramie, 1944, Files of Branch of History, Int.

29. Monthly narrative report, Aug. 10, 1945, Ft. Laramie NM, Monthly Narrative Report, Records of NPS, NA, RG 79.

30. Dabney Otis Collins, "Shrine of the West," *Rocky Mountain Empire Magazine, Denver Post*, May 15, 1949.

31. Porter to Drury, Aug. 28, 1944, Files of Branch of History, Int.

32. Ickes to Mrs. V. G. Simkhovitch, June 25, 1945, Secretary of Int. 12–42, Vanderbilt Mansion, NA, RG 48.

33. Frank D. Quinn to M. R. Tillotson, Apr. 26, 1943, San Jose Mission, Records of NPS, NA, RG 79.

34. Tillotson to Quinn, May 20, 1943, ibid.

35. Erik Reed to regional director, Nov. 18, 1946, ibid.

36. Reed, report for 1946–47, Apr. 30, 1947, ibid.

37. Reed to Mrs. Lane Taylor, Jan. 25, 1949, ibid.

38. Howard Elkinton to A. E. Demaray, June 6, 1947, Old Philadelphia Custom House (CH) NHS, General, Records of NPS, NA, RG 79.

39. Ibid.

40. Drury to Julius Krug, Apr. 27, 1948, Old Phila. CHNHS, Gen., Records of NPS, NA, RG 79.

41. Harry M. Edelstein to Oscar Chapman, May 23, 1949, ibid.

42. Ralph Lewis to Burns, Nov. 16, 1942, Files of Branch of History, Int.

43. Ibid.; Burns to Drury, Jan. 20, 1945, Jefferson National Expansion Memorial (JNEM), JNEM Assn. 871, Records of NPS, NA, RG 79.

44. Kahler to Drury, June 8, 1944, Files of Branch of History, Int.

45. Porter, "The Purpose and Theme of the Jefferson National Expansion Memorial," Nov. 27, 1944, ibid.

46. Kahler to Drury, Jan. 20, 1945, ibid.

47. Drury to regional director, Oct. 17, 1945, ibid.

48. Drury to Julian Spotts, Jan. 5, 1946, JNEM, Gen. 0–35, Records of NPS, NA, RG 79.

49. Drury to Luther E. Smith, Feb. 26, 1946, ibid.

50. Drury to Smith, July 13, 1946, JNEM, Memorials 608, Records of NPS, NA, RG 79.

51. Ibid.

52. Drury to Krug, Apr. 11, 1947, JNEM, Memorials 608, Records of NPS, NA, RG 79.

53. *Architectural Competition for the Jefferson National Expansion Memorial* (St. Louis, 1947), 16.

54. Ibid.

55. *St. Louis Post-Dispatch*, Aug. 24, 1947.

56. Charles P. Russell, W. G. Carnes, and Lee to Drury, Oct. 24, 1947, JNEM, Memorials 608, Records of NPS, NA, RG 79.

57. *New York Times*, Feb. 19, 1948.

58. "A Tour of the Proposed Jefferson National Expansion Memorial on the Mississippi River at St. Louis," JNEM, Reports 207.02, Records of NPS, NA, RG 79.

59. Spotts to regional director, Aug. 25, 1948, JNEM, Memorials 608, Records of NPS, NA, RG 79.

60. Drury to Krug, May 27, 1948, Files of Branch of History, Int.

61. Drury to Krug, Jan. 19, 1949, ibid.

62. Krug to Joseph M. Darst, Aug. 12, 1949, ibid.

63. "Memorandum of Understanding," Dec. 6, 1949, ibid.

64. Ivan D. Parker to Gerhardt Kramer, Mar. 25, 1971, author's collection.

65. *St. Louis Star-Times*, Mar. 29, 1947.

66. John A. Bryan to Spotts, Jan. 21, 1947, JNEM, Roy House, 620, Records of NPS, NA, RG 79.

67. Spotts to regional director, Jan. 23, 1947, ibid.

68. Peterson to Spotts, Jan. 23, 1947, JNEM, Gen. 0–35, Records of NPS, NA, RG 79.

69. Drury to Krug, Jan. 29, 1947, ibid.

70. Lawrence C. Merriam to Drury, Jan. 31, 1947, and Drury to Thomas Vint, Jan. 1947, JNEM, Roy House 620, Records of NPS, NA, RG 79.

71. Spotts to Drury, Feb. 3, 1947, JNEM, Gen. 0–35, Records of NPS, NA, RG 79.

72. "Telephone Conversation," Smith and Tolson, Feb. 6, 1947, JNEM, Roy House 620, Records of NPS, NA, RG 79.

73. Drury (Peterson) to Smith, Feb. 12, 1947, JNEM, Gen. 0–35, Records of NPS, NA, RG 79.

74. Smith to Drury, Feb. 18, 1947, ibid.

75. Spotts to regional director, Mar. 6, 1947, JNEM, Roy House, 620, Records of NPS, NA, RG 79.

76. Peterson to Spotts, Mar. 26, 1947, Roy, J. B., Missouri Historical Society.

77. *St. Louis Globe-Democrat*, Apr. 3, 1947.

78. Howard W. Baker to Julian Spotts, Dec. 16, 1948, JNEM, Educational Activities 840, Records of NPS, NA, RG 79.

79. Vint to regional director, Mar. 12, 1943, Appomattox Court House (CH) NHS, McLean House, Records of NPS, NA, RG 79.

80. Kahler, memorandum, Apr. 13, 1943, ibid.

81. Demaray to Drury, Apr. 16, 1943, ibid.

82. P. P. Patraw to Tolson, Apr. 29, 1943, ibid.

83. Drury to Hubert Gurney, Sept. 13, 1943, ibid.

84. Evison to regional director, Aug. 12, 1944, Appomattox CHNHS, Master Plan, Records of NPS, NA, RG 79.

85. Appleman to regional director, Aug. 29, 1946, Appomattox CHNHS, McLean House, Records of NPS, NA, RG 79.

86. Allen to Drury, Sept. 25, 1946, ibid.

87. Drury to Fiske Kimball, Jan. 2, 1947, ibid.

88. Kimball to Drury, Jan. 7, 1947, ibid.

89. Press Release, Jan. 4, 1948, ibid.

90. Drury, address at McLean House, Apr. 16, 1950, Files of Branch of History, Int.

91. Demaray to Drury, Mar. 2, 1944, Proposed NHS, Touro, 0–36, Records of NPS, NA, RG 79.

92. Francis S. Ronalds to Drury, Mar. 25, 1944, Files of Branch of History, Int.

93. Arthur Hays Sulzberger to Ickes, May 4, 1945, Proposed NHS, Touro, 0–36, Records of NPS, NA, RG 79.

94. Tolson to Demaray, Feb. 28, 1944, Proposed NHS, Misc. 0–36, Records of NPS, NA, RG 79.

95. Minutes of Interim Committee of Advisory Board, Mar. 8, 1945, 1, Int.

96. Kahler to Porter, Mar. 11, 1945, Proposed NHS, Touro, 0–36, Records of NPS, NA, RG 79.

97. Ickes to Roosevelt, Apr. 4, 1945, ibid.

98. Tolson to Ronalds, Apr. 28, 1945, ibid.

99. Sulzberger to Ickes, May 4, 1945, ibid.

100. Ickes to Sulzberger, May 21, 1945, ibid.

101. Sulzberger to Ickes, May 22, 1945, Proposed NHS, Misc. 0–36, Records of NPS, NA, RG 79.

102. Ickes to Sulzberger, July 2, 1945, ibid.

103. Ronalds to regional director, July 27, 1945, Proposed NHS, Touro, 0–36, Records of NPS, NA, RG 79; Drury to Ickes, Feb. 14, 1946, ibid.

104. *Salem Maritime National Historic Site* (Washington, D.C., 1940), 3.

105. Small to regional director, Apr. 18, 1947, Proposed NHS, Touro, 0–36, Records of NPS, NA, RG 79.

106. Memo on Society of Friends of Touro Synagogue, *Newport News*, Feb. 26, 1948.

107. Small to regional director, Apr. 29, 1949, Proposed NHS, Touro, 0–36, Records of NPS, NA, RG 79.

108. Richard B. Wigglesworth to Drury, Jan. 5, 1945, Proposed NHS, Adams Mansion, 0–36, Records of NPS, NA, RG 79.

109. Ronalds to regional director, July 23, 1945, ibid.

110. Porter to Kahler, Jan. 12, 1945, ibid.

111. Interview with Porter.

112. Drury to Ickes, Jan. 16, 1945, Proposed NHS, Adams Mansion, 0–36, Records of NPS, NA, RG 79.

113. Small to Porter, Jan. 22, 1945, ibid.

114. Ickes to Roosevelt, Jan. 24, 1945, ibid.

115. Drury to Charles F. Adams, Apr. 3, 1945, ibid.

116. Waldo G. Leland to Drury, July 10, 1945, ibid.

117. Ronalds to regional director, July 23, 1945, ibid.

118. Ronalds to Drury, July 8, 1946, and Drury to Krug, Oct. 30, 1946, ibid.

119. Interview with Drury and Evison, 130–31, Berkeley.

120. Tolson to regional director, Aug. 30, 1946, Proposed NHS, Wyoming, 0–36, Records of NPS, NA, RG 79.

121. Drury to Kimball, Mar. 12, 1948, Proposed NHS, Perot-Morris House, 0–36, Records of NPS, NA, RG 79.

122. Kimball to Drury, Mar. 16, 1948, ibid.

123. Allen to Drury, Mar. 31, 1948, ibid.

124. Ronalds to regional director, Apr. 9, 1948, ibid.

125. Tolson to regional director, Apr. 20, 1948, ibid.

126. Minutes of Advisory Board, Apr. 28, 1948, 3.

127. Drury to Hugh Scott, May 25, 1948, Proposed NHS, Perot-Morris House, 0–36, Records of NPS, NA, RG 79.

128. Allen to Drury, Aug. 13, 1948, ibid.

129. Drury to Krug, Dec. 6, 1948, ibid.

130. Cox to Ronalds, Jan. 26, 1949, ibid.

131. Allen to Drury, Mar. 18, 1949, ibid.

132. Public Law 386, 78th Congress, H.R. 3524, approved June 30, 1944.

133. Mrs. Frank W. Mish to Lee, Nov. 18, 1947, Proposed NHS, Harpers Ferry, 0–36, Records of NPS, NA, RG 79.

134. Jennings Randolph to Drury, Jan. 19, 1945, ibid.

135. Demaray to W. C. Handlan, May 5, 1948, ibid.

136. Interview with Ronald F. Lee, Aug. 17, 1962.

137. Minutes of Advisory Board, Apr. 28, 1948, 8–10.

138. Interview with John A. Bryan, Aug. 25, 1969.

139. Drury to regional director, Mar. 4, 1948, Proposed NHS, Jefferson Barracks, 0–36, Records of NPS, NA, RG 79.

140. P. Donald Fisher to Drury, Mar. 25, 1948, ibid.

141. Krug (Porter) to Matthew J. Connelly, Apr. 8, 1948, ibid.

142. Kahler to Demaray, July 13, 1948, ibid.

143. Conrad L. Wirth to Bernard F. Dickmann, July 16, 1948, ibid.

144. Lee to Drury, Aug. 16, 1948, ibid.

145. Wirth to regional director, Oct. 15, 1948, ibid.

146. Stanley C. Joseph to deputy regional director, War Assets Administration, June 2, 1949, ibid.

147. Mary Paul Caner, *Governor's Mansion, for Better, for Worse: The Shirley-Eustis House in Roxbury* (Boston, 1941), 8.

148. Roosevelt to Ickes, Jan. 2, 1942, Proposed NHS, Mass., 0–36, Records of NPS, NA, RG 79.

149. Ickes to Roosevelt, Jan. 9, 1942, ibid.

150. William S. Appleton to Drury, Jan. 16, 1942, ibid.

151. Laurence B. Fletcher to Drury, Jan. 20, 1942, ibid.

152. Drury to Fletcher, Jan. 30, 1942, ibid.

153. Appleton to Drury, Feb. 7, 1942, and Caner to Drury, Apr. 22, 1942, ibid.

154. Drury to Ronalds, Sept. 23, 1943, ibid.

155. Drury to Caner, May 27, 1946, ibid.

156. E. C. Russell to Ickes, Oct. 11, 1943, Proposed NHS, St. Ann's, 0–36, Records of NPS, NA, RG 79.

157. Ronalds to Drury, Nov. 20, 1943, ibid.

158. Tolson to Edmund J. O'Keefe, Oct. 20, 1943, ibid.

159. Ickes to James M. Mead, Dec. 20, 1945, ibid.

160. Ronalds to regional director, Aug. 2, 1946, ibid.

161. Drury to Krug, Oct. 24, 1946, ibid.

162. Walter A. Lynch to Warren W. Gardner, Oct. 29, 1946, ibid.

163. Mead to Demaray, Nov. 4, 1946, ibid.

164. Russell to Gardner, Nov. 5, 1946, ibid.

165. Russell to C. Girard Davidson, Nov. 20, 1946, ibid.

166. Demaray to Russell, Dec. 6, 1946, ibid.

167. Russell to Gardner, Mar. 8, May 17, 1947, ibid.

168. Chapman to Lynch, May 19, 1948, ibid.

169. George F. Mand to Harry S. Truman, June 5, 1948, ibid.

170. Chapman to Lynch, May 19, 1948, ibid.

171. Russell to Truman, May 27, 1948, ibid.

172. Drury to Russell, June 19, 1948, ibid.

173. *Post Home News*, Feb. 1949 (Admiral Schley Council No. 122, Junior Order United American Mechanics), ibid.

174. Krug to Everette B. Smith, Mar. 28, 1949, ibid.

175. Interview with Lee, June 29, 1970.

176. Drury to Ickes, Sept. 17, 1945, Proposed NHS, Missouri, 0–36, Records of NPS, NA, RG 79.

177. Ickes to Truman, Feb. 7, 1946, ibid.

178. Lawrence C. Merriam to Drury, Mar. 3, 1947, ibid.

179. Chapman to Richard J. Welch, May 14, 1947, ibid.

180. Drury to Kimball, Aug. 3, 1945, Proposed NHS, Shadwell, 0–36, Records of NPS, NA, RG 79.

181. Kimball to Drury, Aug. 7, 1945, ibid.

182. Tolson to Advisory Board, Sept. 4, 1945, ibid.

183. Abe Fortas to William D. Hassett, Sept. 20, 1945, ibid.

184. William S. Hildreth to M. J. Menefee, Mar. 16, 1949, ibid.

185. Porter to Kahler and Lee, Mar. 28, 1949, ibid.

186. Allen to Hildreth, Apr. 8, 1949, ibid.

187. Kimball to Demaray, Apr. 6, 1949, ibid.

188. Monthly narrative report of the Branch of History, Apr. 1949, Files of Branch of History, Int.

189. *New York Times*, Nov. 7, 1948.

190. Ibid., Nov. 8, 1948.

191. Ibid., Feb. 17, 1949.

192. Ibid., Feb. 18, 1949.

193. *Report of the Commission on the Renovation of the Executive Mansion* (Washington, D.C., 1952), 90–94.

194. *New York Times*, Mar. 23, 1949.

195. Ibid., Mar. 26, 1949.

196. *Report of the Commission*, 43.

197. *New York Times*, Mar. 31, 1949.

198. Ibid., Apr. 16, 1949.

199. Ibid., Apr. 17, 1949.

200. Ibid., May 25, 1949.

201. Ibid., June 1, 1949.

202. Ibid., June 4, 1949.

203. Ibid., June 21, 1949.

204. *Report of the Commission*, 100–101.

205. Ibid.

206. *New York Times*, Aug. 4, 1949.

207. Ibid., Apr. 3, 1949.

208. Minutes of Advisory Board, Dec. 2, 1949, 29–30.

209. *Report of the Commission*, 104–5.

210. *Congressional Record*, 76th Cong., 1 Sess. (July 13, 1939), 9052–9054.

211. Ibid., 9064–9066.

212. A. J. Knox to Drury, Home of Franklin D. Roosevelt (FDR) NHS, 0–36, Records of NPS, NA, RG 79.

213. Henry T. Hackett, Matthew M. Epstein, Ronalds, and Harry T. Thompson, memo for Drury, Oct. 11, 1943, ibid.

214. Drury to Ickes, Oct. 20, 1943, ibid.

215. Roosevelt to Ickes, Oct. 29, 1943, Files of Branch of History, Int.

216. *New York Times*, Jan. 4, 1944.

217. Ickes to Roosevelt, Jan. 28, 1944, Home of FDR, Files of Branch of History, Int.

218. Edgar R. Thayer, letter, Jan. 11, 1944, *New York Herald-Tribune*, Jan. 14, 1944; Clarissa W. Guiler to Ickes, Feb. 6, 1944, Proposed NHS, New York, 0–36, Records of NPS, NA, RG 79.

219. Tolson to Thayer, Feb. 7, 1944, Home of FDR NHS, 0–36, Records of NPS, NA, RG 79.

220. Demaray to Drury, Jan. 9, 1945, ibid.

221. Ronalds to Drury, Jan. 18, 1945, ibid.

222. *New York Times*, Apr. 25, 1945.

223. Allen to Drury, May 5, 1945, Home of FDR NHS, 0–36, Records of NPS, NA, RG 79.

224. *New York Times*, May 15, 1945.

225. W. E. O'Neil, Jr., to regional director, July 9–10, 1945, Home of FDR NHS, 0–36, Records of NPS, NA, RG 79.

226. George A. Palmer to regional director, Oct. 29, 1945, and Drury to regional director, Nov. 20, 1945, ibid.

227. *New York Times*, Nov. 17, 1945.

228. H. I. Brock, "Hyde Park: A New Shrine," *New York Times Magazine*, Nov. 11, 1945, 8.

229. Palmer to regional director, Jan. 31, 1946, Home of FDR NHS, Washington Liaison Office, Records of NPS, NA, RG 79.

230. Frederick L. Rath, Jr., Diary, Jan. 13, 1946, in his possession.

231. Drury to Ickes, Dec. 6, 1945, Home of FDR NHS, 0–36, Records of NPS, NA, RG 79.

232. O'Neil to regional director, Dec. 10, 1945, Burns to Tolson, Dec. 10, 1945, and Kahler to Burns, Dec. 19, 1945, ibid.

233. Burns, "Report on Protective Measures Needed at the Home of Franklin Roosevelt," Feb. 6, 1946, ibid.

234. Interpretive statement for master plan, Feb. 10, 1947, Home of FDR NHS, Wash. Liaison Off., Records of NPS, NA, RG 79.

235. *New York Times*, Apr. 13, 1946.

236. Ibid.

237. Ibid.

238. Palmer to Mrs. Franklin D. Roosevelt, Apr. 29, 1946, Home of FDR NHS, Wash. Liaison Off., Records of NPS, NA, RG 79.

239. Rath, Diary, June 23, 1946.

240. Lee to Drury, July 29, 1946, Home of FDR NHS, Wash. Liaison Off., Records of NPS, NA, RG 79.

241. Rath, Diary, Oct. 20, 1946.

242. Palmer to regional director, Oct. 24, 1947, Home of FDR NHS, Development 600.03, Records of NPS, NA, RG 79.

243. Palmer to staff, Dec. 10, 1947, Home of FDR NHS, Reports 207.01, Records of NPS, NA, RG 79.

244. Lee to Evison, Dec. 15, 1947, ibid.

245. Palmer, "Two Year Summary and Analysis of Administration, Protection, Maintenance and Development," June 1, 1948, Home of FDR NHS, Dev. 600.03, Records of NPS, NA, RG 79.

246. *Philadelphia Record*, Dec. 13, 1941.

247. *Philadelphia Evening Bulletin*, Jan. 13, 1942.

248. Ibid., Feb. 17, 1942.

249. D. Knickerbacker Boyd to Albert Simons, Apr. 22, 1942, City Plan for Charleston, 1939–42, Simons Papers, South Carolina Historical Society.

250. Minutes of meeting of Pennsylvania Committee on Conservation of Cultural Resources, May 8, 1942, 7, Historical Commission, Stevens Historian, General Correspondence, 1941–42, RG 13, Pennsylvania Archives (PA).

251. Ibid., 8.

252. Reminiscences of Isidor Ostroff, Sept. 26, 1969, 9–10, Oral History Research Office, Columbia University.

253. Interview with Sylvester K. Stevens, July 26, 1973.

254. Interviews with Charles E. Peterson, Feb. 9, 1970, and Kahler.

255. Appendix to minutes of continuing meetings, July 14, 1942, Independence Hall, Records of NPS, NA, RG 79.

256. Interview with Stevens.

257. Stevens to Edwin O. Lewis, Aug. 12, 1942, Hist. Comm., Stevens Historian, Gen. Corr., Ind. Hall Assn., President, 1942–43, RG 13, PA.

258. Stevens to Bernard Samuel, Aug. 20, 1942, ibid., Secy. 1942–43.

259. Stevens to Drury, Aug. 20, 1942, ibid., President, 1942–43.

260. Stevens to Lewis, Aug. 20, 1942, ibid.

261. Ickes to Roosevelt, Nov. 9, 1942, Files of Branch of History, Int.

262. Drury to Lewis, Feb. 8, 1943, ibid.

263. News release, March 30, 1943, ibid.

264. Boyd to Kahler, May 17, 1943, Ind. Hall, Records of NPS, NA, RG 79.

265. Reminiscences of Ostroff, 9–11.

266. Minutes of meeting of Executive Comm., Ind. Hall Assn., June 1, 1943, 6, Ind. Hall, Wash. Liaison Off., Records of NPS, NA, RG 79.

267. Ibid.

268. Lewis to Stevens, June 18, 1943, Hist. Comm., Stevens Historian, Gen. Corr., Ind. Hall Assn., President, 1942–43, RG 13, PA.

269. Minutes of Interim Comm. of Advisory Board, Dec. 11–12, 1945, 12–13, Proposed NHS, Philadelphia, 0–36, Records of NPS, NA, RG 79.

270. Chronological outline of events leading to establishment of Ind. National Historical Park (INHP) Project, Dec. 29, 1951, Files of Branch of History, Int.

271. Allen to Drury, Nov. 18, 1946, Proposed NHS, Phila., 0–36, Records of NPS, NA, RG 79.

272. Ibid.

273. Lewis to Drury, Dec. 6, 1946, Newton Drury, INHP, Records of NPS, NA, RG 79.

274. Drury to Lewis, Dec. 16, 1946, Proposed NHS, Phila., 0–36, Records of NPS, NA, RG 79.

275. Lee to Drury, Mar. 4, 1947, ibid.

276. Lee to Drury, Mar. 13, 1947, ibid.

277. Dick Sutton to Drury, Mar. 24, 1947, ibid.

278. Lee to Drury and Kahler, March 21, 1947, ibid.

279. Lewis, "Some Interpretive Possibilities for Independence Hall," Mar. 1947, Ind. Hall, Wash. Liaison Off., Records of NPS, NA, RG 79.

280. Lee to regional director, Apr. 4, 1947, ibid.

281. Minutes of meeting of Philadelphia National Shrines Park Commission, Apr. 18, 1947, Proposed NHS, Phila., 0–36, Records of NPS, NA, RG 79.

282. Appleman to Lewis, Apr. 23, 1947, ibid.

283. Weig, report on inspection at Ind. Hall National Historic Site, Apr. 15–17, 1947, May 2, 1947, Ind. Hall, Records of NPS, NA, RG 79.

284. Lewis to Drury, May 21, 1947, ibid.

285. Peterson, preliminary report, Philadelphia National Shrines Project, June 1947, Proposed NHS, Phila., 0–36, Records of NPS, NA, RG 79; Appleman to Lewis, July 17, 1947, Ind. Hall, Records of NPS, NA, RG 79; interview with Appleman.

286. "Report of Philadelphia National Shrines Park Commission to the

Congress of the United States, 1947," Dec. 29, 1947, xi, Files of Branch of History, Int.

287. Ibid., 317.

288. Ibid., 322–32.

289. Appleman to regional director, Feb. 5, 1948, Proposed NHS, Phila., 0–36, Records of NPS, NA, RG 79.

290. Peterson to Drury, Feb. 6, 1948, ibid.

291. U.S. Cong., House of Rep., Subcommittee on Public Lands, *Independence National Historical Park*, Hearings on H.R. 5053 and H.R. 5054 (Washington, D.C., 1948), 3–4.

292. Ibid., 7–8.

293. Ibid., 9.

294. Ibid., 10.

295. Charles B. Hosmer, Jr., *Presence of the Past: A History of the Preservation Movement in the United States before Williamsburg* (New York, 1965), 84–86.

296. U.S. Cong., House of Rep., Subcomm. on Public Lands, *INHP*, 32–33.

297. Ibid., 43.

298. Ibid., 44–45.

299. Ibid., 55.

300. Ibid., 40–42.

301. Chronological outline of INHP.

302. Press release, July 9, 1948, Proposed NHS, Phila., 0–36, Records of NPS, NA, RG 79.

303. Lee to Demaray, Aug. 23, 1948, ibid.

304. Interview with Porter.

305. Interview with Lee, June 29, 1970.

306. *New York Times*, Mar. 28. 1939.

307. Ibid.; Robert Caro, *The Power Broker* (New York, 1974), 653–77.

308. Caro, *Power Broker*, 671–74.

309. Reminiscences of George McAneny, Jan.-Feb. 1949, Oral History Research Office, Columbia University.

310. Robert Moses, "Some Hard Facts about Practical Preservation," letter, Sept. 19, 1940, quoted in *Journal of American Society of Architectural Historians*, 1 (July-Oct. 1941), 31–32.

311. *New York Times*, Oct. 30, 1941.

312. Caro, *Power Broker*, 678–88.

313. Ibid., 679–80.

314. *New York Times*, June 26, 1942.

315. Caro, *Power Broker*, 683–84.

316. *New York Times*, Sept. 20, 1945.

317. Ibid., Oct. 12, 1945.

318. Minutes of Interim Comm. of Advisory Board, Dec. 11–12, 1945, 13.

319. *New York Times*, July 25, 1946.

320. Ibid.

321. Ibid., July 26, 1946.

322. Interview with Lee, June 29, 1970.

323. *New York Times*, July 30, 1946.

324. McAneny to Mead, July 30, 1946, Proposed NHS, Castle Clinton, 0–36, Records of NPS, NA, RG 79.

325. *New York Times*, July 31, 1946.

326. Ibid., Aug. 2, 1946.

327. Ibid., Aug. 1, 8, 1946.

328. Ibid., Aug. 14, 1946.

329. Ibid., Aug. 16, 29, 1946.

330. Mrs. Arthur H. Sulzberger to Krug, Aug. 29, 1946, Proposed NHS, Castle Clinton, 0–36, Records of NPS, NA, RG 79.

331. *New York Times*, Aug. 30, 1946.

332. Gardner (Lee) to Sulzberger, Sept. 19, 1946, Proposed NHS, Castle Clinton, 0–36, Records of NPS, NA, RG 79.

333. Krug to William O'Dwyer, Oct. 3, 1946, ibid.

334. O'Dwyer to Krug, Oct. 15, 1946, ibid.

335. Davidson to O'Dwyer, Nov. 7, 1946, ibid.

336. Lee to McAneny, Nov. 8, 1946, and Lee to Drury, Nov. 18, 1946, ibid.

337. *New York Times*, Feb. 20, 1947.

338. Ibid., Feb. 21, 1947.

339. Ibid., Apr. 3, 1947.

340. Ibid., Apr. 4, 1947.

341. Ibid., April 5, 7, July 22, 28, and Aug. 7, 1947.

342. O'Dwyer to Krug, May 7, 1947, Proposed NHS, Castle Clinton, 0–36, Records of NPS, NA, RG 79.

343. *New York Times*, July 25, 1947.

344. Ibid., July 28, 1947.

345. Caro, *Power Broker*, 685.

346. *New York Times*, Aug. 1, 1947.

347. Chapman to O'Dwyer, Aug. 1, 1947, Proposed NHS, Castle Clinton, 0–36, Records of NPS, NA, RG 79.

348. *New York Times*, Aug. 7, 1947.

349. Ibid., Aug. 22, 1947.

350. Ibid., Aug. 28, 1947.

351. Ibid., Aug. 29, 1947.

352. Ibid., Sept. 13, 1947.

353. Sulzberger to Krug, Sept. 15, 1947, Proposed NHS, Castle Clinton, 0–36, Records of NPS, NA, RG 79.

354. Krug to O'Dwyer, and Krug to Sulzberger, Sept. 26, 1947, ibid.

355. O'Dwyer to Krug, Oct. 1, 1947, ibid.

356. Sulzberger to Krug, Oct. 16, 1947, and Krug to Sulzberger, Oct. 28, 1947, ibid.

357. *New York Times*, Jan. 29, 1948.

358. Ibid., Mar. 6, 1948.

359. Reminiscences of McAneny.

360. *New York Times*, Mar. 16, 1948.

361. McAneny to Demaray, Apr. 28, 1948, Proposed NHS, Castle Clinton, 0–36, Records of NPS, NA, RG 79.

362. McAneny to O'Dwyer, Apr. 29, 1948, ibid.

363. O'Dwyer to Krug, May 24, 1948, ibid.

364. McAneny to Demaray, May 27, 1948, ibid.

365. *Memorial Meeting in Honor of George McAneny*, Dec. 10, 1953 (New York, 1953), 16.

366. *New York Times*, May 28, 1948.

367. Ibid., May 29, 1948.

368. Ibid., June 18, July 14, 1948.

369. Reminiscences of McAneny; Lee to Drury, Dec. 13, 1948, Proposed NHS, Castle Clinton, 0–36, Records of NPS, NA, RG 79.

370. *New York Times*, Dec. 14, 1948.

371. Lee to Drury, Dec. 13, 1948, Proposed NHS, Castle Clinton, 0–36, Records of NPS, NA, RG 79.

372. *New York Times*, Dec. 16, 1948.

373. Ibid., Dec. 24, 1948.

374. Ibid., Dec. 31, 1948.

375. Demaray to under secretary of int., Feb. 1, 1949, Proposed NHS, Castle Clinton, 0–36, Records of NPS, NA, RG 79.

376. *New York Times*, Feb. 19, 1949.

377. Raymond Walters, Jr., "The Last Word: Call It Oral History," *New York Times Book Review*, Jan. 2, 1972, 23.

378. Reminiscences of McAneny.

379. *New York Times*, Feb. 21, 1949.

380. Ibid., Feb. 24, 1949.

381. Ibid., Mar. 16, 1949.

382. Ibid., Mar. 22–23, 1949.

383. Ibid., Mar. 30, 1949.

384. McAneny to Lee, Apr. 7, 1949, Proposed NHS, Castle Clinton, 0–36, Records of NPS, NA, RG 79.

385. Ibid.

386. *New York Times*, Apr. 11, 1949.

387. Ibid., Apr. 29, 1949.

388. Ibid., Apr. 30, 1949.

389. McAneny to Tolson, June 14, 1949, Proposed NHS, Castle Clinton, 0–36, Records of NPS, NA, RG 79.

390. *New York Times*, Oct. 7, 1949.

391. Ibid., Oct. 8, 1949.

392. Ibid.

393. Ibid., Dec. 24, 1949.

394. Interview with Frederick L. Rath, Jr., July 13, 1970.

395. *Report of the American Commission for the Protection and Salvage of Artistic and Historic Monuments in War Areas* (Washington, D.C., 1946), 3.

396. Ibid., 1–164.

397. Lee to Peterson, Apr. 14, 1970, author's collection.

398. David E. Finley, speech quoted in *Quarterly Report of the National Council for Historic Sites and Buildings*, II (Mar. 1950), Supplement, 4.

399. Minutes of Interim Comm. of Advisory Board, Dec. 11–12, 1945, 8.

400. David E. Finley, *History of the National Trust for Historic Preservation, 1947–1963* (Washington, D.C., 1965), 1; Finley, speech, *Quarterly Report*; Lee to Peterson, Apr. 14, 1970, author's collection.

401. Finley, speech, *Quarterly Report*; Lee to Peterson, Apr. 14, 1970, author's collection.

402. Lee to Peterson, Apr. 14, 1970, author's collection.

403. Interviews with Appleman and Porter.

404. Demaray to regional director, Jan. 30, 1946, Files of Branch of History, Int.

405. Frederick Tilberg, report on Hampton, Mar. 30, 1946, ibid.

406. Allen to Drury, Apr. 18, 1946, ibid.

407. Interview with Porter; Lee to Peterson, Apr. 14, 1970, author's collection.

408. Demaray to Kimball, July 2, 1946, Files of Branch of History, Int.

409. Kimball to Demaray, July 9, 1946, quoted in Tilberg, report on Hampton.

410. Stuart Barnette to Vint, Aug. 9, 1946, Files of Branch of History, Int.

411. Lee to Drury, Nov. 18, 1946, ibid.

412. Lee, memorandum, Dec. 12, 1946, ibid.

413. Drury to Demaray, Dec. 27, 1946, ibid.

414. Demaray to Drury, Jan. 9, 1947, ibid.

415. Lewis to Lee, Dec. 31, 1946, ibid.

416. Demaray to Drury, Jan. 9, 1947, ibid.

417. Donald D. Shepard to Krug, Jan. 10, 1947, ibid.

418. Krug to Shepard, Jan. 25, 1947, ibid.

419. Drury to Demaray, Jan. 17, 1947, ibid.

420. W. E. O'Neil, Jr., to regional director, Jan. 30, 1947, ibid.

421. Cox to files, Feb. 20, 1947, ibid.

422. Lee to Robert Garrett, Mar. 12, 1947, ibid.

423. Lee to Drury, Mar. 12, 1947, ibid.

424. Drury to regional director, Apr. 11, 1947, ibid.

425. Demaray to regional director, Mar. 7, 1947, ibid.

426. Gardner (Lee) to Shepard, Apr. 15, 1947, ibid.

427. Lee to Demaray, Apr. 21, 1947, ibid.

428. Shepard to Krug, Apr. 25, 1947, ibid.
429. Krug to Shepard, May 10, 1947, ibid.
430. Garrett to Lee, May 1, 1947, ibid.
431. Lee to Garrett, May 15, 1947, ibid.
432. Charles W. Andrae to Lee, June 18, 1947, and Lee to John H. Scarff, July 2, 1947, ibid.
433. Truman to Krug, Oct. 6, 1947, ibid.
434. Demaray to Krug, Nov. 6, 1947, ibid.
435. Demaray to Garrett, Dec. 12, 1947, ibid.
436. Scarff to Lee, Dec. 18, 1947, ibid.
437. Cox to Garrett, Jan. 16, 1948, ibid.
438. Cox to Drury, Jan. 16, 1948, ibid.
439. Drury to Scarff, Feb. 25, 1948, ibid.
440. Lee to Garrett, Mar. 4, 1948, ibid.
441. Drury to regional director, May 26, 1948, ibid.; Cox to Drury, July 29, 1948, Hampton NHS, Records of NPS, NA, RG 79.
442. Scarff to Drury, Oct. 1, 1948, ibid.
443. Porter to Drury, Oct. 8, 1948, Files of Branch of History, Int.
444. Sutton to Drury, Nov. 9, 1948, Hampton NHS, Records of NPS, NA, RG 79.
445. Shepard to Krug, Dec. 29, 1948, ibid.
446. Davidson to Shepard, Dec. 31, 1948, ibid.
447. Sutton to Vint, Mar. 31, 1949, ibid.
448. James W. Rader to regional director, May 3, 1949, ibid.
449. *Report of the Avalon Foundation, 1940–1950* (New York, 1951), 15.
450. Finley, speech, *Quarterly Report*.
451. Ibid., 5; Lee to Peterson, Apr. 14, 1970, author's collection.

Chapter 10: *The Formation of the National Trust for Historic Preservation*

1. Charles B. Hosmer, Jr., *Presence of the Past: A History of the Preservation Movement in the United States before Williamsburg* (New York, 1965), 94, 255, 302.
2. Ibid., 246, 252.
3. Minutes of meeting of U.S. Territorial Expansion Memorial Commission, Dec. 19, 1934, 33, Files of Branch of History, Department of Interior (Int.).
4. V. Aubrey Neasham, "Historic Sites of America, Incorporated," Dec. 1941, Neasham Collection.
5. Ibid.
6. Neasham, "The Preservation of Privately Owned Historic Sites," Jan. 1942, Files of Branch of History, Int.
7. Ibid.
8. Mrs. M. McCann Naef to Mrs. Franklin D. Roosevelt, Aug. 22,

1944, Proposed National Historic Site (NHS), Miscellaneous 0–36, Records of National Park Service (NPS), National Archives (NA), Record Group (RG) 79.

9. Newton B. Drury (Charles W. Porter) to Naef, Sept. 13, 1944, and A. E. Demaray to Drury, Sept. 1, 1944, ibid.

10. Mrs. Frances D. Bendtsen to Harry S. Truman, July 24, 1945, ibid.

11. Drury (Herbert E. Kahler) to Bendtsen, Aug. 11, 1945, ibid.

12. Interview with Horace M. Albright, Dec. 2, 1969.

13. Ibid.; Ann Kees, "Washington Square North," *Antiques*, 47 (Mar. 1945), 162–63.

14. Interview with Albright.

15. David E. Finley to Philip B. Fleming, Sept. 1, 1945, D. Finley, Artistic and Educational, "Oak Hill," National Trust (NT) Archives.

16. Minutes of Interim Committee of Advisory Board, Dec. 11–12, 1945, 6–8, Files of Branch of History, Int.

17. Ibid., 8–9.

18. William C. Osborn to George McAneny, Jan. 31, 1946, Geographic File, New York City, Greenwich Village, Washington Square, NT Archives.

19. [Ronald F. Lee] to McAneny, ca. Jan. 1946, ibid.

20. Mrs. George Henry Warren, notes on conversation with Kenneth Chorley, Oct. 10, 1946, K. Chorley Files, Preservation Society of Newport County.

21. Interview with Ronald F. Lee, Aug. 17, 1962.

22. Lee, "The Effect of Postwar Conditions on the Preservation of Historic Sites and Buildings," talk given to American Assn. of State and Local History, Oct. 26, 1946, 1–4, Files of Branch of History, Int.

23. Ibid., 5.

24. Ibid., 6.

25. Hosmer, *Presence of the Past*, 93–100.

26. Frederick L. Rath, Jr., to author, Apr. 1, 1970; *Memorial Meeting in Honor of George McAneny*, Dec. 10, 1953 (New York, 1953), 16.

27. Lee to McAneny, Nov. 8, 1946, Proposed NHS, Castle Clinton, 0–36, Records of NPS, NA, RG 79.

28. Ibid.

29. Kahler to Lee, Nov. 22, 1946, Executive Comm., Meetings, Correspondence and minutes, 1946–50, NT Archives.

30. Interview with Lee.

31. Lee to McAneny, Jan. 24, 1947, Independence Hall NHS, Washington Liaison Office, Records of NPS, NA, RG 79.

32. Minutes of Informal Conference Preliminary to Organization of a National Council on Historic Sites and Buildings (NC), Feb. 5, 1947, N. Drury, NC, Records of NPS, NA, RG 79.

33. Ibid.

34. Lee to McAneny, Mar. 24, 1947, Exec. Comm., Meetings, Corr. and Min., 1946–50, NT Archives.

35. Lee to John D. Rockefeller III, Mar. 24, 1947, NC, 1947, Archives of Colonial Williamsburg Foundation .

36. Rockefeller to Chorley, Mar. 26, 1947, ibid.; William S. Appleton to Lee, Apr. 14, 1947, Headquarters File (Organization), Society for the Preservation of New England Antiquities, NT Archives.

37. McAneny, report at Organization Meeting of NC, Apr. 15, 1947, NC Meetings, NT Archives.

38. Turpin C. Bannister, American Institute of Architects and the Preservation of Historic American Buildings, Apr. 15, 1947, ibid.

39. J. Otis Brew, speech, Apr. 15, 1947, ibid.

40. Minutes of Organization Meeting, NC, Apr. 15, 1947, 3, ibid.

41. Ibid., 4.

42. Ibid., 5–6.

43. Ibid., 7.

44. Ibid., 26.

45. Emil Lorch to Lee, May 16, 1947, Proposed NHS, Michigan, 0–36, Records of NPS, NA, RG 79.

46. Minutes of Executive Board, NC, May 9, 1947, NC Meetings, NT Archives.

47. Helen B. L. Patterson to Finley, June 19, 1947, and William Phillips to Finley, July 8, 1947, D. Finley, Art. and Ed., Restoration of Historic Buildings, NT Archives.

48. U. S. Grant III to chairman of Board of Selectmen, Watertown, Mass., July 18, 1947, Geog. File, Waltham, Mass., Gore Place, NT Archives.

49. Lee to Josiah H. Child, Aug. 5, 1947, ibid.

50. William G. Wendell to Finley, Aug. 15, 1947, D. Finley, Art. and Ed., Rest. of Hist. Buildings, NT Archives.

51. Finley to Wendell, Sept. 23, 1947, ibid.

52. Wendell to Finley, Sept. 30, 1947, ibid.

53. Frank C. Littleton to Finley, Oct. 3, 1947, D. Finley, Art. and Ed., NC—October Meeting, NT Archives.

54. Donald D. Shepard to Finley, Oct. 14, 1947, ibid.

55. Appleton to Lee, Apr. 25, 1947, NC, Misc. Corr., NT Archives.

56. Lee to Appleton, Oct. 16, 1947, ibid.

57. Minutes of Organization Meeting, NC, Oct. 20, 1947, 28, NC Meetings, NT Archives.

58. Ibid., 30.

59. Ibid., 31–35.

60. Ibid., 50–52.

61. Ibid., 67–69.

62. Ibid., 87–88.

63. Ibid., 125.

64. Ibid., 129–30.

65. Ibid., 143.

66. Ibid., 144–45.

67. Ibid., 145–46.

68. Ibid., 151–55.

69. Ibid., 157–59.

70. Ibid., 160–61.

71. Ibid., 161–63.

72. Ibid., 207–10.

73. Lee to Brew, Nov. 4, 1947, NC, Misc. Corr., NT Archives.

74. *Memorial Meeting in Honor of George McAneny*, 16–17.

75. Interview with Ronald F. Lee, June 29, 1970.

76. Interview with Frederick L. Rath, Jr., July 13, 1970.

77. Minutes of Executive Board, NC, Nov. 24, 1947, NC Meetings, NT Archives.

78. Ibid.

79. Interview with Rath.

80. Roy Fitzgerald to Grant, Nov. 28, 1947, Geog. File, Dayton, Ohio, Old Courthouse, NT Archives.

81. Grant to Lee, Dec. 1, 1947, ibid.

82. Grant to Fitzgerald, Feb. 23, 1948, ibid.

83. Grant to associate members, Jan. 26, 1948, NC, Misc. Corr., NT Archives.

84. Report of Committee on Ways and Means, Feb. 10, 1948, ibid.

85. Interview with Frederick L. Rath, Jr., Aug. 5, 1969.

86. Rath, Diary, Mar. 26, 1948, in his possession.

87. Ibid., Apr. 1, 1948.

88. Ibid., Apr. 7, 1948.

89. Ibid., Apr. 15, 1948.

90. Interview with Rath, July 13, 1970.

91. Ibid.

92. McAneny to Lee, Apr. 15, 1948, NC, Misc. Corr., NT Archives.

93. Interview with Rath, July 13, 1970.

94. Ibid.

95. Ibid., Aug. 5, 1969.

96. Ibid., July 13, 1970.

97. Grant to Alexander Smith, Jr., May 7, 1948, NC, Misc. Corr., NT Archives.

98. "Reflections," *Historic Preservation*, 26 (Oct.–Dec. 1974), 23.

99. Lee to Smith, July 29, 1948, NC, Misc. Corr., NT Archives.

100. Draft of Conference on Organization of NT, Sept. 3, 1948, ibid.

101. Finley to Rath, Sept. 22, 1948, NC Corr., NT Archives.

102. Rath to Oliver Bevir, Sept. 30, 1948, NT and NC Headquarters, NC Corr., Aug.-Nov. 1948, NT Archives.

103. Rath to Fitzgerald, Oct. 4, 1948, Geog. File, Dayton, Ohio, Old Courthouse, NT Archives.

104. Rath to Albert Kornfeld, Oct. 10, 1948, D. Finley, Art. and Ed., NC—Public Relations Comm., NT Archives.

105. Minutes of Executive Board, Oct. 21, 1948, NC Meetings, NT Archives.

106. Minutes of Second Annual Meeting, NC, Nov. 4, 1948, 4–16. NC Meetings, NT Archives.

107. Ibid., 6–12.

108. Ibid., 15–16.

109. Ibid., 21.

110. Ibid., 25–26.

111. Ibid., 30–31.

112. Ibid., 35–38.

113. Ibid., 41.

114. Ibid., 43–44.

115. Ibid., 53.

116. Ibid., 73.

117. Ibid., 118–26.

118. Ibid., 131–33.

119. Ibid., Nov. 5, 1948, 7.

120. Ibid., 10.

121. Ibid., 14.

122. Ibid., 18–64.

123. Minutes of Executive Board, Nov. 5, 1948, NC Meetings, NT Archives.

124. Interview with Rath, July 13, 1970.

125. Interview with Mrs. George Maurice Morris, Aug. 22, 1972.

126. Armistead Rood to John N. Brown, Aug. 29, 1948, Woodlawn Foundation, Rood—Misc. Papers, NT Archives.

127. Woodlawn Project, Aug. 29, 1948, Woodlawn Found., Woodlawn Estate, NT Archives.

128. George Maurice Morris, "Statement of Recent Events concerning Woodlawn and the Present Situation," Sept. 15, 1948, ibid.

129. Ray B. Bolton to Morris, Oct. 4, 1948, Woodlawn Found., Misc. Corr., NT Archives.

130. Rood to Morris, Oct. 7, 1948, Woodlawn Found., Rood—Memos, NT Archives.

131. Rood to Grant, Oct. 7, 1948, Woodlawn Found., Trustees Corr., NT Archives.

132. Morris to Bolton, Nov. 1, 1948, Woodlawn Found., Bolton—Rood—Morris Memos, NT Archives.

133. Grant to Shepard, Nov. 19, 1948, NC and NT Headquarters, NC Corr., Aug.-Nov. 1948, NT Archives.

134. Meeting of Board of Trustees, Nov. 30, 1948, Woodlawn Found., Minutes, NT Archives.

135. Paul Mellon to Morris, Dec. 20, 1948, Woodlawn Found., Mellon, P., Old Dominion Foundation, NT Archives.

136. Interview with Rath, July 13, 1970.

137. Ralph P. Wentworth to Grant, Nov. 15, 1948, Seminars and Short Courses, American Univ., NT Archives; Grant to Wentworth, Nov. 28, 1948, D. Finley, Art. and Ed., NC—Public Relations Comm., NT Archives.

138. *Antiques*, 55 (Jan. 1949), 29.

139. Minutes of Executive Comm., Jan. 7, 1949, 1, NC Meetings, NT Archives.

140. Richard E. Bishop to Rath, Feb. 2, 1949, NC, Misc. Corr., NT Archives.

141. Rath to Howard Peckham, Feb. 8, 1949, ibid.

142. Peckham to Rath, Feb. 10, 1949, ibid.

143. Draft of letter from Rath to Peckham, ca. Feb. 20, 1949, and note from Lee, ibid.

144. Julius Krug to Grant, Feb. 16, 1949, Survey General, NPS, NT Archives.

145. Minutes of Executive Board, Feb. 18, 1949, NC Meetings, NT Archives; Grant to Walter A. Taylor, Feb. 24, 1949, NC Corr., Office yellows, NT Archives.

146. Minutes of Executive Board, Feb. 18, 1949, NC Meetings, NT Archives.

147. NC, *Quarterly Report*, 1 (Mar. 1949).

148. Rath to Grant, May 2, 1949, Seminars and Short Courses, American Univ., NT Archives.

149. Rath to Grant, May 11, 1949, ibid.

150. Schedule of meetings, Institute in Preservation and Interpretation of Historic Sites and Buildings, June 6–24, 1949, ibid.

151. NC, *Quarterly Report*, 1 (June 1949).

152. Grant to Ralph T. Walker, Oct. 3, 1949, NC Corr., Office yellows, NT Archives.

153. NC, Third Annual Meeting, Oct. 13, 1949, 43, NC Meetings, NT Archives.

154. Ibid., 79.

155. Ibid., 84.

156. Ibid., 109–20.

157. Rath to Lee, Oct. 28, 1949, NC Corr., Office yellows, NT Archives.

158. NC, Executive Board Meeting, Nov. 30, 1949, NT Archives.

159. Introduction to 1950 budget estimates, NC Misc. Corr., NT Archives.

160. Woodlawn Public Foundation, Meeting of Board of Trustees, Dec. 27, 1948, Woodlawn Found., Minutes, extra copies, NT Archives.

161. Bolton to Rood, Jan. 16, 1949, Woodlawn Found., Bolton—Rood—Morris memos, NT Archives.

162. Rood to Morris, Jan. 18, 1949, ibid.

163. Rath to Rood, Jan. 18, 1949, Woodlawn Found., Suggestions, NT Archives.

164. Anthony C. McAuliffe to District of Columbia Chapter, Military Order of World Wars, Feb. 8, 1949, Woodlawn Found., Publicity, NT Archives.

165. Report to Trustees, Rood, Feb. 17, 1949, Woodlawn Found., F-Misc., NT Archives.

166. Rood to Taylor Burke, Feb. 19, 1949, Woodlawn Found., S-Misc., NT Archives.

167. Woodlawn Public Found., Meeting of Trustees, May 13, 1949, Woodlawn Found., Minutes, Comm. Reports, NT Archives.

168. Morris to Bolton, June 3, 1949, Woodlawn Found., Ford Foundation, NT Archives.

169. Rood to John W. Suter, June 15, 1949, Woodlawn Found., S-Misc., NT Archives.

170. Aubrey R. Marrs, Report of Director, June 30, 1949, Woodlawn Found., Director, Marrs, NT Archives.

171. Randolph Bishop to Rixey Smith, Oct. 13, 1949, Woodlawn Found., Minutes, Comm. Reports, NT Archives.

172. History Division, Monthly Report for Nov. 1948, Dec. 8, 1948, Files of Branch of History, Int.

173. Rood to Morris, Jan. 18, 1949, Woodlawn Found., Rood—Morris memos, NT Archives.

174. Harvey L. Jones to Morris, Dec. 1, 1948, Geog. Files, DC Northwest Woodley, NT Archives.

175. Lee to Frederick Johnson, Mar. 14, 1949, and Rath to Jones, Dec. 3, 1948, ibid.

176. Rath to Albert Simons, Feb. 4, 1949, Office yellows, NT Archives.

177. Rath to Clyde T. Franks, Nov. 23, 1948, Geog. File, Laurens, So. Car., Rose Hill, NT Archives.

178. Rath to Franks, Mar. 11, 1949, NC Corr., Office yellows, NT Archives.

179. Interview with Rath, July 13, 1970.

180. W. Langdon Kihn to H. Alexander Smith, Jr., Feb. 8, 1949, Geog. File, Hadlyme Ferry, Conn., NT Archives.

181. Kihn to Smith, Feb. 19, 1949, ibid.

182. Elmer Keith to NT, Feb. 22, 1949, ibid.

183. Rath to Kihn, Mar. 10, 1949, ibid.

184. Keith to Rath, Mar. 12, 1949, ibid.

185. Rath to J. Albert Hill, Mar. 21, 1949, NC, Office yellows, NT Archives.

186. Ibid.

187. Rath to Bertram K. Little, Mar. 28, 1949, NC, Office yellows, NT Archives.

188. Rath to Kihn, Apr. 7, 1949, Geog. File, Hadlyme Ferry, Conn., NT Archives.

189. Keith to Rath. Apr. 17. 1949, ibid.

190. Kihn to Rath, May 10, 1949, ibid.

191. NC, *Quarterly Report*, 1 (June 1949), 5–6.

192. Kihn to Rath, June 23, July 25, 1949, and Mrs. W. Langdon Kihn to Rath, Aug. 29, 1949, Geog. File, Hadlyme Ferry, Conn., NT Archives.

193. Grant to Chester Bowles, Aug. 2, 1949, ibid.

194. Mrs. Kihn to Rath, Aug. 29, 1949, ibid.

195. Kihn to Rath, Oct. 20, 1949, ibid.

196. Interview with Rath, July 13, 1970.

197. Rath to Grant, May 27, 1949, D. Finley, Art. and Ed., Rest. of Hist. Buildings, NT Archives.

198. Grant to Rath, May 31, 1949, Geog. File, Va., Independent City Alexandria, Old Presbyterian Meeting House, NT Archives.

199. Rath to Bradford Williams, June 17, 1949, NC Corr., Office yellows, NT Archives.

200. Lester C. Simpson to Leon H. Zach, July 14, 1949, Geog. File, Va., Ind. City Alexandria, Old Presbyterian Meeting House, NT Archives.

201. John L. Tilton to Rath, July 25, 1949, Geog. File, Upper Darby, Pa., Jonathan Evans Homestead, NT Archives.

202. Freas B. Snyder to Rath, July 27, 1949, ibid.

203. Rath to Snyder, July 29, 1949, NC Corr., Office yellows, NT Archives.

204. Snyder to Rath, Aug. 11, 1949, Geog. File, Upper Darby, Pa., J. Evans Homestead, NT Archives; Rath to Snyder, Aug. 18, 1949, NC Corr., Office yellows, NT Archives.

205. Erik Reed to Rath, Dec. 17, 1948, and report, Geog. File, Lincoln County, New Mex., Gen., NT Archives. See also chapter 5.

206. Maurice G. Fulton, to Rath, Jan. 5, 1949, ibid.

207. Rath to Fulton, Jan 6, 1949, NC Corr., Office yellows, NT Archives.

208. Fulton to Rath, Jan. 10, 1948 (1949), Geog. File, Lincoln County, New Mex., Gen., NT Archives.

209. Fulton to Rath, Mar. 27, 1949, ibid.

210. Grant to editor, *New York Herald Tribune*, Jan. 13, 1949, Geog. File, New York City, Manhattan, Castle Clinton National Monument (NM), NT Archives; Grant to James M. Cox, July 18, 1949, Geog. File, Dayton, Ohio, Old Court House, NT Archives.

211. Harry C. Durston to Rath, Aug. 30, 1949, Geog. File, Syracuse, N.Y., Leavenworth House, NT Archives; Rath to Durston, Sept. 2, 1949, NC Corr., Office yellows, NT Archives.

212. Rath to Norman B. Wilkinson, May 4, 1949, NC Corr., Office yellows, NT Archives.

213. Grant to Charles van Ravenswaay, Oct. 3, 1949, ibid.

214. Interview with Rath, July 13, 1970.

215. David E. Finley, *History of the National Trust for Historic Preservation, 1947–1963* (Washington, D.C., 1965), 55.

216. Committee Meeting on Organization of NT, Feb. 5, 1949, NC Meetings, NT Archives.

217. Rath to Lorch, Feb. 9, 1949, D. Finley, Art. and Ed., Rest. of Hist. Buildings, NT Archives.

218. Annie Burr to Finley, Aug. 4, 1949, Geog. File, Newport, R.I., Redwood Library, NT Archives.

219. Rath to Wilmarth S. Lewis, Aug. 24, 1949, NC Corr., Office yellows, NT Archives.

220. *New York Times*, July 13, 1949.

221. NC, *Quarterly Report*, 1 (Sept. 1949), 1.

222. *New York Times*, Sept. 8, 1949.

223. Ibid., Oct. 18, 1949.

224. Ibid., Oct. 23, 1949.

225. Ibid., Nov. 1, 1949.

226. NC, Executive Board Meeting, Nov. 30, 1949, NC Meetings, NT Archives.

227. James G. Van Derpool to Grant, Oct. 10, 1949, Geog. File, Scotia, N.Y., Glen-Sanders House, NT Archives.

228. Grant to Van Derpool, Oct. 28, 1949, NC Corr., Office yellows, NT Archives.

229. Grant to Mr. and Mrs. Glen Sanders, Dec. 9, 1949, ibid.

230. John J. Cunningham to Rath, Nov. 21, 1949, Friends of Senate House, N.Y., NT Archives; Grace C. Robinson to Grant, Nov. 29, 1949, Geog. File, New Lebanon, N.Y., Shaker Community, NT Archives.

231. Grant to Robinson, Dec. 7, 1949, ibid.

232. Interview with Rath, July 13, 1970.

233. Paul E. Sprague, "The Wainwright-Landmark Built and Saved," *Historic Preservation*, 26 (Oct.-Dec. 1974), 11.

234. Interview with Rath, July 13, 1970.

Chapter 11: *The Growth of Professionalism*

1. See chapter 1.

2. Mabel Choate to William S. Appleton, Oct. 20, 1926, Mass.—Stockbridge, Mission House, Society for the Preservation of New England Antiquities (SPNEA).

3. Appleton to Choate, Oct. 26, 1926, ibid.

4. Fiske Kimball, *Thomas Jefferson, Architect* (Cambridge, Mass., 1916); *Domestic Architecture of the American Colonies and of the Early Republic* (New York, 1922); Mary Kane, *A Bibliography of the Works of Fiske Kimball* (Charlottesville, 1959); George and Mary Roberts, *Triumph on Fairmount: Fiske Kimball and the Philadelphia Museum of Art* (Philadelphia, 1959), 35–41.

5. Roberts, *Triumph*, 55–70; Marie Kimball, "The Revival of the Colonial," *Architectural Record*, 62 (July 1927), 1–17.

6. Charles B. Hosmer Jr., *Presence of the Past: A History of the Preservation Movement in the United States before Williamsburg* (New York, 1965), 189–90.

7. Ibid., 207.

8. Interview with Ronald F. Lee, Feb. 1, 1971, Archives of National Park Service (NPS) at Harpers Ferry Center (Harpers Ferry).

9. Interview with Charles E. Peterson, Jan. 31, 1971, ibid.

10. Interview with J. C. and Virginia Harrington, Mar. 15, 1971, ibid.; interview with J. C. and Virginia Harrington, May 18, 1970.

11. Ralph J. Lewis, "Ned J. Burns, Educator, Naturalist, and Museum Expert," 1–4, manuscript in Lewis's possession.

12. Interview with Singleton P. Moorehead, 1957, Colonial Williamsburg Foundation (CWF).

13. Interview with Charles W. Porter III, Apr. 20, 1970.

14. Interview with Ronald F. Lee, Aug. 17, 1962.

15. Lee to U.S. Civil Service Commission, Oct. 14, 1936, Personal files of Lee, Harpers Ferry.

16. Interview with Peterson, Harpers Ferry.

17. Interview with Harringtons, May 18, 1970.

18. Lewis, "Burns," 6–7.

19. Interview with Joseph F. Booton, Apr. 17, 1971.

20. Interview with Sylvester K. Stevens, July 26, 1973.

21. Interview with Janet Cooley, July 8, 1970.

22. Ibid.; interview with Louis C. Jones, Aug. 5, 1969.

23. Hans Huth, "Observations Concerning the Conservation of Monuments in Europe and America," 1940, Files of Branch of History, Department of Interior (Int.).

24. V. Aubrey Neasham, "University Training for Park Personnel," Feb. 1942, Neasham Collection.

25. Minutes of 4th meeting of Interim Committee of Advisory Board, Mar. 8, 1945, 2–3, Files of Branch of History, Int.

26. John D. R. Platt, "The Historian and Historical Preservation," Paper given at American Historical Association (AHA) Meeting, Dec. 28, 1963, in possession of Platt.

27. Stuart M. Barnette to Peterson, Sept. 17, 1935, Schneider Report, HABS Headquarters File, Library of Congress (LC).

28. *Journal of American Institute of Architects* (AIA), 14 (Jan. 1926), 46; AIA *Proceedings of 60th Annual Convention* (May 11–13, 1927), 153–55.

29. A. Lawrence Kocher, "Old St. John's," *Journal of American Institute of Architects*, 16 (Mar. 1928), 88.

30. AIA, *Proceedings of 61st Ann. Conv.* (May 16–18, 1928), 124–28.

31. AIA, *Proceedings of 64th Ann. Conv.* (Apr. 11–16, 1931), 135–38.

32. AIA, *Proceedings of 61st Ann. Conv.* (May 16–18, 1928), 127–28.

33. AIA, *Proceedings of 62nd Ann. Conv.* (Apr. 23–25, 1929), 152–54 and *Proceedings of 63rd Ann. Conv.* (May 21–23, 1930), 159–61.

34. *Octagon*, 4 (Apr. 1932), 19–20; 4 (Nov. 1932), 6–7; 5 (Nov. 1933), 8.

35. Ibid., 8 (Feb. 1936), 5.

36. Ibid., 9 (May 1937), 23–27.

37. Ibid., 10 (May 1938), 25, 27.

38. Annual Report of Committee on Preservation of Historic Buildings of AIA, 1946–47 and 1947–48, Committee on Pres. of Hist. Buildings, Earl Reed, 1952–54, Simons Papers, South Carolina Historical Society.

39. Society of Architectural Historians (SAH) *Newsletter*, 10 (Apr. 1966), 4.

40. Hosmer, *Presence of the Past*, 199–203.

41. *New York Times*, June 22, 1948.

42. See chapter 7.

43. SAH *Newsletter*, 12 (June 1968), 3.

44. *Journal of American Society of Architectural Historians*, 1 (Jan. 1941), 20–22; SAH *Newsletter*, 10 (Apr. 1966), 4.

45. *Journal of American Society of Architectural Historians*, 1 (Jan. 1941), 21.

46. SAH *Newsletter*, 10 (Apr. 1966), 4; interview with Charles E. Peterson, Feb. 9, 1970.

47. *Journal of American Society of Architectural Historians*, 1 (Jan. 1941), 23–25.

48. Ibid.

49. Report on session of College Art Association, Jan. 31, 1941, Preservation File, Files of Branch of History, Int.; Peterson, memorandum, Feb. 3, 1941, HABS Headquarters Files, LC.

50. Peterson, memorandum, Feb. 3, 1941, HABS Headquarters Files, LC.

51. *Journal of American Society of Architectural Historians*, 1 (Apr. 1941), 21–22.

52. Ibid., 1 (July-Oct. 1941), 1–45.

53. Ibid., 33–45.

54. See chapter 13.

55. Antoinette F. Downing, *Early Homes of Rhode Island* (Richmond, Va., 1937).

56. Charles M. Stotz, *The Architectural Heritage of Early Western Pennsylvania* (Pittsburgh, 1966), xi.

57. William G. Perry to Congressional Library, Sept. 26, 1928, Historical Data, Letters from Librarians, Perry, Shaw, and Hepburn (PS&H) Archives of Colonial Williamsburg Foundation (ACWF).

58. J. Franklin Jameson to PS&H, Oct. 2, 1928, ibid.

59. *Annual Report of American Historical Association for the Year 1929* (Washington, D.C., 1930), 85.

60. James Harvey Robinson, *The New History* (Springfield, Mass., 1958), 1–25.

61. Thomas J. Wertenbaker, *The First Americans, 1607–1690* (New York, 1927), 283–301.

62. Ibid., 85–86.

63. Arthur M. Schlesinger, *The Rise of the City* (New York, 1933), 286.

64. Donald Millar to Perry, Oct. 24, 1928, Hist. Data, Beech and Dollfuss, PS&H, ACWF.

65. Edward P. Alexander, "Historical Restorations," *In Support of Clio* (Madison, Wis., 1958), 204–6; Herbert A. Kellar, "An Early American Gristmill," *Westerners Brand Book* (Chicago Corral), 4 (Mar. 1949), 1–3, 5–8.

66. Wayne D. Rasmussen, "The Growth of Agricultural History," *In Support of Clio*, 158.

67. Carl Bridenbaugh, *Peter Harrison, First American Architect* (Chapel Hill, N.C., 1949).

68. Ibid., viii, ix.

69. Ibid., xi.

70. Carl Bridenbaugh, *Seat of Empire: The Political Role of Eighteenth-Century Williamsburg* (Williamsburg, Va., 1950).

71. Platt, "Historian"; interview with Edward P. Alexander, May 28, 1970; *Annual Report of AHA, 1939* (Washington, D.C., 1941), 103–4.

72. *Annual Report of AHA, 1939*, 103.

73. Ibid.

74. Interview with Alexander.

75. *Annual Report of AHA, 1940* (Washington, D.C., 1941), 103.

76. Ibid., 106.

77. Ibid., 101.

78. Interview with Alexander.

79. Interviews with Herbert E. Kahler, June 19, 1970, and Ronald F. Lee, June 29, 1970.

80. *Harvard Guide to American History* (Cambridge, 1955), 61–63.

81. Interview with Frederick L. Rath, Jr., July 13, 1970.

82. Frank M. Setzler, "Archeological Accomplishments during the Past Decade in the United States," *Journal of the Washington Academy of Science*, 32, (Sept. 15, 1942), 255, 259.

83. Interview with Harringtons, May 18, 1970.

84. Interview with Clyde F. Trudell, Aug. 3, 1971.

85. Prentice Duell, "The Excavations at Williamsburg," *Architectural Record*, 69 (Jan. 1931), 16–17.

86. Interview with Minor Wine Thomas, July 13, 1970.

87. Interview with Harringtons, May 18, 1970.

88. See chapter 5.

89. Frederick Law Olmsted, *Report of the State Park Survey of California* (Sacramento, 1929).

90. Interview with Robert N. S. Whitelaw, June 22, 1972.

91. Arthur A. Schurcliff, "City Plan and Landscape Problems," *Architectural Record*, 78 (Dec. 1935), 382–86.

92. Interview with Ruth Wells, July 18, 1969.

93. Interview with Peterson, Feb. 9, 1970.

94. Lewis, "Burns."

95. Janet M. Cooley to author, Apr. 5, 1971.

96. Ibid.

97. Interview with Ralph H. Lewis, Dec. 16, 1969; interview with Ralph H. Lewis, Mar. 12, 1971, Harpers Ferry.

98. Interview with Helen McCormack, June 9, 1972.

99. Laurence Vail Coleman to author, July 22, 1965.

100. Laurence Vail Coleman, *Historic House Museums* (Washington, D.C., 1933).

101. Lewis Barrington, *Historic Restorations of the Daughters of the American Revolution* (New York, 1941), 210 plates.

102. Hosmer, *Presence of the Past*, 213–16, 250–51; Hosmer, "George Francis Dow," in Clifford L. Lord, ed., *Keepers of the Past* (Chapel Hill, N.C., 1965), 157–66.

103. Appleton to Coleman, Oct. 3, 1938, L. V. Coleman, SPNEA.

104. George F. Dow, *The Arts and Crafts in New England, 1704–1775* (Topsfield, Mass., 1927).

105. George F. Dow, *Every Day Life in the Massachusetts Bay Colony* (Boston, 1935).

106. Russell H. Kettell, ed., *Early American Rooms* (Portland, Maine, 1936).

107. See the Winterthur section of this chapter.

108. Interview with Kenneth Chorley, July 10, 1956, CWF.

109. Interview with Porter.

110. Interview with Jerome V. Ray, July 12, 1971.

111. Charles O. Cornelius to W. A. R. Goodwin, Nov. 16, 1926, Notes on Wythe House, Mar. 16, 1938, Wythe House, Architectural Reference Library, CWF.

112. Goodwin to Appleton, Dec. 21, 1927, Virginia, Wythe House, SPNEA.

113. Notes on Wythe House, Mar. 16, 1938, Wythe House, Arch. Reference Library, CWF.

114. Goodwin to Perry, Jan. 28, 1927, Hayes Diary, ACWF.

115. John D. Rockefeller, Jr., to Goodwin, May 24, 1927, ibid.

116. Goodwin to Perry, May 23, 1927, ibid.

117. Goodwin, Report, Nov. 19, 1927. ibid.

118. Chorley to Arthur Woods, Jan. 26, 1928, Administration—Architects and Engineers, 1928–32, and Perry to Goodwin, Jan. 30, 1928, ACWF.

119. Minutes of conference held at Williamsburg, Oct. 2–5, 1928, PS&H, Reports of Meetings Monthly, 1928–29, ACWF.

120. Goodwin to John S. Bryan, Oct. 10, 1928, Advisory Committee of Architects, ACWF.

121. Minutes of Advisory Comm. of Architects, Nov. 25, 1928, ibid.

122. Proceedings of Williamsburg Conference, New York, Dec. 11, 1928,

76–77, Conferences—Minutes and Reports, ACWF.

123. Minutes of Antique Committee, Dec. 11, 1928, ibid.

124. Interview with William G. Perry, July 17, 1970.

125. Interview with Trudell.

126. Oral history interview with Singleton P. Moorehead, 1957, CWF.

127. Milton B. Medary to PS&H, Jan. 3, 1929, and Perry to Medary, Mar. 5, 1929, PS&H, Advisory Committee, ACWF.

128. Rockefeller to Perry, July 30, 1929, PS&H, Policy and Procedure, 1928–30, ACWF.

129. Policy–Williamsburg, Sept. 17, 1929, Procedure—Restoration, 1928–30, ACWF.

130. Chorley to Perry, Oct. 18, 1929, PS&H, Policy and Procedure, 1928–30, ACWF.

131. Robert P. Bellows to PS&H, Apr. 25, 1930, and Fiske Kimball to Walter M. Macomber, Apr. 25, 1930, PS&H, Advisory Comm., Paradise House, ACWF.

132. Memo from Thomas M. Shaw to Andrew H. Hepburn, May 18, 1932, PS&H Conference and Arrangements, 1930–32, ACWF.

133. Interview with Orin M. Bullock, July 28, 1970.

134. Interview with Walter M. Macomber, July 8, 1972.

135. Interview with Everette Fauber, Sept. 12, 1972.

136. Interview with F. Paul Houck, Mar. 22–23, 1957, CWF; Duell to Hepburn, May 20, 1929, PS&H, Buildings Wren, P. Duell, 1929–30, ACWF.

137. Duell to Hepburn, Sept. 18, 1930, PS&H, Buildings Wren, P. Duell, 1929–30, ACWF.

138. Goodwin to Chorley, June 5, 1930, Excavations, 1929–35, ACWF.

139. Chorley to PS&H, June 16, 1930, ibid.

140. Interview with Harringtons, May 18, 1970; Perry to Harold R. Shurtleff, Jan. 27, 1931, PS&H (Williamsburg Office), Research General, 1928–31, ACWF.

141. Shurtleff to PS&H, Aug. 18, 1932, PS&H, Research Gen., 1932, ACWF.

142. Kimball to PS&H, May 28, 1932, PS&H, Research, Excavated materials, ACWF; T. R. Goodwin to W. A. R. Goodwin, Sept. 15, 1932, Goodwin Files Research, T. R. Goodwin, ACWF.

143. Chorley to Hepburn, Aug. 21, 1929, Research Gen., 1928–29, ACWF.

144. Perry to Woods, Mar. 29, 1930, Research, Shurtleff, H. R., Goodwin Files.

145. [T. Rutherfoord Goodwin], *The Williamsburg Restoration* (Williamsburg, 1931), 14.

146. Chorley to Woods, July 25, 1930, Research Gen., 1930, ACWF.

147. Shurtleff to Hepburn, July 25, 1930, ibid.

148. Perry to Woods, Sept. 13, 1930, Research, Shurtleff, H. R., Goodwin Files.

149. Shurtleff to Perry, Dec. 19, 1930, PS&H (Williamsburg Office), Research Reports, 1930–31, ACWF.

150. Shurtleff to Chorley, May 28, 1932, PS&H, Research Gen., 1932, ACWF.

151. Ibid.

152. Shurtleff to Chorley, June 1, 1932, Research, Conference of Historians, ACWF.

153. Proceedings of meeting of historians, Oct. 21, 1932, 23–26, Research, Advisory Committee of Historians, 1932–33, ACWF.

154. Ibid., 29, 31.

155. Final Report of Sub-Committee of Historians' Conference, Jan. 28, 1933, Research, Conf. of Historians, ACWF.

156. W. A. R. Goodwin to Woods, Dec. 14, 1932, Procedure—Restoration, 1931–33, ACWF.

157. Ethel Armes to Mrs. Charles Lanier, June 19, 1928, A2–29/Appendix, Binder, History RLMF (UDC), 1928–29, Robert E. Lee Memorial Foundation (LMF).

158. Report of Armes for 1928, B2–3/37, LMF.

159. William L. Bottomley to Virginia Campbell, Jan. 24, 1929, B2–6a/100, LMF.

160. Bottomley to Armes, Feb. 8, 1929, ibid.

161. Armes, Outline General Organization Form of RLMF, Apr. 1929, A2–29/Appendix, Binder, RLMF, 1929, LMF.

162. Mrs. Horace Van Deventer to Lanier, July 24, 1930, B2–6a/7, LMF.

163. Leicester Holland to Van Deventer, June 21, 1930, B2–6a/94, LMF.

164. Van Deventer to Kimball, July 1, 1930, B2–6a/46, LMF.

165. Kimball to Van Deventer, July 15, 1930, B2–6a/46 Restoration Comm., LMF.

166. Van Deventer to Lanier, July 24, 1930, B2–6a/7, LMF.

167. Kimball to Van Deventer, Aug. 16, 1930, B2–6a/46 Rest. Comm., LMF.

168. Erling Pedersen to author, Sept. 23, 1974.

169. Van Deventer to Kimball, Aug. 31, 1930, B2–6a/46 Rest. Comm., LMF; Ethel Armes, *Stratford Hall: The Great House of the Lees* (Richmond, 1936), 501.

170. Van Deventer to Lanier, Aug. 28, 1930, B2–6a/7, LMF.

171. Van Deventer to Kimball, Oct. 24, 1930, B2–6a/46, Rest. Comm., LMF.

172. Armes, General Report of Stratford Survey, Nov. 1, 1931, LMF.

173. Lanier to Mrs. L. N. Bashinsky, Sept. 28, 1931, A2–2a/Appendix, Binder, History RLMF (UDC), 1928–, LMF; Armes, *Stratford Hall*, 500–505.

174. Mrs. Emerson R. Newell to Van Deventer, Jan. 12, 1933, B2–6a/92, LMF.

175. Armes, "Stratford on the Potomac," *Antiques*, 23 (May 1933), 175–77.

176. Van Deventer to Kimball, Mar. 28, 1932, B2–6a/46, LMF.

177. Ulrich B. Phillips to Charles Nagel, Jr., Feb. 25, 1932, B2–3/45, LFM.

178. Everett V. Meeks to Armes, Mar. 3, 1932, B2–2/45, LMF.

179. Meeks to Van Deventer, Mar. 25, 1932, B2–6a/93, LMF.

180. Van Deventer to Kimball, Mar. 28, 1932, B2–6a/46, LMF.

181. Kimball to Van Deventer, Apr. 1, 1932, ibid.; interview with Erling H. Pedersen, Sept. 14, 1972.

182. Kimball to Van Deventer, May 25, 1932, B2–6a/101, LMF.

183. Newell to Van Deventer, Jan. 12, 1933, B2–6a/92, LMF.

184. Thomas T. Waterman to Armes, Feb. 27, 1933, B2–6a/95, LMF.

185. Meeks to Newell, June 3, 1933, B2–3/45, LMF.

186. Hosmer, *Presence of the Past*, 216–33.

187. Charles Messer Stow, "Milestones," *Antiques*, 41 (Jan. 1942), 22–23; Joseph Downs, "The History of the American Wing," *Antiques*, 51 (Oct. 1946), 233–37.

188. Joseph Downs, *American Furniture, Queen Anne and Chippendale Periods in the Henry Francis du Pont Winterthur Museum* (New York, 1952), v.

189. Henry Francis du Pont to Henry Davis Sleeper, July 7, 1925, Sleeper, H., Registrar's Office (Reg. Off.), Henry Francis du Pont Winterthur Museum (Wint.); Hosmer, *Presence of the Past*, 212.

190. Sleeper to du Pont, May 12, 1926, Sleeper, H., Reg. Off., Wint.

191. Du Pont to Sleeper, June 21, 1927, and Sleeper to du Pont, June 27, 1927, ibid.

192. Walter Mellor to du Pont, Jan. 9, 1924, Crowninshield, Mrs. F. B., Winterthur Estate Archives (WEA), Wint.

193. E. McClung Fleming, "History of the Winterthur Estate," *Winterthur Portfolio 1* (1964), 44.

194. Downs, *American Furniture*, vi.

195. Du Pont to Downs, May 16, 1928, Pennsylvania Museum 1928–29, and du Pont to Albert Ely Ives, Aug. 9, 1929, Winterthur, A. E. Ives, WEA, Wint.

196. Du Pont to Sleeper, Sept. 19, 1928, Sleeper, H., Reg. Off., Wint.

197. Du Pont to Bertha Benkard, May 31, 1932, Benkard, Mrs. 1932–33, Reg. Off., Wint.

198. Downs, "Mrs. Benkard," *Antiques*, 48 (Oct. 1945), 232.

199. Du Pont to J. A. L. Hyde, Oct. 6, 1927, Hyde, J. A. L., Reg. Off., Wint.

200. Ives to du Pont, Nov. 1927, and du Pont to Ives, May 7, 1927, Ives, A. E., Reg. Off., Wint.

201. Du Pont to Ives, May 16, 1928, ibid.

202. Du Pont to Sleeper, Sept. 19, Oct. 12, 1928, Sleeper, H., Reg. Off., Wint.

203. Ibid., Nov. 12, 1930.

204. Ibid., Feb. 21, 1931.

205. Barbara Hearn to author, July 17, 1973.

206. Ibid., Aug. 1, 1973.

207. Du Pont to Benkard, May 31, 1932, Benkard, Mrs. 1932–33, Reg. Off., Wint.

208. Du Pont to Francis P. Garvan, July 2, 1931, Garvan, F. P., Reg. Off., Wint.

209. John A. H. Sweeney, *Winterthur Illustrated* (New York, 1963), 8.

210. Isabelle McCoy Jones to du Pont, Aug. 26, 1932, Jones, I. M., Reg. Off., Wint.

211. Du Pont to Charles O. Cornelius, Nov. 7, 1932, Cornelius, C. O., 1931–32, Reg. Off., Wint.

212. Thomas Tileston Waterman and John A. Barrows, *Domestic Colonial Architecture of Tidewater Virginia* (New York, 1932).

213. Du Pont to Waterman, Nov. 7, 1932, Waterman, T. T., 1933–34, Reg. Off., Wint.

214. "A Visit to Winterthur," *Walpole Society Notebook, 1932* (n.p., privately printed, 1932), 22.

215. Du Pont to Waterman, May 19, 1933, Waterman, T. T., 1933–34, Reg. Off., Wint.

216. Ibid., Aug. 22, 1933.

217. Waterman to du Pont, Sept. 3, 1935, Waterman, T. T., 1935, Reg. Off., Wint.

218. Du Pont to Waterman, Sept. 4, 1935, ibid.

219. Du Pont to Benkard, June 22, 1934, Benkard, Mrs. 1934, Reg. Off., Wint.

220. Du Pont to Waterman, Sept. 17, 1935, Waterman, T. T., 1935, Reg. Off., Wint.

221. Waterman to du Pont, Oct. 9, 1935, Bulfinch Stair Hall, Winterthur Museum Archives (WMA), Wint.; Waterman to du Pont, Oct. 16, 1935, Waterman, T. T., 1935, Reg. Off., Wint.

222. Sweeney, *Winterthur Illustrated*, 10.

223. Waterman to du Pont, Dec. 8, 1938, Waterman, T. T., 1938, Reg. Off., Wint.

224. Waterman to du Pont, Mar. 7, 1939, Waterman, T. T., 1939–41, Reg. Off., Wint.

225. Du Pont to Louise du Pont Crowninshield, Apr. 3, 1941, Crowninshield, Mrs. F. B., WEA, Wint.

226. Du Pont to Stephen S. Racz, July 17, 1935, Racz, S. S., Reg. Off., Wint.

227. Waterman to du Pont, Apr. 3, 1940, Waterman, T. T., 1939–41, Reg. Off., Wint.

228. *New York Sun*, Aug. 28, 1942.

229. Du Pont to Benkard, Aug. 3, 1943, Mrs. H. H. Benkard, WEA, Wint.

230. Waterman to du Pont, ca. May 1944, Shop Lane, WMA, Wint.;

Waterman to du Pont, May 12, 1944, Waterman, T. T., 1942–46, Reg. Off., Wint.

231. Waterman to du Pont, Sept. 12, 1944, Waterman, T. T., 1942–46, Reg. Off., Wint.

232. Joe Kindig, Jr., to du Pont, Sept. 12, 1945, and du Pont to Kindig, Dec. 13, 1945, Kindig, J., Reg. Off., Wint.; Hyde to du Pont, Feb. 6, 1946, Hyde, J. A. L., 1946–54, Reg. Off., Wint.

233. Waterman to du Pont, July 1, 1946, Waterman, T. T., 1942–46, Reg. Off., Wint.

234. John A. H. Sweeney, "The Evolution of Winterthur Rooms," *Winterthur Portfolio 1* (1964), 106–20.

235. Downs to du Pont, Oct. 26, 1946, Metropolitan Museum of Art, WEA, Wint.

236. Crowninshield to du Pont, June 18, 1948, Crowninshield, Mrs. F. B., 1942–49, WEA, Wint.

237. Downs and Charles F. Montgomery to du Pont, Sept. 27, 1948, Winterthur Museum–Downs, J., WEA, Wint.

238. Sweeney, *Winterthur Illustrated*, 12.

239. Du Pont to Mrs. E. H. Pringle, May 11, 1929, Pringle, E. H., Mr. and Mrs., WEA, Wint.

240. Du Pont to Cornelius, June 8, 1933, Cornelius, C. O., 1931–32, Reg. Off., Wint.

241. Cornelius to du Pont, June 6, 1933, ibid.

242. Du Pont to Waterman, Aug. 22, 1933, Waterman, T. T., 1933–34, Reg. Off., Wint.

243. Du Pont to Bertha Benkard, Nov. 12, 1937, Benkard, Mrs., 1937–39, Reg. Off., Wint.

244. Du Pont to Waterman, May 31, 1940, Waterman, T. T., 1939–41, Reg. Off., Wint.

245. Du Pont to Waterman, May 19, 1933, Waterman, T. T., 1933–34, Reg. Off., Wint.

246. Kettell to du Pont, Jan. 8, 1941, Kettell, R. H., WEA, Wint.; William G. Wendell to du Pont, Aug. 8, 1941, Warner House, WEA, Wint.

247. Interview with Henry and Helen Flynt, Aug. 1, 1969.

248. Whitelaw to du Pont, Aug. 15, 1933, Whitelaw, R. N. S., 1941–, WEA, Wint.

249. Albert B. Wells to du Pont, Oct. 29, 1940, Wells Historical Museum, WEA, Wint.

250. Walter Muir Whitehill, *Louise du Pont Crowninshield, 1877–1958* (Winterthur, 1960), 29.

251. *New York Sun*, May 19, 1934.

252. Minutes of Delaware Society for the Preservation of Antiquities, Dec. 12, 1937, and Apr. 25, 1938, Delaware Soc. for Pres. of Antiquities, WEA, Wint.

253. Du Pont to Mrs. Henry B. Thompson, Sept. 30, 1938, ibid.

254. J. F. Otwell to Appleton, May 16, 1938, and du Pont to Appleton, June 14, 1938, H. F. du Pont, SPNEA.

255. Du Pont to Appleton, Sept. 1, 1938, ibid.

256. Interview with Charles van Ravenswaay, July 9, 1973.

257. B. Floyd Flickinger to William M. Robinson, Nov. 19, 1931, Colonial National Historical Park (NHP), 1 Conferences, Records of NPS, National Archives (NA), Record Group (RG) 79.

258. Minutes of 12th Conference of NPS Executives, Apr. 3–8, 1932, 59, Files of Branch of History, Int.

259. Verne E. Chatelain to A. E. Demaray, April 21, 1933, ibid.

260. Chatelain to Chorley, May 14, 1934, National Parks, 1932–36, ACWF.

261. Group Conference of Historical and Archeological Superintendents, Nov. 23–24, 1934, 425–439, Colonial NHP Special File, 01.3 General Conference-History, Records of NPS, NA, RG 79.

262. Ibid., 439.

263. Interview with Verne E. Chatelain, Sept. 9, 1961.

264. Chatelain to Arno B. Cammerer, Feb. 20, 1935, Files of Branch of History, Int.

265. John C. Merriam to Harold L. Ickes, July 1, 1935, Historic Sites Act, Files of Branch of History, Int.

266. Ickes to Merriam, July 15, 1935, ibid.

267. Interview with Chatelain.

268. Hosmer, *Presence of the Past*, 140–45.

269. A. P. Stauffer, "The Lincoln Birthplace National Park," Feb. 26, 1936, 12, Files of Branch of History, Int.

270. Cammerer, memorandum for Washington and all Field Offices, June 20, 1938, ibid.

271. Lee, "Objectives and Policies of Historical Conservation," *Regional Review*, 2 (Mar. 1939), 8.

272. [Lee], "Organization and Functions, Branch of Historic Sites and Buildings," ca. 1940, Files of Branch of History, Int.

273. Malcolm Gardner and R. Taylor Hoskins to Flickinger, Mar. 9, 1934, Colonial NHP, 840 Educational Activities, Records of NPS, NA, RG 79.

274. Rogers W. Young, "Recommendations on the Continuance and Expansion of the Historical-Educational Program at Fort Pulaski," Jan. 30, 1937, Files of Branch of History, Int.

275. Interview with Chatelain; Carl P. Russell, "The History and Status of Interpretive Work in National Parks," *Regional Review*, 3 (July 1939), 7–14.

276. Hillory Tolson to author, Oct. 4, 1971, author's collection.

277. Interview with Bullock.

278. Interview with V. Aubrey Neasham, July 26, 1971.

279. Edwin W. Small, "Salem—A Pioneer in America's Sea Commerce," *Regional Review*, 1 (July 1938), 17–18.

280. Lee, "Objectives and Policies of Historical Conservation," *Regional Review*, 2 (Mar. 1939), 3–8; Ned Burns, "Museums: Where-When-Why," *Regional Review*, 6 (May–June 1941), 26–30.

281. "The Significance of Salem," *Regional Review*, 5 (Aug.–Sept. 1940), 19–21.

282. Interview with Frederick L. Rath, Jr., Aug. 5, 1969.

283. Ibid.

284. John P. O'Neill to J. Thomas Schneider, Aug. 26, 1935, HABS Headquarters File, Schneider Report, LC.

285. Ibid.

286. Elbert Cox to Stanley Pargellis, Apr. 24, 1946, Colonial NHP (Special File), Conferences, Records of NPS, NA, RG 79; interview with Harringtons, May 18, 1970.

287. Interviews with Harringtons, May 18, 1970, and Lee, June 29, 1970; list of those attending conference at Colonial National Historical Park, May 6–7, 1946, Colonial NHP (Special File), 1 Conferences, Records of NPS, NA, RG 79.

288. Conference program, May 6–7, 1946, Colonial NHP (Special File), 1 Conferences, Records of NPS, NA, RG 79.

289. J. C. Harrington to regional director, May 10, 1946, ibid.

290. Russell, memorandum for files, May 13, 1946, ibid.

291. Lee to Newton B. Drury, May 15, 1946, ibid.

292. Peterson to Turpin Bannister, Feb. 10, 1941, JNEM, 833.05 Museums, Records of NPS, NA, RG 79.

293. Interviews with Herbert Evison, July 21, 1973, and Philip T. Primm, Aug. 21, 1971.

294. Interview with Primm.

295. Clipping, Aug. 5, 1934, Pearl Chase File, Univ. of California at Santa Barbara (UCSB).

296. Minutes of meeting at La Purisima Concepcion, Aug. 8, 1934, in Frederick C. Hageman, *An Architectural Study of the Mission La Purisima Concepcion*, Apr. 1939, 152.

297. Drury to Pearl Chase, Jan. 25, 1935, and Wallace C. Penfield to William E. Colby, Feb. 1, 1935, P. Chase File, UCSB.

298. Penfield to California State Park Commission, Sept. 24, 1935, La Purisima Mission State Historical Park, 319–513, Division of Beaches and Parks, Department of Parks and Recreation (Cal. Parks).

299. Chase to Lawrence Merriam, May 25, 1935, P. Chase File, UCSB.

300. C. J. Dubrow to H. W. Whitsitt, Aug. 29, 1935, HABS, Files at La Purisima Mission, Lompoc, Calif.

301. Russell Ewing to regional officer, Sept. 9, 1935, Federal Records Center, San Francisco (Rec. Center SF).

302. Lee to reg. off., Oct. 18, 1935, ibid.

303. Ewing to reg. off., Oct. 22, 1935, ibid.

304. Ewing to reg. off., Dec. 2, 1935, ibid.

305. Merriam to Herbert Maier, Dec. 6, 1935, and Erik Reed, undated report, "Methods in Mission Excavation," ibid.

306. Merriam to Cammerer, July 1, 1936, Proposed National Historic Site, California 0–36, Records of NPS, NA, RG 79.

307. Interview with Arthur Woodward, Dec. 29, 1976.

308. Rexford Newcomb to Penfield, Sept. 17, 1936, Rec. Center SF.

309. Mark R. Harrington, "The Right Kind of Restoration," *Masterkey*, 12 (Jan. 1938), 6–10.

310. Report, Apr. 2, 1938 (National Bureau of Standards), Reports (Materials, etc.), La Purisima Mission.

311. Hageman to Edith Webb, May 21, 1938, F. C. Hageman, Architect, CCC, La Purisima Mission.

312. Edith Buckland Webb, *Indian Life at the Old Missions* (Hollywood, Calif., 1953), 105.

313. Olaf T. Hagen to reg. dir., Mar. 8, 1938, Tumacacori NM, 101–General, Records of NPS, NA, RG 79.

314. Hageman, *La Purisima*, 1–171.

315. Hagen to reg. dir., Nov. 7, 1939, Archeological Reports, SP–29, California State Archives, Sacramento.

316. Harrington, Report on Conference, La Purisima Camp, SP–29, July 13–14, 1940, La Purisima Mission SHP, 319–513, Cal. Parks.

317. H. V. Smith to Dana Bartlett, Oct. 22, 1940, Miscellaneous, La Purisima Mission; Bartlett to Smith, Nov. 12, 1940, Index of American Design, La Purisima Mission.

318. Lee to Drury, Dec. 11, 1940, N. Drury, La Purisima, Records of NPS, NA, RG 79.

319. Smith to Drury, Jan. 25, 1952, H. V. Smith, Project Superintendent, La Purisima Mission.

320. Russell to Frank Pinkley, June 12, 1946, Tumacacori NM, 101 General, Records of NPS, NA, RG 79.

321. Six Year Program for Tumacacori National Monument (NM), April 1934, T–12, Tumacacori NM, 600.01 Master Plan, Records of NPS, NA, RG 79.

322. Russell to Ansel F. Hall, Jan. 10, 1935, Tumacacori NM, 101 Gen., Records of NPS, NA, RG 79.

323. Pinkley to Cammerer, Apr. 4, 1935, ibid.

324. News release, Dec. 2, 1935, ibid.

325. Thomas C. Vint to Tolson, June 6, 1935, Tumacacori NM, 618 Publications, Records of NPS, NA, RG 79.

326. Hagen to Chatelain, Jan. 31, 1936, Tumacacori, Files of Branch of History, Int.

327. Kenneth B. Disher to Louis R. Caywood, May 15, 1936, Tumacacori NM, 101 Gen., Records of NPS, NA, RG 79.

328. Woodward, tentative exhibit plans for museum at Tumacacori NM, June 1936, Tumacacori NM, 833.05 Museums, Records of NPS, NA, RG 79.

329. Russell to Pinkley, June 12, 1936, Tumacacori NM, 101 Gen., Records of NPS, NA, RG 79.

330. Russell to Pinkley, Aug. 7, 1936, ibid.

331. Tolson, talk, Apr. 23, 1939, ibid.

332. Cox to reg. dir., Mar. 14, 1938, Files of Branch of History, Int.

333. Cox to Cammerer, June 29, 1938, Morristown NHP, 01 Conference, Records of NPS, NA, RG 79.

334. Edwin W. Small, Oscar S. Bray, and Barnette to Cammerer, July 27, 1938, Salem Maritime National Historic Site, Files of Branch of History, Int.

335. Demaray to Cox, Aug. 19, 1938, SMNHS, 611 Repairs and Improvements, Records of NPS, NA, RG 79.

336. Cox, Policy Governing Furnishing of Washington's Headquarters, May 18, 1938, Morristown NHP, 620 Guerin and Wick Houses, Records of NPS, NA, RG 79.

337. Cox to Vera Noon, June 8, 1938, Morristown NHP, 618 ERA, Records of NPS, NA, RG 79.

338. Vint to Cammerer, June 9, 1938, Morristown NHP, 620 Buildings Gen., Records of NPS, NA, RG 79.

339. Lee to Cammerer, Jan. 21, 1939, ibid.

340. Interview with Melvin J. Weig, Aug. 1974.

341. Weig, Documentary Justification for the Restoration of Washington's Headquarters, Morristown NHP, Feb. 2, 1939, Morristown NHP, 620 Buildings Gen., Records of NPS, NA, RG 79.

342. Cox to Lee and Vint, Feb. 6, 1939, ibid.

343. Waterman, Architectural Justification for the Restoration of Washington's Headquarters, Morristown NHP, Feb. 25, 1939, Morristown NHP, Files of Branch of History, Int.

344. Vint to Cammerer, Mar. 2, 1939, Morristown NHP, 620 Buildings Gen., Records of NPS, NA, RG 79.

345. Dudley C. Bayliss to Cammerer, Apr. 20, 1939, ibid.

346. Waterman, Justification for the Reconstruction of the Main Stair, Washington's Headquarters, May 1939, ibid.

347. Interview with Weig.

348. Porter, memo, May 31, 1939, Morristown NHP, 620 Buildings Gen., Records of NPS, NA, RG 79.

349. Interviews with Rath, Aug. 5, 1969, and Weig.

350. A. F. Hopkins to Kahler, June 22, 1939, Morristown NHP, 620 Buildings Gen., Records of NPS, NA, RG 79.

351. Weig to Kahler, Jan. 25, 1940, ibid.

352. Hopkins to Lee, Apr. 10, 1940, Morristown NHP, 833.05 Museums, Records of NPS, NA, RG 79.

353. See chapter 8.

354. Lee to Cammerer, Feb. 29, 1940, Appomattox CH NHP, Gen., Records of NPS, NA, RG 79.

355. Bullock to regional landscape architect, June 23, 1940, ibid.

356. Roy E. Appleman, memorandum, July 29, 1940, Appomattox CH NHP, Reports, Records of NPS, NA, RG 79.

357. Ralph Happel, McLean House Study, Dec. 1940, Files of Branch of History, Int.

358. A. R. Kelly to regional director, Apr. 7, 1942, ibid.

359. Kahler to Vint, June 22, 1942, Appomattox CH NHP, McLean, Records of NPS, NA, RG 79.

360. Happel to author, Jan. 29, 1970.

361. Kahler to Vint, June 22, 1942, Appomattox CH NHP, McLean, Records of NPS, NA, RG 79.

362. Interview with Lee, Aug. 17, 1962.

363. Interview with Rath, July 13, 1970.

364. Bertram K. Little, selection of historic New England houses for preservation, May 28, 1948, and Lee to Drury, Oct. 22, 1948, Files of Branch of History, Int.

365. Little to G. Edwin Brumbaugh, Mar. 27, 1949, Seminars, 1949, New York State Historical Association, Cooperstown.

366. Ibid.

367. Ibid.

368. Institute in Preservation and Interpretation of Historic Sites and Buildings, June 6–14, 1949, Seminars and Short Courses, American University, Files of National Trust.

369. Ibid.

370. Betty Walsh to Lee, July 5, 1949, Seminars and Short Courses, American University, Files of National Trust.

Chapter 12: *New Restoration Techniques Emerge*

1. V. Aubrey Neasham, "Save the Ruins," *Region III Quarterly*, 2 (Jan. 1940), 29.

2. Interview with Charles W. Porter III, Apr. 20, 1970.

3. Ibid.

4. Ibid.

5. Arno B. Cammerer to Washington officers and field officers, May 19, 1937, Files of Branch of History, Interior (Int.)

6. William Sumner Appleton, "A Description of Robert McClaflin's House," *Old-Time New England*, No. 44 (Apr. 1926), 166.

7. Norman M. Isham, *In Praise of Antiquaries* (Boston, 1931), 21–22.

8. Laurence Vail Coleman, *Historic House Museums* (Washington, D.C., 1933), 54–56.

9. Ibid., 56.

10. Cammerer to Washington officers and field officers, May 19, 1937, Files of Branch of History, Int.

11. Coleman, *Museums*, 55, 160–65.

12. William Graves Perry, "Notes on the Architecture," *Architectural Record*, 78 (Dec. 1935), 369.

13. Ibid., 370.

14. W. A. R. Goodwin, "The Restoration of Colonial Williamsburg," *National Georgraphic Magazine*, 71 (Apr. 1937), 427.

15. Neasham, "The Preservation of Historic Monterey," *Pacific Historical Review*, 8 (June 1939), 215–19.

16. Herbert A. Claiborne, "The Philosophy of Restoration," *Walpole Society Notebook, 1951* (Portland, Maine, 1952), 21–23.

17. W. Duncan Lee, "The Renascence of Carter's Grove," *Architecture*, 68 (Apr. 1933), 185.

18. Ibid., 186.

19. Interview with Kenneth Chorley, July 9, 1956, Colonial Williamsburg Foundation (CWF).

20. Interview with William G. Perry, July 17, 1970.

21. *Baltimore Sun*, Nov. 4, 1924.

22. Goodwin to editor, *Baltimore Sun*, Nov. 11, 1924, Restoration Conception, W. A. R. Goodwin Files, Archives of Colonial Wiliamsburg Foundation (ACWF).

23. Goodwin to Arthur Woods, July 19, 1928, Procedure—Restoration, Goodwin Files.

24. Goodwin, report and recommendations Feb. 4, 1929, Restoration, Its Conception, Rockefeller, John D., Goodwin Files.

25. Goodwin to Woods, June 10, 1929, Procedure—Restoration, 1928–30, ACWF.

26. Goodwin to Perry, June 15, 1929, Procedure—Restoration, Goodwin Files.

27. Goodwin to Woods, Apr. 9, 1930, Policy and Procedure, 1928–30, Perry, Shaw, and Hepburn (PS&H) File, ACWF.

28. Goodwin to Chorley, Apr. 9, 1930, Guide Service, 1930–35, ACWF.

29. Goodwin to Woods, Oct. 11, 1930, Reports, Goodwin, W. A. R., 1928–30, ACWF.

30. Goodwin to Chorley, May 8, 1933, Procedure—Restoration, 1931–33, ACWF.

31. Perry to Goodwin, Oct. 7, 1927, in Elizabeth Hayes, "The Background and Beginnings of the Restoration of Colonial Williamsburg, Virginia, 1933," 139–41, ACWF.

32. Interview with Orin M. Bullock, Jr., July 28, 1970.

33. Perry, report to Williamsburg Holding Corporation, Vol. 1, Sept. 21, 1928, Part 1–3, ACWF.

34. Perry, general statement on restoration of Colonial Williamsburg, Dec. 31, 1946, 8, ACWF.

35. Ibid., 43–44.

36. Minutes of meeting of Advisory Committee of Architects, Nov. 25,

1928, 2, 4, Advisory Committee of Architects, ACWF.

37. Ibid., 5.

38. Ibid., 6.

39. Perry, "Notes," 370.

40. Minutes of Advisory Committee of Architects Meeting, Nov. 26, 1928, 10–12, Advisory Committee of Architects, ACWF.

41. Proceedings of Williamsburg Conference, Dec. 11, 1928, 15, Conferences, Minutes and Reports, 58, 61, ACWF.

42. Caro M. Rhind, Policy—Williamsburg, Sept. 17, 1929, Procedure—Restoration, 1928–30, ACWF.

43. Procedure for Restoration, Aug. 21, 1930, Research, General, 1930, ACWF.

44. Oral history interviews with F. Paul Houck, Mar. 22–23, 1957, and Singleton P. Moorehead, 1957, CWF.

45. Perry, General Statement, 9.

46. Fiske Kimball to Goodwin, Nov. 19, 1927, in Hayes, "Background," 151.

47. Oral history interview with Moorehead; Perry, "Notes," 373.

48. Perry to Edmund S. Campbell, July 12, 1928, Buildings, Wren, PS&H File, ACWF.

49. Perry, Gen. Statement, 69.

50. PS&H to Campbell, Dec. 12, 1928, Buildings, Wren, PS&H File.

51. Campbell to PS&H, Dec. 17, 1928, ibid.

52. Report of Art Commission of Commonwealth of Virginia to J. A. C. Chandler, Dec. 24, 1928, Buildings, Wren, Art Commission, PS&H File.

53. Milton B. Medary to PS&H, Jan. 3, 1929, Advisory Committee, Wren, PS&H File.

54. Kimball to PS&H, Mar. 13, 1929, Buildings, Wren, PS&H File.

55. Perry to Woods, Jan. 10, 1929, ibid.

56. Perry to R. E. Lee Taylor, Mar. 12, 1929, ibid.

57. Perry to Kimball, Mar. 15, 1929, ibid.

58. Perry, Gen. Statement, 19.

59. Oral history interview with Kenneth Chorley, July 10, 1956, CWF.

60. Medary to Walter M. Macomber, July 18, 1929, Buildings, Wren, PS&H File; Andrew H. Hepburn to Kimball, July 19, 1929, Advisory Committee, Wren, PS&H File.

61. Hepburn to Macomber, Sept. 10, 1929, Buildings, Wren, Office Correspondence, 1928–30, PS&H File.

62. Perry to Chandler, Oct. 7, 1929, Buildings, Wren, Advisory Committee, PS&H File.

63. Telegram from Goodwin to Perry, Dec. 23, 1929, Copperplate no. 30, 1930–32, PS&H File.

64. Perry to Woods, Feb. 3, 1930, Buildings, Wren, PS&H File.

65. Woods to Perry, Feb. 25, 1930, Buildings, Wren, Roof 1929–30, PS&H File.

66. Hepburn to Kimball, May 28, 1930, Advisory Comm., Wren, PS&H File.

67. Wren Buildings of College of William and Mary, 1951, Vol. II, Wren Building, Architectural Reference Library, CWF.

68. Ibid.

69. Macomber to Advisory Committee of Architects, Apr. 22, 1930, Advisory Committee of Architects, Paradise House, PS&H File.

70. Minutes of Advisory Committee of Architects meeting, Nov. 26, 1928, 7, ACWF.

71. Memorandum of conference with Woods, Nov. 23, 1928, Reports of Meetings, 1928–29, PS&H File.

72. Kimball to Macomber, Apr. 25, 1930, Advisory Committee of Architects, Paradise House, PS&H File.

73. Macomber to Advisory Committee of Architects, Apr. 22, 1930, ibid.

74. Robert P. Bellows to PS&H, Apr. 25, 1930, ibid.

75. Hepburn to Kimball, July 22, 1930, ibid.

76. A. Lawrence Kocher to Hepburn, Aug. 8, 1930, ibid.

77. Ibid.

78. Interview with Walter M. Macomber, July 8, 1972.

79. Marcus Whiffen, *The Eighteenth-Century Houses of Williamsburg* (Williamsburg, 1960), 115.

80. Ibid., 177.

81. PS&H, restoration of houses, Feb. 18, 1929, Policy and Procedure, 1928–30, PS&H File.

82. Charles O. Heydt to Perry, July 13, 1929, Block 29, Building no. 2, Tucker-Coleman House, 1929–31, ACWF.

83. Hepburn to Chorley, Feb. 19, 1930, ibid.

84. Chorley to Hepburn, Feb. 21, 1930, ibid.

85. Hepburn to Vernon M. Geddy, July 12, 1930, Buildings, Tucker House, PS&H File.

86. Chorley to Geddy, July 17, 1930, Block 29, Building no. 2, Tucker-Coleman House, 1929–31, ACWF.

87. Oral history interview with Mrs. George Coleman, Feb. 22, 1956, written reminiscence, 1932, 48, CWF.

88. Arthur A. Shurcliff to PS&H, Jan. 26, 1931, Block 29, Building no. 2, Tucker-Coleman House, 1929–31, ACWF.

89. Oral history interview with Coleman, Diary, Jan. 25, 1931, 56, 70, CWF.

90. Perry to Chorley, Aug. 28, 1931, Landscaping, Governor's Palace, 1931, PS&H File.

91. Verbatim minutes of Advisory Committee of Architects, Dec. 9, 1931, 9, Advisory Committee of Architects, 1928–32, PS&H File.

92. Perry, "Notes," 370.

93. Perry, report to Williamsburg Holding Corporation, Vol. I, Sept. 21, 1928, Part I-2, Report, 1928, ACWF.

94. Macomber, memorandum of conference, June 16, 1930, Reports of Meetings, 1930, PS&H File.

95. Hepburn to Woods, July 11, 1930, Procedure—Restoration, 1928–30, ACWF.

96. Kimball to Shaw, Aug. 26, 1930, Advisory Committee of Architects, Maupin House, PS&H File.

97. Macomber to PS&H, Oct. 8, 1930, ibid.

98. Addenda I, Minutes of Advisory Committee of Architects, Dec. 9–10, 1931, Advisory Committee of Architects, ACWF.

99. Goodwin to Perry, June 23, 1930, Procedure—Restoration, Goodwin Files.

100. Interview with Macomber.

101. Goodwin to Perry, June 23, 1930, Williamsburg Holding Corp., Suggested Policy and Procedure, 1929–31, PS&H File.

102. Perry to Goodwin, June 27, 1930, Procedure—Restoration, Goodwin Files.

103. Harold R. Shurtleff to Perry, Nov. 17, 1934, Buildings General, 1934, PS&H File.

104. Perry to Chorley, Dec. 7, 1934, ibid.

105. Chorley to Perry, Dec. 18, 1934, ibid.

106. Goodwin to Woods, May 3, 1928, Procedure—Restoration, Goodwin Files.

107. Macomber to Perry, May 19, 1930, Macomber, W., Goodwin Files.

108. Shaw to Macomber, May 22, 1930, ibid.

109. Shurtleff to Shaw, June 4, 1932, Disposition of Buildings, 1931–33. PS&H File.

110. Shurcliff, "City Plan and Landscaping Problems," *Architectural Record*, 78 (Dec. 1935), 383, 385.

111. Perry to author, Aug. 18, 1970, author's collection.

112. Interview with Macomber.

113. Shurtleff, report to PS&H, architects, upon the town plan and other matters relating to the restoration of Williamsburg, Sept. 1928, Vol. III, 7, Report 1928, ACWF.

114. Shurcliff to Chorley, Oct. 18, 1934, Landscaping, Governor's Palace, 1934, PS&H File.

115. Shurcliff to PS&H, Dec. 28, 1934, ibid.

116. Chorley to PS&H, Jan. 2, 1935, Landscaping, Governor's Palace, 1935, PS&H File.

117. PS&H to Shurcliff, Jan. 4, 1935, ibid.

118. Shurcliff to Chorley, Jan. 9, 1935, ibid.

119. PS&H to Chorley, Jan. 16, 1935, ibid.

120. Shurcliff to Chorley, Jan. 16, 1935, and Shurcliff to Anson B. Gardner, Feb. 14, 1935, ibid.

121. Shurtleff to Hepburn, Feb. 16, 1935, Research Report, 1935, PS&H File.

122. Ibid.

123. Interview with Finlay Ferguson, July 1, 1973.

124. Perry to Woods, Dec. 24, 1928, Advisory Committee of Architects, ACWF.

125. A. Edwin Kendrew to Research Dept., Feb. 1, 1938, Research, 1938, ACWF.

126. Elizabeth Hayes to Restoration, Inc., May 23, 1938, Block 21, Building no. 4, Wythe House, 1928–38, ACWF.

127. [Kendrew], Check List for Restoring a Building, 1940, Architectural, 1940–43, ACWF.

128. Francis Duke, Archeological Report, Block 21, Area A (Wythe Lot), Aug. 31, 1939, Wythe House, Architectural Research Library, CWF.

129. T. Rutherfoord Goodwin to Kendrew, Jan. 11, 1940, Block 21, Building no. 4, Wythe House, 1940–47, ACWF.

130. E. G. Liebold to William H. Meadowcroft, June 2, 1928, Acc. 104, Addenda, Box 6, Ford Archives (FA).

131. Oral history interview with Charles Voorhess, April–June 1951, 157, FA.

132. Francis Jehl, *Menlo Park Reminiscences* (Dearborn, Mich., 1941), III, 1135.

133. F. A. Wardlaw to Frank Campsall, June 21, 1928, Menlo Park, Registrar's File, Henry Ford Museum (HFMR); oral history interview with E. J. Cutler, Dec. 15, 1955, Menlo Park, Henry Ford Museum Library (HFML).

134. Wardlaw to Campsall, July 2, 1928, Menlo Park, HFMR; interview with Cutler, HFML.

135. James W. Bishop to Meadowcroft, July 21, 1928, Acc. 104, Addenda, Box 6, FA.

136. Jehl to Campsall, Dec. 3, 1928, Jehl—Edison Laboratory, HFMR.

137. James A. Humberstone to J. F. Perault, Dec. 17, 1928, Menlo Park, HFMR.

138. Jehl to Henry Ford, Feb. 7, 1929, Jehl—Edison, HFMR; Ida Jordan Day to Campsall, May 21, 1929, Jordan House, HFMR.

139. F. R. Schell to Campsall, Mar. 14, and Campsall to Schell, Mar. 19, 1929, Acc. 104, Addenda, Box 7, FA.

140. Wardlaw to Campsall, Apr. 24, 1929, Menlo Park, HFMR.

141. Campsall to Jehl, May 1, 1929, Jehl—Edison Laboratory, HFMR.

142. Campsall to Meadowcroft, July 8, 1929, Edison Laboratory, HFMR.

143. Jehl, *Menlo Park*, III, 1139–40.

144. Ibid., 1144.

145. H. I. Brock, "In His Museum Mr. Ford Glorifies Work," *New York Times Magazine*, Sept. 8, 1929, 9, 20.

146. See chapter 2.

147. Mrs. Horace Van Deventer to Mrs. Charles Lanier, Mar. 2, 1929, B2–6a/3, Robert E. Lee Memorial Foundation Archives (LMF).

148. Lanier to Horace Van Deventer, Mar. 7, 1929, ibid.

149. William L. Bottomley to Lanier, Apr. 25, 1929, B2–6a/100, LMF.

150. Bottomley, report of inspection, Jan. 24, 1930, ibid.

151. Kimball to Mrs. Van Deventer, July 15, 1930, B2–6a/46, Restoration Committee, LMF.

152. Coleman, *Museums*, 56; Newton B. Drury to Aubrey Drury, May 13, 1948, N. Drury, Historic Sites, Records of National Park Service (NPS), National Archives (NA), Record Group (RG) 79.

153. Kimball to Mrs. Van Deventer, May 25, 1932, B2–6a/101, LMF.

154. Kimball to Van Deventer, July 13, 1932, B2–6a/46, LMF.

155. Kimball, "Stratford Yesterday and Tomorrow," Oct. 1932, 1–10, B2–6a/47, LMF.

156. Ibid., 7.

157. Ibid., 24.

158. Kimball to Van Deventer, Mar. 27, 1933, B2–6a/53, LMF.

159. Kimball to Herbert A. Claiborne, Apr. 16, 1933, B2–6a/76, LMF.

160. Kimball to Van Deventer, July 7, 1933, ibid.

161. Kimball, report to Van Deventer, Sept. 23, 1933, A2–2a/197, LMF.

162. Kimball to Mrs. Robert B. Bingham, Feb. 5, 1934, A2–1a/105, LMF.

163. Kimball to Van Deventer, Feb. 23, 1934, B2–5a/Van Deventer II, LMF.

164. Ibid., Apr. 11, 1934.

165. Kimball to Van Deventer, Aug. 11, 1934, A2–1a/128, LMF.

166. Kimball to Erling Pedersen, Aug. 11, 1934, B2–5a/Van Deventer II, LMF.

167. Kimball to House Restoration Committee, May 18, 1935, B2–5a/ Mansion Front Steps, LMF.

168. B. F. Cheatham, sketch of steps, Sept. 6, 1935, B2–6a/5, LMF; Pedersen to Van Deventer, Sept. 17, 1935, B2–5a/Van Deventer II, LMF.

169. Van Deventer to Kimball, Nov. 9, 1935, ibid.

170. Ibid.

171. Kimball to Van Deventer, Nov. 19, 1935, B2–5a/Van Deventer II, LMF.

172. Kimball to Van Deventer, May 1, 1941, B2–5a/Van Deventer III, LMF.

173. Ibid.

174. Charles B. Hosmer, Jr., *Presence of the Past: A History of the Preservation Movement in the United States before Williamsburg* (New York, 1965), 284–86.

175. William S. Appleton to William F. Macy, Dec. 28, 1925, Mass.— Nantucket, Jethro Coffin House, Society for the Preservation of New England Antiquities (SPNEA).

176. Murray P. Course, "The Old Ship Meeting-House in Hingham, Mass.," *Old-Time New England*, No. 61 (July 1930), 19–30; Appleton to Smith and Walker, July 21, 1930, Mass.—Hingham, Old Ship, SPNEA.

177. W. W. Cordingley to George Francis Dow, July 20, 1930, ibid.

178. Appleton to Cordingley, July 23, 1930, ibid.

179. Cordingley to Appleton, July 25, 1930, ibid.

180. Appleton to Cordingley, July 26, 1930, ibid.

181. Appleton to William Emerson, Nov. 10, 1943, Emerson-Howard House, SPNEA.

182. Appleton to D. Newton Barney, June 29, 1934, Conn.—Farmington, Whitman, SPNEA.

183. J. Fred Kelly to Appleton, July 25, 1934, ibid.; Kelly to Appleton, May 24, 1933, Conn.—Guilford, Acadian House, SPNEA.

184. Undated memo, Archives of The First Church of Christ, Scientist, in Boston.

185. Lucia C. Warren to Maude T. Merrill, Nov. 19, 1930, ibid.

186. Warren, memorandum, Feb. 20, 1931, ibid.

187. Warren, memorandum, Mar. 17, 1931, ibid.

188. Warren to George L. Sleeper, Mar. 20, 1931, ibid.

189. Interview with Jerome V. Ray, July 12, 1971.

190. Fern N. Pond to Robert Kingery, July 18, 1937, Pond Papers, Illinois State Historical Library (ISHL).

191. Joseph F. Booton to Kingery, Sept. 22, 1937, ibid.

192. Kingery to Booton, Sept. 24, 1937, ibid.

193. Interview with Joseph F. Booton, Apr. 17, 1971.

194. Booton to Kingery, Oct. 2, 1937, Pond Papers, ISHL.

195. A. E. Henning to Joseph R. Knowland, Aug. 20, 1937, J. R. Knowland, California State Archives (CA).

196. California State Park Commission Minutes, Aug. 27, 1937, 42, Interpretive Services, Division of Beaches and Parks, Department of Parks and Recreation (Cal. Parks).

197. Ibid., 43.

198. Verne E. Chatelain to A. E. Demaray, Apr. 21, 1933, General History Branch, Activities, Functions and Organization, Files of Branch of History, Int.

199. W. A. R. Goodwin to D. M. Bates, Mar. 23, 1934, quoted in General Society of Colonial Wars, *Minutes of the Forty-Seventh General Council Meeting, April 7, 1934*, 12.

200. Demaray [Ronald F. Lee] to G. B. Arthur, Aug. 9, 1934, Colonial National Historical Park (NHP), 620—Restorations, Records of NPS, NA, RG 79.

201. Group Conference of Historical and Archeological Superintendents, Nov. 23–24, 1934, 425, Colonial NHP, 01.3 General Conference—History, Records of NPS, NA, RG 79.

202. U.S. Congress, House Committee on Public Lands, *Preservation of Historic American Sites, Buildings, Objects and Antiquities of National Significance*, Hearings on H. R. 6670 and H.R. 6734 (Washington, D.C., 1935), 5–6.

203. Ibid., 29–32.

204. Lee to Conrad L. Wirth, Oct. 12, 1935, Proposed NHS, Miscellaneous, 0–36, Records of NPS, NA, RG 79.

205. Minutes of Advisory Board on National Parks, Historic Sites, Buildings, and Monuments, Feb. 13–14, 1936, 2, Files of Branch of History, Int.

206. Ibid., 8–9.

207. Olaf T. Hagen to Chatelain, Jan. 31, 1936, Tumacacori, Files of Branch of History, Int.

208. Ibid.

209. Interview with Porter.

210. Projects for Restoration of Sites and Structures of Historical or Archeological Importance, Aug. 26, 1936 (WPA Operating Procedure No. 0–4), Files of Branch of History, Int.

211. Minutes of Advisory Board, Mar. 26, 1937, 11, 56–57, Files of Branch of History, Int.

212. Ibid., 12.

213. Cammerer to Washington officers and field officers, May 19, 1937, Files of Branch of History, Int.

214. Ibid.

215. Ibid., June 20, 1938.

216. "Historical Preservations and Reconstructions," *Park and Recreation Structures*, 1938.

217. Richard Lieber to Cammerer, May 25, 1937, Proposed NHS, Misc. 0–36, Records of NPS, NA, RG 79.

218. Lee, "Objectives and Policies of Historical Conservation," *Regional Review*, 2 (Mar. 1939), 8.

219. Neasham, "Save the Ruins," 29.

220. Interview with V. Aubrey Neasham, July 26, 1971.

221. Interview with Newton B. Drury, July 28, 1971.

222. N. B. Drury to A. Drury, May 13, 1948, N. Drury, Historic Sites, Records of NPS, NA, RG 79.

223. Porter to Herbert O. Brayer, Mar. 8, 1945, Preservation File, Files of Branch of History, Int.

224. William M. Robinson, Jr., Outline of Development, Colonial National Monument, July 12, 1933, 211–12, Colonial NHP, Development Outline, Records of NPS, NA, RG 79.

225. B. Floyd Flickinger to Charles E. Peterson, Mar. 17, 1934, Colonial NHP, 620 Swan Tavern, Records of NPS, NA, RG 79.

226. Peterson to Flickinger, Mar. 21, 1934, ibid.

227. Peterson, The Physical History of the Moore House, 1930–34, Oct. 15, 1934, Covering letter, Colonial NHP, 620 Moore House, Records of NPS, NA, RG 79.

228. H. Summerfield Day to Flickinger, Oct. 11, 1935, Colonial NHP, Ambler, Records of NPS, NA, RG 79.

229. Horace M. Albright (Chatelain) to Fred A. Crane, June 21, 1933, Morristown NHP, 101-General, Records of NPS, NA, RG 79.

230. Interview with Melvin J. Weig, Aug. 1974.

231. Interview with Elbert Cox, May 9, 1970.

232. Ibid.

233. Peterson to W. W. McCollum, Jan. 11, 1934, Morristown NHP, 620 Guerin and Wick Houses, Records of NPS, NA, RG 79.

234. Peterson to Vernon G. Setser, Jan. 19, 1934, ibid.

235. Ibid.; Grace J. Voght to Cammerer, Feb. 5, 1934, 620 Guerin and Wick Houses, Records of NPS, NA, RG 79; Thomas T. Waterman, Restoration of the Guerin and Wick Houses, Jockey Hollow, Jan. 17, 1934, 5, Files of Branch of History, Int.

236. Oliver G. Taylor, minutes of meeting, Feb. 7, 1934, to consider Public Works Projects, Feb. 8, 1934, Morristown NHP, 618 Public Works, Records of NPS, NA, RG 79.

237. Setser to Chatelain, May 22, 1934, Morristown NHP, 620 Guerin and Wick Houses, Records of NPS, NA, RG 79.

238. Setser to Chatelain, July 12, 1934, Files of Branch of History, Int.

239. Meeting at La Purisima, Aug. 8, 1934, quoted in Fred C. Hageman, *An Architectural Study of the Mission La Purisima Concepcion, January, 1935 to April, 1938*, typed report, 152, Interpretive Services, Cal. Parks.

240. Charles B. Wing, report on ECW Projects at Santa Rosa Camp DSP-3, Jan. 24, 1935, no. 6 ECW Camps, Division of Parks, 1935, CA.

241. Herbert Maier, report to district officer, Jan. 1935, ibid.

242. N. B. Drury to Pearl Chase, Jan. 25, 1935, P. Chase File, University of California at Santa Barbara (UCSB).

243. Wallace C. Penfield to William E. Colby, Feb. 1, 1935, ibid.; Penfield to State Park Commission, Mar. 27, 1935, quoted in Hageman, *Architectural Study*, 155.

244. State Park Commission Minutes, Mar. 28, 1935, II, 178, Interpretive Services, Cal. Parks.

245. Harold Fleischnauer to State Park ECW, Sept. 19, 1935, Proposed NHS, California, 0–36, Records of NPS, NA, RG 79.

246. Russell C. Ewing, report on historical field investigation, Sept. 9, 1935, Federal Records Center, San Francisco (Rec. Center SF).

247. Ibid.

248. Ewing to regional officer, Nov. 7, 1935, Proposed NHS, California, 0–36, Records of NPS, NA, RG 79.

249. La Purisima Advisory Committee, preliminary report to State Park Commission, Sept. 24, 1935, La Purisima Mission State Historical Park, 319–513, Cal. Parks.

250. Ibid.

251. State Park Commission Minutes, Sept. 28, 1935, II, 202, Interpretive Services, Cal. Parks.

252. Ewing to reg. off., Mar. 18, 1936, Rec. Center SF.

253. Ibid.

254. Ibid., May 22, 1936.

255. Interview with Neasham.

256. Ewing, The Treatment of Historic Structures, Sept. 11, 1936 (cov-

ering letter, July 3, 1941), N. Drury, Historic Sites, Records of NPS, NA, RG 79.

257. Ibid.

258. Ibid.

259. Rexford Newcomb to Wallace C. Penfield, Sept. 17, 1936, Rec. Center SF.

260. Thomas Plassmann to Hageman, Sept. 26, 1936, F. C. Hageman, Architect, La Purisima Mission, Lompoc, Calif.

261. State Park Commission Minutes, Nov. 14, 1936, 264, Interpretive Services, Cal. Parks.

262. Ewing to Fleischauer, Dec. 17, 1936, Proposed NHS, California, 0–36, Records of NPS, NA, RG 79.

263. Demaray to Herbert E. Bolton, May 25, 1937, Rec. Center SF.

264. Lee to Charles R. Hicks, May 29, 1937, ibid.

265. Bolton to Demaray, July 1, 1937, Proposed NHS, California, 0–36, Records of NPS, NA, RG 79.

266. Ibid.

267. Hageman, review of data used as basis for restoration of La Purisima Church, July 9, 1937, Rec. Center SF; Ewing, Mission La Purisima Concepcion, Aug. 25, 1937, Mission La Purisima Concepcion, Ewing, 1937, Cal. Parks.

268. "Rebuilding the Past," *Union Oil Bulletin*, 18 (Oct. 1937), 8.

269. Hagen to regional director, Mar. 8, 1938, Tumacacori NM, 101—General, Records of NPS, NA, RG 79.

270. Hageman to Drury, Mar. 18, 1938, N. Drury, Records of NPS, NA, RG 79.

271. Ibid.

272. Guy L. Fleming to Henning, June 17, 1938, Fleming, District Superintendent, La Purisima Mission.

273. Minutes of La Purisima Advisory Committee, July 20, 1938, P. Chase File, UCSB.

274. Hagen to regional director, Aug. 18, 1938, Tumacacori NM, 101—General, Records of NPS, NA, RG 79.

275. Neasham to Drury, Aug. 19, 1938, ibid.

276. State Park Commission Minutes, Sept. 23, 1938, 109–10, Interpretive Services, Cal. Parks.

277. Ibid., Mar. 4, 1939, 140–41.

278. Mark R. Harrington, stone structure, supposed infirmary building, furnishings, Mar. 31, 1939, Archeological Reports, Sp-29, CA; Hagen to regional director, Mar. 31, 1939, Proposed NHS, California, 0–36, Records of NPS, NA, RG 79.

279. Hageman, Harrington, and Arthur A. Woodward to regional director, June 15, 1939, Archeological Reports, Sp-29, CA.

280. Harrington to Frank A. Kittredge, Nov. 27, 1939, M. R. Harrington, CCC, 1935–41, La Purisima Mission.

281. Hagan to regional director, Nov. 30, 1939, P. Chase File, UCSB.

282. E. D. Rowe, report of gardens and plants at La Purisima Mission, Aug. 1939, Proposed NHS, California, 0–36, Records of NPS, NA, RG 79.

283. Fleming to Harrington, Jan. 11, 1940, Fleming, District Superintendent, La Purisima Mission.

284. Harrington to H. V. Smith, Oct. 24, 1940, M. R. Harrington, CCC, 1935–41, La Purisima Mission.

285. Woodward to regional director, June 15, 1941, A. Woodward, La Purisima Mission.

286. Hagen, review of consideration in reintroduction of mission arts, crafts, and industries, Aug. 7, 1941, Hagen, O. T., Historian, CCC, La Purisima Mission.

287. Hagen to Harrington, Aug. 14, 1941, Proposed NHS, California, 0–36, Records of NPS, NA, RG 79.

288. Interview with Pearl Chase, Aug. 8, 1971.

289. Fleming to Drury, Nov. 1, 1941, Proposed NHS, California, 0–36, Records of NPS, NA, RG 79.

290. Demaray to Chase, June 4, 1941, P. Chase File, UCSB.

291. Weig, Thor Borresen, John C. Fisher Motz, and Lemuel A. Garrison to regional director, Apr. 11, 1940, Hopewell Village NHS, 101—General, Records of NPS, NA, RG 79.

292. Ibid.

293. Garrison to Francis S. Ronalds, Aug. 27, 1940, Hopewell Village NHS, 101—Gen., Records of NPS, NA, RG 79.

294. Weig to Ronalds, Aug. 28, 1940, ibid.

295. Ronalds to Drury, May 21, 1941, Hopewell Village NHS, 201—Administration, Records of NPS, NA, RG 79.

296. V. R. Ludgate, memo, June 13, 1941, ibid.

297. Roy E. Appleman, memo, June 19, 1941, ibid.

298. Edmund Preece to Branch of Historic Sites, May 7, 1942, Hopewell Village NHS, Reports 207, Records of NPS, NA, RG 79.

299. Thomas J. Allen to Drury, June 8, 1942, Hopewell Village NHS, 620—Buildings, Records of NPS, NA, RG 79.

300. Peterson, "Manuel Lisa's Warehouse," *Bulletin of Missouri Historical Society*, 4 (Jan. 1948), 66.

301. Ibid., 68–69.

302. Ibid., 71–72.

303. Preece, discussion concerning the relation of historical restoration and structural design, Sept. 20, 1941, Files of Branch of History, Int.

304. Ibid.

305. D. Knickerbacker Boyd to Branch Spalding, Nov. 20, 1936, Proposed NHS, Valley Forge, 0–36, Records of NPS, NA, RG 79.

306. Villita Ordinance, 0I–355, Oct. 12, 1939, Preamble, City of San Antonio.

307. Interview with O'Neill Ford, June 29, 1971.

308. Maury Maverick to Alvin Wirtz, Jan. 15, 1940, Proposed NHS, Texas, 0–36, Records of NPS, NA, RG 79.

309. See chapter 5.

310. Lee, "The Effect of Postwar Conditions on the Preservation of Historic Sites and Buildings," talk given to American Assn. for State and Local History, Oct. 26, 1946, Files of Branch of History, Int.

311. Interview with Ronald F. Lee, Aug. 17, 1962.

312. Minutes of informal conference preliminary to organization of National Council on Historic Sites and Buildings, Feb. 5, 1947, N. Drury, National Council, Records of NPS, NA, RG 79.

313. For the development of National Trust policies see Elizabeth D. Mulloy, *History of the National Trust for Historic Preservation, 1963–1973* (Washington, D.C., 1976).

314. National Council Second Annual Meeting Minutes, Nov. 5, 1948, 9, National Trust.

Chapter 13: *Preservation Theory Comes of Age*

1. Henry-Russell Hitchcock, *Rhode Island Architecture* (New York, 1968), v.

2. Hitchcock, "Destruction," *Architectural Record*, 64 (Dec. 1928), 531.

3. "Summary of the Round Table Discussion on the Preservation of Historic Architectural Monuments," *Journal of the American Society of Architectural Historians*, 1 (Apr. 1941), 22.

4. H. I. Brock, "Landmarks Today; They Pass Tomorrow. Progress Submerges, If It Does Not Remove, Things That Have Their Day of Fame in the City of New York," *New York Times Magazine*, Nov. 18, 1928, 10.

5. "Gimcracks and Spizzerinktums," *Pencil Points*, 13 (Mar. 1932), 206, 212.

6. William Sener Rusk, "What Price Progress?" *Art and Archaeology*, 23 (July-Aug. 1932), 195–205.

7. Laurence Vail Coleman, *Historic House Museums* (Washington, D.C., 1933), 17.

8. Ibid., 20.

9. Clay Lancaster, "Save Boscobel!" *Antiques*, 49 (Apr. 1946), 244.

10. Frank J. Roos, Jr., *Bibliography of Early American Architecture* (Urbana, Ill., 1968), 4–5.

11. *Journal of American Society of Architectural Historians*, 2 (Oct. 1942), 35–37.

12. Roos, *Bibliography*, 16.

13. Richard F. Bach, "Early American Architecture and Allied Arts—a Bibliography," *Architectural Record*, 63 (June 1928), 577.

14. Interview with Frederick L. Rath, Jr., July 13, 1970.

15. *Antiques*, 41 (Jan. 1942), 22–23.

16. Lancaster, "Save Boscobel!" 244–45.

17. *Antiques*, 58 (July 1950), 27–49.

18. Charles M. Stotz, *Early Architecture of Western Pennsylvania* (New York, 1936), 9.

19. Philip B. Wallace and William A. Dunn, *Colonial Ironwork in Old Philadelphia* (New York, 1930); *Colonial Houses, Philadelphia, Pre-Revolutionary Period* (New York, 1931); *Colonial Churches and Meeting Houses, Pennsylvania, New Jersey and Delaware* (New York, 1931).

20. Eleanor Raymond, *Early Domestic Architecture of Pennsylvania* (New York, 1931), 158 plates.

21. John Mead Howells, *Lost Examples of Colonial Architecture* (New York, 1931), 244 plates.

22. John Mead Howells, *The Architectural Heritage of the Piscataqua* (New York, 1937), 92.

23. *Great Georgian Houses of America*, Vol. 1 (New York, 1933), Vol. 2 (New York, 1937).

24. Deering Davis, Stephen P. Dorsey and Ralph Cole Hall, *Georgetown Houses of the Federal Period* (New York, 1944), 12.

25. Deering Davis, Stephen P. Dorsey, and Ralph Cole Hall, *Alexandria Houses, 1750–1830* (Cornwall, N.Y., 1946), 5.

26. Interview with Antoinette Downing, Oct. 4, 1974.

27. Norman M. Isham, *In Praise of Antiquaries* (N.p., Walpole Society, 1931), 21.

28. Thomas Tileston Waterman and John A. Barrows, *Domestic Colonial Architecture of Tidewater Virginia* (New York, 1932).

29. Thomas Tileston Waterman, *The Mansions of Virginia, 1706–1776* (Chapel Hill, N.C., 1945), 403–11.

30. Harold R. Shurtleff, *The Log Cabin Myth* (Gloucester, Mass., 1967), 3.

31. Ibid., 186–215.

32. A. Lawrence Kocher and Howard Dearstyne, *Colonial Williamsburg, Its Buildings and Gardens* (New York, 1949), 43–50.

33. Henry Chandlee Forman, *Early Manor and Plantation Houses of Maryland, 1634–1800* (Easton, Md., 1934).

34. See chapter 9.

35. Henry Chandlee Forman, *Jamestown and St. Mary's* (Baltimore, 1938).

36. Charles E. Peterson, Physical History of the Moore House, 1930–1934 (Oct. 15, 1935), Colonial NHP, Moore House 620, Records of NPS, NA, RG 79; Peterson, "Some Recent Discoveries at Jamestown," *Antiques*, 29 (May 1936), 192–94.

37. Peterson, "Manuel Lisa's Warehouse," *Bulletin of Missouri Historical Society*, 4 (Jan. 1948), 59–91.

38. Joseph F. Booton, *Record of Restoration of New Salem State Park, 1932–1933* (Springfield, Ill., 1934).

39. *Architectural Record*, 65 (Apr. 1929), 414–16.

40. Society of Architectural Historians *Newsletter*, 12 (June 1968), 3.

41. Henry-Russell Hitchcock, *The Architecture of H. H. Richardson and His Times* (Cambridge, Mass., 1966).

42. Lewis Mumford, *The Brown Decades: A Study of the Arts in America, 1865–1895* (New York, 1955), 50–51.

43. Hitchcock, "Destruction," 530–31.

44. Hitchcock, *Richardson*, 273.

45. Ibid., ix.

46. Hitchcock, *Rhode Island*, 61–62.

47. Hugh Morrison, *Louis Sullivan, Prophet of Modern Architecture* (New York, 1962), 109–10.

48. Carl W. Condit, *The Chicago School of Architecture* (Chicago, 1964), 74, 77.

49. George Kubler, *Religious Architecture of New Mexico* (Colorado Springs, 1940).

50. Everard M. Upjohn, *Richard Upjohn, Architect and Churchman* (New York, 1939).

51. Ibid., vi.

52. Roger Hale Newton, *Town and Davis, Architects* (New York, 1942), xvi–xvii.

53. Talbot Hamlin, *Greek Revival Architecture in America* (New York, 1944), xviii.

54. Ibid., 3–45.

55. Agnes Addison Gilchrist, *William Strickland, Architect and Engineer, 1788–1854* (Philadelphia, 1950).

56. Thomas Tallmadge, *The Story of Architecture in America* (New York, 1936), 320–24.

57. Ibid., 320.

58. Sigfried Giedion, *Space, Time and Architecture* (Cambridge, 1967), 372.

BIBLIOGRAPHY

The principal source material for this book came from various preservation archives all over the United States and from 85 taped interviews that have been transcribed and indexed. The printed sources, which were important from time to time, are occasionally mentioned in the text. The notes provide a full listing of the books and magazines consulted.

INTERVIEWS

The following individuals are represented by one or more transcripts of taped interviews:

E. Florence Addison
Horace M. Albright
Edward P. Alexander
Roy E. Appleman
William Boizelle
Joseph F. Booton
Paul V. Brown
John A. Bryan
Helen Duprey Bullock
Orin M. Bullock
E. Milby Burton
Josephine and Mary Burtschi
George P. Campbell
Pearl Chase
Verne E. Chatelain
Janet M. Cooley
William King Covell
Elbert Cox
Alston Deas
Paul Delaney
Arthur S. Dewing
Irving Dilliard
Antoinette Downing
Newton B. Drury
Emily Edwards
Albert Erb

S. Herbert Evison
J. Everette Fauber
Finlay F. Ferguson
Helen and Henry Flynt
Mrs. Jules Fontaine
O'Neill Ford
Milton Grigg
Mary Harral
Virginia and Jean C. Harrington
Ethel Harris
Louis C. Jones
Herbert E. Kahler
Harnett T. Kane
Richard Koch
Richard Lawwill
Ronald F. Lee
Ralph Lewis
Bertram K. Little
Theodore Liuzza
Clifford L. Lord
Helen McCormack
Walter M. Macomber
Albert Manucy
Ward Melville
Mrs. George M. Morris
James J. Morrison

BIBLIOGRAPHY

V. Aubrey Neasham
Mayo H. O'Donnell
Philip Dana Orcutt
George A. Palmer
Erling Pedersen
William G. Perry
Charles E. Peterson
Thomas Pitkin
Charles W. Porter III
Philip Primm
Frederick L. Rath, Jr.
Jerome V. Ray
Martha G. Robinson
J. Thomas Schneider
Mary W. Scott
Albert Simons

Edwin Small
Sylvester K. Stevens
Charles M. Stotz
Minor Wine Thomas, Jr.
Clyde F. Trudell
Charles van Ravenswaay
Katherine U. Warren
C. Malcolm Watkins
Elsa Watson
Terrell Maverick Webb
Melvin J. Weig
Ruth Wells
Robert N. S. Whitelaw
Samuel Wilson, Jr.
Arthur Woodward

ARCHIVES AND LIBRARIES

American Institute of Architects, Washington, D.C.
Archives of the Mother Church, the First Church of Christ, Scientist, Boston.
Bancroft Library, University of California, Berkeley.
California Division of Beaches and Parks, Department of Parks and Recreation, Sacramento.
Carnegie Institution of Washington, Washington, D.C.
Charleston City Archives, Charleston, S.C.
Colonial Williamsburg Foundation, Williamsburg, Va., Architecture Reference Library and Archives.
Department of Conservation, Division of Parks and Memorials, Springfield, Ill.
Federal Records Center, San Francisco.
Ford Archives, Henry Ford Museum and Greenfield Village, Dearborn, Mich.
Hammond-Harwood House Association, Inc., Annapolis.
Henry Ford Museum and Greenfield Village, Dearborn, Mich., Library and Registrar's File.
Henry Francis du Pont Winterthur Museum, Winterthur, Del., Registrar's File, Winterthur Estate Collection, Joseph Downs Manuscript and Microfilm Collection.
Historic Charleston Foundation, Charleston, S.C.
Historic New Orleans Collection, New Orleans.
Illinois State Historical Library, Springfield, Ill.
Independence National Historical Park, Philadelphia.
Indiana State Library, Indianapolis.
La Purisima State Historic Park, Lompoc, Calif.

Bibliography

Library of Congress, Washington, D.C., Prints and Photographs Division.

Lilly Library, Indiana University, Bloomington.

Monterey History and Art Association, Monterey, Calif.

National Archives, Records of the National Park Service, Record Group 79, Central Classified Files, Washington, D.C.

National Park Service Archives, Harpers Ferry Center, Harpers Ferry, W.Va.

National Park Service, Files of the Branch of History, Department of the Interior, Washington, D.C.

National Trust for Historic Preservation, Washington, D.C.

Neasham, V. Aubrey, Personal Files, San Francisco.

New Orleans Public Library, New Orleans.

New York State Historical Association, Cooperstown.

Old Sturbridge Village, Sturbridge, Mass.

Oral History Research Office, Columbia University, New York, N.Y.

Pennsylvania Archives, Harrisburg.

Preservation Society of Charleston, Charleston, S.C.

Preservation Society of Newport County, Newport, R.I.

Proceedings and Correspondence, Clerk's Office, Alexandria, Va.

Regional Oral History Office, Bancroft Library, University of California, Berkeley.

Robert E. Lee Memorial Foundation (now Association), Stratford, Va.

San Antonio Conservation Society, San Antonio, Tex.

Society for the Preservation of New England Antiquities, Boston.

South Carolina Historical Society, Charleston.

University of Arizona Library, Tucson.

University of California at Santa Barbara Library, Santa Barbara.

Vieux Carré Commission, New Orleans.

Warner House Association, Portsmouth, N.H.

MANUSCRIPTS

Bullis, Mrs. G. P., "Background on origin of Natchez Pilgrimage," Scrapbook in the possession of Mrs. Balfour Miller, Natchez, Miss.

Charleston Survey of 1941, original cards, Carolina Art Association, Charleston.

Frederick, Robert Allen, "Colonel Richard Lieber, Conservationist and Park Builder: The Indiana Years," Diss., Indiana, 1960, 430 pp.

Hageman, Frederick C., *An Architectural Study of the Mission La Purisima Concepcion, January, 1935 to April, 1938* (Unpublished report), Apr. 1939, 171 pp., Interpretive Services, California Division of Beaches and Parks, Sacramento.

Huth, Hans, "Observations concerning the Conservation of Monuments in Europe and America," 1940 (Mimeographed), 64 pp., Files of the Branch of History, Department of the Interior, Washington, D.C.

Mayo, Chester Garst, Correspondence regarding preservation work in Portsmouth, N.H., 1937–1940, given to the author.

Moore, Mary Lucille, "A Critical and Historical Analysis of the Maurice G.
Fulton Collection of the New Mexicana in the University of Arizona Library," Thesis, Arizona, 1966, 131 pp.

Platt, John D. R., "The Historian and Historical Preservation," paper given at
the American Historical Association annual meeting, Dec. 28, 1963, in the
possession of John D. R. Platt, Philadelphia.

Ray, Jerome V., correspondence dealing with preservation in Illinois, 1937–1941,
given to the author.

Scrapbooks on the history of the Natchez Garden Pilgrimage, in the possession
of Mrs. Balfour Miller, Natchez, Miss.

CHRONOLOGY
1920–1953

1920

Society for the Preservation of Old Dwelling Houses formed May 5 to purchase Joseph Manigault House, Charleston, S.C.

Historical survey of U.S. battlefields conducted by Historic Section of U.S. Army War College.

1922

Antiques magazine begins publication to serve emerging group of U.S. collectors.

1923

Wakefield National Memorial Association formed Feb. 11 to reconstruct Wakefield farm, Va., George Washington's birthplace.

Henry Ford purchases Wayside Inn, Sudbury, Mass., in June as his first preservation involvement.

Thomas Jefferson Memorial Foundation purchases Monticello, Charlottesville, Va., Dec. 4.

1924

San Antonio Conservation Society formed Mar. 22 to prevent destruction of Greek Market House.

W. A. R. Goodwin approaches Edsel Ford and John D. Rockefeller, Jr., June 13 with proposal to recreate Williamsburg.

American Wing of Metropolitan Museum of Art, New York City, opens Nov. 11, focusing interest on historic interiors.

1925

Indiana accepts James Lanier Mansion, Madison, in March for restoration as its first historic property.

First Vieux Carré Commission, New Orleans, formed, becoming one of first local preservation commissions in U.S.

CHRONOLOGY

1926

Vieux Carré Association of local businessmen, New Orleans, formed to promote district's "civic, aesthetic and material prosperity."

San Antonio Conservation Society saves bend in San Antonio River from being drained and paved for parking lot.

Congress authorizes Wakefield Memorial Association in April to build "replica" of Washington's birthplace at Wakefield, Va.

Richard Lieber initiates Indiana state restoration program in August with old capitol, Corydon.

Restoration of Wythe House, Williamsburg, begins with support from Marshall Foundation and Colonial Dames of America.

Greenfield Village, Dearborn, Mich., established by Henry Ford in the fall.

John D. Rockefeller, Jr., visits Williamsburg in November and authorizes preparation of drawings for possible restoration.

1927

California's preservation organizations unite in February to support passage of bond issue for preservation and creation of California Park Commission.

Old Fort Niagara Association formed in June to lobby for restoration of Old French Castle near Youngstown, N.Y.

Richard Lieber negotiates in September for acquisition of Spring Mill area for Indiana Park system to recreate a pioneer village.

John D. Rockefeller, Jr., agrees on Nov. 21 to restoration of key elements of Williamsburg.

1928

Frederick Law Olmsted's *California State Park Survey* published, becoming first state preservation survey.

Role of John D. Rockefeller, Jr., in Williamsburg restoration made public June 12.

Advisory Committee of Architects established at Williamsburg in August to supervise restoration; meets first time in November.

1929

Horace M. Albright succeeds Stephen Mather as director of National Park Service Jan. 12, focusing on historical parks.

Robert E. Lee Memorial Foundation incorporated Feb. 1 to purchase and restore Lee's home, Stratford Hall, Va.

Educational Advisory Committee of National Park Service organized to advise on historical policy matters.

Custis-Lee Mansion, Arlington, Va., restored by U.S. Army; transferred to National Park Service in 1933.

Natchez Garden Club, Miss., formed.

Heyward-Washington House, Charleston, S.C., purchased in the spring with donation and local funds to prevent removal of paneling by museums.

Virginia State Commission on Conservation and Development proposes to National Park Service, on Mar. 27, a Colonial National Monument embracing Yorktown, Williamsburg, and Jamestown.

Charleston, S.C., enacts ordinance Apr. 23 creating temporary City Planning and Zoning Commission.

Pennsylvania acquires Pennsbury Manor site, near Morrisville, for reconstruction to memorialize William Penn.

Spanish Governor's Palace in San Antonio opens in summer, following municipal purchase aided by San Antonio Conservation Society.

Henry Ford purchases old Postville Courthouse in Lincoln, Ill., to move to Greenfield Village, Dearborn, Mich., in September.

"Helldorado" celebration held in October in Tombstone, Ariz., to fund city's plan to recreate the "Old West."

Golden Jubilee of Light at Greenfield Village celebrates 50th anniversary of first commercial light bulb with Oct. 21 opening of relocated Menlo Park, N.J., laboratory of Thomas Edison.

Congressman Louis Cramton in December blocks passage of appropriation bill for Wakefield farm, Va., to renegotiate custodianship from War Department to National Park Service.

Copper plate illustrating Wren Building and other structures in Williamsburg found in Oxford, England, Dec. 23, providing information needed for accurate restoration.

1930

Continental Army's winter campgrounds in Morristown, N.J., Jockey Hollow area, saved from development to later become Morristown National Historical Park.

President Hoover signs bill Jan. 23 creating George Washington Birthplace National Monument, Wakefield, Va., to be administered by National Park Service.

Olvera Street, Los Angeles, restored as a working crafts area and opened to the public Apr. 20.

Leicester B. Holland establishes Pictorial Division of Early American Architecture in Division of Fine Arts, Library of Congress, in June.

Congress authorizes $100,000 June 18 for purchase of land at Appomattox

Court House, Va., by the War Department for Civil War memorial; plans for monument vetoed by National Park Service in 1933.

President Hoover signs legislation July 3 establishing Colonial National Monument, Yorktown, Va., under National Park Service.

San Antonio Conservation Society purchases old Granary at San Jose Mission to preserve crafts of Mexican community.

Excavations at Wakefield in September uncover foundations of U-shaped structure thought to be an outbuilding, but determined in 1968 to be actual birthplace of George Washington.

1931

John Mead Howells's *Lost Examples of Colonial Architecture*, a survey of demolished colonial buildings, published.

Monterey History and Art Association, Calif., formed to restore Custom House, adobe buildings, and other historic sites.

Central City Opera House presented to University of Denver for preservation.

California legislature Apr. 24 authorizes designation and marking of properties for state register of historic landmarks.

Philadelphia Society for the Preservation of Landmarks formed to save Samuel Powel House in Society Hill.

Galena, Ill., citizens convince state to accept Ulysses S. Grant Home in May as state memorial.

MacPheadris-Warner House, Portsmouth, N.H., purchased and restored by Warner House Association in the fall.

Verne E. Chatelain hired in August as first historian in National Park Service.

Yorktown Sesquicentennial celebration held in October, encouraging tourism to Colonial National Monument.

Historic district zoning ordinance ratified Oct. 13 by Charleston City Council, S.C.

Restoration of Tombstone, Ariz., begins in November with town's lease of old courthouse for a museum.

1932

Robert N. S. Whitelaw accepts directorship of Carolina Art Association and leads its growth in preservation planning for Charleston.

First annual Natchez pilgrimage held in the spring by Natchez Garden Club, Miss., to raise funds for preservation of antebellum mansions.

American Institute of Architects annual convention passes motion in April urging museums to refrain from purchasing or installing interiors of American buildings unless their demolition is inevitable.

Wakefield "replica" at George Washington Birthplace National Monument, Va., dedicated by National Park Service.

Opera House Association formed and grand opening of Central City Opera House and a local hotel, the Teller House, held in Central City, Colo., June 16.

Henry Horner, a preservationist, elected governor of Illinois; appoints staff to give Illinois a strong historical program.

1933

Historic House Museums by Laurence Vail Coleman contains full-length statement on restoration and an annotated bibliography.

Research project on mining town of Columbia, Calif., sponsored by Emergency Relief Administration in cooperation with State Park Commission.

Restoration of San Jose Mission, San Antonio, funded by federal Public Works Administration through 1935.

Joseph Manigault House, Charleston, S.C., saved from destruction by contribution from Princess Pignatelli at foreclosure sale.

San Juan Bautista plaza area purchased in January as part of California Park System.

Leicester B. Holland asks architects in February through *AIA Journal* to nominate significant U.S. structures for a Library of Congress master list.

President Hoover signs Morristown Park, N.J., bill Mar. 2, giving National Park Service its first National Historical Park.

Greenfield Village, Dearborn, Mich., opened to the public June 22.

President Roosevelt orders all parks, battlefields, monuments, and cemeteries in U.S. and District of Columbia transferred to Department of the Interior from the Departments of War and Agriculture, effective Aug. 10.

Arno B. Cammerer succeeds Horace M. Albright as director of National Park Service in August.

National Park Service hires historians and puts 800 Civilian Conservation Corps trainees to work in historic sites in the fall.

Gist Blair approaches President Roosevelt in November for assistance in preserving Blair House, Washington, D.C.; begins impetus for Historic Sites Act.

Charles E. Peterson proposes creation of Historic American Buildings Survey to Interior Secretary Harold Ickes; approved Nov. 17 as part of National Park Service; officially begins in December with Civilian Works Administration funding.

1934

Restoration plan for Portsmouth, N.H., proposes formation of federal housing corporation to fund restoration of selected buildings, using unemployed workers.

Seabury-Tredwell House, New York City, purchased and preserved with original furnishings intact.

Reconstructed Capitol and Palace in Williamsburg opened to the public Feb. 24.

Jefferson National Expansion Memorial Association formed in St. Louis in April; plan proposes riverfront clearance for memorial financed by federal government and city.

Henry Ford purchases in May birthplace of Stephen Foster in Pittsburgh for restoration at Greenfield Village, Dearborn, Mich.

Interior Secretary Harold Ickes accepts tripartite arrangement among AIA, National Park Service, and Library of Congress for permanent HABS contingent on funding.

John D. Rockefeller, Jr., on Horace Albright's recommendation, donates $10,000 to Department of the Interior for study of preservation abroad.

Charleston, S.C., obtains federal assistance in the fall for restoration of old Planter's Hotel as Dock Street Theater.

Cooperative plan initiated by federal, state, and county agencies for reconstruction of Mission La Purisima Concepcion, Lompoc, Calif.

1935

Civilian Conservation Corps begins excavation on Jamestown Island, parkway construction from Yorktown to Williamsburg, and restoration of buildings at Colonial National Historical Park; CCC expands to 111 camps in National Parks and 324 in state parks, with an average of 200 men per camp.

Preliminary draft of Historic Sites Act presented to Interior Secretary Harold Ickes Jan. 25; J. Thomas Schneider begins preservation study tour of European countries.

Historic Sites Act introduced in Senate by Sen. Harry F. Byrd of Virginia Feb. 29 and in House of Representatives by Cong. Maury Maverick of Texas Mar. 13. During April hearings major opposition is to federal government's proposed authority to use eminent domain to acquire private property for historical purposes.

Ronald F. Lee becomes historian for State Park Division, Emergency Conservation Work, National Park Service and hires more historians.

Remains of Hopewell Village, an 18th-century rural Pennsylvania iron-making community, discovered by Ronald F. Lee.

Gore Mansion, Waltham, Mass., saved in May from a developer through combined efforts of Society for the Preservation of New England Antiquities, Massachusetts Society of the Colonial Dames of America, Massachusetts Society of Architects and Trustees of Public Reservations.

William Byrd Branch of Association for the Preservation of Virginia Antiquities formed in May to save Craig House, Richmond.

U.S. Territorial Expansion Memorial Commission applies June 19 for $30 million from federal government for Jefferson National Expansion Memorial, to include $7.5 million from a St. Louis bond issue for purchase of river-front property.

Congress appropriates $100,000 in July for reconstruction of McLean House, Appomattox Court House, Va.

Historic Sites Act signed by President Roosevelt Aug. 21; National Park Trust Fund created to hold privately donated funds for restoration work on privately owned properties.

National Park Service initiates classification system in the fall to implement advisory board role in Historic Sites Act and issues regulations; Branch of Historic Sites and Buildings set up in National Park Service to supervise education, research, and policy development for historic and archaeological sites.

Schneider Report making recommendations for U.S. preservation issued by National Park Service in the fall.

Revolutionary war gondola *Philadelphia* found at bottom of Lake Champlain.

Governor of Nebraska creates Old Oregon and Mormon Trails National Parks Area Commission to study possibility of creating national park through most of Nebraska and Wyoming, featuring natural landmarks, surviving trail ruts, and Fort Laramie.

Architect William Perry of Perry, Shaw, and Hepburn summarizes Williamsburg restoration decisions in December *Architectural Record*.

President Roosevelt designates Jefferson National Expansion Memorial, St. Louis, under Historic Sites Act Dec. 21.

1936

National Park Service Branch of Historic Sites and Buildings in January applies historical themes to property acquisition and restoration for all National Park Service sites.

Advisory Board on National Parks, Historic Sites, Buildings, and Monuments, created by Historic Sites Act of 1935, holds first meeting Feb. 13.

Emergency Conservation Work historians employed at National Park Service begin preliminary national survey of historic sites in March.

Henry Ford opens "Wright Brothers' Memorial" Apr. 16 at Greenfield Village, Dearborn, Mich.

Department of the Interior in the summer initiates national historic-sites survey that extends through 1938.

J. C. Harrington, archaeologist at Jamestown, Va., begins development of interpretive museum to educate visitors about excavated artifacts.

Evaluation of fate of 190 buildings documented for Massachusetts Historic American Buildings Survey reveals little preservation benefit for recorded structures.

Verne E. Chatelain leaves National Park Service in September to become director of St. Augustine Restoration Program for Carnegie Institution of Washington.

California State Park Commission convinces federal government in November to complete restoration of all mission buildings at Mission La Purisima Concepcion, Lompoc, Calif.

Amendment to Louisiana Constitution authorizes new Vieux Carré Commission with power to assure preservation of Vieux Carré, New Orleans.

1937

Historical Restoration Committee formed in Portsmouth, N.H., to conduct local survey and seek funding.

Restoration policy drafted by National Park Service Advisory Board in May stresses preservation over reconstruction, urging caution, respect for original elements, sublimation of individual stylistic preferences, and refusal to antique new material introduced into any structure.

California Park Commission develops policy favoring self-supporting system of state historic monuments.

Vieux Carré Commission, New Orleans, officially created in August for members of Louisiana Historical Society, Louisiana State Museum, Association of Commerce, and AIA.

1938

First catalog of Historic American Buildings Survey drawings and photos issued by U.S. Government Printing Office and used as source of information for preservationists around the country.

National Park Service Eastern Museum Laboratory set up in February at Morristown National Historical Park, N.J.

State of California and Monterey citizens raise $20,000 in February to purchase Custom House; Monterey waterfront study prepared as basis for city master plan.

"Phase II" of Williamsburg restoration begins with reconstruction of shops on Duke of Gloucester Street.

Interior Secretary Harold Ickes officially changes Derby Wharf designation to Salem Maritime National Historic Site, Mass., in March, making it first National Historic Site.

Ronald F. Lee appointed chief, National Park Service Branch of Historic Sites and Buildings, in May.

Vieux Carré Property Owners' Association, New Orleans, formed in June as pressure group to influence Vieux Carré Commission.

National Park Service director June 20 orders research to precede all federal restoration work in buildings and sites to assure accuracy.

Wells family incorporates as Quinebaug Village Corporation, Sturbridge, Mass., later changed to Old Sturbridge Village.

1939

Illinois State Architect's Office supervises reconstruction of Cahokia Courthouse with federal funding and professional assistance from Illinois Museum Extension Project, Works Progress Administration.

Frederick Law Olmsted, Jr., undertakes preliminary architectural survey of Charleston, S.C.

Department of the Interior formally applies Jan. 13 for transfer of old U.S. Custom House (2d Bank of U.S.), Philadelphia, from Treasury Department for preservation.

Documented historical report issued in February on restoration of Ford Mansion, Morristown National Historical Park, N.J., becomes model for future National Park Service historic-structures reports.

President Roosevelt donates land from his estate in Hyde Park, N.Y., for construction of Roosevelt presidential library.

Interior Secretary Harold Ickes approves transfer of Sub-Treasury Building (Federal Hall), New York City, from Treasury Department to Department of the Interior in April.

Baseball Hall of Fame Museum opens June 12 in Cooperstown, N.Y., becoming first step toward Farmers' Museum.

Mayor Maury Maverick purchases La Villita district, San Antonio, in July to transform it into arts and crafts area with grant from National Youth Administration.

Louisiana judge rules Aug. 3 in favor of a Vieux Carré Commission decision, establishing constitutionality of Vieux Carré ordinance and commission's right to deny demolition.

Native Sons of the Golden West donate property in mining town of Shasta to California State Park Commission in the fall.

Demolition of St. Louis waterfront for Jefferson National Expansion Memorial begins Oct. 9.

National Park Service Advisory Board Nov. 7 approves donation of Vanderbilt Mansion, Hyde Park, N.Y., to National Park Service.

1940

Kenneth Chorley and Williamsburg restoration staff initiate preservation "advisory services."

Olmsted Report for Charleston, S.C., stresses need for community planning and more thorough survey of historic resources.

John D. Rockefeller, Jr., donates money for purchase and restoration of Philipse Castle, Tarrytown, N.Y., in February as headquarters for Tarrytown Historical Society.

Portsmouth Restoration Project, N.H., ends in the spring because of lack of financial support.

Secretary of the Interior Harold Ickes officially establishes Appomattox Court House National Historical Monument, Va., Apr. 10 with McLean House to be reconstructed in response to local pressure; work halted by war.

President Roosevelt accepts Interior Secretary Ickes's appeal in April to save Old Courthouse (along with Old Cathedral and Manuel Lisa's Fur Warehouse) as part of Jefferson National Expansion Memorial, St. Louis, overruling a November 1939 Advisory Board decision to refuse custody of the building; Warehouse demolished in late 1950s.

American Society of Architectural Historians organized July 31.

Newton B. Drury, acquisitions officer, California State Park Commission, becomes fourth director of National Park Service Aug. 20.

Preservation ordinance adopted Sept. 24 by Monterey, Calif., to regulate construction and alterations but lacks legal enforcement measures.

American Association for State and Local History founded Dec. 27 as outgrowth of American Historical Association.

1941

Proposal by V. Aubrey Neasham outlines nonprofit private corporation, Historic Sites of America, Inc., to assure preservation through public and semipublic agencies of endangered sites National Park Service cannot administer.

First issue of *Journal of the American Society of Architectural Historians* published in January.

College Art Association meeting in Chicago marks increased interest of art historians in historic buildings, including structures by Louis Sullivan and H. H. Richardson.

William Clark Society purchases furnishings of Campbell House, St. Louis, at estate auction Feb. 24.

Acquisition policy for Pennsylvania Historical Commission, presented in March by S. K. Stevens, includes avoidance of properties with large park lands, equitable geographic distribution of state-funded sites, and formation of statewide society (as in North Carolina) to relieve commission of acquisition pressures.

Meeting of federal preservationists, university professors, and private preservation leaders held Mar. 18 to discuss common preservation problems and techniques.

Wealthy New Yorker offers in May to finance stabilization of remaining columns of San Xavier Del Bac Mission, Tucson, with National Park Service supervision.

San Jose Mission, San Antonio, designated National Historic Site June 1.

Extensive survey of historic houses, one of the first, conducted in Charleston, S.C., resulting in exhibit (1942) and book, *This Is Charleston* (1944).

Marine Historical Association acquires whaler *Charles W. Morgan* in November as prelude to construction of New England seaport museum village at Mystic Seaport, Conn.

In honor of Henry Ford's 80th birthday in 1943, alumni of Henry Ford Trade School purchase Ironmaster's House, Saugus, Mass., for shipment to Greenfield Village, Dearborn, Mich.; local group opposes move.

Completed complex at Mission La Purisima Concepcion, Lompoc, dedicated Dec. 7 by State of California.

1942

Ronald F. Lee leaves National Park Service Branch of Historic Sites and Buildings for duration of war; staff decreases to two persons during war years.

Battle begins in January between George McAneny and Robert Moses over demolition of Castle Clinton, New York City, becoming symbol for preservationists battling city planners.

"This Is Charleston" exhibit, based on preservation survey, opens in March at Gibbes Art Gallery, educating Charlestonians in community planning needs.

Collaborative Justification for Reconstruction of the McLean House at Appomattox becomes model for future National Park Service reconstruction research.

President Roosevelt approves Gloria Dei Church, Philadelphia, as National Historic Site Mar. 28, but states that National Park Service historical employees should "be directed into more productive channels for the war efforts."

National Park Service moved in spring from Washington to Chicago because it is considered nonessential agency.

Organization for the Conservation of Historic Sites in Old Philadelphia formed in June to save Independence Hall.

President Roosevelt authorizes purchase of Blair House, Washington, D.C., in August for use by State Department.

1943

Bibliography on Early American Architecture assesses growing interest in early American buildings.

Documentation of Vandalia and Fort de Chartres, Ill., restoration completed; Vandalia report is then most extensive document of its type.

President Roosevelt designates Independence Hall, Philadelphia, May 14 as National Historic Site in cooperative agreement with city of Philadelphia.

1944

Greek Revival Architecture in America by Talbot Hamlin published.

This Is Charleston published, detailing 1941 preservation survey.

Congress authorizes secretary of the interior to accept land around Harpers Ferry, W.Va., to commemorate John Brown's raid; because of insufficient funds, purchase program unfulfilled until 1950s.

Institute of Early American History and Culture created in January from merger of Williamsburg Advisory Committee of Historians and editorial board of *William and Mary Quarterly* to research American history to 1815.

Home of Franklin D. Roosevelt, Hyde Park, N.Y., officially designated National Historic Site Jan. 15.

1945

Georgetown Enterprises purchases and restores buildings in Georgetown, Colo., as shops and encourages restoration of Victorian houses.

Kenneth Chorley of Williamsburg restoration inspires Charleston, S.C., preservationists to form a preservation foundation.

Monterey Foundation, Calif., organized in April to unite area preservation groups.

President Roosevelt signs order May 9 for acquisition of Adams Mansion, Quincy, Mass., by National Park Service.

54 Washington Street Company (later, Preservation Society of Newport County) formed to take over Hunter House, Newport, R.I.

Interest in restoration of Columbia revived because of Gold Discovery Centennial; California legislature appropriates matching funds for property acquisition.

During National Park Service Advisory Board meeting in December, Newton Drury recommends a National Trust to preserve architectural landmarks.

1946

Ronald F. Lee rejoins National Park Service as chief historian.

Touro Synagogue, Newport, R.I., designated National Historic Site by President Truman in March under cooperative agreement.

Congress authorizes creation of Philadelphia National Shrines Park Commission to study area around Independence Hall for proposed National Historical Park.

Interdisciplinary conference on archaeology held at Jamestown and Yorktown, Va., in May.

Congress authorizes New York City to transfer Castle Clinton to National Park

Service as National Monument in August but allocates no restoration funds.

Kenneth Chorley of Williamsburg advises Preservation Society of Newport County, R.I., in October to seek financial support from visitors' fees rather than from "another Rockefeller."

Ronald F. Lee warns at October meeting of American Association for State and Local History that postwar inflation, suburban development, highway expansion, etc., may jeopardize preservation.

Discussion held in New York City on methods of centralizing preservation movement; plans made for meeting of 10–15 key individuals to explore a national conference; Ronald F. Lee, David E. Finley, and Christopher C. Crittenden meet in November to discuss formation of a National Trust, resulting in list of people to attend conference at National Gallery of Art.

Robert N. S. Whitelaw leads group in forming Historic Charleston Foundation, S.C., in December.

1947

State begins restoration of Old Church at Bishop Hill, Ill., 1840s Swedish colony.

Plimoth Plantation, Mass., formed to reconstruct a Pilgrim village.

Architectural competition guidelines for Jefferson National Expansion Memorial, St. Louis, call for mandatory preservation of Old Cathedral, Old Courthouse, and Old Rock House.

Preorganization meeting held Feb. 5 at National Gallery of Art to discuss formation of National Trust; larger conference Apr. 15 endorsed.

Kenneth Chorley in March recommends opening of The Breakers, Newport, R.I., and use of revenue for restoration of other Newport sites.

Meeting in Washington, D.C., Apr. 15 establishes National Council for Historic Sites and Buildings, assigning educational functions to council and property administration to a National Trust for Historic Preservation.

First official letter of protest sent by National Council for Historic Sites and Buildings over Gore Place, Waltham, Mass., in July.

Organizational conference of National Council for Historic Sites and Buildings held in Washington, D.C., Oct. 20; charter of National Trust presented.

"Citizens Community for Preservation of Historic Salem," Winston-Salem, N.C., created to lobby for rezoning of historic Old Salem district.

Bertram K. Little succeeds William Sumner Appleton as director of Society for the Preservation of New England Antiquities in November.

Society for the Preservation of Maryland Antiquities signs cooperative agreement in December with National Park Service to administer Hampton National Historic Site, Towson, Md.; officially dedicated April 1949.

Pennsylvania Historical and Museum Commission conducts state historic-sites survey; report published in 1949.

1948

American Institute of Architects budgets $50,000 to restore its headquarters, The Octagon, Washington, D.C.

War Department declares military posts surplus property, causing organizations to pressure National Park Service and Congress for national recognition and acquisition of old forts.

Eero Saarinen wins Jefferson National Expansion Memorial architectural competition in February with stainless steel arch as focal point.

First expanded house tour of Charleston, S.C., held to raise funds for Historic Charleston Foundation.

Frederick L. Rath, Jr., selected as first executive secretary of National Council for Historic Sites and Buildings.

Restored Ashley House, Deerfield, Mass., opened in April as part of town restoration program.

San Antonio Conservation Society initiates effective fund-raising mechanism with presentation of annual "Night in Old San Antonio" fiesta.

President Truman signs legislation June 28 creating Independence National Historical Park, a partnership between Department of the Interior, city of Philadelphia and Commonwealth of Pennsylvania.

The Breakers, Newport, R.I., opened to the public in July.

Society for the Preservation of Long Island Antiquities founded in the fall.

Master plan for acquisition of Columbia adopted in September by California Park Commission.

Woodlawn Public Foundation formed in September to purchase Woodlawn, near Mount Vernon, Va., working through National Council for Historic Sites and Buildings to raise funds; Old Dominion Foundation offers to match up to $100,000 toward purchase.

President Truman and family move to Blair House while White House is renovated.

National Council for Historic Sites and Buildings holds first annual meeting Nov. 4 at National Gallery of Art; charter for National Trust for Historic Preservation formally presented.

New York Supreme Court rules Dec. 13 in favor of American Scenic and Historic Preservation Society to stop demolition of Castle Clinton, New York City; powers of City Art Commission seen as establishing legal basis for preservation of historic buildings as "works of art."

Winston-Salem, N.C., Board of Aldermen, after studying Alexandria, Va., historic ordinance, passes similar ordinance Dec. 21.

1949

Louisiana Landmarks Society formed as statewide private preservation organization.

New York legislature creates committee to study state historic sites in February.

National Council for Historic Sites and Buildings in March publishes first issue of *Quarterly Report*, forerunner of National Trust magazine *Historic Preservation*.

Commission on the Renovation of the Executive Mansion votes Aug. 2 for restoration plan to maintain existing exterior walls of White House; renovation implemented without advice of National Park Service.

Tombstone Restoration Commission, Ariz., created in September to restore town to its 1881 appearance.

Congressional charter establishing National Trust for Historic Preservation signed by President Truman Oct. 26.

1950

Restoration of Trustees Garden area in Savannah illustrates trend toward preserving districts and neighborhoods.

Old Salem created Mar. 1 to administer financial resources for saving Old Salem, N.C.

Reconstructed McLean House, Appomattox Court House, Va., dedicated Apr. 16 by National Park Service.

Castle Clinton, New York City, designated National Historic Monument May 13.

July issue of *Antiques* magazine devoted to preservation, including restoration principles, preservation problems, and solutions.

1951

Woodlawn Plantation, Mount Vernon, Va., becomes first property accepted for administration by National Trust for Historic Preservation; acquired 1957.

Henry Francis du Pont Winterthur Museum, Winterthur, Del., opens Oct. 30.

1953

National Trust for Historic Preservation and National Council for Historic Sites and Buildings merge July 18.

Index